LABOR WILL RULE

LABOR
WILL RULE

Sidney Hillman and
the Rise of American Labor

Steven Fraser

THE FREE PRESS
A Division of Macmillan, Inc.
NEW YORK
Maxwell Macmillan Canada
TORONTO
Maxwell Macmillan International
NEW YORK   OXFORD   SINGAPORE   SYDNEY

The Free Press
A Division of Macmillan, Inc.
866 Third Avenue, New York, N.Y. 10022

Maxwell Macmillan Canada, Inc.
1200 Eglinton Avenue East
Suite 200
Don Mills, Ontario M3C 3N1

Macmillan, Inc. is part of the Maxwell Communication
Group of Companies.

Printed in the United States of America

printing number
1 2 3 4 5 6 7 8 9 10

Library of Congress Cataloging-in-Publication Data

Fraser, Steve
    Labor will rule : Sidney Hillman and the rise of American labor /
Steven Fraser.
        p.   cm.
    Includes bibliographical references (p.   ) and index.
    ISBN 0-02-910630-3
    1. Hillman, Sidney, 1887–1946. 2. Labor leaders—United States
—Biography.   3. Labor movement—United States—History—20th
century.   4. Trade   unions—United States—History—20th century.
I. Title.
HD8073.H5F73   1991
331.88′187′092—dc20
    [B]   91-6528
                                                                 CIP

Illustration Credits

Bundists; Hillman with his uncle; woman carrying cloth on her head; "Why hire a man for a dollar . . . ": Amalgamated Clothing Workers Records, Cornell University

Lower East Side streets; tenement sweatshop: Library of Congress

Chicago 1910 strike: Chicago Historical Society

Hillman on telephone: The Inheritance, photo courtesy of Lynn and Harold Mayer Productions

1912 New York uprising: Brown Brothers

Original Board of the ACWA; Art Young's cartoon; Amalgamated Bank opening: Amalgamated Clothing Workers Records, Cornell University

Bessie Abramovitz and Sidney Hillman; Leo Wolman with Hillman and Holtz; Hillman honored as "Man of the Year": Courtesy of Philoine Fried

1932 campaign for FDR: The Bettmann Archive

NRA (picketers); Hillman with Richberg, Green, and Lewis: Amalgamated Clothing Workers Records, Cornell University

"Lie-in" at Woolworth's: AP/Wide World Photos

Heads of Labor's Non-Partisan League: Courtesy of Philoine Fried

Fallen worker gets beating: The Bettmann Archive

La Guardia, Hillman, Eleanor Roosevelt: Alexander Archer

Lewis and Hillman; Hillman addressing PAC rally: Amalgamated Clothing Workers Records, Cornell University

North American Aviation strike: AP/Wide World Photos

1943 CIO convention; Kuznetsov addressing meeting; Hillman with journalists: Courtesy of Philoine Fried

Republican Party billboard: Amalgamated Clothing Workers Records, Cornell University

Veterans picketing Texas Company: New York Public Library

Funeral cortege: Alexander Archer

For
Vev and Lillian
Jill and Max

One can hear the footsteps of the Deliverer. . . .
Labor will rule and the World will be free

—Sidney Hillman to his infant daughter, Philoine, 1918

Contents

Preface

I often wondered during the long time it took to write this book whether I was guilty of making both too much and too little of the life of Sidney Hillman. Today, fewer and fewer people remember who he was. Yet during the 1930s and until his death in 1946, Hillman's name was a household word, appearing frequently on the front pages of the nation's newspapers and magazines.

After his death his name receded rapidly from public memory, for reasons having as much to do with the peculiar presentism of American culture as with anything intrinsic to Hillman's character and accomplishments. But it remained alive for legions of aging labor movement militants. It lived as well within families who wistfully remembered and mythologized the thirties and forties as a moment of pregnant social and political promise, full of danger, daring, and self-sacrifice, when Hillman reached the apogee of his prominence and power. Mine was such a family, so I first became acquainted with Hillman's name, casually to be sure, at a time when most of the rest of the country was learning to forget why he'd been so important.

My views about that era—not only the period of the New Deal but the critical decades of Progressive reform that preceded it—have naturally changed a great deal from the hero-worshiping years of my childhood. But still it strikes me as an extraordinary time, a time of irreversible transformations, of ancient promises kept and forsworn. During the upheavals of the 1960s, I naïvely imagined that the organized labor movement might recover the élan and visionary boldness of earlier days. Later, when I retreated into graduate school, it was already settled in my mind that I would seek some more probing insight into this uniquely "proletarian moment" in American history. Along the way I developed the conviction that Sidney Hillman had played an underappreciated but pivotal role in the birth of what might be called the New Deal order.

Whether or not I fell victim to the tunnel vision endemic in graduate school specialization and ended up exaggerating Hillman's significance, readers will have to decide.

But I am certain that from another vantage point I have failed to give Hillman his due. Because, from the beginning, what drove me was a fascination with the larger mysteries of the era, the book that resulted is a biography only in the loosest sense. Hillman's private life with family and friends is scarcely touched on. Attention is paid almost exclusively to his career as a labor and political leader. And even here I have allowed myself the liberty of wandering far afield from the narrative line of his public life. Those who knew him well will realize how much I've missed. Still, Hillman himself measured a person's worth by the quality of his contribution to the community's well-being. If, therefore, the odd proportions of this biography lend an unduly instrumental quality to Hillman's life, then perhaps his own conviction that it was important to be useful can be my partial defense.

Many people have helped me over the years. Walter Lippincott, when he was editorial director at Cambridge University Press, and Martin Kessler, president of Basic Books, generously allowed me the time away from work as an editor without which it would have been impossible to write the book. A fellowship at the Woodrow Wilson International Center for Scholars in Washington, D.C., provided precious time, resources, and congenial surroundings with which to begin drafting the manuscript. The staff of the research department of the Amalgamated Clothing and Textile Workers Union were unfailingly friendly and helpful as I camped out there for months on end. Archivists and librarians at numerous universities and other depositories were equally forthcoming; I want to give special thanks to Richard Strassberg, who is in charge of the Labor–Management Documentation Center at Cornell University, and to his colleague Paulette Manos.

Work on this project began twelve years ago, which is nothing to brag about, but which at least means there were people still alive with vivid memories of Hillman, sometimes even of the heroic days of great garment center strikes before World War I. They were gracious enough to spend an hour or a day talking with me about what they remembered. Some have died since, but I want to thank them here as a group (their names appear at appropriate places in the notes). Especially, I want to offer my gratitude to Philoine Fried, Sidney Hillman's daughter, who is still very much alive and has, at every stage of this undertaking, helped in innumerable tangible ways and, by offering her constant support and encouragement, in less tangible ways as well.

Paul Milkman and Stuart Ewen had little direct involvement with this book, but their reliable friendship over many years meant they too lived with and made it possible for me to live with a project that often proved demoralizing and apparently never ending. Josh Freeman, who "retreated" into graduate school at precisely the moment I did and has been a good friend ever since, long ago read and astutely commented on what amounted to a précis of the book. Debbie Nathan, a comrade from pre–graduate school days, spent weeks gathering material for me about the American Labor Party for reasons hardly congruent with the objectives of the conventional Ph.D. program. Another old comrade, Michael Tinkler, did the same, helping me research the history of collective bargaining in the needle trades.

Together, Gary Gerstle and I assembled a book of essays on what preoccupied us both—namely, the New Deal and its recent decline as the reigning orthodoxy of American public life. In the process we became good friends, and at a very late hour Gary volunteered to read, in record time, the penultimate draft of what had become a truly elephantine manuscript. As I had already discovered him to be in his role as my coeditor, Gary proved a shrewd and candid critic. Earlier, Michael Frisch, Nelson Lichtenstein, and Michael Kazin had also read all or large portions of the manuscript. Their remarks raised my spirits while diplomatically suggesting ways I might become more concise and less pretentious. When the text was fully done, I faced the frightening task of preparing the footnotes. Renée Pearl came to my rescue.

My interpretation of the New Deal particularly and much else besides stems from hours of discussion over many years with Peter Friedlander. Whatever may be considered new or thought-provoking in these pages is to some incalculable degree the product of Peter's remarkably fertile mind.

Peter Agree went very far out of his way on several occasions to help in ways vital to the completion and publication of the book. I salute him.

For years I've known Joyce Seltzer as a colleague. We make our living in the same way; indeed, every now and then we find ourselves competing to acquire the same book for our respective publishing houses. On such occasions I'm invariably reminded of her reputation for editorial excellence. Now, as "Joyce's author," I am an eyewitness to her intelligence, sympathy, and conscientiousness. She displayed great patience as the project dragged on for years past its original delivery date. When it finally arrived, she gently managed to get me to make a whole series of highly sensible cuts and alterations despite my petulant insistence that I was too exhausted to do anything more with the manuscript.

I met Jill Andresky Fraser just about the time I began the research on

Hillman's biography. The three of us have lived together ever since, most of the time good-humoredly, sometimes not. Jill and I are both glad Sidney is at long last leaving, freeing up the backroom of our apartment for Jill's more productive and more remunerative journalism. One thing is certain: Sidney would have hung around forever if it weren't for Jill's assistance on everything from the most tedious clerical tasks to an incisive, critical reading of the whole manuscript. Jill is my great good fortune.

While I was still mired in the final drafting of the book, my son Max Fraser wrote and published two books of his own, one a biography of Superman, the other a duography of that "dynamic duo," Batman and Robin. Remarking that his rate of progress was, to put it mildly, light years ahead of my own, he chastised me for the inefficiency of my work habits, observing that I was too easily distracted from the task at hand. Although I think his criticism was a bit merciless, I take his point. He's offered to become my coauthor on a future book, and so perhaps the next time around I can get it right.

ONE

Rabbi or Revolutionary

A man with an insatiable appetite for practical action in the here and now, Sidney Hillman rarely paused to look back. But many years after fleeing the beleaguered world of his native village in Jewish Lithuania, Hillman contemplated its enduring impact on his later life:

> The rabbis in our family were not outstanding, but the rank and file kind that are called upon more to help than to lead. Concern in the every day problems of working people was their job, so I took it for granted it had to be mine.[1]

It was an artful reimagining of his past, not literally true, but not willfully deceptive either, and above all crafted with one eye trained on the pressing needs of the moment, one on the dimming light from the past. The Hillman family rabbis were neither quite so ordinary nor such helpmates and tribunes of the working poor as Hillman suggested. Moreover, if asked in his late adolescence whether he felt some natural affinity for the rabbinical calling, he would probably have shuddered at the thought of a life so suffocated by obscurantist orthodoxy. Yet he was indeed the favored son of rabbinical ancestors. If he chose, years later, to remember that rabbinical connection, no matter how sentimentalized his recollection, it was because the world of the shtetl, synagogue, and *shul* left its mark in ways perhaps even he, so caught up in the great moments of modern statecraft, failed to realize.

1

Zagare, an inconspicuous spot on the map of northwest Lithuania where Sidney Hillman was born in March of 1887, was like hundreds of other small, fragile villages in the Russian Pale. It was poor and, as the nineteenth century drew to a close, growing poorer. Actually there were two Zagares, Old and New. The latter, where the Hillmans lived, was founded at the beginning of the eighteenth century by Jews who settled on the lands of a Polish nobleman, Umjastowski, to escape the depradations of their gentile neighbors in Old Zagare.

Although separated only by a tiny rivulet which emptied into the river Aa, Jewish residents of the twin shtetls developed intense loyalties and a competitive local pride characteristic of the insular world of the Jewish village. By midcentury there were only 840 Jews living in Old Zagare, a mere 313 in New Zagare. Yet each Zagare maintained its own rabbi, its own ecclesiastical court, its own *shohetim* (ritual slaughtering house), its own *hazan* (cantor), synagogue and schools as well as its own town hall and mayor, village assessor, and ritual baths. Insular rivalries must have been intense indeed to support so much social redundancy. In fact, dwellers in Old Zagare referred to their neighbors as "the New Zagare sinners," while natives of the newei shtetl described the old-timers as "the Old Zagare corpses."

Population grew rapidly in the Pale throughout the nineteenth century. By the time of Sidney's birth there were approximately five thousand Jewish souls living in both villages, representing nearly 70 percent of the total population. As a child Sidney, who was called Simke-ke by his fellow *cheder bucherm,* or schoolmates, was afraid to cross the bridge alone into the old town. For one thing, the bridge was in a perpetual state of disrepair, occasioning interminable meetings and arguments over whose duty it was to fix it. More seriously, the children of New Zagare feared that the dead men in the Old Cemetery would throw stones or choke them to death. Although most of his time as a boy was spent within the narrow and damp walls of the *cheder,* often enough Sidney was caught up in the raging battles between the children of the twin Zagares barricaded on opposite banks of the small stream.[2]

Most of the houses in the Zagares consisted of two rooms set on earthen floors. Throughout the province of Kovno, where Zagare was situated, it was common for several families to share a single room. Most shtetl dwellings were log or mud-and-straw huts of two rooms, three at the most.[3]

The Hillman house, however, consisted of four rooms with wooden floors and a veranda. Measured against the minimal standards of shtetl life, it was a substantial, not to say affluent house, enough above its neighbors to mark its inhabitants as people of a certain modest social significance, but without pretentions to anything grander. Fine shadings of status were after all possible even within the claustrophobic confines of the shtetl, despite the stark simplicity of its material culture: its wooden synagogues and dirt roads and one-room schools; measuring personal wealth in candles and herring and potatoes; where few could afford a cord of wood or a load of peat for fuel to heat the house; where bad roads in bad weather spelled disaster as peasants failed to make the trip to market; and where the *hebrahs* or charitable societies—"The Redemption of the Captives," "Bread for the Hungry," "Visiting of the Sick"—were forever on call.[4]

Four rooms and a veranda meant something in such a world, but on the other hand everything about shtetl life in the Pale in the last quarter of the nineteenth century was becoming precarious. The Hillmans enjoyed what limited social distinction they had because they came from a line of merchants and rabbis. Together merchants and rabbis had constituted, for some centuries, the Jewish community's circle of notables— its judges and legislators, its communal benefactors, its educators and sages, and its cultural arbiters, negotiating its perilous dealings with the institutions of the Czarist autocracy. But the economic position of the Jewish merchant, even the fortunes of those of real national prominence, and the cultural authority of the rabbinic order had both fallen precipitously.

Jewish commercial activity outside the Pale was succumbing both to the pressures of international competition, and, thanks to the hostility of the state and the jealousies of gentile competitors, to the drying up of Russian trade prospects at home. Restricted to the slim pickings of an impoverished shtetl or urban ghetto economy, many merchants began an irreversible slide into the ranks of itinerant peddlers, hawkers, and ragpickers. No great distance separated the hand-to-mouth existence of the peddler from the twilight world of the *luftmensch*—a figure whose enforced idleness and anomalous place in the cramped universe of the shtetl has sometimes been camouflaged by a romantic image of contemplative men pondering the mysteries of life and dreaming of what might be.

Sidney Hillman's maternal grandfather was a petty merchant, the latest in a long line of petty merchants, dealing in buttons, needles, thread, and other odds and ends, who lived and worked in the vicinity of Riga, the capital of neighboring Latvia. If grandfather Paiken managed to survive as a small-time trader, it was only through prodigious acts of frugality and commercial cunning. Hillman's father, Samuel (Schmuel— "Whom the Lord Had Heard"), was also a merchant. He bartered with neighboring peasants for grain and flour, but far less successfully than his father-in-law. Temperamentally ill suited to the life of business, he was drawn instead to the more spiritual pursuits of his own father, Mordecai, a local rabbi widely noted in the region for his piety and saintly disdain for material comforts. Samuel Hillman became in fact a kind of *luftmensch* manqué: the shell of the business remained, but its paltry transactions in flour and grain demanded little of his time, which he spent instead in fervent prayer and meditation.[5]

This metamorphosis of a failed merchant into a *luftmensch*, albeit one who continued to command the respect customarily due the paterfamilias, was not merely a singular disappointing episode in one family's history. As the urban population of the Pale grew denser in the late nineteenth century, the trade sector was saturated, so the percentage of the population engaged in trade (both merchants and small traders called *miezane*) dropped, while the handicraft and casual laboring population increased. Vast numbers of Jewish commercial intermediaries were eliminated, as if by an epidemic. Rapid growth of capitalist industry and trade, the emergence of modern banking, the state's appropriation of the liquor trade and tax collecting (once the lucrative if risky business of tax farmers), and the expulsion of Jews from the countryside produced *luftmenschen* in staggering numbers throughout the Pale. Thus, the private distillation and sale of liquor had once employed thousands of Jews, who now poured into already swarming ghetto towns and cities. The expansion of Russia's previously primitive railroad system was a mortal threat to thousands of Jewish teamsters and draymen. Jewish artisans in the clothing, shoemaking, and weaving trades often found themselves unable to compete against factory-organized and mechanized production. Between 1894 and 1898 the number of Jewish paupers increased by 30 percent, and in many communities nearly 40 percent of all families were headed by *luftmenschen*.[6]

At one time enmeshed in the self-enclosed Jewish economy, where they performed respected and traditional functions, those traders and artisans now became marginal men as that economy decomposed around them. The more fortunate hung on as hawkers of sundries or as petty usurers, although the fall into usury was itself a disgrace: In the customary order of the patriarchal village "free loans" were the norm, and the taking of interest from coreligionists was frowned upon. Those even less fortunate than the ostracized usurer, those more totally marginalized, became beggars, water-carriers, and casual laborers, and at one time or another performed all of those and countless other tasks. With no regular means of support, they lived on hopes and hustle, dreaming always of that miraculous stroke of luck, or *mazl.*[7]

The province of Kovno was a veritable garden of such marginalized *luftmenschen.* Physically enchanting, a region of "ancient woods, tall mountains, dreamy hills, and blossoming valleys through which flowed the Nieman River," it was also miserably poor in natural resources and industrial activity, fertile only in its supply of human surplus. Some victims of this painful uprooting reacted with a newly invented political anger and, like many Jewish students and dispossessed handicraftsmen, went on to join the revolutionary movement against the Russian autocracy. Samuel, however, responded quite differently. He retreated into the consoling orthodoxies of his ancestry. His growing absorption in theological speculation and prayer was neither resented nor disdained by the family, but it was not to be memorialized either, and it contributed little if anything to protecting the family's social position in Zagare society.

Whatever slight social prominence the Hillmans enjoyed, therefore, derived more from its rabbinical connections. Hillmans had been rabbis for generations. Most had served the shtetlach of the Pale, as did Sidney's grandfather, Mordecai, in the neighboring village of Parlich. One great-uncle presided over a congregation in another, equally remote Lithuanian town, Pasvitin, and another served as a *mohel* (who performed the ritual of circumcision) in the provincial capital of Kovno. Other rabbinical Hillmans, however, rose to far greater office, Sidney's later recollections notwithstanding. The *mohel*'s son, Samuel Isaac Hillman, became a noted rabbi in London, head of the rabbinic court there, and a grandfather of Chaim Herzog. Still another relative later went on to become Grand Rabbi of Jerusalem.[8]

Prominent or not, rabbis usually carried considerable communal weight. They functioned not only as priests but as local magistrates, as scholars and educators, as expounders of the law, and as arbiters of communal disputes. Rabbinic juridical writings contained an impressive amount of social legislation—for example, the right of the worker to insist on immediate payment was established in the Mishnah. Together with other town notables, particularly the wealthier merchant stratum, rabbis formed that singular political institution of the Jewish community, the *kehillah* or *kahel*, which regulated the conduct of business and trade, collected local taxes, and monitored the craft guilds and their elaborate codes governing relations among masters, journeymen, and apprentices. It was not unusual for a rabbi to be associated with a particular guild, where he functioned as a judge settling arguments between masters and journeymen. Moreover, for centuries the Czar had used the local rabbinate as a kind of surrogate regional officialdom charged with maintaining order and enforcing the edicts of the state.[9]

Tensions between these town notables and less distinguished resi-

dents, between an "aristocratic" and a "democratic" faction, often simmered beneath the apparently placid surface of village life. Social
divisions among Russian Jewry grew wider with the spread of secular
education and commercial wealth. At opposite poles stood the Jewish
financier with ties to the Royal court and the poor innkeeper on a
provincial estate; the international banker and the village peddler; the
factory owner and the impoverished handicraftsmen; the head rabbi of a
large city and the struggling village tailor.

The *sheyne yidn* (beautiful or fine Jews) expressed a real disdain for
the *proste yidn* (low or common Jews), especially for all those manual
laborers like tailors and shoemakers who were seen as crude and uneducated. Rabbis and Torah scholars, no matter how impoverished, were
always *sheyne*. Rigid social distinctions were observed even within the
confines of the temple; artisans often maintained separate synagogues;
where *proste* worshiped together with *sheyne*, they did so from the back
pews. Status was an abiding concern running through the whole hierarchy of shtetl society—striving, the "chase after *koved*," was ubiquitous.
Tailors and scholars stood at opposite ends of that social hierarchy.
Families like the Hillmans were apt to suffer a chronic fear of downward
mobility and were prepared to mount great efforts to keep their children
free of the stigma of manual labor.

Occasionally the social tensions erupted with great force over the
selection of a new rabbi. The "aristocracy" sought a man of erudition and
solid reputation and was concerned far less with the candidate's ethical
outlook and whether he could be considered truly "incorruptible"—such
a reputation could in fact present certain decided disadvantages. The
"democratic" faction, on the other hand, cared far less about the new
rabbi's scholarship and much more about his conduct. It sought someone
modest and above all approachable, one sensitive to the personal and
social troubles of the poor who would attend their rituals and ceremonies
and be fair in legal disputes.[10]

There were, no doubt, some rabbis in the Hillman line who sympathized with the sentiments of the poorer portion of shtetl society, who
were, after a fashion, the sort of "people's rabbi" Sidney later invoked.
But at least as many were identified with the higher reaches of the
established order. In either case, the heating up of social antagonisms
within the sphere of traditional Jewish life left the orthodox rabbinate in
an increasingly anomalous position.

Fissures in the social order of the Pale grew immeasurably wider in
the nineteenth century, and the authority of the rabbinate declined
accordingly. It was assaulted on the one side by the pietistic, impassioned, and mystical fundamentalism of the hasidic movement, which

flourished particularly among the "democratic" and impoverished segments of East European Jewry. From the other side, rabbinic Judaism
confronted the rationalism and anticlericalism of the Jewish enlightenment, or *haskalah*, which first took root among urban intellectuals and
students and a Russified Jewish bourgeoisie, the *maskilim*. By the last
third of the century it had filtered, in diluted form, well down into the
grassroots of the Jewish school system.

Besieged by *haskalah* and hasidism, the orthodox rabbinate, always
devoutly traditional, became even more conservative and rigid, bristling
with hostility to all forms of secular education. Rabbis struggled to maintain the harsh regimen and obscurantist curriculum of the *cheder* (elementary school) and jealously guarded the portals of the yeshiva. They
often stood in conspicuous opposition to demands for economic and
social reform.[11]

Not surprisingly, the rabbinic reputation suffered further from its
compromising collaboration with an autocratic regime that, except for a
fleeting and frustrating period of liberalization in the 1860s, scarcely
bothered to conceal its contempt for the elementary needs of its Jewish
subjects and tacitly condoned the wave of violent pogroms beginning in
1881. The Jewish quarter of Zagare was itself severely damaged by the
conflagrations that accompanied a second series of pogroms that spread
north from the southern region of the Pale.[12]

Its fragile political authority shattered from without, its spiritual and
intellectual preeminence eroding from within, even its capacity to shield
the community from the avarice and violence of the gentiles reduced to
insignificance, the rabbinate was in a precarious state. If Mordecai Hillman was beloved by the residents of Parlich, he was one of a dwindling
number of "people's rabbis." And for all that, he was no more sympathetic to those secularizing currents of Western thought and culture that
would cause his grandson to break with the family's rabbinic heritage.

Thanks in part to an accident of geography, the immemorial rhythms
of provincial Zagare had been disturbed by the subversive currents of
Western secularism for quite some time. Because of its proximity to
Courland, just over the border outside the Pale in Latvia, tiny Zagare
became one of the first centers of the *haskalah* movement inside the Pale.
Because the Jews of Courland were directly exposed to the cultural influences of the German enlightenment, the *haskalah* penetrated the Courland Jewish community at an early date. Zagare itself soon became known
as "a town full of scholars and scribes." Throughout the nineteenth
century it sustained a circle of *maskilim* who, early in the century, first
gathered around the town's leading intellectual, Hayyim Zak, "the
scholar of Zagare." Included among the Zagare *maskilim* were the noted

Hebrew literary scholars Senior Sachs and Nathan Rabbinowicz, the
Yiddish novelist Jacob Dineson, "extremist" *maskilim* like Benjamim
Mandelstamm, the educator and government official Leon Mandelstamm, and a future leading member of the Zionist and territorialist
movements, Max Emmanuel Mandelstamm. Some of these men only
became prominent *maskilim* after leaving Zagare, but the very fact that
such an unimposing village could nurture such a galaxy of intellectual
moderns suggests what an extraordinary place it was.

For all its preachments about reason and science and progress, the
haskalah was, in its basic disposition, no less elitist and disdainful of the
mores, dress, rituals, and language of the Pale's Yiddish subculture than
was orthodox rabbinic Judaism. The "extremist" *maskilim*, like Benjamin
Mandelstamm, accused Russian Jewry of critical faults that were, he
claimed, responsible for its backwardness: (1) speaking a confused tongue
rather than the Russian language; (2) dressing quaintly; (3) failing to
participate in the arts and crafts; (4) owning no factories; (5) being
neither farmers nor herdsmen. His recommended solution, which depended on harsh government intervention, included "forbidding the
printing of the Talmud, completely removing from circulation books on
the Kabbalah and Hasidism, dissolving the heder, thus removing the
teachers [melammedin] who devour the children, and educating the children of Israel in Russian."[13]

The *haskalah* never marched through the Hillman household to such
martial music. Instead, it made itself felt first through the regular visits of
grandfather Paikin from Riga, that Latvian city whose thriving commercial and industrial life provided a natural environment for the flourishing
of *haskalah* ideas and values. A sense of the excitement of urban life
crossed the border along with gifts for his daughter and grandchildren
and his colorful stories of city characters.

The *haskalah* also entered the Hillman home, but well disguised in
religious costume. In Zagare, the centers of traditional Jewish learning
resisted the secular drift of things, controlled the two yeshivot in Old and
New Zagare, and commanded the loyalty of a great number of the Jewish
faithful. At the same time the province of Kovno, and its provincial
capital located just south of Zagare, became a center of a different kind
of Judaism, one reformulated to take account of rather than repress the
messages of Western enlightenment. One of the leading rabbinical scholars in all of Russia, Rabbi Issac Elkhanan Spektor of Kovno, was exemplary of a new kind of rabbi: open to educational and social change,
responsive to new pressures on his role as community leader. Another
rabbi, a native of Zagare, Israel Salanter, "Teacher of the Diaspora,"
founded the religious reform movement Musar in the mid-nineteenth

century and established a Musar yeshiva in Kovno. Musar made its partial peace with the *haskalah* by emphasizing that the serving of mankind was the highest form of service to God. It stressed that aspect of Jewish ethical tradition concerned with justice and *tikn olam*—improvement of the world. In that respect it was closely analogous to the Ethical Culture movement in America, and in fact Felix Adler, who later founded the Ethical Culture Society in New York, was influenced by Salanter. In combining traditional Talmudism with a certain pietistic social concern, Musar quickly exceeded the reach of the *haskalah* itself throughout Lithuania.

Musar was where Sidney Hillman's spiritual odyssey from orthodoxy to secularism began. The yeshiva of Slobodka, just across the Velikaya River from Kovno, was led by Nathan (Nota) Zevi Hirsch Frankel, "the Old Man of Slobodka." By the end of the century it had become the most renowned center of Musar teaching and scholarship in the Pale. It was also the yeshiva Hillman entered as a young graduate of the local Zagare *cheder*, destined, so at least his parents hoped, to become the newest in the line of Hillman rabbis—if not quite in the mold of his grandfather, Mordecai, a rabbi nonetheless.[14]

Even as a very young boy, Hillman had shown great promise, able at the age of eight to recite four or five pages of the Gemorrah from memory, for which his mother rewarded him at a penny a page. The Gemorrah was the highest stage of the *cheder* curriculum, and the precocious Hillman had mastered it well in advance of his classmates, promising a rapid rise up the ladder of scholarly achievement. For many young boys, the *cheder's* severe regimen, including corporal discipline, dreadful physical conditions, and long hours of remorseless rote learning, was onerous indeed. But Sidney immersed himself in Old Testament texts and soon became known as a solitary and contemplative scholar. On the basis of his remarkable scholastic accomplishments—by the age of thirteen he had committed to memory several volumes of the Talmud—Sidney, along with his older brother Joseph, was chosen by the elders of the Hillman rabbinical clan to go on to yeshiva. Thus began his studies at Slobodka in a shabby little town of the same name across the bridge from Kovno.

He carried with him the hopes of both his parents, in particular those of his mother, with whom he was especially close. As Samuel's business gradually dried up, Judith took it upon herself to open a small grocery store in the front room of the Hillman home. Besides caring for Sidney's three brothers and three sisters, she kept a cow, sold milk, and operated a small bakery, all the while displaying the same ingenious frugality characteristic of her own father, the Riga button dealer. She was a

ın of enormous energy. Yet Judith's labors were by no means un-
ʒal. For generations hard-working shtetl wives had supported Torah
ɔlars like Samuel, often by running small stores selling flour, barley,
sa.t, and other essentials. All of Judith's great exertions were especially
designed to allow "Simcha" (the joyous one), her favorite, to pursue the
rabbinical calling. A yeshiva boy was after all a future *sheyne,* and Judith
spent her few spare moments on Saturday afternoons reading to Simcha
and his siblings from the Bible and Jewish storybooks.

Judith was unaware, however, that Sidney's education had already
veered in a radically different direction even before he left home for
Slobodka. Partly in order to encourage their son's intellectual industri-
ousness, partly because he was precocious enough to exhaust the resources of the local *cheder* while still underage for the yeshiva, the
Hillmans brought a tutor into the home to teach the children Russian.
With the tutor, however, came more than books on Russian grammar;
there were also new books critical of the rabbinical outlook and political
books about democracy and critical of the Czarist regime. By the time the
Hillman elders decided Sidney and Joseph were ready for yeshiva, the
two boys were more than normally eager to go, seeking in the relatively
cosmopolitan world of Kovno (population 70,000) some escape from the
pious homilies of home.

Not long after the two boys left, the tutor's subversion was exposed.
Sidney's younger brother, Harry, apprenticed to a jeweler but quite attached to his older brother, was eager to follow him to yeshiva and the
wider world beyond Zagare. The tutor helped Harry steal money from his
father, enough to make the trip to Kovno, but was soon found out and
dismissed from the Hillman household. But the damage was already
done.[15]

At first Sidney dutifully absorbed Musar teachings: the inate goodness of man, his divinely inspired striving for a better world, and ethical
injunctions to help the poor. The "Old Man of Slobodka" was an appealing figure, by general consensus a saintly man who made it a custom
to give each of the yeshiva's students close personal attention. Despite
the liberal theology and tutorial concern, however, Hillman chafed at
the seminary regimen. Long days began and ended in prayer, punctuated
by four or five hours of sleep a night. The rest of the time was spent in
extended exercises in Biblical exegesis and painstaking attention to legal-
religious doctrine. On the one hand, the Musar yeshiva was itself critical
of the more medieval forms of rabbinical education. On the other, it still
considered subjects ranging from the Russian language and literature to
mathematics and the natural sciences to be impious and excluded them

from the curriculum. Such halfhearted liberalization only strengthened Hillman's interest in secular subjects.

Even apart from those explicitly secular interests first encouraged by his tutor at home, Hillman was drawn to that corner of the Jewish religious universe occupied by a type known as the "Lithuanian scholar." These Litvaks were known for their "cold, rationalistic mind." Averse to fanaticism or pedantry, repelled both by the ecstatic mysticism of the hasidim and the slavish regurgitation of the Biblical commentators, such scholars most often concentrated on the Hashen Mishpot—that portion of the religious code dealing with civil and criminal law. Hillman developed a greater interest in the laws of property than in ritual or ceremonial law. He was fascinated as well by the commentaries in the Talmud for which one needed to develop a quick-witted, logical, and polemical intelligence. Talmud study of that sort was often called "pilpul" (pepper) to suggest its sharpness, subtlety, and logical ingenuity. He loved to dabble in mathematics, algebra and geometry particularly, which called for a kind of mental rigor and acumen. Even his favorite forms of relaxation—debating secular issues, mathematical games, excited discussions of scientific articles, playing chess—were a kind of spiritual and mental calisthenics, enlarging his capacity for subtle argument and polemic that would serve him well later.[16]

Inside the confining walls of the Slobodka seminary there was less and less room for this intellectual style. Within a year of arriving at Slobodka, Hillman was taking Russian lessons in neighboring Kovno from Michael Zacharias. Although not much older than Sidney, Zacharias possessed a Russian education and the ambitions of a Jewish student denied further access to the Russian system of higher education. Such "externs," who spent years trying to gain entrance to the Russian university system, were quite common and formed a kind of intellectual *sans-culotterie* of frustrated ambitions and political resentments.

Lessons with Zacharias encouraged Hillman's scientific inclinations and apparently led him away from a budding interest in Zionism. Before long Sidney joined a semisecret *kruzhok* (study circle) run by Michael's uncle, Dr. Matis, a local chemist whose home also functioned as a clandestine headquarters for political and trade union activity organized by the General League of Jewish Workers of Lithuania, Poland, and Russia, better known as the Bund. The *kruzhki* amounted to a kind of "socialist haskalah" spreading rapidly throughout Russia, formed initially in reaction against the formalism, discipline, and essential irrelevance of the university curriculum. Typically, they were sponsored by already politically active adults like Dr. Matis.

It was in Dr. Matis's *kruzhok*, devoted to the study of literature, social philosophy, and political economy, that Hillman first read, in Russian translation, the works of Darwin, Marx, Mill, and Spencer. He was especially struck by the writings of the German socialist Ferdinand La-Salle, both by his vision of the reformist road to socialism and his pre-occupation with political power. Later Hillman recalled: "I remember well his work on the 'Constitution.' Rights of power make constitutions, not merely legislation." For a boy not much older than fifteen, all this talk of democracy and socialism, the reading and dissemination of pro-hibited foreign literature, and the air of secrecy and danger surrounding the *kruzhok* exerted an irresistible romantic appeal, compounded of real intellectual discovery and resistance to the structures of authority at home, at school, and in the great Russian state.[17]

Inevitably, the "Old Man of Slobodka" became aware of Hillman's illicit activities and at first attempted to bring the young rebel back into the fold. Hillman stubbornly resisted, determined to continue his studies in Russian and mathematics. Rabbi Frankel admonished Hillman for what he considered his "sinful" concern with secular subjects and wrote to Sidney's parents with the news of his transgressions. Judith and Samuel were mortified. Samuel wrote threatening to cut off his meager al-lowance unless Sidney immediately resumed his religious instruction and obeyed the rules of the yeshiva. Gently but firmly, Sidney informed his parents that he intended to pursue his new course, and that if necessary he would fend for himself in Kovno.[18]

In fact, he intended much more than that. Soon he recruited several fellow students from the Slobodka seminary into Dr. Matis's *kruzhok*. At the same time Dr. Matis, who managed to play a delicately diplomatic role in Hillman family affairs, provided Sidney room and board in his own home. In return Hillman performed, rather badly as it turned out, a series of menial tasks in the doctor's laboratory. For someone who was to spend his whole adult life in the labor movement, Hillman was re-markably inept at all forms of manual labor—a typical "yeshiva *bucher*"—but Dr. Matis was more than willing to allow the budding revolutionary to spend the great bulk of his time reading. Sidney thus explored the doctor's well-stocked library, occasionally finding the time to wash a bottle or clean a beaker. Clearly, he had little intention of becoming a chemist, as Dr. Matis related afterwards:

> His free time was spent at the secret meetings [of the Bund]. He was often called upon for revolutionary assignments. In this way he became involved in the revolutionary movement, to which he devoted himself with heart and soul.

Early in 1903 Hillman graduated, so to speak, from the *kruzhok* and joined the Bund. Initially, he carried out a series of minor if largely illegal tasks while participating in secret cultural and trade union meetings. One of his first assignments was to smuggle from one hiding place to another the group's prized hectograph machine, a primitive but invaluable device, the lifeline connecting the circle of Jewish students and intellectuals to the increasingly restive mass of Jewish artisans and laborers. Soon he was involved in efforts to organize the typesetters of Kovno and actively participated in one of their strikes.[19]

Kovno had for some years been a center of Bund organizing. A tailors' *kassa* (workers' self-help organization) there provided the organizational support for strikes in the early 1890s. Moreover, the second congress of the Bund was held in Kovno in 1898. Despite being a fortified town on the western border with a garrison of 30,000 troops, Kovno was a cauldron of antigovernment political activity, honeycombed with *kassy*, *kruzhki*, and highly disciplined Bund cells. It was not a place for mere gestures or halfhearted commitments.[20]

The break with the Hillman family heritage now seemed irrevocable. Sidney carefully avoided arguments with his parents, particularly with his father, who ceaselessly urged him to leave the Bund and with it his dreams of becoming a "politician." In his father's house, he would wear his philacteries and recite the daily prayers. But these had become hollow ceremonial gestures signifying nothing more than his continuing respect for his father.[21]

For Hillman, as for many ex-yeshiva students like him, joining the Bund was a kind of conversion experience. It ruptured ties to the past, including those to family and friends as well as to the ancestral religion. The Bund seemed an entirely separate moral universe, complete with its own educational and cultural institutions, its own songs, holidays, and rituals. Within it were fabricated new men, or rather new Jews, fighters who saw themselves as part of a moral, intellectual, and political vanguard, inflamed with a sense of personal mission, convinced of their historical significance. Yet the secular messianism of the Bund, its spiritual and symbolic vocabulary, bore a distinct family resemblance to a powerful current in traditional Jewish messianism which imagined the Messiah not as a god but as a man of the people, inspired by the prophets, whose mission it was to bring Utopia through reformed government. Redemption was not only inward and spiritual, but a public and historical event. In some respects, then, the Bund's break with the past was more apparent than real.[22]

Sidney's own transformation proceeded with great speed. Even before the outbreak of the Russian Revolution of 1905, he exhibited not only a total dedication but real capacities to lead. On May Day 1904 he led the first public demonstration by the Bund through the streets of Kovno. Arrested shortly thereafter, he spent the next several months in prison, where he was subjected to the usual brutalities of the Czarist gendarmerie. While there his education continued under the tutelage of fellow political prisoners, veteran organizers well-versed in the thought of Marx, LaSalle, Bebel, and Kropotkin, as well as the classical economists.

At first his parents knew nothing about his condition or the disposition of his case. But Samuel, together with Dr. Matis and with the help of a local lawyer, made repeated petitions for his release. Finally, in November, he was freed, returning to Zagare only to resume his revolutionary activity.

When the great wave of mass strikes swept over European Russia in the summer of 1905, Hillman was off organizing near the town of Reshitza on the Latvian border. By then he had become an organizer for the Menshevik wing of the Russian Social Democratic Party. He was arrested and imprisoned again in Kovno, but this second jailing was immensely more pleasurable than the first. Taking advantage of the momentary but incapacitating weakness of the regime, political prisoners had the run of the place, conducted regular classes, exchanged illegal books and newspapers with impunity, and announced political meetings with bulletins posted on prison walls. The tortures and hardships of a year earlier had been banished, along with a great deal of the autocracy's apparatus of repression. Finally, the Czar's general amnesty at the height of the insurrection in November 1905 allowed Hillman to return once again to Zagare. Before long he surfaced as a leader of a local uprising that culminated in the creation of a Zagare Committee of Public Safety.[23]

Those were exhilarating days, and although this revolutionary episode in Sidney's life lasted but a few short years, it was a formative experience that indelibly marked his ideas and character. It left him, at the age of nineteen, a dedicated labor organizer and political leader, prepared to subordinate personal interests to objectives he considered transcendent. Forever afterward, his public commitments would come before his private and family life. Moreover, while Hillman's role in the extraordinary historic drama of 1905 was relatively inconspicuous, he had nevertheless emerged as a figure of local consequence, confident of his abilities to organize and lead men under dire conditions and to command their respect and loyalty as a figure of moral authority. At a remarkably young age he had developed the political self-assurance, the courage that, along with a certain public presence, were to distinguish the rest of his career.

"He was an ardent idealist for the democratic revolution in Russia and showed much courage," his friend Michael Zacharias testified, "but even then he had a quite realistic or practical side." To the degree that Hillman immersed himself in the more pedestrian concerns of the local organizer, for whom leafleting, fundraising, avoiding the police, and haranguing small crowds of Jewish workers made up a day's work, the more remote seemed the airier theoretical problems of the Social Dem-ocratic movement. This "practical side" of Sidney Hillman, already ap-parent at the height of his revolutionary enthusiasm, was to help carry him to heights of political power in decidedly nonrevolutionary circum-stances.

Hillman's revolutionary experience marked him as a kind of marginal man—not, to be sure, in the same sense that his father, the merchant-*luftmensch*, was, but rather as a person straddling the cultural border. His rabbinical training was interrupted in midcourse, never to be resumed. Indeed, the contagion of revolution spread even inside the cloistered confines of the Slobodka seminary, where, amid the turmoil of 1905, students demanded greater intellectual freedom and were excommuni-cated by the "Old Man" for their trouble. This was not at all an atypical pattern for Jewish student radicals, especially among emigrés to the West, who disproportionately turned out to be the sons and daughters of can-tors, rabbis, Hebrew school teachers, and Talmudic scholars.[24]

Yet there endured in the character and psychological style of the newborn revolutionary something of the rabbi: an acute sense of the moral imperative, a painstaking attention to procedural and administra-tive order, a self-certainty dangerously close to arrogant self-righteousness (a charge later leveled at Hillman during his days of national promi-nence). The rabbinical analogy, however, can be carried too far. Hill-man would never show the obsessive concern for doctrinal purity otherwise characteristic of the talmudic radical. But to the extent that the Hillman rabbis, like all good traditional rabbis in the Pale, func-tioned as expounders and guardians of communal law, as practically oriented scholars, as arbiters of community life, to that degree at least Sidney Hillman's later recalling of his rabbinical heritage conveyed a psychological and social truth not belied by its factual imprecision.[25]

Hillman was also marginal to the world of secular learning, especially measured against the serious intellectual aspirations of his youth. In a formal sense, his education was scarcely begun and never completed, having been cut short by the revolution and the education of the streets. He would remain defensively conscious of this "inadequacy" for the rest of his life. Such unfinished scholars were so common in the Russian-Jewish social democratic movement that there were special names to describe them: "Half-intellectual," "demi-intellectual," or *polu-intelligent"* referred to ex-yeshiva students abruptly uprooted from the world of library and synagogue who proved especially adept at transmitting the theoretical precepts of Marxism to the mass of Jewish workers, thanks in particular to their mastery of the popular vernacular of yiddish.

While retaining an affinity and respect for more formal learning, "half-intellectuals" like Hillman dominated the Bund by the late 1890s. They distinguished themselves in practical work as expert organizers, agitators, administrators, and most of all as mediators between the movement's intellectual elite and its less enlightened constituency. They were doers, not thinkers, pragmatic in disposition and organizationally creative, but without the vulgar hostility to ideas and worship of the narrowly practical typical of American-style trade union careerists. Throughout his whole subsequent career, Sidney Hillman remained a "half-intellectual," committed first of all to the palpable dynamics of organized power and uninhibited by any prescribed beliefs that might obstruct the pursuit of that power, yet with a healthy respect for formal intellectual labor and eager to use the discoveries of Western social science to transform and presumably thereby "liberate" tradition-bound peoples.

If Hillman was driven by a distinctly hybrid set of cultural and ideological motivations, so too was the movement within which he came of age. The Bund itself could be called a mass movement of the marginal. While its official program calling for the eight-hour day, a democratic republic, full civil rights for Jews, and peace was ostensibly indistinguishable from the main currents of European social democracy, its rank and file embraced the modern ideology of the industrial proletariat partly in order to defend a much more ancient way of life.

The first Jewish "proletariat" was very much the residue of a disintegrating and impoverished artisan world, but one with a peculiar fecundity of its own. Right up to the outbreak of World War I craft employment continued to increase; the percentage of Jewish artisans was particularly high in the weaving, tailoring, shoemaking, tanning, and cabinetmaking trades. These were men tied by a thousand threads to their traditional fraternal associations, to what remained of their handicraft guilds, to the Yiddish language, and to religious ritual. Although it was a world familiar with organizational life, the traditional regulations characteristic of masters' guilds and journeymen's associations were at most only distantly similar to the precise terms of employment regarding wages, hours, and production quotas of the modern labor contract. Only recently had the Jewish craft guilds of Eastern Europe gained a certain autonomy from the elders of the Jewish community organized in their *kahals.* Furthermore, guild life was still marked to some degree by oligarchic tendencies, including ensconced hereditary privileges, restricted mobility, and social inequality.

To be sure, many poor and "enlightened" craftsmen were in deep rebellion against precisely those immemorial restrictions as well as against the predations of their Jewish employers. Some had been through their own "socialist *haskalah.*" More than half the delegates at the founding convention of the Bund in 1897 were artisans and workers with just that sort of educational background. But when this preindustrial proletariat erupted in a series of mass strikes and demonstrations during the 1890s, its aims were at least partly conservative in nature, hoping to preserve what was left, and perhaps recover some of what had been lost, of their social existence and identity as Jewish artisans. They were, much like Sidney Hillman himself, situated somewhere in between, on the margin between the twilight of one age and the dawn of another.

Thus it was that even apparently modern forms of Jewish worker protest could still be deeply touched by tradition. The first public demonstration of tobacco workers occurred in a factory in Grodno. The workers chose to delay the reading of the Torah at the synagogue to call attention to their grievances—essentially a way of shaming the evildoer by pillorying him before a public assembly of his coreligionists. That was a traditional right; anyone with a grievance against the community, against the rabbi, or against a private individual could, on the Sabbath morning just before the reading of the Scroll from the Ark, mount guard on the steps of the Ark and prevent its removal until he had his say. Similarly, bristle workers in Vilna swore on a Torah scroll not to scab; other strikers swore loyalty by a pair of phylacteries, while strikebreakers were pronounced *herem,* signifying excommunication.

It would be easy to exaggerate the extent to which the rank and file of the Jewish workers' movement was still entrapped by medieval custom and belief. Their great strikes also looked ahead to the future and "aimed at instituting 'modern' relations between employer and employee, relations based on contract, not on habit and whim." The *kassy* and the Bund were the agencies through which revolutionary politics and secular learning first reached large numbers. The Bund, always strongest among handicraft workers, was the incubator of a new morality and character structure that promoted self-discipline, social solidarity, and a sense of mission, one that helped supplant the age-old resignation and apathy of the shtetl.

Swept up in the movements against political autocracy, the stigmata of caste and religion, national discrimination, and the economics of the sweatshop, these declassed artisans—tailors, shoemakers, weavers, print-

ers, engravers, typesetters, watchmakers, carpenters—expressed, albeit
in the language of socialism, the historic aspirations of the third estate for
democracy, equality, and fraternity. Indeed, for a few short years, this
otherwise despised and benighted Jewish semiproletariat rose to a position of preeminence in the movement to transform Russian society and
politics. But it was a brief preeminence. The uprisings of the Jewish
handicraft workers were soon eclipsed by the activities of Russian workers
in modern centers of industry, transportation, and commerce, which in
the end were truly decisive in determining Russia's fate.[26]

Immersion in this deeply ambivalent political culture reinforced Hillman's own marginality. Above all, it demanded a talent for communicating across cultural boundaries that would prove invaluable time and
again throughout the course of his life. By the age of nineteen Hillman
was a thoroughly secularized Jewish half-intellectual working in a far
more parochial milieu of Jewish workers, obliged to translate the message
of the "socialist *haskalah*" into terms more congenial to the continuing
ethnic concerns of his constituents. Jewish workers were at least equally
if not more absorbed by their present predicament as Jews and as artisans
as they were by the more hypothetical problems of their future as an
industrial proletariat.

The tension between the universalist political culture of the socialist
West and the more particularist, ethno-artisan culture of the Pale ran
right through the heart of the Bund, causing a continuing series of
factional battles and a highly erratic relationship with the main centers
of the Russian Social Democratic Party, with which the Bund was in-
termittently affiliated. Many of the half-intellectuals, precisely because of
their more earthbound attachments to the day-to-day concerns of the
Jewish worker, helped create a political culture that turned out to be as
much nationalist, if not actually Zionist, as it was socialist.[27]

Hillman, however, while he shared a great deal with his fellow
half-intellectuals, and while he was indebted most of all to the Bund for
his practical political education, nevertheless identified himself as a Menshevik by 1905. Often enough, mere accidents of time and place determined whether a Jewish social democrat worked for the Bund among the
Jewish proletariat or as a Menshevik among Russian workers. But Hillman quite self-consciously identified with Julius O. Martov, not only a
leading Menshevik but in this period the chief opponent of Bundist
nationalism. His disinclination to empathize with the immediate concerns of the Jewish workers as Jews was an attitude that would distinctively color his behavior in America. It set him apart from his fellow
half-intellectuals who migrated to the New World, and in some measure
it estranged him from the circumscribed world of Jewish socialism and

labor politics centered in New York. It would as well help turn his attention to those more cosmopolitan circles of Progressive reform in America that would make of him a figure of national rather than ethnic significance in the world of labor politics.[28]

Whatever the ambiguity of Hillman's party affiliations, standing as they did midway between the Mensheviks and the Bundists, they exerted a lasting influence on his political and organizational tactics and style. Mixing together marginal Jewish intellectuals and marginal Jewish workers was an incendiary social chemistry, producing explosions not only across the surface of Russian society but also deep within the souls of its participants. If the Bund was, for both the half-intellectual and the declassed craftsman, a rite of passage into a more modern order of things, it did not simply make of them democratic politicians and trade unionists indistinguishable from their counterparts in the West.

Thus, while the Bund may have seen itself as a messenger of enlightenment and emancipation, it did not expect its message to be received with spontaneous enthusiasm or to circulate freely through the open channels of democratic participation. Like its parent organization, the Russian Social-Democratic Labor Party (RSDLP), the Bund was a highly centralized, even on occasion an elitist and secretive, apparatus. It employed such methods not only to protect its own internal discipline and political integrity but also applied them in the wider arena of trade union and mass political organization. Its centralized, secretive approach, which often depended on an informal nucleus of trusted cadre to carry out the policy directives of the top leadership, may have had it origins in the clandestine conditions in which the Bund and the rest of the revolutionary movement were frequently forced to operate, but it proved to be entirely transportable to the New World, where Hillman was to use it repeatedly. Like the half-intellectuals who created and perfected it, the Bund's organizational inventiveness stood halfway between the rationalized and rule-dominated structures of modern bureaucracy and the more personalized, patriarchal command structures characteristic of traditional societies. Thanks to its flexibility and responsiveness to the aspirations of its constituents, this organizational device of the Russian revolution contributed measurably to Sidney Hillman's success in America.

Hillman's whole strategic approach to trade unionism was also permanently colored by his experience in the Pale. The Bund functioned simultaneously as a centralized political organization and as a mass movement, both as a political party and as a trade union (or alliance of trade unions). That was a pattern common throughout much of Western Europe but quite rare in America, where political neutrality was often considered a preferred virtue if not an inviolable principle. Hillman would never give up trying to integrate industrial and political objectives; it was to be the *sine qua non* of his strategy in the United States, but one he was to discover immeasurably more difficult to implement there than in the Russian Empire.[29]

Ironically, it was another facet of his Bundist heritage that found in industrializing America a more hospitable environment than it had in underdeveloped Russia. Bundists and Mensheviks both assigned a progressive political role to the bourgeoisie—merchants, manufacturers, and middle-class intellectuals. In theory such alliances across classes were possible, perhaps unavoidable, in the struggle against Czarism and for democracy. But they were presumed to be far less likely, necessary, or even acceptable in the capitalist West. In practice, however, allying the workers with the Russian bourgeoisie proved problematical at best, whereas circles of "progressive capitalists" not only thrived in America but became Hillman's close collaborators in his most important trade union and political undertakings.

All that, however, lay in the future. The immediate effect of those few feverish years of revolutionary excitement was to commit Hillman to the life of the organizer and extinguish most of his lingering academic or professional aspirations. Moreover, the relationship established between the young half-intellectual and a "worker-intellectual" elite would be transplanted, practically intact, halfway round the world, ready to resume its improbable quest for individual autonomy and social liberation.

Perhaps "transplanted" is too pacific a word to describe the violent uprooting that accompanied the government's repressive counterrevolution in 1906. Arrests, pogroms, and police raids drove the movement back underground. Strikes and demonstrations became all but impossible. Hillman was once again a wanted man in Zagare and spent most of his time in hiding outside the town. With the dissolution of the Duma, the Czarist parliament, in mid-1906, the exodus of revolutionaries began in earnest. Hillman resisted the inevitable: "I will leave only when there is no more hope of doing anything here." By the fall, the Czar had done everything to abolish all such hope. In October Sidney Hillman fled the Pale and traveled, on a false passport, through Germany to join his uncle and two brothers already living in England. Hope, were it to be renewed at all, would have to find its seedbed among the milling crowds of Russian exiles collecting in the great industrial cities of the West.[30]

TWO

"Pauper Against Pauper"

A life of secrecy and danger, trading in banned books and contraband ideas imported from abroad, fired from within by a missionary zeal that lay claim to the world, an exalted worldliness freed of the confinements of kin and community: Sidney Hillman, cosmopolitan revolutionary. Yet he arrived in the West an utter provincial. He was still "Hilkie," a Russian Jew, one of a million "new immigrants" and a green one at that, perhaps with some potential to become a leader of his people, but certainly only *his* people, a voice of the ghetto but not of the world beyond it. Yiddishkeit, his native culture, perhaps the most cosmopolitan and secular of ethnic outlooks, gave him a precocious wisdom and a sense of irony born out of the poverty, fortitude, religious idealism, and sheer materialistic striving of his brethren of the modern diaspora. But it was still a claustrophobic wisdom, and Hillman was still a cultural provincial. Within a few short years of his departure from Russia, Hillman helped found and lead a union of clothing workers born out of mass insurrection, but it was nonetheless one of a cluster of "Jewish" trade unions in the "Jewish" needle trades with its heart and home in the peculiar self-enclosed world of "Jewish" socialism and labor radicalism.*

Hillman might easily have remained a rather minor figure of strictly local significance, the leader of an ethnic union in the "rag trade,"

---

* "Pauper against pauper" was a phrase of Abraham Leisen, quoted in Ezra Mendelsohn, *The Class Struggle in the Pale: The Formative Years of the Jewish Workers Movement in Tsarist Russia* (New York, 1970), p. 59.

21

removed from the main currents of industrial society and politics. His eventual opportunity to enter a far wider universe of national influence and power was due to those great reconfigurations of the American industrial and political order culminating in the New Deal. But it was thanks to his drive to succeed and to other equally compelling traits of character that Hillman managed to recognize and seize his historic opportunity. Even during his first few unpromising years in the New World some of those qualities were apparent.

Sidney left behind him in the Pale his rabbinical heritage. But the mercantile wing of the Hillman family awaited him in England. His uncle, Charles Paiken, was a prospering furniture dealer and textile broker in Manchester. He soon realized his nephew was quick-witted, conscientious, and self-disciplined, qualities bent just as easily to the purposes of business as to revolutionary politics. Within weeks of his arrival, Uncle Charles offered Sidney a position in the family firm and began urging him to give up his "adolescent dreams" of revolution.[1]

Hillman was hardly tempted. His commitment to the causes of Jewish trade unionism and socialism was firm. But his uncle had nevertheless sensed in Sidney's character a single-minded will to succeed that was not to be denied. It was not money that excited him. He was always to live modestly, never owned a car, and drew a salary paltry in comparison to his peers. But he did not disdain mundane success in other terms. A close associate later recalled: "Hillman had the American appreciation of success which was heightened by an awareness of his foreignness, particularly being a Jew." This itch to rise in the world generated a remarkable force of personality, nervous energy, and restless creativity.[2]

During his nine-month stay in England, however, the desire found no outlet. Hillman lived with his younger brother, Harry, now working as a skilled jeweler and carrying the burden of their joint support. Sidney spent most of his time either in endless discussions with his fellow exiles about the current state and future of the movement back in Russia or alone at home reading. His only real friend, aside from Harry, was a former comrade from the Bund.

The refugee revolutionaries, assembled in their own exclusive coffeehouses and lecture halls, sealed themselves off from the wider world of British labor politics. Hillman did attend a few British trade union meetings but seems to have had little contact with the small but active organizations of Jewish immigrant workers. He was intrigued by the British parliamentary system, but otherwise his time in England left little impression. He had considerable difficulty mastering the new language, and in any event his overriding concern was with Russian events. As the

Russian situation grew ever gloomier, he decided to leave Britain for America, where his political tutor from the Bund, Michael Zacharias, had preceded him.[3]

On August 8, 1907, he arrived in New York aboard the Cunard liner *Cedric*, his devoted younger brother Harry in tow. He couldn't have chosen a more inauspicious moment. The country was in the midst of a severe financial panic and depression. Practically penniless, Hillman took what odd jobs he could find but most of the time found himself unemployed. In the Pale, he had of course lived and worked among a desperately poor Jewish working class, but he had suffered its privations voluntarily, so to speak. That had been the deliberate, secretly romantic choice of a revolutionary student. Suddenly he was without any visible means of support, rudely ignored by a world with little use or respect for the arcane learning and intellectual skills he brought with him; no longer a partisan outsider but a permanent resident among the down and out. He gladly accepted the invitation of his friend Zacharias, who was now a pharmacist, to come to Chicago, where there was the prospect of a decent job. At least there was a place to stay with Zacharias's friends, the Halperns.[4]

The job market in Chicago did in fact turn out to be better; never again would he face the destitution he had in New York. But it was a marginal improvement at best, and for the next five years, when he wasn't laid off or unemployed, Hillman worked sixty to seventy hours a week at menial tasks for miserable pay. At first he worked for a very short time as an order picker in a warehouse for $6 a week. Then he spent nearly two years as a stock clerk and wrapper of packages for somewhat more money in the infants' wear department of Sears, Roebuck & Company. During a seasonal downturn in business in the spring of 1909, he was sacked at Sears. Soon thereafter he went to work as an apprentice cutter for Hart, Schaffner & Marx (HSM), his last job as a wage-earner and the one that permanently redirected the course of his life.[5]

Those were years of enormous frustration and unhappiness for Hillman. Michael Zacharias remembered that even then Hillman "believed in his star," that he therefore felt acutely the wasting of his special talents and capacities. He was infused with the ethos of *tachlis*—a need to fulfill grand objectives and ultimate ends—a disposition that perfectly combined social idealism with personal ambition. The revolution had presented a limitless horizon for the working out of his *tachlis*. All of a sudden there was nothing but the cheerless prospect of an interminably slow, lifelong crawl up the ladder of occupational advance. So deep was his inner drive to succeed, however, that for a time he even tried to inflate the significance of his lowly positions by associating them with the prestigious names of Sears and HSM. Charles Paiken had by no means misread his nephew, who wrote to report: "I am working for one of the biggest houses in the United States. There are more than 8000 employees. I am getting $8 a week and the work is not hard. It is a fine place to work. And I am much surprised that management is satisfied with my work. I expect a raise in the near future."[6]

Hillman was rightly surprised at management's satisfaction; according to his friends, he was as inept at wrapping packages as he had been as a chemist's assistant in Dr. Matis's lab. He was right as well about the raise, but it turned out to be an absurdly small one, certainly not large enough to support a real rise in the world. Still, he continued to tell his uncle of his determination to achieve a "real position" in Chicago. He enrolled in night school at the Hebrew Institute to study English and spoke of attending a secular night school, even of preparing himself for the law. "If it will be possible I'll go to night college, when I will know more the language."[7]

While halfheartedly pursuing pipe dreams of professional advance, he resumed the solitary intellectual life of his youth. In the evenings and during periodic bouts of unemployment, he spent long hours alone reading, mainly in Russian literature, especially Dostoyevsky (Ibsen was a favorite among non-Russians), politics, history, and biography, drinking strong tea, and chain-smoking. He was entirely self-effacing, careless about his food and dress, and self-absorbed. When he wasn't in his room reading he made regular visits to the Chicago Symphony and the opera, sitting up in the gallery of Orchestra Hall by himself. Occasionally, he attended Sunday morning socialist lectures at the Garrick Theater, and he became an habitué of the public library.[8]

There was more to all of this than a lonely foreign student's pursuit of enlightenment and high culture, more even than the revolutionary half-intellectual's attempt to catch up on an education long deferred. It was as well a quest for some way out of the occupational ghetto in which he found himself trapped, a goading need to live up to the loftier expectations of his youth and not to suffer forever in some grimy oblivion.

And he was indeed suffering, morally above all else. His work produced a festering sense of indignity, of lost autonomy and self-respect. These were attitudes universally characteristic of declassed intellectuals, as well as skilled artisans and industrial workers who often went on to become dedicated revolutionaries and pioneer trade union organizers. Testifying a few years later before the U.S. Commission on Industrial Relations, Hillman recalled more than just the low wages and long hours customary at Sears:

I especially recall the feeling of fear besides the wages . . . the constant fear of the employee of being discharged without cause at all. There really was no cause at all sometimes. The floor boss, as we called him, did not like a particular girl (Sears employed about 7000 women) or a man, and out they went . . . . I remember we tried, all of us, to get into the good graces of the floor boss."

It was in essence a situation about which "I do not believe it is possible to have the full feeling of manhood." Recollecting this period of life in a letter to a friend a few years later, he described himself as "one who met all kinds of disappointments," who felt a profound humiliation at being denied "the opportunity of doing things that I consider more important than anything else." On a postcard from his mother in the summer of 1909, he scrawled a note to himself that captured both his depression and his growing desire to live up to "our values of life." "Devotion and love your parents can give you but peace you must find yourself. When the crown is on you peace can then be found in the minds of your parents too."[9]

Just about the time he wrote that private lament, his situation began to brighten, almost imperceptibly at first. He moved, this time to the home of Molly Zwhilshi, a Yiddish matriarch from Kiev, and into the neighborhood center of Jewish cultural and political life in Chicago. Molly's home became a haven for young, solitary immigrants who together formed an extended family of sorts. One of them, Bessie Abramovitz, would later become Sidney's wife. It was also in the summer of 1909, when idle again, that he applied for work at HSM on the recommendation of a friend in the Zwhilshi household.

At first little about his predicament changed. Hired as an apprentice cutter, he served without pay for the first six weeks (working without pay or actually paying for one's first job to "learn" was in fact quite common). Thereafter, assuming he succeeded in mastering the craft, he would command the princely sum of $6 a week, with promises, which soon proved empty, of future advances. For ten hours a day he wielded an ungainly cutter's shears, attempting to cut piles or "lays" of cloth ten, twelve, or more layers thick, to conform precisely to the outline traced on paper patterns. It required a physical dexterity and hand–eye coordination that strained Hillman's capabilities. Later on, his legendary incompetence became the object of friendly amusement among his colleagues, but at the time it led to abrasive relations with his foremen. He grew immediately angry when reprimanded for his actual faults and positively furious when a supervisor abused his authority by holding him liable for mistakes he hadn't committed. The humiliations accumulated quickly and inevitably: "I remember when I made the first complaint and I packed up my tools and went out." He couldn't bear the insults, but being out of work was hardly a realistic alternative, so he was back on the job a few weeks later. The feeling of violated dignity, however, wouldn't go away. It was a visceral conviction that he and his fellow workers were "not treated . . . like human beings."[10]

Hart, Schaffner & Marx had a well-deserved reputation for Prussian-style management, but as a matter of fact the company was a distinct cut above most of the rest of the garment industry with respect to wages, hours, and working conditions. Measured against the standards prevailing elsewhere, it was a model enterprise in many ways, modern in its technology and division of labor, sophisticated in its marketing practices, well ahead of its competitors in its management procedures—in all areas, that is, except its relations with its own workforce, and even there its record was not unrelievably bad. The average weekly wage in 1910 was $8.33, better than the norm for the rest of the industry. Joseph Schaffner and Harry Hart prided themselves on the firm's modern, sanitary work-shops, obviously superior to the commonplace filth of the sweatshop.[11]

It turned out to be of the greatest significance that Sidney Hillman went to work here and not somewhere else. The company occupied a special position in the industry, one it shared with a small number of other elite firms engaged in the manufacture of better-quality men's clothing. This "primary sector" of the industry was drastically different from the "secondary sector," composed of many small, technically prim-itive firms and tenement workshops. The differences separating the two sectors were not merely economic but broadly cultural as well and helped shape Hillman's approach to industrial labor relations and labor politics in America.

For years the needle trades comprised a protean sea of tiny enter-prises. They inhabited an economic underworld where chiseling, subter-fuge, and tainted goods were the common currency. Existing perilously close to the edge of commercial oblivion, such small shops were caught up in economic rivalries so intense that they frequently became self-destructive. The difference between victory and defeat in the continuous all-out effort to undercut the competition often depended on practically infinitesimal savings in the costs of doing business, and no cost was more important or more susceptible to cutting than that expended on labor. The petty producer defended his razor-thin margin of profit by means both legitimate and shady, but especially by exerting a constant down-ward pressure on wages and working conditions.

Hence the sweatshop, employing great numbers of impoverished immigrants, including women and children, who worked long hours at low wages in the gloom and dirt of tenement workshops; in badly ventilated, incendiary lofts; or in the cramped quarters of their own apartments. They survived, barely, by combining collective family labor with an extraordinary frugality and an occasional assist from ethnic and religious charities. Testifying before the U.S. Industrial Commission in 1899, Florence Kelley noted that homeworkers in the industry were unable to support themselves without charity. She reported on children "whom I have known to work six months for nothing with the understanding they would later get $1 a week." In 1914 New York City estimated a family of three or four required at least $800 to $875 a year to survive. Most garment workers earned less. Somewhere between 15 and 30 percent were "learners," earning from $3 to $6 a week. Half the workforce earned between $10 and $12 a week and in the busy season commonly labored for sixty hours and sometimes as many as eighty.[12]

Some of these small businesses were contract shops that produced parts of the final product—pants, vests, suits, coats—for other "inside" manufacturers who designed, cut, assembled, and sold the finished garment. Contractors were not only small but invariably undercapitalized and unaware of the most elementary methods of modern business, such as simple cost accounting. Often themselves refugees from the decomposing world of handicraft production in the Pale, they often lived as workers by day and petty entrepreneurs by night. They had mastered, perforce, an extraordinary variety of strategies for economic survival: "An unscrupulous contractor regards no basement as too dark, no stable loft as too foul, no rear shanty too provisional, no tenement room too small for his workroom as these conditions imply low rental. Hence these shops abound in the worst of the foreign districts," Jane Addams commented in 1910.[13]

The contractor avoided heavy fixed costs in machinery, relied on muscle power rather than electricity, and disbanded his workforce as orders slackened during the industry's prolonged slow seasons in the spring and fall. Both contractors and other petty manufacturers exploited the personal relations they maintained with their workers, relations based on kinship, birthplace, and religion. It allowed them to secure the best mechanics and to assemble out of the pools of cheap ghetto labor teams of workers from informal neighborhood groups. Such informal labor markets—like the famous *chazer mark* ("pig market") at Hester and Essex streets in New York or more specialized labor exchanges like the "pressers market" at Ludlow and Grand—were simply New World imitations of the *birzhe* or open-air labor exchange that had operated for generations in the Pale.[14]

Neighborhood work teams were deployed in a simple form of group production known as the "task system," brought to the United States from England by Russian-Jewish contractors in the 1880s. The production team was normally expected to complete its "task" in a week, and owners tended simply to add garments to the "weekly task" as a way of cutting the team's wages. An industrial labor relations investigator, William Leiserson, described the way the "task system" operated:

> There would be a team or "set" composed of a Baster, Half Baster, Operator, Helper, Finisher, Trimmer, Bushelman, and Presser. All these were paid by the week, but the team had to turn out a certain amount of work every day. The contractor took advantage of the absence of the union and constantly added to the day's task. Originally, it had been nine coats a day. It rose to ten and fourteen, then up to eighteen and twenty. Men often came to work at 4 A.M. Ten o'clock at night would usually see the day's task done. But if not, the team would work till midnight or until their powers exhausted. . . . Thus a man who had worked six days of fifteen to eighteen hours might get at the end of the week three and a half to four days pay.

Tenement house sweatshops were also organized according to the "task system." There, women and children were employed at wages 25 percent lower than the rate prevailing in the rest of the industry and for as much as eighteen hours a day. In one Chicago sweatshop an inspector found twenty-nine people and their machines crammed into a room 20 by 28 feet. In another, four men and three women were discovered toiling in a room 14 feet square in a low, dark, fetid basement: "Room contained four machines, stove with fire in it . . . air was intolerably bad; folding doors were open between this shop room and the living room in which Darwut and wife slept and eat and cook and keep boarders; the boarders (two) slept in a low room off shop, unlighted and unventilated." Florence Kelley, working in conjunction with Hull House and the Chicago Trades Assembly to wipe out the "sweating system," wrote to Frederick Engels in 1892 that "the filth and overcrowding are worse than I have seen outside of Naples and the East Side of New York . . . making possible child labor in most cruel forms and rendering tenement house manufacturing of clothing a deadly danger to the whole community." Despite legislative efforts to abolish the system, sweatshop operators successfully dodged the law, and in 1911 there were still 13,000 homework tenements functioning in New York.[15]

Firms in this "secondary sector" were microscopic in size, often employing no more than a few workers, most of the time between six and twenty. Entering the industry in some proprietary way was remarkably easy. Ambitious cutters, salesmen, and others could set themselves up in business, merely by renting a small loft and a cutting table, hiring a cutter if necessary, and shipping out the cut-up cloth to contractors, whose level of capitalization might be no greater than their own. But the cutthroat nature of the trade made it easy to leave the business just as unceremoniously. Bankruptcies were epidemic, and the average life expectancy of a men's clothing firm was seven years. Such enterprises lasted only as long as their desperate hunger for business did not lead them to sell at prices below the level of mere survival.

While larger manufacturers might resent their competition, they nonetheless depended on the efflorescence of petty producers and contractors, especially during the rush seasons, to relieve them of overhead expenses, unpredictable fluctuations in costs, and the anxieties of supervising a sometimes intractable labor force. Thus, the singular advantage of the system was its flexibility. Small manufacturers and contractors produced on a strictly rush-order basis and only after the retailer had placed his order. Because they tended to specialize, contractors sometimes employed highly skilled workers—cutters, pressers, basters, and pocketmakers with a more general, all-around knowledge of tailoring. But work was haphazardly organized, varied widely in quality, frequently arrived late, and often had to be returned. Small shops generally were seldom sanitary, lacked sufficient light and air, and constituted a menace to workers. Garment workers were particularly vulnerable to tuberculosis and other pulmonary diseases, to rheumatism, and to various skin ailments due to the poisonous dyes in the cloth. Even consumers were put at risk to the extent that petty producers relied on homeworkers to perform unskilled operations in tenements where scarlet fever, diphtheria, and measles were prevalent.[16]

This mass of petty producers, contractors, and worker-entrepreneurs in cities like New York, Philadelphia, and Boston dominated the market. Their antique forms of production were strikingly at odds with those trends in technology, the organization of work, and corporate management characteristic of industry not only elsewhere in the national economy but even within the garment trade itself.

HSM was perhaps the best known of a select group of companies whose scale of operations, level of capital investment, technological complexity, and rationalized systems of management placed them recognizably in the twentieth century. This more modern "primary sector" of the industry, while much smaller in numbers, was experiencing its most rapid period of growth when Hillman first went to work for HSM. These firms, including Hickey-Freeman in Rochester, Kuppenheimer and Society Brand in Chicago, Joseph & Feiss in Cleveland, and Sonneborn's in Baltimore, tended to produce medium- and high-priced qual-

ity clothing, which supplied the more predictable component of the
market, leaving to the small-time operators the far more erratic mass
market for cheaper ready-to-wear. The large-volume production and sizable labor forces (HSM employed 10,000) of these elite firms demanded
a continuity and stability in the production process that would permit
reasonable cost estimates, advance planning, and some modicum of control over the oscillations of the market. Management was acutely aware,
as were corporate leaderships in the modern mass production sector of
the wider economy, of the need for a high volume to move continuously
through a plant in order to maximize the profitable use of fixed capital,
materials, and energy. N. I. Stone, labor manager for Hickey-Freeman,
noted that the normal pattern of intermittent, seasonal production was
not only socially harmful but also bad for businessmen, who might otherwise benefit from continuous operations, especially those with "plants
having a large overhead expense, a considerable part of which is in the
nature of fixed charges which cannot be eliminated while the plant is
temporarily shut down." As they matured around the turn of the century,
these elite firms often developed familial and more impersonal connections with mass retailers, with other large manufacturers, and an occasion with financial interests having assets in the clothing business.[17]

At the time of Hillman's employment there, HSM carried out its
manufacturing almost entirely on its own premises, having purchased by
1905 forty-eight former sweatshops and brought their activities under its
centralized supervision. One-time contractors sold their equipment to
HSM and became the company's foremen. The firm pioneered in adopting a system of standardized pricing and was the first to engage in national advertising in 1897. Its system of volume production was achieved
through a series of demometric studies, conducted in 1906, which established fourteen basic male body types, which were then translated
into 253 specialty sizes and shapes. Along with other advanced firms in
Chicago, Baltimore, and Rochester, it had developed an extensive subdivision and simplification of tasks so that, for example, it required 150
separate operations to produce a coat at HSM. Indeed, this modern
sector generally depended much more heavily on semiskilled and unskilled labor than did its premodern handicraft cousin.[18]

Apparently different in every way, the actual experience of working
in either sector was oppressively similar. Hours ranged from an average of
fifty-four in those markets dominated by the "inside shop" to fifty-eight
in cities like New York, where petty producers flourished. Women workers earned on the average between $4 and $8 a week, while wages for
men were about 40 percent higher. The situation facing homeworkers,
however, was considerably bleaker. In Chicago for example, 45 percent

of the home finishers earned less than $4 a week in 1911, and nearly 10 percent earned less than $2. Homework therefore became almost by necessity a system of family exploitation in which young children were employed as helpers at night, on weekends, or after school, assuming they were permitted to attend school.

Of course, homework was not invented in America. It had been quite common, especially among Orthodox Jews in the Pale, for some time, so it was rather easily transplanted to New York, Chicago, Philadelphia, and other centers of Jewish immigration. It was equally prevalent among Italian women, for whom cultural taboos often prevented work outside the home, as well as for the wives of German skilled tailors, who for at least two generations had performed the less skilled tasks during the industry's domestic outwork phase. Investigators reported appalling conditions for homeworkers ranging from malnourishment to anemia and alarming rates of infant mortality. But manufacturers large and small found it commercially useful as a way of escaping burdensome overhead expenses—rent, lighting, fuel, furniture, and shop supervision.

A region of small houses on the Northwest side of Chicago, sunk a whole floor beneath the level of the sidewalk, contained "haggard, sick-looking Sicilian and Southern Italian women sewing anxiously." Almost all home finishing of garments was done in this neighborhood, in "close ill-smelling rooms, fluttering with hostility and badly washed damp underclothes, crowded with half-sick, restless babies, and scattered with piles of finished and unfinished trousers and the remnants of a cold dinner, bread crumbs, banana peels, and sour pickle drippings." Bohemian women doing finishing work with a sewing machine earned about 60 cents a day by stitching coats at 10 cents a pair, but the Bohemians were clearly the elite among homeworkers, living "in good health and . . . in a mortgaged house of their own kept scrupulously clean." Still, family members in such a house might stitch "from before 6 o'clock in the morning till after 10 at night."[19]

Contractors were sometimes fly-by-night hustlers, so well known for absconding with their employees' wages that it was not uncommon for the workers to seize the shop's goods as security. Because contractors were at the mercy of larger inside manufacturers and were under intense pressure to meet rush-order deadlines, they were best known for speeding up their workers. A skilled baster from Russia working for a contractor commented: "We are compelled to work for the inside shops and speed our life out."

In many smaller shops it had long been the custom for workers to own or rent their own machines, and on occasion to furnish trimmings, thread, buttons, and even fuel for heating the huge pressing irons. On top of that, workers were frequently fined for their production mistakes. Thus if a pocketmaker, say, damaged a pair of pants, she was forced to buy the pants at their regular wholesale price, despite the fact that pocketmakers were paid about 7 cents for each pair of pants they worked on. Similar penalties were exacted for the loss of a bobbin or a needle. In one instance a tailor earning $14 a week slightly damaged a pair of pants and was charged $12 by the company.[20]

In factories the pressure of the new industrial regimen was traumatic for many immigrants accustomed to traditional handicraft patterns of intense bouts of labor followed by periods of relaxation and play. The intrusion of the factory clock and the relentless rhythm of industrial work not only destroyed an older sense of daily time but played havoc as well with the Jewish calendar and its traditional holidays, especially offending Orthodox patriarchs attempting to preserve the spiritual integrity of the family. Hours of work were entirely unregulated and potentially endless. One worker explained, "You stopped when the boss told you to stop." Morris Rosenfeld, a pants presser and Yiddish poet, captured the relentless rhythm of the time clock and its assault on an ancient sense of time:

> The clock in the workshop—it rests not a moment;
> It points on, and ticks on; eternity-time;
> Once someone told me the clock had a meaning,—
> In pointing and ticking had a reason and rhyme . . .
> At times, when I listen, I hear the clock
> plainly;—The reason of old—the old meaning—is gone.
> The maddening pendulum urges me forward
> To labor and still labor on.
> The tick of the clock is the boss in his anger.
> The face of the clock has the eye of the foe.
> The clock—I shudder—Dost hear how it draws me?
> It calls me "Machine" and it cries to me "Sew!"[21]

In large factories like HSM, Hillman's experience with the foreman was repeated countless times. Indeed, not only the foreman but even his assistants were dreaded by the workers, since they were possessed of tremendous power not only over the quality of work but especially with regard to discipline. Miss A., a button sewer at HSM, spoke of what it was like:

They used to work sixteen hours at HSM from half past six in the morning to nine o'clock at night . . . These girls cannot make a lot of money because they are reducing the price from month to month . . . The girls buy five, six, seven thousand needles. They give them the thread and wax and they thread the needles at night. They are threading until twelve or one o'clock at night after coming home at six o'clock at night. They just get their supper and then thread needles . . . In the slack season we sit maybe seven hours in the shop and do nothing . . . until the boss gets tired and wants to go home.

Miss D.'s testimony vividly illustrates how even in an apparently rationalized operation like that of HSM, the actual organization and conditions of work remained remarkably irregular, inconsistent, and subject to the personal whim of the foreman: "I learned that in one shop they paid more than in another [both were owned by HSM]. When I asked why do you take less than in other shops they said: 'What can we do when the foreman cuts the wages?' If anybody dared protest, they were put on the blacklist and could not get a job in the shop, in any of the 44 shops." Departments were ruled as if they were the personal fiefdoms of the foremen. Miss E., working as a pocketmaker, was approached by her foreman. "Listen what I will do. You learn somebody else on the machine and don't tell her you used to get 50 cents (per hundred pockets) and tell her 40 cents." Miss E. refused: "No, she's just the same as me. I will tell her just the same." The foreman's harassment continued until Miss E. was forced to leave the shop.

Miss H. described a foreman who deliberately used Italian workers to undercut the higher wages paid to Jewish women: "Afterwards," the foreman said, "we will get Italian people who have just come from the old country and don't know much. Try to get them as cheap as you can. These are greenhorns. . . . The foolish people will pay the smart."[22]

Sidney Hillman thus found himself at work in an industry whose labor practices bordered on the medieval and whose commerce and culture comprised a bewildering array of dualities, paradoxes, and ironies.

Relationships at work, for example, might be familial, communal, or utterly impersonal, depending on where one looked. Artisans plying ancient skills bequeathed by their ancestors and mastered over a lifetime worked alongside "Columbus tailors," recently arrived semiskilled immigrant hands, chained to industrial routines they had mastered in a week. At home, mothers and children toiled for the greater good of the patriarchal household. In tiny shops landsmen (immigrants from the same native shtetl) worked with and for fellow landsmen, bound by ties of kinship and village of origin, where highly personalized, face-to-face dealings between landsman-employee and landsman-employer continued past the threshold of the workshop and into the sanctified space of the neighborhood temple. There, as likely as not, some emblem of their common craft hung above the synagogue door, and the boss could be

counted on to attend his employees' bar mitzvahs, weddings, and funer-
als. Meanwhile, under factory roofs, where work was stripped of much of
its familial, communal, and handicraft character, relationships tended to
become not only impersonal but distant and mysterious. Hillman commented about HSM: "As a matter of fact the working people do not
know who is the real head of the firm, only the people directly above
them."[23]

Mysterious as well was the evolution of the industry. It reversed the
expected linear progression from preindustrial handicraft production to
the modern factory. The proliferation of small, unmechanized shops
where owners were also workers and where all workers were *landsleit*
actually occurred decades after the emergence of the first true garment
factories in the 1870s. And these primitive operations continued to
flourish, like some incongruous growth, alongside firms powered by electricity, organized according to the principles of scientific management,
and administered much like any other modern corporation. Stranger still
was the fact that even within the confines of these otherwise quite
up-to-date corporate giants nested survivals of the handicraft age. Indispensable groups of skilled artisans and their apprentice helpers continued
to carry out functions vital to the life of the modern clothing factory, but
in ways scarcely different from those authorized generations earlier by the
tailoring guilds of the Pale.

Moreover, this industry—widely regarded as a technical and organizational backwater and as an archaic demimonde of labor exploitation—
simultaneously provided the wherewithal for the fantasy life of modern
American culture. In fact, the "inside shop" developed in direct response
to the rise of mass consumption. By the turn of the century democratic
capitalism had begun to translate fashion, once the distinguishing mark
of social class, privilege, and power, into the symbolic vernacular of
popular culture. That happened neither through the conspiratorial manipulations of demand by suppliers nor through the wiles of advertising;
nor did the production process merely respond naïvely to consumer
wants. Rather, every conceivable social distinction—"old" and "new"
wealth, "native" and immigrant, "slicker" and "hick," professional and
tradesman, and on and on—served to differentiate further the production
of clothing.

This fusion of fantasy, fashion, and democracy expanded the mass
market for both quality clothing and clothing that could simulate the
appearance of quality clothing. Sections of the industry began to concentrate on the "effective and cheap reproduction of style goods" as the
highly charged meanings of even inexpensive garments proliferated, performing multiple duties as symbols of leisure and prosperity while em-

bodying deep desires for equality and individual diversity amid industrial uniformity.[24]

What made the business seem so anomalous was not that the preindustrial past coexisted with the industrial present. Rather, it was that their distinctive forms of life—manual and machine technologies, artisan and industrial work routines, patriarchal and impersonal structures of authority, the family enterprise and the anonymous corporation, degraded labor and the "sports jacket"—so completely depended upon one another even as they competed ruthlessly to survive. Elite manufacturers deeply resented the cost-cutting, price-cutting pressures of their Lilliputian rivals. But they also found it expedient and even essential at the height of the busy season to farm out work and the headaches that went with it to those same petty contractors. Skilled cutters and pressers, proud of their craft and attached to its time-honored rhythms, resented the fragmenting and diluting of their skills under the regime of factory rationalization. But they also knew work there was usually better rewarded and invariably more secure. Petty manufacturers envied the wealth and status and resented the demands of the "Giants of Broadway" but secretly dreamed of joining them one day. They fumed about the "uneconomic" pace of work imposed by informal groups of their skilled landsmen and deployed every known means of economic coercion and cultural persuasion to extract more labor, but surrendered quickly to any concerted sign of resistance, so totally did they rely on their highly skilled coreligionists.

This marriage of the medieval and the modern produced odd offspring. Practically a laboratory-perfect specimen of the free market, a living culture of petty entrepreneurial strivings, the industry was also a clinical case of laissez-faire. So marked were its penchant for self-destruction and its extravagant disregard of middle-class sensibilities that, long before Sidney Hillman found work there, the "rag trade" had become the object of public scandal and investigation, social legislation, and state regulation. Those laws, designed to curb the excesses of the tenement sweatshop, especially the abuse of women and children and the threatening neglect of elementary sanitation, were scarcely observed within the industry or enforced from without. Nonetheless, the very existence of such public intrusions into a marketplace as "free" as the one in which garments were manufactured was itself remarkable.

In the industry's tenements and lofts, businessmen acted like frontiersmen with Yiddish accents, accountable to no one and to nothing but the inexorable laws of the marketplace. Such freedom bred a kind of business anarchy, which inspired fear and then restraint. By the turn of the century elements of the industry's manufacturing elite were prepared to police the destabilizing excesses of the free market and to rein in the more unsavory practices of their hard-pressed competitors. Unlimited entrepreneurial ambition, the social dynamo of the nineteenth century, suddenly found itself challenged by the forces of commercial law and order that increasingly dominated the business and politics of the new century.

Within the claustrophobic precincts of the "rag trade" the small-time operator contended against his industrial cousin, the corporate executive who, so long as times were good, could afford to take the long view and looked with disdain on the hustling and grubbing of his less fortunate competitor. What gave this clash a certain poignancy was that the actors in this commercial drama were, if not literally cousins, than at least coreligionists. The "rag trade" was largely an ethnic enterprise embedded within the larger national economy. Indeed, it was the centerpiece of a Jewish economy that also produced, prepared, and distributed much of its own food, personal services, entertainment, housing, health care, and spiritual sustenance. Most garment manufacturers were Jewish, and in cities like New York particularly, the great bulk of its production was centered in Jewish neighborhoods. Many shops, although not all, ceased work on the High Holidays and were closed on the weekly Sabbath. Ancient religious custom and law prescribed the materials to be used and not used in the clothing worn by an observing Jew and had imparted long ago a certain ethnic exclusivity to the clothing craft. Even the gangsters that lived off the industry, and gave it some semblance of order as well, albeit along with some bloodshed, were Jewish. "Dopey Benny," the terror of Brooklyn manufacturers before World War I, could always be found in *shul* on solemn religious occasions.[25]

Yet this ethnic homogeneity was, in many respects, more apparent than real. This industry did indeed embody the Jewish nation in miniature, but it also included dozens of other ethnic groups. At least nine languages were spoken in the shops of Hart, Schaffner & Marx when Hillman went to work there. Italians, Lithuanians, Poles, Bohemians, and Slovaks from among the waves of "new immigrants," and Irish, Germans, and Scandinavians from an older generation of immigrant and native-born workers, dominated whole subregions of the industry's occupational terrain and, on occasion, rose into positions of proprietary prominence. An industrial nation of Jews was thus superimposed on an ethnic universe far more international, giving rise to innumerable ethnic and religious jealousies and animosities. Provincial and cosmopolitan at the same time, it was an industry that necessarily presented enormous problems of cultural orchestration to anyone—manufacturer, retailer, reformer, or labor organizer—who sought to impose on it some coherent and uniform organization.

Moreover, even to the extent that it could be fairly characterized as a "Jewish" industry, the garment business reflected the fierce rivalries and cultural dissonance that left the "Jewish" nation at war with itself. Thus, the "giants of Broadway" were disliked by their smaller competitors from the ghetto not only because they were "giants" but because they affected a German-Jewish aristocratic contempt for their impoverished, uneducated, and Yiddish-speaking coreligionists from Eastern Europe. Tailors from the Pale, on the other hand, were hands-on types who respected and and were intimately familiar with the production process, and who were convinced, with some reason, that their German-Jewish overlords were incapable of telling the difference between cutter's shears and a sewing machine. In fact, many of these "giants" began their careers as peddlers and retailers, as had the principals of HSM, and were well acquainted with the marketing and distribution of clothing, but eager to leave the nastier tasks of "getting the goods out" to supervisors and foremen. Hardly anxious to welcome their uncouth fellow manufacturers as ethnic brethren, the German-Jewish elite disapproved of the shadier and less seemly business and labor practices of the sweatshop operator. Affected as they were by the missionary currents of Reform Judaism and Ethical Culture, they cultivated a guilty social conscience and high-minded philanthropic concern for the well-being of their employees. The struggling entrepreneur from Eastern Europe, on the other hand, tended to be more orthodox, in both his religion and his business, at least in so far as orthodoxy was defined by the Darwinian canons of the free market.

At the lower end of the industrial order, down among the *landsleit* on the shop floor, unanimity among the brethren was just as rare. All might suffer from the exactions of the sweatshop boss or factory foreman, forming a community of complaint against the industry's chronic indignities and immiseration. But the shop floor was also honeycombed with elaborate hierarchies of semiskilled and skilled labor that offered countless opportunities for the exploitation of one's fellow worker and kinsman. These small occupational fiefdoms, governed by immemorial customs as binding as any formally adopted written constitution and sovereign across subregions of the industry, were particularly well-suited to protecting the privileges and prerogatives of cliques of skilled workers. Such cliques monopolized the best jobs, cynically took advantage of less experienced "greenhorn" *landsleit* as apprentices, and in general seized every opportunity to aggrandize their incomes and social position at the expense of fellow workers. Indeed, precisely because newly arrived immigrants depended on kinship networks and shtetl fraternities to find work and negotiate the mysteries of the city, they were especially vulnerable to the manipulations of these craftier veterans of the "rag trade." Even "corporation" or "social" shops, set up by small groups of skilled Jewish workers ostensibly to escape the demeaning and exploitative relationship of owner to worker, were compelled by the rigors of the market to become ingenious devices for taking advantage of "helpers."

But it was not necessary to pit landsman against landsman to break apart the bonds of ethnic fraternity. The most obscure workbench in the most obscure loft tucked away in the most obscure corner of the ghetto was likely to be a breeding ground of unbounded entrepreneurial ambition and self-seeking. As a consequence a kind of moral calisthenics of systematic overexertion developed, a political economy of self-exploitation that divided the needle trades worker not only from his coreligionists and fellow workers, but from himself as well. The system of piecework, which regularly called forth prodigious amounts of labor that taxed the physical capabilities of the worker to the limit, was not only imposed by management from above but often supported by many on the shop floor as the best way to amass enough money either to leave the industry or, better, to set up shop as a contractor. Such dreams were not entirely quixotic, based as they were on the everyday experience of workers who did actually manage to set up in a low-rent loft with a cutting table, if only to fall back into the ranks of the garment proletariat during the next slack season. Realistic or not, the ambition to rise permeated the very atmosphere of the "rag trade." Often enough it short-circuited the currents of ethnic and proletarian solidarity and gave the denizens of the needle trades a reputation for striving more American than Jewish.

Ambition alone did not hold uncontested sway over the conscience of the industry, however. Long before there was a Bund in the Pale, Jewish anarchism, Jewish socialism, and every other variety of labor radicalism and trade unionism thrived among the immigrant clothing workers in Britain and the United States. Those were strikingly different, rarer, transcendent sorts of ambitions. True, they never gained currency with more than a minority of the industry's workers. Nevertheless, as people like Sidney Hillman, refugees from the revolution in Russia, made their way to America, the entrepreneurial spirit, commercial egoism, and self-advancement had to battle for the hearts and minds of the Jewish working class with the spirit of high idealism and collective liberation that inspired the movements for equality, democracy, and socialism.[26]

Both the spirit of capitalism and the spirit of socialism depended on the moral psychology of self-sacrifice—at least that had been the case during the original periods of their more pristine formulations. Both worshiped at the shrine of Progress, finding in it the promise of social and political redemption. Yet they were at war with each other, and the struggle was conducted in an industry riddled with contradictions and anachronisms, in constant turmoil, perpetually poised on the edge of chaos. Whether or not there was some way to master that chaos was to become the great challenge confronting Sidney Hillman over the course of the next decade.

THREE

The Americanization
of "Hilkie"

Sidney Hillman might have toiled on for years in the labyrinthine plants of HSM, slowly working his way up the rather short ladder of occupational mobility. He might instead have found an outlet for his ambitions as an immigrant lawyer or even as a businessman. But between September 1910 and February 1911 the whole Chicago garment trade, the city's third largest industry and largest employer of female labor, exploded in an angry, often violent strike. Beginning at HSM, it spread like a prairie fire through all of the industry's major factories and back-alley sweatshops. It alarmed the city's political and social elite, inflamed its immigrant poor, and decisively altered the course of Hillman's life.

Arguably, the great HSM strike of 1910 was the pivotal event of Hillman's youth. The strike called upon his already apparent talents as an organizer and cultural arbiter. As in the Pale, he played a role as a tribune of the people. This time, however, he spoke not only for oppressed shtetl Jewry but for all the uprooted of Southeastern Europe, and not exclusively in the language of the European revolutionary. Instead, he mastered the meliorative grammar of "industrial democracy" and displayed a remarkable ability to redirect countless outpourings of outrage and rebellion into a system of industrial relations both more equitable and more profitable. For those feats of creative leadership and organization he was quickly singled out and celebrated by the social and political luminaries of Chicago Progressivism, including Jane Addams, Clarence Darrow, and Mr. and Mrs. Harold Ickes. The strike and the few years of organizational work that followed were a crash course in the theory and practice of Progressivism. Hillman graduated a polished apostle of the ideology of industrial democracy, distanced from his native universe of Jewish socialism, and with his gaze trained on those elite circles of industrial and political reform to which he was to remain attached for the rest of his life.

More immediately, the strike and its aftermath began Hillman's mastery of an industry so full of bewildering contradictions, so perpetually poised on the edge of chaos, as to be seemingly beyond anyone's ability to control. Hillman became, in effect, a kind of "hands-on" industrial psychologist and organizational scientist, a social engineer in an industry that defied rationalization.

Similarly, the strike immeasurably broadened his knowledge of the shop floor, that black box of artisan work groups, craft exclusiveness, enserfed homeworkers, militants, scabs, inert masses, and hyperactive revolutionaries, ethnic jealousies and self-sacrificing heroism. The strike thus made him a practicing sociologist of the workplace, a virtuoso of shop floor politics, and a pioneer in a whole new system of industrial labor relations.

Hillman came away from the strike with a permanent set of enemies and friends. For most of the rest of his career as a trade unionist he would be at odds with the American Federation of Labor. That enmity originated in the great HSM strike. At the same time friendships that were to endure long after he left Chicago were first formed on the picket lines and in the meeting halls of 1910. Those founding cadre were to become Hillman's devoted organizational and political deputies, the very few people he trusted implicitly in trying situations. One of them, in fact, was to become his wife.

Long before there were unions of garment workers there were strikes. Since before the turn of the century life in the average sweatshop or factory resembled nothing so much as an intermittent state of civil war, the hostile if intimidated ranks of abused workers massed on one side, the arsenal of the foreman's arbitrary tyrannies deployed on the other. Overexertion, endless hours, the personal brutalities of overseers and contractors, sudden cuts in the rates or unannounced changes in production quotas and work rules unleashed flash floods of rebellion. Between 1880 and 1920, the needle trades were the third most strike-prone industry after mining and the building trades.[1]

Such uprisings were carried off in a mood of near-delirious enthusiasm and exalted idealism. An observer of a May Day mass meeting in 1890 celebrating the strike victory of seven thousand New York cloakmakers commented:

[A] special animation lights up every face. Again hurrahs, again applause and loud exclamations . . . and the godlike sounds of the Marseillaise: words of Liberty, of Equality, of Fraternity . . . the victorious red flags flutter. Everything is joyous and filled with a holiday spirit. . . . Who could have believed that these strikers . . . almost without a cent in their treasury, without a word of encouragement, abandoned by their former allies . . . hounded by the diabolical taunts and provocations . . . of the entire capitalist world, would stand together so firmly, proud and unafraid in the face of hunger and privation. . . .[2]

Such uprisings were contagious and "were organized with the fervor of a religious fanaticism. . . . We were sure the millennium was at hand. . . . We were in ecstasy." Even the "oldest, most backward and docile of all clothing workers . . . loyal to the old orthodox customs who stopped work three times a day to chant their prayers . . . were caught up by the spirit of the time." As this observer suggests, Talmudic aphorisms, Biblical allusions, and all forms of religious ritual were often crucial in those early efforts. Small synagogues became union halls, the *schames* (temple caretaker) a union activist, the local union president was apt to wear peyes (sidecurls), a long beard, and to talk of Moses as the first walking delegate and the Sanhedrin as the first union executive board. But this same observer, aware of how evanescent such triumphs could be, went on to warn the celebrants that "now, after your great triumphs is really the time more than ever to devote yourselves to your unions and to prepare for further and greater struggles." It was not to be. "We had not yet learned how to retain our victory. . . . The proud cloakmakers union lost its power and the other unions vanished almost as quickly as they had come. It was exasperating . . . it was heartrending."[3]

Benjamin Schweitzer, an early and devoted organizer of Jewish tailors, described the entirely informal and occasional nature of those early unions:

Friday evening the vestmakers union would congregate on the street in front of the hall where their union met and hold a weekly fair. . . . The market lasted until 10 or 11 at night. Then the weary vestmakers would come to the union meeting to rest themselves. Of definite working hours the vestmakers never thought, and paying dues . . . was considered useless. The affairs of the union therefore always awaited the beginning of the season so that they could call their yearly strike through which they got the financial means (from employers desperate for the season to begin) to keep up their unions.[4]

Strikes were often impromptu affairs:

When the workers in an outside shop were dissatisfied with the prices, they would gather near their shop in the morning or at noon and one of them would make a motion—today they would not work. The others seconded the motion and all of them immediately proceeded to the Market Street dock. . . . When the boss came to the shop and discovered his workers were absent, he knew just where to find them, and after long negotiations settled the argument. Usually the boss would raise prices 5 cents on the garment and roll out a barrel of beer. Thus ended almost every strike.[5]

In the wake of successful strikes conditions improved temporarily as petty manufacturers and contractors could not withstand the loss of their workers, especially at the height of the frenetic busy season. While work remained plentiful, *ad hoc* strike organizations enjoyed the allegiance of workers, assembled usually along local lines of craft and/or ethnicity. As the season drew to a close, however, manufacturers violated with impunity the terms they had so solemnly agreed to mere weeks or months before. They knew the scarcity of work would demoralize the employees and their provisional organizations. Innumerable unions thus died in infancy. John Commons noted the enthusiasm and determination of those largely Jewish strikers: "They bring in 95% of the trade. They are energetic and determined. They demand the entire and complete elimination of the abuse. The demand is almost always unanimous and is made with enthusiasm and bitterness. They stay out a long time, even under the greatest of suffering." He nevertheless concluded that "when once the strike is settled, either in favor or against the cause . . . that ends the union." By 1900 the Jewish garment workers strike had become an annual ritual.[6]

For years prior to the uprising of 1910, Chicago had been the site of dozens of such strikes and tentative attempts at organization. Those unions which managed to survive, in particular the United Garment Workers, were profoundly conservative. Although founded by the United Hebrew Trades in 1891 with a local in Chicago, the UGW was sanctioned by the AFL as the tailor's national bargaining agency mainly as a device to undermine the national trade assembly of the Knights of Labor. It soon became patently corrupt, nativist, elitist, and anti-Semitic. Top officials of the local union were routinely suspected of embezzling and misappropriating union funds and just as routinely exonerated by the national leadership. Mainly a union of skilled cutters, either native born or the children of Americanized immigrants, it affected a castelike sense of superiority and indifference toward the mass of immigrant tailors. The national leadership scarcely bothered to conceal its contempt for the flood of Jewish immigrants in particular, whose skills they demeaned and whose politics they hated and feared.

The UGW believed in union–management collaboration. More than anything else the leaders were anxious that "tailoring has almost ceased to be a craft . . . and until recently the tailors ranked among the skilled artisans possessing the pride of a thorough worker." The union paper not only inveighed against proletarianization but published regular invectives directed against proponents of independent labor politics and all "panaceas for social ills." Given those anxieties and prejudices, it is hardly surprising that the organization studiously avoided even the pretense of mass organization. The risks were too great. Indeed, the leaders relied instead on the power of the union label, a potent weapon among manufacturers of work clothes whose customers, often working-class union men, were likely to boycott a garment without one. But the label was largely meaningless in the great anonymous mass market for ready-to-wear men's clothing.

Thus, by 1910 the UGW, while practically a negligible factor in the major urban clothing markets, was comfortably ensconced in the trans-Appalachian foothills, where overalls were produced and where it enjoyed a lucrative income from the sale of the UGW label. However otherwise irrelevant to the fate of the Jewish, Italian, Bohemian, Polish, Lithuanian, and Scandinavian immigrant garment workers of Chicago, it nonetheless held the franchise for men's clothing from the AFL. It was therefore in a position to become part of the problem it was ostensibly established to solve.[7]

Despite the studied cautiousness of the UGW, the industry's labor problem grew worse. Although created to exchange credit and other commercial information, the Chicago Wholesale Clothiers Association, founded by the head of one of the city's largest firms, Louis Kuppenheimer, devoted itself as much to maintaining the open shop. HSM was not an Association member, but the firm deliberately avoided hiring union sympathizers. Nonetheless, sporadic efforts at organization, carried out mostly by skilled workers, sometimes under the reluctant leadership of the UGW and sometimes independently, continued. In 1904 the industry's labor bureau launched a campaign against the closed shop as an "Un-American institution" and set in motion a blacklisting and strike-breaking operation, as for that matter did the rest of Chicago's manufacturing community during that period. The bureau's campaign successfully thwarted an eight-and-a-half-month strike. Cutters, trimmers, and examiners were thereafter required to submit in writing their resignation from the union and to register with the Association's labor bureau. Only two UGW locals survived the 1904 defeat, with a membership of less than one thousand. By 1910 the city's garment trade had cured itself of the union virus, or so it seemed.[8]

It was as if some social incendiary device had been carefully planted and set to explode synchronously throughout the garment-making centers of America. Between 1909 and 1915, mass strikes, often described at the time as "uprisings," erupted in New York and Chicago, igniting sympathetic if smaller rebellions in Boston, Rochester, and Baltimore, and elsewhere.

After years of frustrated organizing, these demonstrations of remarkable fortitude, solidarity, and inter-ethnic cooperation, in the face of concerted employer opposition and police intimidation, had an air of almost magical spontaneity. Beginning with the "uprising of the 20,000" in New York in 1909, when a young shirtwaist maker, Clara Lemlich, exhorted her fellow workers to stop talking and "strike, strike, strike," there seemed something elemental and inexorable about these mass risings, as if resistance to the basic miseries of the sweatshop required no planned organization and articulation. The way the events unfolded actually did mimic spontaneous combustion, often beginning in some obscure corner of a factory, spreading from department to department, from shop to shop, from one ethnic group to another, the energy and scope of activity racing ahead of the movement's formal demands and organizational structure, where the very audacity of the movement's social momentum inspired it to be bold in its ideas and programs.

Clara Lemlich, however, was not a "greenhorn" but rather, despite her youth, an experienced organizer for the Women's Trade Union League. As a child in the Ukraine she had read Turgenev, Gorky, and revolutionary literature. She had fled Russia following the Kishinev pogrom and had attended anarchist meetings in London. A skilled, relatively well-paid draper, she was saving her money in the hope of attending medical school. As Lemlich's case makes clear, the appearance of spontaneous rebellion was most often just that—an appearance. Behind it lay not only long-accumulated hatreds for a thousand industrial indignities but the patient, persistent efforts of invisible activists, subterranean groups that managed to survive through the darkest days of the open shop. So when the great HSM strike began, the first sudden outpouring of outraged workers, which elicited shocked surprise from everyone, including management, was welcomed and even prepared for—to the extent such events are ever predictable and controllable—by veteran Jewish and Italian immigrant socialist and anarchist workers.[9]

Sidney Hillman was weaned on the mass strike in revolutionary Russia, witnessed its social explosiveness, and was better prepared than most to help focus its free energies. For months before the outbreak he had circulated inconspicuously among nodules of similarly experienced activists, seeking out potential recruits and even trying to stir up the interest of the lethargic UGW. Yet Hillman was not included within the original secret circle of strike instigators. Indeed, it was only several weeks after the initial walkout that Hillman packed his tools and joined the strike along with his fellow cutters. In fact women, not men, sparked the rebellion, as often happened in the industry generally, where women constituted so large a portion of the labor force. Division of labor by gender was characteristic of the industry. Women were excluded from certain kinds of skilled jobs, particularly those requiring the use of machinery, and were paid less for similar or identical kinds of work. Such segregation and discrimination were widespread, but their extent varied from city to city. In cities like Chicago, where modern factories with extensive divisions of labor were far more common than in New York, a great many more semiskilled positions and machine operations were filled by women. At the same time, the independent female artisan was very much a part of shtetl folklife. Often a seamstress, she occupied a position of respect and economic weight from which she derived a certain amount of personal autonomy as well as responsibility. Jewish immigrant women brought those values with them to America. In the right circumstances, competence in the marketplace, a sense of craftsmanship, and a desire for occupational and social mobility made for an empowering combination. Indeed, young unmarried women constituted one-third of the Bund membership in the late 1890s.[10]

Empowering indeed. On September 22, 1910, Hannah Shapiro and Esther Feinglass refused to accept a one-quarter cent cut in the rates for seaming pants and led fifteen of their fellow pants seamers out of HSM shop no. 5 onto Halstead Street. Yet so inauspicious was the beginning of what was to become a four-and-a-half-month war, involving more than 40,000 garment workers and enveloping the whole Chicago garment trade, that it prompted a certain sympathetic amusement among veteran male organizers, including Sidney Hillman: "I remember we made fun of it, five girls working against HSM, but somehow the girls managed to take out the men after awhile."[11]

Hillman himself had earlier made contact with the Chicago Federation of Labor and its President, John Fitzpatrick, as had, separately, a handful of others, especially a group of cutters, including Frank Rosenblum, Sam Levin, and Anzuino Marimpietri. Disgusted with the passivity of the local UGW, they hoped that the Federation, noted for its aggressiveness, might intervene on their behalf. But the women acted first. Within a week seven of the ten West Side pants shops refused work coming from shop no. 5. In three weeks time most of HSM's seven thousand were on strike. By the middle of October the contagion had spread to other elite firms and threatened the whole industry.[12]

Events galloped ahead of anyone's conscious reckoning. Aware always of the need for careful organization and tactical preparation, Hillman recalled his observations at the outset:

> There were really no definite demands, the demands were that conditions must be changed; nobody knew really exactly what they wanted; they wanted something better of course, or different, and the strike kept on about 18 weeks and it involved the whole city of Chicago . . . our people thought that the closed shop is the remedy for everything, and I daresay that 99 out of 100 never knew what a closed shop meant.[13]

Clara Masilotti, a young Italian baster in the Blue Island shop, described the rather haphazard way in which news of the strike spread:

> I knew they were striking in all the shops, so I told all our girls, I said, "The first whistle we hear in the window, that means for us to strike." So one day it was dinner time, quarter after twelve, and we hear a big noise under the window and there was about 200 persons were all whistling for us to come down and strike, so I was the first to go out and get the girls to come after me.[14]

In those early days of the uprising there was little in the way of formal organization or leadership. Communications were accidental and slow; walkouts of angry workers began and ended in isolation, only to erupt again.

Marie Felski, a pocketmaker, described how the strike came to her corner of the Kuppenheimer empire. When the foreman cut the rates, she and her fellow workers went to HSM looking for work, not knowing the strike was already under way. Not willing to scab, they returned to Kuppenheimer, but

> . . . then the great strike came, not just the separate little strikes, but one whole strike. When the foreman heard us all talking about it, he said, "Girls, you can have your pockets and your cent back again if you'll stay," but just then there was a big noise outside and we all rushed to the windows and there we see the police beating the strikers,—clubbing them on our account and when we saw that, we went out.[15]

In the midst of this apparent "madness," however, there was, if not exactly a method, then at least a discernible pattern of activity. Long before the great strike, HSM had been the site of continuous small skirmishes and stoppages, occurring first in one department or shop and then in another. Many minor irritations inflamed relations: the company's decision to insist on six rather than the customary three stitches for sewing on buttons; its withdrawal of homely privileges like coffee-making and the delivery of milk and beer on the job; and its failure to eliminate production bottlenecks, which idled workers in the piecework sections.[16]

From the outset, when the strike seemed to consist purely of localized outbreaks, those who stepped forward to lead were by no means new-comers. Even Hannah Shapiro, only eighteen at the time, was a veteran of the industry, having begun work at thirteen. For some time she had made a practice of boldly representing her own grievances as well as those of her fellow seamers to the department's overseers. Clara Masilotti was not only an experienced worker but as well a union organizer for the WTUL. Some of the early rank-and-file activists had already been sin-gled out by plant management as prospective foreladies precisely because of their evident skills, aggressiveness, and initiative. A young Italian woman, herself not much more experienced than a "greenhorn" but a fast learner who had quickly mastered several difficult tasks, was ap-proached by the plant manager: "Well I would like to have you be the forelady to teach these greenhorns how to work . . . you just be forelady and tell them to work more and make me good work." A short time later, however, she was ordered to cut the rates: "I'm not going to tell these people twelve cent a coat. He said, 'You got to tell them!' I said, 'No sir, you tell them yourself. I am just ashamed to tell them. . . . I want to be a working girl, the same as the others,' and then I don't speak." Days later she rediscovered her voice, this time to inspire her co-workers to join the Chicago-wide strike.[17]

A disproportionate number of shop strike leaders either were veteran skilled artisans, especially cutters and pressers, or, like Hillman, were in training to become so. Cutters particularly composed one of those semi-autonomous groups of workers, scattered throughout American industry, who enjoyed a degree of supervisory and administrative authority, espe-cially over hiring and training, in otherwise fragmented business enter-prises lacking experienced managerial staff. Such structural independence and control encouraged occupational groups like the cutters to become pioneer trade unionists. Men like Rosenblum, Marimpietri, and Levin—all cutters—persisted in attempts to organize during the bleakest days following the defeated strike of 1907. They were not only dedicated trade unionists and skilled artisans but political radicals as well. Levin and Marimpietri were experienced in the socialist movements of Russia and Italy, respectively.[18]

The biographies of the shop floor cadres suggest those features of character and circumstance which made them likely candidates for leadership. Frank Rosenblum, whose parents had fled the pogroms of the early 1880s, was born in New York City, learned the cutting trade in Philadelphia, and was one of the first to be fired when the HSM strike began. Sam Levin, who was to become Hillman's lifelong friend and comrade, was born in Mogilev, White Russia, in 1884. His father was an overseer on a large farm. Sam left at the age of fourteen and set up a small retail business 1,500 miles from home and outside the Pale. The business prospered, while Sam paid the obligatory bribes to the police and higher officials, until the Russo-Japanese war ruined him. He lost his taste for commerce and joined the Russian Social Democratic Party (SDP). During the 1905 revolution he left for the United States, where he pursued a high school education at night while working first as a laborer, then as a milk wagon driver, a porter, and finally for HSM as a cutter. Anzuino Marimpietri was born in 1881 in Barete, Italy, where he attended night school. He became a highly skilled tailor and composed poetry in his spare time. While working in HSM's "quality shop" no. 3 he met secretly with a group of fellow Italian workers, but suspected he was being spied upon. Jack Kroll, the son and brother of skilled tailors, was born in London in 1885. A cutter in Rochester, he was blacklisted for participating in a 1905 strike there and moved to Chicago, where he worked under an alias. Jacob Potofsky, younger than the rest, was a floorboy in 1910. His father had managed a glass factory in Kiev. His brother was an intellectual and revolutionary. The Potofsky family left Russia in ones and twos beginning in 1905, Jacob arriving in Chicago in 1908. A landsman offered him a job at $3 a week in HSM. He attended the Chicago Hebrew Institute at night, joined the Educational Club, and pursued a course in bookkeeping. Bessie Abramovitz was born in 1890 in a small village in White Russia near Grodno, one of ten children. During the revolutionary upheavals of 1905 she left for America and first found a job sewing on buttons. Blacklisted in Chicago for her organizational efforts, she had gone to work at HSM under an assumed name.[19]

During the strike these men and women displayed a capacity for self-organization, a fighting élan, and a remarkable political sophistication. They gave to the whole Chicago episode a sense of purposiveness and design otherwise missing from its legendary and partly mythological reputation as a righteous and unprompted rising of the oppressed and inarticulate. As a matter of fact, it is practically an axiom of the history of labor organization from the mid-nineteenth century through the creation of the CIO in the 1930s that leadership almost invariably emerged from the ranks of the self-possessed, upwardly mobile, more highly skilled and educated (often self-educated), radically democratic and socialist artisans and industrial workers. Rarely were they the worst abused, the poorest, or the most hopeless.

Hannah Shapiro, for example, did not consider HSM the worst place she had worked. "I thought I have to better myself," she explained, and noted that to accomplish that, "there's nothing like a big place to work." For many women like Hannah the factory represented, both tangibly and symbolically, not only progress but modernism—a kind of urban-cosmopolitan adventure, especially when measured against the ethnic claustrophia of the typical tiny contractor shop. Still, whatever the allures of a place like HSM, as Hannah recalled, "We all went out; we had to be recognized as people."[20]

This fundamental sense of wounded dignity was already deeply implanted in Hillman's psyche:

> I believe that there is such a change that really it cannot be explained. The People really felt themselves a little more like men and women. Before there was not a feeling like that in any non-union shop. Contrary to any statement by people who defend the open shop, I do not feel it is possible to have the full feeling of manhood.[21]

It was that acute sensitivity to indignity, the chronic degradation at the hands of what the Italian workers called "piccoli zars" (little czars), that gave the initial strike its amorphous programmatic quality, that sense, as Hillman reported it, that "nobody knew what they wanted." In fact, there was a veritable tidal wave of grievances: the arbitrary cutting of the rates suffered by Hannah Shapiro; the egregious and whimsical system of fines for lost goods, damaged garments, or disobedience to the time clock; everyday, ordinary insults; and the driving discipline and unchallengeable authority of the foreman. Indeed, while the sophisticated owners of HSM had pioneered in introducing rational, bureaucratic procedures to many facets of the clothing business, the actual organization of work and daily dealings with the company's employees were subject to the personal discretion and remarkably inconsistent judgments of lower-level supervisors.[22]

Thus, hiring and firing were subject to various forms of nepotism and even extortion; they depended far more on personal, family, and ethnic connections than on a set of objective and impersonal requirements. Similarly, tasks and duties departed widely from and greatly exceeded those specified in company rule books, and the rules themselves were often ignored and violations punished at the whim of local authorities. In a department where canvas was spread on coats, "When a girl got sick they would holler at her just for nothing. . . . They would not let her go home. . . . When a girl complained they always hollered at her, and we got to punch two times a day and if we forget they charge us a quarter." In shop no. 21, the foreman, a man named Gorman, was a notorious maltreater of immigrant Italian women. In one instance, dissatisfied with the work of one of the finishers, he fired her and, when she resisted leaving, "he . . . struck her and she had a miscarriage and they didn't tell nobody." A skilled Italian baster suggested to her foreman that she might recruit some of her equally experienced friends to work in his shop:

> Experienced girls? Not in my shop! I want no experienced girls. They know the pay to get. I got to pay them good wages and they make less work, but these greenhorns, Italian people, Jewish people, all nationalities, they cannot speak English and they don't know where to go and they just come from the old country and let them work hard, like the devil, and those I get for less wages.[23]

The atmosphere of sullen resentment produced by these local despotisms was actually best summarized by Joseph Schaffner himself:

> Careful study of the situation has led me to the belief that the fundamental cause of the strike was that the workers had no satisfactory channel through which minor grievances, exactions, and petty tyrannies of underbosses could be taken up and amicably adjusted. Taken separately, these grievances appear to have been of minor character. They were, however, allowed to accumulate from month to month and from year to year. The result was there steadily grew up in the minds of many of feeling of distrust and enmity towards their immediate superiors in positions because they felt that justice was being denied them. If they had the temerity to complain against a boss, they incurred his displeasure, and his word was taken in preference to theirs. In some instances they lost their jobs, and where this was not the case they seldom received any satisfaction. Shortly before the strike I was so badly informed of the conditions that I called the attention of a friend to the satisfactory state of the employees. It was only a few days before the great strike of the Garment Workers broke out. When I found out later the conditions that had prevailed, I concluded that the strike should have occurred much sooner.[24]

At the time of the strike, the company's attitude was somewhat different. It first pretended there was no strike, but then quickly ordered an upward adjustment of the rates in Hannah Shapiro's shop. That did little good, and by the middle of October management hired a private detective agency to "protect" those of its employees still working. The

company, which had earlier deliberately kept its distance from the
antilabor employers' association and had actually considered methods of
resolving workers' grievances prior to the strike, found itself caught up in
the irresistible momentum of events, just like everyone else.[25]

As the movement spread throughout the HSM empire, its tempo
accelerated and emotions heated up:

> *October 12:* An eighteen year old coatmaker, Bessie Abramovitz, at a meet-
> ing of over five hundred coatmakers in Hodcarriers Hall, militant, but with
> restraint belying her youth, argued against the precipitous call for a general
> strike: "What folly you men and women would do here today. Have you
> thought of what it means to call a general strike? Do you know what
> responsibilities you would burden yourselves with. Stop and Think!"

> *October 19:* A parade of 250 strikers, cheered by neighboring
> shopkeeper/residents, were set upon by thugs and police. Bystanders were
> beaten and arrested. Police jeered wounded strikers as they were brought in:
> Dirty Jews, Bohunks, Polaks, Hunyaks . . . This will teach him that he ain't
> in Russia. . . ."

> *October 20:* A jammed mass meeting in Hodcarriers Hall. Storms of
> enthusiasm. Three thousand joined the union. Four hundred cutters from
> HSM, Kuppenheimer, and Hirsch–Wirkere joined the union. Every meet-
> ing marked by huge demonstrations—Hall doors opened, whistles sounded,
> and in marched over 300 men carrying partly opened shears above the
> heads. The cutters had walked out. Deafening cheers.[26]

As the strike wave enveloped the industry, so did the onrushing
waves of violence and counter-violence. "Huskies," "Balagulahs," paid
thugs carrying 3-inch-thick clubs, patrolled the streets itching to "beat a
merry tune on the skulls of the . . . Jews and Hunyaks if they showed
their faces near the shops." A detective agency solicited Chicago's employers offering "secret service men to associate among your employees"
for hire "at the lowest possible cost," and ready to import gangs of fresh
labor from out of town.[27]

Meanwhile, the daily violence of long hours and exhausting speed,
the slow poison of festering irritation for which until now there had been
no outlet or which had been deflected inward or against fellow workers
of alien races, suddenly found more suitable targets. The property of
employers and those "loyal" employees who in effect seemed to belong to
them became objects of loathing. Scabs were persuaded by threats, by
intimidation, and by physical coercion to join the movement or at least
cease obstructing it.

In the dead of night homes were entered and scabs dragged from their beds and beaten. The houses of landlords who evicted strikers were plastered with signs . . . Acids were thrown, plate glass windows shivered, machinery wrecked. . . . A secret night committee of young "terrorists" prowled after dark, spreading alarm.[28]

The unofficial violence of "huskies" and "terrorists" was more than matched by the official and openly partisan brutality of the police—mass arrests of picketers, beatings, shootings, murder. Early in December Charles Lazinskas, a young militant busy arguing with two scabs on their way home and under police escort, was shot and killed. Upwards of 30,000 strikers and strike sympathizers marched through the West Side after Lazinskas's funeral, led by bands playing the Marseillaise. Union teamsters and streetcar conductors doffed their hats in solemn salute. The marchers assembled in the ballpark owned and donated by the owner of the Chicago Cubs to hear passionate speeches denouncing the employers and their hired guns.

When a second Lithuanian striker, Frank Nagreckis, was killed and his companion severely injured by Chicago police on December 15, a pitched battle ensued between the enraged workers and the police and private security guards. This moved Assistant Police Chief Harmon Schuetter to announce: "This is the most vicious strike I have ever seen, except the teamsters. . . . I shall no longer doubt European reports that certain governments there find classes of their people so dangerous that they must get rid of them at any cost." A week later eighteen-year-old John Donnelley, delivering a load of unfinished garments to homeworkers from a nonunion shop, was shot by a squad of three strikers. Days later private detectives retaliated by killing a union supporter, Ferdinand Weiss. Shortly after that Fred Reinhart, a particularly despised security guard at HSM, was ambushed and killed while escorting two strikebreakers home.[29]

This then was the strike as it appeared from ground level: erupting first in this shop, then in that, spreading in ever widening waves, fueled by a thousand harbored resentments, lacking in any apparent centralized organization, fixed programmatic objectives, or hierarchy of leadership. Like the rising of the fascio in southern Italy in the 1890s or the mass strikes that ignited the Russian empire in 1905, the Chicago uprising burst the bounds of conventional conflict. Indeed, a sympathetic if patronizing contemporary observer described "a people's movement, deep-seated, leaderless, marked by all the folly, all the heroism, all the childishness, all the grandeur of a peasant's revolt." Jane Addams was acutely aware of the categorical difference between the

normal trade union strike and the sort of mass strike then unfolding in
Chicago:

> It was in connection with the first factory employment of newly arrived
> immigrants and the innumerable difficulties attached to their first adjust-
> ment, that some of the most profound industrial disturbances in Chicago
> have come about. Under any attempt at classification these strikes belong
> more to the general social movement than to the industrial conflict.[30]

Addams was right. The movement's desires were not yet encoded in
the rational, utilitarian language and psychology of collective bargaining, its energies and forms of activity not yet encased in the bureaucratic
procedures of "modern" trade unionism and contractual obligation. For
many a loyal but orthodox Jewish striker, moved by the same passions
that had transformed shtetl temples into arenas of ritualized combat, the
single uncompromising demand for the "closed shop" expressed a kind of
Talmudic parable in which "Moses became the first walking delegate."
Equally orthodox Polish Catholics responded to the exhortations of their
local priests and solemnly promised in the presence of the crucifix to hold
out come what might.[31]

Alongside those ancient fealties and pietistic devotions, the most
radical currents of free-thinking anticlericalism, anarchism, national liberation, and messianic socialism augmented the movement's expectations and unshakable militance.

From above, it all looked like chaos. George Creel, a noted Bull
Moose Progressive, writing in *Century Magazine* a few years later, remarked on the strike's inchoate, elemental quality:

> The trouble was peculiar in that the workers brought forward no list of
> accurately formulated grievances and presented only vague demands. The
> thing that seemed to possess them, that made them willing to face hunger,
> cold, and even death, was a vast discontent and a very intense unhappiness.
> They were wretched without being able to state exactly the cause of their
> wretchedness.[32]

Creel's puzzlement was shared not only by those manufacturers immediately threatened but by those elements deeply sympathetic to the plight
of Chicago's garment workers.

To begin with, both Harry Hart and Joseph Schaffner seemed genuinely abashed by the extent and fury of the strike. Genuinely surprised
or not, the partners had the most practical interest in seeking some way
of reestablishing stable relations on the shop floor. Alarm at the prospect

of widening chaos impelled the company as early as the end of October to seek a settlement that, while rejecting the demand for a closed shop, would recognize the workers' grievances and institute a vaguely defined procedure for resolving them. Management sensed that its own future, as well as that of the industry, depended on developing a lawful, constitutional framework of labor relations. For the handful of elite concerns like HSM, with high ratios of fixed costs (plant and equipment, energy, materials, managerial staffs) to labor, keeping the workforce steadily employed was vital.

The company's plan devised in October actually envisioned some form of independent unionism "to make shop discipline easier and lead to improved and more economical methods because of the increased goodwill of the employees." In a report to Joseph Schaffner, Earl Dean Howard, an economics professor at Northwestern University, later to become the company's labor manager, recommended compromise:

> From a sales standpoint simply you cannot afford to be classified as "unfair."
> . . . The ideal solution will leave you with the reputation for fairness toward labor, at the same time avoiding any form of organization among your people which will give them power to injure your business.[33]

Faced with a movement whose complex deeper motivations they neither understood nor knew how to address, the partners were irresistibly driven to the conclusion that the company itself lacked the moral authority and the power to impose a permanent order on the wild chaos swirling around them. Only a union, or some similar institution dedicated to the rational adjudication of disputes in terms amenable to conventional business practice while commanding the allegiance of the rank and file, could exercise the sort of constant surveillance over labor markets and shop floor practices without which the industry's natural tendency to dissolve in anarchic competition and uncontrollable labor disorder would continue.

But the company's offer came too early, before the expansive force of the mass strike had exhausted itself and before the movement's desires had crystallized into a set of negotiable, quantifiable demands. On October 26 the company's concessions were read to the strikers in Hodcarriers Hall in English, Yiddish, Lithuanian, Polish, Italian, and Bohemian. With each reading the strikers rose en masse and in unison issued a thunderous "No!"[34]

Meanwhile, pressures to restore a semblance of coherence and order, to give the uprising a language that middle-class citizens, both manufacturers and others, could understand, if not endorse, accumulated at var-

ious points. Jewish employers, especially among the industry's elite, eager
to earn the social esteem their business pursuits rarely gained for them,
were particularly sensitive to the religious pleas of Reform Judaism and to
the secularized pleadings of the Ethical Culture Society. Jacob Abt, who
was to become President of the Wholesale Clothiers Manufacturing Association, typified this circumscribed, assimilationist Jewish business milieu. He had spent some time at the Maxwell Street settlement
ministering to the poor, and was reminded of this by Ellen Gates Starr,
a socialist and leader of the WTUL, when she held him "more accountable than many others for the needless horrors that are taking place."
Given Abt's background, she found it hard to excuse him on grounds of
cultural ignorance:

> Hear, then, the prophets of Israel, in whose teachings you must have been
> reared. . . . When Isaiah rebukes the "oppressor," the unfair employer or
> property owner as we should call him, he does so in these terms. . . . "What
> mean ye that ye beat my people to pieces and grind the faces of the
> poor . . .?"

Starr went on to shame Abt with the words of Ezekiel as well and
concluded:

> Let the God of Israel judge. . . . I daily commend to Him the people whom
> you oppress. . . . A persecution of the Jews by the Jews as relentless as any
> the world affords, is going on in our midst . . . a great protest is rising. You
> will hear the echo of protest and your children will hear it years hence.[35]

Abt, perhaps moved by Starr's admonition, later became a staunch
supporter of collective bargaining. Other businessmen, like Henry Wolf,
the Treasurer and principal stockholder of Kuppenheimer & Co., were
frequent participants in Ethical Culture Society gatherings where the
ethical dimensions of the "labor question" were meticulously examined.
Some of it registered, if subtly.

Almost as alarmed by the uprising as the manufacturers themselves
was the institution that ought to have found in it a great opportunity, the
United Garment Workers. Robert Noren, head of the Chicago UGW,
had actually turned down the strikers' initial request for help. Noren had
consulted with UGW President Thomas Rickert, who expressed a decided "lack of faith in the possibility of organizing these people" and
assumed, or perhaps wished, that "it was just an overnight strike." For
Rickert, "these people"—aliens, Jews, anarchists, socialists, syndicalists,

"Columbus" (unskilled immigrant) tailors, and veteran organizers—constituted an organizational nightmare. They threatened to upset permanently the pacific if severely limited arrangements the union had established with the work-clothing firms and were offensive to its organizational culture of nativism and craft exclusivity. But because the strike turned out to be more than an "overnight" affair, the UGW was forced to intervene, officially proclaiming the strike a general one after it had already become so. In fact, the proclamation was intended less as a prelude to a wider war than as an epitaph for but another heroic lost cause. Mere days after the general strike call, Rickert and Harry Hart initialed an agreement that made no provision for a continuing organization in HSM plants. That agreement was entirely unacceptable to a movement whose strength was just then cresting. Denounced as a "traitor" by, among others, Sidney Hillman, Rickert was forced to flee Hodcarriers Hall in disgrace.[36]

There were others, however, who, unlike Rickert, did not approach the strike and its solution from the standpoint of a social mortician. Chicago was an important center of Progressive reform. Progressive attacks on monopoly, on urban poverty and corruption, on industrial autocracy in the workplace, and on commercial duplicity in the marketplace helped create an environment in Chicago more amenable to the growth of trade unions. Not long after the strike became serious, the Chicago Progressive community mobilized. It made its considerable philanthropic, educational, and civic reform apparatus available to the garment workers, whose normally invisible misery had suddenly become so conspicuous.

Progressives entered into alliances with labor in part because they saw in independent unionism a way of taming the tendencies of laissez-faire capitalism to dissolve into social and economic tragedy. Garment manufacturing presented a lurid foretaste of this possibility. In most cases the socialist or bundist leadership of the unions accepted the aid offered by Progressives but otherwise remained loyal to its traditional ideological beliefs, and practiced a traditional trade unionism. In the case of Sidney Hillman, however, matters developed in a different direction.[37]

Chicago Progressivism was multifaceted. The home of Jane Addams and Hull House, Chicago had become a breeding ground for social workers concerned not only with rehabilitating the victims of urban and industrial expansion but with finding ways of arresting the endless reproduction of new victims. This upper-middle-class milieu of social workers and social reformers paid special attention to immigrants, to immigrant working women in particular. The Chicago chapter of the Women's

Trade Union League (WTUL), in close association with Hull House, was prepared to assist the organizing efforts of female wage-earners in industries like clothing, where they were heavily represented.

The women of the League often turned out to be the blood relations or the social associates of businessmen, professionals, independent and Republican Party political reformers, and assorted patricians who, for a variety of reasons, were seeking ways to regulate the enormous power of big business. Men like Harold Ickes, Charles Merriam, Donald Richberg, and Raymond Robbins feared that in pursuit of its own freedom to accumulate wealth without limit, corporate America might fatally undermine the basis of economic well-being, social stability, and political democracy. They accepted the basic premises of a capitalist society but sought to make it more rational and, to the degree that they shared the pronounced Protestant social conscience of their sisters in the WTUL, to make it more Christian.[38]

However, the concerns of this business and professional elite were not strictly cultural and ideological. They were also more tangibly economic. Chicago was emerging as a critical regional center of diversified, mass-consumption-oriented industries in both manufacturing and distribution. Precisely because those elements were oriented to the mass market and were concerned with the continual expansion of mass purchasing power, they were predisposed to explore new departures in the field of industrial labor relations that promised not only stability but real economic growth.

Thus, the elite worlds of Chicago political, business, and social reform all found repugnant and threatening the specter of industrial exploitation and upheaval. Just as disturbed were those half-brothers and half-sisters of Progressivism who stood to its immediate left: Chicago's active socialist movement and a central trade union federation unusually willing to entertain bold proposals for industrial and political mass organization and reform. All of these circles were prepared to intervene, each in its own way, for the purpose of imparting to the rebellion the programmatic and organizational coherence it seemed to lack.

While the UGW was doing its level best to inter the strike, local militants looked elsewhere for help and appealed to the WTUL. The League maintained a delicate relationship with the AFL and went to great lengths not to offend the parent organization by allying itself with movements the labor leadership considered outlaw. Thus, before acting the League wanted an endorsement of the strike by the Chicago Federation of Labor. Sidney Hillman's dedication had by this time impressed rank-and-file activists. He was delegated, along with three others, to approach John Fitzpatrick and Edward Nockles, leaders of the Chicago

Federation well-known for their support of more daring forms of industrial unionism and independent labor politics. Not surprisingly, the Federation quickly declared that "this firm [HSM] and others of like character were nothing more or less than the slave driving institutions of the worst imaginable kind." A day after the workers' rejection of the Hart–Rickert agreement, the Federation officially endorsed the strike. Quickly a Joint Strike Conference Board was created, including Fitzpatrick and Nockles; Agnes Nestor, President of the Chicago WTUL; Margaret Drier Robbins, President of the national WTUL; and Robert Noren of the UGW. With equal speed the Board announced the strike's demands: a union shop, maximum hours, and a procedure for resolving grievances.[39]

Alongside the Strike Conference Board, Chicago's more pious and reform-minded businessmen established a Citizen's Committee chaired by Rabbi Emil Hirsch, whose congregation included a number of the city's more reputable clothing manufacturers. Ashamed of the behavior of their business colleagues, in some cases their co-religionists, the Committee pronounced the strike to be thoroughly justified. Members of the Committee proceeded to use their influence behind the scenes to mediate the conflict. Young reform-minded lawyers like Harold Ickes and Raymond Robbins, whose wives were meanwhile getting arrested and roughed up on picket lines by the local constabulary, offered their legal services free to the hundreds of arrested strikers. Ickes's mother-in-law, Mary Wilmouth, a member of an old Chicago family as well as the League, was a great help in getting strikers out of jail. She was joined in her efforts by Mrs. Samuel Dauchy and Mrs. Frank R. Little of the Crane family, influential among progressive Republicans in Chicago. When Mrs. Little was herself arrested, Ickes sent Donald Richberg downtown to defend her. Julius Rosenwald of Sears had his personal chauffer deliver Grace Abbott to a garment workers' meeting that organized the picketing of his own factory.[40]

Professor Charles Merriam of the University of Chicago, then a Chicago city alderman, encouraged the municipal government to play a role as umpire and peacemaker. Merriam, whom Theodore Roosevelt considered radical on the question of government regulation of business and who would later spearhead efforts at state planning under the New Deal, saw in the strike an occasion for applying those principles of political and social science which promised to create a functionally integrated and harmonious community out of a normally fractious and conflict-ridden industrial society. While Merriam pursued civic action to end "great suffering upon our citizens and loss of business to Chicago," the Illinois Senate launched an investigation of the strike. Its findings, revealed after the strike's settlement, exposed the blacklisting system inaugurated by the manufacturers' associations. The Industrial Committee of the Churches of Chicago advised the city's garment producers:

> It would then seem to be the part of good business sense as well as social justice and civic righteousness for you to recognize the inevitable trend of civilization. Bow to the inevitable if to nothing else. . . . Tomorrow we will come to a still nobler synthesis, when labor and capital will combine and recognize their mutual interests.[41]

More tangible kinds of assistance—money, food, and clothing—poured in from the city's trade unions, especially from Bakers Union; from the Jewish Labor Federation, from the city's settlement houses, and from Chicago's socialist party, as well as the Women's Suffrage Party and the Teachers' Federation. Chicago's thriving community of dissident writers, artists, and intellectuals lent their moral support and contributed their talents to the Joint Conference Board's agitational work. Carl Sandburg, then a labor reporter for the *Daily News,* not only filed sympathetic reports on the strike but came regularly to strike meetings to play his banjo, sing, and read poetry.[42]

Above all, the activity of the WTUL was critical. The League organized a vast relief apparatus, marched on picket lines, raised money, and provided speakers for innumerable public forums; thanks to their own talents and social connections as well as the ecumenical hostility of the police, League women attracted to the strike continuous and almost invariably favorable public attention. They became the putative conscience of the Chicago middle class and untiringly called upon it to answer "this insistent demand for social justice and human brotherhood."[43]

The mentality of those women was complex. Some were true Brahmins who saw themselves not only as the community's natural moral aristocracy but as its social guardians as well. Ellen Gates Starr, although a socialist, decried the behavior of the police in terms designed to remind her audience of her own connections to another revolution: "The whole thing was to the descendant of a Revolutionary soldier, an American from 1632, a heart-sickening sight." There was, as well, a certain air of *noblesse oblige,* or at least of tutorial patronizing, perhaps inevitably so, given the great gulf of class and culture separating the League's patrician women from the mass of immigrant poor:

> Organization among young girls is brought about in a very simple fashion— the simpler the better trade organization in her craft means for the working

girl . . . a teaching of self-control, fidelity and self-reliance . . . and over the monotony of her daily toil she sees a vision of the kingdom of righteousness.

Visions of the "kingdom of righteousness" and homilies on Christian fellowship, the sanctity of motherhood, and the home were a vital part of the political grammar of the League. Speaking at the WTUL convention of 1911, Margaret Drier Robbins compared the sweatshop girls to "serfs" whose dreams of motherhood were being ruined: "The glory and strength of motherhood; the dream and music of childhood, are many times sold at the bargain counters."[44]

This vision of sanctified domesticity and the accompanying anxiety that industrialism placed motherhood, childhood, and the home in mortal danger were unexceptionable views at the turn of the century, almost the conventional wisdom of the socially conscious middle class. However, for Jewish immigrant women particularly, whose critical role as breadwinners had for generations earned them a modicum of respect and equality of status systematically denied them in religious, social, and familial spheres, the high-flown language of the League must have seemed strange, or at least to have missed the point.

The language of Christian heroism, self-sacrifice, and spiritual rebirth served at the same time as a jeremiad, addressed to League women's peers, about the perils facing the social order and as a call to civic duty and redemption:

Are those Bohemians, Poles, Italians, and Russian Jews to become loyal and law-abiding American citizens? Or shall we allow them, through neglect and misunderstanding to grow embittered and resentful to the prosperity in which they have no part? Despair is the surest road to Anarchy. Indifference to this struggle on the part of the well-to-do is criminally selfish and short-sighted. The political and social as well as the economic well-being of our City depends on the education in citizenship we give to our Foreign population.[45]

The women of the League managed to combine an exalted rhetoric of moral and civic high-mindedness with a very pragmatic and up-to-date awareness of theoretical and practical developments in the field of industrial labor relations. While still committed to the axioms of nineteenth century Republicanism and evangelical uplift, the League, in keeping with broader currents of Progressive reform, had taken the first steps toward transmuting what had once been moral and political questions into matters of administration and social engineering. They had adjudged poverty and exploitation not only inhumane but also seriously inefficient.

During the strike League literature again and again reiterated the idea that "the only practicable method of presenting general grievances is through trade union organization and the recognition of the union is therefore the fundamental demand." It was pointed out to recalcitrant manufacturers as well as the public that "Many employers throughout the country believe in industrial democracy and willingly meet with the accredited and elected representatives of their workers." In an attempt to instruct a public unfamiliar with the workings of a newer kind of trade unionism, the League noted that "a group of union men and women only use the weapon of the strike as a last resort. They can secure a hearing whenever a grievance occurs through their Shop Committee and whatever grievance cannot be adjusted between the workers and the firm is submitted to a permanent board of arbitration."[46]

Some such formalized arrangement for the mediating and arbitrating of grievances, in which labor and management would be equally represented but would defer if necessary to the impartial judgment of a disinterested umpire, was precisely what the League, the Chicago Federation of Labor, the Citizen's Committee, the Industrial Committee of Churches, and Joseph Schaffner—in a word, the disturbed conscience of middle-class Chicago—wanted, and wanted with a growing sense of urgency. Talk about such new institutions of industrial equity and authority, formally democratic and no longer relying on traditional structures of coercive or paternal domination, was part of a wider Progressive search for a new institutional order. In particular, various business and political circles were paying a great deal of attention to all forms of impartial investigation and arbitration, both compulsory and voluntary, that promised to depoliticize and defuse the "labor question," to transform it into a technical and administrative problem. Indeed, shortly before the HSM strike the Ethical Culture Society had recruited the celebrated jurist Louis Brandeis to devise a solution to an equally tumultuous cloakmakers' strike in New York. Brandeis's "Protocols of Peace" quickly became a widely celebrated mechanism of industrial concord that established precise rules for resolving disputes on the shop floor.[47]

But these procedures were completely foreign to the now rebellious and heretofore unorganized mass of immigrant workers. The Joint Strike Conference Board was quickly forced to realize it had reckoned without its hosts. This point in history, where the onrushing waves of ethnic, artisan, and proletarian anger and desire met the more stately currents of bourgeois moral and industrial reform, is where Sidney Hillman emerged into public view.

Attached to the Strike Conference Board, ostensibly acting as a liaison between the strikers and their anointed leadership, was a strike committee of thirty-five activists roughly representative of the movement's occupational and ethnic components. Repeatedly the Board proposed settlements, based on one or another version of mediation and grievance arbitration, which the strike committee found it impossible to sell to the rank and file. Meanwhile, Merriam succeeded in persuading Chicago's Mayor Fred A. Busse to call a conference in early December of the rest of the industry to hammer out a settlement.

So long as the mass strike continued on its upward arch, widening its social reach and extending its moral hegemony, nothing worked. The Conference Board floated a tentative HSM agreement consisting largely of vague promises and insisted that those strikers found guilty of violence be dismissed. In a stormy series of meetings held simultaneously throughout the city, striking workers rejected the proposal. At the same time the city's independent efforts collapsed, largely as a consequence of the killing of the two Lithuanian strikers. In addition, most of the small and medium-size manufacturers refused to participate in the city's mediation conference. Hostile to unionism but with limited stamina and resources to resist, business adventurers were grossly irresponsible in their relations with both the industry and its workforce. While vulnerable to the pressures of weightier industrial forces, whether better-organized workers or larger manufacturers, they almost preferred a state of chronic chaos and crisis. Their peremptory rebuff of the city's invitation further infuriated the movement and undermined whatever slim chance for peace the HSM bargain presented.

The WTUL lamented the rejection of the agreement:

> It would have been the part of prudence for the employees concerned to accept this settlement, and the only organized workers, the cutters and trimmers, did so, but the storm of protest raised by the newer and less responsible members of the union was overwhelming, and feeling ran so high that all efforts to secure quiet consideration of the plan and a representative vote failed.

The League was honest enough to admit that the strikers had more than sufficient reason to be suspicious of a settlement that made no explicit provision recognizing their organization and could easily turn the stipulation against those guilty of violence into a general blacklist of the movement's leadership. Mixing more than a touch of condescension with genuine commitment, the League announced: "Mistakes on their part made through weakness and ignorance, do not minimize our responsibility but rather increase it." But the women also believed that the agreement, "although far from satisfactory . . . was the best that could be obtained under present conditions."[48]

Perhaps they were right. By mid-November Jane Addams privately concluded that "of course there's no chance that the strikers will win." As a matter of fact, an agreement very much like the rejected one did conclude the strike at HSM a few weeks later. What is more certain, however, is that the peculiar bureaucratic apparatus of industrial democracy the League and others had in mind might not have been installed at all had it not found articulate and respected advocates from within the ranks of the strikers, willing to argue on its behalf in the face of vigorous and sometimes vitriolic opposition.[49]

In the person of Sidney Hillman the strike found a bridge over the chasm separating the world of collective bargaining with its rational-bureaucratic institutions, its behaviorist and individualist psychological assumptions, from the closed universe of kin, craft, community, and ethnoculture. If Hillman cannot be counted among the strike's original inspirers, he, more than anyone else, fathered the union which issued out of that strike.

Hillman shared and helped mobilize those deep hostilities felt by the rank and file for the elitism, craft-bounded parochialism, and nativist, anti-Semitic prejudices of the UGW. He made this vividly clear at the time of the proposed Rickert agreement. At a tumultuous mass meeting Hillman, then still an unknown figure, speaking a combination of broken English and Yiddish, and with the help of an Italian translator, denounced the betrayal and helped reinvigorate the strike. The moment instantly transformed him into a popular leader and an authentic moral presence. It also brought him to the attention of the League and, in particular, Jane Addams. Although Hillman had maintained sporadic contact with the Chicago Federation of Labor and may have visited Hull House prior to the strike, after his dramatic debut he was virtually adopted by the strike's Progressive leadership.

During the remaining months of the strike Hillman spent more time at Hull House than anywhere else. He listened attentively to Addams's views on industrial conflict. While Addams defended the strike as "most just and righteous," she was more concerned with devising some permanent system of ensuring industrial peace that would supersede the prevailing law of the industrial jungle. Addams exerted a great formative influence over Hillman's ideas about American labor relations, as did the circle of Progressives to whom she soon introduced him: Ellen Gates Starr, Margaret Drier Robbins, Graham Taylor, Grace Abbott, Clarence Darrow, and Professor Earl Dean Howard.

Darrow took Hillman under his wing and became his principal tutor in English and the latest Progressive thinking about social problems, politics, and philosophy. The essentially tutorial relationships with Darrow and Addams began an extended apprenticeship for Hillman in the social perspective, political objectives, and organizational techniques of Progressivism. The apprenticeship extended over the next several years, first in Chicago and later in New York. This was all happening while Addams was busy behind the scenes reopening channels of negotiation with HSM after the workers' second rejection of a settlement. Darrow, along with Harry Hart and Joseph Schaffner, who both knew Addams, and Professor Howard, an associate of Addams whom HSM was soon to hire as its new labor manager, were the principal negotiators. Hillman attended their meetings, which proceeded to work out a new understanding, one calling for less than the strikers were demanding but at least omitting the threat to discharge those guilty of violence during the strike.[50]

The stage was thus set for Hillman's second critical intervention in the strike, the one that would permanently endear him to the partisans of orderly reform. As formulated, this newest settlement was unacceptable to a very large and militant minority. Led by the Industrial Workers of the World and various free-lance radicals, the opposition issued "A Call for Action." Circulated by a "Committee of Italian Workers," probably affiliated with the Industrial Workers of the World (IWW, or "wobblies"), the leaflet denounced the pending agreement: "Don't hesitate, Don't mediate, Don't arbitrate, Don't wait," it cried, urging the workers not to be "whipped back to work under an arbitration agreement . . . the wounds of the clubbed and the maimed, the blood of the murdered calls aloud for action in the struggle for human rights." This denunciation of the strike's official joint leadership, along with the demand for a closed shop and a 15 percent wage increase, won support among Poles, Lithuanians, and Bohemians as well as among the Italian workers. Then, in the course of an extremely tense mass meeting during which he was at first unable to hold the floor against his infuriated opponents, Hillman finally prevailed. "You can run over my dead body but I shall not leave this platform," he cried defiantly. As the howling continued, he assured the meeting's chairman, A. D. Marimpietri, that he was determined to "hold onto the chair" come what may. Hillman forcefully defended the agreement as a real victory that, if not seized immediately, might be lost for years to come and concluded with a challenge to the opposition: "You may take my life but you shall not repudiate this agreement while I live." Ratified by the assembled strikers, the settlement was signed by all parties on January 14. The strike at HSM, but nowhere else, was over.[51]

Hillman had won a personal victory, however much it might be explained by the tidal shifts of temper in the mass strike. He had already gained a reputation as a dedicated and courageous organizer and spokes-man. His years in the Bund had made him a practiced agitator and public speaker. His public style was strangely compelling, both reserved and dynamic at the same time: "He was no orator and he certainly didn't have any overwhelming physical presence," one colleague would recall. He was small but strongly built. His face looked ascetic, its wide, high forehead modeled by curious depressions above his large, rather lumi-nous, and slightly slanting eyes. His jaw was powerful but not heavy, and the mouth, with full lower and finely curved upper lips, was at once strong and tense. His whole body radiated a tautness that riveted his audience. Earlier training as a *yeshiva bucher* polemicist turned out to be a recyclable resource, so that when publicly pushed to the wall, as he was that day in Hodcarriers Hall, Hillman was capable of extemporaneous adroitness and stinging sarcasm. Unimposing and soft-spoken in private, he nonetheless conveyed an inward strength and self-possession. He conveyed as well a certain intrinsic dignity, which was if anything en-hanced by the thick Yiddish accent that remained with him for the rest of his life. Faced with a situation full of alarms and threats, he showed no fear, either physical or moral. The very timbre of his voice and structure of his speech made that determination audible. By no means polished, he spoke bluntly, with an almost harsh but resonant voice, oddly foreign, and capable of rising in great crescendos of cold-blooded logic, accented sparingly with the more millennial rhetoric of labor's emancipation, and an occasional bit of melodrama:

> After all the tailors are always right. Even when they are wrong they are right. The capitalists have everything and they have nothing but the power of labor. The capitalists make thousands or millions as profits and surplus— why should not the workers be entitled to a few pennies.[52]

Above all, it was his cold realism that made Hillman compelling that day in Hodcarriers Hall. He sensed, as did thousands of the weary strik-ers, that the tide had begun to run out on the movement. No other manufacturer besides HSM was offering an agreement of any kind. The winter was especially harsh, and landlords were showing no mercy. The mass strike had extended its reach across a remarkably wide social ter-rain, but it was getting no closer to victory, at least as victory had been originally conceived. The momentum of events thus lent additional force to Hillman's personal appeal.

Within HSM's empire of needle and thread, the struggle was over, concluded on the understanding that most of the outstanding issues concerning wages, hours, conditions, and—most important—the future status of the fledgling union were to be decided later by a tripartite board of impartial arbitration. Clarence Darrow was to function as the workers' representative. This pivotal act of delicate mediation was what first persuaded Joseph Schaffner that Sidney Hillman was not so much a rebel as "a man of sweet reasonableness, worthy of the highest praise and warmest admiration," for "his great service to the cause of industrial democracy." Harold Ickes remembered that when the HSM partners finally agreed to talk they

> . . . found that the strike leaders whom they had suspected, resented, and distrusted as young hot-heads, had a keen and amazing broad understanding of their common problems and a social vision and idealism. The reports which came back from these conferences . . . invariably singled out for special praise one young man, slight in stature and with gleaming black eyes from which flashed intellectual integrity, indomitable courage, and irresistible idealism. He was, we were told, wise beyond his years and a man destined to be a leader among men.[53]

Hillman himself was under no illusion about the nature of the "victory." Many observers speculated that had there been a formal vote the agreement would have been defeated. Those 30,000 or so still on strike against members of the manufacturers association felt betrayed and were not shy about condemning the HSM settlement. Hillman and his fellow organizer Anzuino Marimpietri decided to remain with the HSM strikers as they filed back to work over the next ten days. "We wanted to accompany the strikers on their way back to the various shops . . . so that they would know that someone was with them and would not feel completely discouraged. . . . On the 9th day we marched with the last returning groups to shops 3, 4, and 5."[54]

The mood of the strikers, demoralized and faced with the belligerent intransigence of the Clothiers Association, grew even glummer over the next few weeks. On February 3 Thomas Rickert, realizing he would meet little resistance, unilaterally ended the strike in the rest of the industry without so much as bothering to consult the Joint Strike Conference Board, much less the strikers. Everybody was angry; Robbins described Rickert's act as a "hunger bargain." But there was nothing to be done. Hillman somberly remembered the grim dénouement as the workers

> . . . were forced to return to their old miserable conditions, through the back door; and happy were those who were taken back. Many who had

participated in the 1910 strike were victimized for months afterward. They were forced to look for other employment and to wait until their record in the strike was forgotten.[55]

Even before this final act of betrayal and defeat, Hillman had wondered aloud to his friend Marimpietri, "What now? Tomorrow you and I must go back to work or lose our jobs. What will become of these people? Who will be there to give them encouragement, to build our union? If one of us can do it there is our opportunity." He was right. Even more important than the skeletal agreement with HSM was consolidating and expanding the group of shop militants. As one of them, Frank Rosenblum, observed, the workers were "licked from a strike point of view [but] it did create a nucleus of an organization." Marimpietri volunteered to donate ten dollars a week of his own wages so that Hillman might devote himself to organizing. That marked the end of Hillman's relatively brief career as a proletarian. Soon his lunchtime visits to the various HSM plants had proved successful enough at recruiting new members for Marimpietri to stop the donations out of his pocket. Before long Hillman was chosen president of a newly constituted local, local 39, and began his career as a trade union official.[56]

Organizing was hard and often tedious work. It required psychological stamina to persevere day after day in the frequently discouraging work of persuading workers, in ones and twos, to enlist in the embryonic local. Many were afraid because the formal agreement with the company's partners had left the dangerous power of foremen over their shop floor fiefdoms scarcely diminished. Others, enveloped in the cultural integuments of the Old World, remained unmoved by the more individuated incentives of trade unionism. Church and synagogue, *landsleit* and *paesani*, still potent institutions and identities, competed for the loyalty of those who worked without yet defining themselves as proletarians. Still others dreamed of rising off the factory floor, of opening up a contractor shop, of peddling; some even indulged airborne fantasies of real estate speculation and great riches against which the modest offerings of a union were laughably irrelevant.

Innumerable meetings, scraping together enough pennies to mimeograph a circular, and petty harassment by foremen and other company officials made up the quotidian concerns of the union's cadre. Hillman was kept endlessly busy traveling from shop to shop to investigate complaints, persuading members to attend local meetings, and drawing up proposals for a new agreement. He visited New York briefly to investigate and report on conditions in the "preferential shop" set up under the Brandeis "Protocols of Peace."[57]

The nettlesome problem of incipient ethnic antagonisms had yet to be overcome. Marimpietri, who was fluent in Polish and Serbian as well as Italian, described the experience of talking to fourteen fellow workers, comprising ten different nationalities:

> We developed friendship of a sort. . . . We used to sing together, each of us a song in his own tongue, but every now and then a sentiment, not very complimentary, was expressed showing plainly that the national feeling was ever present and needed only a spark to make it flame.[58]

Although Hillman and Marimpietri would have preferred to organize locals according to department and job category, the forces of ethnic particularism were too powerful. In short order five language locals— Bohemian, Polish, English, Lithuanian, and Italian—were established. Ethnic hostilities flared anyway. Italians resented Jewish domination of the leadership. Poles threatened not to strike if called upon to do so because "Hebrews" would take their places, and so on. Progress was sometimes discouragingly slow. By 1912 only 2,500 of the roughly 7,000 employees belonged to the union, and many sections remained completely unorganized.[59]

But all that was to be expected. What turned out to be the task of considerably greater psychological and social complexity, demanding a true genius for organizational creativity, was designing and installing the innovative machinery of industrial democracy for which the HSM agreement provided only the barest sketch.

Responding to the influence of Addams and Darrow particularly, Hillman was convinced that the agreement's machinery for impartial arbitration could introduce the rule of law on the shop floor and provide a constitutional basis for equitable labor–management relations. But Hillman was not naïve. He also realized that from the standpoint of the rank and file, who were in any event not wildly enthusiastic about the settlement, the real question was whose law was to rule. Within months of the settlement, walkouts of dissatisfied work groups began. Unilateral changes in work rules and rates prompted numerous short strikes among pants seamers and pants makers, whose faith in the newly established Trade Board for resolving grievances was minimal.

Instances of insubordination caused Hillman and the rest of the union leaders endless aggravation and required patience, sometimes enormous patience. One organizer reported that the workers "make no distinction between the order of a business agent and the order of a gendarme." Even the fledgling union's own cadre, so unaccustomed to their new bureaucratic functions, were not entirely reliable. Sarah

Rozner, a union chairlady, acknowledged that she often precipitated quickie strikes:

> We had specifically written in the agreement, no stoppages. So when I see that the examiner is abusing the workers, although I wasn't an officer if I saw that something is wrong, I would instigate a work stoppage. I would find one confidential person, maybe two, and nobody would ever find out who it was making stoppages. . . . I used to do that. . . . I knew it was wrong, [but] the worker was abused. It was against the union rule. I made my own rules.

Cutters and trimmers obeyed management, union, and impartial authorities when it was convenient to do so. The rest of the time they waged civil war. The Board of Arbitration condemned such "unwarranted rebellion" and expressed its dismay that such occurrences took place among the "most highly paid, the most skilled, and presumably the most intelligent and advanced group of workers." It reflected badly, the Board concluded, on the workers' capacity "for democratic self-government" and suggested the "inability of the local officials to control its members." The Board was determined not to compromise on the issue of unauthorized stoppages and threatened to discharge offenders.[60]

The Board could express its anger and disappointment, and the union leadership could do its best to restore order, but the cutters remained determined to defend their traditional skills and work rules. Thus, for example, when ordered to cut "lays" of mixed fabrics, a departure from past practice and a threat to their control of the job, the cutters first stopped work and then engaged in systematic production slowdowns. Exasperated and operating on the presumption that "efficiency" was in everyone's best interests, the Board described the slowdown tactic as "stupid," "destructive," and "dishonest." But it didn't know what to do, as firing or fining a few offenders would only exacerbate the situation. The problem was clearly cultural as well as economic, and the Board was left with the hope that the behavior was "merely a survival of a policy originating under very different conditions and now decisively abandoned by intelligent and progressive labor."

Other work groups were also capable of displaying displeasure as well as their continuing attachment to older concepts of shop floor justice. Second-basters and off-pressers engaged in frequent stoppages even when severely reprimanded by the union. Pocketmakers, skilled workers who adhered strictly to long established work rules, refused to obey foremen's orders to handle work differently. These work groups maintained a rigid, if informal, jurisprudence all their own. If a member violated a traditional shop floor practice of importance—by exceeding output previously agreed upon, for example—he was punished without delay or ceremony.[61]

In addition to these proud and obstreperous work teams, several well-represented political factions considered the agreement perfidious. The "wobblies" were most vociferous. They enjoyed a bellicose if ephemeral following among Italian workers particularly, as well as among a smaller number of Jews. The IWW assigned a national organizer, Emilio Grandinetti, to oversee the situation at HSM. Jewish anarchists were also present in great numbers. They were not under the auspices of the IWW, but they too opposed contractual obligations of any kind as a bourgeois subterfuge.[62]

Anarchism among Jewish garment workers was a tradition stretching back to the 1870s in Britain and to the 1890s in Russia. Hillman himself had had to contend against the active anarchist circles in Kovno, because the Bund had strict rules against the sort of terrorist tactics some factions of the anarchist movement employed. Partisans of the movement began fleeing the Pale and arriving in America during the few years preceding the wave of needle trades strikes. Sabotage and arson were part of their tactical repertoire, which they were not about to discard in America. One Hungarian anarcho-terrorist, for example, who had seen his brother butchered by the Hungarian cavalry, became practiced in setting fires to nonunion shops as an extreme means of driving cowed workers out of the arms of their intimidating employers. Bearers of a strong populist antipathy to the rich and a conviction that all forms of parliamentary democracy were a sham, this anarchist element on the shop floor was not inclined to volunteer for an experiment in industrial democracy sponsored by the well-to-do and the well-born.[63]

The politics and practices of a generation—in some cases of generations—could not be abolished in a day. Customs governing the pace, organization, and quantity of work lacked the elegant abstractness and precision of a body of law, but they were nonetheless entrenched and persevered, at least to the extent that power could be mobilized on the factory floor to enforce them. This was a most incongruous setting in which to implant a system of industrial democracy, which presumed a certain self-restraint on the part of both workers and management. It depended on workers' willingness to honor work rules, standards of performance, disciplinary procedures, and new codes of shop floor behavior, which they had only indirectly participated in formulating. Most important, it depended on having work groups relinquish their right to strike even when they felt justice or self-interest demanded they exercise it.[64]

Teasing compliance out of this dense web of ethnic, occupational, and political loyalties to a formal, bureaucratic system of representation required the artful orchestration of psychological, behavioral, and cultural currents not absolutely inimical to management and union objectives. Hillman knew the Old World—at least the Yiddish-speaking portion of it—intimately. It was his genius to realize that if industrial democracy, an invention of the new middle class, was to survive and flourish it would have to accommodate a far older, preindustrial artisan democracy. Working closely with Clarence Darrow, and later with Darrow's law partner, William Thompson (when Darrow was called away to take on the defense of the McNamara brothers charged with dynamiting the *Los Angeles Times*), Hillman managed to convince the arbitration board that "the motive of group loyalty is to be relied upon to secure the average production" and that unilateral efforts to abolish "past practice" were seriously misguided. Bureaucratic rationality would have to make its peace with more traditional approaches to work not wedded to the ethos of efficiency. Hillman called it "the new principle of our organization, that if the workers are to be disciplined for any violation, they themselves partly should be the judges." He furthermore realized that militancy on the part of local leaders was not necessarily a bad thing, as it enhanced the credibility of the union not only among the more skeptical segments of the membership but also among elements of middle-level management less inclined to accept the new dispensation without a struggle. Hillman would guess quickly enough what these men would be willing to pay in return for the responsible pledge of uninterrupted production for the present moment, and so would "wring the best price he could get."[65]

Ultimately, Hillman knew, all these popular sentiments and their militant expression would have to be rechanneled, transformed, and encoded in a new rhetoric of workers' demands and perceptions emphasizing economic self-interest and industrial equity: "To see these people, only a few years ago from lands where factories are unknown, meeting to discuss problems of the rights and wrongs of shop discipline, of changing prices, of the rightfulness of a discharge is a thing to fill one with hope for the future of democracy." It provided the workers with an education "no college course in political economy would give them."[66]

In this work of historical and cultural mediation, Hillman was both assisted and applauded by Chicago's social and industrial Progressive elite. Addams made the facilities of Hull House available for many of the early meetings of local 39. The League assigned a longtime needle worker, Mary Anderson, on Hillman's recommendation, as its full-time representative and organizer at HSM. She and Hillman, together with local militant, Bessie Abramovitz, worked closely together "forestalling or ending a succession of wildcat strikes," "training" the workers for "self-government and . . . the importance of presenting their grievances through the appointed representatives instead of going out on strike several times a week." Smothering local brushfires before they spread became especially critical in the spring of 1913, when the prospect of a companywide strike threatened the renewal of the agreement. It was averted when Hillman, in consultation with the impartial arbiter, John E. Williams, formulated a proposal for the "preferential shop" that would not exclude, as in a closed shop, nonunion workers, but rather would give preference in hiring to union members.[67]

The "preferential shop" was a real victory and suggests that no amount of organizational deftness and psychological subtlety could have succeeded if the agreement itself had turned out to be mere empty promises. As a matter of fact, within a short time it delivered tangible benefits. Wages and piece rates improved significantly for all classes of workers, hours were reduced (10 percent for tailors and 3 percent for cutters, a modest decline in hours to 54 in 1911 and 52 in 1913), and perhaps most important, the petty abuses of the floor boss were drastically curtailed.[68]

Mary Drier Robbins was impressed enough with Hillman's abilities to describe him as "one of the leading labor statesmen of this generation" (perhaps the first use of that sobriquet, which stuck with Hillman for the rest of his life) who possessed a "wonderful power over his people." While Drier was congratulating Hillman, the firm itself, represented by Professor Howard, quickly realized how very much more difficult it was to resolve problems in unorganized or poorly organized shops, and actually invited Hillman and Bessie Abramovitz "to go into the shops during working hours and speak to the workers on the need of concerted action and the meaning of the trade agreement." Howard hoped that in strongly organized shops workers would "understand that their grievances must be referred to the Board of Arbitration for adjustment" and that workers would "have learned self-control and self-government and submit their grievances in an orderly and businesslike fashion." Initially suspicious of Hillman, Howard soon admitted:

We learned to like him for his intelligence, his moderation, and his attractive personality. Then too, the reformation in our management came slowly and his criticisms were often found to be justified.

Mr. Schaffner even grew to have as much and even more confidence in him than in some of his own superintendents . . . he was a leader by reason of his obvious fitness. The influence which he quickly and legitimately came to have with the board and the company conferred a natural authority among the workers.[69]

While the profits of HSM shrank in 1911–12 thanks in part to the strike of the previous year, the partners never regretted their decision to recognize the union. Testifying before the Industrial Relations Commission in 1914, Joseph Schaffner enthusiastically described the consequences: "In our business, employing thousands of persons, some of them newly arrived immigrants, many of them in opposition to the wage system and hostile to employers as a class, we have observed astonishing changes in their attitudes during the four years under the influence of our labor agreement."

The whole Chicago Progressive community—its social scientists and economists, its social engineers and Christian socialists, its businessmen and political reformers—celebrated the introduction of what Schaffner called "the rule of reason and justice." They also warmly appreciated the act of industrial statesmanship that had made it possible. Sidney Hillman seemed to them the solution of one vital piece of a larger social puzzle: the search for a competent, responsible elite capable of acting above and beyond "selfish" interests on behalf of social harmony and progress.[70]

That Hillman should find himself among the chosen was a consequence of both deliberate preparation and training by others and a process of self-selection.

No one, not Addams, not Darrow, not Robbins, exercised a more decisive influence over Hillman's apprenticeship than John E. Williams, a pioneer in the relatively new field of industrial labor relations. Williams was a saintly figure of local renown who edited a paper, the *Streator-Independent Times,* in the small coal-mining town of Streator, Illinois. A Welsh-born coal miner who had labored in Streator's mine no. 1 for fifteen years, Williams was self-educated in a fashion peculiar to the prideful independence of mining communities. In 1910 Williams became the official arbitrator between the United Mine Workers of Illinois and the Illinois Coal Operators, his first experience with industrial democracy.

Immersed in the world of Ethical Culture and a practicing Unitarian, Williams was known to be "incorruptible." His reputation as a provincial philosopher of trade unionism brought him to the attention of the principals in Chicago. By 1913 he became the impartial arbitrator presiding over the HSM agreement.[71]

Until his death in 1919, Williams functioned as Hillman's mentor. It was through Williams that Hillman, still in many respects a provincial, ethnic socialist, received his first systematic introduction to both the mechanics and the romance of "industrial democracy" and social engineering.

It is understandably difficult now to think of social engineering as anything but an austere and manipulative view of the world; but at its birth, for people like Williams, and perforce for Sidney Hillman, it represented a new idealism: the idealism of functional integration, of democratic compromise in the interests of greater efficiency and material well-being, and a vision of social cooperation in place of industrial rancor and class struggle. It was, for a historical moment at least, one of the more democratically inspired experiments of Progressivism, but its tacit acceptance of the corporate order poisoned its potential. For Williams particularly, who still spoke the language of Jefferson and Thoreau and remained concerned with "rights," "democratic participation," and the creation of independent citizens, it was an approach still fresh with promise, seeking a way to reconcile the organizational imperatives of corporate-bureaucratic order with the vision of propertied self-reliance that underlay nineteenth-century republicanism.

Williams not only advised Hillman on trade union strategy and tactics but gave him the confidence to explain and defend the ethical accomplishments of the union at gatherings of middle-class reformers. He was convinced that the young immigrant leader possessed an ideal combination of character traits and talents. The "most remarkable characteristic in one so young is his power of restraint," Williams noted. "We expect youth to be fiery, enthusiastic, daring; but we rarely find it coupled with that poise, repose, self-mastery so necessary to great achievements of any sort." As Williams saw it, Hillman was "the most valuable asset that the new unionism possesses. . . . He is the one that in preeminent degree has the vision, the idealism, the genius of leadership, the power of inspiring confidence that is necessary to give a new direction to trade union energies."[72]

The qualities singled out by Williams constituted a kind of characterological ideal of the Progressive mentality. Prodded by a growing fear of the anarchy lurking beneath the surface of industrial society, thinkers and activists alike prized in particular "the power of restraint" and the capacity for "self-mastery" in the face of wholesale disorder.

A "talmudic habit of mind, of looking at all angles of a question" left Hillman psychologically prepared to resolve disputes within the community of workers and to mediate that community's relations with the outside world.[73]

At the same time, Hillman's Bundist upbringing made him a missionary of a different sort. Always a man of the Enlightenment, he saw himself as a messenger of modern thought and culture, bearing the news of scientific progress and political emancipation to the oppressed of the Pale. So too in Chicago, he became the tribune of modernity, in this case the industrial modernism of contractual obligation, economic equity, and productive efficiency. As it had been for all the proponents and movements of the radical enlightenment for a century and more, the war cry of the Bund was *"Raison."* For a much longer time, the rabbinical calling demanded above all "Reasonableness." In the years ahead, one central dilemma facing this visionary of the practical consisted first of all in telling the difference between the two, and then deciding whether *Raison* or reasonableness was to command the course of his life.

FOUR

The Protocols of Power

Baruch Charney Vladek was known, first in the Pale and later in America, as the "Jewish LaSalle." Born in the village of Dookorch, near Minsk, in 1886, he, like his older brother Samuel, attended the local cheder and was then sent on to a yeshiva in Minsk, where his mother fervently hoped the brothers would go on to become rabbis.

It was not to be. Vladek's orthodox studies were soon interupted, first by Zionist appeals, which tended to be strongest in this southern portion of the Pale, and then by secret revolutionary study circles through which Vladek was introduced to the works of Pushkin, Tolstoy, and Turgenev. The Kishinev pogrom made Vladek an activist. By 1904 he had established contact with the Bund, had been jailed twice, and had turned his imprisonment into a postgraduate education in revolutionary doctrine and Western social theory. Vladek's exceptionable skills as a writer and his prophetic powers as a speaker earned him his LaSallean reputation, so when he fled Russia for the United States in 1908, he was already a near-legendary hero. In the New World he became a prominent figure in the Socialist Party in Philadelphia and later in New York, where he joined the *Forward,* first as its city editor and later as its managing editor. His association with the *Forward,* the leading journal of Jewish trade unionism and socialism, and his identification with the world of Jewish labor politics continued until his death in 1939.[1]

The vital biographical benchmarks of Sidney Hillman's early years— birth, maternal breeding, apostasy, political conversion, jailings, revolutionary icons, flight to the West—bear a striking resemblance to

Vladek's. There would be more than a few occasions when they found themselves working together in America. Despite their shared Old World heritage, however, the "Jewish LaSalle" and America's first "labor states-man" established strikingly different presences in the New World, as their sobriquets suggest. If Vladek remained the loyal son of ghetto socialism, Sidney Hillman was later considered by many to be its prodigal offspring, so taken with the urbane and prepossessing world of reform elites that he would deliberately distance himself from the more provin-cial and more strictly Jewish concerns that absorbed people like Vladek.

Hillman, not Vladek, is the anomaly. There were hundreds like Vladek—revolutionary Jewish emigrés from the Pale, who were perhaps less celebrated than the "Jewish LaSalle" but went on to become the architects, organizers, and poets of a uniquely Yiddish working-class cul-ture. They penned its special ethnic literature and newspapers, organized its emphatically Jewish unions and fraternal orders, proselytized for a distinctly Jewish brand of socialist politics, and, as the years passed, made their peace with Jewish nationalism and the Zionist movement. Hillman never entirely lost touch with this world of socialist *yiddishkeit,* especially in his private life, but it became more the shadow than the substance of his being.

Certainly, during his years in Chicago, he thought of himself as an immigrant, a Jew, and a socialist. But those cardinal insignia of his identity, while no doubt still psychologically compelling, lacked a cer-tain social weight. Working in an industry whose ethnic composition was far more heterogeneous and far less Jewish than the needle trades in New York, Hillman's identifying marks as Jew, immigrant, and socialist were not fused, as they might have been in New York, with an actual living community and culture and a set of concrete organizational loyalties. Predisposed anyway to spend a great deal of time by himself, at least before the HSM strike, Hillman never felt enveloped by that nearly infinite array of causes, commitments, and campaigns that consumed the lives of Jewish socialists like Vladek. And precisely because he was not so consumed, he was more susceptible to the blandishments of middle-class industrial Progressives.

Jewish labor leaders, men like Benjamin Schlesinger and later David Dubinsky, Vladek, Abraham Shiplacoff, and others, were also in close touch with the advocates of "industrial democracy." The "Protocols of Peace," under which the International Ladies' Garment Workers Union (ILG or ILGWU) operated, were very much the invention of Progres-sives, of Brandeis in particular. Nevertheless, this Jewish labor leadership was insulated from the values and larger objectives of Progressivism by a dense network of specifically Jewish and socialist organizational affiliations and cultural commitments. Hillman, on the other hand, was exposed at a formative period of his life to an undiluted version of the Progressive persuasion. Addams, Darrow, and Williams left their mark; enough so that when Hillman did finally come face to face with the world of Charney Vladek he came equipped with a developed sense of his own special talents, reputation, and independent associations.

The actual invitation to come to New York arrived late in 1913. It was extended by the editor of the *Jewish Daily Forward* and the godfather of New York City socialism, Abraham Cahan. The "Protocols of Peace" were in danger of imminent collapse, and Cahan thought Hillman could help. The Protocols had been inevitably weakened by the centrifugal competitiveness of the industry itself which undermined all efforts to standardize costs and the conditions of labor. That structural disability was aggravated by what might be called a problem of cultural dissonance, one with which Hillman was already quite familiar.

The ILGWU was led by a conservative trade unionist, John Dyche, who believed improvement ought to come gradually, contractually, and without resort to the strike, which of course the union, as a signatory of the Protocols, had agreed to relinquish anyway. Isaac A. Hourwich, who was both a scholar and a partisan of the labor movement, functioned as the New York Joint Board's Chief Clerk, which meant he had the day-to-day responsibility for seeing to it that the legitimate grievances of the rank and file were satisfactorily resolved by the Protocols machinery. However, a great many of the smaller manufacturers who had ostensibly agreed to abide by the rulings of the grievance and arbitration boards were never really committed to doing so, especially when it meant losing some competitive edge, and even more especially if such self-sacrifice was being called for in the midst of a business recession, which was in fact under way in 1913.

The bad faith with which those "business anarchists" enlisted under the Protocols was matched on the shop floor by an anarcho-syndicalist hostility to all forms of contractual obligation, particularly when such obligations carried with them a promise not to strike. As in Chicago, recently arrived Jewish immigrants were unfamiliar with the bureaucratic procedures and ill-disposed to the self-discipline without which the Protocols were unworkable: A "large number of them have been engaged in fighting autocracy, in fighting ukases of the Czar, and to a great many of them even obeying an order, even though the order comes from the union, is repugnant." Hourwich sympathized with those shop floor sentiments, even as they became obstreperous and seriously disruptive, and did so increasingly as manufacturers made clear their own inclination simply to ignore the provisional jurisprudence of the Protocols. Before long "the Hourwich affair" ignited a small civil war that deeply divided the Jewish labor and radical community.[2]

Cahan, although critical of Dyche's conservatism, thought Hourwich was an embarrassment and would have to go—and he did. Cahan possessed enormous power. The *Forward* was more than a newspaper. It functioned as a kind of Tammany Hall of New York socialism and wielded decisive influence over not only the Socialist Party but over all the Jewish needle unions, the United Hebrew Trades, the Jewish fraternal organizations—especially the Workmen's Circle—and other socialist media. Within the relatively impoverished circles of Jewish labor radicalism, it exercised its considerable financial leverage. More than other newspapers and magazines, it shaped Jewish public opinion even outside the always narrowly circumscribed reach of socialist ideology.

It was Cahan who selected Hillman to replace Hourwich. He did so first of all because John Williams's *Streator Independent-Times* article "The Russian Jew in American History," which had lavished so much praise on Hillman's industrial statesmanship, had come to Cahan's attention when reprinted in the leading Progressive journal *The Survey*. William O. Thompson, Darrow's law partner, who had assumed Darrow's responsibilities in representing the workers at HSM, strongly seconded Williams's opinion and told Cahan that Hillman would make an ideal replacement for Hourwich.[3]

Hillman and his closest friends, particularly Williams, saw in the "Hourwich affair" a great opportunity "to prove himself an able and courageous leader" on a stage more challenging and glamorous and from a position potentially more powerful than anything Chicago could offer. Nevertheless, they agonized over the decision. The core group at HSM had become close friends. Bessie Abramovitz and Hillman were by this time romantically involved. Moreover, Hillman's political sagacity, decisiveness, cool will power, and immense self-confidence had already made him a first among equals and created among his comrades a sense of dependence, especially given the still tentative status of the organization at HSM. They were therefore reluctant to see him go. Knowing that he would most probably accept Cahan's offer, Hillman stressed to Williams how important it was that people like Bessie, Marimpietri, and Sam Levin recognize their own competencies and realize that stable relations in Chicago did not depend on his presence. Still, self-assured as Hillman was, he had some lingering doubts about his own ability to master the tumultuous scene in New York. It took some reassuring words from his mentor, John Williams, about how "supremely gifted" he was to manage it before Hillman made the final decision to accept the new post.

At a homely banquet in a simple workingmen's restaurant, Hillman was toasted by his fellow workers, Mrs. Robbins, members of the HSM management, and the impartial chairman, James Mullenbach. They called him their "young father," and Hillman responded with genuine humility:

> There seems to be a certain Mr. Hillman who has been referred to, but it isn't myself. . . . It is the personification of the new idealism of our organization. It is the result of a movement bigger than any man or locality. Out of the movement for industrial peace and democracy, you and I are getting more than we give.[4]

With some trepidation then, and with more than a touch of nostalgic regret, Hillman moved to New York in January 1914. It was symptomatic of his sense of himself and his place in the complex world of labor reform that he initially established residence at the Henry Street settlement. There he made his first professional friendships with Lillian Wald and Paul Kellogg, editor of *The Survey*. Wald, along with Henry Moscowitz, represented the "public" on the Board of Sanitary Control, established to enforce health and safety standards in the city's garment shops. Hillman's Progressive friends in Chicago, while sorry to see him go, were determined that he not be lost to the cause. Margaret Drier Robbins wrote shortly before his departure to her sister in New York: "We do not know here in Chicago whether to rejoice with you or grieve for ourselves because of Sidney Hillman's election as chief deputy," but she wanted to stress his remarkable qualities as "one of the leading labor statesmen of this generation." She urged her sister to have Hillman in for dinner and "a long quiet talk together. He has wonderful power over his people here in Chicago and I can only hope that he will be able to have the same power with the same splendid self-control on his part that he has had here in Chicago."[5]

However, it was the doyens of Jewish socialism who had hired Hillman, not as a social worker but as a trade union functionary, and it was to the embattled sweatshops of New York's dressmaking industry that he turned his attention. Hillman's previous experience at HSM, establishing and maintaining a delicate equilibrium between the imperatives of managerial efficiency and the informal practices of workers' control of the shop floor, was useful. But it was not the best sort of training for his role as Chief Clerk of the ILG. In that position he was less free to maneuver between the contending parties and was responsible to a bureaucratic hierarchy that scarcely existed in Chicago. Nonetheless, he was at first optimistic and a bit flattered by the appointment. He wrote to his uncle Charles in Manchester:

I am getting along fairly well here holding a position with the Cloak makers Union, a body of 50,000 organized people. Needless to tell you as far as the work is concerned I like it—or rather enjoy it. You know that these were always my desires to be affiliated with the labor movement. I do not know what your views are on the subject at this time, after all the labor troubles in your country, and many other troubles. It may be you feel rather inconvenienced about it, but, that is a matter of geography and I suppose the labor movement in the U.S. would find your approval, if not for the cause, at least for the distance.

Even faced with the bureaucratic tedium associated with the processing of workers' grievances, Hillman retained a sense of high idealism about the undertaking as a whole. His young friend and admirer in Chicago, Jacob Potofsky, thought about quitting and complained: "Idealism—I said it before—it's being drowned in our daily tasks, and becoming more or less a machine. I fear becoming a politician." He went on to muse about returning to the shop and resuming his night school studies. Hillman, alert to the problem, had earlier warned against the danger of turning people into paid functionaries. He insisted to Potofsky that the movement, despite its bureaucratic features, was still the best way to live: "It appears to me that the more I go through those things the more I feel that it is the only thing worth while. It is true in the early days it was more of a romantic feeling, but as time goes on, it becomes a real necessity."[6]

The "Protocols of Peace" were in such an advanced state of disintegration, however, that it was hard to remain sanguine for long. What consensus existed in New York was extremely fragile and was shared mainly by those disinterested Progressives like Brandeis and Walter Weyl of *The New Republic* who presided over the Board of Arbitration, and by people like Hillman. The great majority of the principal actors, among both manufacturers and workers, remained skeptical at best and quite ready to abandon ship. John Williams, who had developed an almost fatherly concern about Hillman's future and was aware of the perilous situation he now faced, allowed his well-intentioned zeal and weakness for the melodramatic to warp his assessment: "Hillman stands like Napoleon as the child of fate, an almost tragic figure, as he surveys the field of battle, with its new, mysterious, and unknown forces and issues." But Hillman was hardly a general, even on this obscure battlefield, and his predicament not so much tragic as it was simply hopeless.

During his brief tenure, which lasted only until September 1914, Hillman never enjoyed the popularity among the rank and file that he had in Chicago. For one thing, he failed to evince the undiluted sympathy for the actions of shop floor militants that had made Hourwich their hero. Indeed, they found Hillman more than a bit aloof, too much the rabbi. Nor were his relations with the ILG leadership and the *Forward* group ever anything more than polite. No doubt a certain resentment over Hillman's fascination with and attachment to people like Kellogg, Wald, and Weyl accounted for some of the frostiness.[7]

For Hillman, however, the only enduring legacy of his otherwise momentary association with the Protocols was precisely his growing familiarity with those fostering the spirit and substance of "industrial democracy," in particular Louis Brandeis. Brandeis, after all, wanted the Protocols to introduce "the element of industrial democracy; that there should be a beginning at least of a joint control and with joint control a joint responsibility for the conduct of the industry." It was through Brandeis that Hillman first became aware of the connection between "industrial democracy" and scientific management, for it was the jurist's intention to combine the virtues of both. Industrial efficiency, he argued, could be permanently achieved only through democratic consent, the mutual responsibility of workers and managers, and through the disinterested knowledge of engineering experts.[8]

For the moment, however, designs for a new industrial order were filed away for future reference. Suddenly, in October 1914, Hillman was drafted by a nationwide group of rebellious tailors, led by his friends in Chicago, to become the president of a wholly new industrial union dedicated to ending the corrupt and conservative regime of the UGW. Trouble had been brewing for some time, and not only in Chicago. As early as 1911 tailors' locals in New York and Baltimore had called a conference in Philadelphia to discuss the future of the UGW and its domination by representatives of overalls workers indifferent to the concerns of urban immigrant garment makers. Delegates from New York, Newark, Boston, Baltimore, Chicago, and Philadelphia listened to a stirring speech by Eugene Debs and then established a "Red" Tailors Council, which the UGW was forced grudgingly to recognize.

But the animosities were deep and irrepressible, at some level striking primeval racial and cultural antipathies. Even at the height of the HSM strike, UGW representatives on the Joint Strike board could hardly contain their nativist and anti-Semitic prejudices, accusing Jewish and Bohemian activists of misappropriating relief funds and supplies in favor of their own ethnic brethren. The UGW leadership was not above instructing convention delegates that it was "their duty as decent American women to stand by their general officers in their struggle against the Jews, who were trying to put Jewish officers in the places of non-Jews."

Most important, the betrayal of tailors' strikes, attempted in Chicago, was repeated and with greater success in Cincinnati, St. Louis, Boston, and elsewhere.[9]

In New York the situation got entirely out of hand. For some years the UGW officialdom had employed a gang of thugs widely known as the "Boys of London" to terrorize militant tailors. The tailors persisted nonetheless. Organized as the United Brotherhood of Tailors (UBT), formally an affiliate of the UGW, they mobilized mainly Jewish workers and conducted widespread although ultimately unsuccessful strikes in 1901, 1902, and again in 1904. Refugees from the 1905 revolution infused the UBT with fresh leadership, younger and in large part ex-Bundist. While politically dedicated, usually to socialism and sometimes to anarchism, they also arrived imbued with a sympathy for the nationalist strivings of the Jewish working class that had followed the Russian pogroms and counterrevolutionary terror. Both yiddishists and secularists were committed to the cultural solidarity of the Jewish proletariat as well as to the universal precepts of socialism and to their own self-improvement. Experienced organizers not easily intimidated, they reinvigorated the UBT and led a series of local strikes in 1907 against the wishes of the UGW. Then the depression of that year made further organizing virtually impossible.[10]

Organizing resumed in 1909 with an upturn in the economy. At a meeting in May 1911 plans were formulated for a citywide general strike. It required meticulous preparation and as much assistance from outside the organization as could be mustered. Although the UGW first sought to forestall such plans, it was eventually compelled to go along and assigned one of its national organizers, Benjamin Schweitzer, to help. Aid came as well in the person of Max Pine of the United Hebrew Trades, a federation of Jewish trade unions that maintained fraternal relations with the AFL. Preparations continued throughout 1912. Substantial assistance was forthcoming from the SP, the UHT, the *Forward*, and the rest of the Jewish trade union movement, as well as from social workers like Lillian Wald and the WTUL. In the case of the WTUL, the tailors asked the League to concentrate their efforts among Italian women workers, which the League proceeded to do with mixed results.

The strike began at the very end of December and followed a course tragically like that of the great HSM rising. More than 60,000 workers responded to the UBT's call for improvements in hours and wages, the abolition of subcontracting and homework, and the elimination of foot-powered machinery. Immediately the strike took on the character of

. . . a great national uprising. The proletariat of the East Side had declared its war of independence. . . . The strike became the chief topic of discussion among all classes of people; it was discussed by the man who sold apples from a pushcart, by the women in the kosher butcher shops as well as by professional people . . . it had the effect of a religious revival.[11]

Affecting as it did the second largest industry in New York, with an annual output in excess of $300 million, the strike naturally alarmed the business and political communities. Once again the *sheyne* of the Jewish business, financial, and philanthropic world, the German *yehudin*, intervened to mediate the dispute and to restore harmony to the "national" community. Indeed, the old world's *kehillah* was resurrected under the leadership of Judah P. Magnes and the banker Jacob Schiff to perform those ancient rituals of arbitration by the wealthy and learned.

To be sure, this *kehillah* was a secularized version of the original. Men like Schiff, the head of Kuhn, Loeb; Louis Marshall, a corporate lawyer and head of the American Jewish Committee; Schiff's partner Loeb; Herbert Lehman of Lehman Brothers; the bankers Maurice Werthkimer and Felix Warburg; and George Blumenthal of Lazard Frères—all members of Reform temples and all assimilationist in outlook—embodied a new faith in scientific philanthropy, preventive social work, and professionalism in general. Eager to extend the ameliorative blessings of the new managerial and social work expertise into the industrial arena, these leaders of the reconstituted *kehillah* established a Bureau of Industry under the direction of settlement house worker, Paul Abelson.

Mediation was in the air, fostered by, among others, Marcus Marks, president of the National Association of Clothiers, and of course actively encouraged by the settlement house circles around Lillian Wald, Henry Moscowitz, and Walter Weyl. It was through the intercession of that milieu in particular that the *kehillah*'s business patricians hoped to establish living ties to the ghettos' workers and perhaps thereby to reestablish their traditional social preeminence. While the *kehillah* seemed to revive an East European tradition essentially religious in nature, for secularists like Schiff and Brandeis the problem was more mundanely one of economic adjustment.[12]

The UBT leadership could be equally pragmatic and therefore welcomed the assistance of the WTUL and the *kehillah* and the public sympathy of the reform Mayor, William Gaynor. But a provisional settlement proved abortive, and with its collapse so too collapsed the formidable-looking but internally fragile edifice of outside support.

As they had done in Chicago, President Rickert and Benjamin Lager

of the UGW moved unilaterally to conclude the strike, sacrificing its
essential demand for union recognition. Rickert and Lager were opposed
by the WTUL, whose relations with the UGW were, if anything, worse
than they had been in Chicago. Surprisingly, the UGW officials were
joined in their act of premature surrender by Max Pine of the UHT, who
acted with the tacit approval of the *Forward* and Cahan. Once the strike
was thus stripped of its aura of legitimacy, Mayor Gaynor no longer felt
obliged to cooperate with it. Instead he ordered police to arrest picketers
and otherwise to obstruct the UBT's organizing efforts.

The strikers were enraged. They marched en masse to the offices of
the *Forward* in Union Square, where they proceeded to smash the windows of its newly erected building and to threaten Cahan when he tried
to speak. The UBT's executive board naturally rejected the settlement,
and the strike continued into late March. Then a new settlement was
negotiated with the help of Fiorello La Guardia, the UBT's lawyer; the
Socialist Assemblyman Jacob Panken; and a Socialist Congressman-to-
be, Meyer London.[13]

As had been the case in Chicago, the strike molded a new leadership
whose political radicalism converged with its bold organizational perspective. Almost all seasoned Bundists, men like Ike Goldstein, Louis
Hollander, Alex Cohen, Joseph Gold, and Abraham Miller were visionary unionists for whom the union served as a principal vehicle not only
of material improvement but of a more general emancipation. For the
Bundist militant the union "constitutes his university, his temple, his
political party, and everything which affects his life socially, spiritually,
and economically is necessarily bound up with it." Their self-confidence
was essential for purging the fear and passivity inherited from the shtetl.
Their combat experience in the Old World endowed them with an
invaluable élan, sophistication, and a feel for the concrete mechanics
and logistics of social struggle. Together with the original Chicago cadre,
and with the important addition of individuals from other key clothing
centers, they went on to become Sidney Hillman's most trusted lieutenants, the indispensable local and national leadership of a new departure
in trade unionism.[14]

The mass strike of 1913 was the first among men's clothing workers
in New York to include sizable numbers of Italians. LaGuardia, the
WTUL, and even the Sons of Italy made concerted efforts to prevent
scabbing by Italian workers and to bring Italian men and women into the
ranks of the UBT. The presence in the strike leadership of the Italian
socialists Frank and Augusto Bellanca and Joseph Catalonotti was of the
greatest significance, not only because they were experienced organizers
but also because it put a period to that phase in which New York City

garment unionism could be considered a strictly ghetto affair. While the problem of organizing Italian workers would continue for some years to be especially troublesome, the mass strike of 1913 was an irreversible breakthrough.

The breach opened up by the strike between the UBT leadership on the one side and the *Forward*-UHT network on the other was never to be entirely repaired. It was the earliest sign of a fateful estrangement of Hillman and his comrades from the rest of the world of Jewish socialism and trade unionism.

Every day in the pages of the *Forward*, Abraham Cahan took the pulse of the shtetl in Babylon. No one was more sensitive to all the subtle nuances of Jewish immigrant culture. No one described in more poignant detail the often painful adjustments and compromises it was forced to make as it tried to come to terms with the occupational mobility, the generational and sexual upheaval, the secularism and self-seeking, the familial and religious dissolutions, and the thousand and one shocks to customs of language, dress, food, schooling, marriage, and so much else introduced by American commercial culture and mass consumption. Intimately familiar with the mores and sensibilities of *yiddishkeit*, Cahan was nevertheless driven to work for its ultimate extinction. He was a master at finding in Jewish traditions and folk religion the premonitions of trade unionism and socialism. Loyal to the universalist principles and the cosmopolitanism of the Second International, Cahan prompted a socialist version of American assimilation at precisely that moment when the several voices of Jewish nationalism were growing louder and more demanding.

When Sidney Hillman arrived in New York, the battle between nationalist and internationalist currents within the house of Jewish socialism was already joined, especially within the ranks of the Jewish Socialist Federation (JSF). Indeed, the very creation of the JSF in 1912 was a concession to that swelling population of Bundist refugees whose experiences in the Pale had convinced them of the need for separate Jewish organizations to represent and protect the special national-cultural interests of the Jewish worker within the larger socialist movement. As early as 1906 there were as many as sixty branches of the Bund in the United States, with approximately three thousand members, more than belonged to the Jewish branch of the SP. Like the leaders of the UBT, they were "nonbelieving, radical, modern, but Jews," who accepted almost everything about socialist ideology except its logic of universal proletarian assimilation.

Even before there was a JSF, those elements within the SP favoring a more ethnic approach to the issues of Jewish working-class life in New

York had succeeded in replacing the rather dour and doctrinaire internationalist Morris Hilquit with the Jewish *folkmensch* Meyer London as
the party's congressional candidate from the Lower East Side. London,
whose father was an Orthodox Talmudic scholar, earned a reputation as
the people's lawyer. For the garment workers he was a hero, idolized not
just because he devoted himself to their struggles, which Hilquit did too,
but because he was never reluctant to speak for the special concerns of
his constituents. That was true even if, as on the question of unrestricted
immigration to the United States, their views ran counter to the more
equivocal position adopted by Hilquit and the national party.[15]

Cahan and Hilquit may have been more doctrinally pure, convinced
that the only hope for the Jewish working class in both the near and the
longer term lay with the general movement for socialism. But such orthodoxy did not necessarily entail a greater militancy or boldness of
organizational conception. In fact, more often than not their Bundist
opponents stood to the left of official Second International policy. As the
scandalous sacking of the *Forward* offices made vividly clear, they were
considerably less conciliatory when it came to conducting a mass strike
and seeing it through to the end.

Indeed, part of what constituted orthodoxy for the American SP was
playing the part of the loyal opposition within the AFL. To sanction and
support a strike against the wishes of Samuel Gompers and the AFL
leadership was to countenance the sin of dual unionism and to risk
excommunication from the only legitimate trade union federation in the
country—even if its *bona fides* was extremely limited in reach, self-
promoted, and morally suspect. Thus it was a matter of party policy
rather than personal faintheartedness or bureaucratic arrogance that
prompted Max Pine and the *Forward* to behave as they did. In the years
ahead, the *Forward* and the UHT would seek, sometimes with the best
of intentions and in the apparent interests of labor unity, to induce the
independently organized tailors to relinquish their independence voluntarily.

However, a declaration of independence was the most fundamental
consequence of the 1913 strike. The formal break occurred a year and a
half later in October at the Nashville convention of the UGW, but
preparations had been under way for some time. The "Red" Tailors
Council formed in 1911 continued to meet and was reinvigorated by the
UBT strike in New York as well as by sympathy walkouts in Rochester.
Earlier, in 1912, Hillman had attended the AFL convention to plead for
a more militant and resourceful organizing policy, one not exclusively
dependent on the moral force of the union label.[16]

Rickert, of course, was well aware of the simmering discontent—the

New York strike made it impossible to ignore—and so deliberately chose Nashville as the site for the 1914 biennial convention. He wanted it close to his only reliable following of workers in the work overalls plants of Appalachia. He also wanted to make it as financially difficult as possible for dissident delegates from the major urban clothing markets of the Northeast and Midwest to attend. Tempers were in such a state that large delegations of angry oppositionists managed to get to Nashville anyway. The Chicago group immediately organized a meeting of all "progressive" delegates, which elected an executive committee of fifteen, including Marimpietri, Rosenblum, and Levin, to provide strategic guidance at the convention. Rosenblum was chosen as the group's floor spokesman.

The general officers felt besieged. Utterly estranged from the ideals and cultural idiosyncrasies of the East Side and all the other immigrant barrios of the "rag trade," they were quite unable to make themselves understood to the alien and alienated tailors. Their political beliefs and trade union philosophy were considered both reactionary and obsolete, and their nativism, anti-Semitism, and capacity for self-indulgence were morally repugnant.[17]

Thus there were really no grounds for compromise, and in any event the general officers sought none. They simply disfranchised most of the opposition delegates on pretexts that were transparently spurious and politically motivated. The tailors were abashed at the preposterousness of a scheme that in a single stroke deprived at least 60,000 workers of representation. They were joined in their outrage by the *Forward* and the rest of the radical Jewish press. A special plea to Gompers was ignored. Two days of futile wrangling over the contested credentials led to a tumultuous walkout by the 110 disfranchised delegates, who immediately reassembled elsewhere and declared themselves to be the "lawful" convention of the UGW.[18]

It was at this juncture that Hillman was asked to give up his prestigious, if embroiled, position with the ILG, and to take command of the new rump organization. It entailed assuming an independent posture within the labor movement. That independence was fraught with risk and opportunity; it was certain to lengthen Hillman's distance from the dominant circles of Jewish radicalism. As an omen of the new group's future, the bolting delegates first elected Joseph Schlossberg as the union's new secretary. Schlossberg, part of the UBT's joint leadership, was a veteran socialist and for years had been a member of the Socialist Labor Party. His selection was an affront to the *Forward* and the UHT, because the SLP was a rival and an acerbic critic of the SP's "gas and water socialism." But the New York Bundists particularly, with the memory of

Max Pine's treachery still fresh in their minds, were determined to protect their freedom of action from the Jewish "socialist central committee"
headquartered at Union Square. Thus, when the delegates next turned
their attention to the presidency of their rehabilitated union, it was
already clear that its future relations with "socialism's Tammany Hall"
were to be, at the very least, troubled.

Hillman's selection was practically a foregone conclusion. His accomplishments in Chicago were widely known by tailors throughout the
men's clothing industry. His contacts with luminaries from the progressive movement were considered valuable in their own right and lent him
a public stature flattering to the new office. At the same time, he was
recently enough of the rank and file not to be considered a creature of the
Forward machine.

For Hillman, the choice was nearly as clear-cut. Indeed, the invitation to become president was more like a command. Levin telegraphed:
"You must accept Presidency. We are majority so decide and wire at
once." A second telegram followed the same day: "Do not hesitate to
take it. It must be done at any cost. I am confident we will go through
with that. But we need you in this situation. We had to act in a Hurry."
Reached in New York by long-distance telephone, he took a day to
decide. His position as chief clerk carried with it, if only in a formal way,
substantial power and a great deal more security. Some of his close
friends advised him against putting his reputation at risk by assuming the
leadership of a secessionist movement. When the telegrams from Nashville arrived, Hillman closeted himself with three friends—George Richter, J. B. S. Hardman, and Hardman's wife, Hannah—to weigh the
situation. Hardman cautioned him that it was an inherently risky proposition and that Gompers was sure to oppose it, and concluded his advice
with an old Yiddish proverb: "You are entering with a healthy head into
a sick bed." Hillman thought for a while and responded:

> I'm sort of persona grata now. The liberals have been lionizing me. And
> other people thought I was a big shot of sorts. But when I was walking the
> streets of Chicago looking for a job as an assistant cutter . . . and I was
> earning $9 a week and probably worth every bit of $6, I wasn't much. So
> whatever I became eventually I got through the tailors. I think I'll give
> them a chance to get some back pay. If they get it or not, I cannot tell
> now.[19]

Moreover, Hillman had never lived up to his press notices in the eyes
of the *Forward* circle, who, it was rumored, considered him a far less

commanding figure than Hourwich and were almost glad to see him go. Finally, his genuine feelings of allegiance and responsibility for his Chicago comrades, together with the enormous opening up of space for the exercise of his ambitions and talents that the new undertaking clearly presented, caused him to accept. At the age of twenty-eight he became the youngest president of an international union in the country.[20]

Just how great an opportunity it would turn out to be depended first of all on establishing the new organization's legitimacy and organizational integrity. Without that the office of president was worthless. In the final analysis, it was the immense practical success in organizing what previously was a largely unorganized industry that would give the new union its authenticity. Meanwhile, for the next several months a legal battle ensued between Rickert and Hillman over the rights to the UGW's name, label, and money. Charges of usurpation and corruption were answered with denunciations for secession and dual unionism. For some time thereafter each group went to great lengths to sabotage the efforts of the other. While Morris Hilquit waged a shrewd defense on behalf of Hillman's group, in the end the courts ruled in favor of the Old Guard; the Nashville "bolters" then assumed the name Amalgamated Clothing Workers of America (ACWA, or ACW). Of more lasting significance, however, was the equivocal position adopted by the Jewish socialist establishment.

Cahan initially endorsed the creation of the ACW as did Abraham Shiplacoff, secretary of the UHT, and Morris Winchefsky, the grandfather of Jewish socialism in the New World. Max Pine, however, stood opposed. As an affiliate of the AFL, the UHT was much more directly vulnerable to the pressures exerted by the national labor federation. Eventually the ACW agreed to withdraw from the UHT voluntarily so as not to aggravate the latter's relations with Gompers. But a residual bitterness remained. The *Forward* and the UHT continued to float propositions that would have seriously compromised the autonomy and authority of the fledgling ACW. The party hierarchy pursued that tactic because Gompers and the AFL were not about to forgive the ACW, which in its eyes remained an outlaw organization, guilty of dual unionism for having dared to abandon the moribund but officially blessed UGW.

Tactical equivocations of this sort probably did little to protect the socialists' already fragile position within the AFL, but they did manage to inspire an abiding distrust of the party's intentions on the part of the young rebels in the men's clothing industry. For his part, Hillman scrupulously guarded the ACW's organizational independence and quietly turned away disingenuous peace overtures while maintaining a public

posture of polite interest. Although he went through the motions of
appealing to the AFL convention, Hillman admitted to Sam Levin that
he harbored few hopes. In any event:

> It isn't our intention to have the matter patched up by the AFL. The further
> things go the more it is obvious that the matter will have to be fought to
> finish. . . . As far as I am concerned it is my intention to fight it out. I want
> you people in Chicago to work on those lines.[21]

Darrow advised Hillman that there was little hope of winning their
case in court and that therefore he ought to hold onto property and local
funds by forming a new association as quickly as possible. Gompers was
no more inclined to compromise than Hillman. He told the ILG president, Schlesinger, that "under no circumstances" was he prepared to
recognize "that hybrid concern which you dignify by the title 'amalgamated.' "[22]

It was an altogether strange situation, full of incongruous animosities, foreshadowings of future conflict, and much irony. From one angle
it was a struggle for bureaucratic power. But beneath the encrusted surface of bureaucratic self-interest lay deeper differences of political and
industrial strategy.

It was to be expected that the AFL would oppose, wherever it felt it
could do so successfully, "industrial unionism." For the Federation, it was
a matter of organizational perspective as well as of obeisance to the
jealously guarded bailiwicks of its craft affiliates. It was also a point of
honor because craft unionism represented not merely a set of lucrative
skills but a social identity, one whose sense of "manhood," honor, racial
superiority, communal status, and self-possession was bound up with the
practice of craft. Moreover, the AFL's growing political relationship with
the Democratic Party depended on respecting the prevailing lines of
ethno-politics, which any venture into industrial unionism would inevitably violate. The Democratic loyalties of Irish and German craftsmen
would be severely strained should the AFL invite despised immigrants
from Southeastern Europe into the Federation, because it was in particular the party's willingness to champion anti-immigrant legislation that
made it attractive to these old-stock urban voters. For socialists, however, who were after all committed to industrial unionism as a principal,
such equivocation was not at all to be expected. At least in this instance,
it was for the party a matter of subordinating the question of workplace
organization to the higher strategic imperatives of politics.

That relations between the rebel tailors and the SP were so brittle was doubly odd since, on the surface, despite the divisions between the Bundists and the orthodox of the Second International, there was naturally a great deal of ideological consensus and real cooperation. The ACW not only was founded by socialists, it drew heavily on the SP, the UHT, and of course the JSF (which with its Bundist leadership was instinctively more friendly) for funds; for organizational, administrative, and educational cadre; and for political support. In return, the union campaigned actively, although often through its own independent affiliates, for local and national SP candidates. Abraham Shiplacoff thus doubled as an SP Assemblyman in Albany and as an ACW general organizer; Jacob Panken, New York's first socialist municipal judge, was a loyal member of an ACW local and provided the union with legal advice; and Baruch Charney Vladek became a member of pressers' local 3, used his LaSallean oratorical and literary skills on behalf of the ACW, and was elected a New York City Alderman from Williamsburg in Brooklyn, thanks in large measure to union electioneering. Yet from 1914 on relations between the men's clothing workers and the captains of Jewish socialism were never truly fraternal. A certain edginess and suspicion were always present, and periodically, over critical issues, they erupted into outright hostility and mutual recrimination.[23]

Hillman's personal situation was if anything even more anomalous and ironic. On the one hand, he had assumed the leadership of a movement that drew much of its energy from a group of inspired radicals whose Bundist affiliations made them acutely sensitive to the Jewish undercurrents and implications of their socialism. On the other hand, there was perhaps no one less inclined, by interest or disposition, not even among the Second International orthodox (with the possible exception of Hilquit), to devote himself to the nationalist awakening of proletarian Judaism. Unlike more conventional Jewish trade union socialists, Hillman pursued industrial union and political objectives without recourse to the communal values of traditional Jewish culture. Nonetheless, the Bundist milieu provided Hillman with a constituency in New York that allowed him to operate in at least partial independence of the *Forward* network.

All that was not simply a matter of calculated tactical maneuvering on Hillman's part. At stake was whether his personal destiny was to be bound up with the intertwined fates of Jewish socialism and Jewish nationalism. Even before fleeing counterrevolutionary Russia, he felt himself drawn away from the ethnic particularism of his Bundist comrades and toward the transcultural outlook of Martov and the Mensheviks. Once in America he studiously avoided active involvement in specifically Jewish causes, and this was at a time when mainstream Zionism, as well as labor or Poale Zionism, was undergoing an explosive growth in the United States.

If there was any variety of Judaism with which Hillman felt increasingly comfortable, it was the Reform Judaism of Rabbi Stephen Wise. But in this case the affinity was not religious or even ethnic, but rather political and cultural. To the degree that Reform Judaism not only eschewed much religious ritual and all forms of ethnic exclusivity and at the same time cultivated a modern civic consciousness and a feeling for secular social reform, it was the Jewish analog of the social gospel. In his way, Hillman translated the cultural imperatives of Reform Judaism into the vernacular of the labor movement. Even as he waged an arduous struggle to master the English language and continued to conduct much of his correspondence in Yiddish, Hillman remade himself in this same cosmopolitan image of the democratic, deracinated citizen. While Joseph Schlossberg became the voice for the labor Zionist aspirations of the ACW rank and file—repeatedly invoking the "fulfilling of a holy duty," and the "spirit of the sacred struggle"—Hillman remained largely indifferent to and detached from Jewish politics.

Sidney and Bessie, who came from a far less Orthodox home, were nonetheless married in a synagogue, but in public Hillman increasingly appeared neither Jewish nor socialist, while repudiating neither. Surrounded on all sides by a flood tide of nationalist sentiments originating in the Jewish working class and middle class alike, sentiments inflamed by the wartime and postwar crises of East European Jewry, Hillman managed, almost by an act of will, to escape its orbit entirely into a desacrilized political culture that deliberately sought to transcend the boundaries of class, ethnicity, and religion. Yet his "Jewishness" lingered on within his psyche, functioning as a stigma, a challenge, and finally as a matter of honor.[24]

The cross-currents of Jewish nationalism and Jewish socialism would continue to impart a distinctive ideological coloring and organizational dynamic to the new union for years to come. In the beginning, however, the fate of the ACW depended less on ideology than on how well it waged industrial warfare.

That it was war it intended to wage was made unmistakable at its founding constitutional convention, held in late December 1914 in New York. The ameliorative and disinterested language of Brandeis and Williams did not yet suit the mood or purpose of an insurgent movement led by anarchists, socialists, Bundists, and syndicalists. Emblazoned on a banner overhanging Webster Hall was a picture of a muscled worker wielding an axe to strike from his body a tangled web of enshackling roots, and inscribed below was the austere imperative: "He Who Will Be Free, Himself Must Strike The Blow." Schlossberg, who for years to come would keep alive a kind of Old Testament socialist rhetoric pristine and martial in spirit, uncompromising and apocalyptic—an eschatology of secular deliverance, delivered the keynote address:

> The ultimate aim of the Labor Movement is to bring the working class into its own, to transform it from a working class within a Capitalist Society into a free and democratic industrial republic. . . . Instinctively, the working class in this country, obeying the dictates of their class interests hew their own path through the fossils of despotism, corruption, obsolete methods and ignorance . . . the Labor Movement, like a phoenix, rises from its own ashes. Though repeatedly thrust to the ground, the tailors drew new strength from the very ground and rose with renewed vigor.

It was the traditional inspirational language of working-class radicalism, part prophecy, part jeremiad, and profoundly moral in its metaphors and injunctions. Thus, Schlossberg described "the forces of brutal despotism" in the former union administration, "who had hatched a devilish conspiracy, which could be conceived only in moral degeneracy and executed in treason" to exclude the great majority of tailors from the Nashville convention.[25]

The convention committed itself to "Industrial Unionism," because "Modern Capitalist production dictates to the working class Industrial Unionism." But it was essential to accompany the form of industrial organization with the "industrial spirit which means the general enlightenment of the workingman, and particularly the teachings of universal working class solidarity and abolition of the wage system." As for the union label, the totem of the despised old leadership, while it could serve a useful purpose under an administration that was not "dishonest and despotic," it was more important to remember that the "power that affords protection to the workingman is not the generosity of the consumers, but the powerful organization of the producers." The newly elected General Executive Board concluded its report by urging the membership to "energetic and courageous action. . . . The time has come for the organization of a Union of Clothing Workers that will become an integral part of the Revolutionary Army that will emancipate the working class! This mission is ours."

Then the convention proceeded to adopt a constitution, which included a memorable preamble. After bluntly sketching the harsh reality of the "constant and unceasing" class struggle, which made trade unionism a "natural weapon of offense and defense," it looked forward to the "inevitable" creation of a

. . . universal working class organization, united along the entire line of the class struggle, economically and politically. The industrial and inter-industrial organization built upon the solid rock of clear knowledge and class consciousness will put the organized working class in actual control of the system of production and the working class will then be ready to take possession of it.[26]

As the founding delegates dispersed, the real question was whether all this muscular idealism would be converted into an equally muscular institution. The answer came quickly and decisively. Over the next few years the ACW managed to organize nearly 90,000 workers and con-ducted several general strikes, major organizing campaigns, and numer-ous local skirmishes in Chicago, Baltimore, Boston, and New York. It did so despite UGW and AFL opposition that on occasion came close to sabotage. In several key clothing centers, the new union not only drove the "sweating system" underground but made the eight-hour day, not long before unimaginable, an industry standard, if only temporarily.[27]

Such summary generalizations fail to convey a sense of how these "gains" actually mattered to people long accustomed to so much worse. For pressers in many small shops it meant the old 35-pound irons, kept heated on red-hot coal-fired stoves "so that no time would be lost," whose gases were a feared danger to health and safety, were replaced by lighter and cleaner air irons. For bushelers, who for years worked in the gloomy basements of Canal Street contractors, the union managed to win more sanitary places of work with at least some light and fresh air. In other shops, "all tools, such as straps, needles, machines, and press towels, etc. were to be furnished to the employee free of charge." The industry's seasonal ups and downs meant a great many workers spent half their time idle, the other half in a feverish, anxiety-ridden rush to work as fast and earn as much as possible. For them, the ACW instituted a policy of work-sharing so that during the slack season work was divided equally, thus reducing instances of extreme hardship. Contractors, no-torious for absconding with workers' wages at the end of the busy season or simply going bankrupt and leaving their employees empty-handed, were now forced to post bonds to ensure payment to workers.[28]

The spirit that sustained the union militant in those early weeks and months was expressed in hundreds of letters to headquarters in New York, of which Sam Gillis's was typical:

I speak to you the words that my bones speak to me. I write to you what my conscience dictates, what my ears hear in the streets: the methods used by the old UGW of A is rank and rotten. I defie them . . . how could a man with common logical sense remain neutral to such a noble battle you people are making? How could a man that hears the voice of probably 60,000 tailors crying "Down with the gang, we want a tailor to represent a tailor. . . ." Pardon me for asking you, pardon my ignorance, answer me, are you in the fight to stay? If you are I am in the battle to fight to a finish.[29]

Hillman, who had presided over the Webster Hall convention and had shepherded through its critical resolutions, but who had allowed others to deliver the inspirational rhetoric, now came into his own. He was everywhere at once, devising strike strategy; negotiating with leading manufacturers; recruiting, inspiring, cajoling, and reprimanding local organizers; conducting merger negotiations with an old craft union of custom tailors (the Journeyman's Tailors Union); conferring with Williams, Wald, and Cahan; fending off attacks from the AFL and even the IWW—in general presiding over an organization that with each successful campaign or strike became less and less strictly Jewish, more and more cosmopolitan, and increasingly difficult to hold together.

Local organizers deluged Hillman with requests to visit their cities, either to encourage an otherwise lackluster organization as in Rochester or, on the contrary, to ward off precipitous strikes by hyperactive rank-and-filers as in Baltimore and Boston. Hillman sometimes had to deflect clamorous demands for citywide or even national general strikes from local cadre frustrated by the limited success of their own efforts. One such organizer accused Hillman of having "fallen asleep at the switch," while another ominously reported: "I hear the funeral march of our organization in Boston if immediate action will not be taken." From Philadelphia came a steady stream of pathetically depressing letters describing what was essentially a dying organization and blaming it all on the *goyim*.

At times Hillman became a kind of father confessor and morale booster, listening to the laments of dedicated but deeply discouraged comrades: "I am most of the time on the verge of collapse and still I do my very best to keep up courage. I am convinced you do not intend to ignore me but I receive no answer just the same and this discourages me more than anything else." So complained comrade Marcovitz from Boston. Moreover, in Boston as elsewhere the situation was aggravated by the inevitable lack of trained cadre in sufficient numbers to carry on the daily work of organization and administration, so that Hillman faced unending pleas for help, which he could scarcely satisfy. Indeed, resources were so spare that Hillman himself went deeply into debt just to keep things afloat. Jacob Potofsky, whose youthful zeal was subject to periodic and melodramatic depressions, wrote gloomily to Hillman about the nasty factionalism inside the Chicago union, where Levin and Rosenblum waged a bitter battle for supremacy: "Boss rule damn it. I am sick of it." He drearily warned that the union already resembled a business or even a political machine and that he'd begun to feel like a politician.[30]

Sam Levin worriedly wrote to Hillman about another chronic problem: "Some demagogues began to play on the National Feeling to give the Polish members to the Polish local, etc." Levin feared that such tendencies would destroy the new union. For a time, however, there was nothing to do but accede to these "national feelings," especially since manufacturers were at the same time deliberately trying "to stir up race antagonism between Jewish and Italian girls for the purpose of retaining the cheaper labor of the Italians." Even in a city like Rochester, where the union was little more than a post office box, provision was made for the creation of Jewish, Lithuanian, Italian, Polish, and English-speaking sections.[31]

Meanwhile Dorothy Jacobs, a key activist in Baltimore, wrote to Hillman observing that women were grossly underrepresented in the union leadership, a critical weakness. Jacobs, a skilled hand-buttonhole sewer and active in local 170 of the UGW while still a teenager, urged the formation of a Women's Department to rectify the glaring imbalance in the union hierarchy. While Jacobs herself was elected to the GEB at the tender age of twenty-two and became the union's first full-time female organizer in 1917, she proved an exceptional case. Hers was the first sign of a chronic failing, never satisfactorily addressed by the union, as the also exceptional case of Bessie Abramovitz indicates.[32]

More than fond of Hillman, Abramovitz kept him informed of her progress and of her work for the ACW and the WTUL. She provided a running commentary on turbulence at HSM and interrogated Hillman about his larger strategic plans: "I am bombarded with questions about what we are going to do next and to my sorrow, I do not know what answer to give them." Were they going to go "independent" or "are we going to affiliate with the Industrial Tailors Union? . . . we must act at once in order to be able to more effective work." Even during the early Chicago days Bessie "had her eye" on Hillman. Some have expressed the belief that she was chiefly responsible for persuading him to take a more active role in the HSM strike. Proud of her position as a union pioneer, she was later to note, not without a certain strain of resentment: "I was Bessie Abramovitz before he was Sidney Hillman." In August 1915 she became the first woman elected to the new union's GEB. Her nomination was to fill a vacancy in between national conventions, however, and was the consequence of a protracted discussion in which pointed references were made to the embarrassing absence of women in the national leadership of an organization so heavily composed of women workers. In

1917, a year after her marriage to Hillman, she gave birth to the first of two daughters—Philoine—and retired from the GEB, and for that matter from the active life of an organizer which had meant so much to her, until, years later, during the Depression, she resumed her role in the union.[33]

Bessie was exceptional and remained remarkably active even after the birth of her second child, Selma, in 1921. Most women activists were expected eventually to fulfill customary domestic roles. As one remarked: "In those days you married, you stayed home, and you got a dining room set."[34]

While Hillman pursued his peripatetic course, racing from one flash-point of strike activity to another, he did not neglect to cultivate relations with friendlier manufacturers and other businessmen. Thus, Leo Mannheimer of the *kehillah*'s Industrial Relations Committee arranged a meeting in Boston with the retailer Edward Filene and Filene's deputy, Louis Kirstein. They were intent on using their influence among Boston's larger producers, especially Frederick Strauss of Leopold Morse, on behalf of the union. Meanwhile, Samuel Weill of the Rochester Clothiers Exchange invited Hillman to address an informal gathering of members of the Exchange. Hillman's willingness to deal with the German-Jewish elite was not shared by Schlossberg, who wouldn't forget "they . . . called us ostjuden. . . . They had nothing but contempt for us."[35]

Developments in Chicago and Baltimore in particular were critical in these formative years and demanded Hillman's special attention. While the agreement with HSM continued to evolve under relatively peaceful conditions, the rest of the Chicago industry remained unorganized. Almost five years to the date of the great 1910 uprising, a second general strike erupted in the fall of 1915. All the same actors were involved, except that now the UGW openly opposed the strike from the outset and put pressure on the Chicago Federation of Labor not to participate. While it failed to intimidate the Federation—"our group of men here have too much red blood in their veins to stand by"—the AFL did manage to prevent a formal endorsement by the WTUL, so the women were forced to channel their assistance through Hull House and various citizens' committees.[36]

It was Hillman's intention to conduct an "organizing strike" to boost morale and to establish the supremacy of the ACW over the UGW in a market of great economic importance in which the new union felt strongest. John Williams, always Hillman's staunchest supporter, reported: "The present strike was planned with a coolness and thoroughness comparable to that of the general staff in Germany." Hillman himself was not quite so sanguine. As the day of the strike approached, he remained unsure of the outcome: While there were certain pockets of union strength, most of the industry remained partisans of the open shop.

In addition to the usual viciousness meted out by private armies of paid thugs, police tactics reached new heights of technological ingenuity and brutality. Olive Sullivan of the WTUL described it as "something fierce. It used to be that clubs were bad enough, but now that we have motorcycles, they are devilish. Think of the terrible things driving right into crowds! And the mounted police too are right on the job, and then Mayor Thompson . . . understands that the police situation is being very well handled." Familiar with both, Hillman actually considered the Chicago police more brutal than those in Russia. He told Williams that while the cruelty of a Russian officer came as a natural outgrowth of his own open rage, "your American police beat or torture a man with cool, calculating fiendishness." By the end of the strike nearly two thousand had been arrested and jailed.[37]

Together with Levin, Marimpietri, Rosenblum, and Potofsky, Hillman plotted strategy, conducted all major negotiations with employers, and marshaled support from among the city's Progressive middle class. Thus, he addressed the Women's Club, where he was warmly welcomed by the city's social elite, including Mrs. F. R. Lillie, Mrs. Medill McCormack (whose millionaire husband was also an alderman and provided the strikers substantial financial help), and Mrs. James E. Field. The Club then penned an open letter to Mayor William H. "Big Bill" Thompson asking him to take steps to "prevent our lapsing into the old evil days of labor wars." Hillman "makes a tremendous impression everywhere," Amy Walker of the WTUL reported. He became adept at suiting the style and substance of his remarks to the tastes and sensibilities of his audience. When addressing a gathering of embattled clothing workers he was capable of rousing deeply rooted historic animosities: "We do not want foremen to become Czars in this land of liberty." Among the city's clubwomen, meanwhile, he was much more the voice of "sweet reasonableness." A great deal of his energy was expended trying "to get some sort of settlement by pressure from the big men in town."[38]

As the strike dragged on into November, Hillman worked at a feverish pace. As was to happen repeatedly at critical, stressful junctures in his career, he became quite ill, this time with the flu, which finally forced him to bed for two weeks. Carl Sandburg provided him with daily reports on the strike, while Bessie carried messages back and forth between the strike leader and Clarence Darrow. What had been conceived of as an "organizing strike" was becoming a pitched battle, and Hillman sought a way out.

At a mass meeting in Cohan's Grand Opera House, Hillman made clear that the manufacturers need only concede the principle of collective bargaining and agree to arbitration to end the strike. A "Citizens' Mass Meeting" issued an open letter signed by Harold Ickes and George Mead, among others, claiming that the principle of collective bargaining was now recognized by "all fair-minded employers, the one point agreed to by all members of the U.S. Commission on Industrial Relations, and even, after bitter Ludlow, by Rockefeller, Jr. It is up to Chicago manufacturers to be reasonable and meet with the representatives of the ACW." Progressive Chicago once again did its part. Jane Addams was everywhere, raising money, speaking to numerous citizens' groups, and using her influence, unsuccessfully as it turned out, to persuade Mayor Thompson to establish a commission to arbitrate the strike. Speaking for the WTUL, Ellen Gates Starr described the strike as a "clear-cut, brave, self-sacrificing struggle" and admired the idealism and cultural sophistication of "these miserable wretches: How they read, those Russian Jews."[39]

In a final impassioned oration, Hillman pleaded for a settlement

by a sane law, not by the law of the jungle invoked by those temporarily stronger to crush and coerce the workers. O' of course there is nothing wrong if 12,000 girls are abused and insulted by foremen. There is nothing wrong if 12,000 girls are put under the absolute charge of examiners and sub-examiners who determine the physical and moral conditions under which they must live.[40]

Neither the millenarian rhetoric of revolution nor the meliorative rhetoric of reform made much difference in the end. The strike continued on fitfully until mid-December and then slowly ended as individual employers capitulated, but without any general agreement. Nonetheless, it was rightly considered a victory. More than ninety houses were now under contract, and although the history of labor turmoil in Chicago was by no means over, never again would this second most important market in the industry be a haven for the open shop. Hillman returned to New York pleased if not exultant. There was no time in any event to reflect on the Chicago events, as strange doings in Baltimore immediately demanded his attention.[41]

Baltimore, along with Chicago and Rochester, was a center of high-quality, high-priced men's clothing, produced in a relative handful of large, technically advanced factories. One, the Sonneborn company, employed three thousand people. In 1914 it laid plans to introduce a version of scientific management, along with an Employees Benefit Society, into its workshops. The Baltimore ACW, led by Hyman Blumberg and Dorothy Jacobs—both of whom had migrated as children from the Pale, the latter from a deeply religious family headed by a shamus in the local synagogue, and both of whom had become skilled workers and veteran trade unionists—angrily objected to the "Taylor Efficiency system with all its features of degradation and most intense exploitation." In response, the company proceeded to lock out its workers.[42]

Sigmund Sonneborn, however, much like Joseph Schaffner, was quick to realize the advantages of labor stability for a company with a large throughput and heavy capital investment in machinery. He further realized that stability and efficiency were probably best achieved under the auspices of an independent union. Thus he was prepared to negotiate with Hillman, who for the first time came face to face with that system of scientific management recently excoriated by the AFL. In an apparently strange reversal of roles, Hillman, the renegade dual unionist and revolutionist, found that he could live with many of the innovations in work organization suggested by Sonneborn, especially as the employer was willing to subject them to the union's scrutiny and approval. The union president actually initialed an agreement to that effect, but, as would happen rarely in his career, he was repudiated by the rank and file. In a second round of negotiations, Hillman persuaded Sonneborn to eliminate the part of the plan calling for "degrading examinations of the workforce," and rank-and-file acceptance followed. In the years to come Hillman's relationship with this more liberal variant of the scientific management movement would become systematic and fundamental to his industrial and even to his political outlook. For the moment he welcomed the understanding with Sigmund Sonneborn because it brought a leading manufacturer within the jurisdiction of the infant union and seemed to set a precedent for industrial peace in Baltimore.[43]

Peace would be harder to come by, however, thanks to a bizarre alliance between the UGW and the Industrial Workers of the World, an alliance designed to stymie ACW efforts at Sonneborn's as well as at the other major manufacturers, Strousse & Brothers and Greif Brothers. The motives of the UGW were hardly mysterious. Its local was not without leverage, as it had managed to organize numbers of status-conscious cutters whose skill gave them certain privileges and who tended to elevate those privileges into a general social disdain for the mass of poorer, less skilled tailors. The UGW campaign was directed by the notoriously corrupt president of the Baltimore Federation of Labor, John Ferguson, who was suspected, not without some evidence, of being in the pay of the Greif firm. Not overly selective in his associations, Ferguson had even fewer qualms when it came to choice of tactics. He was partial to organized violence, a familiar expedient in an industry that for years had been preyed upon by petty criminals, extortionists, and hired thugs.

John Ferguson embodied all that the IWW loathed in a trade union bureaucrat. He was the quintessential "labor lieutenant of capitalism," the kind of functional scoundrel that had to be extirpated as a prerequisite to revolution. Between 1915 and 1917, however, the Baltimore IWW joined with Ferguson and the local UGW from time to time in an orgy of strikes, counterstrikes, shop riots, brick-throwing, stabbings, sluggings, and shootings aimed at driving the ACW out of the city. The Amalgamated responded in kind. Every time the ACW called a strike, the UGW made sure its cutters remained at work, and the IWW did what it could to supply replacements for the strikers. Although the ACW pretended otherwise, it was no more prepared to honor picket lines thrown up by the UGW or IWW. Ferguson went so far as to threaten a general strike on behalf of the IWW, a proposition so preposterous on its face that it was taken seriously by no one. The ACW accused the IWW of anti-Semitism, of "scandalous scabbism," of being a vital link in a "foul chain of treachery," of destroying the tailors' organization in Rochester, of forsaking the silk weavers of Patterson and withdrawing "within its tents like the effeminate Achilles of old," and of repeated failures of nerve and organizational stamina in Passaic and Lawrence, among the piano makers, shoemakers, longshoremen, miners, "everywhere." For its part, the IWW resorted to ambushing ACW members on their way to and from work. On one such occasion Hyman Blumberg was beaten senseless and hospitalized. When J. Friedman, a member of the Amalgamated, refused to join the wobblies, he received the following letter:

> You are written down in our books as a dead man if you don't stop work. Listen, Friedman, you dirty scab from South America, if you keep it up I will catch you—if not today I will get you tomorrow. I tell you to stop, for it will be better for you.

It was signed "Committee, IWW," and was written on condolence notepaper with a black border and enclosed in a black-bordered envelope.

Highly stylized warning letters like the one sent to Friedman were part of the ritual of *omerta*, the ancient Italian tradition of blood revenge for real or imagined acts of dishonor. The letter's ethnic origin scarcely mattered, but its incongruous traditionalism was most striking. It suggested that beneath all the exalted revolutionary rhetoric, all the mutual accusations of betraying the cause of the international proletariat, burned

incandescently a set of far more primordial and petty passions that gave
to syndicalism and socialism meanings never dreamt of by their
progenitors.[44]

At its pettiest, the scandalous mess in Baltimore was all about commercial rivalries and the practice of subcontracting. The Greif and the
Strousse companies both employed subcontractors. The ACW in Baltimore, as everywhere else, struggled to eliminate the practice, as subcontractors could enrich themselves only by exploiting their fellow workers,
often paying mechanics and other skilled workers considerably less than
market rates. The Amalgamated conducted a strike at the Greif company
over this issue, and during it Strousse, a direct competitor of Greif,
benefited. Subsequently the Amalgamated waged a similar and successful
struggle at Strousse's, a firm much like Sonneborn's, willing to deal with
the union and to eliminate subcontracting. It turned out, however, that
a fair number of the subcontractors at both companies, predictably disturbed by the attacks on their livelihood, were Lithuanians. They tended
to employ their blood relations and ethnic brethren, who in turn accorded them a kind of filial loyalty.

Meanwhile the IWW enjoyed a following among Lithuanian nationalists, whose nationalism had taken on revolutionary coloration under
Czarist repression—a national revolutionary amalgam quite common
among various East European populations. It took only the desperate fear
on the part of the Lithuanian contractors that their dreams of entrepreneurial independence were about to be ruined to produce an odd concoction of filial piety and revolutionary syndicalism, which then vented
its wrath against the ACW.

The case of the Chester "factory" was an example. Chester was a
Lithuanian contractor for the Greif company. He was also an investor in
the IWW's Lithuanian newspaper and a rather "big gun" in Baltimore's
Lithuanian colony. Chester actually invited the local chapter of the
IWW, whose secretary was also Lithuanian, to organize his small workforce so that when the ACW, its members concentrated in the "inside"
factories of the Greif enterprise, called a strike, the Chester "factory"
would continue to work. A similar set of events unfolded at the Strousse
& Brothers concern. Once the ACW and management agreed to abolish
subcontracting, the two Lithuanian subcontractors joined the IWW and
"persuaded the majority of their helpers, who are their blood relations, to
go out on individual strike without consulting the other workers in the
shop," hoping thereby to restore the subcontracting system. That was a
course of action simultaneously encouraged by Ferguson, who, given his
moral if not actual financial indebtedness to the Greif company, could

find no more ideal way of discharging his obligations than by engineering a strike at Greif's main commercial rival.

It was indeed an edifying spectacle, an interior view of one niche in the political ecology of the "rag trade." But this instance of conservative ethno-syndicalism should not be construed as a disparagement of the genuinely held anarcho-syndicalist and nationalist convictions of Italian, Lithuanian, and for that matter Jewish workers.[46]

Indeed, socialism, anarcho-syndicalism, and revolutionary national-ism made up a family of beliefs that, by inculcating and exalting modern egalitarian and democratic motivations, provided an inexhaustible res-ervoir of psychological energy upon which the ACW depended. Thus, by late 1916 most of the Lithuanian wobblies in Baltimore had seen through the machinations of Ferguson and their erstwhile contractor-kinsmen and had become loyal and militant members of the ACW, thanks in part to Hillman's prudent decision to allow the formation of an all-Lithuanian local in Baltimore. That experience was repeated in the case of Italian syndicalists, many of whom severed their ties to the IWW, joined all-Italian locals of the Amalgamated, remained staunch partisans of indus-trial unionism, but continued to offer syndicalist resolutions at union conventions like the following: "Scraps of paper signed with all due forms by gentlemen diplomats are of no avail as has been proven so eloquently in the present European conflict."

Bohemian nationalists displayed the same enthusiastic determina-tion, emphatically enough so that Augusto Bellanca, who was sent to Baltimore to oversee the situation, reported to Schlossberg with some surprise on "the loyalty of the several hundred Bohemian strikers . . . who have fought with religious enthusiasm. In their brains, the Amal-gamated will remain forever." And the anarchist tradition among Jewish garment workers long predated the creation of the IWW. Like their ideological cousins among the Italians, Lithuanians, and Bohemians, Jewish anarchists contributed their energy and their idealism, along with their own idiosyncratic and locally bred tactics of action, which in their case included a fondness for arson and other illicit escapades.[47]

What the Baltimore experience therefore demonstrated above all was the deep cultural embeddedness of radical politics on the shop floor. No matter how deracinated, cosmopolitan, and ecumenical they might seem on the surface, the soil of village, shtetl, and handicraft life clung to these cadres even as they made their presence felt in the industrial arena. It is striking that the IWW, whose formal ideological axioms presupposed the most centralized and interdependent forms of economic organization, actually found its greatest strength on the East Coast, in garment, tex-

tile, waterfront, and other relatively small-scale decentralized environ-
ments. In countless ways, radical politics recast and revivified a host of
provincial desires and prejudices, amalgamating ancient codes of private
justice with impersonal conceptions of industrial equity, the insular defenses of the kinship-based community with expansive and nonfamilial
identities associated with citizenship and nation-state, informal *ad hoc*
and even impulsive forms of organization with the more deliberative and
methodical behavior of parliamentary procedure. It is not a matter, then,
of reducing each and every sentiment in favor of human emancipation to
its shabby nesting place in the arena of petty advantage, corrupt dealings,
and racist resentment. If the denizens of revolutionary sects and movements tended to recreate village passions in urban neighborhoods, they
were at the same time pioneers of modernity.

American historians have sought to understand the mentalities
which divided nineteenth-century popular party politics by distinguishing "pietistic" from "ritualistic" cultures. Pietists, found largely in
evangelical Protestant denominations, were committed to an ethos of
self-improvement and moral uplift, to the behavioral postulates of possessive individualism and self-discipline, to the politics of voluntarist
association and the economics of the free market. Ritualists, largely but
not exclusively Catholic, were wedded instead to traditions of social
solidarity, patriarchy, and hierarchical authority, to political quietism
and the economy of moral limits. The analogy is useful. Salient features
of the pietistic psychological profile reappear among refugees from the
polychrome cultures of Southeastern Europe, suggesting that pietistic
social psychologies did not necessarily emerge out of evangelical Protes-
tantism. Jewish socialists, Lithuanian anticlerical nationalists, Italian
syndicalists, anarchists, Bundists, and all the other varieties of immigrant
revolutionaries were the pietists of industrial unionism and the politics of
work. They were a breed apart, a milieu of highly individualized, anti-
authoritarian, and self-assertive cadre, whatever their political affiliation;
they differed from the great mass of garment workers, who remained, for
a while at least, largely untouched by these social, psychological, and
intellectual currents.

Hillman and his circle of most trusted comrades sometimes found it
irritatingly difficult to control the behavior of these shop floor "pietists."
When anarchist-minded pocketmakers and pressers at Sonneborn's
walked out again and again on their own authority, Hillman was finally
forced to reprimand them, explaining that the ACW had the right to
"demand from its members a normal amount of work in a particular
section in order to get concessions from employers when the time comes."
Sometimes official union victories became the pretext for a nearly un-

controllable impulse on the part of the pietistic militants to strike at the slightest provocation. That occurred among groups of Italian and Lithuanian workers, especially among the pressers, in all of Baltimore's major plants after the ACW successfully expunged the UGW and the IWW. Thus Hillman noted after a successful examiners strike at Sonneborn's that "a few more victories of such a nature and our organization will be confronted with a real danger. . . . I realize that the system where the discharge of one man might cause a strike of thousands is very dangerous."[48]

During those formative years, however, the Hillman executive faced a far more intractable problem in organizing those "ritualists" of the factory, sweatshop, and tenement for whom unionism was *terra incognita.* Historical inertia was especially apparent among immigrants from Southern Italy, who composed the second most numerous ethnic component of the industry's labor force. Italians were not only present in great numbers but also tended to congregate in larger factories and were often associated with the more centralized, more capital-intensive sectors of the industry, which were naturally critical to the union's survival. In fact, the high tide of Italian immigration coincided with the renewed growth of the "inside factory."

Some Italians arrived with tailoring skills mastered in the old country and established custom tailoring shops or took up positions in American factories as skilled tailors, pocketmakers, sleeve-sewers, bushelers (skilled workers responsible for making alterations in flawed garments), and occasionally even designers. Marimpietri came from that sort of background, as did Aldo Cursi, who became an invaluable national organizer for the ACW. Born in 1881 in Iesi, Italy, Cursi was apprenticed to a tailor at the age of eleven and became a journeyman custom tailor in Rome, where he was employed making clothes for the King and the Italian nobility. When he moved to the United States in 1902, he continued to pursue his craft and became a custom tailor for Rogers Peet in New York.

These skilled craftsmen were the first to show interest in unionization and supplied the ACW with some of its early Italian organizers, but they also were prone to the same pattern of artisan resistance to industrial democracy exhibited by other skilled work groups.

Most Italians, however, learned the tailoring trade in the United States. They operated sewing machines and performed a wide range of semiskilled jobs. The development of the section system in large "inside" factories made it "possible for a Sicilian peasant that knows nothing at all about tailoring to learn any special operation in a short time." These immigrants from the south and from Sicily tended to behave more like subjects than like citizens or subversives of an industrial republic. Very few knew anything about trade unionism, much less about socialism. They continued to bear the legacy of seigneurial oppression and economic misery. If Jewish and Italian artisans imported the millenarian dreams of the old world, Italian tenant farmers brought with them the passivity, suspicion, and resignation that flourished in the dessicated provinces of the South.[49]

Cultural taboos prohibited Italian wives from working outside the home. Married Italian women thus became the industry's chief source of homeworkers, often supplanting Jewish women, who tended to leave the industry after marriage. (In 1916 only 3.7 percent of female Jewish wage-earners were married, while 38.6 percent of Italian women were—a rate double that of the female laboring population as a whole.) Italian women were subjected to pervasive patriarchal pressure. Homework was a form of family economy in which the young and old participated. Families were often recruited by *paesani* living in neighboring tenements or flats. Typically, those dutiful daughters who were living at home turned over their wages to the head of the household (a father or brother), which was in keeping with the prevailing pattern in Southern Italy, where women were not viewed as autonomous wage-earners and where they remained surrounded by the constraints of propriety and property. Mary Drier Robbins described them as "absolutely under the dominance of the men of their family, heavily shackled by old customs and traditions. They were very much afraid of trade unions." Younger, unmarried Italian women did enter the factory but continued to perform traditional jobs as fellers and finishers in sections segregated from the male labor force, usually under the supervision of an Italian foreman and in factories located close to Italian neighborhoods.

Organizers for the WTUL invariably identified Italian women as the most difficult to unionize. Even those who promised to come to union meetings failed to do so, because "when the meeting nite comes some old superstition or some old tradition that girls ought to be at home at nite keeps the Italian girls away." With more than a touch of ethnic chauvinism, a Jewish female organizer reported: "If [the Italian girls] were more civilized they wouldn't take such low pay. But they go without hats and gloves and umbrellas." Even an Italian seamstress acknowledged that "Jewish girls . . . were much more advanced than the Italians. . . . They fought for us Italians. . . . Oh, they were very advanced. . . . Later on we got our own union and were advanced too." The mass of Italian women remained untouched by unionization until well into the 1930s.[50]

Among Italian men the situation was different but not necessarily in ways favoring the cause of industrial unionism. In contrast to the precocious political and organizational activity of the declining handicraft milieux, the Italian clothing proletariat, with little or no experience of industrial life, repeated a more or less invariant pattern of first generation peasant submissiveness to factory routine and authority. The ethos of *campanilismo,* which inhibited associational life beyond the geographic and psychic frontiers of the village, made labor organization extremely difficult in America, where *campanilismo* continued to dictate the lines of residential and occupational clustering. The even greater power of *la famiglia* not only reinforced patriarchal structures of authority but made all ties except those based on blood and marriage tenuous. Italian trade unions themselves had a tendency to become clannish, ultimately serving as a device for preserving the parochial and patriarchal world of the extended family.[51]

However, the pattern of peasant submissiveness was punctuated by episodic outbursts of mass rebellion, analogous to the rising of the *fascio* in Sicily in the 1890s or the more common village-based bread riots of the *contadini,* which expressed long-festering hatreds with great energy. Frank Bellanca described the perennial rhythms of these industrial *jacqueries:*

> Italians are impulsives, are easy to enthusiasm, but they are also easy to mistrust. And those who know Italians know also that it is more difficult to keep the organization among the Italians than organize themselves. Often is easy to organize the Italians; to call them in strike; but for to keep them, believe me, is necessary constancy, sacrifice, honesty, and big moral and material power.[52]

Not surprisingly, therefore, Hillman was flooded with reports from the field describing and complaining about the extraordinary difficulties encountered when organizing Italians. In St. Louis, Italian inertia was reportedly the biggest single obstacle, and in Cincinnati a combination of Italian sympathy for the IWW and a more widespread resistance to organization of any kind stymied local Italian cadre. Rochester remained unorganized until 1919 mainly because the Italians in the coat trade and the Italian women were unreachable, especially those working for Hickey-Freeman, a flagship company whose paternalist labor policies gave it a popular reputation as the "paradise" of the industry.[53]

Hillman was driven to devise appropriate tactics. It was clear, for example, that if the Italians were to be reached at all, they could not, as a rule, be recruited in ones and twos but only in large groups, and more often than not through the galvanizing effect of a big strike. One woman organizer wrote: "Very often you see in a shop a set of finishers who are nearly all Italians . . . if you can persuade one to join the union, you may be sure of getting them all, if you fail with one, you fail with all." For many Italian workers the concept of organization was synonymous with that of the strike. Often enough, however, even strikes failed to produce the desired result. There were instances of Italian scabbing, which naturally inflamed already tense relations with Jewish workers and sometimes led to retaliatory scabbing. In such serious cases, Hillman called on the help of Italian notables, in particular his friend and union lawyer in the 1913 strike, Fiorello La Guardia, who used his growing political prestige to urge *paesani* to refrain from strikebreaking.

Hillman and the Italian union leadership deliberately used the traditional ties of *campanilismo* and the ethos of *la famiglia*. They instructed organizers to observe sexual and other cultural prohibitions. Union broadsides urged strikers not to "dishonor your name and that of your family by committing treason against your fellow workers" and painted a grim picture of the social ostracism that awaited any Italian scab. But even where organizing succeeded, as in the plants of leading Boston manufacturers like Barron-Anderson following the strike of 1913, the results proved ephemeral. Italian locals were defunct shortly after birth or were subject to rapid turnover. In some cases, where Italians refused to pay dues or to join the union at all, Hillman, who was becoming increasingly tough-minded and martial in his strategic thinking, "virtually forced the Italians to join" through the closed shop and the compulsory dues checkoff.[54]

This historical passivity and insularity had begun to weaken even before the ACW announced its existence, in part as a consequence of the needle trades uprising of 1909–13. More fundamentally, the ongoing cultural transformation of the Italian-American working class community opened up avenues of communication between Italian garment workers and trade union organizers.

The emergence of mutual aid societies and supralocal associations like the Sons of Italy helped overcome the ancient insularity of *campanilismo*-rooted behavior. Sensing the opportunity, the Bellanca brothers sought to ally with or systematically infiltrate the Sons in order to establish a liaison with Italian tailors. In turn, the Sons lent moral support to the 1913 strike and subsequently in Philadelphia and elsewhere provided the union access to its membership lists and enforced the organization's constitutional provision calling for the expulsion of scabs.

Furthermore, Italian nationalism flourished for the first time in the United States among immigrants from the south, partly in response to their own despised position in American society. Less oppressive features of American culture also had their impact, especially upon the second generation, making them more at home in urban and industrial settings so that the union began to experience greater success among the "young, new Italian-American elements." But this confluence of cultural, political, and even religious change developed slowly; for example, it wasn't until the 1920s that Catholic parishes in Italian neighborhoods were visibly "Americanized." In the meantime, Hillman and the ACW continued to wrestle with an Italian milieu for which industrial democracy and trade union discipline were not yet second nature.[55]

"Ritualists" were represented not only by the Italians but by great numbers of Poles, Lithuanians, and Russians. Despite the pioneering role played by Jewish trade unionists taken as a group, it was true of Jewish garment workers as well. Thus, on one side stood the liberated Jewish handicraftsman, for whom *"melakhe iz a malkhes"*—"a trade is a kingdom." He thought of himself as a "head worker"; spent precious moments in and outside of the shop reading and discussing world history, science, art, and politics; and took pride in his self-education, which he saw as the key to personal and social emancipation. There were sizable numbers of such "head workers." Two-thirds of those who emigrated between 1900 and 1925 were skilled workers, and one-half of those craftsmen were associated with the garment industry. Moreover, the largest proportion of these immigrants came from the northwest Pale, where literacy was most widespread, along with higher secular education and a more rationalist religious culture, less influenced by Hasidism.[56]

Across a deep historical divide, however, stood the massed ranks of Jewish traditionalists. Rumanian pants makers working for their *landsleit* contractors made it a practice to consult the boss on their marriages, divorces, children, and daily decorum or to turn to their landsman-employer for a loan to help bring a relative over from the old country. The familial atmosphere sometimes made the shop seem like a home away from home, where workers smoked, ate, and even sent out for a "pint." Orthodox to a fault, such workers were loyal not only to their religion but to the familial and patriarchal codes of the shtetl and *landsmanschaften.* These ties of locale, kinship, and religion constituted a network that penetrated all levels of the industry's occupational hierarchy from the skilled mechanic to the lowly apprentice, so that whole sections of the "rag trade" could be categorized by their place of origin in the Pale. Clustered in small contractor shops no less primitive technically than the ones left behind in Europe, caught up in the demanding syndrome of mutual and self-exploitation, they were better members of the thousands of *landsmanschaften* that honeycombed the Lower East Side and Brownsville than they were recruits to modern trade unionism.[57]

During these formative years, Sidney Hillman's most impressive accomplishment, more important than strike victories, contractual gains, and growing numbers of dues-paying members, was his forging of a group of committed organizers capable of mastering this ethno-cultural Babel. These were not paid functionaries or union bureaucrats in the conventional sense. They were instead organized outside the formal structure of the union in local circles or "activities," consisting of experienced and creative men and women, secular pietists, subject to their own internal discipline, whose mission it was to transmit the policies, practices, and larger purposes of the new union to the workers on the shop floor.

Lazarus Marcovitz was a devoted member of an "activity." His background and peripatetic career in the ACW was not uncharacteristic of the "activity" as a whole. Although he had managed to complete only three grades of grammar school in his home town of Botoshani, Rumania, he had mastered not only Yiddish but German, Hebrew, and Rumanian as well. His father had been a common laborer at a flour mill and later on the railroad and on the docks. Lazarus was apprenticed as a cabinetmaker and worked at his trade for eleven years before deciding to leave Rumania. He joined the Footwanderers group in Galati in 1899, where he wrote poems in Yiddish (and later in English). The Footwanderers planned to migrate to the United States to help found a utopian community, but the Rumanian government prevented the group from leaving, so Marcovitz instead arrived in Boston in 1903 as part of a group sponsored by the B'Nai Brith. He became president of his local of the International Woodworkers Union, but during the depression of 1907 he left the trade and went to work in Boston's garment district, where he once again rose to the presidency of his UGW local. Already committed to the cause of trade unionism, with the creation of the ACW it became his consuming passion. Between 1913 and 1937 he moved dozens of times—to Boston, Montreal, Toronto, San Francisco, Wilkes-Barre, Rochester, Philadelphia, Cincinnati—to wherever the leadership felt his talents and influence might be best used. He was heart and soul part of the "activity."

Actually, the "activity" was Hillman's creative adaptation of the organizational experience of the Bund, whose own highly centralized apparatus was made to work through identical nuclei of self-reliant comrades, depended upon to carry out the policy directives of the leadership. Like the "half-intellectuals" who created and perfected it, this piece of organizational inventiveness stood halfway between the rationalist, rule-dominated structures of the modern bureaucracy and the more personalized command structures characteristic of traditional patriarchal cultures. From the beginning, all the customary paraphernalia of formal trade union organization was in place: business agents, local presidents, citywide joint boards, a national General Executive Board. But Hillman really negotiated the great cultural and social transformations of the rank and file through the immeasurably more sensitive social instrument of the "activity," over which he presided like a father, or perhaps an eldest brother, and which extended beyond the perimeters of the Bund to include pietistic militants from the other ethnic enclaves. The "activity" had not yet crystallized as an impersonal institution subject to the methodical routine of bureaucratic administration. Instead, it retained the fluidity, open-endedness, and roiling inconsistencies of a mass movement.

Indeed, there were even occasions when Hillman found the "activity" itself troublesome: Torn between their devotion to the union and the equally compelling principles of shop floor and artisan solidarity, numbers of these founding cadres remained suspicious of the new machinery of impartial arbitration and had to be constantly wooed by Hillman and the national leadership. Hillman told Schlossberg he had prepared "fresh chocolate for some of the terrible rrrrrevolutionists" (sic) in Baltimore, who were being particularly willful. Men whose years of self-education had left them proud and jealous defenders of their capacity for independent thought and action objected to Hillman's more elitist proclivities: "I strongly protest against having our organization run by a few 'select ones,' " a Syracuse organizer wrote.[58]

Nonetheless, during the critical years following the UBT strike of 1913 the "activity" was the heartbeat of the movement. By 1916 the union's foothold in the industry was still tentative, not only in New York but in all the major markets. Many manufacturers and contractors remained unreconstructed and violent opponents. Guerrilla war on the shop floor was still the norm. The survival of the ACW depended on whether and how the "activity" managed the transformation of what was still a mass movement, inchoate and impermanent, into an institution, and whether it could do so in the face of the global cataclysm that was about to engulf the United States.

FIVE

"The Messiah's Footsteps"

The war turned the world upside down. An unimaginable catastrophe for millions, it was at the same time, especially in America, a harbinger of good as well as great fortunes, not only commercial but also political and social. The largest strike wave in the history of the United States, including a dozen citywide general strikes, swept the country between 1916 and 1922. Trade union membership doubled between 1916 and 1920. All throughout a Western world undone by war and revolution, a crisis of state and society erupted with particular force across the contested terrain of the industrial workplace. Throughout Europe, and even in the relatively quiescent United States, revolutionary parties, trade union bureaucracies, and political and business elites reexamined and struggled over the customary prerogatives of management and the "rights" of the managed. The relationship between democracy and industrial organization, between public institutions of the state and private institutions of the economy, were subjected to an unprecedented social inspection and criticism. While hardly a war to "end all wars," nor one likely to make the world "safe for democracy," the war did become, without anyone's prior contrivance, a war if not for than about "industrial democracy."[1]

"The world is in the midst of a new social era," Hillman proclaimed. "What labor is demanding all over the world today is not a few material things like more dollars and fewer hours of work, but the right to a voice in the conduct of industry." Hillman's plea for "a voice in the conduct of industry" was freighted with ambiguity, evocative and imprecise, pregnant with possibilities and millenarian visions. An invisible immigrant proletarian, subsisting on tea, cigarettes and Tolstoy just a few short years before, and not otherwise given to outrageous flights of fancy, Sidney Hillman now imagined for himself and for his union a prominent role in the re-creation of Western industrial society.[2]

It was the shattering impact of the war that made such reveries seem real. The government was desperate about labor shortages, about escalating rates of labor turnover, especially among precious reserves of skilled craftsmen, and about the rising tide of labor unrest and strikes. Consequently, it actually came forward to champion collective bargaining. For the ACW this proved decisive. Membership increased from 48,000 in 1916 to 138,000 by mid-1919. Prior to the outbreak of war, with the single exception of Hart, Schaffner & Marx, the union had nowhere secured a reliable foothold in the industry. By 1920 the ACW comprised the fourth-largest body of organized industrial workers in the United States, after the miners, machinists, and railroad workers.[3]

Thanks to the war, Hillman was allowed entry, albeit by the back door, into the administrative centers of political power. His wartime dealings with government agencies left him permanently persuaded that collaborations with the state were welcome if not essential. By elevating the question of "industrial democracy" to a preeminent place on the public agenda, the war vastly extended Hillman's associations into the worlds of scientific management, juridical and political reform, and the broad fraternity of social engineering. First formed in wartime, those were pivotal relationships that would shape the rest of Hillman's career. Meanwhile, the war confronted partisans of "industrial democracy" like Hillman with a revolution in the politics of production from below. If "industrial democracy" excited the imaginations of trade union, managerial, and political elites, "workers' control" electrified the anonymous warrens of the shop floor. Artisan and industrial democracy did not always speak the same language; Hillman, finding himself at the confluence of those two social currents, managed momentarily to embrace them both, itself a sign of how the Great War elasticized the boundaries of the socially possible.

Finally, the war was the occasion for a crisis of conscience: Whether to pledge allegiance to "workers' control," socialism, and anti-imperialism; or to "industrial democracy," social engineering, and the "war to save democracy." The Great War was, in part, "Great" just because it raised the temperature of moral life, forcing fateful choices and excruciating evasions. Hillman hesitated, but only briefly, and then decided.

Momentarily, the war reversed the balance of power in the clothing industry. It generated an extraordinary demand for military clothing, thereby improving the bargaining leverage of all garment workers. Moreover, lucrative government contracts, together with a tightening labor market, made even the most stubborn manufacturers vulnerable to the proddings of the union. Still, the military draft had a contrary, disruptive effect, as it depleted the ranks of the young union militants, especially among the cutters, including Frank Rosenblum, who was given a rousing sendoff at the ACW's 1918 convention. The draft also produced an influx of unskilled women workers into a number of job categories, a process accompanied by a general deterioration in conditions. Dorothy Jacobs complained that they were treated like "beasts of burden" by the bosses and even, for a time, by the union.[4] Meanwhile, during the first year of American belligerence the cost of living increased by more than 60 percent, further fueling discontent. On balance, however, for once the invisible hand of the market dealt generously with labor. More important, it was the visible hand of government that proved decisive.[5]

At first the Army bypassed union jurisdiction in meeting its need for uniforms. The Quartermaster's Department simply let contracts to the lowest bidder, a policy that created great pressure to cut labor costs, for which the favored method, predictably, was contracting out work to tenement sweatshops. Whatever minimal labor standards existed previously collapsed almost instantly. The ACW lambasted the Quartermaster's Department for its barbaric violation of "true democracy and civilization"; even "the glory of infancy is desecrated." Middle-class sensibilities were offended as well. New York's Municipal Service Commission, the Mayor's Committee on National Defense, and the National Consumers' League attributed the return of the sweatshop, child labor, homework, substandard wages, and dangerously unsanitary conditions to the government's laissez-faire attitude.[6]

Florence Kelley, Secretary of the Consumers' League, arranged for Hillman to meet with Walter Lippmann, then working for Newton D. Baker's War Department, to discuss the sweatshop problem. Kelley touted Hillman as the most knowledgeable person in the industry. That was a weighty endorsement. Kelley herself stood at the center of a cluster of "social scientific" reform organizations, including the Consumers' League, the National Child Labor Committee, the American Association for Labor Legislation, and the WTUL, whose campaigns on behalf of accident, health, and unemployment insurance, as well as minimum wage and child labor legislation, commanded the attention of both major political parties. Kelley's recommendation was seconded by Henry Moscowitz of the Municipal Civil Service Commission, who told Secretary of

War Baker that Hillman was a "man with an unusual capacity for vision and leadership," one who took a "sound and patriotic point of view."[7]

While most of Hillman's time since coming to New York had been taken up with union business, he still assiduously cultivated his relationships with Kelley and the near-familial network of professional social workers and reformers who worked and often lived together on East 22d Street. The energy invested in building those ties now paid a handsome dividend, and Hillman leaped at the chance to meet with Lippmann and Felix Frankfurter, who had also come to work for the War Department.[8]

Hillman supplied Lippmann with a listing of all those clothing manufacturers performing work for the government who were "notorious for their hostility to organized labor." He provided him as well with detailed reports on which firms were violating government or union standards of wages and hours, and which ones were responsible for the evils associated with subcontracting and homework. He emphasized that the rank and file had already made great sacrifices, both as citizens and as soldiers, but there was a limit to everyone's patience and loyalty. Indeed, in Hillman's view, which he expressed to Brandeis as well, the "labor situation is quite critical." Unless the government acted quickly, the ACW would be unable to honor its no-strike pledge, as discontent was becoming acute: "While we have urged upon our members . . . to refrain from striking on uniform work . . . we feel we shall be doing an injustice to our organization . . . if we stand idly by and permit the enslavement of tens of thousands of people by union hating employers." The forebodings shared by most Progressives before 1917 about the domestic dangers of war seemed to be coming true.[9]

Even while anxious not to jeopardize his sudden entree into official circles, Hillman remained forthright in his criticism of government policy. He wrote directly to Secretary Baker, professing again the union's patience and patriotism, explaining that at "numerous meetings of our members we have pleaded with them to be patient," but that the government's failure to act was "creating a condition where hundreds of thousands of needle workers . . . feel that the government . . . is encouraging non-union employers . . . and is breaking down the union standards long established." He reminded Baker that both Lippmann and Frankfurter had promised relief and that it was urgent for the government to make it clear it "will not directly or indirectly lend its authority to the misconduct of union-baiting employers and will see to it that justice is done."[10]

Hillman told his friend John Williams that Lippmann was a "profound thinker" whose views he respected as much for their political practicality as for their intellectual subtlety. The war, both by opening up avenues of communication with people like Lippmann, and through its practical display of the powers of state intervention and administration, introduced Hillman to a new logic and language of *raison d'état*. Lippmann was drawn to Hillman for similar reasons. Together with Frankfurter and the labor economist–government consultant John Commons, Lippmann had come to regard matters of industrial exploitation and domination less as moral–political dilemmas than as questions of social cohesion. Disorder, inefficiency, and outmoded shibboleths like "individualism" stood in the way of a functional harmony of interests. The social engineering mentality proposed erecting a more powerful, ostensibly disinterested state apparatus devoted to enlarging the nation's productivity and efficiency, a purpose presumably more exalted and self-less than any competing vision of class solidarity. This transvaluation of moral and political issues into matters of social administration was a dream shared not only by Marx and Lenin but by twentieth-century liberalism as well. The Marxists predicted it as the outcome of proletarian revolution, the liberals as the antidote to that revolutionary mood.[11]

Practically speaking, it meant for Lippmann that industrial peace depended on unions "which acquiesce and are compelled to acknowledge the responsibilities that go with power."

Hillman did not all at once abandon his old-time political religion with its jeremiads against capitalist greed and its prophetic vision of a new moral millennium. Temporarily, it immunized him against those Progressive solipsisms which established an all-too-easy equivalency between industrial democracy and industrial stability. Still, he was mightily impressed with the Lippmann viewpoint and even more so with the practical advantages of having people like Lippmann and Frankfurter as allies.

For his part, Lippmann immediately assigned Mary Anderson, then working for Mary Van Kleeck in the Women in Industry Service and an acquaintance of Hillman from her WTUL organizing days in Chicago, to investigate Hillman's complaints regarding the maltreatment of women clothing workers. Soon thereafter, Lippmann and Frankfurter conferred with Secretary Baker, who on August 24 announced the creation of a Board of Control of Labor Standards, operating under his authority and consisting of Louis Kirstein, manager of the Filene retailing complex (and an acquaintance of Hillman); Florence Kelley; and Captain Walter Kreusi of the Quartermaster's Department. The Board was empowered to inspect factories producing Army clothing to be sure manufacturers were upholding labor and sanitary standards. The Board gave its blessing to contracts calling for the eight-hour day, equal pay for equal work, the right of collective bargaining, and the elimination of workers under the age of sixteen. Even before Baker's announcement, Hillman was making preparations for a crash organizing campaign to follow immediately upon the Board's creation, while at the same time he canceled a planned general strike in Boston to give the Board time to complete its investigations.[12]

Samuel Gompers, enjoying a moment of unprecedented power and prestige that would last as long as the war, used his influence to prevent official representation of the ACW on the Board. Indeed, the appointment of Thomas Rickert, an otherwise obscure AFL official of a semi-moribund union, to the War Labor Conference Board, was engineered by Gompers as part of his ongoing assault on the Amalgamated. Within the councils of government, Frankfurter lobbied for Hillman and in general argued against treating Gompers as the sole legitimate representative of labor, but to no avail. The Wilson administration sought to maintain a delicate equipoise in its labor policy, to balance workers' nearly irresistible demand for some formal recognition, however hedged about with disabling qualifications, against the fear of business leaders that such recognition would prove fatal.[13]

Despite his official exclusion, Hillman was pleased with the Labor Standards Board's performance. First of all, although the rivalry between the ACW and the UGW was intense at the outset, the vigorous activity of the former soon left the older craft union a negligible factor in war production. The UGW, sometimes with the connivance of Gompers, periodically complained of government favoritism shown to the ACW. However, a confidential report prepared by the Board conclusively refuted that claim.

The Board's powers steadily increased. At first it enjoyed no official mediating functions. But in December 1917 the Board was replaced by an Administrator of Labor Standards for Army Clothing. Kirstein became the first Administrator (later to be replaced by another friend of Hillman, the labor mediator, William Z. Ripley), and immediately added labor adjustment to his other functions, insisting, wherever feasible, on the practice of collective bargaining. The Board, and subsequently the Administrator and his staff, successfully reduced the innumerable disputes over piece rates and, in those instances where traditionally weekly pay rates prevailed, even managed to persuade cutters to end slowdowns and other methods of deliberately limiting output.

Rather rapidly the Board's surveillance helped eliminate child labor, homework, and unsanitary facilities. The eight-hour day and forty-eight-hour week became uniform throughout the industry. Most important of all, the legitimate status of the union, whatever Gompers may have wished, was no longer in doubt. Indeed, local organizers as well as the national leadership made use of the Board's investigative and mediating powers to embarrass manufacturers who resisted unionization. They trusted the Board's administrators, who were themselves committed to the industrial and social virtues of independent unionism, to withdraw contracts from firms that remained hostile.

Its lack of official representation notwithstanding, the ACW was regularly consulted on labor as well as on more general matters of production. The Board relied on the union's expert knowledge of industry costs, production methods, and prices in carrying on its negotiations with uniform manufacturers. In turn, union officials cooperated with Board initiatives to rationalize the industry, conferring with Frankfurter, Ernest M. Hopkins, and the ex-socialist N. I. Stone about establishing "scientifically" determined standard prices for piecework in New York and Chicago.[14]

Cooperation between Hillman on the one hand, and Kirstein and Ripley on the other was especially close. Kirstein must be credited with the nearly single-handed organization of the Rochester industry. Exercising his commercial leverage, he managed to induce all but one of the major producers there to enter into a general agreement with the ACW. Up to that time the ACW had been mainly unsuccessful in penetrating the ranks of that city's clothing workers. Meanwhile the city's larger manufacturers asked N. I. Stone of the Board to "handle their labor situation," indicating they were "prepared to go all the way up to the actual recognition of the union." They made it clear that Stone "could play with Mr. Hillman on the back stairs," but Stone insisted that the relationship be open and formal. Max Adler of Adler Brothers invited Stone to talk to his foreman "on the 44 hour week and the wisdom of dealing with the union," and the manufacturers Weill, Rosenberg, and Hickey were of the same mind. Stone was able to report that the war experience was having a salutary effect even on "old Bourbons like Mr. Friedman of New York," who had begun "talking industrial policy with him."[15]

Hillman was quick to reciprocate. He emphasized the union's commitment to war production even if it meant temporary suspension of union rules on overtime and Sunday work. He denied charges that the ACW was pacifist and therefore sanctioning deliberate slowdowns. When slowdowns or strikes did occur, the leadership went out of its way to discipline offending workers, ordering strikers to return and sometimes fining or even firing insubordinate members of the rank and file. Hillman made it clear that work on uniforms would continue, "because the position of our organization [is] that no matter what happens there will be no interruptions on the government's work." In fact, after the war ended, Hillman boasted that only prompt action by the union managed to keep wages at a reasonable level.[16]

As the war was drawing to a close, the government created the War Labor Policies Board (WLPB), chaired by Frankfurter. It was designed to "eliminate all those factors . . . reducing the productivity of the workers" in the economy at large. Although created too late to implement policy, its plans were in part formulated on the basis of wartime experience with the clothing industry. Frankfurter convened a conference of New York clothing manufacturers' associations with the ACW at which both sides agreed to submit their differences to an advisory board composed of Frankfurter, Ripley, and Louis Marshall, who was also serving as Director of the Industrial Relations Division of the Shipbuilding Labor Adjustment Board.

In subsequent reports the Board went on to recommend the establishment of impartial arbitration machinery to improve discipline and efficiency and to regulate the discharge of workers carefully, including full rights of appeal, all to be balanced by an understanding that interference with efficiency or a deliberate reduction in output constituted legitimate causes for suspension. But even more significant than its specific recommendations was the Board's strategic plan for modernizing the New York market.[17]

Frankfurter envisioned an alliance of inside manufacturers, Progressive reformers, liberal technocrats, and the ACW designed to eliminate the archaic contracting system. The scheme was a more elaborate and more permanent solution than any previously attempted to the contractor dilemma that chronically unsettled the industry. As early as 1915 the ACW sought to control the situation by actually organizing contractors' associations under the union's supervision. In New York the union was briefly able to determine which contractors received work, but it was a volatile business and, as one organizer from Boston reported, "a dangerous move and I agree with you that we must be on the watch."

The anticontractor alliance fostered by the Frankfurter Board confronted the ACW with a tactical problem: While the union encouraged contractors' associations to exercise a collective discipline over their entrepreneurial members, any such actions, by bolstering the position of contractors, perpetuated the system that lay at the root of much of the union's difficulties, one which the Frankfurter Board proposed to attack root and branch. Hillman was convinced such an assault was necessary and was merciless in his attitude toward these marginal employers:

... I say we are not to be called upon to have here a standing army of unemployed, not fed by the state, so that the small manufacturer who has no credit can come into the field four weeks and have an army of starving men and women ready to do his bidding. I say if people haven't got the capital to go into business, let them stay out of it, better for everybody concerned. And I haven't got sympathy for the underdog. If a man is a small man he doesn't have to go into business. He can work as well at the bench. We are not to suffer and to supply a standing army of unemployed so that someone can go into business.

So long as it proved impossible to eliminate the contractors entirely, the ACW sought to control them by insisting that manufacturers deal only with contractors appearing on the union's approved list or by obligating manufacturers by contract to enforce union standards in those contractor shops they dealt with. By virtue of the new strategy of social cooperation, however, far more was possible. For the higher purpose of what Frankfurter described as "constitutionalizing" the industry, strikes, once feared like chaos itself, now were selectively and conjointly deployed by manufacturers, the union, and the Frankfurter–Ripley Board as a weapon to discipline recalcitrant contractors.[18]

The WLPB's industrial and social innovations were of course not limited to the clothing industry. Its broader plans included a mechanism for controlling national employment through centralized recruiting of unskilled labor by a U.S. Employment Service; training programs; a system of labor priorities; price controls; wage and hour and child labor standards; specialized agencies to deal with housing, transportation, and education; and government mediation of labor disputes. Hillman's dealings with the Board thus immeasurably widened his perspective about the potential role of the administrative state, especially since Board personnel, in addition to Frankfurter, were often at the forefront of the new sciences of industrial organization and labor relations. Many became lifelong associates of Hillman, including the attorney Max Lowenthal, Frankfurter's assistant, who later represented the ACW in legal matters; Mary Van Kleeck, the Board's economic adviser; and Louis Marshall, Dean of the University of Chicago, later to serve as impartial arbiter in the men's clothing industry. Moreover, the Frankfurter-proposed *entente cordiale* among managerial, labor, and technical elites in the clothing industry was a microcosm of larger designs for social harmony that wartime experiences with methods of planning, improved efficiency, and industrial democracy encouraged. Increasingly, Hillman found it easier to identify his own future with these confections of social cooperation than with the more uncompromising imperatives of his socialist youth.[19]

Government policy was exquisitely executed, if not self-consciously formulated, so as never to violate the prevailing lines of industrial power, even though sometimes government functionaries like Frankfurter would press against those limits. Thus, while the National War Labor Board (NWLB), recognized the right of collective bargaining, it gave unions no actual grant of power; it never went so far as to require companies to bargain as a matter of policy, and, in an excess of even-handedness, also encouraged the growth of company unions and shop committees, which by the mid-1920s would grow to one-half the size of the AFL itself. In the business community, where hostility to centralized state integration of economic functions was palpable, Veblenesque visions of engineers supplanting political and corporate chiefdoms—a new disinterested, rationalist, and professional ruling elite—no doubt seemed more plausible when industrial engineers and social scientists suddenly played conspicuous parts rationalizing leading sectors of the war economy. People like the economist Wesley Mitchell believed social science research and planning could restore, or create for the first time, real harmony in social relations through planned industrial development and distribution. But given the enduring realities of corporate power and an antithetical political culture, such visions were, for the moment at least, quixotic.[20]

Indeed, the ambivalence of federal labor policy reflected a wider ambivalence about the role of the state. The war significantly expanded the professional elite of state bureaucrats, but the infrastructure of the national state was still formative and conflict-ridden, and was itself constantly sniped at by Congressional opponents of executive power. Consequently, the role of the new state bureaucrat became less a matter of supervising and directing the private sector through some powerful engine of government than of mediating and coordinating the activities of a powerful private sector through a relatively weak state.[21]

Frankfurter was well aware that the war, precisely because of its putative democratic objectives, had exacerbated the workers' perception of the "disparity of opportunity as a political system and their lack of authority as employees. When it comes to industry, the masses of men have no control, or feel they have no control, over their lives." The war produced a legacy of "spiritual demands and ferment for democratic participation" especially on the part of the "most intelligent and well-paid and skilled," who sought some control over the "disposal of labor power." Industry therefore needed to be democratized and "treated as a social phenomenon," as was already the tendency in Europe.[22]

With those broader concerns in mind, Frankfurter singled out the entente arranged in New York, in particular its machinery of impartial arbitration, as a model of scientific and equitable adjustment of industrial discord, akin to the British Labour Party–sponsored Whitley Councils, which were then attracting enthusiastic attention among American Progressives. He was at pains to point out, often in fraternal criticism of those in the Taylor Society who failed to see the need for independent vehicles of working-class expression, that such organizations were "indispensable." However "scientifically" disposed management might become, it could never adequately represent the needs and point of view of labor, and it was inexcusably imperious to assume they could. As the Whitley Councils had already demonstrated, Frankfurter argued, business, labor, and the public each required its own organs of representation. [23]

As Frankfurter's words do more than suggest, the war turned out to be the occasion for a plethora of experiments in redesigning the architecture of power at the workplace and even beyond the workplace. Works councils, shop delegates, and corporate parliaments, along with more conventional forms of independent trade unionism, all inspired visions, some would say delusions, of "social participation." The political and ideological impact of the British Labour Party's wartime program on Hillman and the whole of the American Progressive community was little less than sensational.

The "British way," to which Hillman was to refer with increasing frequency, was encapsulated in the Labour Party's 1918 manifesto "Labour and the New Social Order." It sketched a quasi-socialist commonwealth comprising essentially a series of social welfare measures, including unemployment insurance; health care; public housing and education; "democratic control of industry" in transportation, communications, and utilities; and an egalitarian tax system. The manifesto's emphasis on planning and class cooperation were particularly appealing to an American Progressive mentality that had for years sought a "northwest passage" to "social partnership." [24]

Above all, the British example was inspirational in its approach to the "labor question." The Whitley Commission report of 1917 recommended the creation of industrial councils comprising representatives of labor, management, and the public, which were to function as the organizational basis for a more total economic reconstruction, a reformed capitalism more equal in its distribution of wealth and power. American Progressives who pondered ways of restoring some sense of creativity and democratic participation to the otherwise stupefying routines of mass production paid close attention. They saw in all the various blueprints for industrial democracy ways to avoid "the bitterness of class war and the horrors that have paralyzed Russia."

All those influenced by the Whitley Report insisted that the state become more active. Industrial concord and equity, they contended, must become matters of public policy. Frankfurter envisioned a government that would exert a "moderating influence" and would persuade reluctant industrialists especially to recognize and cooperate with independent trade unions to achieve both efficiency and social stability. However, the WLPB was no more than a gesture in the direction of a coordinated federal labor policy; it lacked any direct grant of Presidential authority and was otherwise symptomatic of the profound ambivalence afflicting Washington's approach to the "labor question."[25]

Despite the proliferation of government agencies charged with responsibility for dealing with labor problems—the food, fuel, and shipbuilding administrations for example—there was in fact no coherent policy nor any adequate administrative and judicial machinery, especially during the first year of the war. The Wilson administration was itself internally divided on the question. Although President Wilson made Labor Secretary William Wilson the nominal head of the wartime administration of labor policies, actual operational control remained fragmented and subject to the power of jealous, self-aggrandizing production and contracting agencies, including the Emergency Fleet Corporation and the War and Navy departments. Secretary Wilson was, moreover, excluded from the war councils and the Industrial Cabinet established in March 1918.[26]

Briefly, the balance of power tipped in labor's favor. Under the auspices of the National War Labor Board and the WLPB, there was a significant improvement in wages, the eight-hour day became widespread, and the right to unionize enjoyed official sanction. The Wilson administration, its Department of Labor in particular, displayed a distinct friendliness toward independent trade unions, expressed through the creation of a federal conciliation service and especially through its endorsement of the 1916 majority report of the Industrial Relations Commission, authored by Frank Walsh and Basil Manly, which unequivocally blamed the maldistribution of wealth and income for the prevalence of industrial violence and warned that "political democracy" could exist "only where there is industrial democracy."[27]

But the Walsh–Manly report was dismissed as too radical and partisan even by many Progressives, including the editors of *Survey*, *The Nation*, and *The New Republic*, all of whom preferred the minority report of comission member John Commons, which spoke the conciliatory and consoling language of cooperation, harmony of interest, and disinterested professionalism. Moreover, the administration had from the outset felt coerced by the strike wave that erupted in response to the war economy's inflation and rigorous rationalization. Throughout the war the preponderance of business opinion outside the clothing industry opposed even modest concessions to the trade unions, a weighty sentiment the government was neither able nor inclined to ignore. By 1918 the NWLB had already struck a nonpartisan note, offering its proposed shop committees as a workable compromise between the open shop and the unqualified recognition of autonomous trade unions. The government was particularly alarmed about the antiwar and radical political sentiments accompanying many strikes, which not only repudiated the government's war aims but sometimes went so far as to call for the conscription of wealth rather than men. Indeed, governmental probes into the "labor question," whether at the federal level through the Industrial Relations Commission or by state-sponsored arbitration and mediation agencies, were, from their inception, attempts at administrative-technical solutions—that is, responses to labor radicalism designed in part as antidotes to its political passions.[28]

An admirer of Lippmann, Frankfurter, Herbert Croly of *The New Republic*, and other would-be architects of an empowered administrative state, and plainly grateful for those acts of federal labor policy which materially eased the difficulties of union organizing and bargaining, Sidney Hillman was inclined to overlook certain undercurrents of government intervention that were less beneficial. Even during his revolutionary youth in Russia he had gravitated toward a LaSallean view of the political universe, one not so very different from Croly's or Lippmann's, which treated the state as susceptible to the influence of whatever class managed to exert the greatest force at any particular time. Thus it was conceivable that the state might change hands, even through the medium of electoral contests. It was furthermore possible for the coveted machinery of power, prior to its definitive capture by one class or another, to undertake intermediate forms of meliorative action on behalf of the working class. If anything the sometimes ambivalent and even self-contradictory policies of the NWLB convinced Hillman of the need to capture the apparatus of government, at least in the form of cultivating political alliances and populating the bureaucracies with friendly functionaries. If indeed the federal government was to assume an active role in establishing and enforcing the rules of a new industrial democracy, then penetrating the interior of this administrative machinery was essential.

In part because of his upbringing in the Russian revolutionary movement, the advent of the activist state produced in Hillman none of those feelings of bad conscience that troubled some Progressives, whose liberal-individualistic predispositions and traditional commitment to a minimal role for the state caused them to blanch at the rise of the new administrative order. Since arriving in America, Hillman was ministered to and practically enveloped by a network of social welfare and social reform organizations, all of which were engaged in the political arena, pressuring local, state, and federal governments; seeking legislative remedies for industrial disease and accidents, unemployment, and child labor; and advocating public works, statutory minimum wages, and so on.[29]

However the role of the state was plotted—as umpire, arbiter, watchdog, or even avenging deliverer—there was wide agreement that the democratization of American industry was imminent, no matter how violently people might fall out over just precisely what that might mean. Even Herbert Hoover was prepared to countenance, to be sure only briefly, a meaningful role for labor in "a new industrial order." So much was expected by so many from this proposed marriage of industry and democracy that no one could predict with confidence the health or longevity of the offspring or, for that matter, whether a marriage subject to so many cross-cutting desires might not itself remain barren. Industrial democracy might conceivably evolve as a new system of domination, that snare and delusion warned of by the "wobblies" and cynically plotted by more hard-boiled industrialists. On the contrary, however, for those radical and skilled denizens of the factory, carriers of a democratic and egalitarian tradition already generations old, industrial democracy plausibly promised an end to hierarchy, centralized authority, and the degrading fragmentation of skills—in a word, a new system of liberation. For a heterogeneous milieu of personnel managers, social workers, efficiency experts, labor relations professionals, and social science academics; for socialists whose watchword was progress and Progressives whose shibboleth was social partnership; for reformers loyal to the hoary tenets of antimonopoly politics; for reformers like Frankfurter and Brandeis, who deployed the populist rhetoric of antimonopoly to express an entirely new industrial dispensation; and finally, for a small circle of trade unionists, among whom Hillman rapidly became the most celebrated, "industrial democracy" suggested a social compromise, the "British way," a new system of integration for a society so explosively fractious it sometimes seemed, in the superheated atmosphere of war and revolution, on the verge of disintegration.[30]

Sorting out just what "industrial democracy" did and did not mean took years, decades even, of organizational, political, and intellectual struggle. Never again, however, would so many purely visionary schemes occupy the public attention. Where those visions were the least delusionary, as in Hillman's garment industry, on the railroads, and in the coal mines, they frequently entailed some system of centralized and rational-bureaucratic management, endorsed and supported by workers'

organizations in return for their own official recognition. In these instances, the new bureaucratic institutions were installed at the expense
of more direct, less predictable forms of shop floor power. But they also
supplanted the less tenable management practices associated with an
earlier era of absolute entrepreneurial freedom and the feudal-style tyranny of the departmental foreman.

Forms of working-class self-organization (such as the local works
councils among metalworkers, which ignored traditional craft jurisdictions as well as the rules of contractual obligation and were free of the
bureaucratic procedures that turned democratic enthusiasm into organizational routine) naturally provoked great concern. Management circles
alert to these subterranean developments in the politics of production
began experimenting with a form of shop committee more susceptible to
their own control. By mid-1919 the National Industrial Conference
Board could report on the creation of 225 works councils in 175 companies, some consciously imitating the 1911 HSM plan for employee
representation. The Russell Sage Foundation became, in effect, the clearinghouse for all sorts of proposals ranging from rather cautious profit-
sharing schemes to much more daring designs for cooperatives and
co-management. Two leading businessmen-Progressives, Edward Filene
and Henry Dennison, both acquaintances of Hillman, founded the
Twentieth Century Fund in 1919. Its announced focus of attention was
to be in the areas of industry–labor relations and industrial equity.[31]

Councils varied widely in the extent of their authority. The weakest
were limited to a kind of custodial concern with welfare and recreation
matters, while others enjoyed some say in settling grievances and monitoring safety and other working conditions. Few, if any, had any real
influence over questions of factory discipline, hiring, firing, promotions,
or apprenticeship rules. From management's standpoint the councils were
most useful when they focused their attention on reducing turnover and
waste. From the standpoint of the trade union movement, it was possible
to coexist with the councils until they began endorsing the wage cuts and
layoffs that accompanied the postwar recession.

Works councils were an official recognition that industrial relations
were plagued by mutual distrust and bitter antagonism to autocratic
authority. But the attempt to resolve that crisis was largely a formal
one—a great torrent of rhetoric about "sincerity" and the need to "listen
and communicate," or pieties about "harmony," "mutuality," and "participation" that scarcely addressed the entrenched mechanisms of domination at the workplace.[32]

Not all was mere persiflage and subterfuge, however. Industrial relations mediators, personnel counselors, scientific management consul-

tants, and others close to the scene knew that the era of the "Prussian method" had to end. The financial and social costs of industrial discipline achieved through coercion were becoming exorbitant. Industrial authority, they argued, should rest on the consent of the governed, so to speak, not merely because that was only fitting in a society so saturated in the political maxims of liberalism, but also because those precious psychic and social energies unleashed by the process of autonomous, self-imposed discipline were simply not reachable through the imperious commands of others.

In the end, while some of the various schemes for workers' participation were thus seriously intended, industrial government by consent depended on a willingness to share real power with organs of working-class strength, free of management control. Very few businessmen were prepared to take that great risk. Only in industries suffering from declining markets, growing nonunion competition, or new products—for example, garments and synthetic textiles—was top management persuaded, sometimes against its own ingrained habits, to collaborate with reliable trade unionists.

Even when the new breed of professional personnel managers was inclined to accommodate democratic impulses, they faced the resolute opposition of an older group of management functionaries, those traditionally in charge of the production process. So long as labor remained abundant and therefore cheap, there was little the "new class" could do to shift the balance of power or to alter the sacrosanct beliefs of America's characteristically frontier business mentality. However, war-induced labor shortages and strikes, along with the simultaneous growth of quit rates and trade union agitation, worked a wondrously quick change of mind in at least some business circles previously unmoved by reasoned argument. The number of personnel departments among corporations employing at least 250 people more than tripled between 1915 and 1920. For a brief interlude the internal politics of the corporation were infected with the general contagion of social experiment. Personnel and scientific management carried on the fight against laissez-faire inside the factory, while it simultaneously suffered an all-out assault from the outside.[33]

By the time of the war, the internal differentiation of function within the organized business world had proceeded far enough to create real sociological and cultural divisions between owners ("capital") and management. These functionally defined managerial-technical circles were less wedded to the patriarchal, property-rooted rigidities of traditional entrepreneurs and financiers. They were willing to sacrifice some efficiency in the short term for greater stability and enhanced morale in the long run. Indeed, the most prescient among this milieu, including those employed directly as labor managers by corporations as well as management consultants associated with the Taylor Society, even envisioned a socially daring system of joint industrial control by "enlightened" and "responsible" trade unions and a new managerial class presumably educated in the spirit of disinterested professionalism. It was precisely with this distinctive segment of the business world—the nucleus, some imagined, of a new technomanagerial order—that Sidney Hillman developed the closest professional and ultimately political ties.[34]

Frankfurter and Lippmann were only the best known of this fraternity. Included also were government-employed educators, economists, and labor relations experts like Leon Marshall, Henry Seager, and Willard Hotchkiss of the Shipbuilding Labor Adjustment Board; Jett Lauck, research economist for the NWLB and adviser to the 1914 Industrial Relations Commission; and a leading Taylor Society figure, Morris Cooke, then working for the Ordnance Department. Mary Van Kleeck was another. Since her tenure as Director of the Russell Sage Foundation's Committee on Women's Work in 1910, she had best embodied the marriage of social science, philanthropy, and the new scientific social work. By the time Hillman met her, Van Kleeck was committed to some form of real workers' participation. N. I. Stone, another devotee of scientific management, later became labor manager for Hickey-Freeman in Rochester and a close collaborator of Hillman. William Leiserson, a nationally prominent labor mediator, and future chairman of the National Labor Relations Board, would remain a valued colleague of Hillman inside and outside of the clothing industry all through the period of the New Deal and into World War II. He functioned as the young Franklin D. Roosevelt's adviser on labor matters during the first war.[35]

Leiserson, who soon after the war became the impartial arbiter in New York, was perhaps typical of the new industrial relations milieu in that his thinking managed to get beyond the old bugaboos about dangerous aliens and labor radicals. He had first met and had been impressed by Hillman in 1916, and had served as an impartial chairman in Rochester and as an arbiter in Baltimore, Cleveland, Chicago, New York, Boston, and Montreal. An immigrant Jew, born in Estonia to a family active in anti-Czarist politics, he grew up on the Lower East Side of Manhattan in a world populated by radicals and trade union leaders. A participant in the University Settlement, itself immersed in Progressive and labor reform politics, he worked for seven years in a shirtwaist factory before attending the University of Wisconsin. From there he went on to become industrial commissioner of Wisconsin and Director of Research for the U.S. Commission on Industrial Relations.[36]

Leiserson accepted the ACW's liberal use of revolutionary rhetoric as a useful and otherwise harmless disguising of economic objectives that in no essential way departed from other, more "American" trade unions. Moreover, he considered the ACW a particularly important and timely experiment in the "Americanization" of the immigrant working class. Up to that time the new science of personnel management had been applied almost exclusively to the English-speaking skilled, while the new immigrant unskilled continued to suffer under an older, harsher authoritarian regimen. Leiserson was convinced that the ACW's "new unionism" opened up an incomparably more felicitous avenue of acculturation and socialization by inviting the participation of the new immigrant working class in a controlled system of trade union and industrial decision-making. As a student of the labor economist and reformer John Commons, Leiserson became an advocate of a new dispensation in labor relations, which took the term "industrial democracy" quite literally: Trade agreements were "nothing less than constitutions for the industries which they cover, constitutions which set up organs of government, define and limit them, provide agencies for making, executing, and interpreting laws for the industry, and means for their enforcement."[37]

People like Leiserson shared neither the facile belief in some natural harmony between capital and labor nor the fatalism that conflict between them was inevitable and irreconcilable. They placed their faith in a "science of adjustment" as practiced by managers and trade unionists, each exercising their appropriate functional expertise. Leiserson sharply defined the arena within which industrial democracy ought to be practiced. It excluded both technical problems involving distribution of men, machines, and materials, and personnel matters having to do with hiring, selecting, training, transferring, and promoting, all of which he considered properly subject to scientific rather than popular determination. Hillman's perspective was not so narrow; he would insist on the union's right and competence to have a say on many of these matters. But all issues having to do with wages, hours, work rules, and discipline, Leiserson and Hillman agreed, ought to be subject to joint labor–management resolution. In his work in the clothing industry, and in reports to the Taylor Society, Leiserson contended that the overriding objective of democratic industrial procedure was "to obtain the consent of employees to their continued participation in the further development of the capitalist mode."[38]

Even more than Leiserson, Morris Cooke exerted a decisive influence on Hillman beginning in this period. Cooke was working for the Ordnance Department and was responsible for General Order no. 13, which recommended that government contractors adopt collective bargaining, the eight-hour day, and minimum wage, health, and safety standards. An industrial engineer, he was a leading figure in the faction of the Taylor Society that insisted that truly effective management of the production process depended on active input from the shop floor, and that independent trade union participation in industrial planning represented the wave of the future. Even Frederick Taylor himself, while no apostle of Samuel Gompers, evinced a certain hostility to Wall Street and to those elements of big business and finance who knew little about the technology and organization of production. Still, while Taylor expressed a productivist disdain for the idle rich, "Taylorism" was, from the outset, not only a science of management but very much management's science.[39]

At first it made no pretense of disguising its partisan attachments. It was elitist and totalitarian in spirit and emerged as a kind of nineteenth-century Stakhanovism whose rather crude Benthamite Utilitarian psychology lacked any sense of the need for cultural transformation arising out of the destruction of craft culture. It paid little attention to the problem of consent or to the complex social psychology of ethno-occupational work groups.

However, Cooke and others in the scientific management movement who would become close associates of Hillman—the industrial engineers Harlow Person and Otto Beyer, the clothing manufacturer Richard Feiss—never subscribed wholeheartedly to the infamous Taylor dictum: "In the past man was first; in the future the system will be first." While their vision never quite reached beyond the marketplace, in their view still the ultimate articulator of human need, they did free themselves of those myopic class loyalties which made most Taylorites anathema to the AFL. Richard Feiss, for example, whose Clothcraft Shops in Cleveland employed more than two thousand, spent considerable time studying scientific management options that might seem credible to his employees. For that purpose he hired Mary Gilson as his personnel specialist. It became her task to undermine the existing foremen-centered, nepotistic system of patronage and promotion that governed the shop floor. Because Feiss welcomed the airing of workers' grievances; championed a merito-cratic system of hiring, training, promotion, and remuneration; and actually encouraged the formation of shop councils to participate in the formulation and execution of time-study experiments, he, Gilson, and Hillman became firm friends. The friendship grew despite the fact that for years the ACW was unable to organize Clothcraft, a measure of Feiss's serious efforts to be fair and his unwillingness to tolerate the customary tyrannies of his foremen. Health and safety conditions were excellent, the bonus system was generous, and the company's offerings of parties, music, and movies were impressive. Conversely, Feiss's confidence in Hillman wore down his aversion to unions. When the ACW began its first organizing campaign, Feiss expressly forbade discrimination against those workers who elected to join. By the mid-1920s Feiss and Gilson were openly praising Hillman as "progressive," "efficiency minded," "pragmatic," and "democratic." They had come to see autonomous trade unions as indispensable vehicles of self-discipline and stability for which no form of company unionism could substitute.[40]

As for Morris Cooke, even during his prewar tenure as Director of Public Works for the reform administration of Mayor Rudolph Blankenburg in Philadelphia, he insisted that scientific management, properly applied, not only was a centralized command function of top management but needed to encourage a reverse flow of information and consultation from below, if only to prevent the potentially dangerous social isolation and social ignorance of the enterprise leadership. During the war Cooke and the Taylor Society drifted steadily to the left. The Society's formal conception of the industrial polity became increasingly syndicalist, envisioning the democratic integration of functional groups in a rationalized production system. Society members were enamoured of the wartime shop committee system, seeing in those committees schools of worker self-management. Cooke not only encouraged the growth of particular trade unions but also proposed the creation of national unions to facilitate planning in the economy at large. Meanwhile, the Taylor Society endorsed the bituminous coal strike of 1919 and the steelworkers' demand for the eight-hour day. Increasingly, its rhetoric condemning capitalist waste and disorder permeated the language of Hillman's "new unionism."[41]

Cooke outlined his broader perspective in a letter to Hillman written not long after the end of the war:

> Most of us have now come to believe that in itself any increase in the production of essential commodities is a desirable social end. All groups and classes of a society should . . . participate in the cultivation of the arts and science leading thereto. . . . The foregoing constitutes a fundamental . . . argument for labor cultivating a broader interest in the productive process. . . . But perhaps of even more significance . . . is the tremendous impetus which would be given to the labor movement through having it stand out before the country as not only back of a program of production but energetically claiming—first through its leaders and ultimately through its rank and file—a responsible part in scheming out and executing such a program. If . . . labor is to ultimately have a radically different part to play

in industry these new contacts and duties will provide the best possible training for the larger responsibilities which would come to labor under any re-vamping of the present order.

Moreover, Cooke was acutely sensitive to rank-and-file sensibilities that seemingly, but to Cooke only seemingly, presented insuperable barriers to industrial integration. "I am not unmindful of the fact," he told Hillman, "that many Amalgamated workers feel that some other system of industrial organization would be far better for society." But he wanted to suggest

> . . . that even those who advocate a radical reorganization and who hope to profit by the change have everything to gain and nothing to lose through acquainting themselves with the details of our present methods. . . . I can't imagine that even if soldiering or sabotage appears to some as desirable that a highly developed technique narrows the opportunities in any way. . . . Even those of the extreme left who look forward to the time when our present organization is to be completely upset . . . can cooperate in the plan [for workers' participation in improved production methods] and if the foregoing is even measurably true, then every labor organization should have an agency or a division specializing on production and labor's participation in it.[42]

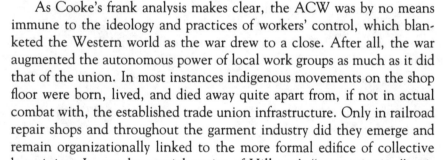

As Cooke's frank analysis makes clear, the ACW was by no means immune to the ideology and practices of workers' control, which blanketed the Western world as the war drew to a close. After all, the war augmented the autonomous power of local work groups as much as it did that of the union. In most instances indigenous movements on the shop floor were born, lived, and died away quite apart from, if not in actual combat with, the established trade union infrastructure. Only in railroad repair shops and throughout the garment industry did they emerge and remain organizationally linked to the more formal edifice of collective bargaining. It was the special genius of Hillman's "new unionism" neither to suppress from above nor to succumb to the centrifugal force of "those of the extreme left."

A tidal wave of shop floor rebellion caused Ripley and Kirstein to bombard Hillman with official complaints about stoppages and slow-downs by pressers and cutters, who simply ignored the government's machinery for resolving disputes. But discipline was hard to enforce when work was plentiful and manufacturers were prepared to concede a great deal just to keep the production stream flowing.

As much as Hillman might have hoped to quarantine the union against the contagion of wartime and postwar revolutionary upheaval, it proved irrepressibly infectious. Ripley reported that with the Bolshevik revolution "anarchy came to prevail to an undreamed of extent in the hundreds of little clothing contractors' shops throughout New York City." Following the armistice, "discipline, production, efficiency, low enough at best, were all shot to pieces." Recollecting his own anxiety, he noted that "in many instances workers took over the establishments."[43]

It all sounded quite ominous. Fortunately, Ripley supplied some homely examples of just what such presumptuous control meant in the claustrophobic precincts of the city's atomized industry:

M. Katz. . . . Told pressers to make the work better and the people went on strike. Katz was fined $25. His people kept on strike until he paid same.

J. Goldstein. . . . Operator opened the window. Bushel girls caught a cold and requested that window be closed. Mr. Goldstein closed the window, because there was a draft in the place. The operator opened the window. Mr. Goldstein requested that the window must be closed. The people went on strike and Mr. Goldstein was fined and he paid the people wages for the day they were not working. His people were on strike until he paid.

S. Adelson. . . . Workers threw a bundle of work on Mr. Adelson's wife and because Mr. Adelson gave the worker an argument, Mr. Adelson was fined $25 and people were kept on strike until he paid.

The fate of private property in the manufacture of men's clothing was clearly not at issue. The industrial and political perspectives of those who "took over establishments" often extended no farther than the horizon of their own tiny shops.[44]

Democratic in spirit, sustained by the tenacity and dignity of veteran craftsmen, artisan democracy was a complex and ambiguous phenomenon that bore all the marks of a culture undergoing decomposition. Anarcho-syndicalist in intent, it was localist in perspective, decentralized, averse to long-term contractual obligations, accustomed to semispontaneous action in a firm-specific context, rarely conscious of the industry as a whole, and sometimes infected with the craft-conscious parochialism it criticized in the AFL. It was demonstrably militant, but its militancy was in large measure conservative, rooted in impulses to defend the work skills and independence still surviving precariously in small shops and under factory roofs, but mortally threatened by a degrading standardization of tasks. In the nineteenth century, unionism often grew up on the basis of such defensive insularity. The "new unionism," however, was predicated on the process of its disintegration and reabsorption into a new institutional and characterological structure of behavior.

Industrial democracy—more precisely the comanagement–workers' participation scheme Hillman, Cooke, and Frankfurter envisioned for the clothing industry—thus emerged in practice as a catalytic agent of managed consent and as a political prophylaxis and therapeutic. In a speech before the prestigious City Club of Chicago in 1919, Hillman called upon all industrial sectors to organize in light of the model created by the ACW. Either American industrial activity would be jointly planned by labor, management, and public representatives in a uniquely "American program" of postwar reconstruction, or else American business would face the economic and social chaos then haunting Europe.[45]

Social liberals generally were well aware of the ACW's contribution to modern management and, more important, its innovations on behalf of industrial democracy. The pages of *The New Republic* and *Survey* were frequently given over to praise of the union's social prescience and responsibility. *The New Republic*'s founder and chief editor, Herbert Croly, was the first to talk about a "new unionism," which would transcend narrow class perspectives and help create a new system based on the dignity and shared value of work. Such unions, Croly advised, must educate workers so that they might become "responsible for the proper organization and execution of the productive work of society." His magazine congratulated the ACW on its dedication to shop floor discipline, scientific management, and participation in the operation of the clothing industry.

Robert Bruere, another liberal Taylorite and head of the Bureau of Industrial Research, summed up the feelings of many when he wrote to Hillman to say: "Many of us have been looking to the fresh developments in the Amalgamated as the most important sign of a new order in the industrial and social world of America that has hitherto appeared."[46]

Men like Bruere were anxious for a success, for some tangible sign that modern industry, despite its taste for the autocratic, could nevertheless be made to cohabit the same social space with a democratic impulse just then at its zenith. Alarmed by the 1915 Industrial Commission picture of a nation nearly overrun with industrial violence, they hoped that the system of industrial democracy would ameliorate the class struggle, lubricate the wheels of progress, and preserve democratic institutions. Thus the "new unionism" commanded intense social surveillance not only because it undertook a major reform in the mechanics of industrial labor relations but also because it promised to transform the social and psychological dynamics of the workplace. The Progressive ideologue Paul Blanshard astutely noted that in order to endure, industrial civility had to sink its roots deep into the social psyche of the garment workers. He reported that the new democracy was "developing trained citizens—trained citizens who are informed, enlightened, and disciplined." Similarly, the *New Republic* editors, aware that democracy was being subjected to "tests of unprecedented severity throughout the world," concluded that its future "depends . . . upon the capacity of employers and workers to harmonize democratic ideals of freedom with the voluntary self-discipline essential to efficient production." The editors could happily report that "no group in America has a keener appreciation of this fact than the ACWA."

Sidney Hillman agreed emphatically. At the height of domestic and global unrest in late 1919, he boasted: "We have actually worked out the moral sanction behind work." That moral revolution, he believed, would "keep our industry isolated from the general unrest." However, Hillman also knew, better than the industrial democrats like Blanshard, Bruere, and the *New Republic* editors, who lived several social strata removed from the industrial fray, that if the new industrial republic had already secured its governing elite, it had not yet secured its citizenry. Before the "rule of law" could be permanently ensconced in the industry's workshops, it first had to be settled whose law was to rule. What made all the scheming and dreaming by industrial democrats so agonizingly imprecise was that no one had any really firm idea of just what the message of industrial democracy meant, first of all to those politically awakened circles of artisans and industrial craftsmen and second, even more mysteriously, to the massed, silent armies of the new immigrant unskilled— indeed, in the latter case no one could even be sure the message had penetrated their ranks at all.[47]

From whatever quarter it emanated, industrial democracy spoke the language of modern Western civilization. It presumed its fundamental existential and moral categories: economic group and individual self-interest; an egalitarianism of "rights"; the motivational priority of the individual; the primacy of instrumental reason; a faith in science and technical progress; and the spiritual calisthenics of disciplined work. Insofar as industrial democracy articulated the aspirations of the labor movement alone, it consisted in an amalgam of artisan-republican and social democratic traditions—all of whose basic premises were part of liberal and/or democratic political culture. It is true that the artisan tradition distinguished itself from entrepreneurial republicanism by its insistence on the "community's" prior right and moral duty to regulate the use of private property. Nonetheless, it expected from this moral economy the individual independence and propertied manliness hallowed by the universal republican mythos.

Still, it would be a great oversimplification to assume that because all industrial democrats shared an ancestral language that the political differences among them were of no great consequence. Even while the middle-class ideologues of "industrial democracy" went about recasting the fundamental premises of liberal capitalism, making room within its juridical and political culture for collectively defined interests and the new practice of administrative law, the axioms of an older ideology of productive labor remained compelling. From the standpoint of the craft militant (and it was almost invariably the most skilled who led struggles for "workers' control"), the advent of bureaucratic-hierarchical management atop a system of mass semiskilled production, represented a root-and-branch expropriation of his social existence and identity.

Partisans of workers' control movements, which sprang up everywhere throughout the industrial world from Russia to America, carried on a final battle against all those threatening tendencies of modern industry for which the war acted as a kind of pressure cooker of change. It was in a sense the last hurrah of the craft militant resisting the inexorable processes of deskilling and the evisceration of what has been called the "culture of control." Incubated by the war and ushered in by scientific management, with its chronometry; its impersonally determined and externally imposed piece rates, bonus systems, and job ladders; and its ingenious designs for serial production to be undertaken by a whole new class of semiskilled operatives, this new industrial order promised the social extermination of a whole social species.[48]

Because those mortal blows to the integrity and autonomy of skilled work groups originated in distant corporate command centers, workers' control extended its animosity to the corporate form itself, to its centralized, hierarchical, and bureaucratic procedures, which were rapidly supplanting contracting and other more personalized, decentralized, petty entrepreneurial systems of labor organization. Not unnaturally, then, "workers' control" assumed the mantle of the antimonopoly movement, sharing its faith in a democratic and propertied egalitarianism and its basic orientation to the primacy of production. It was still very much the age of the "labor question," since the heyday of the social gospel in the 1880s, first of all a moral question of spiritual reformation, redemptive brotherhood, autonomous manhood, and communal rebirth.[49]

The ethos of artisan democracy, however, had very little to do with the toils and troubles of Old World peasants suffering the irremediable process of marginalization. While skilled cutters, pressers, custom tailors, and others hewed to an old democratic faith, for the newer Italian, Polish, and Southeast European casual and unskilled laborers the ideology of productive labor and the program of workers' control exerted little attraction. Indeed, for the most recently arrived unskilled, who were bound together by a more elemental materialism of demands, who lacked political perspective or experience with voluntary, non-kinship-based organizational life—without a vision of a world put together differently—resistance to industrial society was only outwardly similar to their more skilled and assimilated co-workers. Their strikes—Lawrence and Paterson before the war, the steel strike just after it—more closely resembled episodic communal rebellions, peasant *jacqueries,* than acts rooted in the immediate experience of work itself. Socially, these cultures in transit remained profoundly deferential.

From the standpoint of industrial democrats, these marginalized peasants were "uncivilized" or, in the antiseptic parlance of academic social science, "unacculturated." Rousseau observed: "To make citizens is not the work of a day." Proponents of industrial democracy would find this to be true, perhaps even truer in the industrial realm than in the political. But for precisely that reason, industrial democracy as it worked itself out in practice became something more than the fashionings and manipulations of various industrial elites. It had to take account of those countless immigrant agrarians—would-be "citizens of industry"—who were concerned far less with the procedural formalities of industrial due process than with securing the ancient attachments of kin and community corroded by the factory and the market. For those impassive peasants, as for the craft militant, the moral codes of industrial democracy were at first less than compelling.

In the end, however, the power of industrial rationalization proved ineluctable. The worlds of gang labor and industrial handicraft were undermined utterly, especially during and after the war, as the regime of mass production extended its reach across the industrial landscape. The gap between them closed, or rather was filled by a new generation of semiskilled worker, bound neither to the plebian republicanism of the skilled elite nor to the partriarchal traditionalism of the old world.[50]

For a while, however, industrial democracy was a program and ideology in search of a constituency. Shrewdly, Hillman cautioned political and business elites about the dangers of stiff-necked resistance to change. His own youth, the youthfulness and fluidity of his union, and the millennial aura surrounding even the most pedestrian deliberations made Hillman acutely sensitive to the proliferating and free-floating desires abroad in the land. During a visit to Montreal he was warmly received not only by the city's garment workers but by the leading businessmen of the Canadian Club, who listened intently as the union president prophesied industrial democracy as the wave of the future. He warned that if it was opposed, the recent revolutionary events in Russia would be repeated in the West.[51]

Hillman permitted (indeed he would have been hard put to prevent) all the political enthusiasms of the moment to find voice inside the confines of the union. Delegates to the ACW's wartime convention in 1918 listened to the messianic eloquence of Judge Jacob Panken, who spied socialism in the imminent political future; called for the immediate nationalization of the railroads, mines, shipbuilding, and steel industries; and compared the impending final march to freedom to "the flaming pillar, going through the Desert of Sahara." Secretary Schlossberg told the convention it represented the "rising of a new society," that the Amalgamated was the core of a new industrial parliament of a new civilization. Speaker after speaker emphasized that the union was no mere purveyor of material well-being but the midwife of a loftier, more humane order.[52]

Dependent on the government's support, the ACW leadership endorsed the war effort, but only after inventing for it a radical social democratic promise. No issue was more sensitive, and it placed Hillman in an extremely delicate position. He adopted a moderately left-wing attitude toward the war, like that of the British Labour Party, supportive but wary of its hidden imperialist objectives. On the other hand, the tacit understanding between Hillman and his friends in the Wilson administration was that the union would mute its criticisms of the government's war policy. Thus, in a letter to the *New York Times* at the end of 1917, Hillman noted: "The Amalgamated Clothing Workers . . . is not a pacifist organization. . . . Since the declaration of war we have cooperated with the government in every way by suspending our union rules whenever the needs of the government required. . . . We have permitted overtime work as well as Sundays to speed up production." In a letter to the *New York Tribune,* which had accused the union of pacifism, Hillman protested that the ACW was "second to none in its opposition to Junkerdom and Kaiserdom." A few months later Hillman and Schlossberg issued an official statement of support for the war, which included, however, an endorsement of the war aims and program of the British Labour Party and the Inter-Allied Labor Conference held in February 1918. Their statement closed with a flourish: "Long live true social democracy and long live the new working class international," finessing the relationship between the war and social revolution. This sort of social democratic enthusiasm for the war increased conspicuously after the German invasion of Russia in early 1918, so much so that the ACW pledged $500,000 to the third Liberty Loan Drive.[53]

Political ambivalence and division about the war ran like an irreparable fault through the whole of the Progressive and radical world. It was a chasm Hillman's political reach and agility managed to straddle. Personally, he felt no uncertainty. Several months before the United States entered the war, he became an American citizen. At the same time, in an equally significant ritual act, he officially changed his name from Simcha to Sidney. But analogous political rituals for those thousands of men and women who opposed "imperialist exploitation and slaughter" as naturally as they breathed had yet to be invented. Hillman needed to proceed with great caution.[54]

Hillman argued that the original causes of the war were no longer germane. A victory for "German autocracy" would certainly represent a defeat for labor, he argued. Although admitting that the war, from the outset, was antithetical to working-class needs and desires, he crafted a resolution for the 1918 convention which maintained that the war had unleashed "broad democratic forces against autocracy and militarism" and that it might become the catalyst of a "new social order," if only Prussian militarism was defeated once and for all. The convention was filled with such enthusiastic idealism without practical issue. It passed resolutions recognizing the new Soviet government and calling for the public control of industry. It closed with the singing of the *Marseillaise* and three cheers for the program of the British Labour Party.[55]

At the same time, Hillman quietly arranged to table a resolution endorsing the Socialist Party on the grounds that it was not fair to the union's nonsocialist members. Actually, fairness had little to do with it, nor did Hillman fear an outpouring of patriotic indignation from the ranks. He simply couldn't afford to be embarrassed publicly by open endorsement of an avowedly antiwar party. Meanwhile, however, the union was active in numerous local SP campaigns, including Morris Hilquit's 1917 mayoral race in New York, in which the Socialist leader captured nearly one-fourth of the votes. A number of the union's own notables were elected to public office on the Socialist ticket: Judge Jacob Panken of local 156 entered the New York State Assembly; Abraham Shiplacoff of local 213 became a city alderman, as did Charney Vladek of local 3. In Rochester, Jacob J. Levin and George Stahley of local 14 were elected supervisor and alderman, respectively.

Hillman worked at translating revolutionary sentiment into patriotic rhetoric and organizational energy. A leaflet in Chicago, for example, exhorted workers to join the union "thereby voicing your protest against autocracy in your shop. Become an exponent of American standards of Democracy in Industry, of True Americanism."[56]

For many in the socialist movement, the Russian Revolution helped transform the war from an insupportable struggle among equally repugnant

imperialisms into a defensible war for democracy. Still, even after the Bolshevik seizure of power, Hillman was forced to play a delicate game. No
one who had come of age in the Russian social democratic movement
could deny the exhilaration produced by the overthrow of the autocracy
and the seizure of power by a workers' party. October had an electrifying
effect on thousands of garment center refugees from Czarism. Just before
their victory, Jacob Potofsky wondered whether Bolshevik control would
mean disruption and endanger democracy: "I have faith in Kerensky. He
is a leader of genius." Nonetheless, he admitted his attraction to the Bolshevik's tempting call for the abolition of private property.[57]

Potofsky's ambivalence was not atypical. While the socialists who
gathered around the *Forward* thought the revolution gave them legitimate grounds for supporting the war, Hillman's more militant and de-
pendable Bundist comrades in the Jewish Socialist Federation often
remained loyal to their anti-imperialist convictions. Other ethnic radicals were similarly divided. Symptomatic of the widespread, militant
antiwar sentiment was the reception accorded a delegation of Italian
pro-war labor leaders. Welcomed by Gompers, they were denounced as
the king's socialists by the Italian Socialist Federation and by the Italian
leaders of the ACW and other needle unions.

Like Potofsky, Hillman too was uncertain about just what the Russian developments portended. He told John Williams that chaos was
predictable in a situation where "the masses are ignorant for ages and
their experience undermines all faith in the 'ruling class.' " Although he
admitted there was little ground for optimism, he also felt it was too early
to pass final judgment.[58]

His friends and associates lined up on both sides of the war question,
further complicating Hillman's predicament. His mentor, Clarence Darrow, chose to support the Wilson decision to go to war. But elements of
the radical pacifist movement, along with the majority of the SP, formed
the People's Council for Democracy and Peace in September 1917. It
endorsed the Bolshevik peace proposals for an immediate truce without
annexations or reparations. The Council denounced conscription and
war profiteering, welcomed shop committees and workers' councils as the
wave of the future, and was applauded in its pro-labor objectives by
people as moderate in view as Rabbi Judah Magnes. The Council was
immediately successful among the garment workers, which naturally
alarmed Gompers but also worried Hillman. Gompers, assisted by pro-
war members of the SP like John Spargo and J. G. Phelps Stokes, and
with the official blessing of the Wilson administration, organized the
American Alliance for Labor and Democracy, which drew its funds from

George Creel's Committee on Public Information, the government's official propaganda arm. The American Alliance devoted itself to attacking the People's Council's calls for peace negotiations and for independent political activity, and its demands for radical social reform and government intervention in the economy.

While garment center socialists like Max Pine and Jacob Panken joined the People's Council, other close allies of Hillman, including Jane Addams, Lillian Wald, and Rabbi Stephen Wise, refused to do so. With the *Forward* functioning as its headquarters, the Council easily won the contest for the loyalty of the Jewish working class. The Bolshevik revolution reinvigorated the Council movement and led to calls for industrial democracy, the nationalization of the principal means of production, and withdrawal from the war.

All of this left Hillman in a quandary, especially given the importance of his working relationship with various members of the government. From Chicago, Marimpietri worried that endorsement of the People's Council by the joint board might hamper Hillman's dealings with the administration, although he was candid enough to acknowledge that his own pro-war sympathies might be prejudicing his perceptions. Hillman neither joined the Council nor did anything to oppose it, while Schlossberg participated rather conspicuously.

The Council, after all, afforded Hillman his main political defense against Gompers's efforts to break the ACW's near total control of the production of military uniforms. The old guard of the UGW complained to Gompers that "Secretary Baker is forcing our people . . . to recognize the Amalgamated which is part of the SP and the People's Council." Gompers wrote to Baker about the problem and went so far as to call a mass meeting of unemployed garment workers at Webster Hall in New York to protest the ACW's closed shop arrangements and to denounce the Board of Control of Labor Standards. The People's Council, along with the ILGWU, sprang to the union's defense. On May Day, 1918, Hillman returned the favor by addressing a Madison Square Garden rally that proclaimed the virtues of international socialism and demanded an immediate peace.[59]

These few years of war and revolution thus constituted a historical moment when it was possible, indeed almost a psychic necessity, for people like Hillman to maintain two divergent if not absolutely irreconcilable views of the proper and the possible. Hillman could one moment intone the rhetoric of an Old Testament avenger of immemorial injustice and in the next sound like a benevolent bureaucrat armed with the latest dispassionate discoveries of social engineering. He greeted the Bolshevik

revolution with scarcely less public warmth and enthusiasm than he did
the reformist pronouncements of the British Labour Party. There was
more to this than Hillman's formidable talents as a political gymnast or
his admittedly swelling political and personal ambitions. Thus, in January 1918 he wrote to his then six-week-old daughter, Philoine, from a
hotel in Montreal:

> I am just coming from a mass meeting. . . . The hall was crowded with men
> and women who toil . . . in their looks I saw the plea for a word of hope,
> because, my dear, that is the only thing that gives color to their life. Their
> present is so colorless that their only joy lies in the future . . . here in Prince
> Arthur Hall—perhaps the masters of tomorrow—still the Slaves of to-
> day. . . . Here were those who are now waiting for this new Messiah—
> messenger of love, freedom, and plenty to all; those who struck, starved and
> sacrificed themselves to make their hopes possible . . . here were the slaves
> of those rulers, looking for a message of deliverance. As I was looking in
> their eyes, and some of those eyes belonged to young and pretty girls—I
> could not resist, I told them what they wanted to hear—that their Day is at
> hand. Messiah is arriving. He may be with us any minute—one can hear the
> footsteps of the Deliverer—if only he listens intently. Labor will rule and
> the World will be free. And as I was telling them these words, a new fire
> kindled in eyes—the fire of hope, will and determination. A thrill went
> through me at this time—I was watching them and behold, a wonderful
> change took place. At first I only felt his presence and then I actually saw
> him in all his wonderful majesty—strong—determined, full of love. The
> Champion was with us in the Hall, ready to do battle. The people—an
> awakened people—
>
> Dear do you think this could be true—or perhaps it is a vision of a tired
> and inflamed brain. Good night Dear.[60]

Hillman and the ACW came of age at, and were shaped by, the
momentous historical juncture of two vastly different systems of work and
social hierarchy: On the one side stood the circumscribed intimacies of
craft producers and skilled labor, family enterprise, local industries producing for local markets, immemorial customs, and personalized authority; on the other, the semiskilled operative, bureaucratic hierarchy,
functional management of anonymous corporations supplying far-flung
markets with standardized products, the impersonal regime of rules. To
survive the ACW needed to articulate all the distinctive desires and
animosities of people whose attitudes toward work, the family, politics,
and religion formed no unified view of the world as it was or should be.
While clusters of ethnocultural work groups clung to familial and handicraft forms of work organization and labor discipline, whole other sub-

regions of the industry underwent the deskilling and rationalization characteristic of modern technology and corporate organization. So it was that workers' control and industrial democracy, the Bolshevik and British roads, the peasant *jacquerie* and the strategic industrial strike, the class struggle and the politics of administration managed to coexist within the same union, for a moment even within the same personality.

SIX

Bolsheviks and Technocrats

J ust after the war ended, the Chicago market was finally unionized—on the previously only dreamed-of basis of the forty-four-hour week. The victory quickly spread to New York and to much of the rest of the industry, fulfilling, sooner than anyone had a right to expect, a pledge made at the union's 1918 convention. In a telegram of congratulations to Sidney in Chicago, Bessie characterized the triumph as "the greatest thing that happened in the 20th century" and assured him that even his baby daughter, Philoine, would be delighted if only she were old enough to understand. Proudly the *Advance* proclaimed that although "the official Labor Movement does not recognize our existence, our struggles, our victories . . . we have done all this not for ourselves, but for the working class as a whole."[1]

Such hyperbolic euphoria suited the moment. Louis Brandeis observed on the eve of the war: "The labor question is and for a long time must be the paramount economic question in this country." Answering it promised not only permanently to alter the relationship between Labor and Capital, but in so doing to eliminate the immorality of exploitation, the social inequality and antagonisms fostered by great aggregations of wealth, the threat to democratic politics represented by overbearing corporate power and pelf, and even the causes of global and imperial war. Not long after the war ended, President Wilson cabled Congress from Versailles:

> The question which stands at the front of all others amidst the present great awakening is the question of labor . . . how are the men and women who

146

do the daily labor of the world to obtain progressive improvement in the conditions of their labor, to be made happier, and to be served better by the communities and the industries which their labor sustains and advances?

For Wilson, the exalted rhetoric notwithstanding, reform, at least in the arena of labor relations, had always been essentially prophylactic, a way of ameliorating class divisions and avoiding revolution. It was in that anxious frame of mind that he convened the first of two industrial conferences in the fall of 1919.

Other middle-class Progressives, decidedly more sanguine than the President, were prepared to discard outmoded shibboleths. For Frederick C. Howe it was a revelation:

> My own class did not want such a world [a world of equality]. And there was but one other class—the workers. . . . Labor would not serve privilege. . . . By necessity labor would serve freedom, democracy, equal opportunity for all. . . . The place for the liberal was in labor's ranks. . . . My political enthusiasm was now for a party of primary producers.

The leading journals of progressive opinion—*The Nation, Survey, Dial*—all agreed that genuine reform depended on working-class cooperation with constellations of Progressive luminaries like those assembled in the "Committee of 48." The editors of *The New Republic* were swept away: "We have already passed to a new era, the transition to a state in which labor will be the predominating element. The character of the future democracy is largely at the mercy of the recognized leaders of organized labor."[2]

When ancient dynasties perished, empires fell apart, monarchies succumbed to revolution, and colonies defied imperial rule, events seemingly of only local significance were suddenly impregnated with world historical promise. It was a visionary time, Agnes Nestor, a suffragist and social activist, recalled: "We were living in a time of great dreams—dreams of cooperation between the working people of the world, dreams of dignity and plenty for all, dreams of international peace."[3] Yet within a few short years everything would seem immeasurably bleaker, as if some political ice age had descended upon the Western world, leveling the landscape of social and moral possibility. When the new decade opened, the partisans of the Amalgamated imagined themselves a brigade in the grand army of the revolution. Before it was half over the ACW stood practically alone, without serious political prospects, bound to an unstable industry suffering from severe dislocations of technology and taste, and excluded from an official labor movement itself thoroughly intimidated.

While the Red Army vanquished counterrevolutionaries and foreign invaders alike and carried the revolution into Poland, Soviets seized or struggled for power throughout Eastern Europe and even in the continent's German heartland, where a socialist party, albeit one of studious moderation, formed the government. Anticolonial risings in the Middle East, India, China, and elsewhere signaled at the very least the beginning of the end of European hegemony. French railroad workers and British coal miners seemed prepared to challenge conservative governments, while a wave of factory occupations soon engulfed the Italian peninsula. The quotidian antagonisms of the factory suddenly ignited generalized contests for control of the whole production process. Trade unions normally parochial in vision and social reach burst through those boundaries of craft and locale to encompass that pariahdom of the unskilled, forming mass movements for the democratic management of industry. Craft unions that had been too inflexibly bureaucratic, centralized, and exclusionist were bypassed by wholly new shop floor and industrywide councils. Those decentralized, syndicalist organs of industrial control flourished particularly in countries and industries where small and medium-size production units predominated, as in Italy, France, and the American garment industry.[4]

In the United States the social and political order was never threatened that seriously, even if some powerful people were impressed enough by their own propaganda to believe that it was. Nonetheless, 1919 was a year of unprecedented unrest. One of every five workers went on strike at some point during the year. Some of those strikes were not only large and directed at critical industries, as in the case of coal and the railroads, but were socially presumptuous as well. Long-silent Slavic steelworkers defied Judge Elbert Gary and the bastion of the open shop in a strike that lasted through the last quarter of the year. In Seattle, Portland, and Butte, general strikes became municipal soviets, which not only closed those cities down but more alarmingly proposed opening them up again under their own auspices. That the Boston police would even consider striking seemed a mortal blow aimed at the very foundation of civil order and made Governor Calvin Coolidge into a national hero when he intimidated Boston's finest into returning to work. Meanwhile, the wobblies, who had been exciting the lurid and hysterical recesses of the American political imagination for more than a decade, helped lead mass textile strikes up and down the Northeast corridor, proving that news of their demise at the hands of wartime vigilantes and government raiders was premature.

Proposals for reconstructing the social order emanated from all points on the political compass—not only from socialists, populists, and veteran Progressives but from institutions as indubitably respectable as the Academy of Political Science, the National Municipal League, and the Reconstruction Conference of Governors. Even Gompers felt compelled to form AFL committees on postwar reconstruction and social insurance. Many envisioned the continuation of wartime economic controls, new departures in social welfare, and even the permanent nationalization of the railroads. The Plumb Plan, devised by Glenn Plumb, an industrial relations specialist and colleague of John Williams from Streator, Illinois, proposed that the federal government purchase the major trunk lines. The idea was enthusiastically supported by the railroad brotherhoods and the AFL, if only because they sought to continue the government's high-wage wartime policy.[5]

A Progressive–labor coalition, without the name, perhaps, but with at least some of the program of socialism, seemed a real possibility. An American Labor Party, fathered by those perennial black sheep of the AFL in the Chicago Federation of Labor, boldly proposed the socialization not only of the railroads but also of the means of mass communications, most major natural resources, and vital basic industries. Its platform, published one week after the Armistice, included a set of social welfare and labor reform measures—the eight-hour day and federal health, life, and accident insurance—along with a system of progressive and corporate taxation, the democratic management of industry and commerce, and the destruction of "economic imperialism." Its mayoral candidate, the Federation leader John Fitzpatrick, polled a respectable 65,000 votes. Meanwhile, the "Committee of 48," a circle of "advanced Progressives" previously associated with Bull Moose or Wilsonian liberalism, including Amos Pinchot, Herbert Croly, Horace Kallen, Walter Weyl, and Robert Morss Lovett, espoused an antimonopoly democratic politics and saw itself as the vanguard of a liberal–labor party. Its 1919 platform demanded public ownership of rail transport, public utilities, and the principal natural resources, and called for the abolition of labor injunctions, the guaranteed right of collective bargaining, and "equal economic and political and legal rights for all irrespective of sex and color." In the summer of 1920 the National Labor Party and the "Committee of 48" held a joint convention in Chicago to form the Farmer-Labor Party, which emphasized the "right of labor to an increasing share of the responsibility and management of industry." In the pages of *The Nation, The New Public, Dial,* and *Survey,* Progressive publicists all agreed, momentarily at least, that meaningful reform depended on the cooperation of the organized working class.[6]

To be sure, this dependency occasioned a profound ambivalence and anxiety precisely articulated by the editors of *The New Republic:*

> The indispensable political task of liberal Americans in the near future is that of promoting the organization of American workers for the capable exercise of political power. . . . If such a union does not take place . . . American labor will become impatient and fall back on revolutionary agitation . . . the most effective safe-guard against such a deplorable class warfare lies . . . in the formation of a party of workers whose program would be as radical as the proposed programme of the British Labour Party.[7]

Nonetheless, with whatever misgivings, Progressives prepared themselves for root-and-branch change.

Brandeis went so far as to prophesy to Felix Frankfurter that in this new era of Bolshevism and the anonymous corporation the "wage system is doomed." Brandeis was convinced that "no remedy can be hopeful which does not devolve upon the workers' participation in responsibility for the conduct of business, and their aim should be the eventual assumption of full responsibility." That a justice of the Supreme Court could express, if only in private, a prophetic vision that had animated the lives of socialist garment workers long before the Amalgamated's appearance suggests how superheated the political atmosphere had become.[8]

The mood inside the ACW was buoyant and full of great expectations. During the immediate postwar years one-quarter of a million Jews migrated to the United States from Russia and Eastern Europe, many with firsthand experience of the revolution. As they gravitated naturally into the garment industry and joined the ranks of the Amalgamated, they made the otherwise most utopian and improbable revolutionary anticipations seem suddenly palpable, near at hand. The spectrum of Jewish socialist politics shifted dramatically to the left; even the *Forward* initially welcomed the Bolshevik seizure of power, as a necessary if temporary expedient. Although moderate elements within the JSF soon drew back, they were a distinct minority, and Federation leaders, swept along sometimes willingly, sometimes not, severed their affiliation with the conservative anti-Bolshevik SP.[9]

An "Amalgamated Calendar of 1919 Events" (running actually from May Day, 1918, to April Fools Day, 1920) displayed the daily chronology of a cresting militance. It was a chronicle of triumph, of wages raised and hours lowered, of union recognition and victorious general strikes. Previously unorganized markets in Syracuse, Buffalo, Utica, and Cincinnati were penetrated for the first time despite the use of "Czarist methods" in Utica, for example, which included Hillman's forced removal from the city by the local constabulary, mass arrests, and the wounding of several strikers by police gunfire. In Cincinnati the employers' association deliberately provoked a general strike. The police, the city government, the courts, the press, and the local official labor movement hysterically denounced the strike as "seditious" and a "terrifying instance of native Bolshevism." Yet in the end the union's presence was firmly established. Similar inroads were made in St. Louis, Indianapolis, Milwaukee, Louisville, and Minneapolis. The momentum of organization extended the union's reach into the shirt factories of New York and Pennsylvania and the garter-making sweatshops of Streator, Illinois, where children as young as five worked for two cents an hour. In general, between 1914 and 1919 wages rose 70 percent, and hours, which in 1911 averaged 54, dropped to 48 by 1919 and to 44 by 1920. At the peak of the postwar boom, the ACW controlled 50 percent of the industry, as against 23 percent in all other unionized industries, and wage rates in union shops were 25 to 50 percent higher than in nonunion plants.[10]

The union's biennial convention in May 1920 was a carnival of political enthusiasms. It included an endorsement, to "deafening applause," of the presidential candidacy of Eugene Debs, who carried on his campaign from a jail cell in Atlanta. The call to the convention condemned the "statesmen and politicians who threw the peoples of a peaceful world into an orgy of mutual annihilation," indicted their inability "to reestablish order and sanity," and recounted the union's battle to establish the forty-four-hour week and thus eliminate the prospects of a fratricidal competition for jobs between returning war veterans and civilian workers. The forty-four-hour triumph "was the greatest event in this Country since the signing of the armistice." The union was proud that it was the fate of an "illegitimate" and "excommunicated" organization to be "the first labor organization in the country to meet the assault of capitalism upon the Labor Movement." "Are we dreamers and visionaries? Possibly. But it is just such dreaming and vision seeing as ours that moves the world on the path of civilization." The convention sent a message to fellow workers in and out of the official labor movement: "Whatever your attitude towards us may be, we know you only as flesh of our flesh and blood of our blood. We have made a glorious beginning. We hope to see you follow our example. . . . More such victories and more strength to the rising ruler of the world—Labor."[11]

Hillman sensed the mood of uncompromising militance. In an interview with the *New York World* he commented: "The difficulty with most plans of industrial democracy is that they are granted by employers, and what the employers grant they can take away. . . . We have started on the assumption that nothing less than industrial democracy will satisfy the worker, and that none is possible without a genuine and definite transfer of power." The GEB described the newly fashionable "welfare capitalism" as a "deadening anesthetic. It is Delilah's method of robbing Samson of his power. . . . It destroys the self-respecting manhood and womanhood in the American citizen." The version of industrial democracy with which the "welfare system" was often associated "converts the employer into a ventriloquist. . . . It was the growing and irrepressible spirit of our organization among the workers that made the 'industrial democracy' dummy so important." When installed in a plant like the antiunion Kirschbaum factory in Philadelphia, "industrial democracy and justice . . . are like the legend of 'Liberty, Equality, and Fraternity' on the portals of the French prison. They only serve to mock the sufferings of the inmates."

Charles Ervin, editor of the socialist *New York Call*, allowed his imagination to break free of its Marxists moorings, converting an otherwise trendy phrase into a medieval romance. He told the convention delegates that industrial democracy

> . . . is almost the oldest of industrial ideas. And almost the only beautiful industry the world has ever known was the guild industry, which built the temples, the cathedrals, the guild halls that made Brussels, Antwerp, Düsseldorf, Munich, the French and Italian cities the beautiful cities that they are—when a man worked alongside of his master—not his master, but the man whom he expected to succeed. . . . That was industrial democracy and for ten centuries it was the industry of all Europe, destroyed by the industrial revolution, by the machine, by steam, by electricity that divorces the hand and the brain of labor from the tools of production.[12]

Ervin's sentimental elegy to handicraft production suggests how far the fraternal spirit had suffused across the social landscape. The revival of the cooperative movement was equally indicative. Farmer radicalism in the Great Plains, especially the success of the Non Partisan League in North Dakota during the war, led to a rebirth of a cooperative impulse about which organized labor had long been ambivalent, certainly since the days of the Knights of Labor. The ACW, however, greeted the call for a Cooperative Congress in Chicago in 1919 with great warmth, convinced that the farmer now "sees Modern Capitalism or Big Business as a growing menace. . . . The railroad trust, the speculators, the banks, the grain elevator monopoly, are to him so many tentacles of the same monster." As a consequence, property-owning farmers were developing "a spirit of revolt against social conditions not unlike the spirit of propertyless proletarians." Hillman attended the founding Chicago conference, along with delegates from the railroad brotherhoods and the UMW, and decried the absence of the AFL. Beyond whatever practical benefits might accrue from consumer, producer, and financial cooperatives, Hillman emphasized "the human solidarity factor." "That includes not only cooperation and mutual aid in the democratic production and distribution of the necessities of life; it includes also the tremendous possibilities of the cooperative organizations of Labor for serving as commissaries for striking workers" (a potential the ACW would realize later that year during a protracted lockout in New York). While ready to acknowledge that cooperatives "may not free the worker from his present status," the fraternal electricity of the moment still made it plausible that "the Cooperative Movement will bring a large measure of democracy and human happiness into industry" and augment the "resources for the Labor Movement for purposes of offense and defense."[13]

This was perhaps the last time that the cooperative ideal presented itself as a serious historical alternative to the political economy of liberal industrial capitalism. From the vantage point of the rank and file, notwithstanding some opposition from the left, the cooperative idea was an included feature of a broader urban populist antipathy to corporate domination. From the standpoint of the union elite, cooperatives opened up another avenue along which to advance the material interests of the membership while pursuing the possibilities of collaborative economic management with enlightened businessmen, technocrats, and social reformers. Thus, Brandeis was a leading advocate of consumer and producer cooperatives, partly as a strategic weapon against trusts and oligopolies, partly because he viewed cooperatives, along with trade unions, as particularly well suited for institutionalizing industrial democracy. Workers who shared not only in profits but in actual management received the best experience in responsible citizenship. Under the new dispensation of industrial complexity and interdependence, there was no better way to develop a sense of efficiency, justice, and, in Brandeis's view, renewed manhood. Hillman concurred. Impressed by the success of consumer cooperatives in Britain and Scandinavia, and at the same time sensitive to the messianic mood of the membership, he presented the cooperative program as a device for training workers to control production with the ultimate objective of assuming full responsibility for directing the social economy.[14]

Revolutionary ardor was pitched so high, however, that even when depicted in such grandiose terms the call to join the cooperative movement elicited vociferous opposition from many delegates to the ACW's 1920 convention. They argued that it was "based on bourgeois principles" and that the "cooperative movement is a capitalist institution." It required the combined oratorical talents of Hillman and Schlossberg to quell the uproar. Hillman accused some of the delegates of wanting to ride "the express train . . . and the only stops they make are Paris, Berlin, Moscow, and Milan. They forget that our stops are New York, Chicago, Rochester, Baltimore, and Boston. And we must sometimes think about the local train." He urged a sober idealism. "I feel even more strongly that the time of simply talking wages and cost of living—that time, I hope, will soon pass. . . . In time of leisure I indulge in dreams but I don't permit them to become the policy of the organization." This talent for mixing the visionary and the practical was perhaps the most conspicuous feature of Hillman's moral and psychological makeup. That it worked so well so often, however, was no doubt in part due to a peculiarly "realistic" quality of Jewish messianism. That messianism, in both its secular and religious forms, unlike its Christian equivalent, focused its concerns on the temporal, not the supernatural, on political redemption rather than the suprahistorical salvation of the endless days.[15]

Of course, everything depends on just what is considered "realistic," and at the 1920 convention the members were in a generous mood. Abraham Shiplacoff, manager of the New York Joint Board and Socialist alderman, elicited enormous enthusiasm when he recounted the story of a factory occupation by striking textile workers in Turin, depicted the Russian Revolution as a factory seizure on a global scale, and suggested similar doings might be part of the immediate American future. Convention resolutions condemning the Western blockade of the Soviet Union, demanding an amnesty for all political and industrial prisoners, and excoriating various legislative threats to civil liberties reflected the combative spirit.

The Amalgamated offered more than inspirational rhetoric. It not only donated $100,000 to the 1919 steel strike, it also lent the strike organizers the services of its own General Organizer, Anton Johannsen. The union's involvement in the great textile strikes in Lawrence, Paterson, and Passaic was even more direct and protracted, and was touched by the moral as well as the organizational ambitions of "One Big Unionism."[16]

Early in February 1919 a series of mass strikes spread through the textile centers of the Atlantic corridor. They deliberately bypassed the long-dormant AFL affiliate in the industry, the United Textile Workers, which late in the winter of 1918 had agreed to a reduction in wages in return for the forty-eight-hour week. Not surprisingly for an AFL union, the membership of the UTW was at most 10 percent foreign-born, while the industry's workforce was overwhelmingly immigrant in composition and included French Canadians, Poles, Greeks, Bohemians, Italians, and Slavs. The union's leadership frankly admitted its fear that foreign workers were either already under "wobbly" influence or had come to America already "inculcated with radical ideas." The UTW was particularly at a loss in centers like Paterson, Providence, Passaic, and Lawrence, where the proportion of unskilled immigrant workers to native skilled workers was especially high.[17]

UTW political and ethnic prejudices only reinforced divisions and antagonisms built into the organization of work in the industry. Thus, at one American Woolen Company mill English and French Canadian employees were awarded the most pleasant and best-paying work, mending and weaving, while the "dirty" jobs—doffer, winding, jack-spooling, beaming, and so forth—went to Italians, Poles, Russians, and Lithuanians. Overseers, invariably English, German, or French, scarcely concealed their contempt for their ethnic inferiors, particularly the Italians.

At the same time UTW leaders were quite right to be anxious. There were radicals aplenty, including not only "wobblies" but Italian syndicalists, Bohemian freethinkers, Polish nationalists, and Lithuanians like the ones massed at St. Michael's Hall in Lawrence, who opened their meeting "as all meetings do, with spirited singing of the 'Internationale.' " Moreover, the February 1919 strikes, as mass rather than conventional trade union actions, released energies not yet canalized into collective bargaining or socialist politicking. Partisans could be wistful, nostalgic, and pastoral while at the same time violent, uncompromising, and profoundly estranged from all the everyday assumptions of proletarian existence. In a word, those strikes, like the ones that a decade earlier gave birth to the Amalgamated, were unpredictable and therefore feared by trade union officials for whom predictable, rule-bound, and role-bound behavior was axiomatic. No one was more aware of this than the shop floor radicals—themselves but a study circle removed from the cultural ambivalence of their ethnic brethren—who sought to mobilize these energies on behalf of the more formal programmatic objectives characteristic of an industrial strike.[18]

Antonette Bolis, a second-generation Lithuanian spinner in the Everett Mills and during the strike a public speaker among Lithuanian women, described the elemental strangeness enveloping her co-workers:

> There the women go bare-footed. . . . One thing that is very hard for them when they come to this country is getting accustomed to wearing shoes. Most of the Lawrence Lithuanians come from little villages. . . . At home

in the old country these people do not have money to spend; they do not need it. They think they can come over here, make some money, and return and buy a little home if they have not one already.

Mary Grinka had been in the United States for eight years and considered herself a Socialist. Conditions in America were harder than in the old country: "In the mills abroad there is no sense of hurry as here. You can sit down occasionally there; here never." Soon she was "crying all the time to go back home, but [I] has no money. There you can live decently and have fresh air. Better eats there and fresh food from your own farm. Here you buy what you eat every day; there you raise almost everything and have cows, chickens, and so on. A bad way here, running to the store for everything." She was eager to return to Europe if only the chance arose, and her people were "almost of one mind to back to Europe," to their "little homes," although she felt her own experience of traveling a bit gave her "more outlook than most of my country people here have."

Annie Trina was elected by the Latvian strikers to represent them on the general strike committee. She had arrived in New York in 1906. Annie's first thought was "America, wrong country." A country girl with some sporadic education, she became a weaver, was swept up in the great IWW strikes in Lawrence and Paterson in 1912 and 1913, and joined the "wobblies." Despite her many years in the mills, she still "comes home so tired I cannot even read the paper properly," was usually "very hungry to get supper too quickly and eats too fast" and complained about an "awful kind of noise which you hear after you come home if you are tired." She often felt like a piece of machinery herself and "cannot able to move." Annie was skilled, relatively well paid, a firm believer in the union, and a member of the SP. In her country "all the people belonged to the SP and make trouble wherever they go." Discouraged by the failure of many of her fellow workers, both native and immigrant, to stand firm, she maintained, contrary to the prevailing propaganda, that "America last—the working people in this country have no brains." Indeed, as a result of the war, she believed, "at home in the old country there is more freedom. . . . When I was there, it was necessary to hold socialistic meetings in cellars or in the woods," but she noted with pride that her country was the first to grant suffrage to women. "Now our country is free, we all want to go back. We would go—if the gates would be open tomorrow."[19]

An amalgam of bitter anger, provincial nostalgia, and diverse visions of a better life made these men and women implacable combatants. They were the committed, the cadre, what in the ACW would have constituted "the activity." Even while maintaining their own serious doubts about their role and future in American industrial civilization, they needed to concentrate attention on mobilizing their more intimidated brethren and workmates, people like Julie Jaguga, a Polish woman of twenty-eight who "looks at least 40," who seemed "sad and listless," who had never been away from Lawrence after arriving there at age eleven, who spoke no English although she would have liked to, who was "timid about nite school" although she would have liked to attend, who knew "only Polish people," whose clothing was "mostly black. No style, no hint of 'dressing up.' " There were countless others like her who succumbed to the shrill antiunionism of their local priests.[20]

As had been the case for the early ACW, the ethnopolitical complexion of the textile workers was almost insolubly intricate. Thus, the war-induced nationalist wakening exacerbated tensions between Poles and Lithuanians that dated from the rise of Lithuanian nationalism in America during the 1890s. But the Lithuanians were themselves internally at odds, split into a Catholic party organized in "church socities" and the Lithuanian Roman Catholic Alliance led by the conservative clergy; radicals, atheists, and secularists represented in the Lithuanian Freethinkers Alliance; and a moderate national party, the Lithuanian National Alliance, with its own anticlerical and more discreetly radical coloration. Similarly, the radical secularism of Hungarians in Passaic, especially their support for a soviet Hungary, profoundly alienated their highly-churched Slovak neighbors, who hated Magyar cultural and institutional domination to begin with.[21]

Almost from the outset groups of local militants, some of them ex-wobblies, appealed to the ACW for help, in some cases for outright affiliation to the clothing workers' union. It made sense. The Amalgamated, of course, had waged its own successful battle against a nativist and submissive AFL bureaucracy. The confrontations among secularist Hungarians, Jews, and Lithuanians and among ritualist Poles, French Canadians, and Slovaks resembled the internal political chemistry of the ACW's development. Clothing and textiles were kindred industries whose economic fortunes were interdependent. Above all, the Amalgamated was conspicuously advertising its willingness to champion the cause of workers everywhere. Thus the Bohemian leader of the Independent Textile Workers Union in Passaic, for example, sought the advice of the Amalgamated several times a week during the course of the strikes. A similar relationship developed in Paterson, whose mixture of highly educated, radical declassed Jewish and Italian handicraftsmen together with a mass of unskilled Sicilian *contadini* closely resembled many of the garment centers.[22]

Hillman proceeded cautiously, however, preferring to delay any decision about affiliation until the organizational fate of these unpredictable and often desperate struggles became clearer. Nonetheless, the relationship remained close. When the UTW and the city central labor council disowned the strike in Lawrence, emboldening the mill owners to refuse arbitration, the ACW sent money and organizers. After sixteen weeks of the harshest conflict, the principal firms offered a wage increase and agreed to negotiate with the insurgent union's shop committee. Similar developments occurred simultaneously in Passaic and Paterson. In April 1919, under the leadership of the radical pacifist A. J. Muste, the Amalgamated Textile Workers was born, legitimately, if only momentarily, claiming a membership of 50,000 and explicitly modeled after the ACW in its industrial structure and its system of impartial arbitration. Its first convention, held in New York, was essentially run by Schlossberg and Bellanca. It adopted a constitution and preamble almost identical to the ACW's. As Muste noted: "The ATWA had, almost completely, the outlook, approach, and methodology of the ACW."[23]

Muste and the rest of the ATW leadership carefully courted the ACW's approval at every stage. They, like the ACW leadership, were in search of some social solution standing midway between Bolshevism and liberalism. Muste told Anthony Capraro, an ATW and later an ACW organizer: "This whole question of a movement for the 44-hour week in the textile mills is one which will have to be solved . . . with the help of the ACW people and . . . I do not want to see so strategic a place as Lawrence committed . . . without such consultation."[24]

Muste appeared at the 1920 ACW convention to plead for amalgamation, arguing that after all, "the clothing workers are at the mercy of the textile bosses." Since the textile manufacturers obviously controlled the raw material of the clothing industry, Muste maintained, a victory over the ATW by the behemoths of the industry, like the American Woolen Company, would constitute a defeat for the ACW. Muste's appeal for a "powerful industrial organization . . . of combined textile and clothing workers," inspired by the spirit of proletarian solidarity then sweeping Europe, was greeted with great enthusiasm. But Hillman quietly deferred taking up the practical question of merger. In the meantime the convention deputized a committee comprising Hillman, Bellanca, and Schlossberg to advise the ATW. Muste's essential point about the interrelationship of the two industries was not lost on Hillman, who knew that textile unionism was a vital piece of unfinished business.[25]

At least part of the reason for Hillman's hesitancy had to do with the presence of the wobblies. Ever since the celebrated strikes of 1912 and 1913, they had maintained a certain moral favor among some Italian and

Slavic millworkers as well as among the Lithuanians, whose parish in Lawrence the FBI characterized as a "socialist church." However, within the ATW they deliberately adopted a low profile. Moreover, relations between the ACW and the IWW had improved since the vitriolic exchanges in Baltimore, in part because the union had come to the defense of the onetime IWW leader Carlo Tresca when he was accused of murder and had condemned the government's mass arrests of wobblies in 1917. In return Tresca and Arturo Giovanitti assisted ACW organizing efforts among Italians in Syracuse and Rochester. Giovanitti spoke in Lawrence in favor of affiliation with the ACW.[26]

On the other hand, it was clear to observers like David Saposs that the ACW presence in the textile strikes meant that "workers in that industry are gradually led away from the influence of the IWW." And in fact at one point a "wobbly" paper accused the Amalgamated and the Italian Socialist Federation of conspiring with the Justice Department to break the IWW in Paterson. While such rumors were symptoms of a feverishly paranoid imagination, the ACW general office did receive regular reports of the waning of IWW strength and rising sentiment for the Amalgamated, which it naturally found most encouraging. For its part the ATW was careful to dissociate itself from "wobbly" attacks on religion and from any advocacy of sabotage or violence.[27]

The ACW continued to balance its unequivocal support for the strike with a cautious attitude toward the question of merger. Despite Muste's persuasive entreaties that Lawrence presented a ready entry for the ACW into the textile industry, Schlossberg insisted that the purpose of collaboration was not affiliation but victory for the strike. That attitude generated some resentment, particularly from the ACW's most valued on-the-scene organizer, Anthony Capraro, whose brutal kidnapping and beating by a vigilante group in Lawrence had made him a strike hero. He complained to August Bellanca about the ACW's "temporizing," its "vague promises" regarding affiliation. In his view the situation was ripe: "The mass is in a divine state," but everything depended on resolute support by the Amalgamated. Without that commitment the Lawrence organization was too weak to confront the American Woolen Company, and the strike would therefore be lost. The defeat would constitute a "moral disaster" not only for the workers but for the Amalgamated as well.[28]

If in fact the ACW did "temporize" during the Lawrence affair, it was because it was already apparent to Hillman, revolutionary expectations of the rank and file notwithstanding, that the strategic position of the ATW, and for that matter of the labor movement as a whole, was rapidly becoming deeply defensive. To begin with, the clothing and textile industries were similar but not identical. There were really no "friendly capitalists" among the textile magnates, as there were in the garment trade. Nor was there the same urgent need for a union-enforced standardization of labor costs among desperately competing tiny firms. The three key mills in Lawrence, for example, American Woolen, Arlington, and Pacific, were all large, vertically and horizontally integrated concerns. Those companies were quite capable, in normal circumstances, of imposing their will through a combination of welfare programs and city and company repression. Hillman sensed the possibility of creating a huge industrial union—a million or more members—of clothing and textile workers that together would control the whole apparel industry. He was aware that the process of postwar reconstruction would entail a major confrontation between labor and business, that millions of jobs would be won or lost in the event, and that therefore the shorter work week, which was after all at the heart of all the textile strikes, represented the centerpiece of any labor-oriented reconstruction program. But he knew as well that the risks of defeat were enormous, including the overcommitment of resources that might jeopardize the well-being of the ACW itself. Finally, looming in the background were all the signs of a severe economic downturn, which would abruptly alter the balance of power in the labor market and, in the case of the textile industry, would lead to a crushing round of layoffs, wage cuts, and deteriorating conditions, leaving the ATW prostrate in Lawrence by mid-1921 and everywhere else a few years later.[29]

Everywhere the signs were ominous. The great strikes of 1919, steel most fatefully, were lost. Attorney General A. Mitchell Palmer's extraconstitutional raids on left-wing political and labor organizations were symptomatic of a general retreat on the part of the Democratic administration from its prior commitments to labor, social, and economic reform. At President Wilson's second Industrial Conference the business representatives were practically unanimous in their opposition to independent collective bargaining and any form of state social insurance.

Wartime economic controls over prices, fuel, and other raw materials were dismantled with unseemly haste. Frankfurter's call for a planned reconversion to avoid murderous competition for diminishing markets and the predictable decline in labor standards and rise in unemployment was ignored. The railroads were returned to their owners despite all the talk of nationalization. The War Labor Board was terminated in deference to dominant business interests anxious to eliminate any public monitoring of their labor relations. There was a collateral counterrevolution in the field of personnel management. Meanwhile, the recession of 1921–22 led to a series of rearguard struggles in coal, textiles, railroads, and meatpacking, but their failure marked the terminus of the labor insurgency. Turnover, quit rates, and trade union agitation declined together. Membership in the organized labor movement dropped precipitously by more than 1.5 million between 1920 and 1923. Strikes declined in the same period, thanks to the open shop campaign, with its arsenal of blacklists, yellow dog contracts, and armies of spies, provocateurs, thugs, private police, and scabs. The Supreme Court contributed as well, with a defense of the labor union injunction, limitations on the right to picket and boycott, and active hostility to labor legislation generally, including nullification of state child labor and women's minimum wage statutes. Workers even suffered chastisement for their profligate consumption habits.[30]

In such circumstances the apparent need for a costly and unorthodox "scientific" personnel bureaucracy seemed negligible. The authority and prestige of existing personnel departments within the corporate hierarchy fell drastically, with much power returning to foremen and supervisors. Only in a few technically advanced firms in high-profit industries like electrical machinery, scientific instruments, chemicals, and oil; among an equally small group of privately owned, medium-size, labor-intensive industries with particularly stable demand schedules—consumer nondurables, for example; and finally in industries like clothing where unionized firms faced intense competition from nonunion shops did this personnel vanguard retain a foothold.[31]

Even by the time of the Boston convention in 1920 the global currents of political reaction and economic retrenchment had made themselves felt within the Amalgamated. Clothing manufacturers found it expedient to try out their own anti-Bolshevik atmospherics. Andres Burkhardt, the president of the National Association of Retail Clothiers, toured the country in 1920 for the express purpose of red-baiting the ACW. For a while it seemed that Attorney General Palmer's raiders or their local deputies might actually come after those more conspicuous radical aliens in the ACW itself. In Chicago the Illinois Attorney General conducted a raid on union headquarters and arrested the leadership on politically inspired charges of bribery and extortion. In New York those deemed likely targets were transferred to organizing posts in places remote from the city.[32]

In New York State the legislature barred five legitimately elected socialists, including Abraham Shiplacoff, from taking their seats in the state Assembly. Soon thereafter the state Senate established an investigative committee under the chairmanship of Senator Clayton A. Lusk, whose ostensible legislative mission was merely an excuse to conduct an inquisition of alleged syndicalists and Bolsheviks. While the ACW was defending itself against a lawsuit in Rochester that threatened its very existence, the Lusk Committee came to that city and, while never calling on anyone from the union to testify, managed to inflame the atmosphere further with wild talk about ACW syndicalism and sabotage. A Lusk Committee informant planted in the union described the ACW as run "on the Soviet style" and reported that "this organization is known as the banner radical organization in America that is trying to break up the AFL." In a more fanciful moment, the same agent went on to single out a Russian Jew named Shotofsky who "runs the spy system in the organization from his office in back of the telephone operator."[33]

William Leiserson, then functioning as impartial chairman in Rochester, offered to testify. When rejected, Leiserson drafted an open letter to Lusk and sent a copy to Governor Al Smith, along with a note arguing that the Committee's activity was creating rather than solving the problem of labor unrest. Leiserson's message to Lusk was forthright:

> Why did you permit ignorant and incompetent investigators to make your committee ridiculous in the eyes of the people of Rochester? . . . If your investigators had any brains at all, they would know that syndicalist and IWW unions do not sign agreements. They do not believe in them, and the ACW have the most successful of all signed agreements made by labor unions in this country . . . you have made more Bolsheviks than the government can ever deport.

It was easy enough to subject the Lusk Committee to verbal ridicule, but the last laugh was the Committee's. Soon several bills were making their way through the Albany legislature that not only prohibited strikes but made most normal trade union practices illegal in specifically enumerated industries, including "the manufacture of clothing." While the legislature adjourned without taking action, the bills were ominous portents, appearing as they did just a year after the same legislative body had considered statutes designed to protect the rights of strikers.[34]

Meanwhile the judicial system posed a more practical and immediate threat to the Amalgamated. The wartime efforts of Filene's manager, Louis Kirstein, culminated in the complete organization of the Rochester market, with the sole exception of Michaels, Stern & Company. To forestall unionization by the ACW the company provoked a strike in July 1919, described the strikers as "un-American," "alien," and "seditionists who should be deported"; and simultaneously entered into an agreement with the UGW. Next the company was granted a sweeping injunction (actually one of twenty-four issued against the ACW within two years) that prevented not only normal picketing but all efforts to persuade the firm's employees to join the strike. At the same time Michaels, Stern sued the ACW for $100,000.

The case quickly became a minor *cause célèbre* as it actually charged the Amalgamated with being an "illegal organization" and sought to disband the union as an "illegal conspiracy." Handling the case for the company was Judge Sutherland, who acted as counsel for the New York legislature in the expulsion of the five Socialist Assemblymen. Hillman responded by calling upon his allies among Progressive jurists, publicists, and politicians for help.

Felix Frankfurter, back teaching at Harvard, agreed to serve *pro bono*, in part because, as he explained in a letter to Hillman, "I am very deeply interested in the establishment of sound legal principles in the disposition of labor litigation primarily as a scientific student of the law and our legal institutions." By that he meant he intended the suit to become a laboratory for testing the principles and procedures of that legal realism to which he and Brandeis were devoted. He told Hillman, "The Courts should have the benefits of all the relevant facts, the ramifications of the industrial factors." Hillman in turn assured Frankfurter: "As you suggested, we are preparing for the benefit of the court a statement of the economic and other pertinent facts relating to the men's and boy's clothing industry." Indeed, the union assembled a sizable staff of technical people to analyze a great mass of data bearing on the industry's economic anatomy. On the legal side, Frankfurter was assisted by members of Elihu Root's prestigious New York law firm Root, Clark, Buckner, & Howland, including Max Lowenthal, Emory Buckner (a former classmate of Frankfurter), and Robert Szold. To establish the economic bedrock of his sociological jurisprudence, Frankfurter turned to Leo Wolman for advice. Wolman was then working for the newly formed National Bureau of Economic Research. The Bureau was another of those proliferating Progressive think tanks which found much of orthodox economic theory irrelevant to the realities of oligopoly and of a marketplace of administered prices, and to the ambitions of the administrative state.[35]

In the course of the Michaels, Stern affair, Wolman became a valued member of the Amalgamated's inner circle. Partly at Frankfurter's urging, Wolman agreed to create the union's research department, one whose technical sophistication was practically unique among trade unions. Thus began a relationship, lasting for more than a decade, in which Wolman functioned both as the union's most trusted economic adviser and as Hillman's confidant. He was present at all critical negotiations, and Hillman so valued his counsel that at times when he was indisposed or urgently required elsewhere Hillman allowed Wolman to function as his surrogate. Moreover, through Wolman, who sat on Commerce Secretary Herbert Hoover's 1921 Economic Advisory Committee (along with representatives of the Taylor Society, the American Association for Labor Legislation, and the NBER), formed to devise an agenda and set of recommendations for the Unemployment Conference to be held later that year, Hillman kept open lines of communication into influential policy-making circles, even if their actual influence was measurably diminishing.[36]

Wolman's origins were modest. His father, a Polish immigrant, ran a contract tailoring shop in Baltimore. Wolman managed to attend Johns Hopkins, where he specialized in labor economics and statistics and received a Ph.D. in 1914. He first met Frankfurter while working for the Industrial Relations Commission and then met the founder of the NBER and leading institutional economist, Wesley Mitchell, while working for the War Industries Board. After the war, Mitchell offered him a job at the New School for Social Research, where he was influenced by the technocratic views of Thorstein Veblen. He then went to work for the NBER, where he met Frankfurter's acquaintance Robert Szold, who, together with Max Lowenthal, was providing legal help to several garment unions.[37]

Frankfurter and Wolman persuaded Hillman that one way to fight the Rochester antipicketing injunction was through the introduction of new kinds of evidence, as Brandeis had done successfully some years before in the famous *Muller* v. *Oregon* case over the legality of maximum hours legislation for women workers. Frankfurter told Hillman that "the relation of the law's response to the right of picketing . . . depends on the whole industrial context and that's the business not of lawyers . . . but of economists and sociologists, and therefore I want to be free to select not only legal associates but an economic adviser." So Wolman went immediately to work coordinating the gathering of data on wages, hours, arbitration decisions, contract provisions, and the like. In the end, the presiding judge ruled this "evidence" irrelevant, but Hillman's relationship with Wolman persisted and became prototypical of the union's marriage to, if not its dependency on, the world of academic social science and its culture of expertise.[38]

Over the next several years, and periodically thereafter, Hillman surrounded himself with what amounted to a brain trust of economists, statisticians, industrial engineers, and political and social theorists, some of whom worked strictly as free-lance consultants, others temporarily at least as union apparatchiks. He sought their help in gaining better grasp of the intricacies of the clothing industry; in devising systematic solutions to the problem of unemployment; in erecting sound financial structures for the union's forays into cooperative banking and housing; and most ambitiously in penetrating the cyclical mysteries of the national economy, to which the union was subject and often fell victim. Nothing better indicated the way this ex-*yeshiva bucher* was drawn into the orbit of intellectual modernity. Hillman was always acutely sensitive to his lack of a formal secular education. Gathering about him men like Wolman, Bryce Stewart, and Harold Ware was in part a form of psychological compensation. Moreover, Hillman had a practical appreciation for the technical insights of people like Wolman and Morris Cooke or, later Isador Lubin. Such practical knowledge about costs, prices, and profits became increasingly indispensable as the union assumed more and more managerial responsibilities for the industry. But beyond the practical, Hillman shared, to some significant degree, the constitutional illusion of much modern social science: that its special forms of knowledge were privileged epistemologically, thereby neutral, politically incontestible, and thus capable of resolving and controlling social conflict. Hillman was too political a creature ever to become entirely credulous, but he was susceptible, especially at moments when the political environment seemed intractable, to the social scientist's presumptive sense of superiority.[39]

Of course it was precisely this attitude which made Hillman so singularly attractive to the leading lights in Progressive business and politics and made them eager to reciprocate, as they did quite tangibly in the Michaels, Stern imbroglio. Leading manufacturers had long since come to appreciate the union's value to the industry, enough to defend it openly in court. Eli Strousse of Strousse Brothers in Baltimore testified that he "could not get along without the agreement" and that especially during the war his firm "could not have navigated." Productivity had risen, thanks to the ACW. Max Holtz, president of the Rochester Manufacturers Association, confirmed that agreements with the ACW eliminated chaos, raised productivity and "assured a continuous supply of labor." Senator William E. Borah of Idaho pitched in with a preliminary hearing to see if the industry's working conditions warranted a full-scale investigation and gave Hillman ample time to make the union's case. *The New Republic* condemned the judge's refusal to entertain Frankfurter's "sociological" evidence: "The Amalgamated is being tried for its life, and, really its life cannot get into the court room." *The Nation*, similarly disgusted with the narrow literal-mindedness of the court, concluded: "Therefore, it is not in a court of law that the men committed to the making of today's industrial history will find direction . . . the sagacity of the courts is that of an individualism which is growing stale; industry itself must evolve the younger wisdom which shall infuse a new collective program." Meanwhile, Hillman went out of his way to make it as easy as possible, given the red scare atmosphere, for his Progressive friends to defend the union. Thus he disavowed any ties to the Bolsheviks, indicated that the union's revolutionary-sounding preamble was not to be taken seriously, and touted the union's war record on overtime, work stoppages, and Liberty Bond purchases.[40]

It would be a decade and more before "sociological jurisprudence" aired out the American courtroom, the illuminations of enlightened Progressive opinion notwithstanding. Nonetheless, the efforts of Michaels, Stern to destroy the Amalgamated proved fruitless. Far more serious was the worldwide recession, lasting from mid-1920 well into 1922, which fundamentally altered the strategic position of the union as well as that of the whole labor and socialist movement at home and abroad. Together with the postwar suppression of the Bolshevik threat, the advent of a buyers' labor market brought to an end an insurgency that had lasted nearly a decade and had stretched from the Russian Far East to the American Pacific Northwest.

In the clothing industry the signs of serious trouble appeared even before the recession struck. Between 1914 and 1921 the cost of consumer goods doubled, and clothing led the way with prices rising 198 percent between December 1914 and December 1919. There was a furious public reaction against suspected profiteering, including threatened consumer strikes and boycotts. Hillman took the initiative and suggested to the Justice Department that it call a conference of all elements of the industry to investigate high prices and profiteering. Assistant Attorney General Howard Figg convened such a meeting in Washington in February 1920. Hillman, Schlossberg, and Blumberg attended, as did representatives of cotton and wool producers, woolen manufacturers, and clothing manufacturers and retailers. The conferees issued a statement defending the essential fairness of clothing prices given the general postwar inflation. But a month later the speculative bubble collapsed, and along with it much of the industry. There was an avalanche of price cuts and bankruptcies. Suddenly the industry faced an enormous overcapacity of machines, companies, and workers. By May commercial hysteria gripped the trade. In June manufacturers staged a colossal auction at Madison Square Garden hoping to relieve the market of some of its suffocating inventory. Joint attempts by leading manufacturers and retailers to stabilize prices succumbed to overwhelming competitive pressures. All of this was prelude to a longer-lasting secular deflation and restructuring. The dollar value of the industry in 1925 was less than it had been in 1919, while the production cycle became even more erratic as fashion-conscious buying habits penetrated all segments of the mass market. Meanwhile the growing commercial leverage of chain stores and purchasing groups of independents made manufacturers ever more dependent and vulnerable.[41]

Hillman was acutely concerned. The commercial catastrophe directly jeopardized his efforts to rationalize the industry's labor relations. Just a year earlier he had managed, with Frankfurter's help, to persuade the National Association of Clothiers to establish a separate organization—the National Industrial Federation of Clothing Manufacturers—to deal directly and on a national basis with the ACW on all labor matters. The Big Four markets of Chicago, New York, Baltimore, and Rochester were represented, along with Boston. All the talk of the 1920 convention about amalgamating the needle trades unions was in part predicated on this sort of parallel centralization of the industry's labor administration. A Needle Trades Workers' Alliance, comprising the ACW, the furriers, the ILG, the United Cloth Hat and Cap Makers, and the JTU, was briefly formed. Initially hopes were high. George Bell, impartial chairman in New York in 1919, voiced the most sanguine perspective, shared by a good many others: "Eventually, I should like to see a National Joint Council, representing manufacturers and workers equally, formally organized and created along lines similar to the Whitley Councils in England." Although he considered it futile to expect a "complete, static solution of the so-called 'labor problem,' " he placed great hope in the new cadre of labor managers, men of "a new and high type" working not "as the selfish advocate of manufacturers" but in a "new spirit of disinterestedness."[42]

Meyer Jacobstein provided a homelier picture of the advantages of co-management in a speech to foremen at Stein-Bloch (Joseph Freeman delivered a very similar talk to his own foremen at Hickey-Freeman). Jacobstein contrasted the great amount and variety of the foreman's responsibilities under the pre-ACW regime—bookkeeper, instructor, disciplinarian, cost cutter, quality controller, output maximizer, hirer and firer of men.

> Now he was to be relieved of all the multiplicity of things. His job was simply to produce. All the bother about discipline, hiring, and firing and the intimidation connected therewith was given to the Labor Manager. . . . He would not any longer have to go around with a pad and pencil and surreptitiously write down the name of "Tony, good labor union man" and report that to the firm.[43]

But in fact the New York firms had never been happy with the arrangement, so especially vulnerable were they to the deadly competition of hundreds of tiny nonunion competitors who easily escaped the Federation's surveillance. Only the wartime attitude of the government and the related labor shortage had induced them to join the alliance. Their patience was only as buoyant as the price bubble, and they burst together. At first Hillman was approached surreptitiously with a devious plan for a "friendly strike" that would reduce the market glut and shore up prices. When he refused to go along, a group of the most irreconcilable companies hired a veteran labor-baiting attorney, who proceeded to orchestrate a lockout. When the Chicago and Rochester manufacturers refused to join, the New York group officially resigned from the Federation, ending any serious national bargaining for the next fifteen years.[44]

The desperate New York lockout, which lasted more than six months, called into question the Amalgamated's very existence. The union survived, to be sure, but it survived in some ways as a different institution. The struggle in New York widened ethnocultural and political fissures, aggravated differences over matters as fundamental as "workers' control" and scientific management, and led to the only protracted challenge to Hillman's leadership and a decisive shift in the way he would forever after address the "labor question."

In some ways the lockout recalled the great pitched battles of the past, the mass strikes at HSM in 1910 and New York in 1913. The city's trade union and socialist movements seemed to recognize what was at stake, and tangible help poured in from the UHT, the Workmen's Circle, the JSF, various needle unions, and the jewelers' and upholsterers' unions. The ILG offered medical aid through its health center, although it should be noted that mutual suspicions were such that Hillman was convinced the ILG and *Forward* support was at best perfunctory. Five great New Year's parties for Amalgamated children featured Charlie Chaplin movies, music, and vaudeville acts. The Yiddish theaters staged free plays. The ACW itself embarked on its first practical experiment in cooperative "business" by setting up seven commissaries that offered cut-rate groceries to strikers payable in scrip issued by the union.[45]

Hillman sensed that this local skirmish was part of a national assault on the organized labor movement. Months before the explosion he had warned the GEB that "we have to do everything to prevent a general conflagration." In an address before the Nebraska Retail Clothiers Association he noted that cries of "Bolsheviki" and "100 percent Americanism" disguised a policy of postwar reconstruction that depended on "reducing wages," "smashing unions," and "shutting down production." He urged that

. . . we drop the policy of laissez-faire in our industrial life. We are animated by a profound indifference and we leave it to quack physicians to
poison us with their quack remedies. The new patent medicine on the
market now carries the big label "union baiting; labor smashing."

For that reason the New York lockout raised questions of "national
importance."[46]

To the ACW rank and file he spoke in a blunter idiom:

Open shop means arbitrary dictatorship. Open shop means the Un-
American way—open shop means employing the methods of the Kaiser,
Czar, and every other autocrat. Open shop means starvation, death. Open
shop means the slums, it means crime, it means asylums, it means everything that is rotten, it means everything that is inhuman.[47]

William Bandler, president of the renegade Clothing Manufacturers
Association, responded in kind, describing Hillman's pleas for industrial
self-government as a disguised form of "Sovietism." Bandler's accusation
was particularly preposterous because Hillman, aware of the economic
downturn, was tacking away from, as quickly as circumstances would
permit, the sort of supercharged activity "Sovietism" often implied.

Thus, Frankfurter pointed out in an open letter to *The New Republic*,
that,

. . . Mr. Bandler thus fails to note not only the real effort of the leadership
of the Amalgamated to resist temporary advances and the successful self-
restraint, as in the case of the Cutters, but also the weakening of the
authority of the union by wage increases against the opposition of the
leaders.

Frankfurter had enlisted for the duration of the war. Together with
Brandeis and Wolman, he plotted out a series of articles, eventually the
basis of a widely distributed pamphlet, narrating the history of the New
York agreement reached under his auspices, defending the operation of
the arbitration machinery, and assembling testimony by prestigious academics and public figures, all designed to build morale on the one side,
to cause "defections and discouragement" on the other side, and to
demonstrate the "unclean hands of those in control," including their
misbehavior as stock speculators and union busters.[48]

Help came from other quarters as well. When, in the midst of the
strike, Senator George H. Moses of New Hampshire called for a Senate
investigation of the ACW, Senator Borah counterpunched by requesting

an investigation of the entire clothing industry, and the Moses resolution was quickly quashed. Meanwhile, suits filed by manufacturers happy to use the revolutionary phraseology of the union's preamble to call its legitimacy into question were met by an impressive roster of character witnesses, including leading economists and political scientists from Columbia, Florence Kelley of the Consumers' League, and others. Ray Stannard Baker, a muck-raking journalist; Earl Dean Howard; and Jacob M. Moses, the legal counsel for Sonneborn's, all testified that the ACW was hardly radical and violent, but on the contrary peaceful, irreproachably American, and above all rational. Even a portion of the New York press condemned the recalcitrance of the manufacturers and their belligerent unwillingness to negotiate.[49]

By May 1921 the ranks of the renegade employers' association were broken or, more accurately, corroded by commercial self-interest. The perseverance and self-sacrifice of thousands of clothing workers gave greed time to do its insidious work. Never again would the very existence of the union in New York be questioned. The associated attempt to introduce piecework, slash rates, and restore the autocratic power of employers to hire and fire consequently also failed. Thus, the campaign for the open shop, a counterrevolution in labor relations that in many American industries recaptured management prerogatives lost or threatened during the war, was decisively defeated. And yet the lockout reinforced a certain defensive, if not quite siegelike, mentality, which made its outcome less than unreservedly favorable to the union.[50]

Even before the lockout began, Hillman made plain the union's willingness to meet the crisis of the industry by enforcing standards of production, so long as those standards were arrived at through the machinery of impartial adjustment. And indeed, the agreement signed in June ending the strike acknowledged readjustments in the costs of production designed to make New York more competitive with other markets. In that way the lockout marked a critical shift in the behavior and strategic outlook, if not the rhetoric, of the "new unionism." Resolutions celebrated the heroism of the textile workers, but the tangible commitment of union resources dwindled. The cooperative movement was hailed as a piece of proletarian ingenuity and agrarian radicalism, but its emergence was closely correlated with a garment unionism in decline, as in fact it invariably had been since the turn of the century, and moreover pockmarked by those exploitative subcontracting practices endemic to the industry. Production standards, mutually arrived at, were supposed to signal the coming of age of the "new unionism," its full democratic participation in as well as responsibility for managing the industry. That may have been true, but it was also true that union-enforced production standards came at the expense of more autonomous if less reliable forms of shop floor workers' control.[51]

The AFL became infamous in the 1920s, at least in certain circles, for its capitulation to scientific management. The ACW did not suffer the same calumny, even though production standards in the clothing industry were worked out on the basis of a similar collaboration between the Amalgamated leadership and the "left wing" of the Taylor Society. The difference was that while the arrangements accepted by the AFL entailed absolute managerial control over the production process, job classifications, and so on in return for a formalized employment relationship, the "new unionism" successfully insisted that it share substantially in determining all questions affecting the organization of production as well as in those matters customarily defined as falling within the purview of industrial labor relations. The AFL's accord with scientific management, which occurred mainly in declining industries, was thus part of the decade's counterrevolution in employment relations. This was decidedly not the case for the Amalgamated. Still, by gravitating into the orbit of managerial modernism the "new unionism" ruptured its ties to the messianic trade unionism of its birth.

Thus, it was not the "social conscience" of the "new unionism" that was so unprecedented. Indeed, the language of chiliastic brotherhood had long been a vital dimension of prewar Marxism, and in the ACW it continued to find an eloquent exponent in Joseph Schlossberg. Rather it was the voice of the other Marxism, the "Marxism of the parties," of organizational science and its austere, technocratic utopia, that echoed longest and loudest. Within the fraternity of industrial democrats, it was the ACW's remarkable ability to transmute the idiom of the shop floor and the pragmatic designs of socialism into the modern grammar of the managerial revolution that made the "new unionism" truly new.[52]

Between the revolutionary prophet and the social engineer it was not simple to choose the more socially daring. Arguably, Hillman's rupture with tradition was more radical, more anxiety-producing, than the one opened up by traditional Jewish socialists, who often mobilized by reconciling and legitimating new interests with older communal values— what Schlossberg attempted when he spoke of "fulfilling a holy duty" or of "being filled with the spirit of a sacred struggle." Hillman was the true industrial modern: A pioneer of workers' participation as a vital component of managerial strategy, he was an architect of a new moral order of work, one based neither on coercion nor on monetary incentives, but on those intangibles of the psyche and the social then being explored by industrial psychology and sociology. Before it was discovered by academic social science, the practical experience of the "new unionism" revealed the dialectic of the informal work group: that it may on the one hand resist the intrusion of management, but that management nonetheless depends on the subtle influence of the group to enlist the productive cooperation of the workers in what Morris Cooke called "the adventure of industry."[53]

Cooke and like-minded technocrats, all allies of Hillman and proponents of what might be called the "new managerialism," were immediately motivated by a fear of Bolshevism on the one hand and a disdain for the open shop on the other. The world right after the war seemed to them a dangerous place where literate men and women, angered by economic and social injustices, were apt to spark mass turmoil. Social science research and planning offered the best hope of restoring a sense of concord, but Wesley Mitchell, the NBER founder, observed: "That is a task of supreme difficulty—a task that calls for intelligent experimentation and detailed planning rather than for agitation and class struggle." Cooke and others in the Taylor Society were acutely aware that the specter of Bolshevism was creating, at least temporarily, a receptive audience for their own message of industrial reform.[54]

What needed to be confronted, so Cooke argued in 1920 before the thermidor arrived, was the new balance of power between the classes. Working-class defensiveness, symptomatically expressed in soldiering on the job, was a thing of the past, as now workers all throughout the Western world felt prepared to take responsibility for production as a whole. Encouraging this sense of "ownership" in industry, especially through the medium of independent trade unionism, was the best antidote to Bolshevism and syndicalism, even if it seemed to some of the more near-sighted industrialists that they amounted to the same thing.[55]

Progressive publicists agreed and appreciated the delicate dynamics of the Amalgamated from this vantage point. Ray Stannard Baker, commending the "shop council plan" in the clothing industry as a public service, argued: "The chief struggle of the far-sighted leadership among the amalgamated clothing workers is to keep in line the impatient extremists who are not satisfied with steady growth, but want the millennium by tomorrow afternoon." In the eyes of *The New Republic*, the impending choice was between "sabotage and a collapse of productivity or," if the ACW example was widely followed, "a possible advance in productivity," because the union was "not afraid of incurring the risk of the epithet Bolshevik, but neither was it afraid of incurring the risk of collaboration with Capital or fixing standards of output."[56]

Radicalism, however initially worrisome, receded in importance as the postwar reaction picked up steam. What increasingly alarmed managerial Progressives was the philosophy and practice of the open shop. Cooke wrote to Frankfurter suggesting they convene a group of labor leaders as well as "men and women representing science" to establish a "brand new organization perhaps to be called the 'Institute of Labor and Science,' whose purpose it would be to forestall the open shop movement."

The open shop threatened a cherished ethos of professional neutrality and the capacity of administrative expertise to resolve conflict. More than that, for people like Cooke, who had functioned as an adviser to Gompers after the war, the open shop destroyed the evident advantages for efficiency and technological innovation of democratic participation by responsible trade unions. Cooke, Ordway Tead, Otto Beyer, and Robert Valentine of the Taylor Society, together with labor-connected reformers like George Soule, Robert Bruere, and Clinton Golden—all of them Hillman's colleagues—were, to one degree or another, attracted by Thorstein Veblen's critique of the superfluous capitalist and his putative vision of a soviet of technicians. Brandeis characteristically formulated the perspective of this circle in the most far-reaching terms:

> The great developer is responsibility. Here no remedy can be helpful which does not devolve upon the workers' participation in responsibility for the conduct of business; and their aim should be the eventual assumption of full responsibility—as in cooperative enterprises. This participation in and eventual control of industry is likewise an essential of obtaining justice in distributing the fruits of industry.[57]

No wonder Hillman recognized such men as kindred spirits and so welcomed Morris Cooke's invitation to establish a more systematic relationship between the ACW and Cooke's socially minded circle of production experts. It was Cooke, after all, who authored the report on the clothing industry, written under the auspices of Commerce Secretary Herbert Hoover's special conference on "Waste in Industry," which blamed management for 75 percent of the industry's waste of men and materials and applauded the ACW's wisdom in applying scientific management methods to improve efficiency and flexibility. Cooke told Hillman that every labor organization ought to have an agency or division specializing in technical production matters, or else "the technique of the industry actually retrogrades." Convinced that clothing manufacturers could be persuaded to go along in a cooperative effort to improve production technique, Cooke suggested three initial topics for study: "(1) stabilizing employment; (2) cost pricing; (3) individual production standards."[58]

All three items commanded attention, but establishing standards of production quickly became the highly charged focus of deliberations among union, managerial, and technocrat circles and of acrimonious debate on shop and convention floors. Immediately following the Boston convention, Cooke brought together a group of production engineers, including H. K. Hathaway and Harlow Person, to advise and consult with the ACW leadership "as to the implications of week work with standards." Cooke told his fellow Taylorites that the ACW was making progress in its efforts to develop "some measure of democracy in industry" and that it was important that the union's plans in this regard "conserve true production." From the vantage point of these "scientists of work," the overriding issue was efficiency, and it took on added urgency with the recent recession.

As a general solution, "standards of production" raised certain so-ciotechnical problems to be hammered out with union and management officialdom: Should standards apply to a single shop or a whole urban market or even the national industry; should they evolve out of the practical day-to-day experience of the industry or be more systematically formulated in a laboratory-like model factory; what new financial obli-gations should the industry assume; how many "levels of accomplish-ment" ought to be recognized; what rewards and punishments should be applied to those who exceeded or fell below expected standards; and, in keeping with the sensibilities of people like Cooke, for whom "one of the highest aims of factory management is to teach people to do more than one thing," what methods of compensation might be devised to avoid unduly penalizing a worker engaged in a new task? In the end it was decided that standards were to apply to distinct work groups and depart-ments, and only indirectly to individuals, and were to be established through the joint consent of labor and management, each armed with its own battery of technical experts. In many respects production standards made sound economic sense, not only from the standpoint of business but as a device for fixing a limit to overexertion on the shop floor.[59]

However, from the vantage point of the shop floor the issues seemed less technical than they did moral and existential. Production standards, even if dubbed "week work with standards," too strongly resembled a counterfeit version of piecework and even a return to the loathsome "task system" of the nineteenth century, in which manufacturers unilat-erally raised expected output. As such they outraged an artisan sense of autonomy and fueled anxieties generated by the homogenizing and lev-eling tendencies represented by new technologies, by the expanding mass market for cheaper clothing, and by the rationalizing practices of the "new unionism." In New York particularly, the standards threatened to eliminate a system of "week work" that entailed the payment of weekly wages calculated on the basis of hours worked without precise regard for the quantity and pace of production. The "week work system" enhanced the power of informal work groups over the production process; "standards of production" would undermine that power and restore what many characterized as an "old slavery."[60]

"Slavery," a blunt word, elicited from Hillman an equally blunt, indeed brutally frank response: "I believe that what is understood by week work is the privilege of the individual to lay down on the job if he so desires." On the other hand, sensitive to the radical temper of the convention delegates, he was not above deploying a bit of verbal legerdemain. Week work without standards, he claimed, merely mimicked the corrupting ethos of capitalist society—"to do as little as possible for as much as they can get." To those "brothers" apt to jump up and ask "How about the revolution?" Hillman rejoined that for the sake of the labor movement as a whole it was vital the union make clear both to employers and the public that it sought not only "standards of health, standards of living, standards of conditions" but also "standards of production."[61]

Hillman was becoming ever more adept at playing the labor statesman and revolutionary at one and the same time, a talent that matched the moment and the peculiar human chemistry of his union. Thus, he accused the opposition of a criminal attempt on the life of the organization: The "greatest enemies of our organization are those who preach interference with production." Yet anxious to retain his revolutionary credentials, he maintained, "No one opposes revolution in itself. What we are all opposed to is disorder and the interruption of production. . . . By gradually increasing our power and responsibility in the industry we are preparing to be ready to conduct it when the day for complete industrial democracy arrives"—a truly Fabian idyll of the orderly revolution. However, this was by no means a disingenuous argument. Working-class radicalism was of two minds about the inherent virtues of an ever more rationalized production order, attracted by its technical promise but repelled by its bureaucratic rigidity.[62]

Temperamentally and functionally, it was easier for Joseph Schlossberg to pay his respects to a vanishing artisan radicalism while still defending the leadership's policy:

> In New York, however, before we were organized, we had the task system experience . . . the most cruel form of exploitation. . . . Since then every

time a standard or piecework is mentioned, it is generally understood . . . in the terms of the task system. While that is wrong, it is understandable. . . . When we speak of standards today, we speak of standards under the direction and jurisdiction and with the approval of our organization. . . . I have no grievance against the New York members because of their feelings against standards. Those feelings . . . are a perfectly natural result of the reign of terror, autocracy, and chaos which had existed . . . before the advent of our organization. [But] we have abolished absolutism [so that now it] is our responsibility to establish order in the industry.

Judge Jacob M. Moses, a former State Senator in Maryland and impartial chairman in the Baltimore market, gave a homely if more dispassionate account of what was to be lost and gained:

[A]fter all, when a man has been making pockets in a certain way for ten years and has acquired a skill and speed and a fair earnings capacity, he can hardly be expected to submit tamely to a radical change in method which practically nullifies his accomplishment and relegates him to the ranks of the learner or unskilled worker.

For that reason unilateral changes in production methods by employers invariably provoked work stoppages, but the new system would, Moses hoped, solve that problem by guaranteeing that "the individual worker does not suffer because of such change."[63]

Judge Moses's guarantee that no one would suffer under the new regime was made in good faith. Many local activists were persuaded, as one impartial chairman noted: "It is interesting to observe the gradual change that has come over many of the union officials who were formerly the most extreme in their social views. From everyday contact with the orderly processes of industrial government, they have become the most jealous of the interests of law and order." From Rochester, Meyer Jacobstein cited the characteristic example of a rank-and-file militant who was "struggling constantly to hold in check a strong class conscious feeling in order to be fair to the employer's side." Winning such cadre over was of the greatest importance, as they enjoyed the confidence of the workers. Jacobstein was well aware of the excruciating psychological tension this could generate. He told of an Italian leader, "the most radical in the group," who became a business agent, and "then his troubles began; instead of merely delivering keen, sarcastic tirades, he had to put things across for his workers consistent with the principles laid down in our agrteement." For this particular Italian activist the tension proved too much, and he resigned his position.

The struggle over "standards of production" was thus a struggle to create a new man. It demanded a transformation of character and culture. Jacobstein, for one, realized that in its formative stages, when the ACW was more a movement than an institution, the union

> . . . was dominated by men who were the most daring fighters and loudest talkers. They were not necessarily men of careful judgment and responsibility. Now the union is dominated by leaders who know the industry from A to Z, men who are capable of representing the workers before a court which requires reasoned statements supported by an array of facts.

Jacobstein expressed a certain condescension, the normative illusion that behavior too at variance with prevailing standards is somehow, if not exactly primitive, then certainly immature and inferior. However, his observations pointed to an essential truth: The behavioral axioms and moral imperatives of the new unionism's industrial democracy, its apotheosis of rational-technocratic man, called into question all those principles and practices of artisan democracy and peasant traditionalism—kinship and ethnic solidarity; skilled work group exclusivity; customary, informal constraints on time and effort; the legitimacy of charismatic leadership; and the immediacy of direct action. Arguing in defense of the leadership, Abraham Shiplacoff noted there were already standards in New York, but they were set "by two or three of the leading stars in each factory." While his logic was impeccable, Shiplacoff managed to miss the whole point while making it: The real question was not "standards or no standards" but whose standards. With so much at stake, it was inevitable the struggle would assume a political character, testing the otherwise unchallengeable authority of Hillman and his closest comrades.[64]

SEVEN

A *Strange Alliance*

Fratricidal civil wars, fought without mercy, spread through the needle trades unions in the mid-1920s like forest fires. Jewish socialist faced off against Jewish communist, each laying claim to the moral high ground while engaging in every imaginable form of organizational skullduggery and violence, stooping even so low as to hire small armies of Jewish gangsters, always a shadowy presence in the "rag trade," to terrorize the opposition. The ILGWU was practically destroyed, while the Furriers were almost as severely wounded. The Amalgamated, however, emerged essentially unscathed. Factional combat, while generating much rhetorical heat, never became more than a manageable skirmish, because Hillman refused to become a prisoner of that first ideological cold war which made socialist and Bolshevik irreconcilable enemies. Indeed, in an act that would forever leave him morally tainted in the eyes of the Jewish trade union and socialist leadership, Hillman entered into an alliance of convenience with the Communist Party. It was a temporary alliance, but carried with it international entanglements and had an impact on U.S. presidential politics. Arguably, Senator Robert La Follette's quixotic quest to become president in 1924 marked the end of an era of reform. Like so much else that happened to Hillman and the Amalgamated in the deceptively quiet decade of the 1920s, the campaign prefigured relationships later to occupy center stage in the arena of national politics. Immediately, it left Hillman uncharacteristically at a loss about what to do next.

"Standards of production" ignited political passions. Opposition to production standards was voiced principally through the union's foreign-language press. It centered in older groups of skilled workers, especially cutters and pressers, and children's clothing workers, some of whom had experienced the task system firsthand. The creation of the union had fortified the position of these skilled work groups, reinforcing and formalizing their customary rights to regulate the pace of production, to control the level of expected output, to police the introduction of new machinery, and so on. Now, however, the same leadership for whom they otherwise displayed the greatest respect proposed a new system with a repugnant resemblance to the old order. While by no means the only ones alarmed by the attempt to install standards, these older artisan immigrants, concentrated in New York's contracting shops, were overwhelmingly Jewish and socialist.

Torn between their unswerving commitment to trade unionism and their anxieties about the new unionism, the Jewish artisan opposition remained organizationally and politically inchoate until the SP, and especially the *Forward* circle, launched a campaign against production standards as part of a more general assault on the union leadership. Serious differences in political and industrial strategy, as well as struggles for pelf and power, had made relations between the union and the *Forward* apparatchiks brittle from the ACW's inception. It was Bolshevism, however, that transformed a polite if edgy relationship into open antagonism.

Hillman was determined, for a variety of reasons, to maintain the union's political friendship with the Russian revolution. By 1922, however, the *Forward* group had assumed a posture of militant anti-Communism and had found Hillman's attitude insupportable. The crime was compounded when Hillman channeled funds into the launching of the *Freiheit,* a new daily paper of the Jewish left under the joint control of elements close to or in the Communist Party and groupings of independent socialists and anarchists, all of whom had left the SP in 1921.[1]

During the earliest years of the revolution, when the Red Army afforded the only protection to Jews from pogroms organized by White Russians in the Ukraine, the *Forward* group remained mildly pro-Bolshevik. Thus, while the ACW was supplying Russian famine relief with food and clothing as well as machinery and hospital supplies, the ILG contributed sewing machines to help restore the Russian clothing industry. But by 1921 the majority of the Jewish Socialist Federation, led by Moishye Olgin and J. B. S. Hardman, who had become the ACW's educational director, left the party because of the refusal of the Cahan minority leadership to affiliate with the Third International. Hardman

and Olgin envisioned a new party resembling the German Independent
Socialist Party, open to cooperating with the domestic and international
communist movement, of which the jointly run *Freiheit* was one such
instance. Meanwhile, the *Forward*'s Abraham Cahan and the loyal SP
minority established the Jewish Socialist Farband, and Cahan began
publishing pieces highly critical of the Bolsheviks.[2]

In a bitter contest for the loyalties of the Jewish rank and file, the
contentious issue of production standards provided SP functionaries a
convenient stick with which to flay the union leadership. Indeed, the
SP's most devoted followers included those most sensitive to the issue.
Their artisan ethos responded to the pressures of the new unionism by
gradually surrendering to a mentality of craft exclusiveness intent on
defending parochial privileges. Despite the delirious enthusiasm with
which they initially greeted the overthrow of the Russian autocracy, it
was this group as well that was most prepared to follow the SP elite into
the new politics of anti-Communism.

For many others, however, Bolshevism remained a heroic crusade.
Within the ACW they coalesced inside the CP's united-front trade
union formation, the Trade Union Educational League (TUEL). In a
fundamental sense the social makeup and motivations of the Jewish left
was strikingly like those of the right. Not only did they display a similar
artisan militance, but the shop floor cadre of the TUEL were no happier
about the advent of production standards than their factional opponents
from the SP.

The singular difference was that rank-and-file TUEL members accepted the political and organizational authority of a CP leadership that
supported the Hillman elite in its struggle against the right. The price of
such obedience was the muting of indigenous shop floor protest over
production standards, an act of self-abnegation sometimes preferred voluntarily, at other times only under the pressure of party discipline.

Tactical advantages accrued to both Hillman and the CP so long as
the alliance lasted. Hillman could count on the TUEL's factional support; on its core of experienced and dedicated organizers to help domesticate the New York market, then in a state of disintegration; and on its
ability to discipline segments of the membership otherwise apt to oppose
the continued rationalization of the industry. Most important, the alliance meant that the Hillman leadership, unlike its bureaucratic colleagues in the rest of the needle trades, never had to face a united
factional opposition. In return, Hillman warmly endorsed the Russian
revolution and its Bolshevik leadership, mobilized political as well as
material aid on its behalf, and even entered into a joint agreement with
the Soviets to reconstruct the Russian clothing industry. At the same

time, the union extended its administrative protection to a TUEL caucus under attack from the SP right.[3]

Although strongest in New York, the "rights" also controlled the Jewish cutters' locals in Rochester and Toronto; indeed, the struggle against the left in the latter city nearly paralyzed normal organizational activity. As the faction fight heated up in 1922, the perspective of the right narrowed, focusing on a defense of its special prerogatives. The New York cutters resisted efforts to merge them with other elements of the union, as it might "bring them down to the level of the tailors." In a struggle more territorial than ideological, Cahan sided with Harry Cohen, the unsavory leader of the Children's Joint Board, in his resistance to Hillman's plan for merging this administrative structure with the Men's Clothing Joint Board. Similarly, and despite the wide popularity of the strategy, the right did what it could to sidetrack periodic proposals by Hillman and others to amalgamate all the needle trades unions into a single industrial union.[4]

Mutual suspicions spilled over into political matters as well. Abraham Beckerman, a right-wing socialist from the cutters' local, organized opposition to an otherwise benign resolution by the GEB to investigate the possibilities of independent political action, suspecting Hillman might be preparing to endorse the Workers' Party, a concoction of the CP and independent socialists like Hardman.

Hillman, for his part, was convinced that the *Forward* group hated him and had always viewed him as an outsider to whom they would only grudgingly offer help. Nonetheless, to alleviate the chronic uproar in the New York organization, he met with Vladek and Cahan in mid-1922 in search of a truce. At a larger conference attended by representatives of the *Forward*, UHT, Workmen's Circle, and ILG officials, however, Hillman was accused of promoting the cause of the CP and of intervening in the internal affairs of other needle unions. Furious, Hillman told the GEB that if there had to be a fight, "let us fight to the finish" and accused the *Forward* of being more pro-Gompers than the railroad brotherhoods.[5]

Because SP cadres exerted enormous influence in certain critical and vocal Jewish locals, and because party functionaries had for some time filled posts in the union bureaucracy, they could mount the most troublesome internal opposition and contended openly with the leadership for power. But they were by no means the only locus of factional disturbance. Within the Lithuanian branches in Brooklyn a struggle for control took place that pitted pro-Bolshevik syndicalists, allied with like-minded Lithuanian tailors in Chicago and Rochester, against more moderate Lithuanian nationalists and socialists. For a brief period the left was in ascendancy and managed to appoint the best-known Lithuanian radical, Anthony Bimba, as editor of the ACW's Lithuanian paper the *Darbas*, one of the union's six foreign-language publications. Left-wing control culminated in resolutions by the two Brooklyn locals calling on the ACW leadership to abandon piecework and threatening that if it failed to do so they would call their own convention and prevent the leadership from attending. When the GEB suspended *Darbas*, the Lithuanian local in Rochester called upon its kinsmen to "urge those undertaker-officials who have buried our organization" to resume its publication immediately.[6]

Considered extreme anti-organizational types, who in Philadelphia threatened to leave the ACW for the IWW, the Lithuanians were nonetheless not alone on the left. Remnants of the IWW, Jewish anarchists affiliated with a shop delegate league, independent socialists, and Italian syndicalists also opposed the leadership from the left. Italian syndicalism particularly took root in the larger factories of Baltimore and Rochester and in foreign-language locals in New York. However, during the initial period of factional strife lasting through the convention of 1924, the most formidable force on the left, the CP, aligned itself more often in support of the union leadership than against it.

The new revolutionary party was hardly shy in expressing these surprising sentiments. Mike Gold and Moishye Olgin penned eulogies to the union in the pages of the *Liberator* and *Freiheit*. Gold particularly was rhapsodic about the revolutionary kernel germinating within the shell of the "new unionism." He described the work of the 1922 convention as preparation for the "red dawn of labor" and concluded that the union was "bringing in the social revolution in America as fast as it can be brought." The Workers' Party defended the union against attacks by the *Forward* and applauded its commitment to independent political action and aid to the Russian revolution.

The communist left went so far in its endorsement of the "new unionism" as to risk becoming an appendage of the leadership rather than its factional ally. Thus, Mike Gold, who described the union's 1920 convention as a "soviet of the sweatshops," argued that production standards was not a concession to Taylorism, that it was in fact compatible with revolutionary principles of economics. At the 1922 convention, William Z. Foster and Robert Minor exercised stern party discipline to prevent their immigrant cadre and followers in the union from waging a floor fight against standards. The party carefully avoided association with outbreaks of rank-and-file insurgency, and until relations with Hillman soured in 1924 the TUEL caucus in the ACW found it difficult to voice its objections to production standards or other matters in the pages of *Freiheit*, even though its members often deeply resented the loss of control the new production regime entailed. Even as late as 1924, when the party's ties to the union elite were already seriously strained, Foster cautioned TUEL cadre against any open break.[7]

The Party's infatuation with the union was not entirely unrequited. Rhetorically at least, Hillman expressed his affections with no less restraint. He staunchly defended the Bolshevik revolution against the "small imperialistic, militaristic clique" that sought to destroy it. In 1921 he returned from a trip to Russia and the first of a series of meetings with Lenin, Trotsky, Kamenev, and Radek. Hillman was convinced that the Bolshevik leadership was "realistic, practical, courageous," and enjoyed the full support of the people. He pronounced Lenin "one of the few great men that the human race has produced, one of the greatest statesman of our age and perhaps of all ages."

On his way to and from the Soviet Union, Hillman traveled throughout Western and Central Europe, which he described as a political and economic insane asylum on the verge of collapse. France was "full of fear and hatred," Germany a land of the hopeless, and there were "some very violent insane people running amok." Europe was, he reported to the overflow audiences that came to hear about the heroic Bolsheviks, hopelessly corrupt and selfish, its population demoralized and without the most elementary democratic rights. By contrast the Soviets represented the only truly stable regime in all of Europe, and the Bolsheviks the only vehicle of political and social cohesion preventing the sort of political dismemberment that was then well under way in China. He especially admired the Bolsheviks' practicality and flexibility, their concern for efficiency and respect for the "facts"—qualities frequently cited by others to characterize Hillman.[8]

Most of all, Hillman was pleased with the Bolsheviks' new approach to economic reconstruction. He reported the apparent widespread support for the New Economic Policy's departure from the practices of "war communism." The NEP provided economic incentives for all classes and thereby held out real hope for economic revival. It was time, Hillman declared, to dispense with outmoded political labels like "conservative" and "radical," as they were mere shibboleths that obscured the real questions of action and the power to make change, areas in which the Bolsheviks had proved themselves.[9]

Of course, the voyage abroad was as much personal as it was political. Embarking in July of 1921, just after the victory in the New York lockout, Hillman announced that he was taking his first vacation since the founding of the ACW to "see again my father and mother who I left in Lithuania 15 years ago." Traveling first to London and then Berlin, he finally made his way to Lithuania. His parents were still living in Zagare in the same simple home, along with four of his siblings. During the worst years of the war, the family had fled into the Russian interior, but Hillman's mother, always strong-willed, had insisted they return to Zagare to reopen the family shop and resume the life she had always known. She resisted Sidney's blandishments about settling in America while expressing her pride in her son's "mission." Eager to get on with his "mission," he crossed the border into the USSR, anxious about what he might find: "You want sometimes to keep your dreams in this gray world, in this world where there is very little of the ideal and the beautiful . . . and before entering Russia there is the doubt that perhaps that dream will be shattered. . . . I crossed the border and felt a great sense of relief."[10]

The deep affinity Hillman felt for the Bolsheviks in this formative period of the revolution arose less out of admiration for their tangible accomplishments than from his own magnetic attraction to power. Just before he left for Russia, when asked what he wanted to discover there, Hillman explained to Hardman and to the Bolshevik head of the Jewish section of the Russian Communist Party (then visiting the United States): "If I can find out that it can hold power, I don't care very much what you are telling this man [Epstein, the Bolshevik representative] about his party. I'm not interested in his party. But if it can't hold power, even if the party is perfect, what use do I have for it?"[11]

Hillman's open appreciation of Bolshevik accomplishments infuriated the SP and simultaneously attracted the attention of the FBI. In the fall of 1922 Hillman embarked on a second trip to the Soviet Union, during which he established formal relations between the newly created Amalgamated bank in Chicago and the Russian State Bank, thus expediting remittances from Amalgamated members to their hard-pressed kinsmen. Two FBI agents followed Hillman on his return voyage aboard the *S.S. Olympic.* Without identifying themselves, they questioned the union president about his Russian and West European contacts. Hillman volunteered nothing but indicated his willingness to speak to the State Department. Thus began a Bureau file that was to accumulate steadily until Hillman's death. Besides his business dealings with the Russians, the red-hunters were most exercised by his contribution to the American Fund for Public Service, also named the Garland Fund after Charles Garland, the wealthy, Harvard-educated son of businessman James A. Garland. An endowment which grew from $900,000 when established in 1922 to $2 million by 1928, the Fund donated money to the *Daily Worker,* the *New Masses,* the Russian Reconstruction Farms, the International Labor Defense, Brookwood Labor College, and other communist and noncommunist radical causes. Gompers, of course, condemned it as subversive. To the extreme annoyance of the SP, Hillman sat on its board of directors.[12]

If Hillman could befriend the Bolshevik experiment and Communists do likewise for the "new unionism," it was not because either was especially ingenuous or especially cynical. The collaboration was premised on a more basic if temporary affinity between Bolshevik policy, at least during the period of the New Economic Policy, and that of the "new unionism." The most tangible expression of that convergence of historical perspective was the creation of the Russian-American Industrial Corporation (RAIC), a joint Soviet–ACW enterprise whose purpose was to modernize the Russian clothing industry.

Consultations between Hillman and the Bolshevik elite, which began during Hillman's first visit, concerned the urgent problem of reconstructing and rationalizing Russian industrial, managerial, and labor practices, without which the revolution was in imminent danger of perishing. Lenin apparently emphasized in his discussions with the ACW leader the need for Russian workers to master the techniques of modern management. Hillman, for his part, was enthusiastic about the NEP as a great testing ground for the ability of workers to run industry on their own without any sacrifice of productive efficiency.

RAIC was thus conceived as an industrial experiment. Hillman told his colleagues on the GEB that the Russians had great confidence in the ACW, that they were in desperate need of capital as well as technical and managerial experience and that they were prepared to make guarantees with respect to preferential access to raw materials, export licenses, and special banking relations. Hillman had spent part of his visit inspecting clothing factories in Moscow and Petrograd, and apparently it was he who first broached the idea of a cooperative manufacturing venture in his meetings with the Bolshevik leadership. Indeed, in an interview published in *Izvestia* shortly before his departure, Hillman remarked that the ACW was not only interested in the Soviet clothing industry. "Our aims are much higher; we will begin with this industry and then grant credits to the other trusts."

Ideological promissory notes notwithstanding, this was to be strictly a matter of business practicality. Lenin and Hillman "did not discuss the revolution in the U.S. or even in Russia. We did not discuss any theories. . . . It is much more important to have a proper policy than a great deal of noise." The union president told his GEB: "If Russia believed our tendency was to become a communist organization the real government would not make the arrangements with us." He furthermore reassured the GEB members worried about the riskiness of the investment that Lloyds of London felt confident enough about the arrangement to insure it.

Hillman unveiled the actual plan for the RAIC near the end of the 1922 convention. His speech captured the delegates' prevailing sense of revolutionary determination. The Allies were accused of "attempting to starve the Russians into submission to the rule of international financiers." Hillman argued that disaster would result if "the masses were prevented from determining for themselves the course of economic reconstruction." Cooperation with the Soviets was not a question of being "for Bolshevism or against Bolshevism," but of being for or against "the slaughter of millions of people." He expressed his confidence in the Bolshevik approach to labor organization and in the work ethic and "iron discipline" of the Russian proletariat. The latter, together with the great natural wealth of the Soviet Union, made it perhaps the most promising place to invest in all of Europe.

The nine clothing and textile factories set up under RAIC auspices were to install the most modern machinery available in America and would benefit as well from the accumulated expertise in industrial engineering, technical innovation, and personnel relations, which Hillman pledged to make immediately available. Skilled cutters from the more advanced factories in Rochester, Chicago, Baltimore, and Philadelphia were sent to Russia to provide technical advice and training. They reported to the scientific management expert Otto Beyer that in every essential respect Soviet clothing factories resembled modern, unionized plants in the United States. Not only was the machinery up to date, but so was the system of resolving shop floor grievances through arbitration. Workers' representatives participated in the fixing of rates and pored over books by Taylor and Gantt on industrial efficiency. In the process of introducing new production methods and a sense of industrial work discipline, the Soviets had to overcome the same artisan resistance confronting proponents of "industrial democracy" in America.

Paralleling Hillman's ideal scenario for the American clothing industry, RAIC factories were supervised by joint management–union councils, which collaborated in establishing "scientific" standards of production and rates of pay. Ultimate authority resided in the Supreme Council of National Economy of the Soviet Union (the Vesenkha), a scheme of which Hillman approved, as he acknowledged that trade unions by themselves were too parochial and stubborn to take into account industrywide and general economic needs. In a sense, the Bolshevik RAIC and the ACW's "new unionism" were each other's mirror image: the RAIC as the embryo of what Hillman characterized as "state" or "cooperative capitalism" germinating within the womb of war communism, and the "new unionism" as the kernel of state capitalism concealed within the husk of free enterprise.

The RAIC crystallized an outlook shared by both union and CP elites, which made their mutual commitment more than merely expedient. Both groups subscribed to the credo of "scientific socialism," whereby History and its Progress were to be the final arbiters of the class struggle. Sophisticated technologies, the concentration of capital, and the rationalization of the labor process were as necessary to the socialist future as they were hallmarks of advanced capitalism. Collaborations with business and political reformers were scripted prologues in an unfolding socialist or cooperative drama, epilogues to capitalism's denouement. As the ideology of "progress" came to feel more comfortable with and in need of the perspicacious observations of Marxism, much of Marxist practice unambiguously expressed the premises of "modernization."

Lenin had come to appreciate the discoveries of scientific management. Once a bitter foe of Taylorism as the "scientific method of extortion of sweat," he had begun, even before the Revolution, to examine Gilbreth's motion studies, which he came to see as a means to enhance the technical transition from capitalism to socialism. Shortly after October the exigencies of the civil war and acute economic distress produced a fundamental shift in orientation, converging on the politically sanitized approach to Taylorism already adopted by the ACW. Increasingly, Lenin chose to emphasize the virtues of centralized management, efficiency, and labor discipline, and the critical importance of productivity and the intensification of labor if the Revolution were not to starve to death. "We must organize in Russia the study and teaching of the Taylor system and systematically try it out and adapt it to our purposes." Very much like Hillman, Lenin avoided becoming the prisoner of theoretical pronouncements made for other times and purposes.

Naturally, the adoption of "democratic Taylorism," whether by the ACW or in the Soviet Union, accelerated the disintegration of preindustrial craft and workers' control traditions and on occasion prompted serious resistance. For Soviet technocrats, as for ACW industrial democrats, the aversion to industrial discipline and the persistence of seasonal and rural work habits and religious inhibitions among Russia's newly proletarianized peasantry were insupportable obstacles to the application of time and motion studies, incentive pay systems, and other methods of labor intensification. Thus the domestic alliance between Hillman and the party was premised on far more than Hillman's support for the Russian Revolution. The American party's leadership, if not its social constituency, was as receptive to strategies for rationalizing an underdeveloped clothing industry as the Bolsheviks were fascinated with Western administrative and technical practices that promised to modernize an underdeveloped country.

Of course, one must not exaggerate the degree and significance of the resemblances between Lenin's New Economic Policy (NEP) and the "new unionism." By 1924 Soviet trade unions had become in many essential respects the creatures of state and party labor policy. That is to say, their very conditions of existence and their role in the political economy were both more fundamental and at the same time far less independent than those of the ACW or, for that matter, the labor movement at large in the United States. Questions concerning the extent of trade union autonomy and freedom of action continued to interest Hillman throughout the life of RAIC. Initially he had been pleased to report that strikes were not uncommon since he considered them a sign of "democratic vitality." Even late in 1925, when RAIC was coming to an end, he was still sanguine about the prospects. He reassured the GEB that "fundamentally . . . there is trade union control. Nothing can be done without the support of the trade unions. In five years there will be a live trade union with responsibility for production. It is expected that cooperative and government control will remain." The unique relationship between party and trade union in the Soviet Union was only just then emerging, and it would take some time to make clear the special consequences of party domination. [13]

As in the case of the ACW, it is also fair to see the communist accommodation with Taylorism as symptomatic of a decline in revolutionary spirit and purpose. In the Russian case Taylorist methods appealed to a state desperate to rebuild quickly and to reintegrate the Russian economy into the world market. Factory committees dominated by the most skilled, literate, disciplined, and culturally sophisticated, those with developed organizational as well as egalitarian traditions, ultimately succumbed to the external exigencies of the economy and the civil war. The patterns of organizational evolution were strikingly alike. As the state economic apparatus extended its own reach, in a process similar in form to the growth of the ACW's central administration, these original avatars of "industrial democracy," whether on the Lower East Side or in Petrograd, either narrowed their own horizons or were absorbed by factory management staffs or by state or union bureaucracies. In the East, under conditions of extreme scarcity and pervasive patriarchy, this gave rise to the barbarism and cruelty of Stalinism, while in the West, a different logic of compulsive consumption and competitive individualism crystallized in the system of industrywide collective bargaining. Different evolutionary outcomes indeed, yet it is worth remembering their similar ancestries, this fundamental affinity of technocratic mentality and organizational style—the common ground, so to speak of their lives lived within the "iron cage."[14]

This alliance of democrat and communist was a fragile affair and fell apart with the first unilateral shift in strategic outlook. It so happened that political questions, in particular presidential politics, rather than matters of trade union or industrial perspective, proved to be the occasion for a parting of the ways. The union elected to support the La Follette campaign in 1924 and not the efforts of the CP to establish an independent labor party. For the Hillman group, the campaign represented the last best opportunity to extend both the labor and the more general reforms of the clothing industry into the mainstream of national policy-making. For the CP leadership such developments signaled the restabilization of bourgeois politics and a closure of radical options.[15]

After the 1924 election Paul Douglas, the future New Deal Senator from Illinois but then an economist at the University of Chicago in quest of a radical alternative to the two-party system, reflected on the La Follette campaign: It "was in a sense both ridiculous and humiliating to have Senator La Follette dictate to the Cleveland convention which nominated him in 1924 a program which was almost entirely based upon the vanished days of small and independent business." Douglas perhaps exaggerated. There were more premonitions of the future than he might have cared to admit in the aftermath of an embarrassing and disappointing defeat. Still, he had a point.[16]

The La Follette adventure was a long time in the making. Five years' worth of Palmer raids and open-shop union-busting, of anti-Bolshevism and nativist revanchism, of hostile Supreme Court rulings and the seductions of corporate welfare "people's capitalism" had taken their toll. In two years, from 1921 to 1923, the AFL lost nearly a quarter of its membership. The mass strikes and apocalyptic visions of 1919 receded almost as quickly as they had appeared. Year by year the prospects for independent politics diminished. So too did the social imagination, programmatic reach, and tactical boldness of whatever prospects remained.[17]

Those attempts to realign American politics by forging a coalition of middle-class Progressives and labor radicals which had accompanied the end of the war ran afoul of their own social inhibitions. The "Committee of 48," named to suggest and exaggerate its national extent, was really a creature of New York Progressive circles. It was an amalgam of patricians and social radicals, nostrum peddlers and social engineering experts.

Some, like Frederick Howe, were radical industrial democrats, believers in nationalization, and ready to join and subordinate themselves to the wider purposes of a labor party. Many others felt uncomfortable with the language of class collectivism, believing as they did in conciliation and the transcendence of social antagonisms and in some form of mixed economy. They could abide "industrial democracy" only because no one knew for certain what it meant. For some, like Pinchot and Croly, government ownership was a last resort. By late 1919 Pinchot and others pared down the 48ers' program to its antimonopoly core, retaining only a safe endorsement of collective bargaining and a tepid and vague preference for a workers' "share in the management of industry." Pinchot put it bluntly: "Nobody wants to put labor in power, just as nobody is particularly interested in having industry run by and for the employees." Predictably, the proponents of the "Committee of 48" were immediately disappointed at the failure of the 1920 Farmer-Labor Party convention in Chicago, sponsored by the Chicago Federation of Labor, to nominate La Follette and walked out, along with the Wisconsin Senator.[18]

Third-party maneuverings continued over the next few years, but the social and psychological momentum gradually shifted in the direction of liberal moderation. Filene, for example, wrote to Newton Baker about plans to organize groups of liberal businessmen, the aim being the formation of a new liberal party distilled out of the disaffected circles of Democrats and Republicans. Meanwhile, early in 1922 the railroad brotherhoods convened the Conference for Progressive Political Action, attended by three hundred delegates from the machinists' union, other international unions, the Non-Partisan League, the "Committee of 48," the SP, the National Catholic Welfare Council, the Church League for Industrial Democracy, single-taxers, and assorted free-lance radicals. Not surprisingly, an aggregation so enormously diverse found it difficult to agree on a common program and contented itself with attacking monopoly, corruption, and privilege, the metaphoric staples of oppositional politics in America for nearly a century.

Moreover, it was more than symptomatic of the decline in radical influence that the otherwise cautious railroad brotherhoods, never known for their political adventurism, convened the gathering. Indeed, by the time the CPPA assembled again at the end of 1922, the brotherhoods (the Trainmen and Conductors particularly) were actually flirting with the idea of endorsing William Gibbs McAdoo, should the Democrats nominate him. Thus, the SP-sponsored motion to form a third party immediately stood no chance, and even its planks on child labor, the public ownership of utilities, and the nationalizing of the coal mines were defeated.[19]

By 1924 the brotherhoods, La Follette's Wisconsin machine, and the Non-Partisan League and farmer-labor groupings from the Dakotas and Minnesota were firmly in control, so when La Follette was officially nominated in July the convention studiously avoided any commitment to a permanent third-party organization. The program was vintage turn-of-the-century entrepreneurial Progressivism: eventual public ownership of water power and the railroads; a Great Lakes waterway to expedite commerce, along with tariff and freight rate reductions; and the perennial calls for the referendum and initiative and direct election of the President.[20]

The ideological center of gravity within the compressed universe of independent politics converged irresistibly on the moral grammar of anti-monopoly. Delegates to the CPPA founding convention filled the air with talk of "the money power" and "tax-dodging capitalists." "Sons of greed," "corruption," and "betrayal," monopolists sought "new privileges and immunities for capital" while "trampling under foot the rights of man." La Follette told Fiorello La Guardia his real aim was to "drive Special Privilege out of control of Government," and not to create a third party. The CPPA convention of February 1924 depicted itself as a party of "wealth producers," invoking a tradition that stretched more or less continuously from the Workingmen's parties of the Jacksonian era through the Greenback–Labor alliances of the 1870s through the Knights of Labor and Populist insurgencies of the 1880s and 1890s, a tradition that continued to echo not only in the sedated antitrust rhetoric of Roosevelt, Wilson, and La Follette, but also in the producers' eschatology of the IWW. The condemnation of unearned wealth—landed, financial, or, finally, corporate—as parasitic, aristocratic, arrogant, corrupting, and sinful was the venerated form in which the "labor question" had long infused the country's political culture. The struggle seemed ageless. Imagery once deployed to pillory the slavocracy of the South was redesigned and pressed into service again and again. The modern corporation was "soulless" and recreated, behind the façade of bureaucratic impersonality, the hierarchical structure of a feudal authority accountable, however, to no one; a private institution combining the worst aspects of collectivism and private selfishness at the expense of democracy. In many respects the La Follette campaign became the last hurrah of small-town republicanism, a political carnival of purity, invoking the moral calisthenics of "spotless towns" and women as "guardians of ancient sanctities"; the nth crusade, as the candidate's principal slogan put it, "To break the combined powers of the Private Monopoly system over the political and economic life of the American people."[21]

The campaign was safe enough even to win an unprecedented endorsement from the AFL—that is, once the Democrats unequivocally rejected labor's program. Gompers, however, bent over backward to eschew all third-party intentions, making clear Federation support for La Follette and his running mate, Senator Burton Wheeler, was strictly personal, not to be confused with the Progressive movement or party. Moreover, the actual financial and organizational contribution of the official trade union movement turned out to be even skimpier than its rhetoric. By election day some members of labor's official family, still disturbed by the faint echoes of third-party declamations, had deserted the campaign entirely: John L. Lewis of the UMW and William "Big Bill" Hutcheson of the Carpenters Union endorsed Coolidge; George Berry of the Printing Pressmen came out in support of John W. Davis, as did the Executive Council of the Central Trades and Labor Council of New York.[22]

The AFL's caution and coyness was to be expected. Its privileged position as labor's only recognized voice was premised on its special relationship to the Democratic Party, which had come to fruition under the Wilson administration. If the AFL invoked voluntarism as its moral-ideological response to corporate liberal, statist, and socialist calls for political intervention, it was a dogma subject to a kind of strategic relaxation when it came to the Democratic Party. Indeed, voluntarism was premised on that special partisan relationship and its institutional and political rewards. Old-stock craft unionists wanted their organizational integrity protected both against state intrusion—especially by an injunction-crazed federal judiciary—and against the continuing flood of cheap, new immigrant labor toward whom the AFL had long expressed its nativist animosity. Otherwise its ideological voluntarism, which was after all a defensive reaction to a Republican-dominated Congress and court system, made it wary of all forms of state social insurance, state jurisdiction over collective bargaining, and so on.

State intrusions of this sort, however, were at least implicit in the La Follette campaign, particularly among its social worker and socialist elements. Only the withering of AFL ties to the Democratic Party occasioned by Wilson's use of the Lever Act to enjoin the 1919 coal strike and the subsequent elimination of the traditional anti-injunction plank from the 1920 party platform, made the Federation momentarily reconsider its strategy. Still, lingering hopes of recapturing the national party from the DuPonts and Wall Street, and persistent fears of allying with the immigrant unskilled, made the connection to the La Follette movement tenuous in the extreme.[23]

Election day totals reinforced the trade union leadership's caution and demonstrated the shrinking perimeters of the antimonopoly persuasion. With 16.5 percent of the vote (4,826,471) La Follette managed to win only his home state of Wisconsin, and otherwise showed his greatest strength in areas of the Midwest and the Great Plains—Idaho, Iowa, Minnesota, North Dakota, and Wyoming—where populist protest voting was an honored tradition. Not long after the election, the AFL and the railroad brotherhoods quickly interred any surviving hopes that the campaign might be the prelude to a more permanent new political party.[24]

For Hillman the situation was quite different. No matter how much the "new unionism" might at times resemble the AFL's approach to industrial partnership, Hillman's social democratic past, his more recent conversion to social liberalism, the inherent instability of an industry where self-regulation could never become more than a holding action, and a polyglot immigrant rank and file with no liking for the AFL's exclusionary racialism, together meant that no mere tinkering with established political relationships could satisfy the larger needs and ambitions of the "new unionism." Of course, the ethos of Christian fraternity, the political grammar of sin and redemption, the moral vision of nineteenth-century republicanism, was neither common currency in the Pale nor Hillman's adopted language in America. Yet he welcomed this third-party crusade from the beginning.

As one of the organizers of the All American Farmer–Labor Cooperative Commission of 1920, Hillman was already involved fostering liberal–labor political cooperation. He sat on the National Committee of Fifteen chosen by the CPPA in 1922, which included Warren Stone of the BLE, William Green of the UMW, Morris Hilquit of the SP, Agnes Nestor of the WTUL, and William Johnston of the IAM, among others. Briefly, the 1922 elections seemed to augur a Progressive revival. Hillman was encouraged by the victories of senators Burton Wheeler, Henrik Shipstead, and Smith W. Brookhart, and the landslide triumph of La Follette. Shortly after the elections, Hillman, together with John Fitzpatrick of the Chicago Federation of Labor, tried to push the CPPA December convention in the direction of independent politics, arguing that labor "has no future as a tail to either of the two old parties." But even people like Hilquit and James O'Neal of the SP were more cautious, not to mention the railroad brotherhoods. Indeed, long after many of his union colleagues had abandoned ship, Hillman continued to press for a third-party organizing drive. In New York the ACW, along with the ILG, was instrumental in creating the American Labor Party in 1922 as an alliance between the SP and the local farmer–laborites. Abraham Shiplacoff served as vice chairman. This coalition worked diligently for La Follette but kept apart from the liberals of the local Progressive Party.

The ALP platform was distinctly more radical than most middle-class Progressives were by then ready to accept. It involved recognition of the Soviet Union, support for Eugene Debs, and the abolition of the Lusk Committee. It did, however, denounce Bolshevik suppression of rival political organizations, thus scrupulously maintaining its distance from the Workers' Party, which was excluded from the ALP's founding convention.[25]

Hillman felt estranged ideologically and moreover suspected the intentions of the brotherhoods and the AFL. The GEB resolution endorsing the La Follette campaign formally distanced itself from those planks calling for the restoration of competitive industry but dismissed their significance by suggesting they were impractical and anachronistic anyway. His more practical suspicions were confirmed when in New York the brotherhoods went so far as to set up a separate nonpartisan CPPA to counter the formation of the ALP.[26]

Because of his own doubts and the misgivings of others, Hillman kept open the option presented by the Communist Party's first flirtation with united front politics. Thanks to the railroad unions, which controlled the credentials committee, the CP was barred from the CPPA. It organized instead an alliance of the Chicago Federation of Labor, the Farmer–Labor Party of Minnesota, and the Workers' Party. The ACW sent delegates to its first convention in Chicago in mid-1923. Hardman was influential in encouraging this course as he denounced the timidity of the CPPA, the vagueness of its class position, and its abject reliance on La Follette. Hillman too thought La Follette tactically unwise to condemn the CP and to excommunicate those groups who gathered at its nominating convention in St. Paul in 1924. After all, until May 1924, when La Follette denounced the CP as "the mortal enemy of the Progressive movement and democratic ideals," the programs of the CPPA and the National Farmer–Labor Progressive party were nearly identical. Only in 1924, when factional struggles in the Kremlin dictated that the communist parties of the West terminate their collaborations with liberal and social democratic parties, did Hillman end this episode of friendly relations with the domestic Bolsheviks and make clear his unreserved commitment to the La Follette campaign.[27]

If Hillman had no other choice, the commitment to La Follette was nonetheless not as cynical as that fact might suggest. Not all the programmatic elements of the La Follette campaign were anachronistic relics of an endangered political species. Not only did the campaign foster an interest in some form of "co-management of industry" but, more practically, in New York at least it called for the eight-hour day, the abolition of child labor, public works as relief and recovery from the postwar recession, and government-aided old age, sickness, and unemployment insurance—all to become staples of the politics of labor reform in the twentieth century. Addressing the union's 1924 convention, Hillman summed up the imperative for labor political action: "The labor movement in this country has long seen that political power is absolutely essential. . . . We cannot go far enough with the economic power alone." Whatever La Follette's national headquarters might think deserved emphasis, Hillman made clear he intended the Presidential campaign to turn on

> . . . the stand of the Government on such matters as unemployment, the use of the injunction against workers in times of strikes, the standard of wages and similar matters. . . . These issues do not affect the workers alone. The question of a high living standard for the American workers is a matter of vital importance to the entire nation. . . . Any attempt to lower the living standards is certain to bring with it industrial depression![28]

Hillman's concern with the relationship between the level of mass consumption and the well-being of the national economy and his insistence that the federal government accept responsibility for averting industrial depression were all but ignored amidst the torrent of antimonopoly invective. But there were others—Paul Douglas among them—who sensed, like Hillman, that the terrain of social and economic conflict had shifted fundamentally over the previous two decades. They entered the La Follette campaign seeking a political realignment, one not circumscribed by the traditional antimonopoly precepts. Many belonged to the loosely organized circles gathered around Brandeis and Frankfurter. James Landis, for example, later to become the chairman of the SEC, joined the campaign as a "fight against the organized power of finance," surely a turn of phrase with which any upstanding foe of the plutocracy would have felt comfortable. But Landis, like his mentors Brandeis and Frankfurter, was really concerned not with the sheer size of the country's financial goliaths, but rather with the way they undermined efficiency and innovation through rigid rates and prices, unsupported bond issues, stock manipulations, absentee management, and the financial leeching of otherwise productive enterprises. In Landis's view both the political and the economic system were subject to a hardening of the arteries thanks to this coagulation of financial power. He said, "We want [through the La Follette campaign] to give a fair share of representation to other interests that have so far been warped out of their place under the control of government by the present parties."[29]

The Chicago Progressive Donald Richberg was another seeking

a new political economy. As legal counsel to the railway unions, he was naturally involved in the CPPA. When Glenn Plumb died during the 1922 shopcraft strike, Richberg took over and helped implement the Plumb Plan provision for impartial arbitration. Concerned with economic integration and stability, Richberg adopted a quasi-corporatist approach that sought to incorporate trade unions in a process of industrial self-government to maximize production and consumption. As chairman of the resolutions committee at the 1924 La Follette convention, Richberg attempted, without success, to write into the platform measures calling for unemployment insurance and industrial stabilization.[30]

Of course Frankfurter himself viewed the 1924 election as a ripe opportunity to realign the political parties, especially the Democratic Party, whose nomination of Davis certified for Frankfurter its capture by the Morgan interests. For Frankfurter, and no doubt for Brandeis, with whom the Harvard law professor carried on a quiet political collaboration, the La Follette campaign was the best available medium for raising the era's central issue, the "great inequality of property."[31]

Despite the disappointing election totals, Brandeis and Frankfurter, like Hillman, persisted in their quest for political alternatives. The two jurists attempted in 1925 to assemble "a general staff of thinkers" to develop strategy for independent political action. It never got off the ground. Hillman tried to keep his own hopes alive. The election results were after all not entirely discouraging. La Follette did well not only in the heavily industrial counties of the Midwest but also in New York (where La Guardia was elected to Congress on the third-party ticket) and in New Jersey textile centers.

> Considering the circumstances under which the Conference for Progressive Political Action engaged in the last campaign for the Presidency and the speed with which political organizations were thrown together in practically all of the states of the Union no one has any valid reason for being disappointed with the results. . . . They indicate a very substantial proportion of the rank and file of the American labor movement were prepared to support an independent labor-political party.

There were lessons to be learned, however. Such a future party "must be based not on personality alone but on the force of the movement underlying it."[32] For the foreseeable future, however, there was no "movement" with any measurable "force" underlying what amounted to wishful thinking about a "labor–independent" political party. People like Harold Ickes and Frederick Howe were privately quite glum. The postwar red scare and recession, followed by the sharp upturn in the economy and the widely publicized new era of "peoples capitalism," put a period to radical or even mildly reformist politics. Within the labor movement the official reaction reached its height at the AFL's convention in Portland, Oregon, where the Federation declared a war to the death against the TUEL. William Green went out of his way to praise the organization's respectability, its fitness for the New Era, and its conviction that organized labor's "best interests are promoted through concord rather than by conflict." Sidney Hillman was isolated and he knew it.

> It is my firm judgment that when we start taking a selfish attitude, when we assume the attitude that most labor organizations do . . . we and we alone will be the first to pay the penalty. . . . I plead with you to understand that . . . we are a movement of those who have been oppressed, and who have still a great distance to go before we get what we are entitled to get, and that it is our obligation to help those who are still suffering under the iron heel of oppression.[33]

Throughout most of his life Hillman would feel more comfortable chastising the "patent medicine men" of the left, their "abstract theorizing," "revolutionary phrase-mongering," and "dreamy ultimatums." But by the midpoint of the decade, he was on the contrary urgently concerned with the drying up of all social initiatives within and outside of the labor movement. Not unlike the impending Bolshevik decision to build "socialism in one country," Sidney Hillman was compelled to consider the prospects for "socialism" or, if not socialism, then social reform in one union.

EIGHT

⁓

Socialism in One Union

What is the measure of the time elapsed between 1919 and 1929?
J. B. S. Hardman reflected in 1928 that "the language that was
used then no longer sounds familiar to our ears. The emotions that
overwhelmed people in those momentous days fails to excite us today."
A rhetoric far older than Marx, its moral injunctions, its illuminations,
its psychological compensations, its millenarian incantations sounded, to
some at least, suddenly hollow. The metaphors seemed worn out, lacking
sensual power, the idols mortally stricken. If the cultural age of Marx and
Bakunin, of the Jacobins and Chartists, of Debs and Sorel, of the IWW
and the revolutionary General Strike was passing away, unable to renew
itself, a frightening indeterminacy loomed. What multifarious associations, symbols, heroes, villains, memorials, precepts, visions, oaths, and
martyrs could ever provide the same social adhesion? And yet a new
culture—tutelary, contractual, possessive, mobile, and bureaucratic—
was already flourishing inside the ACW before the great social upheavals
of the 1930s and 1940s carried its message to the rest of the immigrant
working class.[1]

Sidney Hillman was the visionary pragmatist responsible for this
precocious exercise in bureaucratic modernism. Had this onetime shtetl
revolutionary fallen victim to some improbable kind of cultural amnesia?
No, Hillman had not forgotten or repressed the ascetic enthusiasms of
embattled yeshivas, Czarist prisons, and garment sweatshops. His commitments, and those of his closest comrades, to the world of the large-
scale, complex organization—the corporation, the trade association, the

administrative state agency, and above all the centralized industrial union—were nourished first of all by socialism's promise to expropriate the fruits of progress and modernity periodically wasted and destroyed by capitalism's compulsive irrationality.

Moreover, in the ACW, and almost invariably in the industrial unions that followed it in the CIO, the trade union bureaucracy itself was initially peopled by the most active, aggressive, and politically articulate cadre from the ranks. They were the bureaucracy, at least in its formative period. So if the bureaucracy was a cage of invisible iron, it was by no means one erected by outsiders but rather a more organic outgrowth of the mass movement itself, including especially its most democratic impulses.

∽

However much the labor bureaucracy might later seem an ossified body, estranged from its own constituents, it began its life as an act of democratic creativity. Indeed, as Irving Howe noted in a different context, "the only certain way of preventing bureaucracy is to refrain from organizing, but the refusal to organize with one's fellow men can only lead to acquiescence in detested power or to isolated and futile acts of martyrdom and terrorism."[2]

That is not to say every rank-and-file militant, every revolutionary loyalist, was an incipient bureaucrat. For some, ancestral certitudes remained inviolate.

Samuel Liptzin, shop floor leader of the CP's caucus in New York, was typical of the indigenous currents of Jewish radicalism. Too quick to act without regard for the strategic concerns that worried the party's elite, Liptzin took up the age-old struggle against "bureaucracy" and "graft," whose basic contours hadn't changed any more than the populist allegory that for generations had provided such struggles with their transcendent meaning. While the party leadership was often drawn from a second-generation and native American milieu more attuned to the workings of corporate capitalism, Liptzin was of a different species, one that survived and even thrived in the fetid atmosphere of patrilineal sweatshops like the one his father worked in as a tailor in Lipetsk and which he too entered at the age of nine before coming to America in 1909.

What modern wonders did New York hold for Liptzin? The "pig market" at Hester Park; primitive little shops run by *landsleit* equipped with stove-heated pressing irons and foot-powered or, if extraordinarily advanced, bicycle-powered sewing machines; a Torah in one corner where boss and worker prayed, played cards together, and deliberated over domestic intimacies; a workaday world riven by a thousand petty rivalries, competitions, jealousies, ingenious little rackets, and recurring cycles of submission, abuse, and sudden, rage-filled work stoppages.

The appearance one day of a new worker, a fitter and also an anarchist, Ike Goldstein, forever altered Liptzin's life. He helped Goldstein write leaflets, smuggled them into shops in bundles of clothes, and was swept up by the great UBT strike in 1913. Joseph Schlossberg, whose honesty and righteousness had earned him the nickname "The Mezuza," became Liptzin's hero. But the time for heroes came to an end, and by the 1920s not only was Liptzin far less enamored of Schlossberg, he was sickened by the behavior of men for whom the union was less a cause than a career, and others who were not above cutting deals with manufacturers, with out-of-town scab shops, or with outright racketeers, especially in the trucking industry.[3]

Liptzin and his fellow shop floor communists and anarchists articulated a popular and traditional ideology whose values, myths, and nostalgic tone remained disconnected from the new processes and institutions of modern industrial society. These transplanted villagers compared the spirit prevailing in the union to that of a pogrom and described a once-militant union leadership as "the pride of priests, princes, and open-shop manufacturers." For them politics and ideology camouflaged a deeper characterological estrangement from the institutions and ethos of the "new unionism."[4]

In his youth Elias Rabkin was every bit as militant and devoted as Samuel Liptzin. Indeed, his political experience was richer, his revolutionary perspective considerably broader. Perhaps for that reason he was better prepared to accommodate the compromises of the postwar era, in fact to become a militant pragmatist, an organizational loyalist feared by factionalists on the left like Liptzin.

Born in the late 1880s in Bobruisk in the southern, most prosperous, more middle-class Pale, Rabkin was the son and grandson of land surveyors. His grandfather owned a fair amount of real estate in the town, so Elias was raised in relative comfort. He attended yeshiva briefly but was soon infected with the revolutionary fever and joined the Bund. There he led several embryonic trade unions, including one of tailors, and became the town's first open socialist. Soon he also became the first to be jailed. In prison he led a hunger strike that nearly cost him his life. Once released he was immediately drafted, but his family used its money and influence to have him appointed to the regimental orchestra, from which post he continued his revolutionary activity. When the Czar dissolved the Duma, Rabkin was incarcerated again, along with sixteen other prisoners in a cell built for four, and he served this time for thirty-three months. Once again he resumed his political work. Tipped off that he was about to be rearrested, he disappeared on his way to the police station with the help of a bribed border guard. Bundist comrades smuggled him out of the country, disguised as a girl, in a wagon.

Rabkin went first to Belgium, where he worked as a coal miner and steelworker. Quickly enlisting as an organizer, he witnessed his first free mass demonstrations, unhindered by the authorities, and was impressed: "I understood what democracy means as compared to bureaucracy under Russian Czarist government." But he was small, and the work was exhausting, so he emigrated to Canada, where he had a sister and an anarchist brother-in-law living in Montreal. There he became an apprentice pocketmaker and then a pants maker and general tailor, tying his fate first to the UGW and then, as a founding member, to the ACW.

In Montreal, with the help of the SP and the Young Socialist League, he conducted a series of strikes, including a partially successful general strike in 1917. During those early years he refused even the paltry wage offered by the union and lived on nothing, "on five cents for a glass of tea." Such extreme asceticism embarrassed even Schlossberg, who fairly begged Rabkin "that you agree to accept an amount of money as your salary, that this office should not be ashamed of. It is not proper for an organization like ours to expect any man to work for $10 a week." When he started writing for the union's Yiddish-language paper, the *Fortschrift*, he again refused any salary, as was customary in the old country.

When the alliance with the CP fell apart over the La Follette campaign, Hillman called upon Rabkin to return to Montreal to deal with the large CP caucus vying for control of the city's union. Confronting five hundred CP members and sympathizers angrily determined to resist the imposition of production standards required toughness, fortitude, and a willingness to engage in unsavory back-alley politics. It was, Rabkin remembered, a "hellish business," complete with street brawls and gerrymandered elections. Local characters strongly suspected of graft were enlisted in the struggle against the communists. On Rabkin's recommendation the resident manager of the Montreal Joint Board was summarily removed for a failure of nerve. Rabkin himself acted without qualms. Within weeks the organization was once again safely in the hands of Hillman loyalists. At the same time, and with similar dispatch, Rabkin dismembered the equally powerful CP faction in Toronto. There a foreman friendly to the ACW was bribed with $800 to help turn his shop over to the Rabkin forces.

It was above all Rabkin's resolute service as an organizational apparatchik in the factional wars of the 1920s that forever established his place in the bureaucratic hierarchy. Forever is hardly an exaggeration, as Rabkin held one office or another until his retirement in 1972. His career exemplified that seamless blending of hopes for collective and for personal fulfillment, the amalgamation of revolutionary enthusiasm and bureaucratic advancement, which to a greater or lesser degree characterized rank and file and leadership alike and therefore supplied the ingredients for a healthy bureaucracy—one not too dissociated from its social and psychological moorings.[5]

While presidential politics provided the occasion for the falling out between the CP and the Hillman leadership, which in turn led to Rabkin's bureaucratic elevation, the La Follette campaign was only the immediate pretext. This second phase of factional turmoil was bound by a thousand threads to earlier currents of shop floor insurgency. Its resolution was part of the process of transforming the "new unionism" from a set of imaginative possibilities into an organization of more businesslike regularity.

The TUEL comprised a hybrid ensemble, combining artisan resistance to production standards and the loss of shop floor control with a more generalized hostility to industrial and union discipline. Once the inhibitions of party discipline were removed, traditions of shop floor militancy reasserted themselves. At the 1924 convention, even while the CP leadership still hoped to avoid a break with Hillman, its local constituents fought for "week work" and supported resolutions calling for one-year contracts instead of the three-year arrangements recently agreed to.

By 1925 relations had grown extremely bitter. During a protracted strike against the International Tailoring Company, TUEL's Amalgamated Joint Action Committee began collecting its own dues from locals like the coatmakers, which it controlled, and the CP began denouncing the union leadership as "class collaborationists." Once the strike was settled, Hillman turned his full attention to the left. The Action Committee was declared a dual union, and the leaders of oppositionist locals were suspended.

Hillman now asked his erstwhile enemies on the right for help in carrying out the purge of the left. The SP was more than willing to forget past differences for an opportunity to strike at what it considered the main enemy, the CP. The apparatchiks selected—Abraham Beckerman, Hyman Nemser, Philip Orlofsky—were leaders of a cutters' local now cleansed of radical politics. They were in many respects indistinguishable from AFL business unionists and were known by many to maintain connections to the criminal underworld. Beckerman was appointed manager of a new, merged New York Joint Board. Local strikes were prohibited unless authorized by the manager, a stricture Hillman intended to apply also to the independent-minded cutters on the right. A representative of the *Forward* now regularly participated in GEB meetings, and steps were taken to expel the most notorious communist in the cutters local, Benjamin Gitlow.[6]

While New York was subjected to a mild form of martial law, factional tensions in Rochester, Montreal, and Toronto became acute. The ethnocultural basis of factionalism in those cities was distinctly different from that in New York. There Lithuanian, Italian, and Ukrainian communists joined Jewish pressers and coatmakers in challenging the national leadership with calls for the forty-hour week, for factional representation in union elections, and for amnesty for suspended leftists. However, the alliances struck between the Jewish left and these non-Jewish insurgents proved to be organizationally unreliable and politically ambiguous.

The Lithuanians were preoccupied with their own bloody nationalist struggles for control of the Lithuanian foreign-language locals. Their nationalism and latent anti-Semitism not only estranged them from the preponderantly Jewish union leadership but for the same reason lent a tentative air to their relations with the TUEL. Their syndicalist traditions also made them reluctant participants in contractual commitments, which the CP and TUEL had, in the end, come to accept as the essence of collective bargaining.[7]

Italian insurgents, who constituted the main body of factional opposition in Rochester particularly, proved even more organizationally and politically undependable. Leading Italian leftists, while associating with the TUEL, maintained a dual loyalty to the world of Italian radicalism, which tended to reproduce a kind of *clientilismo* politics on the left. Thus Italian organizers turned to August Bellanca for protection against the more repressive maneuverings of the rest of the union leadership, and in return were willing to be guided by Bellanca's cautious advice, even if that meant strained relations with their non-Italian comrades in the TUEL caucus. Bellanca proved capable of manipulating the currents of Italian radicalism so that they remained in the end loyal to the ACW without becoming politically and organizationally inarticulate. On a number of occasions he opposed GEB proposals to revoke the charters of Italian locals with the argument that Italian affiliation with the left was a passing phenomenon.

Bellanca was right. The CP was forced to admit its greatest weakness in all the needle unions was that it lacked a real foothold among the Italians. The Italian workers who made up the small armies of the left were often as new to unionism as they were to radical politics. This is not to say that until their arrival in Rochester they lived in glacial isolation. Rochester's *paesani* came not from the miserable and demoralized worlds of the latifundia but from regions of smallholders, agriculturalists, and handicraftsmen, with room, however cramped, for some upward mobility, where fraternal associations thrived, literacy and voting were not unheard of, and an ethos of thrift, sobriety, and moral probity struggled against the more saturnine impulses of Italian peasant life. However, more often than not their anger with the union leadership was sparked not by political differences but by a sense of ethnic discrimination and a general reluctance to submit to industrial routine, whether under union auspices or not. The latter accounted for the epidemic of stoppages that plagued the Rochester market in the mid-twenties. Relations with the left were further strained by Italians who posed as militants in order to cultivate a more traditional *personalismo* politics among their ethnic brethren. Once such personal ties between charismatic leader and followers were established, alliances with the left proved unreliable in the extreme. That was a common problem throughout the Italian labor movement, where Italian bosses "saw to it that no general interlocking movement among Italian workers developed and that whatever leadership was created should remain regionalistic, clannish, and almost feudal in its antiquated form and function." Thus, in a sense the Italians had always been "anti-administration." But they felt comfortable with neither the shop floor perspective of artisan democrats nor the political abstractions of the CP.[8]

The CP–TUEL caucus was by no means reluctant to take advantage of this prepolitical rebelliousness and racial animosity. Indeed, the union leadership was well aware that its own failure to organize the Italian majority, particularly in Rochester, undermined its position there and allowed its leftist opponents to enhance their organizational leverage by fueling the fires of ethnic suspicion. This Italian "problem," moreover, was growing in importance as the industry's workforce underwent a prolonged demographic shift beginning in the 1920s. In 1913 as much as 80 percent of the workforce in New York was Jewish. By 1950 the proportion had dropped to less than 25 percent. Hillman was properly worried and told fellow GEB members the CP had outmaneuvered them by using racial antagonisms and antiadministration sentiments. The appeal of the left was in part neutralized, however, by militant convention resolutions, as well as *Advance* editorials, speeches, and demonstrations on behalf of Sacco and Vanzetti.[9]

Meanwhile, the left contributed to its own downfall by overestimating the extent of its support once the tide turned decisively in favor of the union leadership in 1926–27. The TUEL was compelled to live an underground existence, while party leaders deliberated over ways to reestablish or maintain alliances with Italian insurgents they inaptly characterized as "center groups." The party vacillated on whether to cultivate the Italians by running prominent Italian leftists for union office, realizing that in so doing they risked losing the Jewish vote.[10]

In addition to those deep ethnic and social fissures, the activity of the left was further complicated by the byzantine shifts in factional alignments taking place at the highest levels of the CP hierarchy. As competing factions within the party vied with one another for the most credible revolutionary credentials, they were prone to make impetuous and extreme assaults on the union elite. This bothered independent leftists like Hyman Schneid, a longtime Chicago organizer with syndicalist sympathies, who objected to the union's endorsement of La Follette but could not go so far as to condemn the leadership as class collaborationist. Anthony Capraro complained to the CP directorate: "So far as I know Hillman is not a traitor. . . . Although I have no pretensions to be holding a brief for Hillman's infallibility, I have the deepest respect for his honesty of purpose which I feel ought to receive better treatment at the hands, especially of those who claim to be Communists."[11]

The party grew ever more isolated. Internally divided and politically excommunicated, the status of the party in the ACW was soon reduced to that of a sectarian clique. Its voice was heeded by few as it enunciated the mordant jeremiads of a bygone era and the belligerent platitudes of a revolutionary future not many thought necessary any longer. At the 1928 convention the GEB was able to report: "Factionalism in the Amalgamated has burned itself out. It is no longer a source of danger." With its demise, the last serious internal opposition to the "new unionism" died also.[12]

In some respects the internal life of the ACW thereby lost a certain elan and moral fervor. It began to display an incipient bureaucratic sclerosis. But perhaps that was to be expected. After all, this was a period during which the AFL was so cowed by corporate power that it felt compelled to demonstrate an almost abject commitment to productivity and labor peace. Yet it still suffered declines in membership throughout the decade from a peak of 5 million in 1920 to 3.4 million in 1929.[13]

It is hardly surprising, then, that Selig Perlman, who as a student of John Commons was thoroughly familiar with the radical currents running through the labor movement of an earlier era, chose this time to publish a theoretical explanation for what seemed the unchallengeable and, in Perlman's view, inevitable cautiousness and conservatism of the organized American working class. The symptoms were everywhere. Turnover and quit rates fell, and strikes declined by 70 percent over the

course of the decade. The earnings of union labor, while coming closer
to matching the acceleration in output than did the income of unorganized workers, managed at most to maintain without improving their
share of national income.[14]

However, contrary to Perlman's "American exceptionalism" thesis,
cautious "job consciousness" and security-minded conservatism were not
inherent in American culture but rather a response to a set of contemporary circumstances: a secular decline in the real wages of manufacturing workers, due in part to technological unemployment, generated by a
wave of mechanization expressed as a remarkable 3.8 percent annual rise
in productivity; market saturation, excess capacity, and declining employment in older industries like textiles, shoes, and steel; and a merger
movement among medium and large corporations that both augmented
the shift in the "organic composition of capital" and further weighted the
balance of power in labor relations in favor of business. Inside the firm a
counterrevolution in employment relations allowed the resurrection of
the foreman's empire, the neglect of rules governing promotion and
seniority, and a general decline in job security.[15]

All of these developments, and more immediate contingencies, profoundly affected the clothing industry and the ACW, acting as an incubator of the union's inherent bureaucratic tendencies. But these were
long-standing problems. Features peculiar to the "new era" capitalism of
the 1920s exacerbated the situation. Vertical mergers between the largest
manufacturers and mass retailers sometimes succeeded, as in the case of
Stein-Bloch and Fashion Park in Rochester, but they more often fell
apart, as in the case of Society Brand, which was forced to close all its
retail outlets, as the market for traditional forms of ready-to-wear business suits declined. Meanwhile the mass market for clothing became
increasingly style conscious. Not only did that demand more costly designing, it also generated a big business in style piracy. Producers of
high-quality items were hit particularly hard, forcing some to close and
others, like HSM, to undertake the production of whole new lower-
priced product lines.

Consumer buying habits changed in other ways. Discretionary income was reallocated away from clothing in favor of newer items of
leisure and mass consumption, including the radio and automobile. Purchases were more often made all year round rather than seasonally,
which meant retailers in turn bought for their immediate and not for
their longer-term needs, making the product cycle that much more erratic. A rapid growth in the chain store business and in cooperative
buying groups of independent stores together exerted decisive buying
leverage over manufacturers.

The accelerated mechanization of parts of the industry further threatened the job market. Even the high tariff policy of the Harding administration was a problem, as the 1922 Fordney–McCumber bill raised the tariff on raw wool by 83 percent over the rate established by the 1909 Payne–Aldrich.[16]

For all of these reasons the industry remained in chronic trouble after the postwar recession. Neither wholesale nor retail prices ever recovered from the crash of 1921. The bankruptcy rate, always high given the presence of so many marginal enterprises, soared, and even affected some of the industry's giants, including Strousse Brothers in Baltimore, which was liquidated; Greif Brothers, which fled the city; and even the once-dominant Sonneborn's, which barely hung on through the decade. Between 1923 and 1929 the number of firms dropped from 4,024 to 3,691.[17]

For some, like HSM, the liquidity crunch forced sharp cutbacks in production. For others the favored escape route was a flight to the hinterlands of the New York metropolitan area—New Jersey, southeastern Pennsylvania, Connecticut—which became havens for runaway shops fleeing the union's jurisdiction. Of course, the centrifugal spinning away of firms to outlying cities and towns had been going on for many years, a process facilitated by mechanization, which steadily reduced the need for scarcer, urban-based tailoring skills. But in the twenties the problem became acute enough to warrant the appointment of a general organizer, Clinton Golden, to plan and direct a special campaign in these "frontier zones," populated by callow country women and hostile police. In cottage industry barns where farmers' wives and daughters worked for a piecework pittance; in the homes of Pennsylvania Dutch farmers; in the tenements of Passaic and Paterson, New Haven and Bridgeport; in small factories tucked away in the sleepy towns of Vineland, Rahway, Lodi, and Peekskill, clothing manufacturers evaded the standards and scrutiny of union shop stewards.[18]

While the ACW did not experience the same precipitous drop in membership suffered by the ILG, a steady erosion reduced its numbers from a high of 177,000 to 100,000 by 1930. The proportion of unionized workers dropped from 68.8 percent of the industry in 1923 to 58.5 percent in 1929. Philadelphia, St. Louis, Buffalo, and Cleveland remained centers of the open shop. Every market lost members, with the steepest declines occurring in Baltimore, Cleveland, and Montreal.[19]

In the era of the "new capitalism," direct public intervention on behalf of economic regulation and stabilization was not to be hoped for. What presented itself to Hillman as the next best alternative was a system of micro-industrial regulation, carried out jointly by technical experts, "scientized" managers, and union officials, sanctioned by public

authority, an arrangement standing somewhere between statist collectivism and laissez-faire orthodoxy. What Ellis Hawley had characterized
as "techno-corporatism," or what might be seen as the micro approach
to macroeconomic coordination, was a live idea among economists and
social scientists like Wesley Mitchell at the NBER, social engineering
philanthropists like Mary Van Kleeck of the Russell Sage foundation
and Beardsley Ruml of the Carnegie (and later the Laura Spellman
Rockefeller Memorial), among public-policy-minded businessmen like
the Filenes and Henry Dennison, and most conspicuously Herbert
Hoover at the Commerce Department. This intended marriage of social science, technical knowledge, and practical business experience in
behalf of micro-planning entertained large ambitions: to generate sustained, countercyclical economic growth as a painless remedy for distributive inequality and class conflict—in effect, to replace politics
with administration.

Hoover sponsored a national conference on unemployment in 1921.
The Committee on Business Cycles and Unemployment, which issued
out of it, talked about public policies like unemployment insurance,
Federal Reserve credit manipulations, and countercyclical public works.
But the emphasis was on microregulation. Private management was to
formulate production and sales strategies informed by the latest economic
research and with an eye to reducing the fluctuations in employment and
business activity.

Clearly those formulations, however technocratic in appearance,
tended to accord the dominant influence to a business elite. While the
scientific and eleemosynary objectives of social scientists and social workers respectively informed the fundamental techniques of planning, it was
obviously possible to deploy them far more narrowly, for purposes of
controlling the market for industrial oligopolies or cartels without regard
for the general welfare or even the larger economy. Within the technocratic consensus, a "left wing," with which Hillman enjoyed close relations, worried about these dangerous misapplications of microregulation.

Hillman's economic adviser, Leo Wolman, sat on Hoover's commission and in 1927 was appointed by the Commerce Secretary to the
Committee on Recent Economic Changes. He was the author of a report, "Consumption and the Standard of Living," which focused on the
decade's revolutionary changes in economic structure and the need for a
public policy to sustain mass purchasing power. Mary Van Kleeck, an
associate of Hillman from the war, refused to join the Committee on the
grounds of insufficient trade union involvement in it; she was determined
that social science be used "to help labor achieve greater independence
and more power." Edward Filene, perhaps Hillman's most important

Although his parents sent him to Kovno to join the rabbinical seminary, Sidney Hillman's education quickly took a more secular and revolutionary direction when he became a ready recruit to the Jewish Bund. In about 1904, Hillman is third from the left among his fellow Bundists.

When Sidney fled Russia, a refugee of the 1905 revolution, he settled first in Manchester, England, where his uncle, Charles Paiken, was a prosperous merchant. This was the first stop on his journey into the industrial heartland of the West.

Immigrants like Hillman settled in the teeming ethnic ghettos of America's cities. Hundreds of thousands of Jews particularly went straight from Ellis Island to the Lower East Side of New York, where dirt, discomfort, and disease greeted the new arrivals.

At the turn of the century much of the Jewish community depended on the garment industry for its livelihood. Although Hillman first worked for Sears, Roebuck in Chicago, he soon hired on as an apprentice cutter at Hart, Schaffner & Marx, the largest garment manufacturer in America.

Primitive tenement sweatshops like this one flourished alongside larger, more modern, mechanized "inside" factories like the one Hillman worked in at Hart, Schaffner & Marx.

"Why hire a man for a dollar when you can hire a kid for a dime?" was a commercial axiom that many a sweatshop employer lived by. The industry was notorious not only for its exploitation of children but for the ways it degraded and impoverished its adult employees as well, making it a hotbed of resentment and rebellion.

Simmering discontent over low wages, exhausting and unhealthful conditions, and the dehumanizing abuses of tyrannical supervisors culminated in the mass strike of 1910 in Chicago, where Hillman first emerged as a leader. Here, workers and their allies parade to protest the killing of a striker, Charles Lazinskas.

Following the strike Hillman devoted himself tirelessly to organizing a new union, the Amalgamated Clothing Workers of America. The system of democratic grievance resolution and impartial arbitration pioneered by Hillman and the Amalgamated would later become the model for much of American industry.

The uprising at the end of 1912 in New York displayed how polyglot the garment workforce was. Hillman and his comrades had to overcome dangerously divisive ethnic suspicions and animosities if the new union was to survive.

The strikes in Chicago (1910) and New York (1912–13) prepared the ground for a new militant organization of garment workers. Ten of the 11 members of the original Board of the ACWA are seen here, including General Secretary Joseph Schlossberg and President Sidney Hillman, seated, second and third from the left, as well as A. D. Marimpietri and Frank Rosenblum, leaders of the Chicago group, standing second and third from the left. Hillman's election, at age 27, made him the youngest president of an international union in the country.

Bessie Abramovitz and Sidney Hillman are seen here on the occasion of their engagement. Bessie, a leader of the 1910 strike, later recalled her own notoriety by observing that "I was Bessie Abramovitz before he was Sidney Hillman."

Art Young's cartoon celebrated the union's triumph during the New York lockout of 1921. Although the victory secured the Amalgamated's position in the industry's most important city, Hillman now faced a long period of employer reaction during the era of the open shop.

JULY 1ST, 1922
OPENING OF THE FIRST LABOR BANK IN CHICAGO
AMALGAMATED TRUST AND SAVINGS BANK

During the 1920s Hillman became the leading exponent of the "new unionism," which concerned itself not only with the conventional issues of wages, hours, and working conditions, but also with unemployment insurance, low-cost cooperative housing and consumer cooperatives, and labor banking. Pictured here is the ceremonial opening of the first labor bank, the Amalgamated Trust & Savings Bank, in Chicago in 1922.

A "half-intellectual" like so many of his comrades from the Bund, Hillman was drawn to intellectuals sympathetic to the purposes of the labor movement. He developed a close relationship with economist Leo Wolman of the NBER and Columbia University, who functioned as the Amalgamated's research director and general adviser. Wolman is seen here smoking his ubiquitous pipe with friendly clothing manufacturer Max Holtz at his right.

Hillman was honored as "Man of the Year" by the Harmon Foundation in 1928. While the rest of the labor movement was in deep decline, the Amalgamated was a stable organization noted for its pioneering social innovations, and Hillman was widely celebrated as the country's foremost "labor statesman."

business contact, called regularly throughout the decade for concerted state action to raise wages through minimum wage legislation so as to prevent competitively driven wage gouging. Long an advocate of meliorative forms of industrial democracy, Filene predicted in his 1924 book, *The Way Out: A Forecast of Coming Changes in Business and Industry*: "If they [the workers] cannot settle their issues inside industry by industrial methods, they will go outside industry and settle them by political methods." "Since the war," Filene noted, "the masses everywhere have become more keenly aware of their political and economic strength. There is a new sense of solidarity among the masses."

In 1924 such "solidarity" was largely a figment of Filene's imagination. But it provided at least a rhetorical pretext for arguing for a system of microregulation in which "employees have an adequate voice in the determination and control of the conditions of work, an adequate stake in the results of work, and . . . a guarantee that the management of business shall be efficient."[20]

As the prospects for political and economic reform withered, Hillman grew ever more committed to a system of co-managed microregulation. He inveighed against the prevailing "law of the jungle" and acknowledged that the fate of the industry and its workforce were inseparable. "We cannot wreck the house in which we expect to live . . . we cannot in the end defeat the industry. By that route we can in the end only defeat ourselves." He urged the members to "rise above" the selfish morality of the average manufacturer. "We have to be for the industry, for law and order in the industry, for science in the industry."[21]

At the same time, Hillman was still prepared to "give a stubborn employing concern all the fight they want." Indeed, in mid-1925 he marshaled the resources of the whole organization to conduct a protracted strike against the International Tailoring Company, although only after the most flagrant and violent provocation, including an injunction in New York secured through the offices of a Tammany Hall–connected lawyer in the Bronx with great influence over judicial nominations. Sam Levin and Samuel Rissman, who led the struggle in Chicago, summoned the martial, street-fighting spirit of the rank and file: It was "a real war between the clothing manufacturer and our organization." Faced with the full arsenal of union-busting weapons, including imported scabs, private detectives, and even a raid on ACW headquarters, Hillman let it be known that "the Amalgamated knows no fear; that we are determined to uphold what we have built; that every officer and every member of our organization is ready to face not only Rice [the President of International Tailoring] but every underling of a Judge, and if it is necessary to go to jail and still uphold our rights."[22]

But except for the occasional and uncontrollable explosion, as at International Tailoring, Hillman was ready to "send our best heads to put the firms' productive strength in shape. If they prosper we will secure a share of that prosperity. If they don't, we may as well close shop." Critical of those trade unionists "content to use their power negatively and obstructively," the ACW now boasted that it "identified its own permanent interests with those of the industry, and is concerned to see it grow into ever greater efficiency and prosperity."[23]

What the strategy of microregulation reflected and took advantage of was the fact that the garment trade simultaneously deployed a deservedly infamous form of sweatshop labor and a skill-demanding system of flexible production. The latter system of flexible production flourished especially in urban centers along the Atlantic corridor—Newark, Providence, Brooklyn, Worcester, Philadelphia—but was eroded by the new system of mass production. It was characteristic of style goods particularly—furnishings, fabrics, stationery, jewelry—but also of specialty industrial goods like valves, textile machinery, and machine tools. In these industries rates became the focus of conflict and regulation between skilled workers and their employers. Extraordinarily detailed lists of the price of work were drawn up, debated, and posted, and every new product or variant of an older product evoked elaborate rituals of performance and rate-setting. The introduction of scientific management personnel into this process by the ACW in effect served to formalize and rationalize those customary relations of the shop floor. This "game theory" pattern of "manufacturing consent" coexisted with sweated labor, itself organized as piecework. The two patterns should not be conflated; indeed, that is a reason the ACW developed as an impure form of industrial unionism in which the skilled cutters, especially, jealously guarded their limited yet meaningful jurisdictional autonomy. It was a mark of Hillman's creative practicality that within his own industry he avoided inflexible attachment to either mode of organization, while outside of the industry he became a paramount spokesman for industrial unionism as the only suitable strategic response to the triumphs of mass production.[24]

Microregulation was thus on the one hand a protective device for coveted practices and privileges. It was at the same time a response to ominous undercurrents threatening the system of flexible production in garment manufacturing and elsewhere: the merger movement, standardization and routinization (accelerated by the production crisis of World War I), and the increasing irregularity of employment. In the last case, it meant an assault on seasonality, a key marketing dimension of the flexible system as it responded to the shifting desires of the expanding urban marketplace. Efficiency and standardization were ideologically linked in the postwar Hooverian consensus. The new emphasis on product narrowing and the elimination of "needless" diversity of goods and tastes infiltrated the garment trades. HSM's "X" plan exemplified this commercial and manufacturing modernism: the discarding of a broad product spectrum in favor of a large-run best-seller. Cheapness replaced novelty. Product narrowing promised to lessen dependence on skilled labor, to even out the oscillations in demand, and to promote more full-time employment of machinery and equipment. Chain store buying and national advertising furthered the spread of product narrowing and standardization. It also increased price competition (as product differences meant less and less), and put even greater pressure on labor costs.[25]

The 1928 convention report boasted that the ACW was steadily assuming a larger and larger share of the "functions of management," including the minatory role of labor supervision. Thus the chronic crisis of the industry encouraged the centralization and concentration of both management and union power at the mutual expense of entrepreneurial autonomy and workers' direct control of the shop floor. It meant as well wage concessions—temporarily, it was hoped—the elimination of restrictive work rules, especially among the cutters, and lower piece rates for cheaper lines. The policy of paying cutters on Monday for a whole week's work was dropped; so too the insistence that manufacturers guarantee prevailing income levels whenever new machinery was introduced that threatened customary skills, allowing instead new rates to be set in accordance with the new, diminished skill levels. The union became less vigilant about fighting discharges, so the number of cases brought to arbitration dropped dramatically.

In the case of HSM, which faced serious problems adjusting to changes in mass taste, the union helped plan the introduction of a cheaper "X" line of business suits, which could be produced more speedily and with less skill but at the expense of a great number, as many as one-third to one-half of the existing cutters' jobs. It was testimony to the still substantial power of the union that those cutters volunteering to leave received the then substantial compensation of $500, most of it contributed by the company.[26]

The "X" plan exemplified a profound if subtle shift in industrial relations. Ever since the strike of 1910, while dealings between union and management had proceeded with remarkable smoothness, they were in essence adversarial in nature and understood that way by all parties. Adoption of the "X" plan made management and the union partners in sharing responsibilities and functions once perceived as inherently separate. The company cut down on its staff of quality examiners, turning over that critical task to union functionaries. In turn, the union helped design the new "X" construction garment and the flow of work in the new "X" factory. The union actually allocated the total labor cost of the "X" suit among the operators as it saw fit, while relinquishing long-cherished work rules, in particular the prohibition against cutting "mixed lays" of fabric. The "X" plan was a great commercial success and soon became the company's principal line.[27]

Change was noticeable everywhere. Where once shop stewards had been the union's most visible day-to-day presence, now business agents, expert in some particular operation, moved from shop to shop and performed double duty as production technicians helping to improve methods and reduce costs, providing employers with industrial engineering knowledge vital to the practice of microstabilization. These acts of service and self-sacrifice were offered, however, only on condition that management also make concerted efforts to eliminate its own inefficiencies. Where management lacked the requisite knowledge, the ACW sometimes took responsibility for setting up whole new shops or lines of production. It initiated major changes in garment construction, the layout and flow of work, methods of payment, equipment, and even personnel. Hillman managed to convert the demand for wage concessions and revised work rules into an exacting examination by ACW experts of costs and methods, which in most cases resulted in stabilizing rather than reducing pay rates. The union was even prepared to risk its own financial resources to bail out key manufacturers verging on bankruptcy. Sonneborn's in Baltimore received a loan of $125,000 and sold stock to its employees to keep afloat. A line of credit was extended to Goldman & Suss, a large New York producer. The first entirely union-owned shop was established in Milwaukee to produce low-cost suits for HSM.[28]

While Hillman was still ready to engage in the martial heroics of the union's formative years, as the International Tailoring strike amply demonstrated, a more telling story of uncommon industrial pacifism unfolded in Cincinnati. A peculiar mixture of commercial cunning and hellfire religion, it was a story whose very incongruousness highlighted Hillman's accommodationist approach to industrial self-regulation.

Arthur Nash, a Seventh Day Adventist who had lost his faith while hoboing through the Midwest and then regained it when church members started bringing their business to his Detroit laundry, became a minister in the Disciples of Christ—only to be cast out for preaching a memorial sermon for an unbeliever. He became a clothing salesman and then organized his own A. Nash Tailoring Co., where he quickly became known as Golden Rule Nash for raising wages 300 percent, a token, he informed his workers, of his abiding sense of Christian fellowship. The

Golden Rule turned out to be a smashing success. Organized with a capital of $60,000 in 1916, the business was worth $20 million by 1925 and was the largest direct-to-the-consumer manufacturer in the country.

It was hard to distinguish the firm's corporate from its more spiritual forms of evangelism. Nash salesmen, crucial to his direct-to-the-consumer business, when assembled in annual convention, would sing "Nashional songs," one of which, to the tune of "Throw Out the Life-line," urged the sales force:

> Take out the Nash line, go see the last man,
> Tell 'em and sell 'em wherever you can.
> The Golden Rule first, the clothes will sell too,
> And money and friends you will make if you do.

For the small-town clergymen, schoolteachers, barbers, pool-room operators, and so on who canvassed for Nash in their spare time, the ambience was familiar.

Inside the factory the rule according to Matthew 7:12 meant no time clocks, shorter than normal hours, and frequent mass meetings, at which Mr. Nash addressed his employees as Brother and Sister. Labor peace came easier no doubt because of the sizable number of fellow Seventh Day Adventists (70 percent of the vestmakers for example), along with the presence of a docile group of unskilled Italian women.

It would be inaccurate to call the Nash works unorganized. Part family union, part congregation, it was, or so Nash maintained again and again in evangelical speeches that moved effortlessly from religion to cost accounting, a model of Christian fraternity: "I don't see any place I can build the Utopia of the man of Galilee except in the Labor Movement." Yet he steadfastly refused to allow the ACW to organize his several thousand employees.

For several years Arthur Nash and Sidney Hillman carried on more or less amicable discussions, while union representatives conducted, *sotto voce,* an educational campaign among Nash's workers. Impressed by Hillman's patience and moderation and embarrassed by coreligionists who charged that the Golden Rule as practiced in Cincinnati might not quite meet the standard enunciated in Matthew, Nash once again knew the joy of conversion. As the business exploded volcanically in the few short years following the war, Nash, who had never sewed a button and who knew basically nothing about the work of designers, cutters, pressers, bushelmen, and the like, increasingly lost touch with the manufacturing operations. Morale declined along with workmanship. Favoritism and a primitive and violent competition broke out among cutters and other skilled workers. Nash recognized the need for expert organizational help.

The upshot was a mass meeting at which Nash expended all his revivalist zeal to persuade his otherwise reluctant employees (especially lower-level management) to join the ranks of the Amalgamated. He urged his "Brothers and Sisters" to "join wholeheartedly and unreservedly with this great group of fearless organized workers who are laboring to loose the hands of wickedness, to undo the heavy burdens, to let the oppressed go free and to break every yoke." He denounced anti-Semitic attacks on Hillman: "It has constantly been said to me by the enemies of the Amalgamated that Sidney Hillman is a Jew. . . . My fellow workers, in our whole movement we have been following the leadership of a Jew."

Hillman reciprocated: The "work of the organized labor movement, as the Amalgamated sees it, is to bring the precepts of the Golden Rule into the daily working lives of men and women." This love feast of industrial concord was then blessed by Judge Julian W. Mack of the U.S. Circuit of Appeals, who declared the voluntary venture in union–management cooperation one of the happiest occasions of his life. Consummation was reached at the ACW's 1926 convention, when Hillman introduced Nash with a glowing tribute and Nash responded with a paean to trade unionism and brotherhood and pledged to turn over his property to any labor movement able to demonstrate it could put it to better use. While not quite prepared to expropriate himself, Nash did go so far as to put an ACW representative on the board of management.

In meetings with the firm's manufacturing and sales executives, Hillman had already given more tangible evidence of what cooperation could deliver. Union technicians from Chicago and New York were sent to Cincinnati to reorganize the work procedures of a floundering Nash subsidiary. As one observer noted, grievances were now discussed "not as an ethical but as a technical problem." Nash candidly acknowledged that for the first time he knew in advance the precise cost of each suit, thanks to the union's presence. Hillman publicly predicted that the Golden Rule experiment would establish a precedent for the garment industry and for all industry.

Of course, in the pre-union era there had always been a great deal less to the regime of the Golden Rule than met the eye. Wages were good, but no better than union scale, and were often raised in response to increases won by the ACW in other Cincinnati shops. The profit-sharing and stock purchase plan lasted only a year. A week's paid vacation at Christmas was soon rescinded once a threat of unionization dissipated. A widely publicized no-layoff policy was circumvented in bad times through "voluntary" unpaid vacations. The semiannual mass meetings of the workforce were always convened at management's initiative, were conducted under its direction, and addressed an agenda of its own devising.[29]

On balance, spiritual compensations aside, the arrangements at the A. Nash Tailoring Co. were no better and no worse than the variety of corporate paternalisms then being practiced under the rubric of the "American Plan." Although flawed, they were often serious attempts to minimize problems of industrial discord and, as was evidently the case at Nash, commanded a certain amount of allegiance. As was also the case at Nash, they made three vital promises: property or material well-being (stock, savings, home ownership), security (insurance against accident, sickness, old age, death), and democracy (a galaxy of industrial representation plans).[30]

Democracy, property, security: the watchwords of a new industrial order, the promissory notes of a "people's capitalism," to be honored under the benign auspices of a corporate commonwealth that presumed an identity of interests between the public weal and the wheels of commerce and industry. In retrospect it may seem a vision so transparently threadbare and self-serving as not to be taken seriously. The close proximity of the Great Depression, which instantly destroyed even the soundest corporate welfare programs, certainly reinforces that sense of trading in shallow fantasy. But democracy, property, and security, under normal circumstances, and even to this day, remain animating concerns of domestic politics. In an era of general retreat from public life, but one still sanguine about the unalloyed virtues of science, technology, and economic growth, the corporate commonwealth seemed a plausible response to the vicissitudes of industrial civilization.

Periodically throughout the decade, Hillman called for a more public and political assault on the economy's chronic ailments: cyclical and technological unemployment, declining real wages, and business cycle instability. But his was a lonely if not solitary voice, demanding national action on unemployment insurance, public works, low-cost housing, the five-day week, and minimum wages. Because Hillman was well aware of the increasingly quixotic nature of such rhetorical crusades, the "new unionism" offered its own private alternative to the corporate commonwealth; if not exactly "socialism in one union," then some approximation of the welfare state in one union.

With respect to democracy, of course, the union's achievements, whatever its shortcomings, were immeasurably richer than anything undertaken by even the best-intentioned forms of company unionism. In the cross-pollinated fields of security and property, the "new unionism" pioneered a set of innovations—unemployment insurance, an employment stabilization exchange, labor banking, cooperative housing—which comprised in microcosm many of the essential reforms soon to emerge as the landmark achievements of social liberalism under the New Deal.

Late in 1919 Morris Cooke wrote to Hillman urging him to press forward with a union campaign to measure accurately and reduce unemployment, which, he argued, would "work for the betterment of leadership and management of the industry." He suggested a guiding principle: "The more unnecessary unemployment [by which Cooke meant unemployment due to poor management] there is, the higher the unemployment insurance rate will be." Cooke further suggested that a campaign for unemployment insurance "will also pave the way in the future for the larger participation by the workers in management which we believe it will be in the interests of society and production to bring about." Cooke's broad view of the problem and its solution was echoed by Hillman a year later in a speech to the American Association for Labor Legislation (AALL). Unemployment was no more inevitable or "part of the natural order of things" than was the sweatshop. The welfare of the general public, not merely that of labor, depended on its abolition, and "no real efficiency is possible until such time as the problem of unemployment has been met and solved effectively." The latter consideration was of strategic importance, because public opinion had to be "aroused not alone on sentimental grounds." While the "very price paid for commodities, the tremendously high prices which impoverish all of us, are largely due to the inefficient conduct of industry" to which unemployment contributed mightily, Hillman contrasted the selfish approach of the average manufacturer, for whom artificially generated unemployment might be expedient in a glutted market, to the mature attitude of the ACW: "We believe that industry is a partnership of interests" without whose mutual accommodation and adjustment efficient industry was impossible.

Even at that early date, when political prospects still seemed sanguine, Hillman was realistic about the chances for public action: "Unfortunately for labor the public does not sufficiently concern itself in matters where it cannot clearly and definitely see a public interest. Much as I should like to see legislation enacted . . . I do not believe labor can wait. . . . To make progress, therefore, labor must fight its own way." And in fact in the summer of 1920 the ACW officially raised the demand for unemployment insurance before the Board of Arbitration. There the union mounted the argument that unemployment should be charged against the industry just as wages, overhead expenses, or fire or any other kind of insurance were. If unemployment was symptomatic of managerial inefficiency, then the further consequence of the union's position was that the charge against potential unemployment should be automatically less for the more efficient producers, a position first enunciated at the 1920 convention.[31]

This last notion, with its mechanistic emphasis on prevention rather than relief, was peculiarly American and indicative of how far Hillman had already moved toward assimilating the point of view of micro-industrial self-regulation. In part a reaction against what was disparagingly referred to as the British "dole," it also expressed a more hopeful view about the fundamental strength of the economy and the prospects for business stabilization. It was an approach that dispensed with the need for national legislation and left it to each particular line of business to study closely the nature and causes of commercial fluctuations in order to apply the appropriate antidote.[32] In any event, it was the only line of attack open.

Leo Wolman had visited England in 1922, as a member of the Hoover–NBER–sponsored study of cyclical unemployment, to study the British system of insurance. He returned to help draft the ACW's position. Not surprisingly, an initial agreement was first worked out in Chicago. A special board consisting of John Commons, who was responsible for drafting the Huber unemployment insurance bill in Wisconsin (which just barely failed of enactment), along with William Leiserson and David Friday, formulated a plan for joint employer and employee contributions to a fund that initially covered approximately 30,000 workers in 350 companies. It included a provision obligating companies to continue unemployment benefits even if other contractual arrangements with the union were for some reason terminated. The plan's preventive philosophy was expressed in a feature calling for a maximum contribution to the fund that was not to exceed the total benefits hypothetically payable over a two-year period. That provision was meant to act as an incentive to stabilize employment.[33]

The plan took effect on May 1, 1923, and was immediately applauded by Progressive publicists. *The New Republic* hailed it as "the first substantial attack on unemployment in this country." While the editors noted strong reasons for imposing the whole burden on the employer, given the apparent opportunity for "malingering" they approved the decision for joint contributions as prudent. Although initially the plan provided for only five weeks of benefits (later increased to seven and a half) amounting to 40 percent of full-time wages in an industry notorious for protracted bouts of seasonal idleness, it was, at least the editors hoped, a precedent-setting experiment.

Robert Bruere, writing nearly two years later when a more sober assessment of the plan's limitations was possible, reminded readers that while the relief afforded might never measure up to the need, the plan's fundamental objective, not yet realized, was "to contract the labor force to the limits of known demand . . . and to bring increasing pressure on manufacturers to organize their production programs with reference to predetermined demand," a prescription for the microregulation of a debilitated industry.

Continuing in this vein, Bruere went on to note how the unemployment plan enhanced the performance of the Employment Exchange previously established under the directorship of the scientific management expert Bryce Stewart, former head of the Canadian government's free employment offices. Many veteran workers who viewed bouts of seasonal idleness with fatalistic resignation had failed to register with the Exchange, thus hampering its efforts to compile comprehensive and detailed labor force data for purposes of matching the demand for every variety of skilled and unskilled work with the available supply. The unemployment insurance fund provided the incentive to register—or else lose eligibility for benefits.[34]

When measured against standards later established during and after the New Deal, benefits provided by the Amalgamated plan were undoubtedly spare. In the era of the "American Plan," however, this experiment in social insurance was counted a success, enough so that in 1928 the ACW reached agreement with the manufacturers in New York and Rochester to create similar unemployment funds in those cities. Thus, by 1929 the plan covered approximately 60,000 workers. It provided a real, if limited, form of security to workers facing seasonal, technological, and cyclical unemployment in what was arguably the most unstable of all American industries.

Moreover, the reciprocal relationship between the Unemployment Fund and the Employment Exchange, by strengthening the latter, not only further rationalized employment but helped eliminate those parasitic private employment agencies, and in some cases outright racketeers, who otherwise supplied a perverse kind of law and order to the industry's chaotic labor markets. Finally, the success of the Employment Exchange was conspicuous during a period in which there was a great deal of talk about employment stabilization but precious little corporate action.[35]

The Unemployment Insurance Fund and the Employment Exchange attacked the problem of insecurity from within the precincts of the industry, and they did so as an included feature of its microregulation. Simultaneously, the union pursued experiments with the cooperative movement in an extra-industrial quest for security and property. Schlossberg; Daniel Hoan, the SP mayor of Milwaukee; and Warren Stone of the Locomotive Engineers sat on the Board of Directors of the Cooperative League of America and worked closely with Senator Smith W. Brookhart of Iowa to encourage the growth of cooperative banking. Hillman actually portrayed labor banking as a vital part of the movement to democratize industry, a school in which to initiate workers into the mysteries of investing, underwriting, and lending.[36]

Eventually the union organized two cooperative banks, one in Chicago and one in New York, and a cooperative investment trust, Amalgamated Investors Inc., which by 1928 disposed of $1 million in resources. Inspired by the Filenes, who had pioneered in the field, the banks established credit unions for the members. All of these financial institutions were run with studious caution. Before reaching a definite decision to proceed with the banks, Hillman carried on discussions with bankers like Paul Warburg, Eugene Meyer, Jr., and Bernard Flexner, all of whom approved of the proposition.[37]

In Chicago the bank's real estate department facilitated home-building and home ownership by extending many small loans to ACW and other trade union members at low rates. Dividends to stockholders, who consisted of ACW members, were limited to 10 percent, and bank profits were to be either shared with depositors or reinvested. Finally, the banks facilitated the transfer of desperately needed hard currency from ACW members to relatives in Russia. By 1925 such remittances amounted to $10 million at very low cost.[38]

Only the industry's acute difficulties inspired the banks to depart from their studied conservatism. While initially it was a firm policy not to lend to clothing manufacturers, as the decade wore on and financial troubles spread the Amalgamated banks slowly relaxed that rule but only under conditions that assured the union much more intimate supervision of the company's operations than called for by more conventional commercial transactions.

Hillman was quite proud of the banks' accomplishments and of the broader labor banking movement of which they were a part. By 1925 there were twenty such banks, mainly organized by the railroad brotherhoods and construction trade unions. In an address before the Academy of Political Science, Hillman associated labor banking with the broader desire to share in the responsibilities of management and offered it as an ideal way for such "experimentation with the popular conduct of industry" to proceed gradually so that "mistakes will be corrected without disastrous effects on the industry and the nation in general."[39]

Enthusiastically, the cooperative idea was applied to the festering problem of urban housing. An acute housing shortage followed the war, exacerbated by high rents and inflated building and financing costs. Six cooperative apartment houses, accommodating three hundred families at a cost of $1.8 million, were completed by the union in New York City.

With evident delight, Hillman observed that they not only made available decent housing with sufficient light and air to former tenement dwellers, but were another living demonstration of the social possibilities of the "new unionism"—in this case that "through the cooperation of organized labor, the curse of the slums can and will be abolished."

Hillman drew on his friendships in the business community, including Henry Bruere, vice-president of the Bowery Savings Bank, and Herbert Lehman, to finance the construction costs. Metropolitan Life granted a first mortgage of $1.2 million at 5 percent with no commission, while the Amalgamated Bank loaned prospective tenants money with which to buy their apartments. Belle Moscowitz and La Guardia helped maneuver a tax exemption through the New York State legislature. Once in operation, the Bronx cooperative became a kind of total community, offering a nursery, medical and dental facilities, gymnasiums, playgrounds, a library, a kindergarten, and an auditorium for community functions.[40]

It would be easy to draw the wrong conclusions. The "new unionism" was not an apposite response to the corporate commonwealth, but a channeling of those desires that under other circumstances fueled the factional opposition to the leadership's authority. Between 1919 and 1924 a quarter of a million Jews fled Eastern Europe and Russia for the United States, adding a new radical element to a Jewish labor movement already well supplied with experienced revolutionaries. Temperamentally less prepared to settle for the pedestrian accomplishments of conventional trade unionism, they not only accounted for much of the internal political turmoil but also pressured the union leadership to express its socialist convictions in areas ostensibly peripheral to normal collective bargaining: the rights of women, socialist education, medical clinics, and cooperative housing.

Microregulation and social welfare unionism were thus remedies of the moment. Notwithstanding some overblown rhetoric, Hillman never viewed them as more than second-best solutions to be supplanted by more public initiatives should the time ever again seem propitious. Nonetheless, these strategies produced tangible results both by damping down the unnerving fluctuations of the industry and by softening the impact of material hardship. More than that, they helped produce that eerie sense of cultural distance separating 1919 from 1928.

As early as 1922, one of the industry's impartial chairmen noted: "It is interesting to observe the gradual change that has come over many of the union officials who were formerly the most extreme in their social views. From everyday contact with the orderly processes of industrial government they have become the most jealous of the interests of law and order." A new respect for the sort of law and order preferred by social scientists and industrial relations counselors were indeed a momentous psychological and moral development, one that emerged isomorphically with other fateful transformations in the cultural interior of the union and its constituencies.[41]

The Amalgamated, like other Jewish-dominated unions, had enormously ambitious educational plans which it pursued with great diligence if indifferent success. Members were to be schooled first of all in the basics of trade unionism, parliamentary procedure, and English composition, the standard fare offered by the average AFL union. The Amalgamated was by no means averse to this sort of more mundane undertaking; the Rochester Labor College, the Workers University of Cleveland, and the Baltimore Labor College were all sponsored by the ACW. Moreover, Joseph Schlossberg attended the founding meeting of Brookwood Labor College in 1921, and Leo Wolman became the school's academic adviser. Although Brookwood developed a reputation for labor radicalism, in its early years it was essentially a training ground for union organizers and scrupulously avoided offending the AFL chieftains. ACW students attended courses at Brookwood no more daring than Otto Beyer's and Stuart Chase's on "Labor's Responsibilities in Production," Mary Van Kleeck's on "New Developments in Industrial Relations," and Jett Lauck's on "Recent National Strikes."[42]

What really distinguished education in the Jewish labor movement, and in the ACW, as Irving Howe has noted, was the way it blended the lofty and the mundane, *haskalah* and *tachlis*; its pedagogical amalgamation of a secularized messianism and the hunger for material advance perfectly mirrored the movement's unstable alloy of rebelliousness and assimilation.[43]

For the Amalgamated, in the beginning, the emphasis was on high culture, or more precisely on a democratic variant of that culture. It adopted as its own the landmarks of the arts and sciences of the eighteenth and nineteenth centuries—Mozart, Beethoven, Darwin, Watt, Edison, Dickens, Tolstoy, and Goya—while offering a partly populist, partly socialist critique of the bourgeois political and economic order that eclectically drew on the thinking of Jefferson and Marx, Paine and Veblen. There were classes on labor history, psychology, women's issues, the party system, Shakespeare, and so on. In New York, lectures on the NEP, on "What Is Doing in Europe," on American Imperialism, on the Paris Commune, and on the question "Must We Change Human Nature" were attended by as many as 2,500 people. Classes, as opposed to one-time lectures, tended to emphasize the basics of English reading and writing and civics. But business agents and shop chairmen, the foot soldiers of the new unionism's cultural revolution, matriculated through a sophisticated three-part curriculum: "The Bases of Modern Civilization" included the "fundamentals of psychology," the nature of society, and man and society in history, including historical materialism. "The Labor Movement" sequence emphasized the "problems of leadership and organization," including the problem of "organization forms." "Weekly Interpretation of Current Events," the third panel of this educational tryptich, drew its material for discussion from a broad cross-section of American and European newspapers and magazines. Educational plans for the rank and file were equally grand. "Education at large" included a series of mass lectures followed by a half-hour "musicale" with violin or song recitals. The lectures might include "Three Years of Workers' Government in Russia: An Analytical Review"; "Changing Italy: An Account of the Latest Industrial Revolution"; or "The Murdered Apostles of Labor" on the anniversary of the Liebnicht–Luxembourg assassinations. In the category of "Group Education" classes were projected on "Management of Industry" and "Economic Organization of the United States." In Chicago Sam Levin made sure, once the days of dramatic organizing strikes were over, that part of all regular meetings was devoted to some cultural activity and arranged for visits by the Chicago Symphony orchestra and local operatic and ballet stars. There was a tacitly understood political subtext to this sort of cultural agenda: To appreciate a Shakespeare tragedy or a Beethoven symphony was simultaneously to disdain the inherent shoddiness and vulgarity of the marketplace.

In 1922 the union published the *Amalgamated Illustrated Almanac*, an iconographic sampler of Western cultural history, including inspirational maxims from Debs, Whitman, Tolstoy, Ibsen, and Luxembourg, along with a recommended reading list of the works of Dreiser, Twain, London, Shaw, and Romain Rolland. Brandeis praised it for raising "the industrial struggle out of the grimy slough of materialism and presents generous striving for the good life."[44]

It was a cultural potpourri that recapitulated the intellectual coming of age, in Old World prisons and secret study circles, of the union's founding cadre. These were no less steeped in socialist culture, bearers of enormous respect for social science, the realist novel, and the achievements of modern science and technology. For them the union was to be a carrier of modern culture. The educational program was thus aimed at replacing the multiplicity of cultural agendas articulated by each ethnic constituency with a homogeneous set of values, beliefs, and motivations.

William Leiserson deemed the ACW a great agency of Americanization and, with Italian as well as other immigrant workers in mind, noted that the union replaced the "traditional patriarchal clan leader" with the self-conception of the "independent citizen." David Saposs similarly observed: "The first step in the assimilation of the immigrant is to weaken the old national tie," a process abetted by the ACW in part because the union encouraged the use of English and even more because "the Amalgamated initiates its members into the mysteries of self-government."[45]

The union's effort at reeducation called on a whole roster of Progressive intellectuals, dissident academics, and socially concerned artists. There were lectures by Lincoln Steffens on "The Effect Revolutions Have on Civilization," a dramatic recitation from Hugo's *Les Miserables* by Bertram G. Nelson, talks by Horace Kallen on "Labor and the Washington Disarmament Conference" and A. Philip Randolph on "The Negro and Labor," a course by Charles Beard on the "History of the Worker and the Worker in History," and one by James Harvey Robinson on the "History of Civilization."[46]

The active interest of people like Brandeis, Robinson, and Beard suggests the complex motivations inspiring the Amalgamated's "cultural revolution." Robinson's commitment to the "History of the Common Man," for example, was intimately bound up with an urgently sensed need for social adjustment, an intellectual simulacrum of the cooperative commonwealth and its evolutionary progress. It was "of the greatest moment to society that this class should be recruited from those who have been taught to see the significance of their humble part in carrying on the world's work, to appreciate the possibilities of their position." History should "explain our industrial life and make its impact clear . . . explain the existence of the machine which the operative must tend . . . the very last link in a chain of marvelous discoveries . . . how the present division of labor of which he seems to be the helpless victim, has come about." All of this would work to "give the artisan an idea of social progress and its possibilities."[47]

The Amalgamated, and the radical labor movement generally, were, after all, apostles of modern times, not cultural modernism, believers in the bourgeois utopia of self-fulfilling productivity, discerning in it the ultimate historical fate of the proletariat.

The union's ultimate ideological attachment was to a socialism utterly at home with the modern world's need for bureaucratic organization and a political realism based on scientific objectivity. Culturally, it repudiated the mythic messianism of the syndicalist movement, with its roots in the nineteenth-century romantic rebellion against industrialism. It was as well indifferent to the modernist assault on bourgeois rationalism, committed instead to progressive efficiency with its penchant for treating the body as a kind of human motor subject to the general laws of thermodynamics. Modernism, whether originating in the diffidence of preindustrial social groups or in the dissociation and nihilism of middle-class intellectuals, was fundamentally antithetical to the objectivism, standardization, and realism of modern times, and to its central institutions—the factory and the bureaucracy. As such it found no expression in the Amalgamated's cultural and educational program. For that matter it left no enduring traces anywhere in the labor movement.

Moreover, even the democratic-egalitarian ethos that infused the Amalgamated was subject to certain limits, marked off by the social and psychological boundaries circumscribing the "holy family." That institution once defended by conservatives as the *sine qua non* of established hierarchy and moral order, and by liberals as the locus of private property and its accumulation, and, conversely, attacked by radicals as an anachronism, was by the turn of the century an object of tutelary and defensive protection by the labor movement and the wider world of social welfare reform. The welfare initiatives of the "new unionism" were a kind of genealogical bridge between the Christianized social welfare of the previous century and "scientific welfare" and state capitalism, stepping into the breach when the old philanthropy failed to save the family from material and moral devastation.

Certainly, the radically modernist cry to abolish the family was not heard within the ranks of the labor movement. The ACW's inability to answer the "woman's question" within its own ranks was further evidence that social criticism dared not trespass across the borders of the "holy family." Although Dorothy Bellanca was appointed the first Director of the ACW's Woman's Department in 1924, and although one-fourth of the organizers hired in the 1920s were female, the Department soon folded. The nearly complete male domination of a union at least half female was never seriously challenged.

The pressure to create separate female locals or branches, cutting across occupational and craft lines, began in 1917 in Rochester, where a woman's local was first established, followed by one in New York. But the local male leadership in Baltimore resisted both the creation of a Woman's Department and the formation of a woman's local, enough to demoralize even the most devoted women organizers. The situation was repeated in Chicago. Women activists were shunted aside, expected to perform the union's equivalent of domestic housekeeping. In a city where approximately 60 percent of the membership was female, no more than two hundred women attended local meetings. A resolution at the 1928 convention to reestablish the Women's Bureau was opposed by the leadership, including both Sidney and Bessie, who argued that the women were adequately represented. Usually immune from criticism by the Progressive press, the delinquency of the union was finally addressed in a 1927 issue of *The Survey*. Reminded that its own constitution guaranteed full equal rights and privileges, Theresa Wolfson was critical of the union for having only one woman on the GEB, employing a negligible number of female business agents and local officers, despite the approximately 50 percent female membership, and tolerating traditional forms of wage and occupational discrimination and segregation by sex. Such friendly criticism made little impression, and Bellanca found herself in the compromised position of defending the men while sanctioning an "underground" woman's caucus to carry on the fight.[48]

The woman's question aside, a great gulf separated the audacious educational visions of the leadership from what turned out to be feasible and, for that matter, desirable from the standpoint of the membership. In Chicago, Sam Levin worried that the educational policy of the UHT-sponsored Workers Institute tended too much toward "high browism, in giving lectures on art, on the history of money." He preferred lessons in English and lectures on "practical questions." Hardman, who began his tenure as Educational Director with great optimism, after a few years was conceding his own discouragement in the face of rank-and-file indifference to much of what his department offered. But even from the start he was aware of the enormous difficulties.[49]

One problem encapsulated the irony of the leadership's own sense of cultural mission. J. M. Budish, who chaired a United Labor Education Committee that included representatives of the fur workers, the hat and cap makers, and the Workmen's Circle, as well as the ACW, observed that all the highbrow forums, concerts, and lectures were in part quite consciously offered to counter the "degrading effect on the personality of the worker" produced by mass culture "cheap moving pictures and musical shows." Budish acknowledged that making "few concessions to popular taste" had hurt attendance. But the goal of creating a "new and finer culture" as part of the general process of "spiritual emancipation" would not be sacrificed on the altar of expedience. The irony was that the productivist ethos, the cultural legacy inherited from the nineteenth century, which constituted the bone and sinew of Budish's "spiritual emancipation," was increasingly bound to and insidiously degraded by the new century's consumerist ethos.[50]

Budish's lament was therefore profoundly conservative. It was itself symptomatic of the fading resonance of the "labor question," as the efflorescense of a mass-consumption economy and culture transferred the repository of value from the objective and measurable activity of productive labor to the evanescent tastes of the desiring individual. It foreshad-

owed, in Daniel Bell's words, a "culture no longer concerned with how
to work and achieve" but rather obsessed with a new discipline, a new
moral regime and set of incentives "primarily hedonistic, concerned with
play, fun, display, and pleasure." The anxieties about consumerist civilization expressed by Budish and others drew their strength from the
social democratic variant of an Apollonian order of perfect productive
harmony complete with its own economic eschatology and an almost
superstitious veneration of science.[51]

While Budish worried about the seductions of mass culture and Hardman grew increasingly dispirited in the face of rank-and-file indifference
to his educational exotica, there were those for whom the new, expanded
capacity to consume opened up the prospect that "a capital–labor war
which has been going on now for upwards of 300 years" was about to
end.[52]

The extent of mass consumption and installment buying was far more
limited in the working class than in the middle class. And within the
working class, family budgets among Southeast European immigrants
were noticeably less likely to expand beyond traditional "necessities"
than were the budgets of those from Northwestern Europe. Through the
twenties, working-class consumption habits remained largely traditional,
security conscious, and tied to communal functions. Relatively small
sums were spent on recreation, movies, travel, household help, and
vehicles.

While the technology of mass culture—radio, phonograph, movies,
the automobile—were certainly becoming commonplaces in the material
culture of working-class immigrants, they were embedded within the
intertwined networks of family, church, ethnicity, and even trade union.
The neighborhood movie functioned as a site of social adhesion in immigrant enclaves. Over the airwaves messages of labor, ethnic, and religious solidarity made the radio, at least temporarily, an instrument of
provincial insularity rather than a great homogenizer of secular consumerism. Furthermore, the tenacity of nineteenth-century cultural standards among both the Jewish working class and its tutelary leaders ensured that while consumption might become less parsimonious, it
would be constrained by a sense of "refinement," "respectability," and
self-restraint.[53]

Hillman personally certainly found most congenial an essentially
nineteenth-century middle-class design for living: education and uplift; a
carefully arranged marriage of ascetic idealism and modest material comforts; and the judicious blending of books, magazines, lectures, and music, all some distance removed from both the conviviality of working-
class saloons and from the socially promiscuous emporiums of mass

culture. But he was never guilty of the pious moralizing, sentimentality, and social preaching that often characterized social gospellers and other Progressives anxious about the debauchery of a sated working class. His view of mass culture was increasingly functional, similar to that of the industrial relations counselor Edward S. Cowdrick, who realized that as people come to treat luxuries as necessities, "existing high standards of living will promote enterprise, energy, and stability among all classes."

While the remnants of an older genteel, moralistic culture continued to condemn profligacy, "modern men" like Hillman and his friend Edward Filene bravely pointed to a new connection between a high standard of living and more elevated aspirations. David Saposs, whose study of the Americanization of the immigrant working class drew much of its evidence from the experience of the Amalgamated, also recognized the causal links between material and cultural transformations: "The fact that the Amalgamated succeeds in raising the general standard of living of its members may readily be observed in their dress, behavior, living quarters, manners, tastes, and developed feeling of community responsibility and self-respect." Even without the utopian gloss, by the end of the decade consumption was seen less and less as a moral question or as a matter of character, and more as an activity vital to national economic well-being.[54]

Praised or damned, garment workers were by no means immune to the magical urban worlds of leisure and personal consumption: proliferating fashions; the commercial amusements of matinees, movies, dance halls, theaters, and cafés; the omnipresent spectacle of goods on display. Garment worker Ida Richter remembered: "We used to love the American people, to copy them. . . . I saw people who looked better and dressed better and I wanted to be like that kind." Precisely because most could afford only the cheapest mass-produced clothing, they were particularly vulnerable to the brash allure of "style goods": "It is wonderful to have [a suit] from Wanamakers. I wish I could wear the label on the front." Moreover, the craving for fashionable clothing and commercialized forms of leisure exacerbated tensions over low wages and the dirt and ugliness of the average factory, adding a very modern motivation to the class struggle. Clara Lemlich, heroine of the 1909 rising of the 20,000, noted how the women workers hated to see their new hats ruined hanging on hooks on the walls of their shop: "We're human as well as any other young women." To buy a new hat, "even if it hasn't cost more than 50 cents, means that we have gone for weeks on 2 cents lunches—dry cake and nothing else."[55]

The alchemy of the marketplace, the cultural ministrations of the Education Department, the metamorphosis of foreign-language locals into mixed assemblies, and the ideological cosmopolitanism of the leadership were all channels of "adaptation" and "Americanization." They flowed sometimes swiftly, sometimes glacially, and not always in the same direction, but they inexorably worked to dissolve ethnic divisions and to mute their cultural dissonance. This was no mean feat in a union whose members spoke at least thirty different languages and paid fealty to twenty-six different nationalities.

The work of "amalgamation" was furthered as well by larger social and demographic transformations. The emergence of mutual aid societies and supralocal associations like the Sons of Italy, or in Chicago during the twenties national fraternal organizations like Unione Veneziona and the Italian–American National Union, eroded the more insular familial and village-centered relations of the Old World. Italian nationalism, at least among immigrants from the south, really flourished for the first time in the United States, partly in response to their own despised, caste-like position in American society. The second generation was more at home in urban and industrial settings, hence the union began to experience greater success among the "young, new Italian–American element." Forty-five percent of the initiates into the union in 1921–22 were already U.S. citizens. This confluence of cultural, political, and even religious change developed slowly. For example, it wasn't until the 1920s that Catholic parishes in Italian neighborhoods were visibly "Americanized"; where old country feasts, distinct village liturgies, local patron saints, and processionals were replaced by a more austere and devotional sacramental orthodoxy.[56]

The war and the fevers of the postwar insurgencies accelerated the dissolution of peasant culture in America. The uproarious applause that greeted Schlossberg's stirring eyewitness account of the Italian factory occupations of 1920, as an expression of the international solidarity inspired by the postwar outbreaks of workers' revolution and revolutionary nationalism, was not unusual. The union's early staunch campaign on behalf of Sacco and Vanzetti further strengthened the bonds of Italian nationalism and the ties between the Italian rank and file and the largely Jewish leadership.[57]

Fascism was a more vexed issue. Sympathy for Italian combativeness and hero-worship of Mussolini grew substantially through the decade. The head of the Cincinnati Joint Board informed the GEB about a large number of fascist sympathizers in the city, forcing the Board to ponder how openly it ought to associate its extra-union, antifascist activity with its normal organizing work. The moral psychology of fascism, the appeal to Religion, Fatherhood, and Family, so vividly evoked through Mussolini's artfully crafted symbolic presence, was profoundly antimodern, not merely "anticommunist." But fascism was Janus-faced. In the United States there was a live nationalist current within the Italian–American anarcho-syndicalist movement during the war, before Mussolini's rise to power—in part a reaction against the xenophobic nativism of domestic American politics—which found solace in fascism. It produced acrimony not only within the Italian left, where Giovanitti and Tresca stood adamantly opposed, but throughout the Italian community. The Sons of Italy, for example, split apart over the issue. The same fissures appeared within the organized labor movement. In the ILG the antifascist leadership of the large all-Italian local 89 confronted a rank and file enthusiastic about Mussolini.

The ACW leadership responded promptly to the fascist threat. The 1924 convention adopted a strong antifascist resolution and called for support of the Anti-Fascist Alliance of North America, which included representatives of the ILG, the Italian Chamber of Labor, and the New York Federation of Labor. At the 1926 convention Giovanitti appealed to the delegates to support the antifascist paper, *Il Nuovo Mondo*, which was begun with help from the ACW. At the 1928 convention he delivered a passionate exhortation about the need to destroy fascism, while many locals introduced resolutions against the Fascist League of North America.

Italian organizers anxiously pointed out that fascism was both a foreign and a domestic danger: Members of the Fascist League were serving as shop chairmen and as heads of locals. Rochester became a focal point of antifascist activity. In 1929 the local chapter of the Anti-Fascist Alliance adopted a militant anticlerical and antifascist resolution on the occasion of the Concordat between Mussolini and the Vatican. It called on Italian workers not to repudiate the spirit of independence nurtured by Garibaldi and Mazzini, described the Church as an ultrareactionary institution, and explained that the anticlerical, antifascist, and antimonarchist movements constituted one indissoluble struggle.

The fascist problem did persist, indeed would grow under the pressure of the Great Depression, actually igniting a kind of urban guerrilla warfare in the streets and shops of the garment industry. No doubt it was one measure of the failure of the union's program of cultural enlightenment.[58]

Nonetheless, however violent the clashes between fascists and antifascists, they were different in kind from the ethnic animosities that had roiled the union's internal life during its formative period. Ethnic jealousies and conflicts didn't vanish. Italians at times still suspected the motives of the Jewish leadership. Care was still taken not to raise "inflammatory subjects . . . for example the late Mexican situation, the separation of Church and State, we are careful not to discuss because while as a union we might approve of it, our Italian Catholics naturally would not." But by the end of the decade both *landslayt* and *paesani* were becoming something else entirely: citizens of the factory and the marketplace.[59]

∽

In 1928 the Harmon Foundation, a liberal businessman's group, awarded Hillman its gold medal and a prize of $1,000 for "outstanding service in the year 1927" in recognition especially of the union's unemployment insurance plan and its undertakings in cooperative banking and housing. That same year the *St. Louis Post-Dispatch* noted that Hillman was regarded by friend and foe alike "as the flaming genius of union labor in the U.S." and published a lengthy article by Hillman on the occasion of the paper's fiftieth anniversary, an article entitled "Labor in the United States."[60]

The Harmon Foundation's Man of the Year lived up to his rapidly growing reputation as a "labor statesman." "A high standard of living is no more a mere question of justice," he wrote.

> It is essential to our system of mass production to create a consumers' demand for almost unlimited output. To meet these problems, only the labor movement holds out a constructive program. Its insistence upon a sane and responsible democracy in industry and the progressive improvement in standards of living are essential for the maintenance and progress of our industrial system.

Such sentiments were earning him the accolades not only of social workers and reformers but of the business world as well; a publication of the National City Bank praised the union's experiment in cooperative banking and noted approvingly that Hillman no longer contemplated "violent revolution or change" (as if he ever had). The insurance industry lauded the Amalgamated's venture in cooperative housing, while the *San Francisco Post* editorialized about the union president's sage opposition to communism and his strenuous exertions on behalf of industrial peace. Louis Marshall, corporate lawyer, philanthropist, and sachem of the Jewish community, in a speech at a manufacturers' banquet pronounced Hillman a man of "sweet reasonableness and marvelous tact." At the age of forty, moderately famous, widely respected, and successful, if a bit unconventionally, Hillman had arrived.[61]

For Jewish "half-intellectuals" like Hillman, the world of radical *yiddishkeit* was at most a temporary haven. While the Samuel Liptzins of the garment center would always feel at home in this "culture of transition," people like Hillman faced a choice: to accommodate themselves

to the increasingly dominant influence of middle-class Jewish nationalism, as did Cahan and even David Dubinsky, or to break more fundamentally, at least in their professional and political lives, with their
ethnocultural past and undergo the reorientation necessary for functioning within a more cosmopolitan elite.

The contrast in personality between Hillman and Dubinsky was expressive. Outwardly, Dubinsky was everything Hillman was not: gregar-
ious, warm, earthy, with no intellectual pretensions or ambitions, and
avowedly Jewish, if not religious. Hillman shunned participation in the
organized religious life of the Jewish community (and its civic expression
through the Zionist movement in America). He rarely attended temple
services, even on the High Holy Days, yet at times of personal crisis he
was apt to slip away to a synagogue for a moment of private contempla-
tion. Still, he was essentially indifferent to formal religion, and his
children, Selma and Philoine, received some Jewish education only because Bessie felt it was important.[62]

Yiddishkeit lived on in Hillman, partly as nostalgia for Old World
jokes, Yiddish melodies, and the games he still enjoyed playing with his
close friends; partly through living ties to the family in Russia; partly in
the irrepressible, primordial music of his body so that in the midst of a
fervent exposition his body "takes on the slight rhythmic rocking of the
Talmudic student"; and partly as haunting memory, so that on one
occasion he noted that his experience at the yeshiva of Slobodka was
"good background for public work." But the sequestering of his cultural
heritage in the interstices of his private life and in the silent catacombs
of memory was an expression of a larger, historic project: the transcendence if not the suppression of those provincial cultures that only inter-
fered with the theory and practice of modern collective bargaining.[63]

The psychological strain was palpable and took a toll on Hillman's
emotional and physical health. A workaholic, "bottled up," driven from
project to project, never satisfied, he was chronically subject to real and
imagined illnesses that, however painful, also offered psychic respite.
Repeatedly, when under great stress, he would break down physically.
Before every convention, and especially before his own major addresses,
his ankles would hurt so badly he could barely walk. He was chronically
subject to painful sinus attacks and to bouts of nervous and physical
exhaustion, forcing him into periodic recuperative leaves of absence. He
underwent two minor operations in 1923, and late in 1924 he was forced
to undergo major stomach surgery (an operation that followed by a few
months an equally serious illness and operation on his daughter
Philoine). In the midst of a four-month campaign finally to organize the
Philadelphia market in 1929, he entered the hospital, again for minor

surgery, awoke from the ether at 2:00 P.M., and by four o'clock was holding a meeting of the strike executive in his hospital room. As he grew a bit older his heart became the chief victim of demands that originated deep within him as much as they did from his public functions.[64]

Neat, trim, quiet, consummately self-possessed, reserved, and taut with concentrated energy, Hillman presided over a smoothly running machine. Indeed, one reporter thought his "solidly molded head and body" suggested a "smoothly geared physical mechanism" and thought he detected a visible "correspondence of physique with character," a body well-suited to "an engineer in labor dynamics." Like many a manager, he was less and less inclined to brook interference, especially "revolutionary" distractions. With tart realism he browbeat those for whom every discussion of hours, wages, and conditions had to be conducted from the standpoint of The Revolution. Nonetheless, he never became, nor wished to become, the sort of absolute autocrat that John L. Lewis most certainly was in the UMW. Especially during the height of the factional wars, as well as during the period of reorganization that followed them, he was occasionally opposed by members of the GEB and forced to retreat or compromise.[65]

Hillman never felt entirely comfortable with the English language. He remained throughout his life acutely self-conscious about his thick Yiddish accent and lack of formal schooling and reacted with bitter sarcasm to any implied personal slur or belittlement. He found writing in English an arduous task. He was also temperamentally averse to philosophizing, wary of the danger of preconceived notions, of hackneyed attitudes and petrified programs. He was committed only to the reality of "facts and forces." Yet in 1928 he published an extended essay, to whose composition he devoted many tortuous hours, enlisting the labors of Leo Wolman and Horace Kallen. "Labor's Attitudes" came very close to presenting the Hillman credo.

"Only actualities should be taken into account," he began. People had to free themselves from a slavish loyalty to words, sympathies, and creeds, which "really have no fixed meaning." Scornfully he referred to a labor union so radical "it recognizes no god or master nor common sense, either," and consequently "wields no power in its industry. This very advanced union matters to no one." He contrasted such exercises in verbal pyrotechnics to the sober progress of real, steady accomplishment. "It is not the program or belief one adheres to, but the line of action one follows that matters."

Power was the lodestar, the basso continuo of his thinking and behavior. To be of "practical value" assets of the labor movement "must

be stated in terms of power." "Policies and strategies are only applications of the major concern . . . the exercise of power." Industrial organization was imperative, for "without organization there is no power.
And power is the foundation of effective policy and distant goals." Those
who approached the labor movement with plans for cultural enlightenment and "recipes for rapid salvation" overlooked workers' primary need
for "power to establish themselves as a full-fledged part of organized
society," a task achievable only when trade unionism embraced all
branches of labor, "penetrating all of national industry and business."

Perceptively, he observed that while European labor radicalism "has
been mostly political or sentimental," American workers were more
likely to find "economic radicalism" appealing, even if it lacked "impressive high-sounding formulae." Never one to run from the accusations
of his opponents, Hillman noted, "There has been a lot of loose talk in
some quarters about class collaboration, a term which really means everything and nothing." He shrewdly pointed out that many an otherwise
stolidly conservative trade union had too strictly adhered to "this scare-
crow of lip-radicalism" and had perished as a result. Victory or defeat in
a strike "in themselves don't settle anything," if the cost of the triumphant strike was the bankruptcy of a firm or industry. The only settlement truly accountable as a victory was one that "increases or enlarges
the power of the workers' organization," and such a result sometimes
depended on carefully avoiding the abuse of power by pushing an advantage past the point of mutual interest.

In a blunt expression of the pragmatist's creedless credo, Hillman
wrote that while the objectives of labor education were unobjectionable,
no "program of stereotyped education . . . will teach anybody anything
worth learning." A formalized program of any kind was "really superfluous. Labor itself is such a program. One of achievement and advancement toward a life rich in scope and more vital in outlook than the one
we have thus far been living."[66]

Among his closest comrades—Sam Levin, Hyman Blumberg, Jacob
Potofsky—Hillman was fond of repeating the following maxim: "If I need
the bar that is rusted I'll use it." It not only expressed Hillman's steely
determination, a certain amorality of means, but also implied a selfless-
ness of purpose and moral ambitiousness. Lenin might easily have subscribed both to its studied tough-mindedness and to its less conspicuous
idealism.[67]

After his second trip to the Soviet Union, Hillman was interviewed
by the *Baltimore Evening Sun.* He took the occasion to praise Trotsky and
Lenin as "practical idealists," specifically Trotsky as the admirably "ruthless organizer" and Lenin as a great statesman. In contrast he depicted

the Wobbly exile Big Bill Haywood as a "pathetic figure" who had failed, because of his lack of technical training, at his job of administering an industrial colony in Siberia and was therefore without influence in the Soviet Union, where there was no longer a real place for the mere "propagandist." Shortly after Lenin's death, Hillman eulogized the Bolshevik leader as "one of the outstanding personalities of the century and the greatest statesman that ever arose from the ranks of labor." He showed deep empathy for those qualities of Bolshevik character and behavior which he recognized and cultivated in himself.[68]

Self-effacing almost to a fault—at least in this period prior to his elevation to a position of national prominence—he was nonetheless a powerful speaker. Like Lenin, he was impassioned rather than eloquent, with few rhetorical flourishes, always concrete, even blunt. Even the utterly unpretentious, workmanlike way with which he conducted the affairs of the union was reminiscent of the conspicuous austerity with which Lenin conducted the Revolution. A journalist interrupting him in the middle of a typically crowded day remarked: "There were no papers on his table, no parade of importance of any kind; he has no 'manner.' " The fit between man and organization was seamless. Even as he became a staple object of media attention, he was the despair of reporters trying to penetrate his reserve. About his "hobbies," his private life, his thoughts on that faintly absurd pastiche of popular topics, ranging from immortality to the latest fads and fashions, which journalists seemed to assume notables were obliged to comment on, Hillman kept his silence.[69]

In fact, on first acquaintance Hillman was distinctly stand-offish, an armoring more than surface deep, which left him with few really close friends. That practically palpable sense of distance expressed as well an innate and jealously guarded dignity. Hillman was rarely if ever vulgar in word or behavior, even when under great stress, so acute was his sense of propriety. Even when he gave vent to some impatience or exasperation with Bessie, the children, or his intimate friends, he managed to maintain a dignified mien, the emblem of his complete self-mastery.

He was a conventional doting and indulgent father, and capable of great sentimentality about his friends, but his private and family life occupied a secondary place in his life. His first daughter, Philoine, was born while he was out of town, and he was frequently away all through her childhood, as well as that of Selma, her sister. He had no hobbies and allowed no outside or family interests to interfere with his public function. Hillman's personal circumstances were a study in modesty: an unpretentious apartment in a pleasant but equally unpretentious lower-middle-class neighborhood in upper Manhattan; later a smallish wooden summer bungalow in a Long Island seaside town lacking in notoriety or high society; a taste for food no more "refined" than the fare he'd grown up on in Lithuania; never the owner of as basic an element of American consumer citizenship as the automobile. Off duty, however, when he shed his armored intensity and reserve, he could be warm and relaxed—listening to music, reading (mainly biography and history), dancing with pleasure at ACW affairs, and joining in group folk-singing with friends. [70]

Two decades in the New World by no means effaced Sidney's past, most particularly his ties to the ancestral home. He used the occasion of his trips abroad to meet with political figures—the leaders of the Polish labor movement and Labor Party in 1925, for example—but also to visit the family. In part he assumed the role of paterfamilias. When able, he sent money to a bank in Kaunas, Lithuania, to the account of his old mentor, Dr. Mathis, money to help with his parents' support. Hillman donated half of the $1,000 Harmon Foundation prize money to his old school in Kovno (and the other half to the library of the Amalgamated cooperative apartments). At the request of his brother Motke, he wrote to Armand Hammer, head of the American Industrial Concession in Moscow where his brother was employed as a bookkeeper, to plead his case for permanent employment, since Motke's efforts to immigrate to the United States were blocked by the new immigration law. He tried to use what influence he had to expedite the immigration of family friends as well, but failed thanks to his radical reputation among State Department functionaries. [71]

Ancestral sentiments and familial pleasures scarcely left a trace, however, on the public persona. The compactness of style and the canalized energy were the expressions of a politics of anxiety and order about which Hillman was at times quite explicit: "In Russia I discovered how universal is the fear of chaos. Only a few can nourish their lives on promises alone of things to come. Most of us need to make a living now, mate now, enjoy now a reasonable degree of social stability." The specter of chaos, even the pregnant chaos of revolution, needed to be exorcized with a Leninist discipline, more rational than coercive, that in principle was applicable anywhere—a rational discipline, like bureaucracy, was, as Weber noted, impersonal and "places itself at the disposal of every power that claims its service and knows how to promote it." [72]

As was the case for Lenin and the Bolsheviks, for Hillman the organizational imperative replaced Kant's, its clamorous drumbeat drowning out the more soulful commandments of yeshiva and *Kolkhoz*. Consequently, he became less and less patient with the "inefficiencies" of others as his character took on some of the hardness prized in every bureaucratic machine. A critical observer noted his "decisiveness, cool will power, and an immense self-confidence," but also the ease with which he used and just as easily disposed of people. Indeed, a close associate confessed he "could be ruthless to the point of cruelty" toward his own most intimate colleagues if he felt them to be obstacles in the way of some higher organizational purpose. All the jousting among the comrades for personal favor and position had made him wary of the motives and integrity of others. Under stress he was apt to become unreasonably suspicious, but when convinced of another's organizational fealty he became inordinately credulous.[73]

Hillman's credo of the rusty bar was not that of a cynic, but of a man who, as the British journalist Mary Agnes Hamilton noted after a long interview in 1927, was "no visionary; but he has a vision." It was a vision grounded in the tangible accomplishments of the previous decade. Hill-man contrasted the garment worker of 1914, "a little feared, hardly understood, and never respected, without power to defend his rights and responsibility for whatever rights he had acquired, a worker without a voice in the management of industry, capable of guerrilla warfare, and helpless to make anything of incidentally wrested victory, a worker and nothing else," with his social stature a decade later as "a citizen of industry, respected, self-possessing, responsible to himself and the indus-try, a citizen with a clear view of possibilities and limitations."

Fused to this image of working-class sobriety, responsibility, and self-possession was a still compelling one of man as *homo faber,* of a world where work "is not something one has to undergo as punishment, but something to be proud of. . . . Labor's mission in life is to build." So, if Hillman embodied a new managerial type, one suited to the visionless interior of the modern bureaucratic organization, he was still an early prototype, one whose roughly irregular exterior in language and appear-ance was a window into the moral intensity of his psyche and soul. Hamilton was impressed:

> Determination is there, sympathy also; not a beautiful face, but a highly significant one. The wide-apart eyes hold you; the voice, soft and resonant, and still oddly foreign, holds you; what he says holds you, even more firmly.[74]

The *Chicago Daily News,* in a preelection editorial, called for Hoover's victory in 1928, noting that the Commerce Secretary, like Sidney Hillman, was working creatively to promote industrial harmony and to transcend the class struggle.[75] It was a Fabian moment in Amer-ican history, so evanescent and even fanciful as to be scarcely noticed or remembered. After all, by that time Hoover was so openly identified with the business community that most Progressives supported Alfred E.

Smith. Yet there they stood, in the mind's eye at least, two Fabians, one a renowned capitalist, the other a celebrated trade union socialist, about to transform the angular fractiousness of modern society into its organically harmonious opposite. If Fabianism was perhaps more elitist, more bureaucratic-centralist, more drily academic, and decidedly more mistrustful of spontaneous class struggle than Hillman had yet become, its worship of efficiency and its "experts," its pluralism, and its tempered sense of gradual change were already unmistakably a part of him.

How utterly different the world in 1928 seemed as compared to 1919, less portentous, lacking in apocalyptic electricity perhaps, but also less fraught with anxiety. The catastrophic events of the next few years would make this Fabian reverie of industrial fraternity, this dream of wholeness, seem to have been just that, a dream, or rather a mere optical illusion. Inevitably, both Hoover and Hillman would be drawn irresistibly away from whatever Fabian utopias they might have momentarily entertained.

NINE

"A Great Deal of Disaster"

Neither the fancies of Fabianism nor the shibboleths of laissez-faire survived the Great Depression. At first the union managed a brave face. Delegates to the Toronto convention in the spring of 1930 were presented a rather sanguine assessment, given the circumstances, of the state of the organization. While acknowledging the alarming rise in unemployment, the GEB was reassuring about the solvency of its banks, housing cooperatives, and unemployment insurance. It recounted the union's role in saving financially threatened firms and boasted of its new departures in health and dental clinics, libraries, recreation facilities, and the newly erected cooperative apartment complex on the Lower East Side of Manhattan, which included a grocery, milk distributor, laundry, and preschool center. All in all it came as close to a picture of self-sufficiency in the teeth of disaster as anyone could reasonably expect.[1]

What lent all this brave talk some credibility was the ACW's exhilarating victory in Philadelphia during the previous summer and fall. Philadelphia was the last of the eight major markets to remain adamantly open shop, earning its reputation as the "Siberia of the clothing industry." The city was a haven for both subcontractors and runaway shops from New York. An extensive subcontracting system was run by Italian padrones, who were bitterly antiunion. For years they functioned to subvert strikes and organizing efforts in other cities. Progress, Hillman perceived, depended first of all on breaking up the padrone system. Philadelphia was a piece of vital unfinished business.

The campaign was mounted with military meticulousness in the summer of 1929. Hillman took up semipermanent residence in the city. Top organizers from around the country were imported for the duration. Major retailers were approached, successfully in most cases, to use their influence on behalf of the union. Albert Greenfield, one of the country's largest urban real estate developers and the owner of a chain of retail stores in the South and Southwest, brought pressure to bear on the Philadelphia manufacturers to come to terms with the union.

Weeks of silent, secret shop organization were followed by sudden, selective strikes, directed first at the more vulnerable contractors, then, as the movement crested, against the city's major manufacturers, especially Kirschbaum & Company. Gimbel Brothers and a major Rochester retailer, Fashion Park, exerted pressure on a key Philadelphia supplier to withdraw its request for an injunction against the Amalgamated. Morris L. Rothschild, an important Chicago retailer, actually visited Philadelphia to persuade the head of the Middishade Company to settle with the union. Middishade had previously compelled its employees to sign a yellow-dog contract that Senator Robert La Follette, Jr., characterized as the "yellowest of any that I have ever had called to my attention." The industry was squeezed from above and below. When eight manufacturers obtained a sweeping injunction prohibiting mass picketing, it was greeted by a storm of adverse public opinion. La Follette demanded on the floor of the Senate that the Judiciary Committee investigate the whole subject of labor injunctions and their misuse. U.S. District Judge William H. Kirkpatrick felt compelled to modify the injunction. All in all, it was an unqualified victory about which the Toronto convention delegates were rightly proud. The union, after all, had secured signed agreements with 300 out of 324 firms and had enrolled more than ten thousand members.[2]

Yet the tone of the 1930 convention betrayed a more somber mood, one closer in spirit to the grim economic news. Bold visions of industrial democracy gave way to a new emphasis on security and material well-being. Joseph Schlossberg, for whom the rhetoric of revolution never seemed to grow old, nonetheless suggested a much more modest agenda: collective bargaining rights; a reduction in hours as a hedge against technological and cyclical unemployment; and unemployment insurance. Jacob Panken, whose socialist eloquence had aroused many a union convention, was reduced to civic-minded banalities, remarking that what distinguished the ACW was its "proper moral concept of honesty, decency, and responsibility." J. B. S. Hardman, who would continue his espousal of independent labor politics, was nevertheless more hard-boiled in facing the new age when "many ideals of a former day appear to be devoid of meaning." Lamenting that fact, he pleaded for a resurrection of the power of ideas and ideals.

There was no escaping the fact that the onset of the Depression short-circuited even the most practical-minded undertakings. Plans to use the momentum of Philadelphia to invade other open-shop centers in Cleveland, St. Louis, and Buffalo had to be abandoned.[3]

The crisis for the ACW was acute. Although wages remained steady through 1930, bankruptcies and unemployment spread at alarming rates. By 1931, 60 percent of those working at all were irregularly employed, and 50 percent of the industry's normal workforce were completely without work. Wages had fallen by 40 to 50 percent. The unemployment situation continued to worsen, and by early 1932 Hillman was describing before a Senate subcommittee a "condition of utmost despair" in which less than 10 percent of New York's workforce was at work at the start of the season and perhaps 50 percent by the height of the season. For those fortunate enough to be employed, weekly hours of work declined steadily from 40.6 at the height of the season in 1928 to 37.3 in 1932, while 26 percent worked less than thirty-two hours.[4]

The industry was functioning at 30 percent of capacity, and in 1932 alone nearly one thousand firms went bankrupt. ACW membership dropped by 50,000 from the level reached in 1929, keeping pace with a decline in the number of workers in the industry from 149,868 in 1929 to 109,000 in 1933. The unemployment reserves previously established in the New York, Chicago, and Rochester markets proved inadequate to meet the national catastrophe. The original unemployment reserves were never designed to cover workers entirely out of work and no longer on the employment rolls of any particular shop. In New York the fund was so recently established that its reserves from the outset were completely insufficient. Special relief funds provided by a progressive tax on the earnings of employed workers barely helped meet the emergency. Many of the union's foreign-language papers suspended publication, and the organization was so strapped for funds that it canceled its biennial convention in 1932.[5]

All the worst abuses associated with the preunion era reappeared, including the fratricidal competition, the spread of sweatshop labor, subcontracting, and the proliferation of runaway shops to the small towns surrounding the major urban centers of clothing production. Homework revived also: By 1933 seven thousand mainly women workers were employed working up goods in tenement houses in New York, Philadelphia, and Rochester. In New York, Progressive era legislation governing homework, as well as child and female labor, became practically unenforceable. The same situation prevailed in Baltimore, where an investigation revealed that 23 percent of the industry's female labor force was under twenty years old and working illegally long hours under unlawful conditions. The union conducted rearguard defensive campaigns, as in New York in 1932, just to maintain minimal levels of union organization and labor standards and to quarantine the open-shop contagion before it became epidemic. Plans to recover lost ground, much less to expand the union's organizational reach, had to await a change in the political climate and balance of power.[6]

In the interim Hillman called upon major retailers and leading manufacturers to help stop the spread of sweatshop labor and cutthroat competition by boycotting goods produced under substandard conditions. He conferred regularly with Louis Kirstein of Filene's, Lessing Rosenwald of Sears, and representatives of Montgomery Ward about establishing minimum standards for the industry and a board to supervise their enforcement. This "board of standards" would oversee not only wages but hours, sanitary conditions, and the observance of formal grievance procedures. General Wood of Sears reacted well to the idea and agreed to help persuade Montgomery Ward and J. C. Penney to follow suit. Kirstein was of course also quite cooperative, agreeing to eliminate all buying from firms appearing on the ACW's unfair list. In return Hillman promised a concerted union effort to standardize and equalize costs between competing markets. For their part, most major manufacturers favored a uniform minimum wage and shorter hours to stabilize the industry.[7]

Even in unionized markets the leadership was forced to accede, reluctantly and only after heated internal debate, to an average wage cut of 30 percent between 1931 and 1933, often under the very real threat that the affected firms would otherwise close. By mid-1931, the industry was alive with rumors that even the flagship firm of Hart, Schaffner & Marx was threatening liquidation unless the ACW agreed to a drastic wage reduction. Hillman convened an emergency meeting of forty union leaders in Chicago to impress them with the "need to do something for Hart Schaffner and Marx." It was no easy task, and he wanted assurances first from the firm's board of directors that if he succeeded the board wouldn't come around again in a short while demanding more concessions. He told Rosenthal, the company president, that two of the directors were still talking about liquidation, and he wanted it stopped. Rosenthal assured him that the stockholders were opposed to liquidation. This bankruptcy talk was probably deliberately exaggerated. By late 1932 Henry Goldman of Goldman Sachs was reassuring the board that the Depression had bottomed out, citing reports from the Commercial Investment Trust and various other sources.[8] Still financial straits were severe, not only for HSM but for two other leading Chicago firms,

Kuppenheimer and Alfred Decker & Cohen. Hillman seriously questioned whether any of them could survive. All were forced to reduce factory overhead because of the drastic decline in sales volume and were in addition compelled to shut down retail outlets. HSM directors conferred with the union about the closing of at least one large plant and the reduction of supervisory costs.[9]

The failure of the Bank of the United States in New York at the end of 1930 was a mortal blow to the industry, as one of the bank's directors was also a principal manufacturer and the bank itself had been a primary source of credit, especially for the New York market. New York sales volume declined to 57 percent of its 1929 level, and the number of businesses dropped by 40 percent. Similar or even worse declines occurred in Chicago, Philadelphia, Boston, Baltimore, and Rochester. Sonneborn's in Baltimore, a great friend of the union since 1914, struggled desperately to survive. The firm had borrowed $125,000 from the union in 1927 while simultaneously raising capital by selling stock to its employees. The rescue had been only temporary. At the beginning of 1930 the Amalgamated Bank in New York loaned Sonneborn's $50,000 in emergency funds, but by July 1931 the company was bankrupt, and the union was making frantic efforts, ultimately unsuccessful, to persuade other manufacturers to take it over.[10]

In the midst of all this "chaos," this "condition of utmost despair," Hillman was forced to confront another disaster, a moral one closely related to the economic one and bearing the same mortal consequences for the Amalgamated's integrity.

Jewish gangsterism was as much an outgrowth of the local ethnic social economy as was the garment industry itself. Indeed, what was distinctive about Jewish criminals was their connection, as parasitic racketeers, to the petty business worlds of their ethnic brethren. The "racketeer," however, was more than an ethnic hoodlum exacting tribute on penalty of violence. After all, by such strictly utilitarian calculation it might have been wiser to prey on wealthy individuals than struggling businesses. Moreover, the extortion was often camouflaged as a charitable contribution, an entirely unnecessary ruse. The racketeer called on resources other than violence, and his relationship to the world of Jewish business was not merely a matter of unilateral coerced contract. Rather, he exploited vulnerabilities already built into the social organization of small business and provided very specific services.

Owners were protected against the entrance of new competitors. The more established and successful they were, the easier it was to afford criminal tribute. The criminal demand for "key money" thus functioned as a kind of licensing system. Racketeers also lubricated the gears of municipal–commercial politics. Political machines used clubs of young men to "get out the vote," now and then through open or covert intimidation, and in return local officials turned a blind eye to violations of municipal regulations by small businesses in which these young toughs had an interest. Racketeers were also bankers. Ethnic petty entrepreneurs often depended on intragroup mechanisms for raising capital, often through kin, regional, and religion-based credit associations. Loan sharking had essentially similar origins. Loans to landsmen were subject to the informal but firm exercise of patriarchal authority and were considered profoundly moral and social as well as commercial transactions. More or less naturally, the enforcement of these relations devolved onto groups of enforcer specialists, or *shtarkers*. Industrial labor relations was another specialty. The market for "labor muscle" in New York between 1930 and 1950 covered at least all the following economies where systematic extortion was common: "bread, cinder, cloth shrinking, clothing, construction, flower shops, the Fulton Street fish market, funeral parlors, fur dressing, grapes, hod carriers, kosher butchers, laundries, leather, live poultry, master barbers, milk, millinery, musical instruments, night patrol, neckwear, newsstands, operating engineers, overalls, paper boxes, paper hangers, shirt makers, taxi cabs, and window cleaners." "Labor muscle" was useful in any number of ways: to "break heads" of strikers; to protect scabs; to intimidate competing unions; as liaison to corruptible government officials; and to enforce secondary boycotts. Finally, racketeers regulated the mass market, especially through their control over warehousing and delivery services, above all trucking. Before World War I, for example, many tiny ethnic businesses depended on an easily sabotaged form of delivery. A dozen Jews directed by "Yushke Nigger," known as the "Yiddish Black Hand," began poisoning horses so that by 1910 ice cream manufacturers were losing anywhere from one to five horses each and were more than ready to pay $1,000 for two years' worth of healthy horses.[11]

In all those ways, racketeering had for years flourished throughout the needle trades. Its extortions at first were petty, preying on defenseless, tiny shops and stores, tithing these marginal enterprises in return for a modicum of commercial and labor peace. Into the impersonal chaos of an intensely competitive marketplace they introduced an element of law and order, a perverse kind of "moral economy" constraining employer and employee alike. Their services were available to the highest bidder— sometimes to trade unions seeking to intimidate antiunion employers or to terrorize internal oppositionists, or simply as the enforcers of sweetheart or kickback arrangements between union leaders and their ostensible collective bargaining adversaries. Tactics varied and ranged from arson to tampering with elevator shafts, destroying clothing stock with acid, forcing trucks off the road, beatings, and murder. Jewish gangsters were equally prepared to serve as strikebreakers or strike enforcers.

In those early years especially the degree to which Jewish thugs remained tied to the cultural and even religious customs of their ethnic brethren was remarkable. After the 1910 cloakmakers' strike, the "Dopey Benny" gang became an integral part of the Jewish labor movement, freelancing, if not on the actual payroll of the UHT and the ILG, as strike enforcers against rival thugs hired by management. "Dopey Benny," or Benjamin Fein, refused to work for the bosses, because "my heart lay with the workers."

There were others with similar attachments. The left-wing union militant Samuel Liptzin remembered fondly the gangster who took $500 to beat him up but lost heart because he considered Liptzin a "foolish idealist" whose ideals he respected. Together they fixed Liptzin up with a fake bandage around his head, and no one was the wiser. Arnold Rothstein seemed different. He was considered the J. P. Morgan of the underworld because of his Brahmin manners, his very modern fascination with administrative expertise and bureaucratic organization, and his role as financier for diverse criminal businesses. Even this most "American" of gangsters suffered his own moments of filiopietistic and ethnic longing. His Orthodox father, Abraham, was a wealthy dress manufacturer and a respected member of the Jewish philanthropic-religious community. Estrangement between father and son was more or less total. But in an effort to repair some of the damage, Arnold offered, during the wild garment wars of the twenties, to make his unique mediating services available. Abraham rejected the favor but later arranged for his outcast son to receive a fully traditional religious burial.[12]

Rothstein was for a time the garment underworld's preeminent overlord. In the course of a great life-and-death strike by the ILG in 1926, which at the same time pitted the CP left against the SP right wing of the union, the communist strike leadership hired "Little Augie" Orgen, while the manufacturers turned for help to "Legs" Diamond. Both sides appealed to Rothstein to mediate, and Charles Zimmerman of the ILG actually met with him to discuss the terms of a settlement. Whatever Abraham might have thought about his son's involvement, Rothstein no doubt sensed a chance to enhance his own position. He called off "Legs" Diamond and helped impose a peace accord on management, which temporarily at least left him master of the industry.[13]

The situation in the men's clothing industry never became that desperate. The ACW was a stronger institution. The level of internal factional discord and organized violence never approached that of the ILG. Its position vis-à-vis the industry, in part because its internal life was more stable, was also more secure and commanding. Furthermore, men's clothing manufacture was a less fragmented, decentralized business, even in New York, allowing for a greater degree of administrative surveillance and control by the union, by manufacturers associations, and by the apparatus of grievance mediation and arbitration. Nonetheless, this was still the "rag trade," a world of sharp dealing and ingenious chiseling, always precarious, merciless to those not prepared to engage in a kind of tooth-and-claw struggle for survival. And no market was more savagely competitive than New York.

As the great lockout of 1920 demonstrated, New York was a hotbed of antiunion sentiment. Manufacturers hired underworld mercenaries to terrorize the Amalgamated—and at some point in the mid-twenties elements within the union deployed the same resource in the person of one Louis "Lepke" Buchalter, who would go on to found the infamous "Murder, Incorporated." Lepke was one of Rothstein's subalterns, running a small gang of his own under "Little Augie." Initially, Lepke broke strikes. Soon he was making his services available to either side. Gradually he encroached on Amalgamated territory, working less and less with Rothstein and "Little Augie," and in some instances ended up defending rather than assaulting strikers. Relations with "Little Augie" naturally deteriorated, and apparently Lepke had him killed. Once ensconced, Buchalter proved far less easy to "fire."[14]

Hillman claimed to be unaware of this criminal infiltration before the Depression. It's a hard claim to credit, given his keen intelligence and his almost compulsive monitoring of all union affairs. Graft and corruption among union officials were diseases endemic to the industry. The tales are endless: of manufacturers bribing union officials to take up cut-work from New York to Passaic, where they held auctions among nonunion contractors bidding for the work; of the leaders of a pressers local who made much militant noise about the introduction of a new pressing machine while at the same time the business agent of the local became a salesman for the pressing machine company while his union conferees coerced payments from small contractors who wanted to buy the machines and eliminate workers; of business agents, joint board managers, and clerks who became partners in union related businesses like trimming supplies, sewing machines, pressing equipment, sponging material, insurance, and printing and used them as sources of graft; of the not rare business agent who swore never to take a bribe but left the manufacturer's office at the end of the day with a packet of bills sewn into the lining of his coat; or of the manager of a knee pants local who would get unused

Yiddish theater tickets and sell them to manufacturers for $100 apiece.

Even someone far less knowing than Hillman could not have been blind to such an omnipresent if often petty chicanery. Moreover, much earlier than the Depression he had displayed his concern with the problem insofar as it afforded a point of entry for more organized crime. The case of the Children's Clothing Joint Board of New York was notorious. Harry Cohen, the head of the Joint Board, was long and widely considered a grafter. At a GEB meeting in 1922 Hillman blamed his rise, as well as the growing immunity of the Joint Board itself from centralized union discipline, on the support of the *Forward* group. Cohen himself was an SP loyalist. Implicated as well was the secretary of the Joint Board, Max Gimber, who was charged in 1923 with financial malfeasance and fraternizing with criminal elements. An investigation failed to turn up sufficient evidence, however, and Gimber and Cohen were temporarily exonerated at a union trial. At the time, Hillman acknowledged that graft was widespread throughout the New York organization; in fact in 1928 he estimated that 80 percent of the New York union was infected to one degree or another.

Rumors even circulated that in certain instances Lepke, and his crony Jake "Gurrah" Shapiro usurped the functions of the impartial arbiter, settling disputes between union and manufacturer for a fee.[15]

While not every case of corruption turned up the same strange political-criminal connection as the Cohen case, it is true that the most conspicuous and important cases, especially the one that exploded into headlines in 1931, did. The *Forward* group, contending for control of the ILG against the CP, had already grown accustomed to fighting with brass knuckles. Its criminal partners more or less naturally drifted into the ACW. So long as the *Forward* constituted Hillman's main factional opposition, the union president was prepared to expose its nefarious friends, as he tried to do with Cohen and Gimber. But after 1924, with the shift in factional alignments, Hillman turned a blind eye to those same criminal associations, as SP apparatchiks proved to be enthusiastic red-hunters, not at all squeamish about using the roughest tactics for dealing with Hillman's new opponents on the left.

More than anyone else, the right-wing socialist and *Forward* loyalist Abraham Beckerman emerged as the union's enforcer against the remains of the CP and the TUEL. With Hillman's approval he quickly became a power in the New York union and was even elevated to the GEB, where his open advocacy of strongarm methods sometimes embarrassed others in the leadership. Even more embarrassing, however, was Beckerman's evident toleration of and even connivance with the Lepke gang, which, amid all the internal turmoil, began its penetration of the strategically important cutters' local 4. It is nearly impossible to believe Hillman was in the dark about this. J. B. S. Hardman threatened to resign in 1925 because nothing was being done to stop Lepke. Hillman persuaded him to remain, arguing that the situation, for the time being at least, was hopeless. Although he genuinely wanted to rid the market of gangsters, Hillman told Hardman, employers were too intimidated to testify in court. Others complained as well. Augusto Bellanca opposed Beckerman's initial appointment as head of the New York Joint Board, in part because of his unsavory associations. Anthony Capraro, who admittedly had become too closely associated with the Italian left to suit Hillman, warned the union president about the growing power of rack-eteers. In a 1926 letter he referred specifically to one of the leaders of the New York cutters' local, Philip Orlofsky, who, like Beckerman, was an SP functionary. Capraro asserted that the organization "is slowly but surely passing into the hands of gangsters or gangster-minded executive officers." Later, in 1929, an "Amalgamated Pressers Club," a residue of the TUEL, brought its own charges of union–gangster thuggery to the ACLU and to New York Police Commissioner Grover Whalen. The "Club" issued a leaflet calling Beckerman "a 5 and 10 cents Mussolini," the "prince of thugs," a leader of "Frenchies" and "Little Augies." By 1930 even a loyal union comrade like Hyman Isovitz was angrily com-plaining to Hillman that the New York organization was spiritually dead, crushed by Beckerman, who smothered all dissent while allowing the union's position in the market to disintegrate. But Hillman dismissed all the various suspicions and accusations, reluctant to bring the New York organization—especially the Children's Joint Board and Cutters Local 4—forcibly under the control of the national organization for fear of alienating his socialist allies on the right. Even Harry Cohen, whose corruption was practically a public spectacle, managed to hang on until 1930.[16]

The Depression forced Hillman's hand. Cutters, skilled and better paid, had always maintained a certain distance from the rest of the organization. If not exactly worker-aristocrats, they were nonetheless conscious of their strategic position in the industry—controlling the flow of work to a mass of contractors and subcontractors—and their relative scarcity on the labor market. During the union's formative years, Jewish cutters especially, many of them committed socialists, deployed their power boldly, often risking their own personal and organizational secu-rity on behalf of their more vulnerable, dispensable co-workers. Under the straitened circumstances of the twenties, however, what had once been proud militance and social leadership became a concern with parochial privilege.

Under the rule of Beckerman and Orlofsky, cutters' local 4 became a practically autonomous organization. That freedom allowed the leaders to make deals with manufacturers to establish out-of-town nonunion shops, a process abetted by trucking concerns under the control of Lepke. If cutting rooms represented one point of strategic control over the industry, trucks were the other. Lepke infiltrated both. He organized truckowners and self-employed drivers into a cartel-style association designed to raise cartage costs and share out the profits. At the same time his people penetrated the Amalgamated's own expressman's local. His ambition grew, and he began buying into manufacturing firms—Raleigh Manufacturing, Pioneer Coat Front, Greenberg & Shapiro—through which it was easier to manipulate the employers' protective association. Recalcitrant manufacturers as well as rank-and-file cutters were terrorized into going along, although it was later charged that in the case of the cutters it was more a matter of trading the union's set of enforcers—Terry Burns and Abe Slabow—for a pair of Lepke's own men. As the Depression deepened and the union engaged in a struggle just to survive in New York, the situation became intolerable. The cutters' local, to protect its sweetheart arrangements with manufacturers, actually went so far as to scab on striking tailors.[17]

Finally Hillman acted. Convinced that it was no longer possible to treat the problem as a private matter, to be resolved within the union family, he publicly declared: "We might as well be frank here and say out in the open what we have been saying to each other in private. What the New York market is suffering from more than anything else is the racketeering evil." It was a declaration of war, and Hillman followed through by ordering a strike against a gangster-controlled firm. The other side responded as it best knew how: by shooting and seriously wounding Tony Froise, an organizer for the New York Joint Board, on his way to a strike site in Brooklyn. Hillman raised the stakes in turn. In June 1931 he convened a conference that included, together with the New York Joint Board and the New York Clothing Manufacturers Exchange, Police Commissioner Edward Mulrooney and Mayor Jimmy Walker. Its purpose, Hillman announced, was to destroy the "organized blackmail system." The Amalgamated was "definitely determined come what may that we are not going to recognize the racketeers as the government in the City."[18]

His timing couldn't have been better. The investigations of city corruption by the special investigator Samuel Seabury were already deeply damaging the credibility of Mayor Walker's regime. Of the thirty industries listed by Seabury as infested with racketeers, as many as nine were in one way or another associated with the garment center. By 1930 racketeering was widely recognized as a noisome social and criminal justice problem in New York. The *New York Times* ran prominent stories on extortion schemes in many of the city's businesses—laundry, construction, milk, taxis, slot machines, baking. They were followed by Seabury's lurid revelations of rampant corruption in the criminal justice system itself. From there Seabury's investigations uncovered the power of "Little Augie's" gang in the millinery trade, where unionizing was throttled, and the influence of Joe Mezzacapo in the cloth-shrinking business, where a genuine union was destroyed and replaced by Mezzacapo's own. Seabury's were but the first of an ongoing series of exposés of corruption and gangsterism which fascinated Americans throughout the 1930s as they struck resonant chords in a Depression-era generation—the nefarious role of "big shots," "the money boys," and "the interests."[19]

For all those reasons Hillman could exert real pressure on Walker to act. He confronted the Mayor with the charge that the gangsters were so entrenched in part because they enjoyed political influence. Walker hotly denied it, but Seymour Dreschler, head of the Manufacturers' Exchange, seconded the accusation. Indeed, initially Philip Orlofsky seemed unmoved by Hillman's public offensive precisely because for a long time he had functioned as Tammany's man in local 4, which had campaigned actively for Walker. But times were rapidly changing. Hillman had his own Tammany connections and, more important, links to Lieutenant Governor Herbert Lehman as well.

Finally, Hillman managed to extract from Walker a promise of real help, not just a vague pledge of greater police protection for strikers. The Mayor agreed to take a role in a coup d'état plotted and staged by Hillman. After the conference with the Mayor, Hillman called a massive one-day stoppage and march to protest underworld domination of the industry. Three hundred union officials, manufacturers representatives, and dignitaries proceeded to the steps of City Hall to demand that Walker act. Walker assigned police from the Homicide Squad, instead of the thoroughly corrupted Industrial Squad, to protect the strikers. The mass rally and parade through the garment district and the subsequent picketing of all Lepke-affiliated manufacturers was an unprecedented and daring public act. Privately Hillman's plans were even more audacious. One Sunday night, surrounded by a cordon of city police, Hillman, together with selected members of the New York Joint Board, marched into local 4's headquarters, seized all its records, and deposed its legally elected leadership. At the same time Hillman filed formal charges against Orlofsky and others in the cutters' leadership. The GEB assembled in

emergency session and summoned the local's officials to explain certain
expenditures. They refused to appear before the union tribunal. The
investigation proceeded without them and quickly adjudged Orlofsky and
the secretary of the local, Sidney Machlin, guilty as charged, summarily
removing them from office. The GEB assumed control of the local. Jacob
Potofsky temporarily ran its affairs while convening a meeting of the
local's membership in Webster Hall, which enthusiastically sanctioned
the GEB's coup. Meanwhile Beckerman, who was after all a member of
the GEB, was interrogated by Hillman, in particular about a $5,000 loan
made by Howard Clothes to Beckerman's brother, who was a clothing
manufacturer. Beckerman denied everything but was forced to resign.[20]

The war was far from over. The ousted officers of local 4 applied for
an injunction. Judge Irwin Untermeyer denied the request, leading the
Beckerman group to form the International Clothing Workers Union.
No one took that seriously, not even Lepke, who resorted to less pacific
measures. In November Charles Weinstein, a veteran ACW organizer,
was shot in Philadelphia by a "crazed worker" who was then mysteriously
spirited out of the country. That same month the head of the small
Amalgamated organization in San Francisco, B. Reinisch, was killed by
someone described as a "frustrated Persian office-seeker." Garment manufacturing on the West Coast, at the time still a fledgling industry, was
widely understood to be under the control of organized crime, which in
part accounted for the disappointing performance of the ACW in both
San Francisco and Los Angeles. The shootings naturally alarmed Hillman. He spent several weeks hiding out, moving from "safe house" to
"safe house" under the protective care of his legal counsel, Maxwell
Brandwyn, and union bodyguards.[21]

But Hillman did more than hide. He counterattacked, first with a
flanking assault on the Newark union, long a sink of corruption. There
a coat manufacturer, Joseph Spiotta, was induced to testify that he had
paid off local Newark union officials in return for a cut in the rates. The
payments were made through a representative of the contractors' association, Jimmy Citrano. Spiotta's affidavit was followed by an open letter
from the executive board of local 24 accusing Citrano, along with Harry
Taylor, of graft, appended to which was a list of all those shops then
paying graft. Local officials had essentially converted the union into a
device for extorting money from contractors. Cooperative contractors,
for their part, were rewarded with lowered piece rates ruthlessly enforced
by those same ACW bureaucrats. Hillman used the information to clean
up Newark, in the course of which he admitted to Newark unionists that
he had been wrong to ignore earlier warnings of union corruption.[22]

Rooting out the grafters in Newark was inspirational to a union deeply demoralized by the Depression and the fear-induced selfishness it bred. But it was more a symbolic victory than anything else. The hemorrhaging in New York was still a mortal threat to the organization. Hillman thus next attempted to staunch the flow of blood, in the course of which his relations with Lepke became much murkier.

First, Murray Weinstein, another ACW pioneer, took over as manager of the reorganized cutters' local. The New York Joint Board meanwhile was placed under the capable direction of two other founding cadre members, Louis Hollander and Joseph Catalanotti. Structurally, New York was now a centralized, disciplined machine. In May 1932 Hillman ordered it into battle. The New York Joint Board called a general strike to stop the contracting out of work to out-of-town shops in Pennsylvania and New Jersey, Passaic especially. To stop the reverse flow of worked-up, bootleg goods back into the city, mass picketing on lower Fifth Avenue, during which some of the more courageous threw their bodies in front of oncoming trucks, proved highly effective. Meanwhile, small groups of organizers were assigned to follow the trucks back to their sources. In this way the vital trucking link was severed. The Amalgamated finished the job by creating its own Expressman's local, stopping for the moment at least the transportation of nonunion goods.

Attacking the trucking connection was serious business. While manufacturing facilities were not often owned by criminal groups, trucking concerns were. It was the method favored by Lepke and Gurrah for dictating terms to other equally fragmented businesses within the Jewish economy, like baking, fur-making, flour, and milk distribution. Control was exercised either through direct ownership or by running the local truckmen's union. For years both Amalgamated and ILG officials, not to mention manufacturers, rarely dared interfere with Lepke-operated trucks.[23]

Thus Hillman's surgical strike at the critical transportation link was bold. While it predictably provoked Lepke's counterviolence, it also arrested the disintegration of the New York organization. By mid-1932 the Amalgamated was able to launch a marketwide campaign against the avalanche of wage-cutting and the stampeding of onetime union firms to the open shop small towns of Pennsylvania, upstate New York, and New Jersey. The successful work stoppage in New York reestablished the Amalgamated's presence on the East Coast.

Yet there is also evidence that if a new peace settled over the industry in New York, it was not because Lepke and Guarrah had retreated from the field of battle. A business agent, Sam Katz, and an organizer, Bruno Belea, apparently resurrected the old arrangements. Together with two of Lepke's men, Danny Fields, a former amateur boxer, and Paul Berger, they became "expediters" between the union and the gang. Between 1932 and 1936 these men collected $280 a week in return for coercing manufacturers to resume their tribute to Lepke.

More significantly, there is also some fragmentary evidence that Hillman himself connived in these arrangements, reaching an understanding with Lepke and Gurrah that was a material factor in the union's successful 1932 campaign to restore its power in New York. Subsequent testimony, often by indicted or convicted gangsters and by Orlofsky himself, suggested that Lepke offered Orlofsky as a sacrificial pawn in return for a more permanent accord with Hillman and that Hillman may have paid anywhere from $25,000 to $50,000 as part of the new relationship. Through intermediaries, including Bruno Belea, Hillman let Lepke know he wanted a stoppage of trucks carrying cut-up goods to nonunion contractors in New Jersey. Lepke obliged by ordering local 240, the Clothing Drivers and Helpers Union of the ACW, to cease such deliveries. In effect, a labor statesman and a statesman of the underworld created a private, cartel-style arrangement.[24]

It is at this point that the nature and extent of the relationship, if any, becomes befogged by rumor, post facto journalistic sensationalism, and ulterior political motive. One story went like this: A Joseph Rosen, a trucking operator in New York, refused to abide by Lepke's ukases about transporting goods to nonunion contractors. Rosen then sought to expand his business into Pennsylvania, but Lepke refused him permission. Again Rosen defied the racketeer, and in retribution his goods were damaged and manufacturers were pressured into refusing him business. Finally, in 1932, at the height of the Amalgamated's campaign, Rosen was forced to liquidate, turning over the business to Cooper Brothers, a Lepke-controlled concern. At that point Rosen may have gone to Special Prosecutor Thomas E. Dewey and, off the record, told all, naming Lepke and the business agent of local 240, an ex-cutter named Max Rubin. Rubin, acting as Lepke's emissary, offered Rosen a bribe and suggested he leave town. Rosen did so, but then returned one last time. At 6:50 in the morning of September 13, 1936, Joseph Rosen was found lying in the center of his candy store in Brooklyn in a pool of blood with bullet wounds to the head, neck, and chest, shot to death by four unknown men. The murder was a commercial transaction, carried out by Lepke's "Murder Incorporated." It was for this particular murder that Lepke was convicted and executed by the State of New York in 1944.[25]

Years later, during Lepke's final days on death row, rumors of Hillman's involvement with Murder Incorporated's chief executive were circulated and exploited by the right-wing columnist Westbrook Pegler and later still, indirectly, by circles close to the Republican presidential aspirant Thomas E. Dewey. Lepke, it was claimed, was prepared to implicate the Amalgamated's president in return for a commutation of his death sentence. Dewey, then Governor of New York, demanded that the federal government turn Lepke over to the state, insinuating that in not doing so it must have something to hide. Once he had Lepke in his clutches, Dewey kept delaying the execution, some thought in hopes that Lepke would "sing" not so much about other gangsters as about Hillman. Meanwhile, the Daily Mirror suggested that Hillman had colluded in an earlier murder, in 1931, of one Joseph Ferreri. At that time, the newspaper reported, he was interrogated by the police and was represented by his good friend Fiorello La Guardia. At Lepke's trial Max Rubin, whose falling out with Lepke in 1937 led to his near assassination, admitted, along with Paul Berger, that they were "sluggers" working for the ACW in an operation run by Lepke. The Daily Mirror used their presence to season innuendos about Hillman's complicity. La Guardia, then Mayor of New York, appointed a magistrate, Vincent Sweeney, to investigate the charges against Hillman. Sweeney dismissed them as groundless. Nonetheless, at the end of 1943, as the national presidential campaign began to heat up, a column by Pegler appearing in the New York World-Telegram and syndicated in 121 other papers claimed that Lepke was the boss of local 4 when Hillman procured "the murder of Joseph Rosen."[26]

Hillman's longtime factional rivals on the socialist left circulated the same nasty rumors. Norman Thomas, the Socialist Party leader, accused Hillman of being one of the worst in the trade union movement when it came to dealing with racketeers. He went so far as to say: "I think that was very fortunate for Mr. Hillman that Mr. Lepke went to the electric chair without talking more than he did."[27]

It seems probable that Hillman behaved like a great many other trade unionists facing the reality of highly fragmented, decentralized industries like trucking, longshore, and garment manufacturing as well as numerous branches of distribution and retailing. Precisely because they were composed of intensely competitive firms surviving on the margins of commercial oblivion, these businesses were acutely vulnerable to criminal coercion, so that extortion ceased to be an aberration and became a normal, if illegal, feature of their daily operations. In the garment industry this blurring of the boundaries between illicit and legitimate commercial transactions was made even fuzzier by the role of financial "factors" who provided cash-poor manufacturers with heavily discounted loans on inventory topped off by usurious rates of interest. The "factors" were sometimes tied to the most respectable financial institutions or were themselves these institutions. Just as often, however, their connections were a great deal shadier. Certainly all the needle trades unions accommodated themselves to these facts of life, in most cases, as for example in the Fur Workers union, establishing live-and-let-live or even closer relations with organized crime. Nonetheless, such relations did not fundamentally compromise their integrity as institutions of collective bargaining.[28]

No doubt Hillman was prepared to accept such a truce except when circumstances—Depression and rapacious gangster incursions into the heart of the union—put that institutional integrity in jeopardy. But there is really no substantial evidence he ventured any further. What testimonial evidence there is to the contrary is highly tainted by motives of political animosity and self-interested defense. When Dewey was first appointed Special Prosecutor in 1935, he met with Hillman and Dubinsky over dinner to talk about racketeering in the needle trades. Both men pledged their support for Dewey's crusade but denied any union–gangster connections, a denial Dewey was inclined not to believe. Once the Rosen murder case broke, Dewey clearly instructed his staff to hunt down any links to Hillman. They were more than diligent in doing so. In questioning Esther Rosen, Joseph's wife, Assistant District Attorney William E. McCarthy went out of his way to suggest such connections. While Esther was able to supply some of the details of how local union officials connived with Lepke's thugs, she was a dry well when it came to Hillman. She'd heard his name—he was the "president of some union"— and thought he was associated with Lepke and Gurrah, but when McCarthy asked if he'd ever threatened her husband she said no. When McCarthy questioned Max Rubin, he asked if Hillman was involved: "No, he's a big shot. He knows President Roosevelt—he wouldn't know any of this stuff." In the course of his statement, Rubin further noted that Rosen's former business partner was "looking to get even with Hillman. As far as he is concerned, Hillman is a Russian bastard."[29]

The records of the Kings County District Attorney's office and the minutes of the Executive Board of Local 240 depict the intricacies of ACW dealings with gangsters past the time when Hillman, according to his admirers, had driven Lepke out. One manufacturer testified, for example, that "through their connections with the Amalgamated Lepke and Gurrah could force the manufacturers to give them their business and by violence." That same manufacturer noted that even after Orlofsky's ouster the same arrangements persisted and cutters were ordered to perform work destined for nonunion contractors. But these files nowhere contain evidence actually linking Hillman directly or indirectly to the

Rosen or Ferreri murder. Later, when Dewey finally had the convicted murderer in his clutches, Lepke was interrogated by New York District Attorney Frank Hogan about both Hillman and Dubinsky. Lepke claimed he hardly knew them.[30]

Hillman was a preeminently practical man, even at times a hard one, ready to deal roughly with his industrial and political foes. He was, too, a masterful compromiser, and doubtless he deployed that talent in his approach to Lepke and Gurrah. But he was also a man with a cultivated sense of his own dignity and moral stature. His jealous protection of the institution he, more than anyone else, helped found and lead was after all the reason he so boldly tackled the New York mobsters to begin with. It thus strains credulity to assume he would go so far as to risk everything—his personal, professional, and political aspirations—by colluding in a gangland slaying, which, at the very "best" might eliminate one defiant manufacturer and terrorize innumerable others, but which in the end he knew could do little to alter permanently the profoundly unstable nature of the industry.

In any event, the reconsolidation of the Amalgamated in New York, however achieved, was decisive in reversing the debilitating and demoralizing decline of the union generally. The stoppages in July and August 1932, involving 30,000 and 15,000 workers, respectively, demonstrated its renewed capacity to mobilize the rank and file in aggressive direct action even in the worst sort of economic conditions. It was conceivable now to tackle the other major market whose disintegration was as dispiriting as New York's.[31]

Baltimore, where once the union was solidly ensconced and enjoyed excellent relations with most of the city's major producers, had turned into a disaster area. By 1932, only 10 percent of the market was organized. Sonneborn's, the Baltimore market's flagship concern and a pioneer in union–scientific management cooperation, finally went bankrupt in 1931, despite several efforts by the Amalgamated Bank of New York to bail the firm out. Strousse Brothers, another large-scale manufacturer and ACW stronghold, was barely hanging on. The city as a whole, once a center of high-quality production for the upscale end of the market, became instead a haven for primitively equipped nonunion contractors along with larger producers who together manufactured cheaper, often shoddy goods. Conditions deteriorated precipitously. Young women were earning between $6 and $8 a week, men between $10 and $20, as against an average wage of about $30 a week in the late 1920s. The proliferation of contractors and cut-make-trim shops, operated by out-of-work cutters who rented a floor somewhere or used one in their own homes, devastated standards established over the previous fifteen years. Indeed, in

some respects it was as if the clock had been turned back before the turn
of the century, before the 1902 Maryland law prohibiting just those sorts
of sweatshops. "Sanitation was bad throughout." Toilets "were always
dirty, without ventilation of any kind, and frequently partitioned off in
a dark corner of the workroom." "There were never any safety devices on
the presses," and as gas irons were used, there was always the danger of
carbon monoxide poisoning. At best only one-fourth of the women
workers in 1932 were earning enough to support what a report to Baltimore Mayor Jackson austerely defined as a "decent minimum." Such
workers were partially or completely dependent on city or church charity
and on help from more fortunate friends.[32]

The largest surviving concerns—Schoenman and Greif Brothers—
divided once integrated operations into separate subcontracting sweatshops all housed together in a single commercial building. Inside these
tiny warrens the despised work patterns of an earlier era reasserted themselves.

Marion Vigneri, who worked in the cellar of the Industrial Building,
described a scene out of Dickens or Mayhew. Working in the gloom
below street level for sixty-four hours a week, she earned $6.96. Yet Mrs.
Vigneri was an experienced worker. The cellar was filthy and overrun
with rats and roaches and lacked not only light and air but even a source
of fresh water. Foremen practiced their customary tyrannies and drove
their workers at such a killing pace that fainting spells were common,
especially among the pressers operating their machines in heat that sometimes reached 120 degrees.

Conditions finally came to a boil in September 1932, when the
ACW felt strong enough to call a strike of four thousand directed mainly
against the Schoenman company. The police openly sided with the
manufacturers, as did Maryland's Governor Albert Ritchie. Picketing
was drastically curtailed, and there were hundreds of arrests as the struggle dragged on through the fall and into the new year. The tide slowly
shifted in favor of the strikers. Mayor Howard W. Jackson, who was
sympathetic, ordered an investigation, which was conducted by Jacob
Hollander, a professor of political economy at Johns Hopkins. The appalling poverty, filth, and abuse uncovered by Hollander's inquiry scan-
dalized middle-class Baltimore. Local academics, among them the well-
known economist Broadus Mitchell, and prominent rabbis and Catholic
clergy, including the redoubtable Father Francis Haas, a longtime friend
of the Amalgamated, helped mobilize public opinion and political influence on behalf of the union. Equally important, the "new sweatshops"
were populated by new workers, second-generation Baltimore immi-

grants, "educated in its public schools—almost always through the ninth grade." They were "American to the core. . . . At school they had ground into them from primary grades what personal hygiene means and the importance of sanitation, ventilation, proper dress, and nutritious food. . . . They had been taught the ideals of this country and they subscribe to them." Journalists noted that arrested strikers sang not "Red Flag" or the "Marseillaise" but "The Star Spangled Banner." It was a generational milieu both less alien and frightening to middle-class residents and more familiar with the elementary principles of trade unionism—if also, in some cases, far less committed to the ideological radicalism of its forebears.

While the battle against Schoenman ended in only a qualified victory, as the company was forced to flee the city, the rest of the strike must be counted a more clear-cut success. The ACW was once again established in the Baltimore market. Moreover, following upon the encouraging developments in New York, the Baltimore strike was further evidence of the union's organizational and moral fortitude, tested under the most extreme circumstances.[33]

But after all was said and done, this was more than anything else a case of looking for silver linings. From the onset of the Depression, Hillman used every piece of tactical ingenuity developed over the previous twenty years to prevent the industry from devouring itself and the ACW. Mass organizing campaigns, self-sacrificing concessions by the rank and file in the interests of reduced costs, and institutional retrenchments were skillfully orchestrated with joint initiatives by grateful retailers and manufacturers to maintain minimal standards and to police transgressors. Hillman even went to war with organized crime. But the forces against which he contended were simply overwhelming. Early in 1933 Hillman, deeply depressed, wrote to Felix Frankfurter that "what seems so very sad to me is the fact that whatever constructive work was accomplished in the last two decades in industry is being broken down and our drifting toward chaos is being accelerated almost from day to day." He reported that a number of firms in Chicago and Cincinnati, employing about 10,000 workers, were seriously considering liquidation and that losses in the three largest houses in Chicago ranged from $1 million to $4 million for 1932. The period was, in his view, "the darkest since the Depression began," and he was "fearful that before Mr. Roosevelt will do anything along constructive lines a great deal of disaster will overtake us."

A few weeks later Ben Cohen confirmed the desperation of Hillman's predicament in a letter to his legal and political mentor. Cohen furthermore assessed Hillman's current perspective on the crisis; noting to Frankfurter: "I somewhat doubt that in handing over his problems to the national government he will find the solution he hopes." In the event, Hillman turned out to be more right than Cohen. It was to politics then, the politics of labor and national economic reconstruction, that Hillman now turned his attention. For the rest of his life it was to be his preoccupation.[34]

TEN

In the Antechamber of Power

In the interval between Wall Street's "Black Tuesday" and the advent of the New Deal, the credibility and legitimacy of the *ancien régime* was undermined beyond any real hope of recuperation. The architects of a new order, a critical number of whom were Hillman's political and business associates, assembled in the antechamber of power and engaged in a protracted struggle to recast public policy as well as the very nature of elite and mass politics. From the outset Hillman was an enthusiastic partisan in this effort to unseat the "tories of industry." He lobbied, proselytized, and advised, pursuing down every avenue and byway the elusive prospect of labor's political enfranchisement. On inauguration day, 1933, no one could divine the pattern or meaning of the new administration, so complex was its tapestry, but Sidney Hillman at least had become a figure in the carpet.

From Hillman's standpoint the collapse of the economy presented at one and the same time a specific desperate emergency for the life of the ACW and an inescapable challenge to reconstruct the nation's political economy. Rescuing the union depended on the realignment of national politics and the systematic creation of an enlarged state bureaucracy to regulate and reorient the economy. Ben Cohen may have doubted Hillman's wisdom in turning to the national government for a solution, but for Hillman this was no sudden, panic-driven panacea following three long years of Depression. On the contrary, it had informed his behavior from the earliest days of the crash.

259

The recovery of any particular industry, including the manufacture of men's clothing, Hillman believed, was not within the power of that industry to accomplish, even where all the elements of production and distribution were prepared to cooperate in a concert of interest for that purpose. Hillman argued, "No one industry can stabilize itself entirely by its own efforts. Regularity in production and employment depends on the general state of industry and agriculture, in short on the economic health of the country as a whole and that means national planning." Moreover, Hillman distrusted the kind of planning envisioned by industrial corporatists, who preferred a system of self-regulation by trade associations and leading corporations. "In the absence of leadership in private industry, we must look to the Federal Government to check the continuous and rapid breakdown of our industrial machinery."[1]

Underlying his conviction about national economic planning was a "Keynesian" intuition, which he had voiced before the stock market crash: A "high standard of living is no more a question of mere justice. . . . It is essential to our system of mass production to create a consumer's demand for almost unlimited output." Business cycles and their disastrous downturns were not inevitable, he averred, but were amenable to adjustment, if only the government was allowed to extend its authority to plan and balance aggregate levels of production and consumption. Even after the Depression was well under way, at a time when the immediate problem was somehow to meet the elementary material needs of the population, Hillman continued to emphasize the peculiar dynamic upon which the revival, expansion, and consequent stability of the new "people's capitalism" depended: "Greater needs and desires must be created to take care of the rapidly developing technological improvements and efficiencies in the management of industry." Such a complex and delicate mechanism could no longer be entrusted to myopic, self-interested corporate managements, but "implies planning on a national scale."[2]

Every specific remedy Hillman submitted for public debate he self-consciously offered as part of his proto-Keynesian, underconsumptionist outlook. Unemployment insurance, for which he campaigned actively in New York and nationally, was, he maintained, designed not only to relieve immediate distress but to provide a critical cushion of demand that might blunt the impact of future depressions. By the late 1920s, in fact, Hillman was proselytizing for unemployment insurance not only as a way to reduce joblessness and promote efficiency but also in the expectation that it "will establish that balance-wheel between the consuming and producing powers of the country without which the social functioning of industry is not possible."

Similarly, his proposals for a shorter work day, coupled with an expanded volume of production and countercyclical public works, were intended to offset the arrhythmias of the economy as well as to reemploy people. Maintaining and expanding levels of mass consumption was, Hillman was convinced, even more vital than industrial efficiency. His initial call for the universal five-day week emphasized how important it was to expand the mass market by increasing leisure time.[3]

Hillman was certainly no economic theorist, but underconsumptionist diagnoses of the Depression were common enough. Indeed, it is remarkable how far these views had disseminated. Hillman himself cited "Professor Keynes" as saying "every two people re-employed at a decent wage make employment for another person." Years before the publication of his General Theory, Keynes's underconsumptionist analysis was familiar to reform circles in the United States. Frankfurter, for example, quoted the British economist on the tendency of interest rates to fall in a climate of business confidence to support his own conclusion that "the important desideratum is the encouragement to an all-around high standard of living and a relatively shorter working day." Rexford Guy Tugwell, an acquaintance of Hillman since the mid-twenties, shared the views of another British economist, J. A. Hobson, who located the basic flaw in capitalist economies in their tendency to depress purchasing power. Indeed, in 1931 even the Taylor Society drafted an Industrial Employment Code emphasizing the systematic connection between technology and expanded production on the one hand and the growing capacity to consume on the other.[4]

Everyone in the world of Progressive reform, including Hillman, was familiar with those damning social statistics buttressing the underconsumptionist case. According to a Brookings Institution study, "America's Capacity to Consume," the income of the top 0.1 percent of American families in 1929 equaled that of the bottom 42 percent. Seventy-one percent of all families had incomes under $2,500. Between 1920 and 1929 the disposable income of the top 10 percent increased by 75 percent; yet 80 percent of all families were without any savings whatsoever. Meanwhile, output per worker in manufacturing rose 43 percent between 1920 and 1929 while wages climbed a mere 8 percent. Even someone as improbable as the AFL sachem John Frey of the machinists' union was exercised by these numbers and by the crying need for new investment in wealth-producing activities, arguing that government fiscal policy ought to be geared to the business cycle, not the otherwise artificial fiscal year. The great problem, according to Frey, was the relationship among consumption, production, and distribution: "There is no human

problem which compares with it in difficulty, in magnitude, in hopeful-
ness. It is world-wide in its impact. . . . What is being contemplated is
nothing less than a purposeful changing of the course of history."[5]

It is unlikely that a man of Frey's studied caution was truly contemplating changing the course of human history. But others with whom
Hillman was familiar, either personally or through their work, were.
Earlier, in the 1920s, Hillman had clipped for further study portions of
Profits, the 1925 book by the two widely known economists and investment counselors, Waddill Catchings and William T. Foster, in which
they made the case for countercyclical government spending. He was
equally attentive to Foster's and Catchings's next book, *The Road to
Plenty*, published in 1928, which defended the efficacy of federal public
works spending for combating unemployment and the business cycle. He
also found appealing the views of the social critic Stuart Chase, particularly his rather technocratic proposal for an economic general staff or
"Peace Industries Board" of technical experts with authority to make
basic economic decisions. Hillman and Mary Van Kleeck of the Russell
Sage Foundation testified before the Senate Finance Committee early in
1933, where Van Kleeck mobilized an army of statistics to buttress their
underconsumptionist argument.[6]

Some of these social scientists—Foster and Catchings, for example—
moved easily and often between academe and certain segments of the
business world most interested in their orientation to mass consumption
capitalism. Beardsley Ruml was another such figure; he doubled as head
of the Rockefeller Foundation and adviser to Jesse Strauss of Macy's.
Hillman had dealt with all the Strauss brothers for years. They, along
with an entire circle of Hillman's business associates, shared this "Keynesian" view. Edward Filene was perhaps the best known; an incipient
underconsumptionist outlook was already apparent in his 1924 book, *The
Way Out*. Even before the 1929 crash Filene had contemplated the
prospect of industrial expansion predicated on the cultivation of new
needs and desires, embodied in new products like the radio, airplane,
household appliances, and the telephone. By 1931 his remedies for the
Depression included the six-hour day, the five-day week, unemployment
insurance, and banking reform that would contribute to the "buying
power of the masses." Filene's good friend Henry Dennison of Dennison
Manufacturing, with whom he founded the Twentieth Century Fund,
presented a similar analysis in a 1931 publication of the Foreign Policy
Association entitled *The World-Wide Depression: Ways Out*. Dennison
was himself advised by a young economist, later to become a prominent
proponent of left-leaning Keynesianism, named John Kenneth Galbraith.
Ralph E. Flanders, the president of Jones & Lamson Machine Company,

was another prominent business reformer whose testimony before a Senate subcommittee chaired by La Follette in 1932 argued the underconsumptionist view. Understandably less sanguine than Filene had been eight years earlier, Flanders urged a large public works program not only to reemploy people but as a device for drawing out savings and investment capital that were otherwise inert as long as no new mass production, mass consumption industry like automobiles appeared on the horizon. Flanders co-authored a "Progress Report of the Committee on the Relationship of Consumption, Production, and Distribution" for the American Engineering Council. The tract emphasized new investment in wealth-producing activities in contrast to the trading of old securities, and recommended a "Keynesian" fiscal policy organized around long-term government budgeting geared to the business cycle; deploying public works to offset unemployment and to soak up accumulated saving; and higher taxes in boom years to reduce purely speculative capital flows.[7]

There were other such reform-minded businessmen, well-known to Hillman, sharing his "Keynesian" concern with the dynamics of mass consumption. Morris Leeds of Leeds & Northrup, an associate of Flanders and on the board of the Twentieth Century Fund, was a staunch advocate of public works for those same reasons. Henry Kendall, a key figure in the New England textile industry, an associate of Frankfurter, was an activist in the Taylor Society, as were Leeds and Flanders. There were others: Milton Florsheim, the president of the Florsheim Company, a confidant of the HSM top management and many of the mass retailers with whom Hillman was in frequent contact, and Ernest Hood of the Naumkeag Steam Cotton Company, another Taylor Society activist and, together with Flanders and Mark Cresap of HSM, an advocate of wages and hours legislation to stop the downward spiral that was eviscerating the mass market.[8]

All of these businessmen, and others, would go on to become supporters of the New Deal, in some cases architects and administrators of its critical legislation in labor relations, social security, investment banking, public utility regulation, taxation, and deficit spending. They were no more economic theorists than was Hillman; many were even less directly familiar with the scholarship of Professor Keynes. Yet together they articulated the attitudes and interests of a much broader network of manufacturing, distributive, and financial elites in the arena of mass consumption. Politically dominant business lobbies associated with nineteenth-century infrastructural and heavy industrial development—railroads, utilities, basic steel, raw materials producers, manufacturers of superannuated consumer goods, capital goods suppliers of these industries, along with their financial underwriters and creditors, preeminently the Morgan and Kuhn Loeb group of investment banks—were scarcely concerned with the mass market; if anything their impulse was to shelter their investments in the capital goods sector by limiting productive output. The new, rising milieu of mass-market–oriented producers, distributors, and financiers was far more amenable to "Keynesian" approaches to shoring up aggregate demand. It was not a homogeneous group, uniform in interests or beliefs, and was often divided by regional and commercial rivalries. But there were nevertheless organic connections between newer, often technologically innovative manufacturing enterprises, associated for example with the burgeoning mass market for housing and building supplies (Armstrong Cork and American Radiator Company, for example) and household appliances, and major retail concerns. Together, they depended on the regular expansion of the universe of mass distribution and consumption. They were linked financially to newer investment houses, commercial banks, and real estate concerns— Goldman Sachs and Lehman Brothers; the Giannini diversified and consumer-oriented banking empire in California; the Greenfield real estate and retail interests headquartered in Philadelphia; and the Bowery Savings Bank of New York, all of which rose to positions of real power in the 1920s.[9]

Thus Hillman was swept up in a secular reconfiguration of the American political economy. During the period between the two world wars, the rate of increase in infrastructural and heavy capital investment slowed, as did the rate of population growth and immigration. That, combined with a glaring maldistribution of income and antiquated technologies, aborted new sources of demand and investment opportunities. Recovery, a new era of capital accumulation, depended then on decisive government action to break the stranglehold on the flow of capital and new competitive enterprise. Oligopolistic heavy industry, dominant railroad and utility groups, and their allied investment banks together constituted a parasitical "securities bloc," more concerned with the trading of inflated paper than in the underlying operating companies hypothetically represented by those partly "fictitious" securities. Renewed economic expansion would entail new markets, product innovations, and new product mixes as well as new marketing efforts, especially in the nondurable goods sector, to take advantage of a long-term secular rise in national income. Demand had shifted in the direction of "higher ticket" items and into industries like appliances, cigarettes, recreation, medical care, and processed food. Newer "basic" and raw materials industries— petroleum and chemicals especially—were themselves implicated in this rising mass-consumption–oriented economy as suppliers of the processed food and appliance industries, for example. Meanwhile, demand steadily shifted away from older producer goods industries, like lumber, iron, and steel.

Shifts in demand could also effect consumer goods industries, as Hillman knew all too well. Clothing declined between 1923 and 1929 from 17 to 15.1 percent of consumer spending, while sizable, sometimes unimagined, increases were occurring not only in food, appliances, medical care, insurance, tobacco, and recreation, but in a variety of consumer service industries—domestics, barbers, dry cleaners, laundries, hotels—and also in certain kinds of producer services, hence the picture for office machinery and supplies, where Henry Dennison's company was quite active, along with Otis Elevator and Thomas M. Watson's IBM (Watson turned out to be a staunch New Dealer), brightened considerably.

Between 1929 and 1938 the food industry, for example, introduced thirty-eight new primary products, due in part to advances in canning, refrigeration, packaging, and distribution; supermarkets therefore experienced enormous growth. The petroleum industry did more than grow, it diffused across a changing economic landscape, discovering the most varied uses: in automobiles, of course, but also in aviation and in home heating, thanks to the introduction of the oil burner in the 1920s. The chemical industry showed similar vitality thanks to the discovery of rayon and the expansion into the rubber, paper, drug, photography, and movie industries. Glass manufacturing was invigorated by processed food packaging and, via the light bulb, by the rapid electrification of America. Rival transport modes grew stronger, especially trucking (Adams Express Company and Mack Truck would become loyal corporate New Dealers). Even in a heavy industry like steel, certain subsectors did well, including lighter strip steel and tin plate for food containers, new alloys for fabrication and finishing for new auto designs, transmissions, and gears, while steel plate and rails continued their secular decline.

This new industrial network exploited an extensive development of new markets rather than the intensive development of old ones. Its central concern was not with the preservation of property titles to the means of production—the preoccupation of the "securities bloc"—but with the dynamics of the mass market. In an emerging economic universe of new markets, new industries, and new patterns of consumption and distribution, this Keynesian milieu was preoccupied with the creation of new values, not the buttressing of old, fictitious values. This transformed the geophysics of economic life. A truly national market and economy appeared for the first time. Although obviously in the nineteenth century goods were purchased in the marketplace, those markets were largely local and often supplementary. That century's modern in-

dustry did not, for the most part, sell to consumers. Instead it produced
and sold securities, along with primary metals and producer goods, to the
financial system, to the railroads, to the manufacturers of rails, power-
generating equipment, copper wire for electricity, and so on. It produced
the framework for a national economy, but not that economy itself. In
that formative era of large-scale industry, the modern consumer did not
really exist.

The newer frontier industries and technologies of the twentieth century were tied to exponential increases in the size and depth of the urban
mass market, to the emergence of whole new regional political economies, especially in the West, and to the further transformation of rural
society. This new milieu was therefore open to the possibilities of macroeconomic control and regulation through the mechanisms of planning
and antitrust enforcement, as surgical devices for clearing the clotted
arteries of business and finance. But this perspective did not arise as a
natural by-product of some daily economic metabolism.

An industrial profile, after all, is a far cry from a political action
committee of businessmen; it is even farther removed from the sort of
shadow government that began to gather in the corridors of the Democratic party and around the statehouse in Albany. In the mass, businessmen were scarcely more politically articulate or active than other
functional groups, oscillating between apathy and political routine, often
informed by nothing more elevated or enlightened than habit and tradition, or the myopia of self-interest. The mere fact that a particular
business displayed certain salient characteristics did not automatically
mean it enlisted in the New Deal crusade. Some, like Watson, Dennison, Filene, or Robert Johnson of Johnson & Johnson, did. But even at
the height of the "second New Deal," the newly empowered "Keynesian"
elite enjoyed at best limited support among the great mass of entrepreneurs and practically no support among older industrial groups.

Rather, the Keynesian instinct was given coherence and political
form by men and women who stood outside the marketplace: industrial
engineers, social scientists and economists, foundation administrators,
"scientific" social workers, lawyers, "Progressive" legislators, and even,
on occasion, a labor leader like Hillman.[10]

Hillman was a nodal point along the complex circuitry of this network of institutional and personal associations. Connections radiated in
various directions. The Bruere brothers offer an example. Robert, a
founder of the NBER, on the board of the Twentieth Century Fund, and
affiliated with the liberals in the Taylor Society, was one of the earliest
celebrants of the "new unionism." Through Robert, Hillman first met
Henry Bruere, president of the rapidly expanding, consumer-oriented

Bowery Savings Bank. Henry was a former social worker, an officer of Metropolitan Life, and a member of the Taylor Society's Industrial Commission. In the fall of 1928 Henry proposed to Hillman the Bowery's financial involvement in a new cooperative housing project on the Lower East Side. Bruere spoke not only for the Bowery but for his longtime business associate and friend, Herbert Lehman (with whom he consulted frequently on the need for banking reform). The Amalgamated's second venture into low-income housing thus put Hillman in touch with the firm of Lehman Brothers, a key financial institution in the mass distribution sector.[11]

Lehman Brothers, along with Goldman Sachs, did a great deal of joint underwriting of the newer, larger, riskier retail operations—Associated Dry Goods, Gimbel's, American Stores Company, W. T. Grant, Abraham & Strauss, Stern Brothers, and Allied Stores. Through Sidney Weinberg of Goldman Sachs, it financed Sears, National Dairy Products, and others. For some years in the twenties Goldman Sachs employed Waddill Catchings as its chief economist. Those two houses and others, particularly Lazard-Frères, were not only closely linked in the business world but had begun migrating into the orbit of the Democratic Party at the time of Woodrow Wilson's ascendancy. The Lehman Brothers interests extended widely throughout the brave new world of mass consumption and mass culture, including such major moviemakers and stalwart future New Deal companies as Paramount and RKO. Lehman was tied to Federated Stores as well. Federated, of course, was controlled by the Filene brothers, pioneers of the movement for "industrial democracy" and a high-wage, mass consumption economy. Louis Kirstein, who was responsible for day-to-day operations at Federated, sat on the boards of Lehman Brothers and RKO.[12]

Hillman's dealings with the Filenes and Kirstein dated from the earliest days of the union. At the same time Lehman also maintained strong business and personal ties with another Hillman associate, Jesse Strauss—actually, all three Strauss brothers, including Nathan and Oscar, who ran Macy's. Jesse Strauss was a director of the Bowery and was linked by blood to the firm of Goldman Sachs as well. Jesse also cultivated political interests. He was appointed by Governor Franklin D. Roosevelt to help administer the state's Temporary Emergency Relief Administration, in part an experiment in work relief and public works. At the same time Macy's was advised by Beardsley Ruml, who would go on to direct the National Resources Planning Board, the New Deal's main executive vehicle, in the late 1930s, for promoting the most far-reaching proposals for state-directed economic development and social welfare.[13]

Lehman Brothers employed the economist Alexander Sachs as its chief of research and planning. Sachs, who would become a dissenting member of Hugh Johnson's staff in the early days of the NRA, was a caustic critic of the old "securities bloc," accusing it of "sterilizing wealth and credit resources." He was also sympathetic to industrial unionism, which points to another dimension of the underconsumptionist outlook and to another circle of Hillman's personal and organizational associations that drew him into the center of this formative Keynesian elite.[14]

The Taylor Society had drifted steadily to the left after Taylor's death, particularly during and after the war. Within the engineering profession, Morris Cooke was a long-standing opponent of the bloc of railroad and utility interests and their kept engineers and financial allies who opposed scientific management. As Harlow Person noted: "In contrast to mass production, scientific management had its origins in and is to be found today [1928] chiefly in small and medium-sized plants making variable items." He was unimpressed with "welfare capitalism": The "more I study the company union movement the less sympathy I have for it . . . a very high percentage of the company unions are fakes, pure and simple." Anyone who failed to see the utility and necessity of collective bargaining was not a worthy associate. "I make collective bargaining as essential to the proper conduct of industry as modern tools."[15]

By the mid-1920s the Taylor Society had become a crossroads not only for democratically minded efficiency experts and for those rather rare labor leaders like Hillman, but also for a diverse assortment of mass-consumption–oriented merchandisers, manufacturers, and investment houses and banks. The Society's manufacturing membership comprised primarily mass-market–oriented firms in dry goods and housing along with groups of diversified, mass-oriented machine and instrument firms—capital goods suppliers to mass production firms, including IBM and Eastman Kodak, with highly developed marketing functions—and paper, packaging, printing, and publishing enterprises (Dennison's homely company made labels) similarly linked to the mass consumption sector. The single largest sectoral group of manufacturers came from clothing, clothing-related, and dry goods producers. But only 54 percent of the Society's members were manufacturers. The other 46 percent comprised what Peter Friedlander describes as "producer services," including management consultants, periodicals, foundations, and legal and technocratic groups, all tied in one way or another to the same broad sector. Certainly there were plenty of firms within the Society that couldn't abide all or even part of what people like Cooke and Person were proposing. Concerns like AT&T, Western Electric, Westinghouse, and so on tried but failed to make the Society subordinate to the much more conservative views of the American Management Association. But a sizable portion of the membership contemplated along with Cooke a new role for labor in a new economic order.[16]

Cooke's 1928 presidential address to the Society (during which a number of infuriated executives walked out) anticipated the next decade's agenda of industrial reform:

> The interests of society—including those of the workers—suggest some measure of collective bargaining. . . . Effective collective bargaining implies the organization of the workers on a basis extensive enough—say nation-wide—as to make this bargaining power effective.

Inevitably, he argued, in an economic world of complex interdependence, one populated with "national trade organizations; national and even international standards and sales syndicates; the vertical and horizontal integration of widely different industries; inter-industry research organizations; and in combinations of one sort or another," adversarial industrial relations must "gradually give way" and labor organizations would be given "that functional status in the industrial process which is now denied." It was essential, from the standpoint of management, Cooke maintained, "to look upon some organization of the workers, such as labor unions, as a deep social need." It was not enough for sympathetic employers and management consultants like himself to adopt a position of benign disinterest. The point now was to assume active responsibility "for forwarding such movements," to "direct some of our energies . . . toward the problem of the organization of the workers," to work to eliminate yellow-dog contracts and "grossly unfair injunction practices and obviously unnecessary unemployment or peremptory wage cuts."

In this "new day of scientific management, high wages and standards of living, mass production, quick changes, cooperation, mechanical improvement" it was necessary to have strong labor organizations—"very probably national in scope—ready to grapple with any group of employers guilty either of cupidity or industrial illiteracy." A mass consumption economy and culture, Cooke observed, was recasting the immemorial struggle between the haves and the have-nots. It was no longer a matter of "the full dinner pail," but the "full garage"; now gasoline rather than bread and perhaps later "a share in the world's highest culture" was at stake. So long as "property essentially controls the avenues to these things," it seemed desirable that the relatively propertyless be organized "as a balance of power." It was critical, Cooke insisted, to encourage an independent presence for labor to ensure "a proper distribution of the rewards of productive enterprise" and to check the "ineffectiveness and inefficiency of those who control through their property rights."[17]

As a premonition of the new industrial and political order, including mass industrial unionism, one could scarcely ask for more, or from someone better positioned to assess simultaneously the internal dynamics of labor and industry. As the Depression descended over the country, the Taylor Society pursued an approach to recovery distinctly at odds with that of the major trade associations: one at home with centralized, industrial unions, rooted in mass production, informed by scientific management, developing within the context of mass consumption, and guided by an activist government.[18]

Cooke and Hillman both were political creatures, acutely aware that the "industrial future," Keynesian or otherwise, was at bottom a political question. What made this incipient reform elite into a real political threat to the old order, and not merely a plaintive assortment of renegade businessmen, perfectionist engineers and social scientists, and disgruntled trade unionists, were those activist political circles gathered around the jurists Louis Brandeis and Felix Frankfurter and such men of influence as Senators Robert La Follette, Jr., and Robert Wagner. Hillman had relied upon and worked with these people for a decade and more. They constituted something far less formal than a shadow government and far less disciplined than a central committee. Yet they managed to integrate these networks of businessmen, industrial unionists, labor-minded social scientists, unorthodox economists, managerial scientists, and foundation administrators into a strategic alliance potent enough to upset the balance of power in American politics.

Conventional wisdom about Brandeis and Frankfurter and the circle of lawyer-politicians that assembled around them—most notably Benjamin Cohen, Tom Corcoran, and James Landis—held that they were bearers of an antiquated tradition of antitrust political economy, blind to the advantages of complex organizations and mass production. Yet, beginning with Brandeis, they had all represented large corporations and investment houses, although invariably ones outside the orbit of the Morgan interests. Brandeis's clients included New England consumer goods manufacturers, retailers, and scientifically managed midsize companies like Brighton Mills, Link Belt, and Tabor Manufacturing, along with associated investment houses like Lee Higginson & Company, a longtime rival of the Morgan group. Morgan's control of railroad transportation and power generation and distribution (including municipal traction and utility companies as, for example, represented by the Belmont, Whitney, and Ryan interests in New York) presented a serious obstacle to the growth of the mass market merchandisers and manufacturers. Brandeis's celebrated brief in the Eastern Rate case was exemplary of these relationships.

The brief, argued in 1910 before the ICC, mounted a compelling argument against the Morgan-controlled New Haven railroad and its stultifying effect on commerce and manufacturing in the Northeast and Midwest. It also showcased Brandeis's commitment to scientific management. It united shippers everywhere, except in the South and the Great Plains. The Chicago group within the Shippers Association comprised an especially diverse milieu of modern firms oriented to the mass market (shoe and processed food producers). It included such leading companies as HSM, Rosenwald & Weil, and major urban retailers like Marshall Field and Montgomery Ward, along with Sears, Beech-Nut, Libby, McNeil & Libby, and National Biscuit. As a proponent of the new science of management, Brandeis contended that the trunk lines could afford to raise wages and improve profits without a rate increase if they applied the latest organizational techniques. At the same time, he maintained that the rates affected not only specific firms but the ability of a whole sector to market and accumulate by depressing and restricting the mass market, especially its poorer working-class segments.[19]

The indictment of the Eastern trunk lines and their financial keepers as obstacles to the further expansion of the market was to be echoed again and again in the views of Frankfurter and in the legislative innovations authored by his students. The enemy against which they contended was not "monopoly"—a metaphoric abstraction—but a concrete ensemble of corporations and banks. The antimonopoly politics of the nineteenth century grew out of a quite different environment, out of the soil of early capitalism, a market economy in which economic institutions were still closely linked to product and personality or family. Thus the great petty capitalist movements of the Gilded Age—the Greenback-Laborites, the Populists, the Knights of Labor, the innumerable local struggles against the encroachment of corporate power—organized the resistance of familial, craft-based capitalism to anonymous, corporate-bureaucratic power. By the twentieth century the "big business" targeted by populist rhetoric was rooted in the provision of basic services and primary materials, dominated by a tightly knit network of banks and insurance companies. As a consequence, the market and private property, once perceived as mutually reinforcing, became separate and antagonistic as the preservation of existing property titles entailed the restriction of a market clogged with overbuilt railroads, watered stock, and so on. A social milieu far wider than the immediately advantaged banks, insurance companies, savings associations, and investment houses had a stake in the protection of these inflated values. It included a broad spectrum of white, middle-class petty investors, normally Republican in politics, individualist in ideology, driven by envy and anxiety. Coagulations of capital, consolidated by leading fiduciary institutions, sought to restrict the dynamic of the market through competitive restraints, government favors, and the informal regulation of prices and production. Thus, the antimonopoly movement of the nineteenth century and the modern antimonopoly animus of the Brandeis–Frankfurter elite were generically different.

Certainly the circles around Brandeis and Frankfurter were aware of the economies of scale realizable through standardized mass production. But they retained a wise skepticism about the morals and motives of the "securities bloc." Federal coercion seemed unavoidable to prevent a fatal case of economic arteriosclerosis. Adolph Berle, a member of Roosevelt's Brain Trust who earlier worked for Brandeis's law firm and with Edward Filene at the Social Science Research Council and the Twentieth Century Fund, argued that economic coagulation, the stifling of innovation, and the maldistribution of income resulting from the concentration of business generated economic disaster and needed to be controlled by forceful state planning. James Landis, a Brandeis disciple, joined the ill-fated La Follette campaign of 1924 as an attempt, misguided as it turned out, to break the grip of the "securities bloc" on the political system. It was not "bigness" *per se* that was anathema, but a certain kind of corporate structure, targeted in some New Deal securities legislation and later the Public Utility Holding Company Act, which rested on a shaky foundation of bonded debt, absentee management, and the financial draining of productive enterprise. It was just this sort of "monopoly" that in 1933 was the object of an investigation by the Senate Banking Committee, run by Ferdinand Pecora, for which Max Lowenthal, a Frankfurter associate and onetime ACW legal counsel, provided legal advice regarding potential securities legislation.[20]

Other Frankfurter students, Cohen and Corcoran particularly, were scarcely naïve trust-busters, inexperienced with the world of corporate finance. Benjamin Cohen had made an earlier legal career out of corporate reorganizations and sophisticated stock market manipulations. Tom Corcoran, who was to become Cohen's co-author of key pieces of New Deal legislation, was a shrewd strategist of stock promotions and pooling arrangements for a Wall Street law firm. That firm, originally under the leadership of Woodrow Wilson's son-in-law, William Gibbs McAdoo, developed extensive ties with Progressives in both major parties. Their clients included the Bank of America, Lehman Brothers, Dillon Reed, and Lee Higginson—all rivals of the Morgan interests who deliberately used the Pecora investigation to embarrass their foe. Corcoran was single-minded in his pursuit of the House of Morgan. He was convinced that opposition to the Securities Act by the U.S. Chamber of Commerce was organized by Morgan people.[21]

This animus was deeply felt and long-lasting. At the outset of the Depression, Frankfurter wrote to Bruce Bliven of *The New Republic* (and board member of the Twentieth Century Fund) to express his disgust with Morgan, Thomas Lamont, and even Owen Young of General Electric: "After all, we tried his great remedy . . . finance and industry ruled politics. . . . And now look at the damn thing! Where were all those great wise men from 1925 to 1929—including Mr. Young and Mr. Morgan and Mr. Lamont?" Frankfurter told Bliven and George Soule that it was time to go after Young "hard," "to take Owen Young's hide," to expose his slick talk about the public interest as a cover for his "really undemocratic and fundamentally plutocratic" outlook, an outlook Frankfurter characterized as a kind of "subtle fascism."[22]

This latter perception, that people like Young were undemocratic in inclination, whether accurate or not, suggests that the connection between democracy and the new economic order was, for the Brandeis–Frankfurter group, organic. Because the "securities bloc" exercised enormous influence within the Republican Party, segments of the pre-Roosevelt Democratic party, key parts of Congress, state legislatures, and municipal governments, it was able to stymie democratic reforms like collective bargaining and income redistribution, reforms essential and not incidental to these avatars of industrial democracy.

Their sympathies for labor, for democratic procedure, and for mass consumption were Hillman's own. From the onset of the Depression he dedicated himself to the programmatic objectives and political scheming of this emergent coalition. When, for example, the union's own unemployment reserves proved wholly inadequate, he joined with Progressives like Paul Kellogg and John Andrews of the American Association of Labor Legislation to campaign for publicly mandated unemployment insurance. Hillman testified on behalf of the Association's legislative proposal at hearings in Albany on the Mastick–Steingut Unemployment Insurance Reserve Fund bill. New York was an especially hospitable environment, as the executive branch of state government was seeded with friendly faces. By 1931 Cooke was ensconced as the governor's adviser on electric power, and various other Taylor Society personnel provided State Labor Secretary Frances Perkins with help in devising an employment stabilization plan. Hillman himself, drawing on the technical expertise of Leo Wolman and the advice of William Leiserson,

helped draft reports for Roosevelt and Perkins on legislative solutions to
the problem of unemployment insurance.

In addition to relief and some system of public unemployment insurance, Hillman advocated the shorter work week, public works, and a
national standard of hours and wages. The widespread interest in minimum wage legislation in many states as well as nationally was in part a
response to the revival of the sweatshop and draconian wage-gouging in
the garment industry, in the cotton, silk, and woolen branches of the
textile industry, and in restaurants, shoe manufacturing, hosiery, hotels,
and canneries. In New York, after the passage of a minimum wage law,
Wolman and Hillman were appointed by Labor Commissioner Andrews
to an advisory commission of eleven that included manufacturers as well
as representatives of the Consumers League and the WTUL. Hillman
urged that "the government should step in and use its power to compel
reluctant or enlightened industrial leaders to accept this program as a
national policy."[23]

In formulating plans for relief and recovery, including the most ambitious schemes for tripartite labor-management-government councils to
plan production and distribution, Hillman expressly drew on the path-
breaking experience of the "new unionism." The union's principle of
equal division and sharing of work during slack periods and the ACW's
unemployment insurance exemplified what ought to be done nationally,
he argued. Hillman drew close to Senator Wagner, whose efforts in favor
of unemployment insurance and countercyclical public works (as well as
a public employment exchange and an enlarged state statistical capacity
to diagnose and predict economic trends) prefigured a variety of state
capitalist planning with which Hillman felt quite comfortable. Indeed,
since the late 1920s Wagner's own thinking had been influenced by
"Keynesians" like Leon Keyserling, who helped draft his recovery legislation.

Hillman's proposal for a tripartite board to regulate the conditions of
labor was modeled after the arbitration machinery installed in the garment industry over the previous two decades. Industrial democrats like
Frankfurter and Cooke knew how important such formal, democratic
arrangements were to help translate the fissionable rhetoric of the class
struggle into the less threatening language of consumption, economic
self-interest, and political pluralism. Thus, Frankfurter invited Hillman
to speak at a Harvard conference about the need for a "constitution for
industry" like that established by the "new unionism."[24]

Never one to ignore the sometimes intractable realities of industrial
and political power, Hillman did not offer his proposals for national
industrial democracy, social welfare, and income redistribution without

considering the means for their realization. He advocated the creation of emergency authorities, supported measures to enlarge the executive power, and insisted that any national planning body needed to be equipped with powers of enforcement or else risk irrelevance. [25]

It was of course one thing to propose, quite another to dispose. Hillman above all attended to the realities of power. Jacob Potofsky remembered about this period: "His consuming interest was the power of labor. He foresaw in the establishment of wage boards, fixing maximum hours and minimum wages, and so on, the increase of power for labor." [26]

But the "power for labor" was then at its nadir. Even at the height of "prosperity" in 1929, trade union membership amounted to only 3.4 million, a decline of 1.7 million from its postwar peak. By 1933 membership was less than 3 million. For years the Amalgamated valiantly if futilely floated proposals to arrest this fatal decline. At a meeting of progressive unionists convened by the ACW in 1928, Schlossberg asked rhetorically:

> What are the [AFL craft] unions doing with their own to withstand the attacks of company made [works] councils? Do they realize how much the employer is stressing factory solidarity as against craft solidarity? Do they realize this argument sounds persuasive to unskilled workers, with no trade or craft who work in . . . increasingly mechanized industry? The answer is clear in the experience of the [AFL craft] unions during the last few years, and in their failure to launch any drives against the big steel, rubber, electric, and automobile companies. [The AFL crafts] are trying to use a wooden plow to cultivate a modern 5,000-acre farm. . . . The confusion and disillusion bred by craft union failure in the worker's mind has made him easy prey for the personnel expert offering salvation in the form of the company union. That confusion and dismay will not be lifted until the unions move towards real amalgamation rather than general, generous, but meaningless expressions of good will toward one another in times of strikes.

Such pleading—shrewd in detecting the mutual attractiveness, to employer and worker alike, of "factory solidarity"—fell on deaf ears. The AFL hierarchy feared that a serious campaign to mobilize not only the immigrant unskilled but also, and more worrying, the newly emerging milieu of second-generation, semiskilled machine tenders would jeopardize both what little was left of its favored position in the Democratic Party and its own credibility in the eyes of its skilled and often nativist rank and file. [27]

Besides Hillman, John L. Lewis was the only other labor leader supporting the idea of federally sanctioned labor boards to monitor the conditions of work and to arrest the auto-cannibalism of labor-devouring competition. But Lewis was still officially a Republican; his sympathy for planning was largely a function of the desperate plight of the soft-coal industry, plagued by overproduction. He had spent the better part of the 1920s ruthlessly suppressing and purging all those elements in the UMW who shared Schlossberg's sense of urgency. Indeed, Hillman had gone so far as to involve himself in efforts to undermine the mineworkers' patriarch. Early in 1930 the SP, along with the Brookwood Labor school, helped foster a reorganization movement within the union, centered in the Illinois district, with the hope of including as well miners from Ohio under John Brophy and Powers Hapgood as well as the Kansas miners led by Lewis's foe, Alex Howat. Hillman attended a conference in Chicago for this purpose. Factional squabbles between the SP, Brookwood cadre, communist members of the purged National Miners Union, and various local potentates of the UMW left the movement stillborn. Only because he felt so trapped by the organizational and political timidity of the official trade union movement did Hillman allow himself to get caught up in this misadventure to begin with.[28]

Within the needle trades he could no longer count on the assistance of fraternal unions; all were barely surviving, and the ILG particularly was practically in ruins. Politically, the AFL remained the prisoner of its voluntarist ideology. It continued to oppose minimum wage legislation and as late as 1932 was still equivocating about unemployment insurance despite the persistent lobbying of members, the meatcutters, the needle trades, and the miners. The leadership feared the creation of a social welfare bureaucracy that might compete with the labor movement's own insurance services, inadequate as they obviously were. They feared as well, and not without reason, the moral imperialism of middle-class welfare bureaucrats, especially given their association with a tradition of progressive reform, including charitable "uplift" and "good government" that frequently attacked those urban political machines with which many AFL leaders collaborated. Intimidated and in a state of disarray, the AFL could do no more than add its vote of confidence to Senator Hugo Black's Thirty Hour bill. A piece of legislative simplicity, the bill momentarily enjoyed great popularity because it was usefully vague on those issues—most pointedly the redistribution of national income—most likely to generate the greatest political heat.[29]

Nothing, not even the greatest economic calamity, seemed capable of shaking the trade union bureaucracy out of its profound torpor. Mass production industry remained for it a black box, not only because the steel, auto, rubber, and other industries resisted its infrequent incursions, but because its own internal organizational culture and the politics of work it sustained were premised on the continued subordination of the immigrant unskilled. Moreover, its "most favored" institutional status within the national Democratic Party, or what was left of that status by the late 1920s, was bottomed on an aversion to state and judicial interference with free market labor relations. The political imagination of the trade union hierarchy extended not much farther than a call for federal sanctions against the use of the labor injunction.

For Hillman the message was clear. The balance of power in industry would remain fixed without a change in the balance of power in Washington. Just how to strike a new balance, however, was not at all obvious, especially at the outset of the Depression, when the Democratic Party was still very much the creature of Southern landlords, railroads, nativist agrarians, Wall Street lawyers, the Dupont interests represented by John Raskob and Jesse Shoup, and the urban patronage machines. Even Al Smith's nomination in 1928, while undoubtedly signaling an immigrant political awakening, was by no means unequivocally "progressive." Smith's welfarism contained a heavy admixture of Catholic paternalism, which deferred to the prerogatives of the propertied and was on guard against the intrusions of the state into matters it considered the proper province of the family and the church. While Hillman dealt regularly with Belle Moscowitz, Governor Smith's alter ego, his contact with the Governor himself was minimal.[30]

Some realignment of the Democratic Party, where Hillman enjoyed powerful friendships, was thus to be hoped for but was scarcely a foregone conclusion. Therefore, despite the disappointment of the 1924 La Follette campaign, Hillman did not shut the door on independent politics, the prospects for which were multiplying. *The Nation* issued a call for a new third party at the end of 1928. Hillman allowed his election to the National Committee of the League for Independent Political Action, organized by John Dewey; Paul Douglas; James Mauer, president of the Pennsylvania Federation of Labor and SP vice presidential candidate in 1928; and Oswald Garrison Villard of *The Nation*. The League, created in 1929 with the active participation of J. B. S. Hardman, attracted a host of social critics and intellectual luminaries, including Reinhold Neibuhr, Paul Blanshard, W. E. B. DuBois, and Stuart Chase. Committed to some amorphously defined version of the British Labour Party, it attacked the unequal distribution of wealth and advocated national economic planning, industrial democracy, social insurance, public works, the public control of transportation and utilities, a national minimum wage, and collective bargaining protections. However, while the League made gestures in the direction of labor, it really envisioned a kind of cooperative consumers' democracy. At its 1933 convention labor was scarcely represented.[31]

Meanwhile, Hillman's confederate from the days of the Amalgamated Textile Workers Union, A. J. Muste, organized the Conference for Progressive Labor Action. The Conference was more strictly labor-oriented. It lambasted the AFL and called for a mass campaign for industrial unionism and national unemployment insurance. It felt more at home with the traditional language of labor politics, which emphasized the worker as producer, not consumer. At first LIPA and CPPA were not drastically different in political temperament, but Muste became increasingly sectarian, unwilling to continue relations with mainstream political figures, which might compromise the Conference's commitment to a "workers republic." Hillman therefore kept his distance.

While the League was, on the contrary, anxious to open up channels into mainstream Progressivism, it was not successful in doing so. The godfather of Progressivism, Senator George Norris, declined to accept the titular leadership of the League. By 1932 it was fairly well isolated. Fewer and fewer Progressives were opting for the risky alternative of independent politics.[32]

Proposals, programs, and platforms were everywhere. In 1933 Hillman, along with David Dubinsky, joined the "Continental Congress of Workers and Farmers," convened by the SP and the leadership of the Minnesota Farmer–Labor Party. The Congress was a congeries of all those whose hopes were still invested in a third party. Both the League and the Conference attended, as well as the Farm Holiday Association, the Non-Partisan League, and the various needle unions. Emil Rieve of the Philadelphia hosiery workers' union was present as well. However, by 1933 the political landscape had altered considerably, and the terrain within the Democratic Party suddenly seemed much more hospitable. When Hillman and Dubinsky attended the Continental Congress, they did so not to foster its independence but to convince it that its future lay with the New Deal.[33]

The relationship between independent and major party politics was always a vexed matter for the labor movement, especially for those socialists, or lapsed socialists like Hillman, who presided over institutions saturated in socialist sentiment. The SP aside, most of the fledgling third-party movements of the twentieth century carried on, in one form or another, the antimonopoly oppositional politics of the nineteenth century. Those original antimonopoly parties—beginning with the Greenback-Laborites of the 1870s—by no means ignored the "labor question." On the contrary, these parties were avatars of that "question," burdening its solution with the moral, political, and economic fate of the nation. But it was not the "labor question" as formulated by socialists and their putative proletarian following. The polarities of antimonopoly political morality were not embodied by capital and labor, property and the propertyless, but by parasitic as opposed to productive ways of generating and acquiring wealth. In the legions of social virtue, agrarian smallholders, petty entrepreneurs in business and commerce, and independent artisans occupied the front rank; the position of factory operatives, whose work was certainly productive but also collective and anonymous, was ambiguous. This social and political dissonance continued to trouble the farmer–labor party murmurings of the early 1920s and were in part responsible for the nostalgic atmosphere that haunted the La Follette campaign.

While Hillman remained loyal to the bitter end of that campaign, he would never again seriously countenance this species of third-party or labor-party politics. It was more than a practical reckoning with the enveloping pressures of America's two-party system and more than disgust with the factional hair-splitting typical of third-party ideologues. It was as well Hillman's intuitive sense that the "labor question" had undergone a metamorphosis. If at one time it interrogated the moral legitimacy of the relations of production, indicting those who lived off the labor of others as "parasites," in the future the "labor question" would instead challenge the prevailing relations of consumption, finding in their inequity both a moral flaw and a systemic malfunction. As the axis of the political economy shifted from production to consumption, from the asceticism of productive labor to the narcissism of manipulated desire, the politics of class and caste, always at least implicit in antimonopoly political culture, gradually gave way to the politics of the mass. Some groups, like John Dewey's League, attempted a radical reformulation of this new consumer-oriented labor politics. Others, including the SP, remained wedded to the old verities. On ceremonial occasions even the New Deal invoked an older populist rhetoric, redolent with "economic royalists," "money-changers," and "the tories of industry." But the existential center of national politics was moving steadily away from the workplace and toward the marketplace. Although the principal actors were seemingly the same farmers, workers, and capitalists, they no longer struggled as intensely over the possession of land, surplus value, and corporate enterprise, nor mounted their battles animated by visions of moral redemption or social revolution.

Hillman felt at home with this new political persuasion, notwithstanding his socialist heritage. Years before the Depression, he was recognized as one of its pioneers. He sensed that the traditional centers of popular protest were out of touch with the new politics of economic growth and mass consumption. However, given the still-live convictions of many union militants, for whom the Democratic Party was anathema, it was initially impossible to embroil the ACW directly in various efforts at elite regroupment converging around FDR. So, while Hillman kept the lines open to Dewey's League, to Muste's Conference, and to the Continental Congress, his serious intentions were directed elsewhere, toward the political mainstream.

In March 1931 Senators Norris and La Follette, along with Costigan, Cutting, and Wheeler, convened a "bipartisan" conference, presumably to establish a Progressive legislative agenda and plot strategy. Norris made clear from the outset he would entertain no third-party options. To make his meaning unmistakable, he exclaimed that what the country needed was "another Roosevelt in the White House." The two hundred or so who attended, including Hillman, were of the same mind. They were more or less agreed too on a disparate set of legislative planks— unemployment insurance, public works to settle the business cycle, utility regulation, farm credits, and tariff protection. But it was perhaps premature to expect more. No consensus emerged on a recovery program. The Conference could not even manage to establish a permanent organization. John Dewey was quick to call the conveners to task for failing to force a special session of Congress to act on the emergency and asked: "What has paralyzed Progressive Senators into acquiescence in the plan of exploiting interests to reduce the American people to a state of industrial feudalism and serfdom?" He accused them of betraying the heritage of the senior La Follette. Nonetheless, the conference was an important moment in the slow crystallizing of a reform coalition.[34]

The junior La Follette was raised on his father's populist invocations of "the people," "the interests," and "the trusts." But even for La Follette Senior the latter were principally obstacles to economic development and diversification. By the late 1920s his son was acutely concerned about the way excessive stock speculation was depriving "legitimate" business of adequate credit. Even before the Depression he, together with Robert Wagner, addressed the neglected problem of regional and structural unemployment in an attempt to bridge the gap between rural and urban Progressivism. Unlike his father, he had no aversion to concentrated state power and no longer worshiped the panaceas of traditional "Progressivism" nor trembled at its plutocratic villains. "Of all the progressives of that time," Rexford Tugwell wrote, La Follette "had made the most complete transition to modernism." Like his father, he was a foe of the labor injunction and a good friend of the ACW.[35]

Together with George Norris, La Follette took the lead in assembling the "bipartisan" conference. He proposed to unite it around a legislative agenda whose priority was the creation of a national economic council representing all the principal economic functions—finance, transportation, agriculture, industry, labor—as well as the public. The council's purpose was to restore mass purchasing power through the deft use of public works and a tax structure expressly designed to reapportion wealth, the severe extent of whose maldistribution the Senator cited from a New York Taylor Society study.

Many of Hillman's associates attended, including Wolman, Bruere, Bliven, George Soule, Lillian Wald, Florence Kelley, and Charles and Mary Beard. William Green was also there, but out of phase with other conferees, still equivocating about unemployment insurance, taken aback by the idea of national economic coordination, and, to the consternation of many, arguing vigorously against recognition of the Soviet Union. With equal vigor Soule and Wolman made the case for centralized planning, Soule seconding La Follette's call for a national council. Hillman too spoke on behalf of national unemployment reserves modeled after the Amalgamated's experiment and proposed the five-day week. He was blunt: "I believe today the industrial and financial leaders of the country are bankrupt." He too favored an economic council, urging that it include labor representatives and that it be endowed with executive powers, suggesting that the old War Industries and War Labor boards were analogous to what he had in mind. There were already recommendations aplenty filling the air, but the nation's business and banking leadership seemed deaf to them all. "I have given up hope," Hillman confessed, "that you are going to get it through enlightenment and education."[36]

Enlightenment and education, however, was about all the "bipartisan" conference had to offer. It established committees on agriculture, the tariff, and public utilities, and one chaired by La Follette on unemployment and industrial stabilization. Hillman was a member of the last, along with his old friends Florence Kelley, Soule, Wolman, and Meyer Jacobstein (by then head of the First National Bank and Trust of Rochester). After the conference the committee was enlarged to include Basil Manly (co-chairman with William Taft of the old War Labor Board), Edwin Smith (adviser to Dennison and Filene at the Twentieth Century Fund), and Tugwell. But like all the other committees, its preliminary report was rather vague and without issue.[37]

This very vaporousness pointed up the need for more concrete stratagems. Even before the conference convened, Charles Ervin, socialist, future editor of the *Advance*, and ACW operative in Washington, received a call from Hillman asking if "there's someone in the Senate to put in a bill for an economic council or at least to hold hearings to get

the real picture of the economy of the country." La Follette, as chairman
of the Senate Committee on Manufactures, was the obvious candidate,
and he readily agreed. The hearings were carefully choreographed well in
advance in small gatherings organized by La Follette that included Hillman, Soule, Harlow Person, Wolman, and Isador Lubin, an economist
at the Brookings Institute who served with Hillman on the unemployment
and industrial stabilization committee. The group discussed who was to
testify and what questions were to be asked; they plotted the sequence of
testimony to display first the ideological and programmatic exhaustion of
the business community and then to follow that exhibition of incompetence with "expert" analysis by friendly economists and industrial engineers in support of the committee's predictable recommendation: a
national economic council to be composed of fifteen representatives of
industry, finance, transportation, agriculture, and labor.[38]

The hearings were conducted between October and November of
1931 and proceeded according to plan. La Follette questioned Hillman
about the recently released report by Henry Harriman, president of the
U.S. Chamber of Commerce, which came out in opposition to a representative council on the grounds that it would be paralyzed by the con-
tradictory interests composing it. Harriman, like others in the business
community, was desperate enough to countenance some collective monitoring of commercial activity but was determined that in any such venture business remain the senior partner. Hillman noted that the
Depression had gone on long enough to convince even the most myopic
that a national view of the economic crisis was essential if only from the
standpoint of enlightened self-interest. La Follette next afforded Hillman
a chance to launch his first public attack on the Swope Plan for industrial
self-regulation, then attracting much attention. Hillman echoed Frankfurter's anxieties about Swope's confederate, Owen Young. He warned
that less democratic organizational formulae, including the Swope Plan,
could conceivably lead to fascism.[39]

Gerard Swope was an unusual man, and his plan was a strange
concoction. The President of General Electric, Swope, like Harriman,
presumed the preeminence of business. Unlike Harriman, his origins
were far less prepossessing. He was a poor boy who had made good. As
a young man in the 1890s he had taught classes at Hull House on algebra
and electricity. He had lived at the House and had come to know Jane
Addams, Florence Kelley, and Ellen Gates Starr. There he had met as
well the Webbs and Ramsay McDonald. The impact of these earlier
associations, and GE's own experiments with welfare capitalism, especially company unemployment insurance, were detectable in the "Plan"

announced by Swope. For example, it called for a federal workmen's compensation act and unemployment insurance funded by voluntary employee contributions to be matched by the employer. Because of its social welfare appeal, and because it declared the need for conscious coordination of production and consumption—an imperative vague enough to command broad agreement—the "Plan" was endorsed by Walter Lippmann and Stuart Chase, and was even critically supported by *The Nation*. Indeed, Swope's credentials were impressive enough so that even before the "Plan" was unveiled Jacob Billikopf, an ACW adviser and Jewish labor conciliator, actually explored the chances for Hillman and Swope to collaborate.[40]

Billikopf's was a well-intentioned dream, but a dream nonetheless. Hard-core support for the "Plan" remained confined to the business community, among those like *Business Week* who applauded its call for the suspension of antitrust law. The Swope Plan was essentially a version of business syndicalism plus the police. It was genealogically connected to the trade association movement of the previous decade, but the Depression proved that movement's vision of voluntaristic self-regulation of capital to be a chimera. Gerard Swope was not the first to convert to the belief that in conditions of shrinking markets and declining profits sterner political measures and legal sanctions were perhaps the only way to prevent the autocannibalism of American business.[41]

Hillman was not alone in decrying the "Plan," along with similar, if less legally coercive, arrangements sponsored by the USCC and the NAM. Tugwell pronounced business incompetent to manage the economy in the public interest, as the Swope Plan proposed. He called instead for social—i.e., state—control over profit margins as well as investment and pricing decisions. Both Hillman and Tugwell dismissed schemes like Swope's because of their focus on price competition and on the arguably fraudulent problem of overproduction rather than on questions of aggregate demand. The Swope proposal was, Hillman asserted, critically flawed, as it contained no provisions for proper wage and hour standards, deliberately neglected to afford a place for labor representation in the regulatory mechanism, was niggardly in its estimate of unemployment reserves, depended essentially on a process of voluntary compliance, and was intrinsically inefficient. At best it would permit price-fixing and the restriction of production in those industrial sectors subject to monopolistic or oligopolistic domination.[42]

The struggle over whether corporatism was to determine the contours of public policy lasted from the time of the La Follette hearings to the creation of the NRA and beyond. While often presented publicly as an attack on low wages, long hours, unemployment, and child labor, in fact the operative core of this corporatist program of guildlike cartelization was a system of production controls, the regulation of new entry into industry, price-fixing, and the cooperative sharing out of the remaining market. Strategically, its outlook was intrinsically parochial, consisting of the arithmetical summation of individual corporate and trade association self-interests. Hillman was willing to grant the usefulness of cartelization under government auspices in special emergency cases, in particular for those industries that even in the 1920s were generally recognized as "sick"—textiles and mining, for example. But those exceptional cases never led Hillman to adopt a more global corporatist orientation. As a practical matter, what schemes like those promoted by Swope, Harriman, and especially Bernard Baruch entailed was mortgaging the moral and political authority of the state to distinct blocs of concentrated industrial and financial power whose needs under the extraordinary pressures of a depressed market could no longer be adequately accommodated within an unpredictable parliamentary system susceptible to the pressures of mass politics. Adolph Berle put it well. He told Roosevelt that Bernard Baruch's recovery program, once looked at closely, essentially ceded to 600 to 800 large corporations the freedom "to fight out among themselves the ultimate mastery of the situation."[43]

Yet it is also true that Hillman was directly involved in all the political maneuvering preliminary to the creation of the NRA, and immediately accepted appointment to its Labor Advisory Board and later to the National Industrial Recovery Board itself. He did so despite the fact that the final draft of the NIRA was regarded as a triumph, if not a total one, for corporatism. No doubt this betokens his single-minded pursuit of power, but it is also true that in the actual "eating" the NRA turned out to be far less an unadulterated form of big firm corporatism than the original recipe may have called for. Such anomalies were to be expected, given the liquified state of national politics. In any event, as the presidential election year began, the struggle to shape the recovery policy of the Democratic Party's front-runner heated up. In the process, Hillman drew closer to the inner sanctum of the new regime.[44]

Hillman's general views about planning and purchasing power as well as his specific recommendations for unemployment insurance and public works became known to FDR principally through Felix Frankfurter, Frances Perkins, and Rexford Tugwell. Tugwell consulted Hillman, along with others, in the summer of 1932 regarding a seven point program of industrial reconstruction then being discussed within the Brains Trust. Later that year Hillman drafted a memo, with the advice of Wolman and the encouragement of Perkins and Frankfurter, addressed to the recovery problem. It prescribed industrial regulation, national planning, and a

federal labor board to enforce wage and hour legislation. Hillman recalled the efforts of the WLB and WIB to establish rules "subordinating
the interests of the group to the welfare of the country," and suggested
that the President-elect convene a small group to work out a specific plan
"for protecting the purchasing power of our industrial communities."
Frankfurter presented the substance of the memo to Roosevelt, who
indicated his high regard for the ACW's accomplishments in the field of
cooperative housing and noted not only Hillman's policy recommendations but his specific suggestions for personnel to administer the proposed
labor board. "I put your views very strongly to the President-elect, with
a sympathetic response on his part," Frankfurter reported. Frankfurter
advised Hillman to put together a small group, including Wolman and
Henry Bruere, to formulate a concrete set of legislative proposals for a
forthcoming Senate inquiry.[45]

But Roosevelt's views on these matters remained far from settled.
Hillman grew anxious for some more concrete indication of administra-
tion plans. Wolman contacted Perkins just as she was about to leave for
Washington to tell her that "Hillman and the boys are restive that
nothing's being done for labor." "The boys" had worked hard for
Roosevelt's election in the face of the long-standing socialist traditions of
the Jewish labor movement. They wanted something tangible in return.
Wolman arranged for Hillman to meet Perkins at Penn Station, where
the union leader was "trembling with excitement, his nostrils dilating."
While offering his moral support for Perkins's overall program, he feared
it would take considerable time to implement, and that in the interim
what was required was "a signal, a symbol" of the labor sympathies of the
new regime. He suggested a conference of labor leaders, which Perkins
reluctantly agreed was probably wise. Isador Lubin, together with the
Taylor Society activists Otto and Clara Beyer, helped Perkins plan the
conference. That it included Hillman at all was for Perkins a somewhat
risky departure from established practice, as the ACW still remained
outside the official labor movement. But she was anxious for Hillman's
support for her legislative program, and in particular expected his help in
engineering protective legislation for women workers.

When the conference gathered it discussed unemployment and old
age insurance, child labor, and the Black bill. Hillman then joined a
conference delegation, chaired by Dan Tobin, Teamster President and
Democratic Party labor chairman, to meet with FDR. There Perkins
raised a Frankfurter–Hillman proposal for government-enforced standards
of wages and hours on all government contracts. Roosevelt was noncommittal. Meanwhile Hillman, together with Donald Richberg and in consultation with Frankfurter, drafted a series of amendments to the Black

bill (amendments later identified with Perkins) designed to create an adequate enforcement mechanism of regionally based tripartite labor boards. The boards would have the power "to fix or alter wages, hours, and other employment conditions," with hours to be set initially at thirty. By April Frankfurter was urging the wisdom of "someone holding, as it were, a watching-brief for the ideas of Hillman, which if I understand it aright, have been the governing impulse behind the present effort for wage boards, etc."[46]

This whole scheme for executive-administrative intervention into the labor market was vehemently opposed by AFL voluntarists like William Green and Matthew Woll. Indeed, part of Green's enthusiasm for the original Black bill stemmed from his antipathy for Hillman's, and now Perkins's dangerous amendments. Green found himself in alliance with Henry Harriman and John Dickinson, Roosevelt's Assistant Secretary of Commerce, who also opposed federal intervention in the labor market. Despite its AFL support, however, Hillman was not bashful about criticizing the Black bill for its lack of an enforcement mechanism and its neglect of a complementary minimum-wage provision. Unamended, Hillman warned, the bill might "merely have the effect of sharing the misery." Alexander Sachs articulated this broader, "Keynesian" critique of the bill:

> In sum, the Black bill, with or without a minimum wage, will have repercussions in the direction of making current operations of business unprofitable . . . and narrowing the margin of mass income that can be spent for articles other than bare necessities, so causing a discontinuous or slumping drop in demand for the articles produced by a great many of the larger employers of labor for the making of semi-luxury or intermediate goods from biscuits and articles of new apparel with every change in fashion to automobiles.[47]

In the absence of an administration alternative the Black bill attracted surprisingly wide Congressional support. The Hillman–Richberg amendments offered by Perkins were in part designed to stall the bill's momentum while contending factions within the administration struggled to formulate a more comprehensive and politically viable program for industrial revival. Hillman was recruited into one of the working groups, chaired by Senator Wagner, drafting recovery legislation. It included Isador Lubin and Meyer Jacobstein, as well as Harold Moulton of Brookings, and the Progressive businessmen Malcolm Rorty and James Rand of Remington Rand. Also in attendance was Jett Lauck, a Taylor Society member and economic adviser to John L. Lewis, who together with Richberg would help formulate the labor provisions of the recovery act. The Wagner group favored a moderate form of "Keynesian" economic management emphasizing the interim usefulness of countercyclical fiscal policy. In turn they conferred with Perkins, Tugwell, and Jerome Frank, who were similarly inclined in favor of public works, government loans, and the guaranteed right to collective bargaining. Paul Mazur of Lehman Brothers, a "satellite" member of the Brains Trust and an associate of Louis Kirstein, added the weight of the consumer-oriented investment banking community to these circles advocating some form of "Keynesian" economic policy.[48]

Corporatists under the leadership of Bernard Baruch, Swope, Hugh Johnson, and others turned out still to carry greater political weight than their foes. The command centers of the Democratic Party remained densely populated with proponents and practitioners of corporatism and fiscal conservatism. Baruch himself leaned toward state-sanctioned cooperation among producers to avoid overproduction and price-cutting competition, hoping an administrative elite rather than a more popularly vulnerable Congress might resolve the crisis. While he favored the eight-hour day and a minimum wage, he sought a private, essentially voluntary solution. Fred Kent of Bankers Trust, a Morgan Guaranty ally, lobbied for support to the capital goods sector together with a government guarantee against losses. Within the NCF, support poured in from older, lower-profit makers of basic producer goods, primary materials, and undifferentiated consumer commodities like textiles. Business opposition to any federal law regulating labor standards was widespread and determined. In late May the Senate Finance Committee heard Robert P. Lamont of the Iron and Steel Institute, James Emery of the NAM, and Charles P. Hock of American Rolling Mills denounce the collective bargaining provisions of the prospective recovery bill. They were equally intent on excluding from the legislation any manifest connection between hours of work and the problem of reemployment.[49]

As the NIRA crystallized, pessimism in the Frankfurter circle grew. Only the labor provisions of the act, which they viewed as genuine devices for reemployment and recovery, commanded their wholehearted support. Frankfurter pinned what hopes remained on the bill's separate public works section and observed: "The labor clauses at once assume a commanding importance as part of any industrial code." Jett Lauck also expressed reservations. He told Roosevelt he was worried about business domination of the NRA and drafted a memo warning that the bill would be "temporizing, ineffective, and ultimately (within two or three years) disastrous" unless it was all-inclusive and mandatory and based on a sense of a permanent new order to secure expanded purchasing power. "The point is—not that we wish to secure advances or higher standards or power for labor and salaried workers—but in order to save and maintain capital and the capitalistic system in an enlightened way, we must do this. There is no other alternative."[50]

Alexander Sachs, the economist from Lehman Brothers who would soon go to work for the NRA's research division, warned Hugh Johnson about the dangers of the corporatist thinking inspiring much of the NRA. He cited as causes of the Depression "policies which had the effect of sterilizing wealth and credit resources" as well as a lack of flexibility and initiative on the part of large corporations "sicklied o'er by the pale cast of laissez-faire and liquidity complexes." There was an "imperative need for Government intervention to stimulate activity." Large corporations had "interposed rigidities and put resistances to the very adjustments that laissez-faire capitalism requires." He suggested a hefty government investment in capital goods in construction, railroad maintenance and rehabilitation, slum clearance, and a major homebuilding movement mobilized by reorganizing and enlisting the insurance and savings bank business "in the way Keynes has in Britain and a big program of consumer credit for consumer durables." Sachs feared instead that what was to become the NRA would, like the German cartel system, have the effect of "congealing the inflated capital values of the speculative era."[51]

As the NIRA became the law of the land, it remained an open question as to whether or not a real remedy had been found for an economy "sicklied o'er" by "liquidity complexes," whose sclerotic arteries were all but dammed shut by "inflated capital values." Hillman went about bravely claiming that "the old order had passed—no matter how much its adherents may regret it." But as a matter of hard fact, for those who, like Frankfurter, Lauck, Sachs, and Hillman too, had fought tirelessly to bring it to an end, the "speculative era" was by no means dead.[52]

ELEVEN

❦

"Washington Merry-Go-Round" or "National Runaround"

William Green hailed the NRA as the "Magna Carta" of organized labor. John L. Lewis compared it to the Emancipation Proclamation. Both men undoubtedly knew better. After all, the act's celebrated clause 7a, legitimating the right of collective bargaining, was hardly a credit to the labor movement's strength. *Fortune* magazine reported that the emancipatory provision was essentially drafted by Jett Lauck and Harold Moulton of the Brookings Institute and that the AFL was nowhere to be seen at the critical meetings in Wagner's office when the bill received its final formulation. Instead, 7a expressed the independent political strategy and economic theorizing of an emerging elite, which more often than not had to encourage an otherwise intimidated labor bureaucracy to think as boldly as it did.[1]

Hillman also publicly supported the act, especially its separate public works section. He preferred the amended version of the Black bill, which "would have put labor onto the ground floor of the new industrial structure." Nevertheless, the NRA "restores, if only to a degree, the possibility of labor recovery." Privately, in discussions with the GEB, he was franker, if still cautiously optimistic. He told them that the bill was not intended to help labor and had been drafted by major banking and manufacturing interests. While noting that he, along with Richberg and Wagner, had managed to incorporate a collective bargaining clause, he acknowledged the failure to have it made mandatory. He recognized General Hugh Johnson's open shop inclinations but felt he might be flexible, especially as Wolman and Richberg were to work closely with the General. Most important, he speculated that the ACW could count on its "extraordinary contacts within the Administration" and that the bill's rhetorical support for collective bargaining could be used to mount a mass organizing campaign.[2]

Hillman expected little to happen through the machinery of the act by itself. Everything depended on the response of organized labor. "Labor must think in terms of the whole working class and base its policies upon inclusive, all-encompassing organization." He proposed to the GEB a joint organizing drive by all the needle trades unions. The NRA would create, he predicted, a buoyant and militant spirit and a shift, if only temporarily, in the balance of power, which might make militant struggle once again possible not only in the garment industry but across industrial America. In a radio address in June, Hillman prophesied that mass industrial unionism was the only way to combat the growing organization of business. Signs were for the first time propitious: a new administration, new legislation, a new spirit of resistance. He was, moreover, ready to pioneer the effort. If the ACW acted decisively and immediately, the AFL would follow. He told his confidant Jacob Potofsky: "You don't transfer power by statute. Section 7a can be enforced through strikes. You don't expect the Government to send the American working class to Labor Unions. That is the union's job."[3]

Hillman was as good as his word. His intuitive sense about a sea change in popular attitudes was on target. The Amalgamated immediately launched a major drive to organize the shirt industry, centered in the Appalachian foothills of Pennsylvania.

New York City was once the heart of the shirt industry, much of it unionized. But by the late 1920s it had deserted the city, drifting out of town into the farming communities and tiny hamlets of rural Pennsylvania, New Jersey, Connecticut, and upstate New York. Only the skilled design and cutting operations remained in the city. Conditions and wages in the hinterland were horrible. Wages ranged from $2 to $10 a week for eleven-hour days. The union assigned its most experienced and talented organizers, headed by Potofsky. Because farm women and the wives and daughters of anthracite miners constituted so much of the workforce, women organizers—Dorothy Bellanca, Mamie Santora, Gladys Dickason—played a conspicuous role. It was the occasion too for Bessie Hillman's return to active duty. Having spent the previous decade caring for their two young daughters, Bessie was more than eager to resume a place in the movement and institution she rightly felt responsible for founding.

The Amalgamated general staff decided to tackle first the most notorious sweatshops of Connecticut and Pennsylvania, in towns like Allentown and Northampton. Next the battle plan called for organizing small, independent, but sympathetic manufacturers as a way of tightening the noose around the larger shirt companies like H. D. Bob and Phillips-Jones. An "Anti-Sweatshop Committee" was established in Allentown, headed by the Mayor, to mobilize citizens outraged by the sweatshop labor of children. Meanwhile, the New York cutters called a general strike and refused to prepare garments for out-of-town contract shops in Connecticut. In New Haven, where many such shops were located, Yale students helped man the picket lines. That was a sign of some vaster shift in the climate of public opinion, as unions were hardly accustomed to sympathy from students at elite universities. By May the union was proclaiming victory across much of Connecticut. While the Yale undergraduates marched they were heartened by news of a great triumph by three thousand workers in Elizabeth, New Jersey. It was a particularly notable victory because it involved a large number of black workers, a relative novelty in the industry, and because the strikers were actively aided by Elizabeth's Mayor—another sign of something astir in public life.

The anthracite region of Pennsylvania was the toughest to penetrate. Miners and their union were of enormous help, both politically and by providing critical manpower, especially in the strategically vital center of Hazelton, where a major manufacturer, S. Liebowitz & Sons, operated one of its thirty branch plants and where the UMW exerted real municipal power. The Liebowitz firm quickly agreed to arbitration, in part because Samuel Rosenman, a Roosevelt confidant, was providing the company with legal advice. The drive in Hazelton coincided with and complemented a mass campaign of hosiery workers in nearby Reading. This joint organizing drive established a relationship between the Amalgamated and a militant wing of the UTW under Emil Rieve which would mature and bear fruit later.[4]

The shirt campaign culminated in an assault on H. D. Bob and Phillips-Jones, both with shops organized in chain-store fashion throughout the mining country. They were defiant and dominated municipal politics; local officialdom went so far as to prohibit union meetings and the distribution of union literature. Union flying squadrons sped from town to town in trucks spreading word of the strike, bolstering picket lines, and intimidating scabs. H. D. Bob succumbed. Two thousand workers joined the union in Hazelton. Phillips-Jones chose instead to sign a contract with the UGW, doubtless a less expensive option, as the UGW remained ready to oblige if it meant thwarting the maddening ambitions of the Amalgamated.

All in all the shirt campaign was a creditable victory. By May the union could report six thousand workers in Pennsylvania alone— Allentown, Shamaking, Bangor, Mt. Carmel, Roseto, and Northampton. In June the *Advance* reported 13,000 shirt members nationwide. Solid inroads the following year were made in Rhode Island, West Virginia, and Maryland, as the union chased the industry from state to state.

It was a victory made possible in part by the country's new political chemistry and the announced purpose of the new regime's recovery legislation. In Pennsylvania, for example, Governor Amos Pinchot, an acquaintance of Hillman and a loyal friend of the New Deal, pressured manufacturers to negotiate with the union. The union itself made it unmistakably clear that it was acting in accordance with the wishes of the President and the NRA. A leaflet distributed to Bob Company workers in Sunbury, Pennsylvania, warned: "The Industrial Recovery Act is here for *ONE* year *ONLY.*" "Unionization of your shop is your part in making the Industrial Recovery Act a success." It concluded by exhorting workers to "Exercise your American Rights and organize." A similar leaflet distributed in Morgantown reassured shirtworkers, "The law is behind you. The NRA protects your right to have a union and will punish the boss if he tries to stop you. . . . The President is behind you." Another pamphlet informed workers that Hillman had just been appointed by the President to the Labor Advisory Board under the NRA, a board chaired by the onetime ACW research director, Leo Wolman. Clothing workers at open-shop Keller, Heumann, Thompson in Rochester learned that the "National Industrial Recovery Act is the greatest victory organized labor achieved since the Civil War." In Boston the union proclaimed that President Roosevelt "has given us a republic in industry, and abolished industrial despotism."[5]

As in the case of the shirt drive, the NRA became a usable instrument of labor organization. The whole city of Cleveland, led by its paternalistic chief employer, Richard Feiss, succumbed to the union in 1934 during a strike that its leader, Gus Strebel, acknowledged was not planned but was rather a testament to the "moral strength provided by the NRA." In 1933 and 1934 ACW membership increased by 50,000. The ILG, a practically moribund organization in 1932, was healthy again by 1934. There were similar results elsewhere, as for example in the growth of the UMW, where John L. Lewis proclaimed it a patriotic duty to enlist in the union. Millhands in the Southern textile industry, long among the most abused and intimidated, overwhelmed an otherwise comatose UTW with their demands for organization so that within a year the union grew from 40,000 to 270,000 members. In steel, automobiles, and rubber, in the electrical and longshore industries, and almost everywhere, even among despised and powerless migrant workers, the NRA proved inspirational, even if the results turned out to be less tangible. A great flood of strikes followed the promulgation of 7a—indeed, more than in any year since 1921. Just in the few months from June to October 1933 the AFL established 3,537 new federal locals. In 1933 and 1934 the trade union movement recovered all the membership it had lost since 1923. While only 17 percent of the labor force in 1929, trade union membership increased to 27 percent in 1933 and to 33 percent in 1934.[6]

Yet on the whole the NRA, so far as the labor movement was concerned, amounted in the end to the "national runaround." Nor were trade unionists alone in their disappointment. Even those elements of business who greeted the passage of the NRA with enthusiasm were bitterly aware, within a year or less, that it could do little to eliminate the endemic fractiousness of a capitalist economy in crisis.

The NRA was born in contradiction and would never escape that fate. Its various godfathers and midwives, its critics as well as its champions, imagined an utterly improbable administrative creature, one capable of social reform and economic recovery; of production curtailment and expanded production; of restricted private investment in new capital goods and expanded investment in public works to stimulate capital goods investment; of establishing minimum wages while avoiding plant shutdowns; of reducing working hours while raising the standard of living; of fixing prices while maintaining the competitive marketplace. The guildlike corporatist collaboration envisioned by Swope, Harriman, and Baruch; the fantasies of state capitalism dreamed by Tugwell and Berle; and the labor-oriented mass consumption industrial democracy prophesied by Frankfurter, Perkins, and Hillman all disintegrated in an acid bath of acrimonious self-interest, administrative ineptitude, and political vacillation.

If Hillman too grew discouraged, he could scarcely claim to be surprised. From the inception of this anodyne recovery administration he was embroiled in the industrial and political machinations that paralyzed its machinery.

Soon after the bill was passed, Roosevelt appointed industrial and labor advisory boards to assist the NRA's administrator, Hugh Johnson, and to formalize channels of communication with the government. Frances Perkins consulted Leo Wolman about a list of nominees for the Labor Advisory Board, a list that did not include Hillman. She feared his appointment would antagonize the AFL. Wolman, however, insisted that Hillman be included: "I knew it would break his heart if he wasn't on." Perkins had worked with Hillman for years. She knew he felt jealous, left out, and yet "superior to the AFL," and therefore bitter that

despite the achievements of the ACW the Federation continued to exclude it. Moreover, it was in Perkins's political and bureaucratic self-
interest to promote the unity of the labor movement. So she relented and
sponsored Hillman's appointment to a board that also included Green,
Lewis, Rose Schneiderman, Frey, and Father Francis Haas. She never
regretted the decision: "Hillman behaved beautifully through this
period"—by which she meant he was diplomatic and did his best to
suppress what the Secretary considered his pronounced tendency to display his superiority.[7]

Hillman in turn was gratified by the official recognition of his real
standing in a trade union movement that still formally treated him as a
renegade. In fact, soon afterward the AFL felt compelled, given Hillman's new status, to accept the outlaw Amalgamated. Jurisdictional
negotiations with his old nemesis, Rickert of the UGW, were concluded
by September and, for a while at least, Hillman enjoyed this besting of
an old foe.[8]

As the shirt workers' campaign demonstrated, the Amalgamated was
quick to exploit the illusion of Hillman's new-found power. Hillman
himself doubted that a board with strictly advisory powers could have
much effect on industrial codes that were clearly, in most cases, to be
designed by trade associations. Nonetheless, he was determined to make
the most of the opportunity.

Almost immediately the LAB moved to assure labor's right to representation at all conferences preceding public hearings on prospective
code provisions. Soon thereafter, in August, the Board issued a statement criticizing industrial "merit" clauses. Open-shop industrialists
sought to include such "merit" clauses in codes as a way of circumventing
Section 7a; union sympathizers could then be fired for "merit" rather
than for their sympathies. Indeed, bad omens appeared everywhere. Hillman denounced the forty-hour maximum and $10 minimum proposed for
the Cotton Textile code, calling instead for a 50 cents per hour wage and
a thirty-six-hour week. The textile hearings were critical first of all to
Hillman personally because of the industry's proximity to his own; whatever standards were established there would undoubtedly affect the prospective garment code. More important, because the cotton textile
industry was the first to promulgate a code, it could, Hillman feared, set
a bad precedent. He was right, and it did. Eighty-three of the first
hundred codes established forty-hour maximums. Six actually allowed for
more than forty hours.[9]

If the textile code was a disappointment, the avalanche of worker
complaints, petitions, and strike demands that poured into the offices of
the NRA and the Labor Department presented a real crisis. The flood-

waters rose even higher when the President issued a blanket model code for all industries. It practically invited a torrent of grievances, strikes, and lockouts with no administrative machinery in place to handle it all. General Johnson convened a joint meeting of the IAB and the LAB early in August. Walter Teagle of Standard Oil, who chaired the meeting, wanted a statement urging workers to be patient, to accept the status quo at least temporarily while the NRA devised means for adjudicating disputes. The conferees were paralyzed with fear and indecision. Johnson himself was ambivalent. There were times when he actually lectured the LAB on the need for "vertical unions" in modern industry, a phrase he had borrowed from his adviser, Alexander Sachs. At other times he championed the avatar of the open shop. Meanwhile Teagle's stand-pat view was shared not only by the other members of the IAB but by William Green as well. Hillman insisted instead that "special examiners," "men of reputation and standing," be appointed immediately to handle the most urgent matters and that whatever joint statement issued out of the meeting guarantee the "right to organize."[10]

Green, who made no secret of his hostility to Hillman's very presence on the Board, denounced his views as "extreme." A joint statement was issued, pleading, essentially as Teagle wished, for industrial peace until the codes were installed. Rhetoric, no matter how conciliatory or aggressive, was clearly by itself insufficient. In September the President created a tripartite National Labor Board. Teagle, Swope, and Hillman's old friend Louis Kirstein represented business; Wolman, Green, and Lewis spoke for labor; Senator Wagner chaired. From Hillman's standpoint this was a promising development. Wagner was a political ally, as was Kirstein. Neither Teagle nor Swope was inveterately hostile. William Leiserson, Hillman's friend and clothing industry arbiter, was active behind the scenes in defining the procedures and functions of the new board. Leiserson consulted frequently with Wolman, who was not only chairman of the LAB but remained Hillman's closest economic adviser, even though he had returned to teaching at Columbia University in 1931.[11]

The Board's initial interventions were largely successful and pleasing to Hillman particularly. At his urging the Board took an active interest in the shirt and hosiery strikes. In fact, its first strike settlement came in the hosiery mills of Berks County, Pennsylvania. More generally, the Board brought its power to bear in decentralized, competitive industries—clothing, jewelry, hosiery, laundries—where internal pressures to establish uniform standards complemented its work. Wagner even tried to bring to heel the ACW's most implacable opponent, William Curlee of St. Louis, who led a national trade association of open-shop manufacturers. Curlee refused to negotiate during a three-month strike in St. Louis. At Hillman's request the NLB announced a public hearing to be conducted by Kirstein, Father Haas, and Berry of the Printing Pressmen's union. Curlee remained defiant and boycotted the proceedings. Nonetheless, the responsiveness of the Board was encouraging.[12]

So too was the presence of Father Haas. Haas's admiration for Hillman and the ACW began with his 1922 Catholic University dissertation on the union's innovations in collective bargaining. Thanks in part to Hillman's influence, Haas was appointed to the LAB. He was a typical social action priest whose views were shaped by the the papal encyclicals of 1891 and 1931. The latter particularly not only pleaded for protective labor legislation but sketched a corporatist vision of the tripartite determination of economic life more generally. Haas blamed the Depression on the maldistribution of income. He not only approved of trade unions, but considered it a sacred obligation to join one. Naturally, he advocated unemployment insurance, a minimum wage, and health insurance legislation.[13]

Friendly faces and friendly decisions, especially the Reading Railroad case, in which the Board enunciated the principle of "majority rule" for determining the sole legitimate collective bargaining representative, made these early months of the NRA hopeful if not harmonious. Two Taylor Society engineers, Ordway Tead and Harry Metcalf, published a guide, *Labor Relations Under the Recovery Act,* to demonstrate the wisdom of bargaining through either independent or credible company unions and called for nationwide labor agreements arrived at through national industrial councils. Theirs was a benign corporatism which could be given life by the NRA, or so they hoped.[14]

But there were forebodings. Few were ready to be guided by Ordway and Tead. Frankfurter wrote to Richberg in July noting the "growing attitude on the part of some major industries, now that an upswing seems to be definitely under way, to give the Industrial Recovery Act the quiet go-by in order not to yield a jot or a tittle of their intransigent attitude against collective bargaining." For many industrialists fealty to the Blue Eagle was as fickle as the most recent upticks in the stock market. Frankfurter remained optimistic, however, that the President still intended to impose codes covering hours and wages, which, in his view, were the two critical areas for recovery: "If those standards indispensable for re-absorption of labor are enforced by the government, the gentry can take their own sweet time about other subjects."[15]

But neither Roosevelt nor Johnson was ever prepared to take that step, nor was either about to assume the political risk of supporting agencies like the NLB when it ran into the concerted resistance of heavy industry, as it did in the corporate presence of Budd Manufacturing and Weirton Steel. Industry launched a counteroffensive in the name of collective bargaining "pluralism," a principle of "proportional representation" that effectively nullified the bargaining leverage of independent unions and gave company unions a new lease on life. The principle initially had been rejected by the NLB, but Johnson and Richberg connived to get Roosevelt to endorse it in the case of the auto industry in the spring of 1934, thus terminating the viability of the ill-fated NLB. A boom in company unionism followed. By 1935 there were about six hundred or seven hundred of them, covering 2 to 3 million workers, many purely cosmetic, others, as at AT&T, GE, Goodyear, and Standard Oil, that actually engaged in serious consultations over wages and grievances.[16]

Over this issue Hillman lost an erstwhile ally in Richberg and, more painfully, a valued friend in the person of Leo Wolman. Like Richberg and Johnson, Wolman was deathly afraid of alienating the politically potent and vengeful titans of heavy industry. Besides, he had married into wealth and increasingly moved socially in those circles. Hillman was grievously hurt by what he considered Wolman's betrayal. He felt acutely the loss of intellectual support, but he was also quite fond of Wolman and had shared confidences with him that he had with very few others. Another good friend, in looking back, thought "some of Hillman himself was lost with Wolman's defection from his small circle of trusted associates."[17]

As Wolman's defection suggests, federal labor policy was incoherent mainly for lack of political will and wherewithal. The LAB was an excellent example. It was saturated with good intentions. Its key administrative aides working under Wolman, including Solomon Barkin, Gustav Peck, and Howard Meyers, were all committed to independent unionism. In a memo to his staff, Barkin defined "company or individual plant unions" as beyond the pale, "not even to be considered in the problem of representation." Similarly, Peck recommended that his staff engage in a mild tactical subversion by deliberately boycotting code authority meetings lacking "true labor representatives." Underconsumptionist analysis and ideology pervaded the Board's approach to recovery. Its briefs argued that through a reduction in hours

> . . . the leisure provided will foster greater consumption of durable goods and new services and culture industries. The broader base provided for mass

income and the greater time for the utilization of the income may facilitate
vertical growth in mass standards in contrast with the concentrated profit
inflation of the late New Era.

Barkin, Peck, and Meyers were diligent enforcers of health, safety,
and age limit regulations encoded by industry authorities and were te-
nacious in pursuing complaints, especially those many well-founded
charges of discrimination for union activity, or merely for complaining.
In the area of health and safety, and in protecting skilled wage differentials, the Board was on the offensive. Thus, it fought hard over the issue
of wage-sex differentials: 456 codes included equal pay for equal work
provisions. But on the matters of basic wages and hours and union
recognition, the LAB was almost invariably on the defensive, responding
to the incursions and defiance of basic industry.[18]

Despite its valiant struggle against "merit clauses" as "screens behind
which employers opposed to any organization by their employees have
intimidated or eliminated wage-earners forming organizations of their
own," the Board's warning was heeded only in smaller peripheral industries. Although a resolution in September 1933 asked for Board representation on all code authorities, Johnson stalled, and the principle died
from disuse. Once codes were adopted, the Board was in most instances
helpless to affect amendments in basic wage and hour provisions. The
very process of code adoption was often an exercise in hypocrisy and
sham.[19]

The AFL spent a great deal of its time in endless administrative-
bureaucratic wrangling, meanwhile trying to forestall strikes and to control rank-and-file militants in the auto, aluminum, steel, and rubber
industries. But even someone as cautious as John Frey was moved to
complain that many codes arrived on the desks of Johnson and Roosevelt
claiming approval by the LAB when in fact the Board had little or no
knowledge of what they contained. Part of the problem, Frey observed,
was the part-time participation of the Board's busy members. He suggested the employment of full-time trade union representatives. The
whole NRA did indeed suffer from administrative amateurism, a symp-
tom of the underdevelopment of the American state bureaucracy and of
its civil service cadre more generally.[20]

But the problem at bottom was political, not administrative. The
compliance mechanism was after all motivated to maintain "fair competition," whether or not that coincided with the needs of working
people. So long as compliance was a function not of the government but
of each industry's code authority, little could be expected, unless there
happened to be a strong union presence on the authority itself. However,

even in some of those relatively rare instances where the preexisting strength of the trade union movement allowed for labor's official representation, the practical results were hardly different. Jacob Potofsky complained to Bertram Oppenheimer, the Deputy Administrator of the Cotton Garment Code Authority, that the Labor Complaints Committee set up to adjust labor provisions was little more than a "rubber stamp for approval of the acts of the officers of the Code Authority . . . who we feel are merely carrying out the designs and wishes of the International Association of Cotton Garment Manufacturers."

Here was a code with active labor representatives and an industry with an active, if weak, union. Yet an anonymous New York worker, one among many who chose anonymity for fear of retaliation, wrote to Frances Perkins to report how his employer, a member in good standing of the code authority, had compelled him to train workers in a scab plant, workers destined to replace him and his fellows. "There is a bellicose attitude on the part of the employer and very threatening of dismissal." In a pointed and poignant depiction of the conundrum facing sympathetic bureaucrats, Clara Beyer, wife of the scientific manager Otto Beyer and Perkins's assistant director of the Labor Department's Division of Labor Standards, replied that as long as the employer was abiding by the provisions of the code, "there is little that can be done by the Government. The improvement of conditions in general will probably only come through organization of the workers." In the coy parlance of the self-censoring functionary, Beyer noted that "I should think you would be justified in developing this possibility in your plant." If the administration lacked the political fortitude and unity of purpose to take on industrial lawbreakers, it fell to their victims to take up the challenge.[21]

Potofsky himself actually threatened to resign unless something was done to investigate the accumulating pile of reported violations. Typical was a letter to Johnson, Wagner, Green, and Senator Black from a group of red ore miners in Alabama, officers of the Bessemer Council of the Mine, Mill, and Smelter Workers. They charged "every method, including coercion and victimization, has been practiced by the companies in an effort to install and promote company union activities." The writers professed not only great patience but a patriotic loyalty to national recovery policy and to the local instrumentalities of the NLB. But patience was running out, particularly in the case of Republic Steel, which seemed determined to defy both the NRA and the NLB. The LAB was powerless to do anything about this. Already by the end of 1933, the Board was more often than not ignored, hearings held without its notification or participation, codes adopted despite its protests.[22]

A reasonably dispassionate appraisal of Federal labor policy concluded: "In most cases, the LAB could not accomplish much more than rendering advice and striking an attitude." At bottom, this Brookings study decided, was "the reluctance of the Administration to face the fundamental issue raised by the statute, namely the part to be played by trade unions in American industry."[23]

Defeat followed defeat and depleted what morale remained from the Board's early days. Its enemies were legion. The Industrial Advisory Board, while not a monolithic body, nevertheless consistently argued against any strict rule of equal pay for equal work, demanding instead a flexibility in work time that made a mockery of maximum hour provisions. Although the LAB opposed the creation of multiple industry-specific labor boards because they weakened the already fragile jurisdictional authority of the NLB (and subsequently the NLB's successor, the NLRB), General Johnson proceeded to set them up anyway. When the Board was rebuffed once again in March 1934 on the question of lowering maximum hours below the unofficial and self-defeating norm of forty, most trade unionists lost heart. Solomon Barkin reluctantly admitted that labor advisers had failed in their mission to reduce hours by 10 percent and raise wages by 10 percent; success, he noted, was not only infrequent but a credit not to the Board or the government but to the rougher persuasions of strong labor unions. By the end of 1934 the Board, with a note of sarcasm, observed it was wishful thinking to believe that the majority of workers were covered by codes calling for "equitable adjustment" of wages, adding that code minimums often became industry maximums and that some companies reduced the wages of their skilled workers to compensate for the raise in the minimum wage. If anything, noncompliance grew as the act neared its expiration date.[24]

Hillman was at the forefront of the Board's many, mainly losing struggles. He quickly emerged as its most resourceful and influential member, as labor's most audible voice in the NRA and in Washington. According to one report, "the Administration turns to Hillman for advice on labor problems rather than to any old-line AFL leader." He was everywhere at once, running back and forth from New York to Washington, where he shared an office with Rose Schneiderman, manfully keeping pace with the deluge of requests from trade unionists to track down violators of the labor codes, to pursue amendments exempting certain classes of workers from code protections like those on maximum hours, to adjudicate jurisdictional quarrels and claims for representation, and to advise on price-fixing provisions. He was available to represent labor at public hearings and private conferences; to coordinate activities with other parts of the NRA bureaucracy; to advise Johnson when the General was in the mood to take advice; to recommend amendments; to nominate labor representatives to codes, and so on. Manufacturers too approached Hillman for help in disciplining "chislers" seeking to evade labor standards. He served on numberless subcommittees to study competitive conditions, scales, apprenticeship rules, and industrial stagnation.[25]

Moving often in strange circles, certain insecurities in Hillman came to the fore. Never one to put himself conspicuously forward, he was sensitive about his thick accent and its public effect. When he could, he avoided public speaking engagements or arranged for "the goyim" to take his place—or perhaps someone like Hyman Blumberg, whose mastery of English was superior to his own. The consequences were sometimes comical. At a meeting with Johnson, Hillman had Blumberg do the talking. After a while, however, Sam Levin, notoriously emotional and hot-tempered, whose speech was no closer to the King's English than Hillman's, couldn't restrain himself and joined the debate with an armada of Yiddishisms. "How did I do?" he asked Hillman later. "Fine," his leader responded, "but it doesn't compare to not talking."[26]

❧

The lion's share of Hillman's time, however, was spent on home turf in the clothing and textile industries. His experience in the first highlighted those rare circumstances in which labor could expect to fare well under the NRA; his experience with the second just as convincingly demonstrated why in most cases it could not.

The men's clothing code, created in early September, was the first to include full labor representation from the start—Hillman, Blumberg, Levin, and two representatives of the UGW sat on the code authority. This was indicative of the union's commanding position in the industry, which even in the best of times depended on the Amalgamated to control its internecine struggles. Mark Cresap of HSM was chairman of the code authority. Its first Executive Director was George Bell, an executive of the Caterpillar Tractor Company, secretary to Frankfurter's War Labor Policies Board, and a former arbiter in the New York garment industry. Bell was succeeded by Morris Greenberg, also from HSM.[27]

All was not harmonious, however. Open-shop manufacturers, led by Francis Curlee of St. Louis, who employed his own strikebreaking agency, Industrial Investigators and Engineers, Inc., were implacably hostile. They defied not only the union but the code authority as well, precisely because the ACW carried such weight in that body. Indeed, during public hearings held in late July to formulate the code's basic provisions, Curlee, representing the Industrial Recovery Association of Clothing Manufacturers, opposed the plan offered by the Clothing Manufacturers Association of the United States, the pro-union trade group. Cresap spoke for the major manufacturers of Chicago, New York, Philadelphia, and Rochester. He welcomed the NRA's efforts at stabilization and called for uniform standards, including the end of child labor, asking for government help in dealing with a "destructive minority" of unfair competitors. He proposed a 35-cent minimum wage in the North, 32.5 cents in the South, and 80 cents for cutters; a minimum weekly income regardless of the piece rate; the phasing out of homework after one year; a forty-hour week and an eight-hour day; no workers under the age of sixteen; no selling below cost except for seasonal clearances of excess inventory at specified dates; and finally the creation of a "Planning and Fair Practices" agency.

Curlee's association, which included among its principal members old foes of the Amalgamated: the infamous Greif brothers of Baltimore; Heumann of Rochester; and Schoenman of the same city, barred from membership any firm that recognized the closed shop. It opposed all regulations governing output, as Curlee denied the industry suffered from anything comparable to the "stretch-out" in textiles. He accepted the forty-hour maximum and 35-cent minimum but adamantly resisted the 80-cent wage for cutters. Finally, Curlee strongly objected to the heavy representation of labor on the code authority.

Hillman first attacked Curlee as an exploiter of low-wage labor and the Association as a rump body of runaway shops. The Deputy Administrator, Lindsay Rodgers, admonished him not to cross-examine witnesses. Hillman persisted, not only against Curlee but against his friends as well. He had warned General Johnson at the textile hearings that the approval of a forty-hour maximum would create a dangerous precedent, and here was proof. The Amalgamated proposed instead a thirty-five-hour maximum as the only way to absorb some of the industry's vast labor reserve. He also argued for a 50-cent minimum, noting that Cresap conveniently overlooked the seasonal nature of employment. Thirty-five cents was after all as low as the textile code, an industry with traditionally lower wage scales and one less subject to seasonal shutdowns. This was no mere commercial challenge, he maintained with some eloquence, but a desperate battle to end "chaos," "ruination," and "social decay." Moreover, he reminded Kirstein and Rosenwald as fellow NRA officials that the purpose of the act was, by definition, to raise wages and purchasing power, and so, eventually, prices.

As finally codified, the provisions were a testimony to Hillman's power and persuasiveness. Forty cents became the code minimum (37 cents in the South) and thirty-six hours the maximum. Homework was abolished—on paper at least—as was the hiring of anyone under sixteen. The authority adopted a health and safety code. Perhaps most

significantly—and in opposition to the Curlee Association, which nonetheless was accorded a place on the code authority in the interests of
commercial peace—cutters received a dollar an hour, and pressers 75
cents. This last maintained a hard-won wage classification system based
on skill; it did so in the face of a widespread contrary tendency, one
sanctioned by a growing number of NRA industrial codes.[28]

Many codes sought to finance the increase in wage minimums by
closing the wage gap at the top between the skilled and the unskilled.
What was being accomplished, more often than not, was a redistribution
of wages rather than a redistribution of income as between labor and
capital. Hillman was well aware of this tendency to redistribute wages
from the skilled to the unskilled. He pushed the LAB to recommend a
new code clause providing maintenance of weekly earnings at least at
parity with full-time weekly compensation prior to the NRA; a schedule
of minimum wage rates for skilled occupations; and provision for upward
adjustment of wages with rises in the cost of living. Because the skilled
were also vulnerable to layoffs, Hillman encouraged the NRA to adopt
unemployment reserve plans and industrywide protections against not
only unemployment but sickness, death, and accidents.

The import of all this was of course economic, but not merely economic. The NRA tended to nationalize labor standards in order to eliminate some of the wide dispersion within plants, industries, cities, and
regions. Where hours, for example, once ranged from forty to sixty and
over, they now tended to settle around forty. This leveling threatened a
relative decline in income for skilled tradesmen and industrial workers
and thereby generated growing anxiety over social position and status.
Many of the militants responsible for the first great wave of strikes and
organizing drives in 1933–34, and again later during the rise of the CIO
in 1936–37, were skilled cadre angered and anxious about the threat to
their status and security. It was notable therefore that Hillman's position
was dominant enough to staunch this social hemorrhaging at least in his
own industry.[29]

Hillman himself later acknowledged that in most cases "the labor
provisions . . . are very, very meager. In our code we have just about 5%
more than in some of the other codes. Fate was kind to us." Yet as it
became ever clearer that code violations were occurring wholesale across
the country, that it had become a kind of legal game for businessmen to
evade these regulations, Hillman's accomplishments seemed all the more
distinctive and impressive. Thus, clothing code enforcement, almost
uniquely, took place before and not after complaints and violations were
registered. There were tangible results: 94 percent of all homeworkers in
the men's clothing trade were reemployed in factories, their wages more

than doubled from about $6 to more than $13 a week. Child labor was effectively eliminated, at least so long as the NRA lasted. On the industry's side, Morris Greenberg noted the sharp drop in the bankruptcy rate between 1932 and 1934 and credited the NRA. Defiant manufacturers faced the whole weight of the code machinery. Thus, L. Greif & Brothers, the second largest producer in the country with ten plants, refused to obey a code authority order to raise wages and restore $100,000 in back wages. The Compliance Division pursued the case, and eventually Greif was stripped of its Blue Eagle (although characteristically the company continued to display it).[30]

Within the code bureaucracy Hillman's position was unassailable. Deputy Administrator Lindsay Rodgers disliked him and complained to Cresap that Hillman nagged him about enforcement problems. To Hillman's face Rodgers cautioned that the authority had little legal power but was mainly a moral authority, which required it to tread carefully and seek cooperation with management. Hillman, furious, threatened "a showdown on enforcement." He threatened to go to Johnson and Richberg and ask them "whether the Code was a joke or not." He did just that. The General confronted Rodgers, and the deputy was forced to explain a telegram from a New York manufacturer, quoting Rodgers to the effect that Johnson and Richberg didn't care about enforcement. Rodgers told Johnson it was all a lie and in a subsequent meeting accused Hillman of writing the telegram himself or at least of putting Riesenfeld, the New York manufacturer, up to it. Hillman denied the accusation; Johnson in turn made various noises in favor of enforcement, and Hillman left "satisfied." According to Rodgers, once the union president left the room, Johnson confessed: "It's just the kind of stunt that a . . . likes to pull," a remark that would not have been out of character, given the General's notorious impulsiveness, vulgarity, and prejudice. In any event, Rodgers later told Hillman not to "try it again" or else risk hurting his own chances "to be someone in Washington." But it was Rodgers, not Hillman, who would see his ambitions thwarted. Although the deputy went to Wolman and threatened to quit unless something was done, nothing was. And later on, when Rodgers was under consideration for the post of Code Authority executive director, Hillman's opposition proved fatal.[31]

Hillman's experience with the textile industry and its code machinery was, by contrast, frustrating and futile. His concern was nearly as acute, given the intimate commercial connections between the two industries and Hillman's abiding interest in textile unionism stretching back to the days of Muste's ATW. His original condemnation of the code's labor provisions was a position echoed by William Green and Senator Black, as well as John L. Lewis, with whom Hillman was becoming friendly. Elements within the industry, especially among some New England manufacturers, shared his concern. M. D. C. Crawford, editor of Fairchild Publications, including *Women's Wear Daily*, sought to collaborate with the ACW to reorient production toward finer, high-quality goods and improved marketing. Crawford argued against production restrictions, speed-ups, and the debasement of the labor force; he proposed instead technological innovation accompanied by environmental adjustments to control humidity, ventilation, and lighting. Acknowledging management's failure, Crawford urged the government to save the industry from self-destruction. Some might call that "socialism," he said, but actually "it widens the field for the essential individual initiative and control by creating new industries and wants."[32]

But the views of Hillman, Crawford, and others counted for little. The code authority was dominated by managements who not only despised trade unions but who were prepared as well, under market pressure, to violate their own solemnly agreed-to understandings for controlling competition. Thus production quotas rose inexorably, and the eight-hour limit was ignored as often as it was observed. The LAB asked Johnson to investigate worker complaints. The General referred the matter to Robert Bruere's Cotton Textile National Industrial Relations Board. The Bruere board proved to be congenitally indecisive, cowed by the code authority and wary of the majority rule principle in collective bargaining. As Johnson and the Bruere board vacillated, Hillman grew more alarmed. He warned Roosevelt that unless something was done there was bound to be a strike. He cautioned about a similar situation in the closely allied cotton garment industry, an industry with close to 250,000 workers, mainly in the South, whose abysmal labor standards were an immediate threat to the dress and men's clothing centers of the North.[33]

The President responded with an executive order establishing a thirty-six-hour week and a 10 percent wage increase. The President's proclamation thrilled Hillman, proving the NRA "to be a living, flexible statute, adaptable to real conditions," and promising to create ten thousand new jobs. However, the industry had no intention of complying and contested the order in court. Hillman led the fight on behalf of the President's right to impose code terms. He furiously denounced the NRA's decision later in December to allow the Cotton Garment Code Authority to stay the raising of wages: "They've been getting away with this for fifteen months and it must stop." At the same time, he struggled mightily to keep the cotton garment workers from striking before the court issued a final ruling. That ruling came, finally, but so late that it

was soon made moot by the outlawing of the NRA. In the textile industry proper, no courts came to the rescue, and Hillman possessed
neither the wherewithal nor the will to prevent the strike he had warned
Roosevelt was inevitable.[34]

On or about Labor Day, 1934, a general strike—or more accurately
a series of semi-spontaneous, spasmodic local walkouts constituting not
so much a single event as a set of related incidents—broke out across the
country from the mills of New England to the company mill towns of the
Deep South. The strike, conducted by the UTW under the leadership of
Francis Gorman, demanded the elimination of the stretch-out, a thirty-
hour week, and the recognition of the union. Hillman did what he could
to lend it organizational coherence. Dorothy Bellanca and Leo Krzycki
were loaned to the UTW for the duration of the strike, and ACW
headquarters in Allentown, Pennsylvania, became the center of the
textile drive in that area. Hillman met with Gorman and Emil Rieve in
Washington to cement the ACW's support for the strike, which included
a check for $50,000. With some regularity, Hillman attended and ad-
vised UTW Executive Board meetings.

But the strike suffered a thousand wounds. Gorman was certainly
militant enough, particularly as he launched a "flying wedge" of Northern organizers to crack the ferocious resistance of the South. But he was
strategically naïve and undercut by forces he neither controlled nor understood. Frances Perkins tried to quiet things by arranging an investigation of conditions under the auspices of the liberal Republican ex-
governor of New Hampshire, John Winant. Meanwhile, the Labor
Secretary maneuvered behind the scenes to replace Gorman with the
more tractable and aged UTW president, MacMahon. She also arranged
for Hillman to meet with the head of the Avondale Mills in Alabama to
discuss the trade union situation. (Perkins was careful to warn the textile
magnate not to be offended by Hillman's accent, but in any event he
actually found this exotic creature from the New York rag trade "charm-
ing.") Meanwhile, the President appointed yet another special board,
the Textile Labor Relations Board, to pursue a settlement.

Neither the Winant Board nor the TLRB had much effect, however,
because the strike that gave rise to them was a failure. In the South
especially, the political establishment—governors, congressmen, and
mill town potentates, together with the militias at their disposal—
combined with local managements and their private armies of strikebreakers to break the strike. Within three weeks workers were streaming
back to work. It was a devastating defeat, not only for the long-suffering
millhands but for the New Deal's incipient labor policy.[35]

The textile strike was of course a personal disappointment for Hillman, so different was it from his experience with the clothing industry. It was as well the culminating crisis leading to the basic reorganization of the NRA, which catapulted Hillman into a position of some national prominence.

∽

The textile strike was only the last of a series of labor upheavals during 1934, beginning with a strike at the Toledo Auto Lite Company in the winter and continuing through the Minneapolis and San Francisco general strikes of the spring and summer. The NRA played a negligible role in all of these events. Indeed, the strikes themselves were, at least partly, responses to the evident impotence of the NLB after its emasculating decision against the majority rule principle in the automobile case of March. The collapse of the NLB meant the end of the tripartite approach to resolving labor disputes. Its successor body, the first National Labor Relations Board, adopted instead a neutral, administrative, and quasi-judicial strategy and consisted of "public" representatives only. The new "board" was promising indeed to Hillman: William Lloyd Garrison as chairman; Harry Millis, who had served as chairman of the Chicago Board of Arbitration in the men's clothing industry from 1919 to 1923; and Edwin Smith. Smith had served for years under Mary van Kleeck at the Russell Sage Foundation, as personnel director at Filene's, and as secretary to Lincoln Filene.

In the Houde Engineering case in August, the board tried to live up to the reputation of its members by reviving the majority rule principle despite the opposition of Johnson and Richberg. But with such open division within the administration itself, it was easy enough for manufacturers to boycott the board. Especially after the textile general strike national labor policy was in a state of all-sided confusion. By then, Hillman was confiding in Lewis that he was "sick of Richberg" for undermining the NLRB's authority. As for Lewis, he had been afflicted with that sickness for some time.[36]

The business community meanwhile was fast losing confidence in the recovery adminstration, and not just because of its maddening equivocation on labor policy. By mid-1934, auto and steel industrialists, for example, were quickly developing their attachments to the violently anti–New Deal American Liberty League organized by Al Smith, the DuPonts, Alfred Sloan, and John Raskob of General Motors. At a dinner meeting of the IAB at the home of Edward Stettinius, the president of United States Steel, in the fall of 1933, Gerard Swope warned that any concerted effort by the government to coerce the regime of industrial self-government would be viewed with great alarm. As the Blue Eagle boomlet fizzled out, every statistical index, every qualitative report, every curbstone conversation carried an ominous undertone of fatal pessimism and rebellious disaffection.[37]

One popularly held view at that time and since was that the NRA was the vehicle of oligopolistic industry determined to make use of price and production controls to destroy their competitors and cartelize the market. However, the disaffection of the corporate interests represented in the American Liberty League, the BAC, and the IAB makes that position untenable. Contempt for the NRA was epidemic and nonpartisan. The USCC was a "peak" organization of peripheral smaller industries, yet it too found the Blue Eagle increasingly obnoxious. Such peripheral enterprises as cleaners and dyers, for example, hated the NRA not for what it tried to do but for its failure to succeed. High stabilized prices, an NRA objective, was after all in the interests of these marginal competitors. But the recovery administration was never able to exercise sufficient control over the economy's wild oscillations.

Indicative of how the NRA often merely mirrored the heterogeneity and fractiousness of the commercial world was the fact that its principal support from within the business community came from competitive, less capital-intensive consumer goods industries in textile, apparel, and retail, including the Consumer Goods Committee of the NRA under its chairman, George Sloan. This milieu was much more willing to accept government regulation of prices—indeed, depended on it to save it from bankruptcy.

Unanimity of business opinion was thus a fiction. Even within the ranks of elite business groups like the IAB and BAC there were serious divisions. Ralph Flanders addressed the IAB in mid-1934 to condemn "malignant financial and speculative growths" in the business system, which were hampering economic expansion and mass consumption. He warned his industrial colleagues against the dangerous search for "illusory and unsocial speculative gains." Instead they had to be willing to distribute fair returns to labor and consumer interests as well as management and capital. Flanders blamed the Depression on an

> . . . inflationary credit structure built up to finance the securities speculation of the period ending in 1929. . . . These credit specie are not a necessary feature of the profit system. They are wasting fevers, malignant tumors in its body. . . . It is by means of these malignant credit structures that wealth is maldistributed to elements in society which had no part in producing and distributing it; and it is the bank indebtedness underlying this credit which during the long years of the Depression absorbs purchasing power faster than it can be produced.

Flanders believed that precisely the same milieu was undermining the NRA. Edward Filene agreed. In a report to FDR based on a cross-country investigative tour, Filene noted the severe criticism of the administration's labor policy; its failure to enforce its own encoded standards for fear of confronting the Supreme Court was emboldening corporations to use company unions to crush independent ones. The whole recovery program was threatened as a result. Filene, together with Morris Leeds, carried on a rear guard effort within the IAB and BAC to grant the administration real enforcement powers over hours, wages, and child labor. "American business cannot recover unless the wage levels are raised," Filene lectured an unfriendly audience at the USCC.[38]

The NRA was a morass. Johnson and Richberg lacked coercive power adequate to the task. Even those oligopolists most favored by the NRA's encoded cartels proved unreliable. Every significant shift in the domestic and world market encouraged them to break free of whatever restraints they had momentarily agreed to. Meanwhile, the universe of excluded interests—labor as well as peripheral enterprises—was so vast, so frangible, and so often endowed with its own countervailing political resources that no conceivable amount of executive authority that still preserved the essentials of a democratic polity and the free market could have produced the desired accords.

Among the more incongruous results of this commercial and social impasse, one which deepened the crisis of the recovery administration and presented Hillman with a second personal loss, nearly as great as the one he'd just experienced over the falling out with Leo Wolman, was the creation of the National Industrial Recovery Review Board under the chairmanship of Clarence Darrow in the spring of 1934.

From the beginning the NRA was subjected to a familiar Midwestern populist assault led by Senators Borah and Nye. The NRA was indicted as a tool of dominant corporations intent on crushing smaller independent businesses. Consumer groups concerned about artificially high prices joined the antimonopoly campaign. Thus, Johnson was forever trying to bury Consumer Advisory Board hearings on NRA pricing policy. But this only infuriated Borah and Nye, who in turn increased the pressure on the President at least to investigate charges of monopoly control and trustification. The Darrow board, appointed in March 1934, was the result. Long before its final report was issued in June, the Board quickly became a predictable vessel of small business resentment, of "all Farmers and Businessmen outside of the Trusts and Chain Stores and Department Houses . . . the Neglected and Forgotten Men . . . who are struggling along making a brave dying effort for existence." Letters and witnesses poured forth a litany of monopolistic oppression. Typical was a letter from a businessman in Joliet, Illinois, to Darrow:

> The underlying cause of all the trouble seems to rest with the code author-
> ities who are under the direct or indirect control and influence of the
> brainless trusts and their slick paid agents. Together with the rotten kept
> press which is . . . working under the direction of the greedy manufacturers
> and unrestrained monopolists with their congressional underlings along
> with their legal minds, the New Deal is being undermined from within.

The writer, no less than the members of the Darrow Board and Senators Borah and Nye, was inclined to forget just how often opposition to the NRA's codes was an excuse for price-gouging and union-busting on the part of desperately hard-pressed businessmen. Nor were they apt to notice how often small businesses, especially in industries with dominant producers, did quite well under the NRA; indeed, they were often saved from certain liquidation by price regulations and codes of fair competition, including a provision against selling below cost.[39]

Hillman was not about to forget these matters and was stung by what he considered the betrayal of his onetime mentor, Clarence Darrow. Appearing before the Board in May, Hillman bluntly described the Board as a "haven of the sweat-shoppers." He cleverly cross-examined a shirt manufacturer from North Carolina and trapped him into admitting that he discriminated between the parts of the law that smiled on business, which he liked, and the ones that seemed to favor labor, which he didn't. The testimony was becoming embarrassing when Hillman was interrupted and prevented from further questioning by the two Board members: W. W. Neal, a hosiery manufacturer, and Lowell Mason, a former attorney for the Insull interests. Later Darrow himself stymied Hillman by instructing him that the Board was not interested in the labor provisions of the codes. Hillman rejoined that such a position was absurd and charged Neal with running a "star chamber." He went on to describe conditions in the cotton garment industry, Neal's own, as "shameful."

> Obviously, the Darrow Board has secured its information regarding specific
> codes from the rag-tag and bob-tail elements of industry. Irresponsible mal-
> contents, sweat-shop employers and business interests which had lost spe-
> cial privileges found the latch string out and a warm welcome awaiting them
> before the National Review Board. . . . The NRA codes of fair competition
> were attacked without any input as to the benefits to wage-earners.

The LAB, at Hillman's urging, followed up with a resolution that "The Darrow report has rendered a disservice. . . . It has pandered to the worst elements in our political and economic life."[40]

Hillman would never forgive Darrow. No doubt Roosevelt and Johnson regretted the original decision to create the Review Board. But in the end it made little difference. The antimonopoly sentiments for which it provided a forum were abroad anyway, infusing such disparate discontents as Huey Long's "Share the Wealth" movement and Father Coughlin's invectives against the "money-changers." The great strikes and pervasive labor turmoil, the collapse of the NRA's labor policy and of the NLB, and the wholesale violations and ignoring of code provisions were by themselves mortal wounds. With or without the Darrow board, the NRA was headed for some sort of crackup, mirrored and personified by the mental disarray of its commander-in-chief, General Johnson.

Despite Johnson's volatility and sometimes even friendly gestures, he was considered by Frankfurter "the most influential single individual in the United States," whose influence he despised and who in turn despised the growing influence of the "Keynesians" around Roosevelt. Even before the textile strike in September, it was clear Johnson would have to go, and that it wasn't only his "enemies" who thought so. Bernard Baruch wrote to Roosevelt's secretary, Marvin McIntyre, in June arguing it was imperative to get rid of Johnson because he was wild and impetuous and dangerously unpredictable. Baruch suggested that in his place the President ought to appoint not another "general," but an administrative board. He recommended a group of nine from which to choose five. Hillman was on Baruch's list, along with Wolman, Leon Henderson, Clay Williams of Reynolds Tobacco, L. C. Marshall, Henry Harriman, the NRA legal adviser Blackwell Smith, Walter Teagel of Standard Oil, and Walter Hamilton. Richberg followed up two months later with a memo to McIntyre:

> The General himself is, in the opinion of many, in the worst physical and mental condition and needs an immediate relief from responsibility in order to improve health and relieve the mental strain of present conditions. . . . The situation is highly explosive.[41]

By mid-September, in the confusion and anxiety generated by the textile crisis, Richberg outlined a proposal to the President for a new board like the one suggested originally by Baruch. His list of potential members also included Hillman. He told McIntyre:

> In view of the General's radio speech of last night with its blazing indiscretions, the President will be very anxious to act as soon as possible. Insanity in public performance, added to insanity in private relations, is pretty dangerous. . . . I only hope it does not produce an outbreak of

violence paralleling the one he helped produce by a similar speech in San
Francisco.

Richberg went on to suggest that an industrialist should chair the
new board. He thought either Teagle or Arthur Whiteside of Dun &
Bradstreet might make a good choice as chairman. Whiteside, he argued,
was not as conservative as many assumed and was a good executive,
"sound on the New Deal." He would have proposed Kirstein as well, "but
the presence of Hillman—and other reasons—makes him inadvisable."[42]

Soon afterward Roosevelt arranged for the general's departure from
the NRA. In his place he appointed a National Industrial Recovery
Board comprising Clay Williams, Leon Marshall, A. D. Whiteside, Walter Hamilton, and Sidney Hillman. Williams, the president of Reynolds
Tobacco, was elected Board chairman. He was conservative enough to
reassure the business community, had represented industry on the old
NLB, and was a member of Commerce Secretary Roper's Business Advisory Council (BAC). He came from that conservative, but internationalist, export-oriented milieu of commodities producers which
remained loyal to the Democratic Party with its roots in Southern agriculture and with ties to the Harriman Brothers railroad network. Marshall, a distinguished professor at Johns Hopkins and an associate of the
Brookings Institute, had also served on the old NLB. He became the new
NIRB's executive secretary. Arthur Whiteside's affiliations included, besides Dun & Bradstreet, the National Bank of Commerce and A. G.
Hyde & Sons. Walter Hamilton, a liberal political scientist from Yale,
quickly became Hillman's most reliable ally on the Board.[43]

The political chemistry of the Board was thus fairly clear. Williams
and Whiteside represented the right; Marshall and Hamilton the center;
Hillman the left. The tilt was to the center-right, as Richberg secured
Williams's appointment as chairman over Hillman's opposition; the
ACW president had lobbied hard for Robert Hutchins of the University
of Chicago. The *New York Times* pronounced the Board a purely administrative body. It assumed the actual work of policy formulation would be
carried out by Richberg in consultation with an industrial policy committee that included Ickes, Perkins, and Hopkins. The *Times* was right,
and such a division of authority left the NIRB in an anomalous position.
Not only was its statutory authority ambiguous, but its composition almost guaranteed immobilizing standoffs between its business-minded and
more liberal members.[44]

Hillman told Kirstein he was surprised by his appointment, that he
hadn't solicited it, and that he was favorably disposed toward the group,
although he wanted Kirstein's advice about Williams. He was in fact

honored by this elevation and, driven both by his nature and by the steadily deteriorating position of the labor movement, pushed the Board to act. Indeed, Drew Pearson in his "Daily Washington Merry-Go-Round" described Hillman as the "strongman" of the NRA, a leader as "strategist and negotiator." "Hillman dominates the Board working closely with Leon Henderson." There was some truth, albeit exaggerated, in all this. But the role of "strongman" on an inherently weak board was nothing but frustrating.[45]

Examples were legion. A code for the banking industry that had already been found defective was amended and referred to Hillman and Hamilton. Their report strongly recommended against approval but was ignored. Again and again Hillman decried the lack of code enforcement. He and Hamilton pushed for a thirty-six-hour provision in the telegraph code. Industries, Hillman declared, "who are sitting back and laughing at us while making big profits," engaged in endless judicial delaying tactics. He was referring to AT&T in particular, but it was Hillman's constant refrain. Thus, he denounced the auto code, its ignored provisions, its "merit clause," and its poor wage standards. As Solomon Barkin observed, Hillman was the sole member of the Board who "bore down day after day upon this aspect of policy"—Barkin was especially concerned with maximum hour provisions—"but his efforts in that body were practically single-handed."[46]

The clash of wills between Hillman and Williams became a recurrent feature of the Board's deliberations. Thus, the tobacco code was a scandal in its original form. At a public hearing on the code in October, Hillman and Williams skirmished. When it came before the Board again early in 1935, it was not much improved. Although Williams, as a Reynolds Tobacco executive, officially removed himself from its formal consideration, he and Hillman had it out anyway. Supported by Hamilton, Hillman said he couldn't approve a forty-hour provision as it would reemploy nobody, especially given the industry's new technical developments, which were bound to produce additional unemployment. He lambasted the major tobacco companies for their exorbitant profits and noted that labor accounted for a small percentage of their costs. He asked Williams why the tobacco industry could not shoulder its fair burden of reemployment like other consumer goods industries, for example, clothing. Williams retorted that the capital goods sector had to lead the way to recovery. Hillman reminded him that the big four cigarette makers paid more in stock dividends in 1932 than the tobacco farmers received from their entire crop and noted that recently introduced machinery was saving those companies millions of dollars in wages. Approving the code in this form would make the NRA seem "ridiculous." "I would not be faithful to my trust as an Administrator of the NIRB if I gave my assent to the proposition of the industry . . . there will not be the faintest possibility of re-employment on the forty hour basis."

A letter to Frances Perkins from a Brown & Williamson Company worker in Winston-Salem punctuated Hillman's point:

> Now how can we be considered in the President's spending program when we don't make enough to live on and pay our just and honest debts . . . we are piling up millions for the firms we work and the sad part of it the majority are afraid to make an out cry about conditions.

The real trouble, he suspected, was that

> . . . the greatest portion of us are colored people and I think everyone hates a colored man. How can we support a family of seven or eight send our children to school and teach them citizenship when capitalist choke us and make criminals out of some of us that might be a bit weak. . . . Now most of my people are afraid to complain because some few years ago the R. J. Reynolds Tobacco Company discharged every one that joined a union."[47]

Isolated once again, Hillman watched as his fellow Board members approved a code they tacitly acknowledged as inadequate. It was another instance in which the administration drew back at the prospect of frightening away its skittish allies in the Southern wing of the Democratic Party.[48]

The NRA's multiple disabilities were debilitating for everyone. As always the "labor question" threatened a terminal crisis. But it was just then that Hillman managed his one triumph. In the event, however, it turned out to be no more than a brief resuscitation of a doomed institution. Jacob Potofsky remembered Hillman returning from a trip to Washington early in 1935, "tired but full of glee. He succeeded in effecting a rapprochement between labor and the President. He succeeded to make the President take his coat off and get into the fight to save the NRA." The rapprochement took place at the White House in a meeting attended by Lewis, Green, Richberg, and FDR. The President agreed to make the extension of the NRA "must legislation" and, most critically, to add a labor representative to the NIRB. Hillman, Potofsky remembered and others would corroborate, had brought this off, but "All he would say [was] it was a tense week. It was dramatic. To make men and women cry in a matter as business-like and matter of fact as NRA is a great emotional achievement."[49]

This emotional climax was a long time building. Hillman encouraged the LAB to persist in its quest for greater labor representation, which the Board did, noting that only twenty-one out of five hundred code authorities included "legitimate" representatives of labor. In late 1934 the Board submitted a set of amendments for the NIRA should it be given a new lease on life in May, when it was due to expire. The amendments called for equal labor representation, minimum wage scales for skilled and semiskilled workers, and improved enforcement. The recommendations, which reflected the thinking of Frey and Wharton as well as Howard Meyers and Hillman, also sought to give union labor the right to open codes and compel their amendment, and to apply 7a to any industry not yet codified.[50]

Richberg stalled, rationalized, and did nothing. The labor leadership grew angrier and angrier. Then Richberg, in pursuit of his own political ambitions, told Marvin McIntyre it was urgent to reorganize the NIRB as the Board was functioning badly. It was too weak, and the legislative situation in Congress was bad; a bad bill or no bill at all might be the result of its current deliberations. The recovery administration needed a strong chairman with authority from the President. Then the punch line: "Hillman, the best informed, most level-headed labor adviser, strongly urged today that I should be given and accept active responsibility for heading NRA." After a coy demurral, Richberg went on to suggest that the NIRB should be reorganized to include two labor representatives: Hillman and John L. Lewis's lieutenant, Philip Murray. With two industrialist members to be nominated by the IAB and the BAC and two public members, Marshall and Hamilton, there should be a neutral chairman. Richberg left little doubt who he thought that should be. He confessed that while labor had cooled to him, that was due to Lewis's friendship with General Johnson. In any event, Hillman gave assurances that under this new arrangement everything would be okay.

There is little doubt that the plan Richberg presented to McIntyre was in fact authored by Hillman. When the President announced Richberg's promotion, it initially infuriated Lewis. It was Hillman who, at the meeting from which he returned "tired but full of glee," won the inclusion of Murray on the NIRB, thus equalizing the weight of labor and industry. He also managed to wrangle the President's rhetorical endorsement of the pending Wagner Act. The Nation and the World-Telegram gave Hillman full credit for saving the Blue Eagle.[51]

∽

He deserved the praise, but more than anything else it was the desperate political situation that forced the action. As the NRA expiration date approached, its chances for renewal were in obvious jeopardy. Hillman was everywhere, pressing for its extension, properly amended, he hoped, to include the recommendations of the LAB, but without them if necessary. For Hillman, matters came to a tumultuous head at hearings held by the Senate Finance Committee in late March. Chaired by Senator Pat Harrison, the committee was a hotbed of anti-NRA sentiment. Clarence Darrow testified at length to make the case that the NRA was a foe of small business. He dismissed its accomplishments in the area of labor relations, arguing that trade union organization and the elimination of child labor would have occurred with or without the act. Richberg was only trying to scare its critics by intimating that responsible labor organization and collective bargaining were the antidote to "a class struggle for political domination."

Hillman followed in rebuttal. He cited the NRA's attack on sweat-shop and child labor as well as the fact that between March 1933 and December 1934 3.5 million people returned to work, presumably thanks to the Blue Eagle. He was openly bitter about Darrow, depicting him as someone who could afford to indulge in speculations about some perfect future and who simply ignored the way child and sweatshop labor were rife before the advent of the NRA; someone "who can afford to wait two hundred years but the men and women out of work cannot afford to." In a friendly exchange, Senator Hugo Black offered him the chance to elaborate on his claims. The NRA fostered reemployment, Hillman maintained, in five ways: through maximum hours, minimum wages, child labor prohibitions, price, and production controls. But even Black was not entirely convinced. He sought instead separate labor legislation and tried to get Hillman to acknowledge that price and production controls were far less important and often unfair.

On his second day of testimony, Hillman confronted a hostile Senator William H. King from Utah. King badgered the union president about the old ACW preamble. Hillman dismissed it as a piece of expunged utopianism. In a moment of excessive cleverness, he reminded King, "It was a time, Senator, when a number of our people were impressed with the beautiful constructive thought of Mr. Darrow." But the Senator wouldn't relent. He baited Hillman about his Russian birth, noting that the preamble was "put into your organization after you had come from Russia." Then he taunted him with the fact that for years the ACW was excluded from the AFL "with some of your radical views or bolshevistic views." King presented his own statistics to prove that the NRA actually reduced employment between 1933 and 1935, but he refused to allow Hillman a rejoinder. The contention that volume and continuous production actually allowed for price reductions, which Hillman offered in contradiction to King's assertion that the NRA's labor provisions and price regulations artificially inflated prices, the Utah legislator dismissed without even the pretense of a counterargument.

The atmosphere was heated and nasty. Senator Edward Costigan from Colorado interrupted to tell King that the hearings were not a "court trial" and that Hillman should be permitted to answer. Senator Black followed with a long speech in defense of Hillman's claims about volume and continuous production lowering unit costs, therefore allowing for improvements in wages and hours. Costigan chimed in with corroborating evidence from the Rocky Mountain Fuel Company's experience with raising wages and reducing hours, claiming it saved the company from bankruptcy in the late 1920s. After finishing his lecture on the economics of trade unionism, Costigan accorded Hillman a chance to talk about the Amalgamated innovations in unemployment insurance.

But the anti-NRA camp was not through. Whatever legitimate grievances excited critics of the recovery administration—and there were many—took a back seat to the anti–New Deal, antilabor prejudices of people like King and his colleague from Delaware, Senator Daniel O. Hastings. Hastings hardly even pretended any interest in Hillman's views about the NRA. Instead he interrogated him about past ACW economic and financial relations with the Soviet Union—its loans, banking exchange services, and especially the cooperative clothing factories run by the RAIC. Hugo Black gave Hillman a chance to note that the Chase Bank had also loaned money to the Soviets and that numerous major American manufacturers sold them machinery and even whole industrial plants. Hillman told Hastings that the Bank's remittance service was used by 1,100 other banking institutions, including American Express and the Mellon Bank of Pittsburgh. Disingenuously, Hillman made it seem that the Amalgamated's dealings with the Russians involved nothing more than facilitating the transfer of machinery by providing financial credits. But he could hardly be faulted for whatever way he responded to a question that was not only irrelevant but asked in bad faith and for discreditable reasons. In any event, Hillman finally had enough. He replied to Senator King's ethnic aspersions: "At least I can say, Senator, that this country is not with me merely a matter of accident, but it is the country of my choice."[52]

This last acid retort, like the ones before it, was greeted with great applause, prompting threats by the Senator to clear the chamber. Immediately afterward there was an outraged response to King's performance by lawyers, trade unionists, and NRA officials. But if King was momentarily silenced, the more general animus against the NRA took its toll. While Hillman went on to defend the act, he admitted there were trends abroad to "make of NRA an instrumentality for an economy of scarcity" and called for greater public control and surveillance. He even voiced his own grievances. The low minimum wages adopted by most codes was a kind of opiate, he charged, "giving them some opium while the sweat operators were operating on them."[53]

And so, after nearly two years of embattled life in the Washington bureaucracy, during which his stature in the official labor movement and in national public life appreciated considerably, Hillman was no less ambivalent about the New Deal's recovery policy than he had been early in 1933, when the struggle to formulate the NIRA was first joined. From the beginning he assumed the role of the loyal opposition. Assessing the NRA's accomplishments early in 1934 in the *Annals* of the American Academy of Political Science, he awarded it unduly high marks for its record on minimum wages, maximum hours, and reemployment. Still, he called Johnson to account for the shamefully low standards approved in the textile and cotton garment codes, for his resistance to planning, for the dearth of labor representation, and for the clear failure of 7a to foster truly independent unions.[54]

At the Amalgamated's convention in May 1934, he again congratulated the New Deal most profoundly for its spiritual impact. Inadvertently perhaps, the New Deal and the Blue Eagle had lifted the torpor that had surrounded the labor movement for a decade and more. He praised the NRA and even lauded Johnson, while accusing those who attacked the recovery administration of abetting the sinister designs of big business. For those who sought to wound the New Deal with charges of radicalism, he was ready with a telling response: "People talk about the Roosevelt revolution. They make me laugh. A year ago a revolution was a distinct possibility. Today, we hear no more of that sort of thing. The New Deal has changed all that." He was exaggerating, of course; revolution was never on the agenda, not in 1933 and not even when Hillman made those remarks at the time of the Minneapolis and San Francisco general strikes. Still, the New Deal, and 7a particularly, channeled widespread frustration and anger in manageable directions, an accomplishment someone with Hillman's experience in controlling radical insurgents in the garment industry would not be likely to underestimate.

NRA weaknesses were too glaring to ignore, however. While he publicly recognized a minority within the USCC that was fighting for "the social point of view," in most instances "the Tories of industry" were brazenly defying 7a, and the NRA was powerless to do anything about it. It was up to Congress, Hillman maintained, to rise to the task of enforcing its own legislation. Thus, in the spring of 1934 he testified on behalf of the Wagner–Connory labor relations bill as the only way to make 7a a reality, and thereby to increase mass purchasing power and save the NRA. Otherwise, he warned, the recovery administration would become a "purely monopolistic organization."[55]

By the time of the Richberg imbroglio and the confrontation with Senator King, Hillman was irretrievably committed to the defense of the NRA despite all his criticisms and reservations. During the month preceding the Supreme Court's *Schecter* decision (*Schecter v. U.S.*), which made the whole issue irrelevant by outlawing the NRA, he campaigned tirelessly for its renewal, cautioning that otherwise the economic recovery, such as it was, would collapse together with the living standards of the nation's workers. The Amalgamated staged a mass demonstration for the same purpose in Madison Square Garden, endorsed by the AFL. "Labor," Hillman declared at the rally, "has been altogether too patient. Too patient for its own sake as well as for the sake of the country."[56]

All the ambivalence, the second thoughts, the guilt about what might have been, and the anxieties about the future came to a head in a long, defensive, self-justifying peroration before the militant members of local 4 in April 1935. Hillman began by defending the progress made under the NRA, but he quickly admitted it was too slow. He pointed to the ACW, the ILG, the UMW, the 150,000 children no longer working, and the millions of adults who were working again, and at higher wages. "I tell you in all sincerity, and it is my firm belief: If the NRA continues, and if we have a labor movement vital and moving, we will make more progress than the dreamers can look to." He was proud of his newly realized influence. Just a few weeks before, he told the cutters, the NRA had been all but doomed, but, thanks to Hillman's bureaucratic ingenuity and craft, "the President took his coat off. And when he takes his coat off and goes to work, I feel better." He advised the President that if he didn't get behind the NRA, mass unemployment and wage cuts would inevitably follow.

Then he recalled his appearance before the Senate Finance Committee, the memory still sour: "Then an old friend of mine, whom I had loved and respected for twenty years, Clarence Darrow, joined them. He went on record against the abolition of child labor, against collective bargaining, against minimum wages and maximum hours!" But it wasn't only the "Tories of industry" and turncoats like Darrow one had to worry about. Hillman felt the still-warm breath of his past, of other "old friends"—"of course the liberals and left-wingers could have told us—well, wait till the revolution—but we might have had to wait a hell of a long time! And in the meantime we would have destroyed what we had built up throughout the years."

Hillman spoke as that "man of sweet reasonableness," the practical idealist and consummate opportunist who had earned the plaudits of middle-class Progressives years ago for his remarkable ability to navigate between the antipodes of social class and to get from power what could at the moment be gotten. The NRA had to be saved because it was the best available option. He denied that he was a pure and simple trade unionist. He too believed the movement required ideals and vision, but not perhaps any longer the visions dreamed by a more mythopoetic age. "The ideals of the labor movement must be security for every man and woman in the country. If capitalism can't give us security, then let another system do it."

It was a pregnant formulation, this narrowing onto security, one that was apt for the times and that promised to alchemize the "labor question," to channel primordial concerns with production, profit, and power into the calmer channels of security and the standard of living. And if indeed this was what the labor movement was ultimately about, then quibbling about names was foolish and even dangerous. If your political organization was viewed as a religion, then one could be righteous and sectarian. "But if the labor movement is to make progress politically, it must be a mass movement." Granted, the two parties were not trustworthy, but "until we have a mass movement we cannot hurry things beyond their natural course." After all, it was an important break with the old order when the government assumed, if only in theory, responsibility for unemployment and for creating jobs at decent wages. GM would "rather see the country go to hell than give more power to labor," and the Raskobs and DuPonts would get their way unless the labor movement stepped into the breach. "The NRA will go as far as the labor movement pushes it forward. . . . These are days in which we have an opportunity to change our social system, to try to bring equality, justice, in industrial relations, not just in words." Now was the time to organize in the millions and tens of millions. "There's no need talking about Leninism, Trotskyism, and other theories and theoreticians. . . . We must get out of our little circle, and get into national life. . . . I am happier now than in the good old days." Admitting that just a few months earlier he had considered quitting official Washington, he was convinced that "things have turned around. . . . I must be at the post."[57]

Character and circumstance conspired to keep him "at the post." Hillman's ambitions were subtle, even, it might be said, self-effacing, but he was nonetheless driven by a quest for power and influence. It was not so much whatever notoriety accompanied his appearance on the stage of national politics, but rather the more private access to the channels of power that drew him on. Rarely seduced by the flattery of friendly media or honorary appointments to blue ribbon commissions and advisory councils, never one to put on "napoleonic airs," he valued instead the confidential telephone call or conference with the President, the sort of hidden maneuverings in the White House that temporarily salvaged the NRA during the Richberg–Lewis controversy. Among his closest comrades he took evident delight in his privileged access to the President as well as to others in the upper reaches of the Washington bureaucracy. He also discovered along the way that one back channel of power led to another. For example, the President of the Title Guaranty & Trust Company, George McAneny, invited him to a working meeting of the metropolitan elite to discuss the business and general economic future of New York City. Such invitations to join in the closed-door deliberations of the mighty were an outgrowth of his new public prominence. Hillman had a "healthy respect for our industrial empire builders and their achievements," a close acquaintance remembered, but "so far as he personally was concerned, he invariably laughed at the high places he had reached in his career" and "always made cynical remarks about being made much of, laughing it off among his intimates." The shutting down of the NRA would necessarily curtail both kinds of opportunity: to be flattered, about which he cared little, and to be listened to, about which he cared a great deal.[58]

There was as well a practically organic connection between Hillman's character structure and the public project into which its energies flowed. Hillman was a craftsman at work erecting the skeletal infrastructure of the modern administrative state. The bureaucratic impersonality, the efficiency-mindedness, the judicial supercession of social antagonism—all hallmarks first of the "new unionism," later of its accomplishments writ large in the CIO and welfare state—were mirrored in his own depersonalized pursuit of power, in his steely impassiveness in the face of internal opposition, in his cultivated talents for meliorative persuasion and compromise, and in his chronic seeking out of new avenues of institutional aggrandizement. He was, to be sure, an imperfect mirror of what he created or, rather, of what became of what he created. For example, he was notoriously sloppy and disorganized when it came to administrative detail. His energies were always too politically charged to pay the necessary attention. In addition, he would never forgo the possibility of action outside the bounds of the trade union and state bureaucracies, a confinement practically taken for granted by a later generation of labor officialdom. He was not then an idolator of the state, but he was nonetheless a true believer in its social potential. Through its latent organizational capacities the administrative state could assume indispensable functions, accomplish feats no ensemble of private associations, no matter how cooperatively disposed, could ever hope to undertake. Valid in so many respects, especially when all the normally energetic elements of civil society seemed utterly lacking in imagination and initiative, this disposition also reinforced a tendency to reify the new state, to endow it with enormous authority and a kind of *sui generis* and divine status, a *deux ex machina* to be called upon by its supplicants to resolve apparently insoluble contradictions. Hillman's loyalty to an otherwise misconceived, crippled, and ultimately nugatory bureaucracy was the first sign of an attitude that would grow more pronounced.

Above all, what he hoped the new state might achieve, and what the Depression seemed to prove was beyond the reach of any private concordat, was both material and social security. In his anxiety about the looming chaos of the Russian revolution fifteen years earlier, in his daily wrestling with the chaos of the garment industry, as far back as the Talmudic legal logic-chopping in the obscurity of the Kovno seminary, Hillman repeatedly demonstrated an extraordinary sense of the orderly and stable. No greater chaos than that of the Great Depression, not even that of the 1905 revolution, had ever confronted him. He, along with millions of others similarly unmoored, were prepared to engage in titanic struggles against intimidating authority and immemorial custom in quest of some lasting security. Security became the leitmotif of Hillman's political vision. In a BBC broadcast at the end of 1934 entitled the "Quest for Security," he described it as "the central issue in the life of modern man." And a month later, in an address to the Wisconsin Bar Association, he asked rhetorically: "Is it any wonder that the worker is bent on an insatiable quest for security" given the unpredictability of the marketplace, disruptive technological innovation, and the malign indifference of management? A job was the worker's only form of property. He pointed to the "striking and omnipresent fact of the insecurity of hired labor and the inequalities of income as between labor . . . and management, employers, and owners." Like his belief in the socially capacious and conscious state, this singular identification with the "quest for security" would also grow more pronounced, leaving little room on the social agenda or in his political psyche for competing ideals, binding him ever closer to the converging purposes of the Keynesian elite.[59]

And yet on May 27, 1935, when the Supreme Court in a unanimous decision declared the NIRA unconstitutional, the state from which he expected so much seemed to have failed utterly. The fact that another idol of his political apprenticeship, Justice Louis D. Brandeis, concurred in that infamous ruling only made the wound angrier. What was to be done? After cresting in the spring and late summer of 1934, the labor movement was once again in disarray, at the top divided over strategy, at the bottom demoralized, as thousands let lapse their affiliations with the craft and new federal locals that had mushroomed during the heyday of 7a. In a memo to Hugh Johnson a year earlier, Adolph Berle aptly summed up the state of the movement:

> Unfortunately, organized labor is a pure abstraction in a great many industries. There is not "organized labor." There are "organizations of labor" in many cases and in many other cases there are not even those.

Berle noted that organized labor had never assumed responsibility for a major national policy because it conceived of itself as a bargaining group and thus failed to put itself forward as "a champion of the popular rights." For this reason labor never emerged as a unified counterfoil to business under the NRA. "[W]e over-estimated the potential statesmanship of American labor."[60]

Sidney Hillman was a labor statesman in waiting, waiting for a movement to represent and a regime to invite that representation. Just days before the *Schecter* decision, at a White House meeting attended by Hillman, Wagner, Perkins, Richberg, Green, and Lewis, where Wagner debated Richberg on the wisdom of his National Labor Relations Act, the President announced his support for the act. But whether it would make it through Congress, and if it did whether it would be obeyed, and even if obeyed whether it would survive the scrutiny of the Supreme Court were all worrying unknowns. When the Court delivered its stunning blow three days later, the labor movement seemed, to Hillman, naked, with no government statute or bureaucracy standing between it and the "Tories of industry." What was to be done?[61]

TWELVE

∾

"We Are Going Ahead
on Our Own"

"Sweet reasonableness" gave way to anger in the wake of the *Schecter* decision. Nothing embittered Hillman more than the apparent betrayal of Justice Brandeis, pioneer of industrial democracy and of so much else that had become part of the union president's credo. One week after the infamous ruling, Hillman told the New York Joint Board:

> I am glad that labor now knows that it cannot depend even on a man like Brandeis. It is a great shame that the man who presided at the signing of the anti-sweatshop Protocol should put on his robes and sign a decision to bring sweatshops back again. . . . That was what the Constitution was used for, to protect the man who sells stinking, sick chickens.

Striking a tone of belligerent defiance absent since the days of the postwar insurgency, he rallied his comrades:

> Well, we won't listen to the Supreme Court of the United States and those judges cannot do anything about it either. . . . Perhaps there is going to be a new law, fixing minimum wages and maximum hours, but we are not going to take a chance on it. We are going to forget about it and go ahead on our own.

The years of "labor statesmanship" seemed suddenly irrelevant; instead, Hillman reminded his listeners of a more distant outlaw past: "It was my privilege when just a boy of sixteen to go to jail fighting against tyranny in Czarist Russia." That moment beckoned again.[1]

There was more than a touch of theater in all this, but Hillman also meant what he said. The strategy of the "statesman"—diplomatic forays into the state bureaucracy on behalf of the labor movement, ambassadorial tete-a-tete's with the chief executive—was for the time being exhausted. The friendlier subdivisions of the bureaucracy were closed down, and the Supreme Court seemed determined to keep them that way. Besides, the labor movement itself was, despite its recent numerical growth, so racked by internal turmoil, so demoralized and at cross purposes with itself, that functioning as its ambassador was a little like being a man without a country. "Going ahead on our own" was as much a concession to reality as it was an act of will. Hillman accepted that fact without complaint and boldly pursued its consequences. The creation of the CIO just six months after *Schecter* required great courage. Even though the CIO depended on the New Deal—and so it did, profoundly and in multifarious ways—it nonetheless threatened to rupture the main lines of authority all across American basic industry. No matter how thoroughly underwritten by the New Deal regime and the state apparatus, it was an inherently risky undertaking, comparable if not exactly commensurate with the dangers confronting revolutionary youth in Czarist Russia.

In the weeks immediately following the *Schecter* decision, Hillman seemed not at all prepared to forge ahead in solitary defiance. He had long dreaded what life after the NRA, for all its faults, would be like— and, it turned out, with good reason. Child labor, for example, which had increased sharply with the onset of the Depression and then fallen off through 1934, rose sharply again after *Schecter*. Children under sixteen left school in droves to work sixty-hour weeks for a median wage of four dollars. Even the extent and forms of worker militance shifted from the offense to the defense. In 1935–36 there was not only a tapering off in the number of strikes—29 percent fewer workers and 10 percent fewer man-hours lost than in the previous year—but most were fought to prevent wage cuts rather than for union recognition and wage hikes, as in the NRA years. The slashing of code standards post-*Schecter* was the rule, not the exception.[2]

Initially, Hillman spent an inordinate amount of time trying to revive the NRA, which was a bit like trying to resuscitate an unloved corpse. Actually, within the clothing industry itself it was not nearly so difficult. After all, the most effective part of the code machinery had always been the Amalgamated anyway. Hillman promptly gathered man-

ufacturers together in voluntary codes. He enlisted the help of major
retailers as well, confessing to the head of Allied Stores in Seattle that he
still hoped for the revival of the NRA. He called on Louis Kirstein and
Percy Strauss to mobilize retailer cooperation, especially through the
National Retail Dry Goods Association. What months earlier had been
code provisions were transposed, more or less intact, into collective
bargaining contracts. Even longtime holdouts, like Rogers Peet in New
York, were finally won for the union.[3]

Flexing a bit of organizational muscle and calling on trusted and
influential business associates when pressed was enough to recreate a
miniature NRA in the clothing industry without a government presence.
Here it was truly possible to "go ahead on our own." The "outside
world," however, proved far less manageable. Indeed, the collapse of the
NRA constituted a regime crisis. It left the government without a recovery program. The President seriously contemplated restoring the
NRA and wished for ways of doing it. So too did Hillman.

Just days after *Schecter,* Hillman and the New York trade union
movement mobilized a quarter of a million people to march in protest. A
rally following the march at Madison Square Garden heard Lewis, Green,
Hillman, and others call for the continuation of the recovery program. A
week later Hillman, along with Philip Murray of the mineworkers,
pleaded for quick action to reformulate the NRA. Anything, they were
reported as arguing, was better than nothing. As late as the AFL convention in October Hillman, along with Lewis, Dubinsky, and Howard
of the Typographers union, rammed through a resolution, just before the
delegates adjourned, calling for a constitutional amendment allowing
Congress to reenact economic and social legislation along the lines of the
NIRA.[4]

Earlier, at a speech in July at the Tamiment Economic and Social
Institute, Hillman, still furious, called for curbs on the Supreme Court
and assailed both radical and conservative critics of the NRA, including
Borah and Darrow. He went so far as to warn that the "people" might
compel changes through the creation of a labor party. But that was
largely rhetoric. Labor party plots, rife at the time, amounted to "going
ahead on our own" with a vengeance, something Hillman at the time
was not prepared to do, especially not in the political arena. Instead, he
scouted the political and industrial landscape for signs of NRA rescue
and rehabilitation parties. He conferred with Mordecai Eziekel, an economic adviser in the Agriculture Department, who was working with
Dennison and other "liberal businessmen" on devising a successor to the
NRA, one conceived from the standpoint of expanding the mass market
for mass production. More statist than anyone except perhaps Tugwell,

Eziekel envisioned expanded national output and income occurring under a fairly rigorous regime of government regulation of prices, production, and the national budget. He proposed an industrial analog of the ever normal granary. If anything, Eziekel was too statist for Hillman's liking. While he approved of most of the economist's suggestions, Hillman balked at the idea of compulsory arbitration. But Eziekel was otherwise openly friendly to industrial unionism and to labor's desire for full representation in government economic bodies. Both men agreed that success depended on overcoming the opposition of the "securities bloc." Hillman served as an intermediary between Eziekel and potentially sympathetic clothing manufacturers, an entry eagerly pursued by the economist as he went about assembling business support for a "second New Deal."[5]

In mid-1935 such support was, if not rare, then painfully difficult to mobilize. As always, there were the Filenes, who labored tirelessly on behalf of the New Deal. As chairman of the BAC's committee on unfair trade practices, Lincoln Filene persistently tried, together with Frankfurter, to work out a collaboration between the manufacturing and distributing trades, one that might recast the NRA codes and have them enforced by the FTC. But the NAM, the USCC, and the ABA were all swept by waves of hysteria directed especially against the government's welfare spending and all hints of government planning or regulation. Not so much elite as mass organizations of smaller, often local businessmen, the USCC and the NAM seasoned their Protestant individualism with a provincial suspicion of all centralized, concentrated power in a toxic political brew. By May 1935 rabid right-wing elements in control of the USCC were denouncing administration efforts to "sovietize the country." Meanwhile, Hillman took on the NAM's general counsel, James Emery, in a Town Hall debate, broadcast live over NBC radio, during which Emery painted a Hooverian picture of an economic utopia undisturbed by nettlesome and incompetent government functionaries, a world where such matters as labor's rights, standards, and social security would be attended to by the corporate commonwealth. In an earlier debate over CBS, Hillman challenged C. L. Bardo, President of the NAM, who took the negative position on the faintly preposterous proposition, "Is the American worker's high standard of living a myth?"[6]

The upwelling of provincial restorationism excited its own opposition. A friendly BAC delegation to the President was heavily weighted in favor of the mass consumption sector: Sidney Weinberg of Goldman Sachs, Lincoln Filene, Lew Hahn of the National Retail Dry Goods Association, Charles Kendall, Charles Cannon of Cannon Towels, Morris Leeds, H. H. Heinman representing consumer credit associations,

Robert Lund of Lambert Pharmaceutical Co., and R. R. Dupree of Proctor & Gamble. RCA and CBS also weighed in on the side of the "second New Deal." If people like Emery or the notorious Ernest Weir of Weirton Steel remained adamantly opposed to practically every form of government intervention, particularly its intrusion into the labor market and the arena of industrial labor relations, these BAC moderates were at least not quite so implacable. Together with labor leaders like Hillman, they were willing to search for some semiprivate accommodation of interests despite the bitter disappointment of the NRA. It was better than having everybody "go ahead on their own."[7]

Some months after the NRA died, Roosevelt appointed George L. Berry, a sometime businessman and leader of the Printing Pressman's union, who had served on the LAB and who was on the best of terms with the trade union officialdom, to serve as Coordinator for Industrial Cooperation. The idea was to explore once again the prospects for reviving the Blue Eagle. Berry created a Council for Industrial Progress, an entity lacking authority and public presence. Hillman accepted an appointment to it, as did William Green, A. O. Wharton of the machinists union, and AFL secretary Frank Morrison. On the business side were Dennison; D. G. Sherwin of Caterpillar Tractor; Flint Garrison, the managing director of the Wholesale Dry Goods Institute; and representatives of Johnson & Johnson and Proctor & Gamble. The Council became a place for the well-intentioned to talk, but the talk only crystallized how improbable an undertaking it was. Hillman was at his most accommodating, willing, for example, to exclude any discussion of public ownership from the Council's agenda. "We are here to find a way to clear the present system," he remarked in reference to the legacy of speculative debt that still clogged the economic arteries. Nonetheless, he fell into an argument with Sherwin, who opposed any wages and hours legislation. This was typical of the Council's predicament, as it made repeated if tepid attempts to skirt the ambivalence of business about government regulation.

The Council was the ghost of the NRA, and it scared nobody. It hung around into 1937, by which time the legislative reforms of the "second New Deal" and the Roosevelt landslide of 1936 had made it practically invisible. But long before that Hillman made it clear he had given up on pious hopes. He told Berry: "I believe that we have passed the stage where we can believe you can educate an industry . . . unless we can address ourselves to compulsion by legislation we say nothing."[8]

The real question was how to achieve such statutory coercion. Publicly, Hillman faulted the "Tories of industry" and "turncoats" like Wolman, Darrow, and Brandeis for the failure of the NRA. More privately, however, he blamed the abject abdication of the trade union movement in the face of unprecedented opportunities to organize millions of industrial workers. A few weeks after the *Schecter* decision Cornelia Bryce Pinchot wrote Hillman to commiserate. Lamentable as that ruling was, she noted, it would at least compel workers "to realize that the building of strong and progressive looking unions is in their own hands, that no one can do it for them, that they alone are responsible." Hillman, of course, agreed. It was what he meant when he talked about "going ahead on our own." But he meant more than that. For Hillman, mass industrial unionism—what would soon announce itself as the CIO—was the pursuit of politics by other means; another, if not the royal, road to state power.[9]

Indeed, from the vantage point of rising new trade union, managerial, and political elites, the CIO was a quintessentially political creature whose origins and fate were entirely bound up with the rising and receding of the "second New Deal." Strangely enough, the view from below was not all that different. The great strike waves and daring forays into the heart of heavy industry of the mid-1930s seem practically inconceivable without the prior sea change in mass political attitudes inspired first by 7a and then by the legislative breakthroughs of the "second New Deal," and registered with irresistible force in the Democratic landslides of 1934 and 1936. Already in 1932 it was clear that several new kinds of voters—principally urban immigrants naturalized in the 1920s, along with the offspring of the immigrants who migrated to America between 1890 and 1910—were transforming the electoral landscape in favor of the urban-Progressive wing of the Democratic Party. Before 1932, for example, the Pennsylvania Democratic Party was largely a rural phenomenon. It was the massive shift of urban Italian immigrants and their children into the Democratic Party, along with the potent influence of the UMW, that with lightning speed led to the state's "little New Deal" under Governor George H. Earle. Similarly, La Guardia's 1933 reform victory in New York City was replicated in Philadelphia, Pittsburgh, Cleveland, and Bridgeport, signaling a cultural and social revolution in mass politics.[10]

The strike wave of mid-1933 and the one in the spring and summer of 1934 were inspired by the rhetoric if not the actual achievements of the new regime; again and again the Blue Eagle and 7a were invoked to sanction acts of resistance and rebellion. Among the many indications that the CIO was but a dependent variable in a more complex political chemistry is the remarkable fact that, with the exception of the Fair Labor Standards Act, all the essential pieces of New Deal reform—not only in the areas of social welfare and labor relations but in the tax, banking, securities, and public utility fields as well—were in place before the CIO erupted as a mass movement. Thus the "second New Deal" was not the outcome of an insurgent labor movement, but rather emerged out of the broader processes of mass politics, orchestrated by the President.

Unlike John L. Lewis, who allowed the CIO's early triumphs to feed his own sense of political independence, Hillman always recognized that it was the electoral arena, not the shop floor, that again and again proved most decisive in molding workers' political and organizational behavior. There an egalitarian resentment supplied the energy and *frisson* of a new politics of consumption. Moreover, the "welfare state" was expressly designed by its chief architects to stimulate mass consumption: State intervention into the labor market, along with the state's credit policy, urban renewal, and so on, were tactical salients for consolidating a new consumerism. Frances Perkins noted as early as 1933:

> As a Nation, we are recognizing that programs long thought of as merely labor welfare, such as shorter hours, higher wages, and a voice in the terms and conditions of work, are really essential economic factors for recovery, and for the technique of industrial management in a mass production age.[11]

Similarly, the Wagner Act was expressly designed by the Senator; Leon Keyserling, his chief economic adviser; William Leiserson, a protégé of Tugwell at Columbia (who would become NLRB chairman in 1939); and Isador Lubin, Hillman's close associate, as a device with which to civilize and stabilize the politics of production and as part of a more general exercise in demand management. The act's preamble proclaimed that purpose: "to insure a wise distribution of wealth between management and labor, to maintain a full flow of purchasing power, and to prevent recurrent depression." The bill itself was introduced after the 1934 elections at a high tide of New Deal mass electoral strength, and at a time when the NRA had evidently failed to augment purchasing power enough to match the rise in prices, profits, and production. Wagner and Keyserling conceived of the act as a vital element in a broader design for centralized and democratic planning, functioning to redistribute wealth and not merely as a device for countervailing power. In an address to Congress, Wagner made these purposes clear:

> When wages sink to low levels, the decline in purchasing power is felt upon the marts of trade. And since collective bargaining is the most powerful single force in maintaining and advancing wage rates, its repudiation is likely to intensify the maldistribution of buying power, thus reducing stan-

dards of living, unbalancing the economic structure, and inducing depression with its devastating effect upon the flow of commerce.[12]

The Twentieth Century Fund, the vehicle of scientific management and mass consumption–oriented business, sponsored a report on government–labor relations that closely paralleled and supported the Wagner Act. While the fund's report did include penalties for trade unions as well as managements who engaged in "unfair practices," the fund's founder, Lincoln Filene, labored long and hard to persuade old friends from the Progressive movement, especially Newton Baker, to support the legislation. The average cupidity and narrow-mindedness of his fellow businessmen infuriated Filene. He began delivering scathingly sarcastic tirades against their anachronistic fondness for the ethos of frugality, their inability to formulate anything but the most immediately selfish policies, and a provincialism he warned would lead to revolution, a grim prospect to be avoided only by encouraging industrial unionism on a nationwide scale. Evans Clark, the director of the fund, conferred with Wagner about lining up businessmen to testify on the bill's behalf. Meanwhile, Edwin Smith, a Filene protégé, who was to emerge as the most radical of the original NLRB members, was active, along with William H. Davis, Sumner Slichter, Leiserson, and Governor Winant, in the fund's campaign on behalf of the Wagner Act. John Carmody, who was recommended to the NLRB by Wagner, emerged from the same networks. He was a Taylor Society associate of Morris Cooke and his deputy at the socially daring Rural Electrification Administration, which challenged the power and prerogatives of dominant utility holding companies of the "securities bloc." He was experienced as a labor mediator in the steel and coal industries, had functioned as a superintendent of a scientifically managed and unionized clothing factory, and was chief engineer of the New Deal's most radical effort at transforming relief into a mechanism of social engineering (and union recognition), the Civil Works Administration. David Saposs, who was to head the NLRB's Economic Research Division, was another employee of the Twentieth Century Fund who before that had worked for the ACWA as its educational director. A student of John Commons, Saposs quickly hired the CIO's first secretary, Kathryn Pollack Ellickson, a longtime socialist and a proponent of scientific management cooperative productivity schemes among the railroad shopcraft workers. A Frankfurter student and member of the CP, Nathan Witt, became the NLRB's secretary.[13]

These institutional and personal circuits, with their lineages stretching well back into the 1920s, suggest something more: A decade before the Flint sitdown strike and the Memorial Day Massacre, a Great Depression away from the general strikes of Minneapolis and San Francisco, and several AFL conventions prior to John L. Lewis's celebrated assault on William Hutcheson, the CIO already existed (the romantic mythos of popular liberalism notwithstanding). It existed, that is, as a strictly managerial-political formation.

It had a strategy, national industrial unionism; a social perspective, functional integration within an interdependent economy of complex, large-scale bureaucratic organizations; and a political economy, planned, expanded production and state sanctioned redistribution of income in the interests of security and consumption. It possessed as well a general staff: not only Lewis and Hillman, but their key economic and social engineering advisers, including, in Hillman's case, Cooke, Harlow Person, Otto Beyer, and William Leiserson; in Lewis's case, Jett Lauck. As early as 1934 Lauck urged Lewis to consider leaving the AFL to set up a new labor federation devoted to industrial unionism, which "would also make communism and subversive movements impossible." At the same time Lauck reiterated the need for government intervention to regularize expanded production in part through government credits, as well as to redistribute income.

This embryonic CIO even had a cadre school—Brookwood—where such key future CIO operatives as Kathryn Pollack Ellickson, John Brophy, Eli Oliver, David Saposs, Clinton Golden, and dozens of anonymous trade union militants, largely drawn from the needle and metal trades, who would go on to become the organizers of the Steelworkers Organizing Committee, the Textile Workers Organizing Committee, the Packinghouse Workers Organizing Committee, and so on, either taught or studied. Cooke did his best to introduce a proto-Keynesian perspective into Brookwood's "curriculum." Last but not least, this new labor movement waiting in the wings had an ideology: industrial democracy, the Marxism of the professional middle class, wise to the class antinomies of industrial society but sanguine enough to believe in their pacific supersession by science and abundance.[14]

Most of all, the CIO already existed as an embryonic strategic alliance, its incipient leadership integrated, via the left wing of the scientific management movement, into the political circles around Frankfurter and Brandeis. What this putative mass organization lacked was a membership, and the strength of will among its self-designated leaders to make those risky overtures into the unknown without which there would be no membership. But forces were converging to make that decisive next step possible and necessary, if not inevitable.

For the immediate future, the death of the NRA foreclosed the use of executive agencies and federal statutes as surrogate organizers. But a sizable economic upturn, which was to last two years, began propitiously in the summer of 1935. The index of production rose from 87 to 115, and unemployment declined from 10.6 million to 7.7 million thanks in part to the Emergency Relief Appropriations Act. As the WPA and the PWA soaked up some more of the labor surplus and consumption rose, the balance of power in the marketplace shifted in favor of labor, not only because there was more work around, but because the revival of domestic and world markets made businessmen less willing to tolerate long, competitively destructive strikes. And coincident with and inspired by Roosevelt's turn to the left in mid-1935, unmistakable signs of discontent with the trade union *status quo* appeared yet again in industrial centers all across the country.[19]

In April Hillman received a letter at the NRA from the president of an Oldsmobile local of the Automobile Workers Association of America in Lansing, Michigan. "We have heard rumors that you may lead a movement to build an organization of industrial unions independent of AFL craft unionism. . . . We are hoping it is true because it will be a life preserver thrown to the workers in the automobile industry." The local had withdrawn from the AFL when William Green announced that they would have to recognize craft jurisdictions in the plant. The membership deserted practically overnight, falling from 1,500 to sixty. Spirits rose again when the union reconstituted itself independently, but the proportional representation ruling of the NRA's Auto Labor Board, which granted the plant's company unions twelve representatives to the union's nine, produced another wave of "apathy" and "inertia." The local president told Hillman that the ACW served as a model of industrial unionism and mentioned that there was sentiment in the local for a labor party like the ones in Britain and Scandinavia. Hillman responded warmly but was noncommittal on his plans to foment opposition to the AFL.[16]

According to Frances Perkins, however, Hillman was restive and contemptuous of the AFL hierarchs from the moment he entered the federation. By her account, he confided to her in 1934 his plan to form a committee inside the AFL to foster the mass organization of the unorganized. Just what Hillman confided to Perkins is open to question. He never entirely trusted her and jealously competed with her for access to FDR on political matters having to do with labor. Nonetheless, his sympathies for industrial unionism and his antipathies for the AFL old guard were well known. When he conveyed his fraternal regards to the Oldsmobile local president, he undoubtedly meant it. It was to the automobile industry, after all, that many, including Hillman, looked for signs of a new unionism.[17]

The strike wave of 1933 swept through at least a hundred auto plants. By the thousands, auto workers swarmed into the AFL. The federation did nothing, and the same thousands streamed back out. Then, in the spring of 1935, a second wave of "wildcat" strikes spread from Toledo to Cleveland and Norwood, Ohio. The AFL representative, Francis Dillon, exerted every effort to abort the strikes, and once again thousands of workers walked away in disgust. Finally the pressure even got through to the AFL Executive Committee, and a national union, under Dillon and Homer Martin, was created in August 1935.

Similar insurgencies spread across the industrial Midwest. Akron became a clinical instance of the disintegration of the old order. Long a town dominated by its tire manufacturers, fiercely Republican in its political loyalties, boosteristic, nativist, and fertile territory for the Klan thanks to its large population of Appalachian migrants, Akron began to come apart under the impact of the Depression and the New Deal. The NRA particularly galvanized dormant populist sentiment and class resentments, especially among the skilled machinists at Goodyear—a highly literate group, readers of Marx and Debs—as well as among the city's electricians, plumbers, and printers. As in the auto industry, the AFL federal local became, in the fashion of a religious revival, the site of mass conversions, recruiting more than 12,000 members in sixty days. Tire-builders, who represented a newly emerging milieu of industrial skilled workers appearing in many industries over the previous twenty years, their jobs and skills closely tied to recent technological changes and transformations in the organization of work, were all too typically ignored by AFL officials. After they walked out on their own, the NRA's NLRB spent time in fruitless investigation and mediation while Goodyear sped up the pace of work and terminated the tire-builders' six-hour day, a Depression-bred attempt to share the work. Finally, William Green abandoned the rubber workers early in 1935. Despair, however, soon gave way to a new international industrial union, the creation of communists and other radicals, which manifested an implacable hostility to the NRA, the AFL, and the rubber companies.[18]

Events in Akron, Toledo, and the auto centers of Ohio and Michigan, and signs of restiveness in the steel mills of Chicago and Gary were worrying to everyone. Lewis had already despaired of real progress within the AFL back in February, when the executive council quashed plans to organize in the auto industry. He was no friendlier to a compromise, offered by Hillman and Howard of the Typographers, to delay a jurisdictional confrontation until after the industry was unionized. Meanwhile Hillman and Frey talked about getting together in the summer to discuss their differences over the appropriate structure for the trade union movement. Frey lamented that "personal and theoretical considerations are playing a part which is undermining," but Hillman was quick to point out that "personal" and "theoretical" differences were not at all the same thing.[19]

The October convention of the AFL in Atlantic City proved his point. The federation leadership fought off a resolution calling for the formation of a labor party that was supported by 104 delegates, including those from the needle trades as well as the hotel and restaurant workers, auto workers, and the recently formed Cleaners and Dyers Union. Tempers then exploded over Lewis's resolution calling on the AFL to sever its ties to the National Civic Federation. That in turn led to a fight over industrial unionism that featured fiery speeches by militant auto, rubber, and other workers. Hillman spoke on behalf of the UAW's right to representation and reiterated his proposal for a moratorium on the jurisdictional question for three years, the time he estimated was necessary to break the back of GM. The debate was capped by fisticuffs between Lewis and Hutcheson, fitting punctuation to mark a fateful parting of the ways. A few days later Lewis, Hillman, Charles Howard, Dubinsky, Max Zaritsky, John Brophy, Tom Kennedy, and Thomas McMahon of the UTW gave birth to the CIO at a meeting also attended by Harvey Fremming of the Oil Workers and Thomas Brown of the Mine, Mill, and Smelter Workers.[20]

Was it in fact a fateful gathering, or something less significant, the outcome of mere personal rivalries and jealous contests over institutional turf? Some argue the latter, noting that the CIO was led by conventional trade unionists, that despite the pyrotechnics and politically adventuresome rhetoric surrounding its formation, it did in fact engage in conventional trade unionism, and that the AFL for its part was not in principle opposed to industrial unionism and contained such unions, most conspicuously the UMW, within its own ranks. The reluctance with which the principals approached the split, until very near the end, and the subsequent and frequent efforts to compose differences discreetly through confidential bureaucratic channels add weight to this view. So long as the discussion is confined to convention speeches and resolutions and the backroom maneuverings of ambitious bureaucrats, the view of the CIO as a radical rupture in labor organization and labor politics does seem a bit overdone.

When one recognizes that the strategic leadership of the CIO was connected by a thousand threads to a newly emergent managerial and political elite, an elite which in collaboration with the CIO would foster a permanent change not only in the national political economy but in the internal political chemistry of the Democratic Party and in the prevailing politics of production in basic industry; and when one further-more recognizes that the AFL old guard not only lacked those same strategic political and managerial connections and objectives, but more-over often adamantly opposed, in the industrial, political and adminis-trative arenas, essential elements of the New Deal–CIO agenda, then the histrionics of Atlantic City appear as more than pure theater.

The major institutional blocs of anti-CIO and pro-CIO voting strength at the convention are suggestive: 90 percent of the anti-CIO vote came from a cluster of unions representing the building trades, various urban service occupations, and the railroad brotherhoods. Those were the strongholds of the traditional urban craftsman and an industrial skilled elite, native or old-stock immigrant in ethnic makeup; they tended to be localist in orientation, often depending on the patronage and commercial largess of the old Democratic Party metropolitan ma-chines, themselves threatened by the rising political power of the "new immigrant," a phenomenon they rightly blamed on the New Deal. Across the aisle, 85 percent of the pro-CIO vote was cast by unions in the needle trades, mining, and printing. The interconnections between the needle unions, most prominently the Amalgamated, and the circles pro-moting scientific management, industrial democracy, and mass consumption–oriented industrial and fiscal policy scarcely need further elaboration. It is worth noting that the printing industry, where the pro-CIO Printing Pressmen and the International Typographers were ensconced, had for years been the site of similar union–management collaborations. As for the miners, Lewis enjoyed his own relationship with the Rocky Mountain Fuel Company under the Frankfurter favorite Josephine Roche. And through Jett Lauck he was in touch with the same reform milieus with which Hillman maintained such cordial relations.

Moreover, the test of parliamentary strength in Atlantic City left out of account the sentiments of militants in the rubber, electrical, auto, steel, and numerous other industries who had come painfully to the conclusion that the AFL was morally, not to mention organizationally, bankrupt. During the next several years the contending sides would become so at odds on so many grounds, it is hard indeed to ascribe it all to bureaucratic infighting. The differences over what the government should or should not do, over who was to control the Democratic Party and for just what purposes, would not only provoke bitter territorial disputes but would profoundly upset the internal equilibrium of the Dem-ocratic Party and vitally affect the fate of New Deal legislation, including the FLSA and attempts to amend the NLRA. Indeed, prior to the actual split, AFL chieftains were still equivocating about the Social Security act, still worrying it might threaten the power they derived from union pension schemes. This is not to say that all the talk about trade union structure, jurisdictional boundaries, tactics, and timing didn't matter. It did, and so too did all the mud-slinging. Frey was convinced Lewis was bound and determined to become AFL President or ruin the federation trying. Charles Ogburn, the AFL legal counsel, thought Hillman wanted to become the "Lenin of America." But these vituperative outbreaks could also obscure more fundamental, less visible social divisions—one might go so far as to call them anthropological divisions—over power and authority concealed within the black box of the factory and the working-class neighborhood.[21]

During the two decades preceding the Great Depression the very category of common labor and its ganglike structure became far less common. A new species of semiskilled machine tender emerged, whose work demanded a new repertoire of talents: judgment, observation, control, and measurement as opposed to the undifferentiated routines of the unskilled. The electrification of production, Cooke and Philip Murray observed, created a new emphasis on "sustained attention; correct perception, quick reaction." By its very nature such work was subject to the more systematic and finely tuned external control and monitoring at which scientific management excelled. It also elicited new habits at and away from work. Together with the alchemical powers of the mass market and mass culture, whose impact on the desires and behavior of the second-generation immigrant was already conspicuous by the 1920s, it helped fashion the new labor force, different in kind from its industrial forebears: in what it did at work and thought about work; in where it lived and with whom; in its amusements as well as its attitudes toward the sacred. It was this new species—often the urbanized sons of immigrants and urbanized blacks, as well as "native" Protestant workers—who, precisely because they were losing their moorings in the closed cultural worlds of kin, craft, community, and culture, became the natural constituency of industrial democracy and the CIO.[22]

At the same time the social and cultural dynamics of the CIO were further complicated by the conspicuous and articulate presence of older subspecies of industrial and urban craftsmen. If semiskilled operators made up the CIO's mass constituency, it was a certain kind of skilled worker, experienced politically as well as in trade union matters, who supplied the movement's élan and organizational genius. Tool and die makers, for example, persisted and resisted the ravages of the depressed economy. In the auto and electrical industries tool and die makers and the machinists especially constituted the indispensable cadre of the new industrial unions, the UAW and UE.

But skilled workers were a heterogeneous milieu. They included both production and nonproduction workers. Some were quite secular and even anticlerical. Others were attracted by liberal currents of Catholic social thought, the modernist Catholicism of Fathers Charles Owen Rice, John Ryan, and Haas. Still others were moved by the more ambivalent Catholic populism of Father Coughlin, which penetrated the ranks of urban tradesmen. Both "catholicisms" were inspired by the papal encyclicals calling for restraints on the use of private property. The modernist variety especially felt an affinity for the new labor movement and the New Deal, but only up to that point where the secularizing and bureaucratic-centralizing incursions of the government and the CIO began to threaten the moral integrity of the Catholic family and community.

Even the most committed to "modernism" were not without their own ambivalences. Skilled workers, originally from the British Isles or from Southeastern Europe, frequently were experienced trade unionists and were often acquainted with some version of radical labor or nationalist politics—the pan-Slavic revolutionary nationalism of the Serbs and Croats, for example, or the syndicalism of Italian artisans, or the belligerent atheism of Lithuanian or Bohemian "free-thinkers." And yet their motivations could often be deeply conservative at the same time. The Depression and the attendant downgrading of skilled jobs (with respect to both pay and job content, a process accelerated by the NRA) presented a mortal threat to their social status, about which they were acutely sensitive. "We were just part of the common mass, you might say. And that's what got us really thinking a lot about unionism," an early UE activist remembered.[23]

Machinists and tool and die makers of the auto and electrical industries, for example, invariably formed the militant and radical democratic core of the CIO. In the front ranks of the AFL, however, other industrial craftsmen, especially among urban tradesmen and non–production line workers, were more tradition-bound and less deracinated. Their status-consciousness was embedded in patterns of neighborhood, ethnic, and familial solidarity. For them, shop floor politics were an extension of the politics of civil society. In even the most cosmopolitan and industrialized urban centers—the "Back of the Yards" neighborhood of Chicago for example, or the self-absorbed ethnic worlds of Pennsylvania steel towns with their own saloons, groceries, butchers, bankers, newspapers, and clothing stores—small-scale, self-contained ethnic social economies reproduced, in relative isolation, social hierarchies in which craftsmen enjoyed an honored position, even if employed by the corporate world outside the ethnic community. Members of the Steelworkers Independent Union, for example, men of skill and self-conscious dignity, were also opposed to the centralizing tendencies of industrial unionism and were bound up in the exclusionary fraternal world of the Knights of Pythias. In Flint, a self-conscious labor aristocracy dating from the carriage and wagon-making era maintained close relations with the local business elite and was separated by a wide gulf of material possessions, social status, and security from the emerging migratory milieu of Southeast European and Appalachian rustics.[24]

The influence of the skilled traditionalists on shop floor politics extended far beyond their own circle, precisely because of their social and cultural hegemony within the circumscribed universe of working-class neighborhood and ethnic life. Within the factory, first-generation unskilled immigrants—for whom work was an unadulterated curse from which they withdrew into the worlds of the tavern, the fraternal lodge, and the family's religious and secular rituals—were tied by customary relations of deference to their more worldly skilled brethren. Skilled gang leaders exercised nearly absolute power over the nature, duration, and pace of work, which imparted an intimidating vulnerability to the work experience of these immigrants. Thus, there was a hard practicality to these deferential relations, as through their observance the immigrant often managed first to secure and then to hold onto a job. A network of authority thus linked the top and bottom of the occupational hierarchy and generated a deeply conservative community with an abiding respect for the institutions of private property, if not capitalism. For many, the fatalism, restricted mobility, patriarchy, and moral and educational parochialism of the Old World village were thus reinforced by the exigencies of industrial and urban life.[25]

The CIO insurgency immediately threatened the customary power and prestige of these shop floor elites. New occupational groupings of semiskilled machine tenders were often eager to perform a variety of jobs and to advance up the job ladder. Ambition about work—they "wanted better jobs, cleaner, mechanized, with some skills"—extended into the realm of consumption. Such ambitions were threatened by the Depression. Especially as the wage differential between the skilled, often German and Irish tradesmen, and the semiskilled narrowed, the former sensed a threat to established patterns of power and status, a mortal threat to the prerogatives of a craft-based and ethnically homogeneous elite, self-conscious about its purported racial and cultural superiority.[26]

In contrast, a newer, historically more fluid sector of the shop floor—the semiskilled—was more ethnically dissociated, less enmeshed within networks of kin and community. For second-generation Italians, for example, the structures of patriarchal authority were already decomposing through exposure to schools and work outside the family and community.

For many Rumanians nationalism had for some time supplanted more parochial attachments. Among various Slavic populations the courtship and marriage patterns of the second generation became noticeably less rigid and endogamous. Neighborhood ethnic parishes were gradually "Americanized." The workplace became a site of social and racial resentment, as the universalist criteria of merit and individual performance clashed with the real structures of racial-ethnic authority: "We didn't want to live like Hunkies any more . . . treated like trash." Quintessentially urban, with a functional and instrumental but not existential relationship to their work, far more integrated as consumers into the mass market and more influenced by the media of mass culture than their parents, this new species of worker came closer to resembling Marx's "proletariat"—rootless, dispossessed, functionally interchangeable—than anything yet seen in America. Precisely because they were often alienated from the extended family, excluded from the charmed circle of craft, and instead integrated into the public worlds of work and citizenship more by bureaucratic than by primordial ties, they were receptive to the message of industrial unionism.[27]

AFL bureaucrats often were overwhelmed, but Hillman's whole previous life and career had uniquely prepared him to command the disorderly social and psychological energies unleased by the dismantling of the traditional framework of working-class life. The "new unionism" foreshadowed the CIO, and not simply because it adopted an industrial rather than a craft form of organization. More significantly, the internal development of the ACW anticipated a range of problems that now confronted the new unions of the 1930s. In the first instance, in the interests of internalizing a sense of industrial discipline, the Amalgamated had to overcome the resistance of ethno-work cultures unaccustomed to the centralized, bureaucratic procedures that made industrial unionism a valuable asset to business as well as to labor. A similar process of resistance, rationalization, and cultural transformation accounted for the turbulence that characterized the early years of most of the CIO unions.

But no matter how well prepared, Hillman did not have the power to call a mass movement into being, nor would he have willed it into being had he had the power. He had become increasingly determined to impose order on inherently entropic labor and social insurgencies. As he helped erect the "iron cage," so he came to identify with his creation. Moreover, he was acutely sensitive to the unpredictability of mass movements, that upwelling of long-repressed desires and resentments which articulated no prescribed program, fitted no prefabricated institution.

Above all, recognizing that the fate of this new venture was irrevocably tied to that of Roosevelt and the "second New Deal," Hillman plotted and watched and worried about every new CIO development, assessing whether it would enhance or jeopardize the lifeline to Washington.

Lee Pressman, the future CIO chief counsel, another Frankfurter student, remembered that in the early days Hillman was anxious that each campaign be meticulously planned and conducted with military precision, while Lewis felt more at ease with autonomous movements from the ranks. Lewis's sympathy for democratic enthusiasms, Pressman's memory notwithstanding, is by no means self-evident; never did anyone run a union more autocratically, nor create one—the Steel Workers Organizing Committee (SWOC)—so patently suited to his own culti-vated patriarchal charisma. But that Hillman was ever cautious is beyond doubt. If he was careful, however, he was also determined, now that it had finally come to it, to "go ahead on our own."[28]

At the first CIO meeting it was Hillman who came closest to Lewis in his willingness to complete the rupture and create a new labor feder-ation. Howard of the Typographers defined his objectives far more nar-rowly, while Dubinsky and Zaritsky, reluctant to sever their ties to the AFL bureaucracy, vacillated. They wanted a conciliatory statement, one emphasizing the educational and advisory status of the "Committee" within the AFL. On the attitude to be taken toward the AFL, Hillman consistently supported Lewis's toughness and independence. For exam-ple, after the AFL Executive Council officially suspended the ten rene-gade unions in the fall of 1936, Lewis and Hillman urged the rest of the CIO to reaffirm its position and move ahead with its organizing plans, to forgo time-wasting legal battles over jurisdictional rights, and to ignore the AFL's upcoming convention in Tampa. Hillman was emboldened by what he considered the amazing progress of the SWOC, to which the ACW immediately donated $10,000, and by the reports coming to him from Hyman Schneid about high levels of CIO sentiment as workers abandoned company unions in the Carnegie steel mills of Chicago and Gary. Together Lewis and Hillman worked out the CIO's response to Green's attacks and decided that none of the suspended unions would honor Green's summons to appear before him in person. Hillman issued a statement defending the CIO's legitimacy and indicting the AFL for its failure to organize.[29]

But on the logistics of mass industrial unionism itself, Hillman was decidedly more cautious than Lewis, or perhaps more focused and sys-tematic. Early in December 1935 he argued that the "Committee" ought to confine its efforts to the auto and rubber industries (especially the former) and stay away from steel and the big radio and electronics manufacturers. He did not want the young "Committee" to "dissipate our forces." The situation in auto was ripe. He had confidence in Adolph Germer, a longtime socialist and onetime labor representative on the NRA's compliance board in the Midwest, who was the CIO's man in the auto centers and later Hillman's contact in Flint. Auto, Hillman maintained, could have fallen some time ago, as Alfred E. Sloan was "scared by the Toledo strike." Moreover, he said, improving business conditions would aid the drive. It was important to act decisively, quickly, and with plenty of resources or else risk being discredited in the eyes of a sophisticated group of auto worker militants. Still, his auto tactics were a study in moderation. While he invited the fledgling UAW to join the "Committee," he still preferred simultaneously to carry on their fight for industrial unionism inside the AFL, believing it still possible to negotiate with federation moderates. Further, Hillman argued, even if the radio workers left the AFL, it might be wiser to stay away from that industry for a while. Here Hillman was being less than candid, concealing the fact that he counted on reaching an agreement with Swope of GE that would avoid the need for mass organization and the danger of a strike.

With most of this Lewis agreed, while Dubinsky was more timid, fearful of AFL reprisals, which Hillman now accepted as a new fact of life. Hillman stood firm in the face of the creeping timidity infecting his needle trade colleagues. As early as October 1936, just as the CIO was about to erupt in a series of mass insurgencies, Zaritsky pushed for peace negotiations. Even after the New Deal's exhilarating triumph in November, Zaritsky, together with Dubinsky, forced the CIO executive to reconsider peace talks. Dubinsky worried that Lewis was too intransigent, allowing the AFL no graceful way to retreat. Hillman agreed that peace was important, but the new opportunity opened up by Roosevelt's reelection was more important and was perhaps the last great chance to penetrate basic industry. "Are we going to surrender?" he asked accusingly.[30]

However much Lewis might have preferred a more diffuse and flexible policy of pursuing organizing opportunities everywhere at once, particularly in steel, events in the rubber and auto sectors reinforced Hillman's strategy of concentration. As 1935 drew to a close, the intransigence of the rubber companies in Akron elicited denunciations not only from Lewis but from Secretary Perkins as well. Early in the new year a sitdown strike by truck tire builders at Firestone soon spread to Goodyear and Goodrich. The strike was conducted with evangelical fervor, inspiring workers outside the industry, and took on the character of a mass strike spreading throughout the city, especially once the tire builders compelled the rubber companies to restore the six-hour day. Lewis's aide, John Brophy, wrote to Hillman at the height of the strike, desperate for help in a situation he described as "very tense," asking him to send Leo Krzycki, ACW Midwest organizer and national chairman of the Socialist Party. Krzycki arrived and kept Hillman abreast of developments. Hillman urged the CIO to capitalize on the Akron victory through a wide publicity campaign throughout the auto centers of the Midwest.[31]

Over the next eighteen months "very tense" situations like the one in Akron became nearly normal. Whether sitdown strikes or not (and after the victorious Flint sitdown against GM in early 1937 a tidal wave of sitdowns engulfed the country), these were embattled affairs in which private corporate arsenals and vigilante committees—often assembled with corporate money and personnel—along with the forces of law and order and public propriety, including not only the police but the local media, together managed to convert industrial disputes into metropolitan civil wars. Precisely because these situations were as open-ended as they were, and because they could not, at least in many critical instances, be called into existence or directed to some foreordained resolution by CIO strategists in Washington, they became "very tense" for those who assumed their titular leadership, for Lewis and Hillman particularly.

At the moment of greatest fervor, during the sitdown waves of 1936–37, the New York Times put the issue succinctly: It "is the young hotheads who have been coming to the front in recent weeks" challenging the authority and institutional legitimacy of the CIO hierarchy. Lewis and Hillman could reassert control, the Times surmised, only if management proved willing to negotiate. Just there was the paradox. Mass action was often essential to bring management to the table, but it was at the same time the source of the greatest anxiety. The presence of political radicals—communists, socialists, and various subspecies—in the strike leadership was not the real problem. These were highly disciplined cadre, employed by both Lewis and Hillman at all levels of the organization and relied upon to carry out the broader strategic purposes of the CIO with which they were in any event in basic agreement. In case after case, from the assembly lines and parts plants of the auto industry to the electrical equipment manufacturers of Schenectady and Pittsburgh, in the rubber factories and on the wharves of the West Coast, underground in New York's subways, in a pattern so invariant as to suggest a law of collective behavior, radicals, both from among the skilled denizens of the shop floor and "colonizers" from the outside, provided the critical leadership not only when the insurgencies were at their height, but also during the long periods of painstaking organization-building that preceded and followed them. These cadre brought to the movement invaluable experience, administrative and bureaucratic talents, and moral self-confidence. As much as Hillman, they were committed to the integration of labor into democratic institutions of collective bargaining and industrial work discipline, to government regulation and income redistribution—that is, to the axioms of the "second New Deal," which infused the CIO at all levels. Hillman's attitude toward Joseph Curran, CP leader of the National Maritime Union, presumed this more general view of the party. He told Len DeCaux, the CIO press secretary, after meeting with Curran: "Joe's a good boy. He has to act red in his set-up. But he's all right. We can handle Joe."[32]

It was not radicalism *per se*, then, that was the cause for concern, but rather the more inchoate, sudden eruptions of desire and power capable of overflowing the boundaries of property rights, the rules and regulations governing daily life on the job, the social hierarchies and rituals protecting those who commanded from those whose lot it was to obey. Many corporations were reluctant to accede even the most elementary rights of collective bargaining mandated by the new Wagner Act, and in fact ignored its provisions until its constitutionality was confirmed by the Supreme Court in 1937. But even those companies that took a more conciliatory approach still jealously guarded what they defined as the inviolable prerogatives of management to control the actual organization and pace of production. A mass movement whose very tactics seemed at times to call basic property rights into question, whose hubris on the shop floor went so far as to circumvent or defy the customary authority of foremen and departmental supervisors, was alarming. It was alarming to management, and for that reason it alarmed Hillman and Lewis, as it undermined the basis for stable collective bargaining and more broadly could and did become a political liability, straining dangerously the lifeline to the Roosevelt regime.

To avoid such dangers, Lewis and Hillman erected, when they could, organizational devices like SWOC, TWOC, DSOC, and PWOC, through which they tightly monitored internal union policy and proceeded with all due deliberation, while dealing directly with corporate chief executives like Myron Taylor of USS. In effect, these were attempts to call mass movements into being by bureaucratic-administrative fiat. The SWOC was a model for this sort of organizational orderliness and command from the top. Hillman followed its progress lovingly and generously contributed organizers and financial resources to its success. J. B. S. Hardman was sent out west to help put out the SWOC paper. That day in early March 1937 when Myron Taylor agreed, without a shot being fired in anger, to recognize the steelworkers union was for Hillman a day of exhilarating triumph, confirming him in his indictment of the AFL's complacency.[33]

Hillman fabricated two bureaucratic siblings of the SWOC, designed to secure him the same unquestioned power enjoyed by Lewis and Murray in the steel industry. The first, the Textile Workers Organizing Committee (TWOC), although born early in 1937, was so bound up with the strategic rise and retreat of the "second New Deal" that its story must wait. The second, the Department Store Workers Organizing Committee, was a case study of the CIO as a mass movement from above.

Attempts to unionize various classes of department store workers predated the CIO. Percy Strauss of Macy's, although by no means a militant advocate of trade unionism, nonetheless had tried to point out to his fellow retailers just after World War I that the solution to their commercial difficulties lay in greater inventory turnover and operating efficiencies, not in the cutting of their clerks' salaries. Later, under the NRA code, hours were reduced and wages rose, although no real union appeared. Then Samuel Wolchok, a Russian-born onetime ILG organizer, later a dissident RCA local leader, and a social democrat, became the chief spokesman for the United Retail Employees of America, affiliated with the CIO. No creature born out of CIO headquarters, this early department store union included remnants of a TUUL group created by the CP in the early 1930s. It had rebelled against its AFL international and was chartered by the CIO in May 1937. Immediately it was enveloped in the sitdown wave, first at Woolworth's in Detroit, then in a particularly spectacular sitdown at Woolworth's in New York, where Mayor La Guardia intervened to help mediate a settlement both at Woolworth's and at the H. L. Green chain. Strikes spread to Philadelphia and elsewhere. An *ad hoc* CIO committee comprising unions with a strong interest in the retail industry—the ACW, the ILG, the hosiery workers, and the UE—lent the drive additional force and led to a new series of sitdowns. At this point the insurgent character of the movement was altered through the joint intervention of managerial and CIO officialdom. The November 1937 CIO convention established the DSWOC under the leadership of Wolchok and Hillman. Hillman was actually reluctant to take over, as he was fully preoccupied with the TWOC campaign and with a critical Congressional battle over the FLSA. But he assented at the request of the New York department store managements, who by now recognized that unionization was inevitable but wanted to deal with Hillman rather than a less "responsible" leadership. It made sense from the Amalgamated's point of view, as historically the union was already linked to the retail arena through its inclusion of department store tailors working in alteration rooms and through its prior organization of a clothing salesman's local. Matters did not look quite as reasonable to Wolchok. It took two days of intensive discussion with Lewis, Hillman, and Pressman before Wolchok agreed to step down and let Hillman run the department store drive. The CIO triumvirate argued specifically that Hillman's "vast contacts" made him better qualified. Everybody knew where these "vast contacts" lay and how valuable they could be. Not long before, Hillman had done a favor for Louis Kirstein by cooling down the ardor of a CIO drive in Boston. He could expect some help in return.[34]

The DSWOC, TWOC, SWOC, and so on represented a social engineering version of how to run a mass movement. Elsewhere, however, in the auto, rubber, and electrical industries most conspicuously, but also in lumber, longshore, and maritime, it was the mass movement that preceded the institution, leaving the latter more expressive of and vulnerable to all the cross-cutting ethnocultural and sociotechnical tensions on the shop floor and less easily molded to fit the higher strategic objectives of the CIO executive.[35]

Julius Emspak, the left-wing leader of the newborn UE, first met Hillman in mid-1936. The CIO vice president quizzed Emspak about UE activities at the GE complex in Schenectady, probing, Emspak remembered, for signs of a strike. Suspecting that Hillman was inquiring on behalf of the GE President, Gerard Swope, as well as for the CIO, Emspak told Hillman nothing much more than that the Schnectady cadre were building toward union recognition. Hillman's mission was approved by Lewis, and in fact Emspak's surmise about its purpose was correct. Hillman had been in touch with Swope for some time; although highly critical of the pre-NRA "Swope Plan," he still considered him a potential friend of industrial unionism—if only from the standpoint of bargaining and production efficiencies—a friend he didn't want to risk alienating through "precipitous" action from the shop floor. Later that same year Elinore Herrick, regional director of the NLRB in the New York area, asked Hillman to approach Lewis on the GE situation, as "Mr. Swope expressed to me the hope that Mr. Lewis would give the union his help and guidance. The scene is all set for successful and harmonious negotiations."[36]

Such "help and guidance" from above was sometimes welcomed and sometimes not, but it was always forthcoming. Two men, variously ambitious, equally firm and determined, and playing for high stakes, gripped the reins of power as tightly as they dared. R. J. Thomas, who would become the president of the UAW in 1938, recalled: "The early Sidney Hillman, I think, was an idealist. The later Sidney Hillman was a very shrewd, able, calculating man . . . interested in power, I think, still interested in the general movement of the workers. His iron hand was in a velvet glove." Thus, through the eyes of Adolph Germer and Leo Krzycki, Hillman monitored the tumultuous life of the UAW. Krzycki, who was sent to Detroit early in 1936, was especially valuable for his extensive contacts among Polish and other Slavic workers. Later in the year, just after the Roosevelt landslide, which excited everyone's emotions and expectations, Germer told John Brophy he was doing his best to mute all the wild talk about a strike against GM by the UAW executive board. Germer pressured the rambunctious board to consult with Lewis, Hillman, and Brophy first. Hillman subsequently spoke to UAW president Homer Martin in Washington and then informed Germer that he was "a little disturbed about the feelings which appear to be prevailing among the officials of that organization at the present time." The group led by Wyndham Mortimer and George Addes bothered Lewis as well, and when they resisted a formal endorsement of Roosevelt, Lewis went so far as to threaten to withdraw the CIO's $100,000 contribution to the auto drive.[37]

The Flint sitdown, which soon followed, was even more disturbing. Perkins pleaded with Hillman and Lewis to intervene, as she was convinced the UAW leadership on the scene was unable to control its people and apt to make unreasonable decisions. When the GM president, Alfred Sloan, apparently indicated, through Myron Taylor, his readiness to negotiate—although only in the struck plants and not for the company as a whole—Hillman thought it was an excellent way out of a situation that every day grew more polarized. Without mentioning its provenance, Hillman conveyed the idea to the rest of the CIO leadership, while Perkins won Roosevelt's support for the compromise. The Hillman–Perkins plan worked until Sloan backed away from what was originally his own idea. Then, in a transparent maneuver to buy time, Perkins advised Sloan at least to meet with Lewis and Hillman as a visible act of good faith, designed to quell rank-and-file anger and a growing suspicion that a sellout was brewing. Sloan agreed but stipulated there would be no negotiations until the occupied plants were vacated. It was a measure of how desperate they were for some evidence of movement that Lewis and Hillman were willing to make themselves available for what was patently no more than a "photo opportunity." Once again, however, Sloan drew back, a final act of pusillanimous equivocation for which he was mercilessly excoriated by Perkins.

Through it all, Perkins remembered, Hillman and Lewis feared the momentum of the sitdown and were "frantic to get the men out of the plant." Hillman was acutely aware, however, that without real negotiations the men were not about to leave even if he and Lewis asked them to. Perkins sensed the same thing, and therefore distrusted the presence of the Communist Party-connected lawyer Lee Pressman in all key negotiating sessions. As for Pressman, he thought Hillman was frightened by the sitdowns and the explosive, disorderly growth of the CIO in its formative period.[38]

Flint was just the sort of predicament Hillman sought to avoid. Nor was it an isolated event. Frank Bowen of the NLRB reported from Detroit that it was common for thirty-five to forty sitdowns to occur at the same time, that more than a half-million were involved in strikes that were often spontaneous, with no union on the scene. Walter Chrysler had already convinced Hillman that a reasonable settlement at GM would be followed by a strike-free one at Chrysler. Waves of unpremediated strikes innocent of any institutional guidance were not going to reassure Chrysler. Meanwhile, close business associates like Kirstein and Filene stayed in touch with Hillman on developments at Flint. (Filene actually attended mass meetings of UAW members in Detroit.) Sympathetic to industrial unionism, but at the same time worried about whether it could be controlled, their impressions mattered. Not only were they personal friends, but in a sense they functioned as advance scouts for a whole sectoral milieu of mass consumption–oriented businessmen, industrial engineers, and social science foundation executives who long before there was a CIO appreciated the potential benefits of "responsible" industrial unionism.[39]

So, even as Hillman and the CIO high command marshaled their industrial armies, they were preoccupied with what others were thinking. The CIO was an irreducibly political undertaking. Hillman's antennae were especially sensitive to every shift in the currents of national politics. Thus, many months before the CIO's first victory on any industrial battlefield, while it was still little more than a blueprint and a bank account, Hillman spent most of his time establishing its political presence, not its *bona fides* as an agency of collective bargaining. Thanks in part to his efforts, in 1936 the Democratic Party came closer than it ever had or ever would to becoming the party of organized labor in America.

THIRTEEN

"All Saw Ghosts"

From late 1935 through the summer of 1937, the CIO's political instincts proved infallible. Everything seemed possible, as industrial
unionism was nourished by and in turn fed the fusing elements of the
"second New Deal," as institutions of the state, Congress, the Democratic Party, and the "new unionism" meshed in frictionless pursuit of
their joint ascendancy. For Hillman the Roosevelt landslide and the
exchanges of mutual affection flowing between the CIO and the White
House were particularly gratifying. They confirmed him in his decision
finally to sever those ties of sentiment and faith still binding him to his
political past. By the end of 1936 he could instead savor the fruits of a
mainstream electoral victory for which the CIO could credibly claim the
credit.

CIO industrial strategy, tactics, and timing were synchronized with
the activities of the NLRB and with Robert La Follette's Senate investigation into the violation of civil liberties. The Board was honeycombed
with radical sympathizers of industrial unionism. David Saposs hired
socialists to man the Economic Research Division, while Nathan Witt of
the Communist Party, a poor Polish-Jewish immigrant who had studied
under Frankfurter, used his position as Board secretary to bring party
comrades on board so that they dominated the Review Division through
a group led by Herbert Fuchs, a party functionary. Witt, together with
Lee Pressman, worked to coordinate CIO activities with those of the
Board so that, for example, during the SWOC drive to organize "little

steel" and in particular its campaign at Inland Steel, the initiating of complaints to the Board was timed to coincide with union organizing efforts.[1]

The staff displayed missionary zeal, tending to idealize the CIO and contrasting its incorruptibility to the AFL's torpid careerism. Following the electoral landslide of 1936 and the ensuing explosive growth of the CIO as a mass movement, the Board operated at full throttle. Exposing labor abuses at many of the country's major corporations, it openly promoted unionization, industrial unionism particularly, by promulgating extremely liberal requirements for proving representation and bargaining rights. By early 1937 AFL chieftains like Green were already attacking the Board for its CIO favoritism. The AFL lost 75 percent of the representation elections in those early days. Moreover, not only did the Board's jurisdictional rulings go against the AFL, but it often found against managements who had rushed to sign up with the federation rather than deal with the CIO. Most galling was the Board's definition of the ideal bargaining unit as the largest practicable one, which was in effect a legal-administrative analog of the CIO's assault on the preeminence of the AFL's craft elite and the prevailing politics of production. This transparent sympathy between the Board and the "new unionism" led Frey to remark bitterly: "There is an impression growing every day that your agents are definitely CIO."[2]

Jealousy and fear motivated men like Frey at least as much as high principle. But his accusation was more than fair. The networks of industrial unionism, scientific management, and Keynesian political reform formed branches of a single genealogical family. It is no accident, for example, that one of the suits that decided the NLRA's constitutionality in 1937 was filed against the Friedman–Harry Marks Clothing Co. Selected by Hillman for its abundance of unfair labor practices, including the transparent firing of union activists, it was systematically pursued as an ideal test case for the Board.[3]

Incestuous relations proliferated up and down the Board's organizational chart. For example, Elinore Herrick, the director of the Board's New York region, collaborated closely with Hillman. Before the 1936 election, during which Herrick took a leave of absence from the NLRB to work for the American Labor Party in New York, she asked Hillman to find a job for Francis Goodell, formerly with the NRA's National Labor Board in New Jersey, working for the UAW, advising the new union on pay rates at General Motors. Goodell, Herrick noted, had a "splendid background of accomplishment in the field of scientific management" and could be vouched for by Harlow Person, who knew his work well. Hillman immediately wrote to Homer Martin, President of the UAW, asking him to hire Goodell. Such were the emerging mechanics of the administrative welfare state at ground level.[4]

To survive, the act and the Board needed to create a political constituency that stretched beyond the ranks of embattled industrial workers. Senator La Follette's civil liberties subcommittee was expressly designed to do just that. Indeed, its investigations and public hearings were, in effect if not by design, part of a broader assault on the redoubts of the "securities bloc" that included Nye's investigations of munitions profiteering, Pecora's peering into the shady dealings of the banking community, and Black's exposé of the public utility manipulators. Together they held the "economic royalists" at bay while La Follette's hearings contributed the concept of "fascist predators" to the superheated political histrionics of 1936. The Committee displayed the same personnel matrix of unionists, Frankfurter lawyers, and New Deal radicals that peopled the administrative grid of the NLRB. The Committee's investigation, which targeted antiunion activity from the outset, was artfully crafted to win public opinion to the side of the CIO. It was planned in February 1936 by Lewis's principal aide, Gardner Jackson, by Lewis himself, and by La Follette and Heber Blankenhorn, who had worked for the first NLRB and earlier as head of the Interchurch World Movement investigation of the 1919 steel strike. Through Gardner Jackson, other Frankfurter and left-wing lawyers came to work for the Committee, including Jerome Frank, Lee Pressman, Edward Prichard (a Frankfurter law clerk who came later, in 1938), and John Abt. The last, the son of that Chicago clothing manufacturer once excoriated by Ellen Gates Starr, maintained close ties to the CP and would later become Hillman's personal legal counsel. Abt functioned as the Committee's chief counsel.[5]

Like the NLRB, the Committee orchestrated its probings to converge with those of the Board and the organizing initiatives of the CIO. Hearings began in the fall of 1936 as election fever crested. They focused on industrial espionage, strikebreaking, the marshaling of private corporate police, and the stockpiling of munitions. During the steel, auto, and mineworker drives all the pieces fell into place. Public hearings in Ohio and Pennsylvania made it possible for SWOC to convene meetings in industrial towns and cities otherwise violently hostile to union organizers. Incidents were carefully selected for public exposure to fuel the campaign's zeal. The hearings into GM's daunting antiunion preparations were timed to coincide with Lewis's December announcement of the CIO's auto campaign. The Committee's staff in Flint reported on company spies and briefed the UAW organizer, Travis, on the doings of the Flint Alliance, a company-sponsored vigilante group designed to intimate the sitdowners. In Harlan County, Kentucky, the Committee helped the UMW fan popular outrage over the gestapo methods used by mineowners and the capitulation of local police. This first phase of the Committee's life culminated with the "Memorial Day massacre" at Republic Steel, where its findings proved beyond doubt the ruthlessness of the Chicago police attack.[6]

With so many potent friends strategically situated, not only in Congress and at the NLRB but throughout the New Deal state, including the Labor Department; the Interior Department under Hillman's onetime Progressive benefactor in Chicago, Harold Ickes; in the multifaceted relief apparatus run by Harry Hopkins; and in the inner sanctum of executive power, where Corcoran, Cohen, Frankfurter, and others could be counted as thoroughly reliable allies, it is hardly surprising that the CIO sought to institutionalize its relationship with the New Deal Democratic Party itself. Yet exactly what the terms of that partnership ought to be was a vexing question. Just as the mood of insurgency and overt class antagonism lent an air of unpredictability to industrial labor relations, so too the efflorescence of populist political protest on both the left and right made it excruciatingly difficult, for New Deal and CIO elites alike, to plot the political future.

Between 1934 and 1936 there were innumerable conferences, conventions, proclamations, and press releases promising, threatening, pleading for one or another variety of third party. In some instances— Upton Sinclair's EPIC movement in California, the La Follette brothers' Progressive Party in Wisconsin, a Farmer–Labor Party in Minnesota, a Political Federation in the Commonwealth of Washington—real or proximate third parties were actually born and thrived. The deep disappointment with the paralysis of the NRA and its termination, together with the depressed economy, falling prices and wages, agrarian disasters, frustrated unionism, and the murky future of such vital pieces of legislation as the Wagner Act fomented discontent. Even someone as sober as George Soule, Hillman's friend and *New Republic* editor, who in the early thirties eschewed the third-party salient, was bitterly disappointed. Convinced that the NRA was becoming an American version of economic fascism, Soule was ready to contemplate a new party dedicated to social planning and welfare. Early in 1935 *The New Republic*'s sister publication, *The Nation*, commented that labor, and in particular Hillman, held the key to the administration's future, and that it was as easy to imagine Roosevelt moving in a reactionary direction as the alternative. Alarmed, David Niles, onetime director of the League for Independent Political Action and a New Deal functionary under Harry Hopkins at FERA, wrote to his mentor, Felix Frankfurter, to urge some decisive action before the readers of *The New Republic* and *The Nation* opted for some independent political alternative.[7]

John Dewey's League for Independent Political Action, whose hopes were submerged by Roosevelt's victory in 1932 and the ensuing 100 Days, was once again actively waving the third-party banner in 1934, encouraged by the success of farmer–labor candidates in Wisconsin and Minnesota and the election of Bronson Cutting to the Senate in New Mexico. After the 1934 midterm elections, third parties held two governorships and ten House and two Senate seats, while the majority of newly elected Democrats spoke boldly about public ownership and income redistribution. A year earlier, anticipating such developments, the Farmer–Labor Political Federation was founded to foster independent farmer–labor parties. But "independence," floating free of the amiable embrace of the administration, made many Progressives nervous. Thus, the emergence of the Progressive Party under Philip La Follette in 1934 constituted a federation achievement, but only a partial one since the Progressive Party was itself not prepared to strike out on its own. Its strategy instead was to promote a national realignment of the Democratic Party. That perspective was shared by the Minnesota Farmer–Labor Party under Governor Floyd Olson. It meant walking a fine line. In 1934, for example, the Minnesota party was daring enough to suggest that "immediate steps must be taken . . . to abolish capitalism." Talk like that was hardly calculated to sweeten relations with the Democratic Party's power brokers.[8]

Talk like that became even more commonplace, however, early in 1935, in response to FDR's passivity, his apparent surrender to right-wing business hysteria, and his dogged faith in some business-led economic recovery that might save his own political future. The Wisconsin Congressman Tom Amlie, Paul Douglas, Alfred Bingham (the editor of *Commonsense*), and others created the Farmer–Labor Progressive Federation as a faction within the Progressive Party to serve as an organizing center for farmer–labor parties committed to a program of "production for use" and the public control of "basic monopolistically controlled industries." The federation staged a conference in Chicago and established the American Commonwealth Political Federation. Its announced purpose was to launch a new national party committed to government ownership of basic industry, aid to the cooperative movement, social welfare legislation, and generous federal loans to hard-pressed agrarians. More specifically, the federation demanded immediate and comprehensive social security; union wages on all public works; bans on the use of police in strikes, on yellow-dog contracts, and on company unions; a steeply graduated wealth tax; and federal ownership of the banking sys-

tem. Its social vision was a bit harder to pin down, as it talked vaguely
of the cooperative commonwealth, a mixed economy, and public control. This was less a sign of fuzzy thinking than a stratagem for courting
the middle classes by skirting the question of private property, emphasizing instead security of income, employment, and retirement; health
care; and protections for the home and family. There was an unmistakable aroma of piety and patriotism exuded by federation pronouncements. Meanwhile, locals of the ACPF were created in California and
Washington; an Illinois Labor Party took shape as a collaborative undertaking by the federation and the SP; and finally Governor Olson and
the Minnesota Farmer–Labor Party officially endorsed the federation's
program, although they drew back at the prospect of an actual presidential nomination.[9]

Third-party formations of middle-class intellectuals like the ACPF
were intensely interested in the political inclinations of the labor
movement—understandably so, as they recognized their own social isolation. By mid-1935, which marked the high point of all the probings
into the politically unknown, the signs were promising. Sixteen separate
third-party resolutions were introduced at that year's AFL convention.
Local labor groups vigorously promoted third-party developments in
Ohio, Michigan, Illinois, New Jersey, Indiana, Massachusetts, and Connecticut. The United Textile Workers and the Newspaper Guild pronounced for a new national party, along with UAW locals in Michigan,
Ohio, and Indiana. ACW locals in Minnesota worked closely with the
Minnesota Farmer–Labor Party. These proliferating signs of political rebelliousness were encouraging to people like Bruce Bliven of *The New
Republic*. Early in 1936 he asked Hillman for his confidential advice on
the question of farmer–labor party prospects: Would they be supported by
organized labor? Would there be support for Congressional candidates?
Was it conceivable that FDR might head a labor party ticket? The
incalculable political promise of the new CIO made the attitudes of
people like Hillman and Lewis a vital consideration.[10]

From late 1935 through the presidential election of the next year,
Hillman craftily concealed his real intentions. That is to say, he found it
expedient to keep alive the hopes of those who desired a clean break with
the Democratic Party while never seriously contemplating such a rupture. Realignment was what he really sought, a perspective he shared
with the whole left wing of the New Deal. The road to state power
seemed straighter and shorter if all energies were concentrated on driving
rival power blocs—the labor and landlords of the South, the old urban
patronage machines, and the corporatist old guard of the business
community—into submission or out of the Democratic Party entirely.

Building a new party from scratch was infinitely more circuitous, arduous, and full of danger, and to Hillman's sensitive political nose carried with it the faint aroma of futility. On the industrial battlefield, Hillman proved as good as his word, ready to "go ahead on our own." But that was so only as long as the new unionism could count on its friends in high places. And that relationship was mutual. There would be no friends in high places, Hillman believed, if the Liberty League, the Supreme Court, and the armies of right-wing populism commanded by Huey Long and Father Coughlin were not vanquished. That was the "great fear" of 1935, a specter that could be exorcised only by convoking the armies of labor and social liberalism in defense of the "second New Deal."[11]

Yet there was no denying that long-dormant sentiments for a new political beginning were reviving everywhere, in and outside of the CIO. To ignore them or, worse, to suppress them would be short-sighted in the extreme. Hillman could not forget his own most immediate constituency, the Amalgamated, where disdain for the "two capitalist parties" and a fealty to some form of socialist or independent politics had forever been part of the sacred creed. It might even be possible to use the threat of third-party rebellion to improve the bargaining leverage of the CIO within the policy-making councils of the Democratic Party. After all, as the election approached party strategists were already worrying about the impact of populist protest on their political right and left. Roosevelt himself feared a sizable opposition that couldn't win but "who are flirting with the idea of a third ticket anyway, with the knowledge that such a third ticket would be beaten but it would defeat us, elect a conservative Republican, and cause a complete swing far to the left before 1940."[12]

Typical of Hillman's approach to this delicate problem was the way he handled relations with the ACPF. At its May convention in 1936, the federation debated whether to run a presidential candidate. The convention was red-baited and boycotted by Dubinsky and the right wing of the SP. Hillman himself avoided attending despite repeated invitations from the Governor of Minnesota, Floyd Olson. But rather than boycott the proceedings, he sent J. B. S. Hardman to represent the ACW. It was Hardman's assignment, which he carried out successfully, to kill the idea of launching a third-party presidential campaign. That might be warranted in the future, in 1940 perhaps, Hardman argued, but not now. The threat from the populist right, from Coughlin, Long, and Townsend, was immediate and urgent. Political experimentation under such circumstances was a form of self-indulgence, a luxury labor and the left could ill afford; better instead to concentrate on key Congressional races, which is what the convention decided to do.[13]

Hardman's powers of persuasion derived from more than just the fact that he spoke for Hillman and the ACW. Only a month before the ACPF convention the CIO made the fateful decision to enter the electoral arena itself. On April 4 Lewis, Hillman, and George L. Berry announced the formation of Labor's Non-Partisan League, whose singular, unambiguous purpose was the reelection of FDR. When Hardman arrived in Chicago, all the conferees knew he spoke as the unofficial voice of the new League and that without the support of the CIO a third-party presidential campaign was all but doomed.

With the creation of the League, the farmer–labor formula, once a volatile mixture of insurgent elements, was rendered chemically inert. People like Amlie, Bingham, and Douglas, not to mention La Follette and the Minnesota farmer–laborites, genuinely credited the "fascist" threat, or at least a willingness on the part of the Liberty League and the Republican Party to use it cynically to undo the New Deal. But the danger was more organic than that. Farmer–laborites recognized they were in a life-and-death competition with Lemke's Union Party for the soul of agrarian radicalism. Indeed, insurgent farmers were not the only ones displaying this political ambivalence. Significant numbers of urban Catholic workers, in the UAW for example, were moved by the corporatist-populist imagery of Father Coughlin. The farmer–labor chemistry could scarcely work if its constituent elements were being depleted of their critical mass, suffering defections from what had once been a formidable populist community of sentiment locked in combat with the "plutocracy of Eastern money and monopoly."[14]

For these reasons, the appearance of the League proved irresistible to many farmer–labor activists who were swept up in its presidential electioneering. Even in Minnesota, where the Farmer–Labor Party dominated state politics and continued to issue vaguely worded calls for the cooperative commonwealth, the party drew closer and closer to the New Deal Democrats. Governor Elmer Benson, who assumed office after the death of Floyd Olson, openly befriended the CIO and the League. By the middle of 1936, Dewey's League for Independent Politics was in the Roosevelt camp as well. While pockets of third-party sentiment remained and even thrived among the auto and electrical workers and within the Newspaper Guild, by and large the trade union sources of the political rebellion evaporated in the presence of the League. Meanwhile, Douglas and Bingham, the leaders of the ACPF, tried negotiating with the League, offering support in return for a pledge to collaborate after the election in creating a permanent farmer–labor party. Lewis and Hillman were hardly tempted, as the federation had little to offer. After the election Bingham and Harry Laidler pressed Lewis, but he evaded the issue. Informed by John Brophy of these new third-party proposals, Hillman made it clear that it was imperative to maintain CIO–League ties to the administration and for that purpose to nip the movement in the bud.[15]

And yet the League was never so single-minded. The insurgent labor movement on which it rested was criss-crossed by multiple desires and resentments, and unaccustomed to the regimen of party discipline. CIO strategists had to worry about radical labor party sympathizers as well as the contrary appeal of Father Coughlin and Huey Long. Moreover, even if all they sought was a recognized position within the Democratic Party, that was not so simply accomplished. The party apparatus was, at first, impervious to the new labor politics; indeed, if that had not been the case there would have been no need for such a strange hybrid as the League to begin with. And so, from the day it was born the League simultaneously depicted itself as a cog in the Roosevelt electoral machine, as a salient into the heart of the Democratic Party that would result in its social realignment, and, despite its quiet quashing of actual labor party forays, as the embryo of an American labor party.

Hillman himself became a study in calculated public equivocation. About his own course he had few doubts. Jacob Potofsky recalled that while at one time Hillman hoped to create an American equivalent of the British Labour Party, he "soon realized that a third party in the U.S. was unreliable." Given that pessimistic conviction, what he sought was a "realignment of all progressives into one party and the basis for that kind of realignment ought to be the organization of labor in the political field," for which purpose the League was created. The objective, he pointed out to the founding gathering of the League, went beyond the passage of specific legislation; the point was to establish labor's permanent place in the national political community and within the infrastructure of the state—those agencies and departments especially responsible for economic planning and social welfare. Certain about what he was after, he could not be so sure about the sentiments of others, first of all those men and women of socialist principle within his own union. For that reason he perfected a sort of verbal gymnastics that seemed to leave open an option he had already concluded privately was foreclosed by the trajectory of American history. Neither entirely disingenuous nor completely sincere, this rhetorical dance, part apologia, part rationalization, alternately defensive and pleading, was a poignant and, in one regrettable instance, shabby personal moment in the odyssey of the revolutionary turned "labor statesman."[16]

Soon after the League was announced, Hillman had to face his own people at a GEB meeting in mid-April. There would be no serious opposition here—the Board was his creature—but it was a confrontation nonetheless with himself, with the history of the Amalgamated, and with the socialist credo. Hillman began by acknowledging the union's previously inviolate prohibition against endorsing either of the two major parties. It is well known "we are for a labor party" and bound by all previous conventions to foster independent political action. But the last two years had changed everything. "We have participated in making the labor policy of this administration," particularly on the question of wages and hours. He reminded the GEB members that the revival of the ACW had once rested on the NRA. Then the *Schecter* decision jeopardized all that had been achieved. It was imperative to retrieve this vital legislative loss. "We know that the defeat of the Roosevelt Administration means no labor legislation for decades to come." Hillman sketched the stark alternatives facing the clothing and all other industries: recovery or disaster. The situation was so dire because labor had abdicated its responsibilities. "The NRA was not repassed because labor was supine. . . . In my judgment up to a few years ago we had no labor movement in this country. . . . I consider that the CIO is the beginning of creating a real labor movement. That I am sure would have been impossible without the NRA." For Hillman, the subordination of the new labor movement to the fate of the New Deal was a fundamental first fact of political life. "But I think now that if we could get another situation like the NRA, even if it were only for two years, that with this group of people in the CIO, we could really get somewhere."

Here then was the possibility of a real historic breakthrough. The question was whether the "activity" would let antiquated shibboleths, fixations from a dead political past, blind them to this main chance. It would be a criminal shame to "wait until the SP comes into power—there is no labor party—let us not fool ourselves about that. And since there is no labor party are we to just sit down and admit that we cannot do anything just because to do something new violates certain notions . . . ?"

Charles Ervin, a confidant, once observed, "Above everything else I should say Hillman hates futility. He also hates mere 'gestures.' " For Hillman, who in 1924 avidly worked to make Robert La Follette, Sr., President, who earlier campaigned for Debs and Hilquit, the talk about independent politics had taken on an air of futility, amounting to a set of ritualized "gestures." Dreams of a labor party would remain no more than dreams without an economic labor movement, and "the defeat of Roosevelt putting in a real Fascist administration, as we will have, is going to make the work of the organizations that are interested in building a labor movement impossible." The steel and auto drives would be lost. The CIO itself would be lost. The AFL once again would envelop the trade union movement in a deathly embrace.

Moreover, Hillman was genuinely exercised by the ethnic as well as the political dimensions of the fascist threat. "Here are the Sentinels, financed by Raskob, supported by Smith. Right in their communications they talk about 'the threat of the Jews.' Sloan was on the list of contributors." While he normally kept his distance from the worlds of Jewish philanthropy and Zionist politics, Hitler's rise to power secularized those concerns and made them of global importance. As early as 1933 he had agreed, along with Gordon Battle, to lead a fundraising drive for the American Jewish Congress to raise $1 million to combat Hitler's anti-Semitic offensive. He appealed to "liberals and the fair-minded that world economic recovery and peace depends upon the defeat of Hitlerism."

If fascism was an urgent mortal danger, why then should the ACW blindly follow the hollowed-out formulas of the socialists Norman Thomas and Louis Waldman, advice as simon pure in principle as it was purely irrelevant? Hillman had tried to get the needle trades leadership together: "All were for Roosevelt, but all saw ghosts, Norman Thomas and this one and that one." Doctrinaire socialists might remain embalmed in the lifeless language and rituals of another epoch, but signs of common sense were appearing elsewhere. The United Front formula, whether as in France with conservatives, or in America where "it must be with the communists," was a practical and potent response to the fascist threat.

But Hillman didn't want his old comrades to misunderstand and to suspect him of trading his heritage for Presidential favor. He was not going to "underwrite Roosevelt." Hillman denied that the League was a creature of the administration. He told the GEB that no one in the administration knew about the League until it was announced. "Only three persons knew," referring to Lewis, Berry, and himself. Indeed, those three deliberately kept the administration in the dark for fear that pressure would be brought to bear by Jim Farley and Dan Tobin (the Teamster President and the head of the Democratic Party's labor committee) to stop it. It was, he argued, the logic of industrial events, not the political machinations of Democratic Party chieftains, that led in this direction. "The more progress the CIO makes the more the logic of the sit-downs drives them into politics." He went further. In creating the League "today we are laying the foundations for a labor party."

Finally, Hillman confessed a personal stake in this peroration. "I wanted to get this off my chest: it has been there a long time. . . . If those who want a labor party will take the opportunity now, when they have a way to the masses of the people and will talk to them, not Marxism, but economic power, I believe that we will have a real chance of getting one." He still found it necessary to reach a commodious ac- commodation with his past, for reasons that were no doubt partly *real- politik* but also because too much of his life had been spent on the social margins ever to feel spiritually at home at the center of power. Indeed, if one considers that Hillman was speaking to a completely sympathetic and comradely group (with one exception) among whom all this self- justification was entirely unnecessary, then it seems an even more poi- gnant soliloquy with his own social conscience, with the "ghosts" of his own past. [17]

.The sole dissent, through which the past found its solitary voice, came from Joseph Schlossberg. For many years the General Secretary had played his part as the union's Jeremiah, reminding the "activity" of its once sacrosanct socialist scruples, invoking its prophetic promise to wage holy war against the capitalist system and its political minions. His whole life had prepared Schlossberg for this last gesture. Born in 1875 in the Pale near Minsk, he bitterly remembered the pogroms of his youth. His father fled, then migrated to America alone in 1883. Joseph followed in 1888. Thrilled by his initial exposure to public school, his hopes soon collapsed as he was apprenticed to his father's trade, ladies' cloakmaking, in a sweatshop of average misery in which he abandoned all his educa- tional dreams and even the petty ambitions of his fellow workers to become "sweaters" in their own right. A boarder introduced him to a terrorist version of socialism, and soon he was caught up in a shirtmaking local led by Jewish anarchists. He and his fellow strikers adopted a practically reverential attitude toward Marx, thinking of him as a mod- ern Moses, a savior and inspirer. Soon he began his long career as a socialist ideologue, for whom socialism was an imperishable ideal, a beacon of social justice in a world overrun with selfishness. [18]

Because of his unwavering fidelity to socialist scripture, and because since the war Schlossberg had become immersed as well in the world of labor Zionism, he and Hillman drifted farther and farther apart. Schloss- berg alone had refused to go along with the endorsement of La Follette in 1924. Hillman made him pay for that disloyalty. He maneuvered to remove Schlossberg from any effective control of the Amalgamated's publications, and as the years passed the General Secretary was system- atically if unofficially excluded from all policy-making deliberations of the inner circle. Exile only stiffened his resolve to maintain his purity of principle. So when the time came to vote on Hillman's resolution en- dorsing FDR, Schlossberg was once again ready to voice his defiance:

Some of us may find ourselves in a difficult position in the present political set up. I am in the least difficult. I am not a member of any party. I do not have to please any group and have only my conscience to guide me. . . . I have been a believer in a Labor party—in a Labor party as distinguished from a Socialist party . . . My devotion to a labor party is no less than it ever was, and it is because of that that I am unable to endorse a candidate from a party that is a capitalist party.[19]

Out of respect and affection, fellow Board members tried to reason with the General Secretary, but to no avail. Hillman's irritation turned to anger when Schlossberg publicly declared his opposition the following month at the union's biennial convention in Cleveland. In words as familiar to the Jewish delegates as the *brucha* before meals or the *kaddish* for the dead, Schlossberg pronounced the Democratic Party to be inherently, genetically, and irretrievably the party of capitalism, one that therefore could not do the bidding of two masters. For Schlossberg this was a simple act of conscience. He was well aware that the audience, excluding some small pockets of skepticism, was entirely captivated by Roosevelt and would enthusiastically support Hillman and the League. He spoke briefly and was wildly applauded, not for his words but for his singular presence as a moral icon, and then ignored as the delegates voted their fealty to the New Deal.[20]

Still, despite the overwhelming enthusiasm for the New Deal exhibited by the delegates, there was enough unease at the abandoning of an honorable tradition to bring out the acid in Hillman. Responding to the labor party resolutions, he contemptuously dismissed them as "a child of idealism; not of Practical Politics." Murray Weinstein, a trusted member of Hillman's circle, reiterated the indictment:

We are practical people. We represent tens of thousands of members. They cannot live on traditions of 30 or 40 years ago. They are looking for wages and conditions. They are looking for the right to bargain collectively. They are looking for a chance to educate their children. . . . If FDR's administration is going to give us what they have given in the past four years, we are for him.

Then Hillman vented his rage at Schlossberg. He attacked the General Secretary for wasting the convention's time. Schlossberg was presumptuous in suggesting only he was an idealist. The ACW as a whole was a great body of collective idealism. For the good of that honorable organization Schlossberg ought to lay aside his ancient obsessions. The General Secretary offered no alternative to meet what Hillman characterized as a racist-capitalist-fascist offensive. "We claim that this is an emergency. We claim that in this emergency the Amalgamated must take a position. Let those who disagree come forward and say whom we shall support. The CP? The SP? Any other party? What party?" Besides, and here Hillman subtly shifted emphasis, tacitly acknowledging the enduring power of "ancient convictions," the LNPL was in reality the beginning of a labor party, even if Schlossberg was too numbed by dead doctrine to notice.[21]

Biting in tone, Hillman's remarks presaged the effective end of Schlossberg's career as an Amalgamated leader and was fair warning to anyone else foolish enough to resist this most vital of all policies. Despite his sympathies and beliefs, Schlossberg was pressured to turn down all invitations to speak at third-party gatherings. Similarly, Leo Krzycki, then chairman of the executive committee of the SP, who felt he couldn't possibly endorse Roosevelt and told Hillman so, was forced to resign as chairman of the SP or else leave the ACW; Hillman assigned to him the painfully humiliating task of shadowing Norman Thomas around the country as a way of intimidating ACW and other potential labor supporters of the SP's presidential candidate.[22]

Of course, Hillman knew that Schlossberg was not alone in doubting the labor party intentions of the new League. The League existed in large measure to channel such rebellious sentiments into the safe harbor of the New Deal democracy. Precisely for that reason it was tactically important to play a double game: In one breath a Roosevelt partisan in struggle against fascism and reaction, in the next, a partisan of the class struggle too wise to be ensnared by the delusions of the two-party system:

> I believe in independent political action for labor. I have always believed in it. I believe in it more today than ever before. But the building of a labor party must be begun by the labor movement, not by those who have taken the book and read chapter so-and-so. . . . Labor knows . . . that the Democratic Party is not an instrumentality that can be depended upon to right the wrong. Labor needs its own party.[23]

That was enough to convince those who needed to believe. J. B. S. Hardman reported in *The Nation* that the 1,200 delegates at the ACW convention were certain that a labor party would issue out of the League and cause "a great shake-up" in 1940. *The Nation*, its past reservations now forgotten, hailed the LNPL as "the coming Labor Party." Hillman fueled such speculative hopes. Addressing the SP old guard in June, he assured them: "There ought to be a Labor Party, no question about it," but there was none, and it was an emergency. The

LNPL could become one, however. Zaritsky, Algernon Lee, and Louis Waldman all agreed.[24]

It was in New York, the ever fecund breeding ground of socialist and independent politics, that this cross-fertilization of realignment and labor party strategies produced an actual institutional offspring. At a meeting at the Hotel Brevoort in Greenwich Village in the late spring, Hillman proposed the formation of an American Labor Party. Present were the sachems of New York needle trade unionism and socialism: Dubinsky, Zaritsky, Cahan, Vladeck, and Antonini. It was an idea Hillman had previously worked out with key presidential advisers, including Eleanor Roosevelt, Adolph Berle, and Fiorello La Guardia. Roosevelt approved the plan despite the opposition of Jim Farley and Ed Flynn (Bronx Democratic Party boss). Indeed, Hillman was partly motivated by a desire to prevent Farley and the Democratic National Committee from dealing exclusively with the AFL–Democratic Party machinery in New York. Farley later frankly admitted, "I was against the formation of the ALP" and blamed La Guardia for selling the idea to the President. That is quite probable. La Guardia and Roosevelt both felt threatened by the traditionally large socialist vote in New York City and the growing support for the Union Party candidacy of Lemke among urban Catholics in the North. FDR feared that Jews and Italians might stay home rather than vote for their nemesis, Tammany Hall, particularly if Herbert Lehman chose not to run again for Governor, which seemed not unlikely. Such a "boycott" was not only a matter of ideology and idealism but, more tangibly, would also be due to the dense network of Jewish fraternal, trade union, charitable, and nationalist organizations, which rendered Tammany's patronage and social service machinery somewhat superfluous. FDR also suspected that the Hall might seek revenge for the President's quiet support of La Guardia's Independent–Republican mayoral race in 1933. The creation of an ALP as an adjunct of the LNPL, under the trusted leadership of Hillman, might be a way to accomplish all these purposes: capturing New York City for the President; winning over the partisans of independent politics; and realigning the state and city Democratic Party machines.[25]

Charles Zimmerman, a pioneer member of the CP and then a converted loyalist of the ILG, retrospectively considered the ALP unnecessary, as most of its constituency was already won heart and soul to the New Deal Democratic Party by 1936. Certainly the collapse of the SP vote in New York (from 122,000 to 38,500) adds weight to that view and suggests that at most the ALP made the transition easier, psychologically and culturally, for a lower-middle-class and working-class milieu whose

aspirations were being attended to by the New Deal. The socialist ideological coloration of the ALP leadership created a misimpression about
the radicalism of the rank and file. Even the ACW Jewish membership
was staunchly Democratic; substantial segments of the Italian rank and
file were contaminated by fascism, despite Antonini's determined opposition; ethnoreligious, territorial, and utterly nonpolitical loyalties further confused the picture, according to Zimmerman, so that the ALP was
always far from being an independent political party.

But the ideological orientation of the ALP's founders, their social
identity within the world of needle trade unionism and socialism, could
not be dismissed easily. On the contrary, it had to be catered to, especially because those meeting with Hillman at the Hotel Brevoort—the
old guard of the SP and their brethren from the needle unions, Workmen's Circle, the *Forward, The New Leader,* and radio station WEVD
(an institutional network on whose resources Hillman counted for the
new party)—were then being accused by Norman Thomas and his SP
"Militants" of betraying the cause of independent politics. It was for that
reason that Hillman deliberately cultivated the notion that the ALP
would someday evolve into a real labor party locally and act as the
catalyst of one nationally. The SP strategist Louis Waldman pressed
Hillman to appoint official Social Democratic Federation representatives
to the LNPL state organizations in Massachusetts, Pennsylvania, Connecticut, New Jersey, Michigan, Ohio, Illinois, and Maryland to make
this labor party talk credible. Even someone like Elinore Herrick could
be wooed in this way. Hillman invited her to become the ALP's campaign manager. On the one hand, Hillman persuaded her that the ALP
could capture 200,000 votes for FDR that would otherwise be dispersed
among minor parties or never be cast at all. On the other hand, when
Herrick questioned him about whether it was to be a permanent party or
merely a tail on the Democratic donkey, Hillman assured her that the
ALP represented a future national labor party.[26]

True, Hillman was more than ready to sacrifice outmoded tradition;
indeed, he considered it essential to do so and had always been so guided
in his pursuit of power. Nonetheless, he and Lewis did anticipate a new
future for labor, one that would supplant its customary political subordination. At the LNPL founding convention Hillman imagined "a great
realignment which will mean liberal forces on one side opposed to the
forces of reaction. . . . I do hope you . . . will see the wisdom . . . of
making LNPL a permanent and effective instrument for labor to fight for
a constructive political program in the years to come." Writing in the
Forward shortly before the election, Hillman justified the break with

independent politics as part of labor's "historic opportunity to play a determining part in the shaping of the nation's destinies. A realignment of political and social forces . . . is now in the making . . . instead of being confined to the part of a pleader for desirable but only remotely realizable dreams," labor could become a major player if only well-meaning people would stop their "theoretic disputations about political pie in the sky."[27]

To be sure, this was some distance from the old labor party dream. But realignment was after all no mean undertaking, unpredictable in its outcome, and not necessarily at odds with the perspective and accomplishments of European social democracy or the British Labour Party. Most important, it coincided with the aspirations and strategic calculations of the Keynesian–New Deal elite which increasingly had the ear of the President.

Hillman claimed the administration knew nothing of the League until its birth in April. It's hard to be sure. Certainly to have notified it beforehand would have incited the opposition of powerful elements in the Democratic Party. The urban and state machines, often intimately associated with the local business community, were bound to be unhappy. For example, the League, led by Amalgamated and ILG cadre, was immediately locked in combat with the Hague machine in New Jersey, which was busy trying to kill a state anti-injunction bill displeasing to business. Jim Farley, party chairman and Roosevelt's chief election strategist, was not only conservative in view, but orthodox in practice when it came to tampering with the power and prerogatives of party machine regulars. Of course, the League was not yet a rival machine, but it might easily become one. Farley, along with Ed Flynn, was deeply disturbed by the formation of the ALP. Then there was the AFL, which also enjoyed some influence in party councils. Dan Tobin told Roosevelt months before the League was founded that all the railroad brotherhoods as well as the AFL hierarchy were opposed to the new unionism and that he feared the political impact of a split. AFL headquarters ordered all federation affiliates to boycott the League.[28]

But the forces of realignment were in the ascendancy. Adolph Berle noted that it was about time labor stopped being a mere lobby and became instead the center around which all Progressives could coalesce. At the same time, even the guardians of party orthodoxy were worried about the universal political disequilibrium, which was making all projections for 1936 a hazardous business at best. Indeed, realignment thinking within the administration was impelled by the rather obvious moribund state of the regular Democratic Party in places like New York and Michigan, where, according to various reports, including those of

Eleanor Roosevelt's confidante Lorena Hickock, workers were deserting en masse, seemingly prepared to support a new political venture. Berle noted that there was a real danger that the Democratic Party might break up into factions; polarized groups of Southerners, followers of Henry Wallace, and patronage hacks. He told his father that it was all coming down to two men: Philip La Follette and La Guardia, who, together "with Sidney Hillman of the Labor crowd, have got to carry the ball." Eleanor Roosevelt told her husband: "More and more my reports indicate that this is a close election and we need very excellent organization."[29]

While Farley and Roosevelt were concerned about rebellion on their left, above all they feared that the populist mobilization on their right might throw the election to the Republicans. The League could serve as antidote for both. The *lingua franca* of the followers of Huey Long and Father Coughlin was not identical to, but did share a core political grammar with, that of the middle-class constituents of the antimonopoly third-party movement as well as segments of both the CIO and the AFL. For that reason Dan Tobin, for example, feared Coughlin's influence among AFL workers. In their purest form, perhaps, the Long and Coughlin movements echoed a dying culture of small-town patriarchal and personalized wealth and property overwhelmed by nationwide industry, national markets, the modern state, and the impersonal bureaucracy of the corporation. But the moral condemnation of concentrated wealth, Wall Street, "the Money Power," and parasitic gain; and the depiction of the enemy as slothful, profligate, cunning, sensual, and sybaritic, yet distant, impersonal, malevolent, and conspiratorial were music to the ears not only of local merchants, bankers, and petty businessmen and storekeepers. It resonated as well among Irish and German Catholic craftsmen, uprooted Appalachian Protestants, and East European immigrant Catholic industrial workers. In the case of those last, both the 1891 *Rerum Novarum* of Pope Leo XIII and the more recent *Quadragesimo Anno* of Pius XI declared it a moral emergency to preserve the traditional institutions of family and local community against the predations of unrestrained industrial and financial capitalism and against the atheism and mammon worship they bred. Many a Polish auto worker, Slavic steel worker, and German carpenter listened intently both to the social Catholicism of Father Coughlin and the social democracy of John L. Lewis. While the leaders of those movements bristled at each other from afar, members of Share the Wealth clubs or the National Union of Social Justice often enough found themselves together with fellow craftsmen in the AFL or with their insurgent brethren in the CIO. Anticommunism, of course, increasingly preoccupied the ranks of the Coughlinites. But the "communism" they really feared displayed a striking resemblance to the centralizing, bureaucratic, and statist orientation of the New Deal itself. What these anticommunists hated far more than the Soviet Union, about which they knew little, was precisely those more recent transformations in American political economy: the advent of mass production and mass distribution and the emergence of an intrusive administrative state regulatory apparatus. It was this equation, at the level of mass politics, between anticommunism and anticapitalism that helps to explain the fraternal relationship between movements that otherwise seemed so at odds.[30]

What the vector of such a political malestrom might turn out to be was not at all clear. It was worrying enough to drive the Catholic allies of the CIO in the liberal wing of the Church into open opposition to Coughlin for fear of the political damage he was doing to the New Deal coalition, including to the League. Once Coughlin and Lemke displayed some real power in the 1936 primaries in Michigan and Massachusetts, Father John Ryan, at the behest of the Democratic National Committee, publicly urged his congregants to vote for Roosevelt. He denounced Coughlin's insinuations that Hillman, Dubinsky, Frankfurter, and Tugwell were tied to the CP. Liberal Catholics like Ryan supported the new labor movement, although with reservations, careful always to respect the sanctity of private property; to censor all signs of class hostility, violence, and radicalism; and to offer instead a quasi-corporatist vision of a state-mandated living wage and a "just price," even at the expense of profits, to protect the integrity of the community. While Ryan worried about the CP, uncontrolled militants, and the political future of the CIO, he recognized in the populism of the right an emergency the CIO and its League were best situated to address.[31]

Neither Ryan nor Farley needed to worry. The League was designed as a vehicle of realignment and for the purpose of containing the winds of rebellion. Lewis's and Hillman's choice of George Berry as League chairman was by itself reassuring. Head of an AFL union, the Printing Pressmen, but friendly to the CIO, and a onetime official of the NRA, Berry was as sagacious as he was safe. He spelled out the prospects for realignment in a memo to Hillman, noting all the fissures in the political topography that seemed promising: Jeffersonian Democrats and Progressive Republicans deserting their parent parties; the split in the SP between the pro-Roosevelt old guard and the Norman Thomas "Militants"; and the Long, Coughlin, and Townsend upheavals. In June he wrote to the President citing as the League's initial great accomplishment "the prevention of a third party farmer-labor candidate." In September Berry sent Steve Early at the White House a progress report emphasizing that the ALP in New York was a tactical device for corralling the independent and socialist constituency. He promised as well that the League would make such FDR critics as Senator Borah and Baltimore's Mayor Jackson pay unless they became more friendly.[32]

The executive board of the League comprised eminently respectable trade unionists, including Hillman, Lewis, Berry, Dubinsky, Rose Schneiderman, Gorman, Clarence Swick of the Painters and Paperhangers, M. S. Warfield of the Sleeping Car Conductors Union, Woodruff Randolph of the Typographers Union, and Elinore Herrick. Key staff personnel were equally reliable and committed to the broader objectives of the "second New Deal." Gardner Jackson, a Frankfurter acolyte, functioned as liaison between the CIO Legislative Committee and the League. He owed first loyalty to Lewis and in part was appointed to balance the influence of Hillman's chief aide, Eli Oliver. Oliver at various times in the past had been an ACW organizer, Research Director of the Railway Clerks Union, and a teacher at Brookwood. He was Hillman's creature at the League, appointed as its first executive vice president at a salary paid by the ACW and responsible on a day-to-day basis for ensuring that the League did not stray from the moderate straight and narrow.[33]

And stray it did not. A League pamphlet, "He Fights for Labor," designed for League and trade union organizers as a kind of source book, painted an embarrassingly roseate view of the President's record on collective bargaining, hours and wages, child labor, relief, housing, and social security. Perceptively it suggested that League literature and speakers emphasize "security" as the encompassing premise and promise of the New Deal. As the tempo of the campaign picked up, the League marshaled all its resources on behalf of the President. It raised more than three-quarters of a million dollars, 80 percent of it from the new CIO unions. Some of that money was spent to cosponsor with the Progressive National Committee supporting FDR (which included La Follette, Norris, La Guardia, and Costigan) nightly radio programs on CBS. Hillman appeared on several. In Ohio the League staged 344 rallies, fielded seventy speakers every day, and sponsored a half-hour radio program in five cities every day for thirty days. In Chicago it organized more than a hundred rallies, and in Pennsylvania its activities were equally intense. Although its proselytizing was directed mainly at working-class voters, the League hoped to reach beyond them. In New York City it established, through the ALP, a "law committee" of luminaries like Arthur Garfield Hayes and Morris Ernst and an "Actors, Artists, and Professionals" group; and it recruited educators like Henrik Van Loon to prepare its pamphlets.[34]

Given its idolatry of the President and its obvious willingness to police the borders for political independents, the League could scarcely come forward as a party in its own right in quest of policy, power, and patronage. On the other hand, its relationship to the Democratic Party and to the state was fundamentally different from that of the AFL. The League and the CIO were by origin and inclination statist in orientation, while the AFL's political engagements were historically aimed at fending off dangerous state incursions into the labor market. Moreover, in its approach to politics, the CIO and its League adopted the standpoint of the working class as a whole—or at least some fair approximation of it—while the AFL self-consciously pursued the political interests of a fragment, one often openly exclusionist, racist, and nativist.

Certainly, the League spoke the language of universal class solidarity. Not since the election of 1896 had the political universe been so polarized by the symbolic arsenal of class enmity. From platform and pulpit, broadcast booth and billboard, a veritable dictionary of injustice and resentment poured forth: "Entrenched greed," "resplendent economic autocracy," "static wealth," "malefactors of great wealth," "forces of selfishness and of lust for power." All through the year political accusations and counteraccusations grew more acerbic and unrestrained. The Wealth Tax Act particularly unleashed a violently hysterical reaction, a combination of calcified social Darwinism and free market maxims informed by a malignant distrust of government. A siege mentality pervaded the roster of organizations and the broad masses of resentful middle classes that found the act repugnant. Finally exasperated with the obtuseness of the business community, Roosevelt and his closest advisers realized that the expulsion or excommunication of "Big Business" was the key to holding together a coalition subject to disintegration from both the left and right. Shortly after the election the Economist frankly characterized the Roosevelt victory as a triumph for the propertyless against the institutions of concentrated wealth. The rhetoric of reform deployed by the League confirmed the Economist's view. In New York State, for example, the League painted a grim picture of bitter conflict between "two encampments"—in one, "the nation's Tories, the reactionaries of all stripes and kinds, the manipulators of other people's money and the exploiters of other people's labor," and in the other, the people who only want to "live and let live, asking for privileges to none and for equal rights for all." The election was "a battle of the masses against the classes, of the people against the economic royalists." Talk like this undoubtedly was warmly received in a state that was practically overrun with strikes in hotels, restaurants, construction sites, and all sorts of service industries, a state in the throes of legislating its own "little New Deal."[35]

As the campaign progressed, it was the "labor theory of value," albeit the one once articulated by Abraham Lincoln, not Karl Marx, that the League invoked. In a radio address Hillman emphasized Roosevelt's solicitude toward labor, his belief in "the right of labor to the whole produce of his labor," and condemned the capture of the Republican candidate, Alf Landon, by "Tory industrialists and financiers." He excoriated the "whole sinister company of reaction and special privilege," holding them responsible for the misery of the Depression. Roosevelt, the ACW concluded, would be a real bulwark against fascism. At one point Jouett Shouse, realizing that these reiterated references to the fascist and racist disposition of Roosevelt's opponents were meant with deadly seriousness, wrote in protest to Hillman. Shouse denied that the American Liberty League maintained any connections to the Sentinels of the Republic (a radical right wing group), decried Hillman's reference at the Cleveland ACW convention to a racist-fascist-capitalist offensive against the New Deal, and piously recorded the Liberty League's official position against anti-Semitism or racism. Hillman replied to Shouse that that was all well and good, but noted that some of the Liberty League's members and biggest donors were involved with the Sentinels, about which the Liberty League said and did nothing.[36]

What was so remarkable about this uncompromising stance, its adamantine tone, its open invocations of the class struggle, and its polarized dramaturgy—all utterly alien to the AFL—was that it was not the embittered outpouring of some despised outcast group but the vocabulary of power. At the zenith of the New Deal's reform zeal, the language of the new labor movement and the language of executive power were practically indistinguishable. The spiritual sympathy that generated this legitimating rhetoric of reform was more than a happy coincidence. What is sometimes credited to a resurgent populism and a new American social democracy received its specific political direction from the policy objectives embodied in the "second New Deal" and its Keynesian elite. The common rhetoric of humanitarian liberalism that resulted was thus the fusion of populist and democratic imagery with the more efficacious organizational and functional language of mass capitalism.

Whatever its exact molecular structure, it was the recombinant rhetoric of victory. Roosevelt swept the country in practically unprecedented numbers. It was an exhilarating time for Hillman, a personal and political triumph. The League, which was as much his creation as anybody's— sitting on every state committee of the LNPL was an ACW representative nominated by Hillman—was widely credited with contributing to the landslide. Locally the results were immediately apparent. League-sponsored candidates ended the reign of rubber and Republicanism in Akron. In Pennsylvania the election of Governor Earle meant the rule of the coal and iron police was over and that steel, mining, and other corporations might finally contribute to the state's revenue. Berry himself was elected Senator from Tennessee. In New York the ALP delivered more than 275,000 votes to the President—only 4.9 percent of the state total, but 11.7 percent of the city vote. Not only did that facilitate the passage of the "Little New Deal" agenda in New York, but from then on Governor Lehman would consult regularly, often through the offices of Lieutenant Governor Charles Poletti, with Hillman and Dubinsky on all important labor and social welfare legislation. The *New York Sun* declared Hillman to be one of the administration's "most important links with urban workers."[37]

His star was rising. Soon after the election he was invited to become a member of the elite Council on Foreign Relations. Not long after that the Foreign Policy Association arranged a meeting between Hillman and a member of the French Chamber of Deputies, who was a principal drafter of Léon Blum's labor legislation, to discuss the political futures of the New Deal and the Popular Front. Frances Perkins thought Hillman had lost his head, that the League's success had made him pompous and self-important, "puffed-up like a peacock," "smirking," "vain," and "disdainful," and that there were loud whispers among his CIO colleagues about his obsession with being a "labor statesman." There is probably an element of truth in Perkins's remarks; similar traits of character—a certain imperious brusqueness—would be whispered about again during the early years of the war when Hillman reached a new apogee of power and influence.[38]

But if it was true, it was also understandable. Doors were opening everywhere, and everything seemed possible. Just days after the election, Berry wrote candidly to the President about the *quid pro quo* anticipated by the League, asking, for example, to be consulted on the appointment of a new Secretary of Labor and on other matters and implying that the CIO was now expecting the President's public support in dealing with GM and Little Steel. Lee Pressman and Hillman conferred on the League's legislative agenda for Pennsylvania and plotted a national conference on labor legislation to promote new laws on collective bargaining, further restrictions on the court's injunctive powers, improved workmen's compensation, civil liberties protections, the banning of private industrial spies and police, outlawing the evictions of unemployed strikers, and a national statute covering hours and wages. Meanwhile, Hillman was meeting regularly with Perkins and with the President to sketch plans for national labor legislation.[39]

Those were heady days indeed. Hillman conveyed some of what he felt to his daughter, Philoine, then a senior in high school. Catching a few moments from his frenetic campaign schedule, he penciled a note aboard the Twentieth Century Limited to describe his state of exhila-rated exhaustion and his skepticism about the labor unity talks Dubinsky and others were promoting with the AFL. Now was not the time to negotiate, he boasted; it could only work to slow down the CIO's forward momentum. Writing a month later, a few days after the great landslide, he confessed that although he had been fairly certain of victory, a shadow of doubt lingered as "so many things worthwhile in life were dependent on the outcome." Now it was back to business. After all, "What's the use of winning an election if its benefits are not felt in the pay envelope?" With Roosevelt's reelection won, "next on the program is CIO—its next course is in the making right now." A month later Philoine learned from her father that he "had a very satisfactory conference with the Chief in the White House about labor legislation," and that he was entirely preoccupied with the GM strike. Clearly, he was proud. For the first time in many years he was also confident about the future. In a word, he felt empowered.[40]

FOURTEEN

∾

Southern Exposure

November's triumph was stunning, portentous, and exhilarating. The year 1937 opened euphorically. Hillman, confident beyond the limits of his customary caution, abandoned his strategy of industrial concentration and urged the armies of industrial unionism into the field everywhere and all at once. For six months the social momentum of the CIO seemed practically irresistible. In a contagion of mass rebellion, waves of strikes and factory occupations rolled across the country, over-turning once and for all the *ancien régime* on the shop floor. Meanwhile the CIO high command plotted a final political assault on the redoubts of reaction in Congress, in the federal judiciary, and in the rotten bor-oughs of the Democratic Party.

Yet by the end of the year a mood of grim defensiveness had settled over the movement. July's Republic Steel "massacre" in Chicago shocked the CIO, less because of its brutal display of corporate and official vio-lence than because of the President's wounding public indifference. It was a bad omen. All the grand plans of the CIO seemed in jeopardy: to organize the Southern textile industry and thereby transform the political economy of the South; to purge the Democratic Party of its agrarian Bourbons and its metropolitan fixers; to mandate a national wages and hours standard; to extend and consolidate the industrial position of the CIO and protect its organizational integrity against attacks by the AFL; to defang the Supreme Court. A precipitous collapse of the economy in the fall accelerated the rate of retreat. By November 1937, crushed by the pressures of recession and reaction, Hillman lay in an oxygen tent in New York battling double pneumonia, hovering near death.

Hillman was emboldened, first by the November presidential land-slide and then by the triumph at Flint. The tempo and timing of the CIO seemed perfectly syncopated with the rhythms of national politics. Thus, SWOC was created and relations with the AFL were severed as electoral fervor crested. The audacity of the auto workers followed naturally from the populist enthusiasms of November's presidential mandate. The bal-ance of power had altered fundamentally, Hillman told his CIO com-rades. Rather than concentrate on one or two key industries, the organization needed a more elastic policy, capable of responding to the insurgencies erupting everywhere. He pointed to the sitdowns in Roch-ester's optical industry and to the restiveness at Kodak as evidence of the need for organizational flexibility. He urged that the Executive Office be granted full authority to certify organizations at all levels and to create on the spot a broad institutional network, leaving jurisdictional and other proprietary matters to be settled later.[1]

Hillman was naturally encouraged by the breadth and buoyancy of the mass movement. The ACW itself benefited, as it expanded rapidly into the laundry and dry-cleaning business and into the manufacture of bathrobes, pajamas, shirts, and overalls. In 1937 it signed its first na-tionwide agreement, which included a 12 percent wage increase in the clothing industry. Growth for the CIO more generally was explosive.[2]

Even more than the robustness of the trade union movement, Hill-man was inspired by the warmth of the administration and its apparent determination to pursue its reform agenda. Just before the new year Hillman met with Roosevelt to discuss the erosion of labor standards since the abolition of the NRA. The president intimated that some federal action was in the works. In April 1937 Hillman conferred with Frances Perkins and Roosevelt on the progress of the textile organizing drive and the need for minimum wage/maximum hour legislation. Even after the Fair Labor Standards Act ran into its first congressional road-block and was tabled in August, Roosevelt reportedly told Tom Cor-coran, "I will never let Hillman down."[3]

Given that sort of White House encouragement, Hillman pressed ahead with the immediate and more long-term legislative and political objectives of the LNPL. Early in the new year he and Lee Pressman discussed arrangements for a conference on national labor legislation to promote state "Wagner acts," a bill to limit further the injunctive power of the courts, and an omnibus bill to protect the civil liberties of strikers against company evictions, the brutalities of private detectives, and the denial of elementary constitutional freedoms. George Berry and Hillman plotted the League's legislative agenda in the areas of housing, relief, wages, and hours, as well as the realignment of the Democratic Party by 1940, perhaps sooner. They were ready to take on the Hague machine in New Jersey, including its allies among the state's AFL officialdom and its friends in Washington, Jim Farley especially.[4]

In rookeries elsewhere in New Deal Washington, plots were hatched to do in the "securities bloc." Hillman's legal associate, Max Lowenthal, reviewed plans with Corcoran and Benjamin Cohen for hearings to expose the strangulating power of "Morgan, Kuhn Loeb, etc.," over the railroads, and envisioned a similar investigation into the insurance industry. Meanwhile, David Stern, publisher of the *New York Post* and another of Hillman's allies, enlisted I. F. Stone to help prepare an editorial "on these power cases to show that the Court's liberalism doesn't exist when they get up against the real economic royalism of the power trust issue." Thomas Watson of IBM, a reform-minded businessman, helped marshal support for the undistributed corporate profits tax, while Federal Reserve Chairman Marriner Eccles argued that taxing corporate surplus (as well as high-bracket individuals) was a way to neutralize the "inherent instability of capitalism." The NLRB and the La Follette Committee felt equally assertive and together stepped up their exposure of corporate abuses, providing the CIO particularly with precious political and bureaucratic support. The bureaucratic infrastructure of the emerging welfare state—agencies responsible for human capital and infrastructural development, for planning and regulating the flow of public and private credit—was seeded with friendly representatives of the newly empowered Keynesian elite: the Labor Department under Perkins and the Interior Department under Harold Ickes; the NLRB; all the agencies of relief and public works; the TVA, the National Resources Planning Board (NRPB), and the REA under Cooke; the various housing and mortgage finance agencies; and of course the Federal Reserve under Eccles.[5]

For a moment anything seemed possible. *Post* publisher David Stern's denunciation of judicial cowardice was a piece of Roosevelt's ill-fated attempt to pack the Supreme Court, a crusade in which Hillman, the CIO, and the LNPL enlisted with relish. In fact, the President apparently confided in Hillman a month before he announced his plans, and Hillman was delighted. Even before this presidential confidence, Hillman had discussed with union and political associates various legislative approaches to the Court problem. He compiled opinions and proposals on ways to circumvent the Court and gathered material to demonstrate the corporate, Wall Street, and railroad affiliations of the Justices. Hillman was especially exercised by the fact that no one paid any attention to the Wagner Act: "High-priced counsel advised their clients to disobey it. They told them it would never get by the Supreme Court."

Once the President declared war on the Court, Hillman campaigned everywhere, venting all the anger he'd accumulated since *Schecter*. On a CBS network broadcast he proclaimed the urgency of the President's proposal, "if the Supreme Court is to be deprived of pretexts of one sort or another to shackle labor." Like David Stern, he accused the Court of sharing the economic and political predilections of Wall Street: "The present Administration has succeeded in breaking the financial and industrial dictatorship. Shall we continue to subject ourselves to a judicial dictatorship?" In the present emergency there was no time to wait for a constitutional amendment to break the Court's "stranglehold over our economic life." The League issued a three-page flyer, "Packing the Court or Petting the Sweatshop," which lambasted the Court's defense of industrial autocracy. It also issued with fair regularity a "Supreme Court Calendar," a running account of the campaign for judicial reform embellished with exhortations to the rank and file to quash the Court "dictatorship."[6]

League and CIO strategists plausibly perceived the 1936 electoral victory as the prelude to a permanent realignment of the Democratic Party and of American politics more generally. Local activists in dozens of industrial towns and cities drew similar and, at times, even more daring conclusions. Across the country the existing Democratic Party machinery led an increasingly shadowy existence. Paralyzed by the convulsions of the Depression and the transformations in political demography, it was weak and growing weaker, vulnerable to invasion and purge. In the spring, in Akron, Kansas City, and Detroit, for example, experimental League slates for municipal office attracted considerable support, as did CIO-backed mayoral candidates in Pittsburgh, Boston, Bridgeport, Buffalo, and, of course, New York. Issues of the League's *Bulletin* noted that in cities like Detroit, New York, and Akron the League was establishing real ground-level ward and precinct organizations with union cadre serving as League organizers and on local papers and radio stations, in preparation for local elections in 1937 and for the congressional campaigns of 1938.[7]

After the presidential election the ALP in New York was reorganized so as to enhance trade union control, reflecting the CIO upsurge. The party clearly wielded the decisive balance of power in the mayoral contest, delivering 21.6 percent of La Guardia's vote, electing as well five state Assemblymen and five members of the City Council. It was a crushing defeat for Tammany Hall, whose efforts to win back the AFL through the Irish-Coughlinite ranks of the International Longshoremen's Association (ILA) failed miserably. In fact the Democrats were in such a debilitated state that Hillman plotted a covert infiltration of the party's nominating machinery until Adolph Berle, by then functioning as part-time brains-truster and liaison between La Guardia and the Roosevelt administration, informed the ACW President that such a coup was not at all what FDR wished. The ALP bragged openly about a national third party in 1940 if the Democrats failed to purge their conservative old guard.[8]

Outside of New York the fall municipal elections proved many of those hopes ill-founded. Until then, however, brave and defiant talk was not hard to find. Lewis, angered when the House Rules Committee blocked the Black–Connery fair labor standards bill from coming to the floor, issued some ominous mutterings about a third party. He coyly refused to prophesy but hinted at accumulating dissatisfaction with both major parties, especially with Democrats who reneged on campaign pledges. Hillman too talked encouragingly of a gathering network of labor parties that would make its impact felt nationally in 1940. At a United Textile Workers convention in September he denied that the LNPL was married to the Democratic Party as such, "for we know that there are still reactionaries walking around active as Democrats." Like Lewis he was coy and provocative: "I don't see a third party at this time," he said, "but of course no one knows what 1940 will bring forth."[9]

Truly no one did know. Richard Nixon adopted a "Southern strategy" in 1968 to enlist the hostilities of a conservative populism against "limousine liberals" in his attempt to overturn the New Deal order. Thirty years earlier, however, the original "Southern strategy" emerged as the brainstorm of Democratic liberalism. It was the approach favored by the left wing of the New Deal for permanently uprooting its enemies within and outside of the Democratic Party. It was grander in conception than anything imagined by the Nixonites, aiming at nothing less than the overturning of the South's prevailing social and political order.

The offensive consisted of three salients. First, the TWOC, created in the spring of 1937 under Hillman's leadership, although mandated to organize nationally, devoted most of its energies to the South, where the textile industry's center of gravity had steadily shifted. The TWOC became more than an attempt to extend modern labor relations into the country's largest industry; it threatened the region's oligarchy at its weakest point, where rural and small-town textile potentates enforced a rough-and-ready patrimonial and pietistic order over the dispossessed multitudes from Southern agriculture. As TWOC chairman, Hillman naturally counted on the administration's assistance as well as on help from the

NLRB and the La Follette Committee, but he banked even more heavily on the second salient of the Southern strategy, the effort by "Keynesian" liberal congressional Democrats to pass fair labor standards legislation aimed principally at the Southern textile industry and at the South's latifundist agribarons. In fact, Hillman spent almost as much time in legislative skirmishes on behalf of the Fair Labor Standards Act (FLSA) as on the industrial battlefields of the South. In turn, the FLSA and the TWOC were to facilitate the third, the most explicitly political, salient of the Southern strategy: the presidential purge of the conservative wing of the Democratic Party, concentrated in the South and Southwest, whose reactionary denizens, allied with congressional Republicans, were managing with growing effectiveness to stalemate New Deal initiatives. Under Hillman's direction, the League devoted itself to the defeat of these Southern Bourbons in the 1938 primaries. Together, the purge, the FLSA, and the TWOC's mass organizing campaign would, it was hoped, recast the Democratic Party, making of it an unequivocal instrument of economic and social reform.

Arguably, this "Southern strategy" also expressed the accumulation logic of the "Keynesian" elite. For example, the Rural Electrification Administration, from Morris Cooke's perspective, was designed to generate not only electricity but the social energy that would sweep otherwise isolated agrarians into the orbit of modern mass consumption. The REA and TVA thus collaborated closely with the Federal Housing Agency and the Electric Home and Farm Authority to provide the credits for domestic lighting, indoor bathrooms, plumbing supplies, refrigeration, hot water, heat, electric cooking and so on. Electricity, deployed by far-sighted social engineers, would flush out the calcified arteries of an antiquated rural order by creating large pools of industrial employment in local capital goods industries; by mechanizing farming operations in and around the barn; by recruiting and training skilled and semiskilled workers from the swelling surplus of agricultural labor; by subsidizing the market for appliance dealers, plumbing suppliers, and others; by standardizing and reducing the costs of refrigerators and other appliances; and by uprooting all the invisible routines of rural life: diet, dress, hygiene practices, tastes and desires. At the same time, unionizing the South's key industry, textiles, together with passage of minimum wage and hour legislation, would transform the closed Southern labor market and help break the political stranglehold of the planter and merchant-manufacturer oligarchy.[10]

America's oldest and by far its largest factory-based industry— employing 1.25 million workers in the cotton goods sector alone, comprising 15 percent of all manufacturing workers and more than either the automobile or steel industries—textiles was the scene of chronic shop floor conflict. But only rarely did that hidden strife erupt to the surface of public life, as in the legendary prewar wobbly-led insurrections at Paterson and Lawrence or in the strikes that swept through the Northeast corridor immediately after the war. Although the industry was well established in the South by the late nineteenth century, for generations no similar outbursts occurred there. After the war the industry was plagued with excess capacity, the loss of export markets thanks to the government's tariff policy, and style changes, all of which generated downward pressure on wages and fostered production economies. Then in the 1920s new machinery and production monitors, like the Veeder–Root counters deployed by the imported Bedaux system of scientific management and the individual motor drives that replaced the older central belt drive system, produced a killing speedup and "stretchout," which permanently soured labor relations. Perpetual acrimony over these new technosocial relations in mill life culminated at the end of the decade in a violent series of strikes in the Carolina Piedmont, in East Tennessee, and in Danville, Virginia. The belated "revolt of the Piedmont," its martial overtones notwithstanding, was a profoundly defensive struggle to prevent a worsening of conditions. While Lawrence and Paterson would endure as mythic moments of labor heroism, on the eve of the Depression the practical accomplishments of organized textile labor, discounting isolated exceptions, as in Pennsylvania's full-fashioned hosiery industry, were meager.[11]

The early years of the New Deal only deepened the sense of demoralization and defeat. In the words of one historian, for textile workers the NRA experience was one of "mind-numbing business-dominated bureaucracy and empty hopes." On paper the textile code halved the North–South wage differential, but the murderous "stretchout," production curtailments, shorter hours, and job reclassifications, which particularly undermined the standards of skilled employees, deprived two-thirds of Southern workers of their ostensible gains.

Even more devastating, of course, was the crushing of the 1934 general strike, which left Southern workers suspicious of the New Deal, government officials, UTW bureaucrats, and unionism in general. The UTW was a shambles, its best cadres gone, thousands of its supporters purged. A local union official in North Carolina wrote to Francis Gorman:

> Our local is gone and it dont seem there is any use to try now as they have lost faith in the union. We have had so many promises and nothing done

I myself am almost ready to give up . . . What is wrong[?] Have the whole works sold out[?] We as a poor hungry people cannot live with[out] something to eat and something to wear and to keep us warm. How do you people in Washington think we can go on living on air and promises[?] What we need is help and if you cannot get that for us then say so and we will not depend on promises any longer . . . it looks like Cannon Mills are running the whole thing. We want to know if they run the whole country it looks like it. . . . Please . . . do something that we may be able to still have faith in our Government.[12]

Despite a surfeit of brave talk, the period between 1934 and 1936 witnessed a series of successful company offensives against all signs of unionism, so that by 1937 the UTW, in both the North and the South, was a largely hollowed-out shell, with a bona fide membership of 37,508 in an industry employing more than a million and a quarter people. Its largest affiliate, the American Federation of Hosiery Workers, numbered just 21,203 members, while among silk, rayon, carpet, yarn, and wool workers as well as dyers, bleachers, printers, and finishers the figures were positively embarrassing. By mid-1936 the organization's impoverishment and vacillation led some executive council members to talk openly about the need to collaborate with the CIO. Always a balkanized union whose federated structure mirrored that of the industry's diverse product lines, the union's authority was vulnerable to the whims and jealousies of its federation chieftains. Emil Rieve of the hosiery workers and George Baldanzi, head of the Dyers Federation, began denouncing Thomas McMahon and Gorman for their inaction. Rieve threatened to secede. While the union's organizational wherewithal withered, President Gorman forlornly depended on passage of the Ellenbogen bill, drafted by the UTW and the Labor Department mandating the thirty-five hour week, which industry lobbyists so emasculated that even Gorman ultimately lost interest. At the eleventh hour the Executive Council, desperate, proposed an organizing campaign concentrated among woollen and worsted workers in the North and among synthetic fiber—mainly rayon—workers in the South. But it was more a collective hallucination than a plan, far beyond the capacities of a bankrupt, apathetic, and internally divided UTW. Beaten down, lacking in imagination, factionalized by meaningless squabbles over title and position, and insensitive in its few Northern redoubts to the peculiarities of Southern working-class culture, the union had become contemptible even in its own eyes.[13]

At that moment of acute crisis the CIO intervened. Intervention hardly describes the peremptory way in which Hillman and his lieutenants simply enfolded the frail remains of the UTW into the TWOC under terms that the textile leadership, as Gorman later acknowledged, was neither materially nor morally able to resist. The first formal overtures occurred in August 1936, when McMahon, a charter member of the CIO, asked the CIO to collaborate in a joint organizing campaign in the South. Discussions continued through the balance of the year among Gorman, Hillman, and John Brophy, and contractual arrangements were confirmed by the following March. The CIO immediately scrapped the UTW's federated structure, creating in its place an umbrella organization, the TWOC, for the whole industry, its officers to be appointed by Lewis. Although technically two—Gorman and Rieve—were to represent the UTW, in fact they would be paid by and responsible to the TWOC. Hillman and the CIO harbored no illusions about the UTW "saddled with factional fights, incompetent organizers who eat up what few dollars reach the UTW treasury, a president who has not the confidence of any of the dominant leaders of the Federation." Despite the pretense of formal collaboration, at no point was there ever any question that the TWOC was solely a creature of the CIO and that Hillman was in charge.[14]

As soon as the ink was dry, in a burst of grandiose optimism, Hillman brashly predicted that the TWOC would immediately enlist 300,000 new members in the South alone. This was an instance of calculated morale-boosting rather than idle bragging, for Hillman knew better than most the forbidding complexity of the crusade upon which he was about to embark.[15]

Even discounting their most recent experience of deceit and defeat, Southern textile workers displayed a tenuous attachment to trade unionism. The mill village, which on average employed fewer than five hundred people, was an isolated and isolating culture, homogeneous, ingrown, insecure, ill-educated, and castelike in its rigid social distinctions. Mill village culture was physically rooted in rural life, kept alive in private and communal gardens and barnyards tucked away behind crude shelters. Into the Depression, textile workers retained diverse ties to their recent agrarian and Appalachian Mountain pasts, often moving seasonally between small town and countryside, carrying with them the legacy of the hinterland, its mores and hardy sense of mutual aid, its kin ties and neighborliness, but also its defensive provincialism. Slavery and the retrograde industrial development of the region bequeathed a sickly craft tradition and ensured that for a long time the South would produce coarse goods with the least skilled labor for the cheapest markets.

For generations millworkers were subject to a pervasive paternal surveillance, both communal and industrial, an admixture of Southern patrician patriotism presided over by millowners whose sense of "stewardship" reached far beyond their own factory walls to encompass the whole region. Villages were often entirely company-owned: houses, company stores, water and power, even church land and buildings where Baptist and Methodist preachers sermonized about work discipline, sobriety, and thrift and sanctified the caste distinctions and taboos of village life. Ostracized from within by village elites—millworkers were "lintheads" disparaged by the rest of the town's social order and left to survive on its margins—and increasingly cut off from the rural worlds of mountain and farm, millworkers were inescapably conscious of their social vulnerability. Women made up 40 percent of a workforce that suffered the lowest hourly earnings of all major industries. The "family wage" system, in which women worked for less than subsistence, aided by their children, reinforced the familial myopia of life on the margins, breeding an insular cautiousness and suspicion of strangers.

After 1920 there was loosening in the totalitarian fabric of mill village society. Company stores and other "amenities" were increasingly abandoned in the face of the industry's chronic depression, as paternalism simply became less cost effective. A semi-underground religious life, surviving in small sects and bursting out in mass revivals, expressed a more populist and less subservient morality expressive of millworker solidarities. A newer generation of workers were psychically more removed from the countryside, and in any event less able, thanks to the steady enclosure of the Southern "commons," to return physically had they wanted to. They had lived through the war and its effusions of democratic rhetoric and were becoming familiar with the paraphernalia of mass culture including the car, the radio, and the daily newspaper. A breed of more modern, scientific-minded management had even made an appearance. Bernard Cone of the Cone Mills and J. Spencer Love of Burlington Mills (soon to become the world's largest textile concern) led the way in technical as well as managerial innovation, in Love's case applying stratagems learned at the Harvard Business School. But even this new breed depended on the destruction of small-scale agriculture to supply tractable help and never deviated from the oligarchy's bedrock antiunionism.[16]

Indeed, all the indigenous inhibitions of millworker culture were fostered and exploited by their fatuous overlords, who viewed trade unionism as inimical to the region's mythic hierarchic and racial harmony. They were, after all, part of an ingrown elite accustomed to their rightful place at the pinnacle of the South's class structure. Mill village industrialists were frequently intertwined, by family or more impersonal connections, with commercial and landed wealth. Often founding capital for the mill had originated in agriculture or trade and then spilled over into local banking and railroads. Kannapolis, North Carolina, which *Fortune* called a "medieval city," was typical. Cannon Mills was not only the largest towel manufacturer in the world but controlled the town's communications, political, and religious institutions. There were many advantages: community subsidies of various kinds, including tax incentives, free land, water, power, and so on. Paternalism in Kannapolis, as elsewhere, had gradually devolved into a cynical conceit, a rhetoric and ideology perpetuated by people like Donald Cone of Avondale Mills in Alabama or the president of Bibb Manufacturing in Georgia, William Anderson, the "Bishop of Georgia," who simultaneously used every conceivable device to undermine trade unionism and thwart the NLRA. Inside the mill, work discipline, once an informal set of patriarchal dispensations, alternating autocratic and ameliorative, became with the onset of the Depression subject to the impersonal, cost-conscious calculations of the personnel manager, an occupational subspecies previously rare in Southern industry.[17]

Outside the factory the mill masters enjoyed enormous ideological and spiritual influence through their ties to local publishers and especially through the vassalage of local Protestant churches, which depended financially on this mercantile-industrial elite. The churches reinforced both the boosterism and the paternalism of mill village culture and helped knit together the network of established families and their deferential inferiors. While it is true that the transformation of the traditional paternalist mill community dissolved many of those sentimental ties, solidarities were just as often corroded by familial, racial, religious, and regional prejudices as well, as xenophobia touched everything not certifiably home-grown. A regionally rooted one-party system, presided over by businessmen and planters operating within the confines of an agrarian social economy suffering from both its isolation and its acute dependency, left the system nearly impervious to change.[18]

In a sense the culturally embedded reticences of the millworkers and the predations of their employers were "appropriate" responses to the deeply distressed Southern economy, in which the textile industry precariously survived between periodic declines and depressions, and where the countryside disgorged an endless stream of dispossessed and desperate agrarians, forming a labor reserve so vast it overwhelmed trade unions wherever they appeared (except in the privileged sanctuaries of the urban crafts). If anything, the New Deal exacerbated the predicament. The AAA acted as a kind of grand enclosure law, favoring large landowners at the expense of tenants and sharecroppers and eventually encouraging the mechanization of plantation agriculture. Off-farm employment was a common enough feature of Southern rural life before the Depression; with the AAA enclosures, however, the ranks of the textile proletariat swelled.[19]

Meanwhile, the anomalous structure of the textile industry, both regionally and nationally, left it financially imperiled and uniquely difficult to organize. In the South, while there was some carpetbag capital present, even it usually originated in contiguous enterprises and was enveloped quickly in the region's business provincialism. In general the industry was closely held and controlled locally by commercial and professional families, sometimes tied to regional bankers, merchants, and railroaders. Mills were often small undertakings in a highly fragmented business, each one accounting for an infinitesimal fraction of the market. The four largest manufacturers, for example, controlled 4.9 percent of the spindles and 12 percent of total assets. Two-thirds of all textiles were produced either in small towns or in rural areas, 60 percent in towns of less than 5,000. There were predictably a great number of companies—about 3,500 in 1938—but very few stockholders; the largest company, American Woollen, whose stock was more widely distributed than most, had only 25,000. The familial nature of the business also accounted for the very small turnover in stockholders; the market for textile securities was restricted and stagnant. The divorce between ownership and management that characterized large sectors of the American economy was not typical of textiles, so the industry was left more impervious to outside pressures. Especially in the South, widening the circle of ownership to include "outsiders" was resented.[20]

By and large, Southern textile managements were influenced by a weblike network of local interests: owners, bankers, selling agents, factors, public utilities, and equipment companies. There was far less of the sort of long distance steering practiced by J. P. Morgan over U. S. Steel. Bankers did indeed exercise leverage as the suppliers of critical short-term credits and on occasion took seats on boards of directors. Nationally important banks—First National Bank of Boston, the National Shawmut Bank (also Boston), National City Bank of New York, and Chase National, as well as Kidder Peabody, Lee Higginson, Brown Brothers Harriman, and Lehman Brothers—were all interested in or invested in textiles, mainly in the North. But in the South financial connections ran mainly to local concerns, and half the cotton mills relied more on factors or commission houses, which assumed credit risks, specialized in sales, and provided working capital. This was also largely true in wool and silk.[21]

Extreme dispersion, small firm size, and capital resource constraints made the production process labor-intensive, lacking in standardized materials, and therefore lacking the advantages of large volume through-put, all of which discouraged major improvements in productivity. A good deal of the textile machinery in New England was old and obsolete, in part because management there was often of the "widow and orphan" type—that is, enterprises were run by conservative estate trustees who were not about to spend family reserves on risky capital improvements. Tariff protection, which the industry enjoyed thanks to its political clout, especially in the Northeast, inhibited export development. The South's predatory low wage–low technology system similarly discouraged real improvements in efficiency and quality, and instead flooded the national market with cheap cotton goods, producing an environment of Darwinian competition with frequent bankruptcies, wage cuts, and general commercial instability.

Instability was further aggravated by the flight of Northern producers to the South, a migration common to light, labor-intensive industry and one abetted by loans, tax abatements and exemptions, bond subsidies for plant and equipment, and guarantees of nonunion labor offered by town elders throughout the South. Out-migration from the North accelerated in the 1920s. Already by 1923 the South accounted for 51 percent of cotton textile manufacturing. North Carolina especially became a haven for New England cotton and Pennsylvania hosiery mills fleeing higher-wage, unionized labor. In Mississippi towns like Natchez, Gulfport, and Picayune, local chambers of commerce built factories, charged no rent or taxes, recruited country women, and segregated black pressers eager for any work—all under the auspices of Governor Hugh Lawson White's "Industrial Plan." Mississippi became a "sweatshop paradise." Its rural isolation, together with a chorus of red-baiting by sheriffs, local businessmen, and the Governor, made organizing practically impossible. By 1938, 70 percent of the cotton textile industry, 280,000 of its 400,000 workers, was located in the South.[22]

This pattern prevailed throughout the staple sector of bulk cotton goods but was not the rule in the specialty firms working in damask, lace, upholstery, hosiery, and silk, which operated in places like Providence, Philadelphia, Paterson, and Lawrence. Those flexibly specialized sectors of the industry, based on multiple products and markets, employed more skilled and versatile workers. There the "stretchout" was an unfeasible managerial tactic, as shop floor relations were too fluid and too contested, subject to numerous skirmishes over job control and rival codes of factory justice. Here the flight to the South was less pronounced. Silk and rayon manufacturing remained based in New England, Pennsylvania, and New Jersey, as did the production of woollens and worsteds, carpets, rugs and hosiery. Hosiery remained singularly prosperous, as the craze for full-fashioned hosiery never abated even into the Depression. It was better paid, easier, and healthier work, and therefore the basis of more robust union strength and stability in both the North and the South, where skilled knitters and loom fixers constituted an industrial elite.[23]

However, the balance of power shifted steadily in favor of the bulk manufacturers, who dominated the main regional and national manufacturers' associations. American Woollen, for example, gradually encroached on the preserves of flexible firms in the medium and high-grade segments of the men's wear trade. By blending their staple base with a specialty capacity, these innovative bulk producers threatened to eliminate the niche occupied by the older flexible firms.

Thus the TWOC confronted a dauntingly complex labyrinth, about which Hillman, his brave words notwithstanding, was well apprised. TWOC faced not so much a discrete set of industrial enemies as it did a whole social ecology. Everything conspired against success: the hostile phalanx of property, pulpit, press, politics, and racial populism; the sad and scarring history of textile worker defeats, North and South; an amorphous industrial structure so fragmented and dispersed it presented no obvious corporate target, like General Motors or USS, whose defeat might bring with it the surrender of the rest of the industry; an industry so chronically plagued by "overproduction," cut-throat competition, and technological obsolescence, so absorbed in its day-to-day struggle to survive, that it could scarcely contemplate the longer-term advantages of collective bargaining. To make matters worse, Southern textiles especially menaced the ACW directly. With the death of the NRA, Hillman's nightmare about what would follow became an ugly reality as garment manufacturers, especially cotton garment producers, freed from any obligation to observe code standards, fled South in search of cheap labor. In part, then, the TWOC was a desperate act of self-defense. Yet despite everything, Hillman was genuinely optimistic. The time was right, and he had a plan.

Hillman's strategy was grand indeed. It was simultaneously industrial and political, alert to the cultural sensibilities of both Northern and Southern workers, sensitive to the structural peculiarities and vulnerabilities of the industry, inviting to dissident elements within the business community, choreographed to elicit the sympathies of liberal opinion, and coordinated with the actions of friendly federal agencies. Hillman brought to bear all his talents at mass organizing, his elite business connections, his political acumen, and his bureaucratic finesse. And his planning was meticulous.

Given the nature of the industry, unlike auto or steel or meatpacking, the campaign would have to be decentralized, but not without tactical focus. TWOC would first of all establish a fortress in the North-east, where textile unionism already enjoyed a real if restricted presence in wool, silk, and synthetic fiber production. Success there was likelier and might inspire the tougher struggle to come in the cotton textile South. In the South, TWOC was to focus initially on the synthetic fiber sector, where firms were larger and production more concentrated. Still, these were points of emphasis rather than concentrated attack. The logistics of the campaign were inescapably affected by the industry's atomistic anatomy. Eventually TWOC sponsored drives in six thousand plants in twenty-nine states. Hillman's penchant for order and system inevitably gave way to the protean realities of the industry.[25]

The CIO made the necessary resources available, and Hillman deployed them carefully. Between 1937 and 1939 the TWOC spent $2 million, second only to the SWOC, of which the ACW contributed $800,000 (and its headquarters) and the UMW about $200,000. From the outset there were six hundred organizers in the field, relatively well paid and remarkably experienced. Many were not only veteran trade unionists but graduates of Brookwood; members of the SP; social workers; labor relations students from Wisconsin, Chicago, and Columbia universities; LNPL activists; La Follette Committee and NLRB functionaries; and earnest young people from the worlds of Christian fellowship and the YMCA. They worked closely with UMW cadre and SWOC organizers, especially in the Appalachian regions of Virginia and Tennessee. They were supplied with exhaustive data on firm size, job classifications, wage and hour scales, marketing connections, profits, gender divisions, production methods, types of machinery, and so on, through an imposing research operation run by Solomon Barkin and assisted by Jett Lauck.[26]

In the North, ACW cadre monopolized nearly all the command posts. In the South, however, Hillman studiously avoided fostering the impression that the TWOC was a radical import of Northern, specifically New York, Jews. Early on Hillman made it clear he would assign no Jewish organizers or men of "foreign extraction" to the South, nor people who might be mistaken for "typical" Yankees. A. Steve Nance, head of the Georgia state federation of labor and of the state's typographers' union, ran the drive in the lower South, assisted by the ACW's Franz Daniel. In the upper South the UTW's John Peel and, later, the 1934 strike veteran Roy Lawrence were in charge. Of the 112 organizers initially assigned to the South, most were Southern-born, many were women, and some were deliberately chosen by Hillman to exploit their ties to the genteel circles of Southern reform.[27]

Two of the best known of these patricians were Lucy Randolph Mason, descendant of two of Virginia's oldest and most honored families, and Katherine Du Pre Lumpkin, offspring of a similarly notable Georgia family. Both women assiduously cultivated the vineyards of Southern liberalism on the TWOC's behalf. Mason, who could boast George Mason, John Marshall, and Robert E. Lee as her ancestors, was onetime General Secretary of the National Consumers League and a lifelong proponent of the social gospel who could address the Southern ministry as a "Christian lady," free of the taint of atheistic communism. She kept Jacob Potofsky apprised about prospects for winning over South Carolina's Governor Olin D. Johnston, the "millboy" attorney, born to tenant farmers, who had defeated the demagogic racial populist Coleman Blease in 1934 and whose sympathy for the New Deal and labor reform was widely rumored. Mason and Lumpkin collaborated with the Southern Conference on Human Welfare. The Conference was the single most significant gathering of Southern liberals. It consisted largely of urban white middle-class professionals, including politicians, businessmen, and even CIO representatives, dedicated to the proposition of regional economic development and social transformation, who recognized the improvement of the South's "human capital" as its prerequisite.[28]

Above all, Hillman tried to conduct a mass organizing campaign while anesthetizing the commercial and cultural anxieties such a campaign naturally provoked among industrial communities that had resisted such incursions, in some cases, for generations. In High Point, North Carolina, the TWOC portrayed itself as the second coming of the Amalgamated, a union noted for its responsibility and sensitivity to the needs of business, one that posed no threat to management prerogatives over production. Any challenge to millowner hegemony would come obliquely, through LNPL infiltration of the Democratic Party, a dim prospect at best in the Carolina Piedmont. Everywhere, the TWOC emphasized the mutual benefits of collective bargaining and labor–management cooperation, its reluctance to strike, and its willingness to discipline overzealous militants. Steve Nance, following Hillman's lead, instructed his Southern organizers that "cooperation with industry to stabilize it was to be the prevailing motif" in the region, that they were to persuade the industry it needed a strong labor movement to deal with its "chiselers." Hillman wrote an article for the conservative business publication *Barron's* on "why textile unionism means profits," arguing its value as a weapon against the industry's ruinous overproduction and competitive self-destruction. Soon after the TWOC drive began, *Business Week* reported that employers in the silk and rayon sectors in New

York, New Jersey, and Pennsylvania were acknowledging that the TWOC could indeed help end the long history of chiseling and were anticipating Hillman's help with problems of production and even merchandising. The National Association of Cotton Manufacturers reportedly "were less concerned when they learned that Hillman was going to lead the drive. . . . They felt further that Hillman would seek to reduce the differential between the North and the South."[29]

As he had throughout his career in the clothing industry, Hillman vigorously cultivated allies and potential allies within the business community. Far and away the most important such friend was Robert Johnson, President of Johnson & Johnson, owner of "captive" textile mills (the Chicopee Mills) furnishing his surgical supply business, located in Massachusetts and Georgia. Johnson actively supported the TWOC and the CIO in general. The TWOC adopted as its own objectives the wages and hours then prevailing at the Chicopee Mills. Johnson brought whatever pressure he could muster to bear on his fellow manufacturers on behalf of TWOC.

Johnson was not alone. Hillman's longtime acquaintance from the worlds of the Taylor Society and mass consumer-oriented business, Henry Kendall, also controlled "captive" mills in the South. Like Johnson, Kendall welcomed TWOC's attempt to rationalize, standardize, and stabilize the chaotic textile trade. Certain Southern textile magnates were close to FDR and so also open to appeals from Hillman: Donald and Hugh Conner of American Cotton Manufacturing (Avondale mills), Robert West of Riverside Cotton Mills, and Bernard Love of Burlington. David J. Mendelsohn of Fairchild Publications made sure Hillman and the ACW were presented in the best possible light in the pages of the *Daily News Record (DNR)*. M. D. Crawford of the *DNR* notified sympathetic manufacturers—Austin T. Levy of Stillwater Worsted Mills in Harrisville, Rhode Island, and Robert West of Riverside and Dan River Cotton Mills in Virginia—of a carefully composed interview with Hillman and pointed out that they knew Hillman well enough to have no doubt "as to his sincerity nor of course as to his ability." Crawford suggested they should treat the interview as Hillman's full view and seek to meet with Hillman, as that way "the entire textile industry can be placed upon a more secure social and economic basis." Harold Whitman of Clarence Whitman & Sons and Gibs Hounsdale of Chase Mills in Wilkes-Barre arranged for Hillman to address other millowners and acted as "missionaries" for a Hillman-proposed "preventative conference" to ward off strikes. Another old friend, Donald M. Nelson of Sears, assured Hillman that if the Hardwick Woolen Mills failed to maintain standards, Sears would refuse to deal with them. In fact, Sears used its formidable commercial leverage to interrogate labor conditions at a number of textile plants.

Most such help from the business world originated as a matter of coolly calculated self-interest, a dawning realization that the commercial and industrial stability of an otherwise anarchic, self-destructive business might be materially enhanced by the presence of a strong "responsible" union. For most manufacturers, however, beset by the pressures of daily survival, pietistic about the inviolable shibboleths of free enterprise, long accustomed to the exercise of unlimited power, righteous about their alleged solicitude for their millworker minions, and as limited in their social intelligence as the mill villages they dominated, the dawn never came. Together they sustained a bitter resistance to the TWOC, and those few deviants among them, however locally powerful and occasionally successful in defending the TWOC, were in the end a weak reed, on which Hillman was by no means foolish enough to rely.[30]

In part, Hillman affirmed and reaffirmed the TWOC's reasonableness and sense of responsibility not only to win adherents within the industry but to reassure its more efficacious friends in the national political community. Hillman genuinely sought a collaboration with enlightened businessmen; he hoped Southern liberalism might discover the courage of its convictions; he counted on the fraternal instincts of Appalachian miners and the commitments of the CIO leadership. But above all, and insofar as he was convinced that the textile conundrum could not be cracked from within by mobilizing the angers and esprit of the millworkers, he turned to Washington.[31]

"Law and Power are on our side," he proclaimed wishfully. Naturally, the NLRB was a willing ally. It did what it could to expose the multifarious forms of illicit antiunionism, especially in the South. The NLRB examiner Charles Whittemore reported that the company "controls their bodies and minds, their living and dying." Fundamentalist preachers, Whittemore noted, organized intensely emotional "religious-drink prayer bands," which went from company house to company house attacking the CIO and prophesying the end of the world when the devil, incarnate now in John L. Lewis, would rise out of the sea, bearing the "mark of the beast," communism. If fundamentalism failed, Whittemore observed, company thugs were available. David Saposs, the Board's chief economist, produced a comprehensive report on "Current Anti-Labor Activity," almost all of it directed at one time or another against the TWOC: propaganda encouraging defiance of the NLRA, injunctions against Board rulings, company unions, spies, strikebreakers, red-baiting, vigilante citizens' committees, back-to-work movements, and the artificial creation of "independent unions" to replace those now illegal and discredited company unions. The La Follette Committee investigators unearthed similar practices, especially the prolific use of spy agencies by textile firms.

The initial phase of the campaign was premised on stimulating sufficient interest among the workers to justify an NLRB election. The TWOC made that easier by not insisting on dues from new enlistees, while the Board liberally interpreted the grounds for holding representation elections. In North Carolina, the Board ordered Cannon Mills to cease interfering with TWOC activities and to reinstate fired union organizers.[32]

Help came from elsewhere within the New Deal bureaucracy and from beyond it. Secretary Perkins made known her willingness to assign a Labor Department conciliator, Charles L. Richardson, to the South. Richardson was a native of the region, sympathetic to the TWOC, who had widespread contacts among public officials and millowners, particularly in Virginia. Governor Earle of Pennsylvania helped resolve a two-week silk strike by insisting that the largest mill owners meet personally with Hillman. Cornelia Pinchot made appearances in the South on the TWOC's behalf, noting that textile organizing was part of a broader programmatic effort to promote a new, mass consumption-based economy. But even more than his friends in high places, it was the second leg of the strategic tripod—the legislative campaign for a national wages and hours bill—on which Hillman counted to help crack the solid South.[33]

⸎

Ever since the *Schecter* decision, in fact, Hillman had plotted and agitated for legislation that would, in effect, reconstitute the best of the NRA. Even before *Schecter* the Depression had sparked renewed interest in minimum wage legislation despite the constitutional obstacles erected by the Supreme Court. The revival of "sweated labor" in textiles, garments, hotels, canneries, shoes, and elsewhere led to a spate of state laws in New York, New Jersey, Connecticut, Ohio, and New Hampshire. However, proponents of such legislation, like Felix Frankfurter and Ben Cohen, despaired at the political and legal prospects for extending its benefits to the national economy and beyond those groups—women and children—traditionally found deserving of such special protection. But after *Schecter*, Frances Perkins told the President she had already drafted, with Hillman's help, a comprehensive labor standards bill.[34]

For the circle of "Keynesian" reformists gathered around Frankfurter, national labor standards legislation ranked high on the political agenda. Perkins's draft legislation was prepared in consultation with Frankfurter, Corcoran, Cohen, and Charles Wyzanski. In turn, Corcoran, who became its chief political manager, recollected that "Ben Cohen and I worked on the bill and the political effort behind it for nearly four years with Senator Black and Sidney Hillman." For Frankfurter, Corcoran, and Cohen, the FLSA was to work in concert with the Public Utilities Holding Company Act and the Securities Act to dismantle the financial and political power of Roosevelt's foes within the party—a continuation by new means of an old war against the Morgan interests and their allied holding companies and railroads, who together dominated the capital resources and commercial infrastructure of the South.[35]

Hillman's collaboration with Robert Johnson exemplified the coming together of Keynesian elite and labor reform objectives. Johnson systematically sought to eliminate the enemies of the New Deal–CIO coalition both in New Jersey (where Johnson & Johnson was headquartered and where he worked closely with the LNPL to unseat the Hague machine) and nationally, where he targeted the whole constellation of urban machines and their business and trade union allies, the Southern land and labor lords. He proudly told Hillman that his group in New Jersey politics was responsible for all the progressive legislation of the last few years. He lobbied tirelessly on behalf of the FLSA and the TWOC and claimed with some justice that he was personally responsible for a general increase in textile wages without any help from Roosevelt or the CIO. As the campaign for the FLSA ran into one roadblock after another, Johnson deluged the country's business and political leadership with communications supporting a high mandatory minimum wage. It would be best, he argued, to establish a high wage as a precedent. Even though Southern textile interests opposed this, "[a]ll the political background for this move has been set up. I have seen to it that everyone in the White House was notified but I am never satisfied with events in Washington until they are 'in the bag.' "

In the spring of 1937 Johnson conferred with James Roosevelt and Corcoran about ways to promote wages and hours legislation, offering to mobilize key figures in the business community: J. M. Patterson of the *Daily News*; the presidents of Strawbridge & Clothier, Kimberly-Clark, and Otis Elevator; leading clothing and textile manufacturers of the North; David Sarnoff; Walter Chrysler; Myron Taylor; Robert Roos of Roos Brothers in San Francisco; and others. Johnson told Corcoran the legislation was "the key to the political and economic situation. . . . These textiles are on the run and don't let them fool the President." By raising standards the bill would force technical improvements, thus achieving a larger objective: "It is the only way we can increase the wealth of the nation," which, he pointed out, was precisely where the corporatist NRA code with its limitations on the use of machinery had failed. He went on to argue the need for "properly organized, well directed unions to represent the industrial and commercial technicians of the present and the future. . . . I am sympathetic with John L. Lewis and a good many of the things that the CIO wants to do." Johnson expressed some cynicism, as business opposition mounted, about what it would take to pass the FLSA. While contemptuous of most of the members of the Business Advisory Council—"Main street boys who like to be under the main tent"—some of whom he considered "pretty bad fellows" who wanted to remain close to New Deal headquarters to "aim their torpedos more accurately," he now thought it might be wise to cut a deal. In return for BAC support for the FLSA, which would counterbalance the attack by the NAM and the USCC, the administration might revise its undistributed profits tax. More broadly, Johnson suggested a triparty "agreement between the farmer, the labor interests, and the business-men" to save the bill. He wrote to Roosevelt recommending a White House meeting of labor, agriculture, and business to promote the FLSA, the farm bill, and the tax adjustment bill as one package. He wanted the President to lock the representatives in a room and demand agreement.[36]

For Johnson, as for Frankfurter, Cohen, Corcoran, Morris Cooke, Harold Ickes, Mordecai Ezickel, and others on the Keynesian left, the New Deal, the FLSA, and the TWOC were ingredients of a complex chemistry whose reactive elements had to be meticulously monitored. Just before the November election, Hillman received a detailed memo-randum from his legislative adviser, Merle Vincent, arguing that instead of the industry-specific remedies of the corporatist NRA, the wisest course would be the promulgation of one blanket law covering all or most industry. Such a national statute would make it easiest for Congress to reassert its authority against the presumptions of the Supreme Court, Vincent maintained. He went on to draft a bill creating both a Federal Economic Commission and a legal strategy justifying congressional reg-ulation of hours and wages. Those drafting the legislation for the admin-istration considered it part of the President's challenge to the Supreme Court, as it would confront the justices with the same essential question raised by the NRA, namely, the government's right, under the com-merce clause of the Constitution, to police the economy.[37]

FDR met with Lewis and Hillman in May to plan the campaign for the Black–Connery wages and hours bill. In June Hillman testified before a joint session of the Senate and House labor committees to urge that the bill empower a Labor Standards Board to establish maximum hours and minimum wages in industries where collective bargaining was still rare and ineffective. Implicitly, at least, he was emulating the British legis-lative model, which expressly identified certain industries as "sweated trades"—in particular shoes, garments, and textiles, and more generally

"the submerged third of our working population." Unlike the British
regulations, however, Hillman and the architects of the FLSA sought a
categorical statement of the principle that the state had the right and
responsibility to guarantee basic labor standards, to establish a universal
egalitarianism of rights and not merely to protect specially defined subsectors of the labor market. In theory at least the new law would disallow
all the regional, racial, and sexual differentials permitted by the NRA.
The Black–Connery bill, Hillman argued, was the key to reconciling
industrial progress with industrial democracy, because it would function
as an antidote to the instability of cyclically competitive, low-wage industries. Senator Tom Walsh and Representative Robert Ramspeck of
Georgia chimed in with confirming commentary. "No more important
labor legislation has ever been introduced into Congress," Hillman
proudly claimed. The FLSA finally made it through the Senate, and
Hillman was elated.[38]

Outside of official circles as well, Hillman did his best to create in the
mind of the political public an intimate connection between the miserable plight of the textile workers and a crusade for national labor legislation. Thomas Stokes authored a series of articles in the *New York
World-Telegram* on sweatshops in the South. The series, which ran
throughout the Scripps-Howard chain, was timed by Hillman and the
publishers to coincide with the initial legislative push for the FLSA.
Stokes described how the destruction of tenant farmers fed an already
obese labor supply. He recorded the hatred of textile workers for the
driving and demanding pressures of the Bedaux system and chronicled
the shameless auctioning off of Southern resources by regional boosters
desperate for the favors of Northern capital. Hillman had the series
compiled into a pamphlet, "Carpetbaggers of Industry," and sent it to
governors and congressmen to elicit support for the FLSA. At the same
time friendly businessmen like Jacob Asher of Fitchburg, Massachusetts,
an employer of two hundred textile workers, were solicited for help.
Asher was recruited to lobby among his state's Republican congressmen.
A power in the state party, Asher could compellingly argue that the
Massachusetts minimum wage law put the state at a disadvantage in
competing with Southern textiles. Asher was not alone. Many other
Northern textile producers endorsed the bill, just as they had promoted
the Blue Eagle's textile code as a way to restrain their Southern rivals.
All over the country ACW functionaries and their friends were similarly
active in applying pressure on congressmen who were themselves sensitive to the textile interests of their districts.[39]

Of course, however comprehensively plotted and judiciously pursued
the campaign was, much fear and loathing were to be expected from

regionally and even nationally based business, mercantile, transport, and utility interests; from party apparatchiks ensconced in all the rotten boroughs of Southern Democracy; from Southern feudalists and non-Southern agribusinesses, and petty producers as well, threatened by the loss of a "captive," underpaid, seasonally exploitable labor pool; from racists and regional patriots, with as many village aristocrats as mill village "lintheads" among them, who sensed how difficult it would become to preserve the South's "peculiar social institutions" in a labor market no longer exclusively controlled by traditional elites and in a political arena invaded by the CIO; and from cultural reactionaries in command of the press and pulpit for whom trade unionism and federal intrusion were a curse practically Biblical in nature, an atheistic collectivism and cosmopolitanism worse even than popery in its insult to the region's religiosity and religious purity, its patriarchalism and romantic individualism.

Still, when Hillman made his audacious pronouncement about the TWOC's future at its inaugural press conference, he at least knew that everything that could conceivably be done from the outside to prepare the ground for its success had been or was being done. In its design and execution, the TWOC revealed Hillman's mastery of the mass movement *qua* political-bureaucratic institution. If an uprising could be stage-managed to conform to the orderly instructions of a single maestro, Hillman was that conductor. Money and an experienced staff were in place. Researchers were dissecting every facet of the industry, probing its vulnerabilities. Publicists already in the field were "enlightening" or "managing" public opinion. Sympathetic and self-interested business-men were extolling Hillman's virtues and the commercial wisdom of collective bargaining. Formidable personages and centers of administrative and congressional power publicly aligned themselves with the TWOC. And finally, even that most imponderable element in this grand equation, those millworkers so long despised, abused, and intimidated, showed signs of rebellious promise, still infected with fear to be sure, but also with a hope excited by the populist fervors of 1936.

A letter to the President written early in 1937 from the Appalachian Cotton Mills in Knoxville described conditions "no less than slavery . . . worse than coercion" that would force "men and women to steal." The correspondent found it inconceivable "that this great big civilization is going to stand for such intolerable conditions." An anonymous mill-worker in South Carolina (anonymous for fear of losing his job) told Secretary Perkins about the deterioration of conditions since the death of the Blue Eagle and looked to the passage of the FLSA for some relief. "J.P.C." from the Danville Knitting Mill Company in Bon Air, Alabama (a subdivision of the big Danville concern in Virginia), expressed a more militant mood. After informing Perkins about the mill's extraordinarily long hours, a shop floor regime "so bad we have no freedom nor rights," and a general manager who was "one of the hardest men on labor I have ever seen," who assumed the position of "Preacher, Doctor, and Boss," and who fired anyone who dared to complain, "J.P.C." noted: "We have been hoping there would be a labor organizer come around and help us out," but until one showed up he hoped Perkins might provide some assistance.[40]

Soon enough, labor organizers did indeed "come around" and were greeted gladly by people like "J.P.C." In fact, the TWOC got off to an auspicious start. In short order it was claiming bargaining rights for 215,000 workers in the North. Right away Hillman managed to organize about nine hundred textile manufacturers into two groups—the United Weavers Institute and the Textile Converters Association—and signed a contract with them in theory covering a quarter of a million workers. Quick, if sometimes bitterly contested, victories were registered at key mills: American Viscose; North American Rayon; Bigelow-Sanford Carpet (the third-largest carpet manufacturer in the world, employing six thousand); Alexander Smith, another large carpet maker; the Celanese Corporation; two key synthetics producers; J. P. Coats & Company, the largest thread mill in the world, employing four thousand; and the International Braiding Company, also the largest in its field. Especially gratifying was the victory at the venerable American Woollen company in Lawrence, the U.S. Steel of that sector of the industry, employing more than 12,000 people in Dover, New Hampshire, and Skowhegan, Maine, as well as Lawrence. The victory at American Woollen, whose president, Moses Pendelton, was rumored to harbor union sympathies, was duplicated at other woollen mills in Lawrence, New York, New Jersey, and Pennsylvania. Elsewhere a silk strike in August resulted in negotiations with the Silk and Rayon Manufacturers Association and agreements with half the industry establishing the union shop, the forty-hour week, and time and a half for overtime. The TWOC won important NLRB elections at Duplan Silk in Pennsylvania, at American Woollen, at Alexander Smith in Yonkers, and at the Merrimack Manufacturing Company in Huntsville, Alabama.[41]

Part of the reason for the triumph at American Woollen particularly, but elsewhere as well, was the TWOC's sensitivity to the religious sensibilities of the largely Catholic workforce. An editorial in *The Textile Worker* appealed to Lawrence workers: "As Catholics you certainly ought to recognize the necessity to work as a body" and not rest till the group's goals were satisfied. In a town where church fathers "tabooed the drive" and refused to let priests speak on the same platform with Hillman, such talk worked like a rhetorical purgative. There were many cities like Lawrence, where the Church hierarchy sensed in the CIO a threat to its moral and institutional preeminence. Reprints of Father Charles Owen Rice's praise for the CIO appeared in textile towns throughout the Northeast. In New Orleans, where 95 percent of the workforce was Catholic, Franz Daniel, a TWOC lieutenant, emphasized winning the sanction of local priests together with Catholic figures of national renown. Jacob Potofsky approached the redoubtable Father Ryan for help.[42]

Elsewhere in the South, textile country was of course Protestant. The TWOC did all it could to tailor its propaganda accordingly, making liberal use of biblical passages exalting the poor and chastising the rich. Such rhetoric resonated with an indigenous evangelical populism, a hidden transcript of resentment and rebellion simmering beneath the surface of mill village life that now surfaced with righteous indignation. A local preacher in North Carolina inveighed against the wealthy with verses from James and told his congregation:

> Do the multi-millionaires of our country have a hard time now? No, they have their palaces, they have their servants, they can write a check for a million dollars. But the day will come, brothers and sisters, the day will come. You run their looms, you run their cards, and you live on a little weekly wage. . . . But what does the Holy Bible teach? Hellfire is waitin' to receive the rich man who gives no thought to his soul but spends his time fillin' his storehouses with earthly goods, and you, you the faithful are storin' up treasures in heaven.[43]

But despite the shrewdness of its appeals and the boon provided by its early victories, the TWOC's momentum soon slowed. Len De Caux, the CIO publicity director, frankly chided members of the New England cadre for the poor state of organization in the region. Joseph Salerno, a local ACW–TWOC leader in Rhode Island, stressed the urgent need for new blood, free of the taint of the UTW. NLRB election victories often proved hollow, especially in the South, as few companies actually sat down to negotiate contracts. By October the TWOC could boast no more than nine contracts in cotton covering five thousand workers, a truly pitiful number.[44]

Southern manufacturers reacted to the TWOC's opening salvos by raising wages 10 percent, a calculated generosity facilitated by the industry's momentary prosperity. More customary paranoia and violence soon followed, however. Lucy Mason reported to Hillman that the TWOC was "regarded by many people who thought they were in sym-

pathy with organized labor as a dangerously radical and subversive movement." Local police, mayors, vigilantes, and the Klan mobilized
accordingly, engaging in an orgy of nativism, racism, anti-Semitism, and
antiradicalism. Mason's first report to Hillman was a grim account of
fierce resistance by Southern politicians, state bureaucrats, and the kept
press, inviting the wholesale violation of civil liberties. The *DNR* reported on Klan night terror raids throughout the mill villages of South
Carolina, spreading demoralization in their wake. Mason would later
document connections between the head of the Klan and independent
employee associations set up to oppose the TWOC at the Columbia
Duck Mills. Nineteen Southern organizers were killed between 1936 and
1939.

Southern provincialism was a resource exploitable by everybody. A
manufacturers' publication prophesied patriotically that Hillman "has
been very successful in dominating the foreign born employees who
operate the clothing factories in the North, but will find it different when
he tackles the Anglo-Saxons who operate the cotton mills of the South."
Evangelists of a more conservative cast of mind than the rabble-rousing
preacher from North Carolina helped pump up this Anglo-Saxon fortitude by sermonizing that the CIO meant "Christ Is Out." George T.
Stephens, a Tennessee evangelist and self-proclaimed moderate who was
considered merely anticommunist, not antilabor, nonetheless announced: "They are having a very bad time to set the revival rolling back
home and the answer is Communism and John L. Lewis. . . . A city
can't be saturated with strikes, etc. and a revival also." As the fall
approached, Franz Daniel breathed a sigh of relief: "Thank goodness the
revival season is over and you can find people at home."[45]

Charles Handy and Roy Nixon, organizers in Tennessee and southern Kentucky, candidly admitted to August Bellanca that they were
wearied by the deep fear, ignorance, and inertia pervading the border
states. By mid-1937 Franz Daniel was writing off Mississippi as a lost
cause. Zilla Hawes expressed her amazement from Wilmington, Delaware, at the deadening fatalism of Southern women, who suffered appalling conditions and paupers' wages but nonetheless displayed a fealty
to antiunion town fathers and church elders. It seemed, sadly, that
whatever stirrings of class solidarity were aroused by the predations of
Southern businessmen were almost as quickly neutralized by the paro-
chialisms and deflected resentments of family, religion, regionalism, and
race.

Solomon Barkin discouragingly reported that workers were "extremely provincial—completely isolated," but at the same time "explosive and unpredictable." Workers, for example those at the Cones' White

Oak Mills, often erupted in strike actions en masse, displaying great moral courage and determination, but then just as suddenly surrendered en masse. The mythic memory of Caesar Cone's vow to shut down forever rather than recognize a union seemed to hover over the proceedings, fostering an attitude prevalent throughout the Piedmont: "Folks can talk all they want to about their right to join a union but right don't count much when money is against you. The government can say it'll make the Cones let everybody that wants join the union but the Cones is still totin' the keys to the mill." When strikes did break out, as in 1934, those most recently evicted from family homesteads enclosed by the AAA, who lived outside the hard-won solidarities of the mill village, were recruitable as scabs.[46]

As the TWOC's forward progress slowed and ground to a halt, people like Franz Daniel concluded that only legislative intervention from Washington could reinvigorate the movement. But much like the TWOC, the FLSA was running into serious trouble. Dorothy Bellanca informed Buck Borah, the Senator's son, then organizing for the TWOC in Roanoke, Virginia, that the Southern campaign was suffering mightily from congressional opposition to the bill. Opposition was formidable from the outset. It included many national business organizations—the NAM, the USCC, the Cotton Textile Institute, the Anthracite Institute—most businessmen in the South; a Catholic Church hierarchy made anxious by federal and state intrusion into the area of child labor, sensing a threat to its control over parochial education and family life; and the AFL, which retained even at this late date much of its traditional hostility to state-mandated minimum wages. Frey and Hutchinson sniped at the bill, exposing it to crippling amendments and exemptions. Representative Martin Sweeney complained to Roosevelt that the split in the labor movement placed the bill in dire jeopardy.[47]

The bill soon fell hostage to the spreading conservative reaction against the New Deal. Roosevelt was compelled to turn to the farm bloc for help and to open the door to the Southern demand for a regional wage differential. When it became clear, by the end of the summer, that the House would fail to move the bill out of the Rules Committee, Hillman denounced both Southern and Northern conservatives. He was in turn assailed by Representative Cox of Georgia for his "moral effrontery" in presuming to speak for the Democratic Party. That turn of events led Hillman and Lewis once again to flirt publicly with the idea of a third party and to raise the temperature of League rhetoric.[48]

❧

Above all, the precipitous and unexpected collapse of the economy in the fall of 1937 was a blow from which the TWOC, the FLSA, the

CIO, and the left wing of the New Deal never recovered. Between August 1937 and June 1938 industrial production fell 30 percent overall and 50 percent in the durable goods sector. Between August and January alone the drop in industrial production equaled that experienced during the first thirteen months following the 1929 collapse. National income declined 13 percent in nine months and payrolls 35 percent. Unemployment rose quickly by 4 million. The speed and depth of the calamity was unprecedented, the steepest economic crash in U.S. history.[49]

The impact in textiles was practically instantaneous. The TWOC simply crumbled like a sandcastle in the rain. Mills closed all over the South; jobs and wages vanished. New organizing became virtually impossible. The devastation spread to the Northeast. American Woollen laid off three-quarters of its workforce. The UTW in New Bedford was forced to accept a 12.5 percent wage cut without the TWOC's permission. Like a prairie fire, cuts like this spread wildly throughout the cotton, woollen, and carpet industries. The recession acted like a purgative, so when the economy brightened a bit in mid-1938, the whole Southern oligarchy of planters, merchants, bankers, publishers, utility magnates, and millowners felt a renewed confidence in their ability to fend off a dispirited labor movement.[50]

Hillman tried to rally his troops too, launching a campaign in June 1938 to consolidate the TWOC in mills where it showed some strength. He met with TWOC representatives in Charlotte and tried to inspire them with grandiose claims about 130,000 members in the South and forty NLRB election victories. But in fact progress was depressingly slow. By early 1939 Barkin could report "no new drives have been recently undertaken." By 1941 there were at best ten live contracts in the South, most of them outside of the cotton sector and accounting for less than 5 percent of the region's spindles, affecting at most 20,000 workers. Drastic cuts in staff and finances accompanied the decline in organizing opportunities. Contracts expired without renewal, and dues became a thing of the past. The situation was not much better throughout New England and Pennsylvania, where the TWOC ruefully consulted on the size of wage cuts. The TWOC, and then its successor, the Textile Workers Union of America, became less and less concerned with rectifying the miseries of textile labor—the "stretchout," heat, exhaustion, foul air, subsistence wages—than with proving itself as a competent and cooperative collaborator with management efficiency experts. Indeed, if anything the TWOC accelerated the speed of modern management into the backwaters of the Southern industry, an irony suffered by the architects of the "new unionism" left now to mourn an entirely one-sided cooper-

The Great Depression was a disaster of unprecedented proportions for the Amalgamated and the whole labor movement. Hillman admitted to feeling "a great deal of despair," but soon focused his hopes on the political arena and the 1932 campaign of Franklin Delano Roosevelt.

The National Industrial Recovery Act was hailed as labor's "Magna Carta." Hillman's presidential appointment to the NRA Board signaled his growing political influence within the New Deal administration.

The NRA was born in controversy and for two years led a politically precarious existence. Despite his own reservations, Hillman did all he could to preserve the "Blue Eagle." Here he is seen leaving the White House in April 1935—a month before the Supreme Court ruled the NRA unconstitutional—after a meeting with the President about how to salvage the recovery act. On his left is Donald Richberg, head of the NIRB, and on his right William Green, AFL President, and John L. Lewis.

With the death of the "Blue Eagle," Hillman knew the labor movement would have to "go ahead on our own." Together with John L. Lewis he created the Committee for Industrial Organization (CIO). A wave of CIO-supported sitdown strikes swept the country during the first half of 1937, like the "lie-in" pictured here at Woolworth's in New York.

Even as the CIO prepared to engage in industrial warfare, Labor's Non-Partisan League was created by Lewis and Hillman in the spring of 1936 to mobilize the labor vote for FDR's reelection. League leaders, including Major George L. Berry of the Printing Pressmen's union, here seated between Lewis and Hillman, were convinced that forging a political alliance with the Roosevelt regime was the prerequisite to the CIO's success on the industrial battlefield.

Roosevelt's electoral landslide in 1936 and the sitdown victories early in 1937 made the CIO a power to be reckoned with. But the defeat of the "little steel" strike arrested the movement's forward momentum. Here, a fallen worker is mercilessly beaten during the strike at Republic Steel in Cleveland, where 18 workers lost their lives.

New York City Mayor Fiorello La Guardia and Eleanor Roosevelt were valued allies of Hillman's as the CIO struggled against the growing anti–New Deal coalition in Congress.

Very different in temperament and style, Hillman and Lewis nonetheless nurtured a mutual respect. But as the Roosevelt administration retreated in the face of conservative reaction, the two men developed deep differences. By 1940 the hostility was palpable, as is evident in this frosty handshake at the CIO convention where the Lewis and Hillman factions attacked each other without restraint.

Hillman's prestige peaked when FDR appointed him to the National Defense Advisory Commission in 1940. A year later, however, his moral authority within the labor movement reached its nadir when, as Associate Director of the Office of Production Management, he acceded in a presidential decision to dispatch the army to check a wildcat UAW strike at the North American Aviation plant in Inglewood, California.

As the war subjected Hillman's labor statesmanship to its most extreme trial, he sought to institutionalize the "liberal-labor" alliance under the auspices of the CIO's Political Action Committee, which he chaired. Here at the 1943 CIO convention, Vice President Henry Wallace and Eleanor Roosevelt are flanked by Hillman to the right and CIO President Philip Murray and R. J. Thomas, President of the UAW, to their left.

The presidential campaign of 1944 made Sidney Hillman a household name in America. Addressing a PAC rally, Hillman declared: "It is within our power to make 1944 a year of decision for the common man." The Republican Party warned that the year might be decisive in a more ominous sense, and erected billboards like this one in Pittsburgh.

While struggling to preserve the New Deal coalition at home, Hillman and the CIO sought to continue the international, united front against fascism into the postwar era through the World Federation of Trade Unions, which Hillman helped create. This meant working closely with the head of the Soviet trade union delegation, V. V. Kuznetsov.

Wartime resentment over defense production profiteering exploded in a wave of strikes as soon as the war ended. Hillman and the PAC sought a political resolution while workers such as the picketers at the Texas Company oil refinery in Port Arthur made clear they expected just treatment in return for sacrifices on the beaches of Guam and Salerno.

As labor unrest crested, Hillman appeared at his last Amalgamated convention in May 1946, speaking extemporaneously to a group of journalists who asked him to sketch the kind of world the American labor movement envisioned. His simple remarks about a world free of want and injustice constituted a last testament: Two months later Hillman was dead.

News of Hillman's death interrupted regular radio broadcasts and commanded eight-column headlines. Thousands came to pay their final respects as his body lay in state at Carnegie Hall, and later as his funeral cortege passed Union Square .

ation, lacking even a scintilla of democratic participation or social melioration.[51]

While the recession paralyzed the TWOC, it emboldened opposition to all elements of the New Deal, including the FLSA. Not only reactionary Southern Democrats but the established leadership of the party in Congress became flag-bearers of counterrevolution. Vice President John N. Garner, along with Senators Pat Harrison, Joseph T. Robinson, and James F. Byrnes, were all associated with the "securities bloc," with Baruch, and with the political economy of the *ancien régime* in the South. They hated everything about the CIO. Byrnes made it his mission to expunge the sitdown from the lexicon of legitimate labor tactics. They feared CIO penetration of the Southern textile industry. They feared that the TWOC and the FLSA, together with the WPA, might severely weaken the grip of the party machinery, deplete the reserves of emiserated labor from which the oligarchs prospered, and undermine the racial order upon which both party and economic elites depended.

As the new "Roosevelt depression" deepened, the FLSA polarized conservatives not only in the South but in the Rocky Mountain West, in rural New England, and across vast stretches of the grain belt, where the exploitation of seasonal migratory labor had long been a way of life. It was enough to bury the bill in 1937, despite the support of the administration and the concerted efforts of the CIO and the LNPL. Robert Johnson hoped the White House might broker a deal among farm, labor, and business interests to save the bill, but he confessed to Marvin McIntyre: "I think that in many respects we may have missed the boat, and just now I cannot see any blue sky." On New Year's Eve the *New York Times* editorialized its opposition to excessive federal intrusion into affairs best left to the states, arguing that a national minimum wage would force drastic industrial adjustments, would generate unemployment and a mammoth federal relief bill, and would be unfair to the South and unwise for the nation. Moreover, the administration retreated from earlier commitments to public works and relief as the recession momentarily resuscitated the reputation of economic orthodoxy.[52]

Recession and reaction had an immediate chilling effect on the CIO's industrial initiatives and strategic planning. At GM, for example, after the euphoria following Flint, management mounted a determined resistance to further encroachments. Then the CIO's defeat in the Little Steel strikes during the summer further encouraged GM in turn to demand that the UAW discipline its shop floor militants, who since Flint had engaged in hundreds of wildcat work stoppages. Just as the earlier upturn in the domestic and international economy had put pressure on companies like GM and USS to settle with the CIO if they were not to lose out on expanding markets, so the "Roosevelt depression," by cutting auto production in half, undermined CIO leverage at GM and elsewhere.[53]

Simultaneously, CIO strategists worried about how to counteract the toxic fear and hostility circulating through the arteries of public opinion. Adolph Berle ruminated about Hillman's attempts to make peace with the Democratic machine in New York: "All that the Labor Party has learned out of this is that they are not very well liked by both old parties. The Republicans hate them on principle; the Democratic machine hates them because they threaten supremacy. The only person who likes them in the Democratic Party is the President." Ever sure of himself, even when all he had to offer was pious advice, Berle thought it best for "Labor people to learn that their inherent strength has to rest with the people and not with political alliance." Shedding political alliances, however, was hardly the prudent thing to do for an industrial union movement that from its inception had depended on powerfully positioned political allies, allies whose reliability under pressure was suddenly in question. If anything, the CIO felt compelled to move in the opposite direction, anxious to prove its loyalty. Already by the end of the year the UAW was backing away from farmer-labor party groupings in Michigan and Illinois.[54]

Gardner Jackson, Jett Lauck, and Lewis discussed a twofold program directed at (1) the nonlabor population—the "middle classes and the farmers"—and (2) CIO members and "other labor," including, Jackson noted, the Newspaper Guild, "who tell me they cannot afford to remain as members of an organization hated by the public at large." Jackson suggested a campaign focused on two of the most damning charges: "irresponsibility" and "violence." Instances of CIO responsible behavior—for example, Philip Murray's exercising "high powers of persuasion to control and prevent general strikes in Ohio and possible slopping over into sympathetic strikes in areas where they would have violated new CIO contracts"—needed to be highlighted as part of a general propaganda demonstration of the CIO's probity and of its contribution to the economic health of local communities through the expanded dissemination of purchasing power. Jackson and Lauck proposed a tactical arsenal: (1) press releases, (2) personal cultivation of key columnists, (3) regular press conferences, (4) assembling of material for friendly legislators, "feeble and shivering as the majority of our friends in Congress are," (5) recruiting sympathetic artists to prepare graphic pamphlets and leaflets embellished with patriotic pieties from the Founding Fathers implying the un-Americanism of corporate "Tories," (6) motion pictures, "the most effective medium of expression known to our society" (Writers, technicians, producers associated with Frontier Films would help portray the "working man's life against the stark cruelty of the greed-run machine." Similar films on sharecroppers' struggles and on the Spanish Civil War had already proved their value.), and (7) radio programs distributed through union channels, the LNPL, and the Federal Council of Churches. Jackson promised to renew his own ministerial contacts from the days of the Sacco and Vanzetti case. Jett Lauck broached the idea of an Economic Security League to organize the professional middle class, ministers, writers, artists, and educators to defend the CIO.

The problem was to convince a broad political public that the CIO was indeed committed to tactical and strategic respectability and to make sure that unauthorized action originating within its own ranks did not subvert that effort at mass political sedation. The fact that Jackson and Lee Pressman cited the danger of general and sympathetic strikes in the steel country of Ohio was no doubt especially alarming. After all, the highly centralized and meticulously planned SWOC campaign afforded far less freedom of action to local militants than was the case in automobiles, for example. Moreover, the SWOC's hierarchical structure and style were far more congruent with the deferential patterns of behavior characteristic of the first-generation Slavic immigrants who populated wide stretches of the industry. Yet even there the social logic of mass mobilization displayed a real resistance to the logic of bureaucratic discipline. For the next few years following the sitdowns, the main task of the new institution, as an institution, would be to domesticate the popular insurgency, to contain its inchoate but anti-authoritarian energies, a task made all the more urgent by the accelerating retreat of the New Deal.[55]

Some of Jackson's proposals were executed, cosmetically improving the image of the CIO, no mean achievement in an age already sensitive to the blandishments of the mass media. But however shrewd, they were hardly antidotes for the recession. About that the CIO high command was no less befogged than the administration. In December Adolph Berle, Tugwell, and Charles Taussig met with Lewis and Pressman about the gloomy state of the economy. The CIO participants were frankly at a loss. They thought a federal housing program of some substantial size might be a way out, but Lewis made clear that he would accept lower than union wage scales only if the government guaranteed a certain level of employment. Berle proposed a conference between Lewis and business statesmen like Owen Young, Thomas Lamont, and Edward Stettinius to find a workable basis for government-run projects in housing, railroads, and construction. Later that month they met, minus Stettinius, at the

Century Club to see if they might reach agreement on a counterrecession policy. All acknowledged the need for immediate relief and agreed that the Federal Reserve ought to reverse its tight credit restrictions. Heavy industry seemed starved for new capital, and everybody thought lowering the capital gains tax might open up capital markets and increase liquidity. Public utility development would undoubtedly stimulate heavy industry, and to do this Young suggested that government competition be eliminated and that when the government did enter the field it ought to buy out existing private interests. The utilities issue provoked argument, but the formula "all public or all private" struck everyone as fair enough. Furthermore, all agreed on the wisdom of a vigorous housing program, or programs, organized by the RFC, spending $2 billion to $3 billion. Lewis repeated his earlier pledge that the CIO could abide lower wages if the new government agency would guarantee 225 to 250 days of work a year. The assembled businessmen apparently accepted the legitimacy of the NLRA and the need for a wages and hours bill.

Surprisingly, Berle observed, Lewis, more than anyone else, "is the man who now wants peace in the country." The leonine Lewis, notorious everywhere for the thunderous Shakespearian periods with which he excoriated reprobate businessmen and denounced the Judases of the labor movement, was in private a much worried man, presiding over a social movement no longer sure of its bearings or confident about its future. Moreover, as Berle perceptively noted later, "the extreme left faction in the CIO want to block any agreement between Lewis, Lamont, and the White House." Most frustrating was the fact that all this maneuvering among Lewis, Thomas Lamont, and the White House came to nothing, symptomatic of the impasse gripping Washington.[56]

Only the AFL took delight in the atmosphere of gloomy indecision enveloping the CIO, scenting a chance for counterattack. William Green telegraphed the NLRB chairman, John Madden: "There is an impression growing every day among the officers and members of the Federation that your agents are definitely CIO." Green was furious that in its jurisdictional rulings the Board apparently went out of its way to prevent managements who feared the CIO from signing on with the AFL; 75 percent of Board elections were won by the CIO. John Frey intimated that the federation might invite the CIO's congressional enemies to join with it in an effort to "remove the tyrannical hand of bureaucracy from the shoulders of organized labor."[57]

Hillman responded promptly, warning Heber Blankenhorn that the CIO would not tolerate amendments to the NLRA and, half-facetiously, that the Committee was equally critical of the Board for its alleged instances of favoritism toward the AFL. Frey soon raised the political stakes by telling New Jersey Representative Mary Norton, floor leader for the FLSA, that the AFL was unsure of its position given its experience with other federal labor agencies. Green testified in Congress against granting the projected wages and hours board the right to raise the minimum wage above whatever was legislatively mandated, wary of granting another administrative agency such discretionary authority over the labor market. For the same reason he wanted the new board squirreled away in the Department of Labor, where the AFL enjoyed an established presence. Hillman, on the contrary, defended the autonomy of the proposed board, arguing that only in that way could it protect the integrity of collective bargaining at higher-wage firms against the wage-gouging of their competitors. Meanwhile, the AFL decried Lewis's veiled hints of third-party intrigue and warned its affiliates to stay away from the LNPL. A. O. Wharton of the machinists was unrestrained in his vitriol, calling the CIO a "gang of sluggers, communists, radicals, and soap box artists, professional bums, expelled members of labor unions, outright scabs and the Jewish organizations with all their red affiliates." A resolution at the AFL's Denver convention dubbed Lewis and Hillman "Caesar and Machiavelli."[58]

While accusations and recriminations fouled the air, more subterranean currents moved events in quite a different direction. As the recession stymied and disoriented the New Deal and the CIO, the administration cast about for ways to shore up its political defenses. Healing the breach in the labor movement became a priority, and Hillman naturally emerged as the figure most likely to accommodate the administration's desires. Elements within the CIO had always been queasy about the break and were perpetually in the mood to talk. Dubinsky and Zaritsky, for example, actually began privately promoting peace negotiations one week after the November landslide. Dan Tobin, head of the Democratic Party's Labor Committee, warned Jim Farley and James Roosevelt that the administration risked alienating the AFL by being too conspicuously friendly toward the CIO. At the same time Representative Martin Sweeney of Ohio told the President that the split in the labor movement was jeopardizing the FLSA and needed to be repaired.[59]

Hillman's old friend Father Haas met with Frances Perkins to examine the feasibility of reconciling the two labor movements. Haas agreed that the time was ripe. He told Perkins that Hillman had intimated as much, noting that the CIO was perforce entering a period of consolidation. Haas and Perkins then proceeded to convene a gathering of notables to include Daniel Willard of the B&O Railroad, Gerard Swope, Henry Harriman, and Edward Stettinius (whom Perkins preferred because earlier he had helped open negotiations between Myron Taylor and Lewis and was on good terms with Lewis and Hillman from NRA days), along with such recognized spokesmen for the putative public interest as William Leiserson, Harry Millis, and Elmer Andrews. At the end of October peace negotiations began in earnest—and then ended abruptly.[60]

Hillman's sound mind inhabited an unsound body. Time and time again over the previous two decades he had broken down physically at moments of acute stress. His psychic and intellectual resilience was remarkable; his stomach, ankles, heart, lungs, and other limbs and organs took the punishment instead. In the fall of 1937 the pressures were punishing indeed. The recession deepened and sapped the administration's political fortitude. Under siege, the TWOC lost ground everywhere. The FLSA was hostage to the conservatives in Congress. Kindred spirits atop the AFL and the old urban patronage machines spied a chance to regain ground recently lost to the CIO, unsavory immigrants, and maverick intellectuals from New York and Georgetown. Signs of dissidence and faint-heartedness were now noticeable even within the CIO.

In those circumstances "labor unity" contained a sour irony; it was no longer the rallying cry of an embattled mass movement, but on the contrary the plaint of a frightened bureaucracy. Peace talks were the misbegotten offspring of recession, retreat, and reaction. It was an ersatz sort of "unity" sponsored from on high by those for whom a revolution in the politics of production in American industry was scarcely the driving motivation. Perhaps this stage-managed "labor unity" might serve as an antidote for a sickened body politic—or so Hillman may have imagined. Still, it was a bitter pill to swallow. But before this form of "labor unity" had any chance to display its curative powers, Hillman himself fell victim to the pathology that produced it.

On the night of the first negotiating session, Hillman became ill. He was confined to his home with a "grippe," which seemed to get better but then suddenly worsened into bronchial double pneumonia. Dr. Alexander Miller, a lung specialist, examined Hillman as he hovered near death in an oxygen tent with a temperature approaching 106 degrees. Dr. Miller treated his patient with newly discovered sulfa drugs and insisted that he must once and for all give up his heavy smoking. The doctor ordered Hillman to undergo a prolonged convalescence in Florida. While the TWOC languished in the fields and the FLSA festered in Congress, Hillman lay immobilized at the Strath Haven Hospital in Miami Beach.[61]

FIFTEEN

The Fall to Power

"Time is heavy on me," Hillman complained to his daughter Philoine from his enforced idleness in Miami Beach, "but when I read about the constant snowstorms and zero weather up North, I come to the conclusion that it is wiser to follow a sensible course and stay here a little longer." More candidly he confessed to Bessie his growing anxiety about being away from the center of action, his apprehension when Lewis failed to report on the progress of the unity talks, and his subsequent depression when he learned that the negotiations had fallen apart almost as soon as he took sick. Dorothy Bellanca and others wrote to plead with him not to worry and rush back prematurely. A stream of visitors—Isidore Lubin, Leon Henderson, Wagner, Farley, Dubinsky, Lewis, Anna Rosenberg—kept him sedated with the latest intelligence from all fronts. He needed more, however, to feed his insatiable hunger to be busy. At the Strath Haven only a month, still bedridden, Hillman began mobilizing the Amalgamated for a concerted fight against congressional reactionaries. Joseph Schlossberg was commissioned to muster all the Joint Boards and locals for multiple campaigns to excavate the FLSA from the House Committee on Labor, to kill AFL and other crippling amendments to the NLRA, and to quash the raft of bills threatening hostile investigations of the NLRB. Equally worried about the collapse of the unity negotiations, Hillman misled Tom Corcoran into believing that he was about to come north to revive the stalled talks. Actually it was only by early February that he was well enough to be moved from the Strath Haven to the Miami Battle Creek Sanatorium in Miami Springs,

407

where he spent nearly two more months recuperating. But by the end of March the *New York Times* was reporting that Hillman was back in action, conferring with his colleagues in the LNPL and his allies in Congress on the fate of the FLSA.[1]

The prolonged rest had done him more than good; it had rejuvenated him. Joseph Gollomb interviewed Hillman for the *Atlantic* in the Florida sanatorium near the end of his convalescence. Gollomb was struck by the CIO leader's health and mental vigor, "an engineer in labor dynamics" who laughed easily and spoke in a richly modulated voice capable of

> . . . power and passion that make him another man when he is crusading. Then his body becomes compact with everything in him mobilized and in action. His pleasantly molded chin and jaw take on a bulldog thrust and aggression. His voice rasps and rings, his consonants are hard and sharp. He uses few gestures with the result that what he says acquires an impact almost muscular.

Illness had done nothing to dim the essential pertinacity of his character.[2]

Muscularity, however, could not hold off the counteroffensive that assaulted all the outposts of reform in the halls of Congress, in the agencies of administrative justice, and even within the insurgent ranks of the CIO. Hillman had to tack and veer accordingly in a period that became less and less susceptible to the force of his "power and passion." His friends among the Keynesian elite became ever more timid, shedding their earlier intentions to perform structural surgery on the economy. Federalizing labor standards became a matter of suturing up the thousand cuts inflicted on the FLSA, preserving at least the principle if not the practice of universal protection for the working poor. The NLRB, besieged, persecuted, and purged, required round-the-clock surveillance to defend it against an unnerving axis of AFL bureaucrats, chamber of commerce attorneys, and bilious legislators who sought to amputate the Board's powers through a series of devastating amendments. Echoes of the persecution reverberated as well inside the CIO. The TWOC took on a spectral appearance, an apparition Hillman sought to perpetuate in the teeth of vituperative resistance. Hillman, Lewis, and Murray contended with outlaw insurgencies on the shop floor and with radicals frustrated by the deceleration of the New Deal, as well as with the suspicions of pious Catholic and anticommunist rank-and-file members alarmed by the CIO's egalitarian secularism. There were also increasingly successful raids by a revivified AFL. Tensions already detectable before Hillman's illness now bubbled to the surface as the pressures became intense to conform to the calcification of the New Deal. Perforce, Hillman became a statesman of retreat.

The left wing of the New Deal was still capable of rhetorical fireworks. Ickes, Eccles, and Assistant Attorney General Robert Jackson decried the "60 families" and the "chiseling 10 percent" for their avaricious indifference to the commonwealth, while accusing "big business fascism" of perpetrating a conspiratorial "capital strike" against the administration's recovery program. But that recovery program was itself fast becoming little more than rhetoric; at least there was precious little surviving of the Keynesian social democracy to which Hillman had dedicated himself since the earliest years of the Depression.[3]

Collaborators in the business community grew increasingly cynical or faint-hearted. After congressional conservatives managed to bury the FLSA, Robert Johnson suggested cutting a deal by dumping the undistributed profits tax. Time was running out. "Business is collapsing—look at the general business index in the Sunday *New York Times*," Johnson said. He told Corcoran that retail sales best predicted the future, and "the consumers of the country are frightened." As the index continued to drop, he grew more despondent. By the spring of 1938 he was lamenting: "I have a feeling that it is now too late for ever a realistic, modern social program to be put forward." An edginess, tinged with mutual suspicion, infected Hillman's relations with Johnson. The corporation president testily took offense at Hillman's implication that he had shirked his duty. In turn he blamed the LNPL for the failure to elect Lester Clee to the governorship of New Jersey. Hillman lost no time patching things up, but the souring of relations even to that extent was an ominous sign that a coalition was cracking up from within.[4]

Johnson's pessimism was echoed by other Keynesian-minded associates of Hillman. Bernard Gimbel, for example, supported the pump-priming efforts of the New Deal and was in touch with people close to the President. But he was surrounded by "a host of ultra-conservative friends" and, as the reaction set in, became increasingly circumspect about making his views known. Albert Greenfield, who had materially contributed to the Amalgamated's 1929 victory in Philadelphia, hoped that "the gains made by the country under the Roosevelt Administration" would continue but feared that war in Europe "might distract us from that steady improvement."[5]

Others in the business community—Filene, Morris Leeds, Henry Dennison, and Ralph Flanders—issued a report in 1938, prepared with the academic assistance of John Kenneth Galbraith, entitled "Toward Full Employment." While it defended the economic efficacy of deficit spending as well as progressive taxation keyed to the oscillations of the business cycle, the report largely abandoned the forward outposts of what might be called "social Keynesianism"—an executive planning mechanism endowed with the authority to trespass the boundaries of industrial property in order to direct the flows of the nation's capital resources. Endorsed by Marriner Eccles, Henry A. Wallace, and Jerome Frank, as well as Beardsley Ruml and Charles Merriam of the NRPB, "Toward Full Employment" was a promise of painless prosperity through a commercialized Keynesianism still insistent on allowing the government to monitor and minister to the economy, but from afar and through mechanisms of fiscal and monetary policy less capable of mounting surgical strikes against offending industrial and financial targets.[6]

More daring undertakings were afoot. Mordecai Eziekel invited Hillman to an informal meeting with Henry Wallace's assistant, Paul Appelby, and some Keynesian-minded businessmen for an off-the-record discussion of economic policy and planning for agriculture and business. But Eziekel's Industrial Expansion bill languished at the shrinking sidelines of social democratic reform. Indeed, Eli Oliver, Hillman's chief lieutenant in the LNPL, told John Brophy that Representative Amlie's call for a "committee to promote the Industrial Expansion bill" was the purest utopianism and not worthy of support.[7]

Pump-priming became the fallback position for the chastened circles of "left-wing" New Dealers. Eccles for one was gradually persuaded that there were no new industries visible on the horizon massive enough to soak up the stagnant pools of idled capital, leaving public investment in housing, urban renewal, rural electrification, schools, and hospitals, along with a more egalitarian tax system, as the only road to recovery.

While Eccles's spending program placed its greatest emphasis on a housing program to help revive the capital goods sector, no such construction was undertaken in any substantial way. Treasury Secretary Henry Morgenthau blamed the monopoly in the cement industry for killing the housing industry. His rhetoric complemented Robert Jackson's acerbic attack on monopoly and administered prices but otherwise left the situation unchanged. This was particularly bitter for the CIO to digest, as it had lobbied on behalf of mass subsidized housing as a lever for raising the rest of the economy as well as for its obvious appeal to their own often ill-housed following. The CIO's Committee on Housing cited the impact of the Depression on fabricating industries like steel, glass, and lumber, arguing that a substantial public investment in low-cost housing was the antidote.[8]

So too in taxes, administration policy quickly retreated from any attempt to redistribute income and idled capital and savings. Instead of real measures to broaden the tax base to include business and the more prosperous middle classes, the administration increasingly resorted to populist pyrotechnics, declaiming against plutocrats and tax-dodgers, mobilizing in its own way a politics of resentment analogous to the social emotions exciting its right-wing opponents. The income tax remained a kind of moral nightstick rather than an economic tool.[9]

Hillman adjusted readily enough to the new politics of moderation and compromise. He marshaled the troops from the Amalgamated and the League to resume the fight for the FLSA. He and Perkins carefully orchestrated spring hearings on the disgraceful wage policy of the cotton textile industry, hoping to stoke up sentiment for the bill. The ACW sent its top cadres to Washington, and Hillman himself spent a week there. At the same time the ALP worked hard to counteract the determined opposition of Democratic Representative John O'Connor from New York. But Hillman knew now that the bill would never deliver the comprehensive protection he once dreamed of.

The prognosis for the FLSA improved with the Florida primary victory of Claude Pepper, who had openly campaigned on its behalf. But even while public opinion seemed to warm, the legislation was being defanged in the back alleys of private deal-making. John Frey of the AFL and Harriman of Brown Brothers, an odd couple, carried on a correspondence about the inflationary dangers of minimum-maximum labor standards that resulted in the AFL's own bill in opposition to the administration's proposal to establish labor–management boards in sweated industries empowered to adjust standards beyond those mandated by statute. As the administration's bill made its tortuous way through the House, amendment after amendment narrowed its coverage, weakened its administrative authority, limited its investigative powers, and lowered its standards.[10]

An impressive armada of industries escaped coverage entirely—retailing, agriculture, dairying, food processing, fishing, seafaring, personal services, and nearly all transportation workers, including rail, airline, and trucking. In the end only 11 million workers, or one-fifth of the labor force, was protected, and of those a mere 300,000 stood to benefit from the act's initial 25-cent minimum (which was to rise to at least 40 cents in six years). Women and black workers, because they labored disproportionately within the borders of the exempt industries, were left largely defenseless, belying the bill's universalist pretensions. Only 14 percent of women workers, as against 39 percent of men, were covered. Southern landlords and Midwestern and West Coast agribusinesses escaped unscathed in return for the help provided by the congressional farm bloc. Some did indeed benefit—those 1.4 million laboring more than forty-four hours a week (after a few years the maximum hour limit would decline to forty) and those 200,000 or so children whom the bill now excluded from the labor market. The act trebled the number previously protected by state laws, and its time and a half for overtime provision helped everybody, especially better-paid workers. In the textile industry, perhaps 35,000 mostly Southern, rural mill village workers saw their wages rise, but that was, after all, a pathetic number. Many large mills already paid more than the miserly minimum. While the act narrowed somewhat the regional wage differential in the cotton garment industry, that gap remained and continued to destabilize the market and the foundations of collective bargaining. Rarely did the legislation lead to collective bargaining as the TWOC had always argued it would, although the ACW for one did its best to milk the law for its propaganda value, leafleting workers that "The Wages and Hours Law Is Here: Let's Make the Most Of It."[11]

Still, Hillman doggedly pursued what was left to be had. The act provided for the creation of industrial committees under the Wages and Hours Division of the Labor Department. In textiles, Hillman lobbied the President successfully to have Donald Nelson of Sears appointed chairman of Textile Committee no. 1. Nelson, along with Averell Harriman, had earlier maneuvered the BAC into an expression of full cooperation with the new act. As a member of the Committee himself, Hillman worked with Robert Johnson, who urged: "Let us try for 40 cents in the textile industry. . . . It seems to me that the fight will be lost unless we succeed in this. . . . The unions can then strive to move the minimum up to 50 cents within a short time, and later to 60 cents, and then we will be doing a worthwhile job." Johnson fought strenuously at the Committee hearings for a higher minimum wage. The South might fear this, but he was confident that the political spadework had been done.

In the end they managed a 32.5-cent minimum in textiles, a victory of sorts but far below their hopes and expectations. Very much as with the NRA, Hillman was able to seed the committees set up to monitor subsectors of the clothing and textile industries with friendly industrialists, professional labor mediators, and public interest spokesmen. Moreover, Hillman became intimately involved in selecting the first administrator of the new Wages and Hours Division, John Andrews.[12]

Victories, then, were few, infrequent, and hard won. As the FLSA was eviscerated and the TWOC routed, administration and CIO schemes to purge and pacify the Democratic Party became more urgent and more desperate. It was an unprecedented attack launched against incumbents in twelve states and with little effort to work through regular party channels. An "Elimination Committee" targeted all those whose 100 percent loyalty to the President was in question. The LNPL committed itself to Roosevelt's purge of conservative congressmen in the primaries. League and Labor Party sources dropped ominous hints about a third party in 1940 if the purge failed. Especially after the Rules Committee had the temerity once again to bottle up the FLSA, League threats grew more strident. Hillman began gearing up for the 1938 elections by condemning conservatives in both the North and the South as traitors to the party and the people.[13]

There was a deadly synergy at work: The rapid decline of the TWOC and the crippling of the FLSA amid the 1938 recession inspired the Southern Democratic reaction against the Roosevelt purge, producing a convergence of failure, further weakening CIO allies like the La Follette Committee, which began to suffer savage attacks from the right, especially from Representative Martin Dies, and producing the largest congressional turnover since 1894. Prominent conservative Democrats—Millard Tydings of Maryland, Cotton "Ed" Smith, and Senator Walter George—targeted by both the administration and the CIO, triumphed nevertheless. The Republican Party victories in the Senate, together with those of the conservative Democrats in the House, would permit their coalition to frustrate all new New Deal legislation, to block administration attempts to expand the TVA and relief, and to rearm for assaults on the NLRA and the undistributed profits tax.[14]

For third-party partisans, even those who aspired to become little more than the Democratic Party by another name, the 1938 elections were devastating. Not only was Philip La Follette defeated in Wisconsin, but slates of candidates in California and Iowa running as National Progressives of America, La Follette's reveille for radicals, state planners, and trust-busters, lost as well. For people like Representative Amlie, the 1938 elections signaled conclusively the indifference of both labor and farm organizations to third-party adventures, and he promptly took up the urgent call to defend the New Deal. Despite some tough talk, the CIO was fast tacking away from currents of third-party sentiment. Adolph Germer let it be known in Illinois and Michigan that the UAW was not willing to get embroiled in farmer–labor party maneuverings. When Philip La Follette announced the National Progressives of America, the CIO leadership remained silent for fear of jeopardizing the FLSA. With the passage of the act in April, along with the reincarnation of the AAA, renewed public works spending, and the antitrust fireworks ignited by Robert Thurmond Arnold and the Temporary National Economic Committee, much of the wind went out of third-party sails months before the elections.

The Minnesota Farmer–Labor Party was shocked when Governor Benson lost to Harold Stassen, and the CIO was bitter. Hillman had spent months trying to get Jim Farley to exert pressure on the Democratic state chairman, Joe Noonan, to endorse Benson, but to no avail. Governor Murphy's defeat in Michigan, Maury Maverick's in Texas, and the ex-UMW officer Tom Kennedy's failure to win the gubernatorial nomination in Pennsylvania were likewise demoralizing. In New York, all ALP candidates for the state Assembly lost, as did party congressional candidates, including Dorothy Bellanca, with the single exception of Vito Marcantonio. Herbert Lehman's margin of victory over Thomas E. Dewey was small, and the Republicans won control of both houses of the New York State legislature. The elections demonstrated as well that the League's impact in rural areas was negligible, confounding its efforts to conclude the most pragmatic of alliances of mutual self-interest with farm organizations like the Farmers Educational and Cooperative Union in St. Paul. The purge had long since become the exclusive preoccupation of the League and the hard core of Keynesian New Dealers within the executive branch. [15]

Meanwhile the AFL turned up the pressure on its affiliates to shun League candidates. In Pennsylvania the state's "little New Deal" was rapidly eclipsed as the AFL openly championed the Republican Party in its struggle against CIO—"Communist"—Democrats. Hillman was dismayed as he watched support erode for designated liberal successors to Roosevelt—Harry Hopkins, Indiana's Governor Paul V. McNutt, and Governor Earle of Pennsylvania—while the fortunes of Vice President Garner, Jim Farley, Secretary of State Cordell Hull, and Senator Champ Clark of Missouri, precisely those elements Hillman hoped the purge would disempower, soared as the 1940 presidential election drew nearer. [16]

Immediately, the AFL took advantage of the CIO's political misfortunes, focusing its simmering hatred on the NLRB. Led by Green, Frey, Hutcheson, and Woll, who was still acting head of the NCF, the Federation concluded a strange alliance with the USCC and Virginia's Representative Howard Smith. They endorsed Smith's bill to separate the Board's jurisdictional prerogatives from its prosecutory powers, to allow employers to petition for representation elections and to appeal the Board's bargaining unit decisions, to limit the size of a bargaining unit so as to open the door to craft-based unions, to weaken the prohibition against company unions, and to dilute employer obligations to bargain. This counteroffensive picked up steam in June 1938, when a Board ruling effectively turned over the West Coast longshore industry to Harry Bridges and his ILWU. The AFL chieftains vented their fury, denouncing Lewis and the Board as coddlers of communists. The AFL convention resolved to amend the NLRA, and AFL legal counsel proceeded to develop appropriate language in close consultation with lawyers from the Liberty League and the "little steel" companies.

Hillman was naturally alarmed. Tom Corcoran told the President that Hillman was "a little unnerved with the NLRB stories" and recommended that FDR make some time for the CIO leader to register his concern personally. Roosevelt was willing to pet Hillman and to resist the move to amend the act. But typically he also wanted to mollify the AFL, and so he appointed the more moderate William Leiserson as the Board's new chairman with a mandate to cleanse the labor relations machinery of its Communist Party sympathizers, including Victor Fuchs and Nathan Witt. Leiserson proceeded to do just that with the help of two former students, Elinore Herrick and David Saposs.

The conservative reaction was not so easily appeased, however. Representative Smith launched a special investigation of the Board, which filled the air with innuendoes about its radicalism. William Green denounced the Board's "unholy alliance with the CIO" as an "attempt to weaken and destroy AFL unions." The AFL president blamed it all on a "flood of radicalism into the country-wide set-up of this agency," which, he slyly observed, "paralleled infiltrations of the Communists into the CIO." The CIO Executive Board charged in turn that "officials of the AFL conspired with representatives of reactionary big business to destroy the NLRA." The "Committee on Legislation," which Hillman chaired, mounted a campaign to defeat all the proposed amendments by distributing pamphlets to its affiliates throughout the country and by flooding Congress with letters. Propaganda emphasized the sinister links of the AFL with the NAM and the USCC. Hillman appeared before the Senate Committee on Education and Labor to refute all the perverse talk about "union coercion of employers." He argued that the NLRA as currently written helped to quell conflict and cited as proof American Woollen in Lawrence and American Bemberg in Elizabethton, infamous sites of earlier industrial wars. He warned that the AFL's craft union amendment would destroy stable labor relations in many plants; noted to Senator Allen Ellender that some of the nation's largest industrial firms, including GE, USS, and RCA, now recognized the wisdom of collective bargaining and of the Wagner Act; and registered his opposition to Senator Burke's bill outlawing the checkoff and union shop.[17]

An industrial counteroffensive accompanied the AFL's political assault. The Federation, after all, also benefited from the NLRA, from the

La Follette Committee investigations, from the Walsh–Healy and Davis–Bacon acts, and from other instances of federal intrusion into the labor market. Naturally, it felt the competitive sting of the CIO. Its own organizing activities and militance thus increased measurably. By 1938, moreover, it was ready to challenge the CIO on its own heavy industrial turf, sponsoring "dual union" secessionist movements among auto, textile, flat glass, and mine workers. Some of this bore little more than nuisance value. The "Progressive Miners" union, for instance, was designed to irritate Lewis. But together with the resurgence of the conservative coalition in Congress, of which the AFL had made itself a limited partner, it called into question the durability and dependability of the CIO's special relationship to the New Deal state.[18]

Vast regions of the executive branch, not to mention substantial portions of the Congress, remained hostile to the "Keynesian" New Deal's public policy perspective and program. Moreover, the mass consumption–oriented strategy had yet to win a following among the mass of entrepreneurs and wide sections of the middle class. Thus, the state itself became a locus of activity for contending elites, for the suddenly articulate armies of the shop floor, for the organizational dynamics of electoral politics, and for the brute force of the marketplace. It was a dangerously centerless structure, tending toward dispersion. Any shift in the fortunes of the new regime would immediately reverberate within the CIO.

Defeat in the "little steel" strike during the summer of 1937 was a harbinger of greater misfortune. The recession that quickly followed aborted the CIO's presumptive momentum. A certain self-confidence returned to the business community, at least with respect to labor relations. Auto production was cut in half, reversing the balance of power on the shop floor; companies like GM suddenly felt muscular enough to confront the ringleaders of rebellion who had made the wildcat stoppage a recurring feature of company life. But even apart from the recession's demoralizing effect on the steel, auto, textile, and all other organizing campaigns, it was already apparent by late 1937 that the associated rise of the CIO and the New Deal were generating powerful countercurrents within the working class.

A fratricidal civil war erupted within the infant UAW, disabling the union just when it had to meet GM's counterattack. Hillman soon became embroiled in the internal life of the CIO's flagship union, seeking to staunch its internal hemorrhaging while importing a new institutional discipline to govern its dealings with GM and the rest of the auto industry. What made it all a ticklish business was that while the main threat to the union's internal coherence came from the right, the stability of its dealings with the car companies was being undermined from the left. It was a task demanding all of Hillman's accumulated wisdom and toughness as an organizational tactician, cultural arbiter, and industrial statesman.[19]

The UAW was fissured by ideological and ethnocultural divisions. Homer Martin, the UAW President, led a diverse "Progressive" group. It was strongest among semiskilled, Protestant, "native" Americans, many of them recent Appalachian migrants now living in Flint, Lansing, and auto centers in Indiana and Kansas. Raised on fundamentalist religion and racism, once up North they were sometimes recruited into the ranks of the Black Legion and the KKK, and they harbored a deep hostility toward the Polish Catholics with whom they often worked and lived. But Martin's "Progressives" included as well a heavy admixture of urban-bred Irish and German Catholics, admirers of Father Coughlin, who worked as mechanics, bricklayers, carpenters, electricians, and plumbers, and in other non–production-line jobs, who were first organized in 1934, with Father Coughlin's help, into the Automotive Industrial Workers Association, centered in Chrysler's Dodge division. They were attracted by the corporatist authoritarianism of the Little Flower's priest.

Leaders of the "Progressives" were implacably hostile to their radical co-workers and unmoved by appeals to class solidarity. Although at times they found themselves directing waves of illicit shop floor militance, "Progressive" cadre were more often accommodationist in mood and approach, ready to conclude deals with local plant managers that may or may not have coincided with the broader purposes and plans of the UAW and the CIO. Martin's followers felt a deep antipathy toward the more secular, cosmopolitan, racially mixed, and often anticlerical, even irreligious, milieu assembled under the radical leaderships of the socialist Reuther brothers and Adolph Germer and the communist caucus led by Wyndham Mortimer and George Addes.[20]

The "Progressive" faction warred against the "Unity" coalition, tenuously allied cadres from the SP and the CP. The left was strongest in Cleveland and Detroit among Polish, Italian, and Hungarian workers. "Unity" caucus radicals had been unflappable and iron-willed at Flint and again in the fall of 1937, when Reuther's group in particular frustrated GM's efforts to fire wildcat strikers—heroic deeds repaid with the gift of fealty. The marriage of the SP and the CP was at best a troubled one. CP influence was resented and resisted not only by SP cadre but by unaffiliated figures like Richard Frankensteen, who complained to Adolph Germer as early as the spring of 1937 about the party's alleged plot to capture the union's upcoming convention. But Hillman and Philip Murray were determined to preserve this fragile unity until Martin's "Progressives" were dealt with.

Homer Martin was emotionally unstable, careless in his approach to administrative duties, wildly impulsive as a negotiator, and subject to delusions of grandeur and paranoid suspicions easily manipulated by cooler heads. All in all he was hapless and ill-equipped as a factional commander. The rivalry between the "Progressive" and "Unity" caucuses, because it exposed to the light of day a subterranean sea of fears and phobias, nevertheless jeopardized the integrity of the UAW, creating a real crisis for the CIO leadership.[21]

Lewis and Hillman were not willing to entrust the fate of the Committee's singular achievement to local cadre. Beginning in mid-1938, when the faction fight imperiled its very life, the union was in effect run by Sidney Hillman and Philip Murray. Commissioned by Lewis to resolve the UAW's internal civil war, both men realized that unless they did so the institution would collapse as an effective vehicle of centralized collective bargaining. For Hillman and Murray the task was to fashion a consolidated executive, which only then could establish uniform relations with an industry emboldened by recession and reaction.

They left for Detroit early in September and called together the rival caucuses for nine days of continuous negotiations. The two CIO leaders announced that they would exercise the real executive power, overruling earlier decisions by Martin to suspend "Unity" caucus members of the UAW Executive Board. Hillman hammered out two agreements with Martin, which the UAW President first repudiated and then reluctantly assented to. A committee comprising Hillman, Murray, R. J. Thomas, and Martin was to resolve all future disputes. Hillman and Murray went off to extinguish local factional fires in Wisconsin, Michigan, and Tarrytown, New York. After the briefest respite, Hillman received reports that Martin was about to hatch a separate tool and die local and that he intended to erect a parallel bureaucracy so as to circumvent the authority of the vice presidents representing the "Unity" caucus. Martin was heard on radio stations in Cleveland, Detroit, and Chicago decrying "a conspiracy to destroy the UAW" and accusing Lewis, Hillman, and Murray, as well as Mortimer, Richard Frankensteen, and John Brophy, of being co-conspirators. Martin was moving rapidly toward secession while proffering a friendly hand to business by charging that it was the CIO that "defended and protected the perpetrators of a welter of chaos of indiscriminate unconstitutional stoppages of work, wildcat sit-downs, and other strikes." Lewis, he noted, had allied himself with the CP. "We are fighting a battle in a great war of world politics." That call to arms, for all its melodramatic grandiloquence, contained a certain measure of truth. [22]

In preparation for the 1939 UAW convention, Hillman kept himself regularly informed about factional maneuverings in the various regions. Germer let Hillman know that Martin was telling his confederates that the international executive board could "go to hell." There were rumors abroad that Martin was conferring with Father Coughlin and with the notorious Harry Bennett, the despised director of Henry Ford's security force, about seceding to form a new auto union, independent of the CIO. Early in the new year, in a report to the UAW membership, Hillman and Murray characterized Martin as an irresponsible and chaotic administrator. Then, in an open letter to the CIO, the two warned of Martin's "dictator-mania," pronounced him a hopeless factionalizer, and, most damning of all, publicly aired their suspicions about his "negotiations" with Harry Bennett. [23]

By this time it was clear the "Progressives" were on their way out of the CIO, headed for the fatal embrace of Father Coughlin, Harry Bennett, and the AFL. For the Homer Martin group to find its way back into the AFL eventually was only natural, as the AFL remained the principal institutional embodiment of the *ancien régime*, both on the shop floor and in the community. The UAW was perhaps cleansed but nonetheless diminished, its once massive membership eroded by recession and reaction, barely clinging to life thanks especially to the fortitude of its tool and die cadre. Thus, even with Martin out of the way, the CIO was not ready to relinquish operational control of this vital union. Everyone knew Martin was the incubus keeping the "Unity" caucus unified. All feared what might happen once he was gone.

As the 1939 convention approached, Hillman and Murray issued a press release pledging the CIO's unqualified support for a new international executive board to be headed by R. J. Thomas. Thomas was himself frankly shocked when Hillman and Murray designated him to be acting President. Maurice Sugar, a UAW lawyer, and Adolph Germer considered Thomas too inexperienced, and Thomas agreed. But for Hillman his callowness made him nearly a perfect choice. What he sought was someone pliable enough to carry out the strategic purposes of the CIO leadership without asking inconvenient questions, someone free of sectarian-factional allegiances, which also meant someone without the necessary independent social and organizational strength to act on his own. As in the 1920s, Hillman again sought to block the CP's advance, not because he considered it a carrier of some moral cancer—he rarely delivered ideological diatribes, and when he did it was a matter more of expedience than of conviction—but because he was determined that the fount of power remain where it was, in the hands of the CIO. Moreover, Hillman's tactical calculations were formulated with one eye on the paranoid symbolism of the national distemper; the convention coincided with a chorus of red-baiting directed at the CIO not only by the AFL and its congressional friends but by the press as well, in particular through a series of stories by the onetime Hillman admirer Benjamin Stolberg and by Louis Stark in the *New York Times*.

Hillman came to the UAW convention in Cleveland to prevent what seemed like the probable election of George Addes to the union's presidency. Hillman's and Murray's letter to the convention urged Thomas's investiture as a way to avoid open hostilities between Walter Reuther and the CP. Hillman chaperoned Thomas and instructed him on how to run the convention. At a breakfast meeting he educated the rather naïve acting President on the delicate issue of getting him elected despite Addes's substantial following. They even mused about the possibility of recruiting a more appealing candidate, perhaps Dick Leonard of the De Soto local. When Richard Frankensteen shifted his support to Thomas, however, Thomas's election was secure. At the same time, CP Chairman Earl Browder, fearing that a split in the UAW would help Martin and undermine the party's position throughout the CIO, instructed the group led by Mortimer to back Thomas in return for Addes's election as Secretary-Treasurer. And so Thomas, an unlikely choice even by his own estimation, became Hillman's hand-picked President of the UAW. But he was not permitted to entertain any illusions of glory. Shortly after the convention Hillman told him not to imagine that his presidency would last long, "because Walter Reuther will be the next president. I don't know how long he will sit still but he's bound to go after it." For all of that, Thomas admired Hillman's courage, firmness, tenacity, and dynamism.[24]

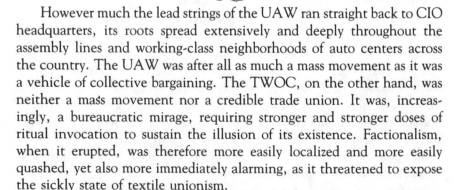

However much the lead strings of the UAW ran straight back to CIO headquarters, its roots spread extensively and deeply throughout the assembly lines and working-class neighborhoods of auto centers across the country. The UAW was after all as much a mass movement as it was a vehicle of collective bargaining. The TWOC, on the other hand, was neither a mass movement nor a credible trade union. It was, increasingly, a bureaucratic mirage, requiring stronger and stronger doses of ritual invocation to sustain the illusion of its existence. Factionalism, when it erupted, was therefore more easily localized and more easily quashed, yet also more immediately alarming, as it threatened to expose the sickly state of textile unionism.

Undoubtedly Hillman's prolonged illness exacerbated the TWOC's predicament as the recession dragged on into 1938. It did not help matters that for a long time after his recovery he was occupied elsewhere, in Washington and Detroit, and left day-to-day operations in the uninspiring if capable hands of Solomon Barkin. In June, however, Hillman resurfaced to announce a renewed campaign to consolidate the TWOC in Southern mills, where it had established a toehold. But in fact progress was deadly slow. Only the TWOC's apparent strength in the North stood between it and oblivion. So when a factional war erupted in New England, as nasty as anything seen in the UAW, Hillman treated it with military gravity.[25]

Francis Gorman, the mercurial and maladroit leader of the 1934 general strike, had resented from the beginning the peremptory way Hillman and the CIO swallowed up the UTW, relegating its chief functionaries to positions of dwindling influence and prestige. But living on borrowed time in 1936, Gorman and others in the UTW had kept quiet and had allowed themselves to be swallowed. Only Emil Rieve among the UTW old guard retained real power under the new regime, thanks in part to the resilience of his hosiery workers' federation, whose large complement of skilled workers clung to the union through the bleakest days of the Depression. Alliances between Hillman and Rieve predated the New Deal, and it became obvious that it was Rieve, not Gorman, who was destined to become Hillman's first lieutenant and eventual successor. Frustrated, jealous, and boiling over with characteristic impatience, Gorman was an apostate waiting for an opportunity to defect.

Opportunities were available in embarrassing profusion. By 1938 the TWOC was dispirited and demoralized. In the South it occupied a few lonely outposts but was everywhere else a defeated army. In New England, where it had begun with great promise, the TWOC organizers candidly acknowledged a debilitating stalemate, while some complained acidly about what they considered the excessive prudence of the national leadership. Finally, the febrile emotions of French-Canadian and Italian workers boiled over, aroused, like their coreligionists in the UAW, by the CIO's conspicuous secularism and deliberately excited by patriarchs of the Church, who feared for their positions as community elders, not to mention the spiritual well-being of their parishioners. Gorman rode this wave of retreat and cultural counterrevolution.

John Brophy was importuned by Gorman, who in a typical burst of hyperbolic audacity argued that the best remedy for the TWOC's passivity was a mass strike, presumably to be led by Gorman. Brophy suggested a meeting to formulate national policy on the wage cuts then sweeping through the industry, upon which Gorman was seizing to upbraid the TWOC executive.

Then Gorman boldly told Hillman it was time to restore the old departmental form of organization. Exploiting a widely shared sense that the organization was foundering, Gorman urged a national conference of all cotton textile locals to launch a new Southern drive as well as a coincident campaign to protect the unemployed. To accomplish all this, Gorman demanded that the TWOC chairman convene an emergency meeting of the Executive Council. Gorman staked his own precarious future on the passions of rebels in Rhode Island and elsewhere. The Providence and Woonsocket Woollen and Worsted District Council issued a statement highly critical of the TWOC and addressed its complaints directly to CIO President Lewis. Tempers grew short, and a bust-up seemed inevitable.[26]

By late 1938 the faction fight was public business, as Hillman made it clear that Gorman was not to be his heir. Gorman hurriedly marshaled about fifty old UTW locals for the short march back into the AFL. He cemented his alliance with Joseph Sylvia and the Rhode Island rebels, who by this time were actually suing the TWOC in the state courts. As Francis Gorman exited the TWOC to reconstitute the UTW, he congratulated his confederates in Rhode Island for their two-to-one margin of victory over the TWOC in the Atlantic Mills of Providence: "The textile workers are through with Hitlerism; no more Goerings, no more Goebbels," Gorman fumed. He promised instead a return to the UTW's old federated, balkanized regime under the consoling rubric of freedom and democracy. The TWOC was equally acrid. Its expulsion order lampooned Gorman as "a pathetic little Napoleon without an army." This exchange of verbal artillery could scarcely conceal the underlying impotence of both organizations. Gorman's reconstituted UTW faded into obscurity, unable even to retain the loyalty of its Woonsocket allies, who were themselves so evenly divided between CIO partisans and French-Canadian conservatives that they remained locked in splendid isolation as an independent union.[27]

At CIO headquarters Gardner Jackson confessed to Hillman his concern about the flood of resignations following the reorganization of the New England district, about TWOC defeats in Sylvia strongholds in Rhode Island and Maine, and about Hillman's too frequent absences from the scene of battle. Jackson had little confidence in the generalship of Rieve and Barkin. Hillman too was alarmed by the defections from a frail and failing movement. For want of anything more tangible, he rushed to give it a paper permanence before it vanished. He knew this was premature but felt he had no other choice. Thus in a ritual incantation in Philadelphia in May 1939 he merged 302 newly minted TWOC locals with 126 ex-UTW locals to concoct the Textile Workers Union of

America under President Emil Rieve. Hillman presided in a mood of absurd optimism, claiming a membership of 424,000 and predicting that in a year the industry would be 100 percent organized, this at a time when there were fewer than thirty organizers and 20,000 members in the South, and when the organization was still financially insolvent. Having performed his midwife duties by ushering the new institution into the world, Hillman quickly distanced himself from a defeat that even the most roseate press releases couldn't transform into victory. In September he attended his last TWUA executive council meeting. Until the war rescued it from stillbirth, the TWUA was less a trade union than a spectral lobby, haunting the corridors of the Wages and Hours Administration and the offices of the RFC, where it sought funds to bail out textile firms.[28]

As the cases of Homer Martin and Francis Gorman suggest, the CIO was a veritable minefield of combustible ethnocultures, which established definite limits beyond which the CIO leadership dared not venture politically. Steel and coal workers from Eastern Europe, for example, even of the second generation, no matter how acclimated to the gains-oriented behavioral norms of industrial capitalism, were still enmeshed in communal, kinship, and occupational networks—"deference societies"—that insulated them from the radical secularism and individualism of other CIO cadre. On the one hand, the proliferation of semiskilled mechanical jobs—hoist, crane, and switch operators, for example—freed the second generation from the occupational purgatory of their fathers. English-language schools and newspapers and new forms of mass entertainment inculcated the value of individual achievement, merit, and the "rights" of citizenship, stoking the fires that gave the CIO its volcanic impact.

Still, castelike occupational divisions and cultural disdain separated the masses of immigrant steelworkers from their betters among native American and West European industrial artisans. Impermeable curtains of ethnocultural isolation fatally divided immigrants from "Americans" at Bethlehem during the "little steel" strike. Parochial schools helped reestablish the unsettled structures of patriarchal authority in home and Church, and reinvigorated the ethnic language and with it respect for traditional moral codes and social hierarchy. The courtship and marriage patterns of second-generation steel and meatpacking workers in Chicago were still subject to the mores and rituals of Old World arranged pairings. Moreover, the domination of the Democratic Party in the "Back of the Yards," based on patronage and ethnic fealties, remained largely intact, although reoriented to plead the causes of its constituents before the new panoply of federal social welfare agencies. The PWOC caused splits within the Church: younger priests endorsed the CIO and its strike against Armour, while their elders and superiors drew back, a situation requiring delicate handling by CIO strategists.[29]

Until the very end of the decade steel and meatpacking unions led a tenuous existence in Chicago. A Steelworkers Independent Union thrived partly on the basis of its anticommunism, its ties to the Knights of Pythias, and its animus against the centralizing logic of the CIO. The SWOC by late 1938 was in danger of withering away in Chicago. Indeed, the city remained an AFL town through the 1930s and experienced few sitdowns, and the CIO was studiously avoided by the Church fathers until the outbreak of war in Europe. The United Electrical Workers (UE) counted for little until 1940, while the UAW was largely confined to parts plants.[30]

Even the most openly partisan CIO circles within the Church hierarchy expressed reservations. Father Charles Owen Rice of Pittsburgh was Phil Murray's valued adviser. Through the ACTU he marshaled Italian and Polish workers in the auto, steel, electrical, and transport industries on behalf of the CIO. Father John Ryan's Christian Front vociferously defended industrial unionism as an instrument for achieving a just social order compatible with Catholic teachings. Ryan, Rice, and other liberal theologians did their best to neutralize the anti–New Deal preachments of Father Coughlin. Father Francis Haas, of course, was always ready to help. At Potofsky's request he wrote to Monsignor Tourenhart in St. Louis to put a stop there to the red-baiting of the ACW. He told the Monsignor that Hillman and Potofsky had "rendered a genuine public service in abolishing sweat shops" and asked him to aid the ACWA "in their great crusade for social justice."[31]

Yet these same elements worried about the influence of the CP and the secular individualism of the New Deal. The ACTU was formed to function as a kind of magic bullet to wipe out centers of the red contagion as it coursed through the ranks of the CIO. Red-baiting of the CIO became a pastime for many Church patriarchs in the late 1930s. The administration's child labor amendment further undermined the Catholic social consensus. Even liberal elements of the hierarchy viewed it as a threat to parental and Church authority. Father Ryan actually opposed a federal housing project in Pittsburgh as a threat to the integrity and autonomy of the family and the community.[32]

The social friction that slowed the CIO was as much demographic as ethnocultural. In 1939 J. B. S. Hardman blamed some of the CIO's problems on the mass influx of "NRA babies," untutored workers with no previous trade union experience who required, in Hardman's view, painstaking education and discipline. The 1938 ACW convention reflected that generation gap as "NRA babies" and those even "younger," recruited through the great campaigns of 1937, accounted for one-third of the delegates.

Arguably, the acculturation of this new generation made the CIO possible by leveling the barriers to cross-cultural cohesion. Intermarriage increased across the whole spectrum of the second generation—among Poles, French-Canadians, Italians, and all the refugees of the Russian Empire. Membership in provincial fraternal societies likewise declined, along with the absolutism of parental authority, abetted by the disintegration of local ethnic economies. But the CIO could never ignore the salience of its ethnocultural infrastructure. Thus, the UAW established a special Hamtramck district to cater to its Poles, broadcast regularly in Polish, and assiduously cultivated relations with Polish fraternal organizations and Polish community elites, including storekeepers and merchants who reciprocated that support during the Chrysler sitdown of 1937. Polish politicians in turn were careful to solicit the counsel of Dodge local 3 in Hamtramck. Later, during the organization of Ford in 1940–41, a similar "ethnic strategy" led to the creation of separate Polish and Italian organization committees. For its part, the SWOC resembled a clearinghouse of fraternal and ethnic societies as much as it did a trade union.[33]

Contending ethnic loyal ties, racial and religious phobias, and political and moral passions left the CIO emitting the sights and sounds of lightning and thunder but without the internal force to duplicate their effects. Even while it assembled the polyglot armies of second-generation semiskilled industrial workers, the CIO behaved like a social centrifuge, its energies dissipated through the rivalries of faith and social status. It became a luxuriant breeding ground for factional turmoil and rank-and-file rebellion from the right and from the left. From the standpoint of the CIO's leadership, resolving these localized civil wars, like those in the UAW and the TWOC, became an increasingly urgent precondition for normalizing relations with industry. In some instances faction leaders stood to enhance their own prestige by championing outlaw outbursts against management. So long as the CIO could be credibly accused of harboring hotheads of workplace anarchy and radicalism—not always the same thing—its relationship with the administration was also imperiled. The chemistry of the New Deal sought a new equilibrium, a "normalization" in which the CIO leadership, Hillman especially, would prove its unwavering conformity to the imperatives of bureaucratic and commercial regularity. All of this helps account for the historian David Brody's observation that as a mass movement the CIO enjoyed an extraordinarily short life and that in general one can't help but be struck by

the impressive strength of conservative elements within the labor movement even as it was transforming the terrain on which labor relations
would be conducted for the next half-century.

It would be wrong to conclude, however, that some moral polarity
separated the uncontaminated, pure-minded militants of the shop floor
from the tainted precincts of bureaucratic and political deal-making. If
Hillman's commitment to large-scale, bureaucratic, complex organization called forth a new form of domination, it also entailed the dissolution of primordial structures of ethnic and patriarchal subordination in
favor of the formally democratic regime of rules. Moreover, this regime,
with its impersonal and elaborate provisions for hiring, firing, promotion, and seniority, was hardly an alien intrusion. The very same un-
tainted and heroic local leaders of embattled strikes and sitdowns,
precisely because they were the uprooted of the factory and the forge, less
bound to the detritus of familial, ethnic, and communal patrimonies,
became the most dedicated and aggressive builders of the "new unionism." They became in effect the bureaucracy, channeling their suddenly
free energies to converge with the higher purposes of Hillman and his
colleagues at CIO headquarters, and did so as an outgrowth of their own
democratic aspirations for individual advancement, self-possession, and
material acquisition. These soon-to-be apparatchiks of the CIO were
sometimes drawn from and more frequently spoke for the semiskilled
denizens of a new industrial order, a new politics of production that was
determined to unseat an older craft aristocracy and install itself as the
decisive formation on the shop floor. If Hillman and Lewis drew back at
the specter of unleashed aggression, if they feared risking all by invoking
an anti-authoritarian tempest, they shared those anxieties with millions
of their newly mobilized constituents. So much of what ignited the CIO
was reactive, defensive, and resentful. The quest for security—again and
again singled out by Hillman as the *zeitgeist* of the epoch—was embedded
deeply across wide stretches of the new immigrant working class, among
their skilled betters from the old immigration, and among the uprooted
of Appalachia and others.[34]

Again the experience of the UAW encapsulated the larger story.
Hillman anointed Thomas not only to dispose of Homer Martin but in
order to rescue the auto union from the brink of extinction. Immediately
after Flint, there was considerable truth in the romantic image of the
UAW as a union of shop floor solidarity, militancy, and democratic
participation. Because stewards were prepared to act boldly, to lead
strikes if necessary, grievances were settled rapidly and workers powers
expanded without regard to contractual formalities. In the auto body
plants of the Midwest, among metal finishers and welders and others

there was an explosion of "quickie" strikes and other forms of shop floor war, where stewards deployed their followers in brash attempts to control and slow down the pace and quantity of production. Just who was running things on a daily basis in the country's most important industry was a seriously contested question.

This sort of behavior was inimical both to the national leadership of the CIO and to GM management. The union sought institutional stability and the regularizing of the collective bargaining relationship. The corporation expected maintenance of order and discipline and recognition of its prerogatives. Factional and shop floor turmoil permitted neither. This worried Washington as well. Thomas Corcoran warned the President about the "serious incipient labor situation in the automobile unions of Detroit," which he felt required the "immediate attention which Sidney solicited this morning." But even while militants flexed their muscle, the union as a whole grew weaker, thanks to the recession and the way it emboldened management to encroach on union entitlements established in the aftermath of Flint. By early 1939, as Hillman and Murray prepared to install the new UAW regime, the UAW's position had become precarious. No longer recognized by GM, its dues payments so far in arrears no one kept count, the infant union could scarcely tolerate more civil war.

To restore its credibility as a combat organization, Walter Reuther shrewdly bypassed the mass of now intimidated and disoriented production line workers and instead called upon the always reliable shock troops of skilled tool and die craftsmen. They struck successfully in the summer, blunting GM's offensive before it became fatal. A year later the company and the union concluded a meticulously detailed agreement designed to pacify life on the line, an agreement that reprised in its essentials the "impartial umpire" system invented by the ACW twenty-five years earlier. Indeed, it was an agreement hammered out in close consultation with Hillman, and its first umpire, Harry Millis, had performed that function in the clothing industry of Chicago. Finally, the agreement for the first time transposed what was perhaps the most enduring achievement of the "new unionism" into the heartland of American heavy industry. In part because it was introduced in the country's flagship industry by its flagship company, it quickly spread to all the core sectors of the national economy, arguably making it the model of industrial jurisprudence for the next half-century and Sidney Hillman's lasting legacy.[35]

On Hillman's advice, Reuther recommended to the UAW Executive Board as early as 1938 the appointment of a permanent arbitrator to resolve grievances. He pursued this line anew in 1939, again under

Hillman's tutelage, and mustered the courage to speak out unequivocally against the rage for wildcat strikes. Reuther described his recommended "umpire system" with explicit reference to the ACW's, noting to the GM Council of the union that "they have made more gains with an impartial umpire, more gains without a strike, than any other group of workers in America." The new UAW leadership acknowledged the need to discipline the rank and file and recognized that many grievances "are not worth a damn," that it was their responsibility "to educate our committeemen to do a job." At the same time Hillman was meeting with GM's Charles E. Wilson to clarify and encourage the company's own studies of the umpire system in anthracite coal, hosiery, and, of course, clothing.[36]

And so a second conflict, pitting the international union and GM management against shop floor militants, supplanted the more celebrated battle between union and corporation. The emerging bureaucracy of the UAW took steps to dismantle the shop steward system, reduced the authority of local unions while augmenting the powers of the International, appended a no-strike and management rights clause to the contract, and perfected the modern grievance procedure and committee system.

What the umpire system did was immunize Reuther, the UAW, and the CIO more generally from the unpredictable and dangerous effusions of shop floor energy. Reuther cited the experience of the Chicago clothing workers to persuade local bureaucrats that the "new unionism" would shield them from corporate reprisal as well as acute factionalism. At the same time, for Reuther and others it was, as it had been for Hillman and the "activity" a quarter century before, the most expedient way, the middle or "British" way, of introducing the rule of law onto the shop floor. It was what "industrial democracy" had become after passing through the cauldron of Depression, mass insurgency, and reaction.[37]

Many personnel managers, reflecting the functional disaggregation of the firm, were quite sympathetic to the Wagner Act: "After a long struggle . . . the principle of representation in employer–employee relations is definitely established. It has become increasingly clear that modern, complex, large-scale corporations no longer admit of satisfactory and individualized control and management." Growing segments of the business community accepted that basic arrangement. Hillman testified at congressional hearings that core companies, including USS, GE, American Woollen, and RCA, had long since recognized the wisdom of the Wagner Act. Walter Chrysler told Frances Perkins of his sympathies with the purposes of the CIO. At U.S. Rubber, Cy Ching met secretly with the URW President, Sherman Dalrymple, to work out the details of union recognition in return for union-imposed discipline and efficiency.

Carle Conway, chairman of the board of Continental Can, delivered a synopsis of the way corporate thinking had changed:

> Certainly anyone who has been in business during the past 30 years would have to be naïve to think that management by and large desired collective bargaining or certain of the other reforms which labor has finally won. . . . But isn't it also likely that better understanding of the basic fundamentals involved in the struggle over the last thirty years between labor and management can work toward harmonizing the two viewpoints into a common objective and so make collective bargaining and many of the other reforms operate in the interests of both labor and management?

Nor was it merely the giants of American industry that began to accept industrial unionism as a feature of modern management. In the late 1930s specialty steel mills on the verge of bankruptcy began to cooperate with the SWOC, especially with Clinton Golden. In return for stabilized and secure employment, Golden showed how the SWOC could improve productivity by sharing in the determination and enforcement of production standards, more or less exactly in the manner that Golden first witnessed in the Amalgamated after the war. Indeed, this scheme for codetermination of production standards, including the elimination of waste and improvement in quality standards worked out by Golden and another SWOC organizer, Harold Ruttenberg, by relieving workers' anxieties about petty discrimination and arbitrary punishments and firings, promised to release as well an untapped body of technical knowledge that workers were otherwise afraid to share with management.

On the eve of the war Philip Murray co-authored a book with Morris Cooke which singled out finance as the group whose interests and motivations were most responsible for blocking real cooperation in the interests of maximum production and a guaranteed annual wage, which would provide the basis for "a home market of almost limitless possibilities." The common ground for close collaboration between modern management and centralized industrial unionism had emerged by the end of the decade. The mutual recognition of "the rights of management" (control over the work process and discipline) and the "rights of the union" (recognition and on-the-job dues collection) amounted to an industrial compact between two institutions each interested in protecting its own power and stability, and together prepared to bargain away the popular rights and power of shop floor militants.[38]

Hillman presided over the maturation of the "new unionism" and seized every chance to broadcast its virtues. Frank Rising of *Business Week* arranged for Hillman to address a group of New England business-men who were, according to Rising, sophisticated and aware of "ad-vanced liberal thinking." Rising contended that "the policies and methods of Hillman . . . will make sense to this crowd," as long as the case for collective bargaining rested "on factual evidence that it is nec-essary" and could lead "to a realization of the proper desires of both capital and labor." He advised Hillman to make ample use of his garment center experience to prove the point that "radicals did not destroy the handiwork of our forefathers."

Hillman hardly needed the promptings of a Frank Rising. His whole career since arriving in Chicago constituted a kind of apprenticeship in the arts and sciences of labor statesmanship. Now all the perils and predicaments of the New Deal and the CIO called upon those talents to salvage what remained of America's flirtation with social democracy. Indeed, the more perilous the situation, the more salubrious his states-manship became. Hillman's remarks to the New England business com-munity were practically olympian as he labored to explain that a whole historical epoch had passed away, that the mechanisms of cyclical, au-tomatic renewal no longer worked their old magic with the vanishing of the frontier, with the leveling off of population growth, and with Europe and the rest of the world walled off into armored spheres of influence. To revive the economy and develop the domestic market now required deliberate, collaborative planning by industry, agriculture, and labor under government supervision.[39]

"The Promise of American Labor," appearing in *The New Republic,* was Hillman's elegiac rendering of the age of the iron cage. Complex industrial society, he argued, had to solve its problems not through individual action but through "strong, responsible, and independent or-ganizations" representing the decisive forces in national life. Disunity was once necessary to bestir an anesthetized labor movement, but now that the CIO was established unity was essential, if only because of the ominous signs of war abroad. Under the tutelage of the ACW and the UMW, the CIO had become a model of responsible unionism from which everybody stood to benefit—not only management but the whole country—thanks to the expansion of purchasing power and production under the disinterested direction of government planners. Labor's para-mount task now was "to assure the continuance in office of a liberal government."[40]

To sustain a "liberal government" in power had long been Hillman's abiding purpose. Chronic civil war between the AFL and the CIO, however, posed a dire threat to the longevity of New Deal liberalism.

Certainly the administration felt that way, and once Hillman returned from his Miami convalescence pressures mounted for him to earn his statesman's spurs as a diplomat of labor peace.

Failure to clear out the centers of reaction within the Democratic Party during the 1938 primaries heightened anxiety within the administration and among its friends. Gerard Swope informed administration insiders about the encouraging talks he was carrying on with Hillman and Lewis. Swope's view, excessively sanguine, was that if the AFL and the CIO selected representatives to meet with two outside neutrals, the breach might be repaired. He urged the President to help.[41]

The humiliations suffered in the 1938 general elections made labor unity all the more an essential item on the political agenda. In Pennsylvania the defeat of Earle for Senator and Kennedy for Governor could clearly be attributed to the AFL–CIO split. Frances Perkins again tried to heal the wound, this time through the offices of Hillman's clerical friend, Francis Haas. At first Hillman anticipated the best. Corcoran reported to the President that Hillman was eager to talk with him about labor unity, that he had never seen a more propitious moment, and begged "for the first time in my acquaintanceship" to give "time enough to really talk things out regarding labor peace and the 1940 elections." Hillman told his daughter Philoine that the CIO had achieved an encouraging unanimity, that the "confused, revolutionary ideas" of Harry Bridges had been peremptorily "deflated," and so the CIO could now approach the AFL from a position of strength. Still, he confessed that "industrial conditions are very disturbing," which made labor unity more urgent but at the same time less easily achieved.

Finally, Haas brought Hillman together secretly with George Harrison at the Pennsylvania Hotel in New York. Hillman was more than accommodating, agreeing to meet without a prior pledge from the AFL to respect the charters of the new CIO unions or even a commitment to create a Department of Industrial Organization after the hypothesized merger. But Harrison refused Hillman's request that the AFL halt its attempts to amend the Wagner Act. Green went so far as to spread the rumor that Hillman was contemplating defecting, a malicious piece of nonsense but also a sign of Green's confidence that the CIO was weakening fast and ripe for attack.[42]

At that point Roosevelt himself got involved. He sent a letter to Green and Lewis asking that they appoint peace delegations empowered to fix the terms of unity. The AFL continued to flex its muscles, insisting that the President support its Wagner Act amendments, which Roosevelt refused to do. He did appoint William Leiserson as the NLRB chairman, but that in turn infuriated Lewis. At a subsequent peace conference

Lewis managed to upstage a personal appearance by the President when
he made an audacious proposal that he and Green step down in favor of
a new president, to be chosen from among the railroad brotherhoods,
who would head a new American Congress of Labor. It was a sensational
gesture and a bit of a gamble, but one Lewis was confident of winning.
When Green spurned the offer, Lewis was delighted; he was aware that
the CIO, beset by multiple disabilities, was hardly in the best position to
enter serious negotiations.[43]

Lewis's relations with the administration having long since soured,
he was not eager to do the administration's bidding. Lewis warned the
CIO Executive about the insidious dangers of peace negotiations, which
had "reduced the fighting spirit" of the CIO. Murray echoed his mentor's
pessimism, as did Harry Bridges, Powers Hapgood, and Alan Haywood,
who chided Hillman: "I hope Brother Hillman's hopes have some foundation but I would rather have division and action than unity and decay." Hillman acknowledged that he might be overly optimistic, but
still, he argued, it was vital to press for unity under militant leadership.
He pointed out that at least the AFL was apparently now ready to
concede that the eleven original CIO unions had to be readmitted without any questioning of their present membership and jurisdictional rights.
The CIO's negotiating position would hold inviolable the full and complete recognition of the principle of mass industrial unionism in mass
production industry.[44]

If Lewis took secret pleasure in the collapse of negotiations, Hillman
did not. Rumors soon circulated that he and Dan Tobin, as point men for
the President, were once again out scouting the landscape for new signs
of peace.[45]

As peace negotiations festered, so too did relations between Lewis
and Hillman. An odd couple under any circumstances—the leonine
Welsh rhetorician of the class struggle and the cerebral-looking rabbi of
industrial concord, Hillman as simple in style as Lewis was extravagant—
they had in fact grown to respect each other during the combative days
of the NRA and afterward. But the clash of their dispositions and outlooks began to surface almost as soon as the tide started running out on
the New Deal and the CIO. When Lewis angrily chastised the President
for his wounding neutrality during the "little steel" strike and made
veiled threats about a third party, Hillman was privately dismayed and
told Lee Pressman that as CIO counselor he should have prevented it.
Lewis's outburst, however, expressed more than verbal posturing or sty-
listic idiosyncrasy.

Len De Caux aptly, if with some exaggeration, contrasted Lewis's commitment to labor organization free of government and/or corporate entanglements with Hillman's preference for state planning and social mediation. Lewis's allegiance to the New Deal "administrative state" was always more pragmatic and provisional, less ideological and programmatic, than Hillman's. If it took the strong arm of the government to stop the coal industry from destroying itself, Lewis was prepared to welcome its participation in the marketplace. But he was a onetime Hoover Republican with an abiding faith in trade union voluntarism and an equally deep skepticism about the benign intentions of the state. Above all, Lewis was perpetually wary and temperamentally indisposed to compromise his own freedom of action through binding alliances, no matter how august the person or party. Fealty to Roosevelt, to the Democratic Party, and to the institutional creatures of the New Deal became an indigestible bone of contention, opening up a field of irreconcilable differences between the lion and the fox.[46]

Officially, the CIO campaigned unreservedly for the FLSA. Privately, Lewis was far more reserved. Along with his titular opposite, William Green, he objected to granting the proposed Wage and Hour Board the right to raise wages above the statutory minimum for fear such an intrusion would undermine trade union authority. Lewis's reluctance was strategic as well. He felt Hillman counted entirely too much and too exclusively on the FLSA to bail out the labor movement. Heated arguments erupted among Hillman, Pressman, Lauck, and Tom Kennedy over whether the CIO should invest its resources so heavily in the FLSA. Only because Lauck and Kennedy insisted that it was the key to organizing the South and vital to organizing efforts generally did Hillman's view prevail. Even then the tepidity of Lewis's support for the act was noted by insiders like Robert Johnson, who complained about it to Corcoran.[47]

Mutual suspicions naturally hardened in the icy atmosphere surrounding the unity negotiations. During Hillman's recovery personal jealousies began to aggravate political tensions. The President was extremely solicitous about Hillman's well-being: "To be deprived of your counsel even very briefly at a time like this is a serious loss to the labor movement and to the people of our country. I do hope you will be well again soon." The President continued this stroking after Hillman returned to work, scheduling occasional lunches or other get-togethers with Hillman, "preferably alone." Corcoran impressed upon Roosevelt that Hillman was taking a pounding from Lewis precisely because even such exemplary New Deal institutions as the NLRB seemed suddenly unreliable. A vote of personal confidence from the President would help shore up his position as an administration loyalist within the CIO.

Roosevelt offered more than a vote of confidence. After Lewis went out of his way to thwart an endorsement of a third presidential term at the CIO's 1939 convention, the President refused to reappoint Donald Wakefield Smith, Lewis's favored candidate, to the NLRB, further freezing relations with the CIO chairman. Instead he appointed Hillman's longtime associate Harry Millis, further irritating the growing estrangement between Hillman and Lewis. The President honored Hillman with appointments to the advisory council of the National Youth Administration, to the Board of the U.S. Employment Service, and to the advisory council on social security.[48]

Lewis was stung by what he considered Roosevelt's obvious preference for Hillman. He let Lee Pressman know that unlike Hillman he "didn't consider it a favor to be permitted to come to the White House." Rightly, Lewis felt like an excommunicant and vented his frustrations with characteristic melodrama. Complaining that Hillman enjoyed the ear and trust of the President, he threatened late in 1939 to quit as CIO head until Hillman persuaded him to stay on for at least another year, during which, Hillman speculated, a compromise might be worked out if only Lewis would quiet his criticism of the administration's foreign and domestic policy.[49]

But other issues poisoned relations as well. None was nastier than the "red" question. Unlike his conferees in the needle trades union leadership, Hillman's relations with the American Communist Party were never ideologically fixed. Although he preferred that party members stay out of the TWOC and the ACW, he appreciated their contribution to the CIO more generally and recognized their genuine commitment to the New Deal—at least so long as the "Popular Front" lasted. But all of that, of course, changed in 1939 with the signing of the Nazi–Soviet nonaggression pact. Once the CP abandoned the administration on orders from Moscow, its value plummeted in Hillman's eyes. Instead, in league with Lewis the party represented a real and present danger to the administration and to hopes that Hillman cherished for the CIO: that it be invited permanently inside the highest policy-making and strategy-making circles of the Democratic Party and the national regime. For that decidedly practical set of reasons Hillman began to criticize, within the CIO's Executive Board, the role of the party and, by implication, its ties to Lewis. Hints were dropped that the Amalgamated might leave if the party's activities were not severely curtailed. Already the Amalgamated in Wisconsin, along with a portion of the UAW, a UE local, and the hosiery unionists, had chosen to remain outside the CP-dominated state CIO Council. If the party had a well-earned reputation for Leninist ruthlessness, so too did Hillman display a *sang-froid*, a Machiavellian purposiveness in his attitude toward the party. For Hillman all that mattered was first that the party serve a purpose useful to industrial unionism and not presume to seduce others to its own purposes, and second that it do nothing to upset the CIO's relations with the administration. Hillman excluded both personal and ideological considerations from his calculations, which is why, beginning in 1938 and continuing on through the years of the Nazi–Soviet pact, John Abt, whose close ties to the CP were widely known, remained Hillman's chief legal adviser on antilabor legislation and other matters of great moment. Within a few years Hillman would again demonstrate his extraordinary flexibility when it came to working with the CP, but for now, and so long as it encouraged Lewis in his cold war with the President, the party represented an enemy Hillman intended to disarm even if it meant worsening relations with Lewis.[50]

Lewis for his part seemed determined to paint himself into a corner. It was as plain to him as to anyone else that all the liberal heirs-apparent to Roosevelt were receding from view, eclipsed by a bevy of conservative hopefuls. Lewis was alarmed enough to go out of his way to derail the Garner bandwagon, publicly flaying the Vice President as a "poker-playing, whisky drinking, evil old man who would destroy labor." Yet in the face of the President's retreat from domestic reform, Lewis could not abide the prospect of a third term. Meanwhile, Hillman continued to do the President's bidding. He doggedly pursued elusive peace negotiations with the AFL and reported his progress to Roosevelt on the President's private train shortly after the CIO convention.[51]

And so the two men seemed caught up in a deadly dance in which every step carried Hillman deeper into the smothering embrace of the administration while Lewis drifted inexorably into open opposition.

Late in 1939 Hillman confessed to his confidential secretary, Teccia Davidson, that he felt anxious if not despondent about his largely secret war with Lewis, about his more public confrontations with Dubinsky and the AFL, about disarray and civil strife within the Amalgamated family, and about nasty innuendoes making the rounds in Washington implying abuse of power. It was all, in a sense, the price of success. Hillman's stature in public life seemed to swell even as that of the New Deal diminished. Any doubt that he was fast becoming the country's preeminent "labor statesman" was officially put to rest when George Soule published a celebratory biography, aptly entitled *Sidney Hillman: Labor Statesmen*, full of dithyrambic praise for his "creative and democratic leadership." Like almost everything else then happening in Hillman's public life, Soule's ritual anointment was probably a carefully conceived political event, designed to burnish his reputation as Roosevent's confidant and adviser. Naturally enough, however, it irked Lewis and others jealous of Hillman's elevation. [52]

Sometimes his eminence was on public display. In Des Moines early in 1939, in a joint declaration with Agriculture Secretary Henry Wallace, he announced "a national conference of labor, agriculture, industry and government for the reconstruction of our economic life." In stately troupes he proffered the fraternal hand of labor in a great national crusade against the "special interests" and "great aggregates of capital." Des Moines typified Hillman's double life: Within the labor movement he naturally lived in Lewis's shadow; in the outside world, however, Hillman was more often than not the labor leader of choice. When Virgil Jordan, president of the National Industrial Conference Board, sought someone to address the members on how labor, management, and government might collaborate in the interest of prosperity and social stability, he turned to Hillman. When Governor Philip La Follette planned a series of radio talks during the 1938 campaign, he turned to Hillman for advice. When *Fortune* magazine organized a round table to examine the question "How Can America Put Its Unemployed Back To Work?" the editors invited Hillman to participate along with Paul Mazur of Lehman Brothers, Ralph Flanders, Nelson Rockefeller, and Wilkie Burgess of National City Bank. [53]

Hillman's stature and influence for the most part were displayed more privately and quietly, as was his custom. He shuttled back and forth between administrative agencies like the Wages and Hours Board and the executive quarters of Cohen, Corcoran, Perkins, and Ickes, passing judgment on policy and personnel. Power occasionally produced quite tangible rewards. In June 1938 the *New York Times* reported that the WPA had agreed to buy $10 million worth of ready-made clothing for distribution as relief. It was a bold stroke, concocted and executed by Hillman at a time when the volume of clothing manufacturing had dropped by one-third, leaving thousands in desperate straits. [54]

All these accolades, and the more material rewards that sometimes accompanied them, annoyed many people besides Lewis. Benjamin Stolberg, who in the 1920s could scarcely find enough good things to say about Hillman and the "new unionism," now expressed the less generous sentiments shared by many others in a spiteful piece in the *New York World-Telegram*. Hillman lacked David Dubinsky's "tough and homey democracy," Stolberg noted. His main fault, Stolberg concluded, was "his own self-overestimation." Hillman wasn't content to be just another trade union leader. Instead he fancied himself an "industrial statesman," but his reputation for "statesmanship" was part pure fraud, part public relations hyperbole. Rather, Hillman was a supplicant, seduced by FDR, who tickled his "Brains Trust proclivities, making him feel that he was a sort of Felix Frankfurter of labor."[55]

For many years Stolberg had functioned as a factotum for the New York world of Jewish trade union socialism, at various times its publicist, adviser, sympathetic critic, and journalistic ambassador. When he compared Hillman unfavorably to Dubinsky, Stolberg articulated those long-fermenting resentments that had periodically bubbled to and receded from the surface of public life ever since Hillman arrived in New York in 1913. What grated was Hillman's pragmatic independence; his expedient indifference to the ideological fixations of the SP, especially with respect to the Party's adamant anticommunism; and his studied aloofness when it came not just to Zionism but to nearly all forms of Jewish-centered politics. At bottom what they found most insupportable was the way he sedulously cultivated his own reputation among "outlanders" among the *goyish sheyne* of national power and intellect, apparently trying by force of will, and in the face of his own talmudic mien and the guttural Yiddishness of his English, to escape the "tough and homey democracy" from which he came. Fueling all the percolating unease at the time was an abiding suspicion of Hillman's "unnatural" ambitiousness. And then in 1938 Hillman did something that seemed to validate all the envy and mistrust. He announced his interest in running for the Senate.

Royal Copeland, Senator from New York, had died in office. It was the year of the purge. For the ALP, filling the vacancy therefore became an open invitation to take on the regular Democratic Party. Hillman floated the idea of a ticket to include Robert Wagner and either Lehman or McGoldrick for Governor (Lehman had talked openly about retiring, and some believed Roosevelt wanted Lehman out anyway because he had opposed the Court-packing plan), and to replace Copeland with either LaGuardia or himself. The brethren from Union Square were shocked and appalled. Abraham Cahan, Dubinsky, and the SP "Old Guard" reacted in fury. Indeed, they overreacted.

Did Hillman ever seriously entertain the idea of his own nomination? Or did he instead mean it as a signal to Tammany Hall that the ALP would not let itself be taken lightly in bargaining over the ticket? Early in July the ALP placed Hillman's name in nomination. Momentarily, perhaps, Hillman was taken with the idea. A few days later, however, the CIO vice president met with FDR and Jim Farley to discuss strategy for the New York elections. Both the President and his chief political adviser made clear that they still hoped Herbert Lehman could be persuaded to run for the seat vacated by Copeland. One hardly needed to point out to someone as savvy as Hillman his own disabilities as an immigrant Jewish radical and CIO leader. The predictable reaction of the AFL alone would have been enough to make him a drawback. His name was quickly withdrawn.[56]

Veteran political operatives like Cahan and Dubinsky were unlikely to have missed the point of Hillman's maneuvering, but it riled them nonetheless. Hillman had grown so audacious, so supremely confident of his own position within the pantheon of New Deal heroes and wise men, that he now displayed the chutzpah to put himself forward brazenly and without consulting the doyens of New York socialism. Almost immediately the ILG announced its opposition to Hillman's candidacy. Cahan blasted Hillman in the *New York Times,* waving the red flag of anticommunism: "In common with the majority of Jewish trade unionists, I feel that Mr. Hillman's attitude toward the Communist movement is objectionable and irresponsible." Consequently, Cahan concluded, Hillman's nomination would constitute a disaster for the ALP and would further aggravate the split between the CIO and the AFL. The *Forward's* sage aired all the ancient grudges, reminding *Times* readers that Hillman's trafficking with the devil went all the way back to the RAIC and his subsidizing of the *Freiheit.* Hillman's proven willingness to "play with the communists" was, for the elders of American social democracy, no mere venial but a truly mortal and unforgivable sin.

The Amalgamated's New York Joint Board responded instantly, labeling Cahan's attack criminal, comparing it to the reprehensible antics of William Randolph Hearst and sundry fascist demagogues. Alex Rose tried to defuse the situation by blaming it all on a naïve reporter from the *World-Telegram* who took too seriously Rose's own jocular reference to a Hillman senatorial candidacy. But, Rose then added, he and Dubinsky were subsequently shocked when Hillman seemed to take to the idea and even went so far as to claim that the White House and John D. Rockefeller, Jr., of all people, liked it as well. Once Hillman withdrew, other attempts were made to cauterize the wound. An editorial in the ILG's *Justice* denied that there was any serious rift over Hillman's candidacy. Dubinsky, however, did admit that he redoubled his efforts to get Lehman to run if only to stop Hillman.[57]

So far as Hillman and Dubinsky were concerned, this senatorial sensation served to inflame further an already raging series of jurisdictional border wars between the ACW and the ILG. Recession and unemployment, as they ate away at the core sectors of men's and women's garment production, made each side greedy to recoup losses by nibbling away at the edges of its rival's weak spots in manufacturing subsectors where gender divisions were not that obvious, bathrobes, for example. Once the ILG quit the CIO, the skirmishing escalated, especially since part of the reason SP-linked unions like the ILG returned to the AFL was their fear of growing CP influence within the CIO. Shops were raided and counterraided, elections contested, and pickets thrown up around rival union shops, and even around union headquarters. There was sporadic violence. By the end of 1939 Dubinsky was proclaiming the end of a twenty-five-year friendship with the ACW because of "unjustifiable and deliberate" invasions of his union's jurisdiction. He declared open warfare, but Hillman refused to rise to the bait and declined comment.[58]

In part his reticence came from the necessarily higher priority he placed on quelling discord within his own union. The historic national agreement entered into between the ACW and the industry in 1937, which seemed at the time the long-sought solution to the industry's endemic competitive chaos, proved vulnerable to the corrosive efforts of the "Roosevelt recession." Soon union apparatchiks in local markets began behaving like feudal potentates, cutting their own deals with hard-pressed manufacturers, luring work to their own cities by undercutting standards established by their union brothers elsewhere. Such dealmaking was both commercially treacherous and demoralizing, enough so that Hillman felt compelled to turn his attention away from his feud with Dubinsky.[59]

Some would argue that it was all symptomatic of a decline in the moral tone and the cultural aspirations of the union. By the end of the decade no one could fairly describe the Amalgamated or any significant portion of its membership as socialist. Many, both among the founding generation and among the "NRA babies," sought nothing more elevated than an expansion of the welfare state. Jewish socialism as a kind of religion of progress had always been both visionary and realistic. But always the practical was measured against the ideal and found wanting. As the Amalgamated matured, however, and was abetted by the gestation of the ALP, practicality tended to become the ultimate measure of things. The Depression reinforced primordial fears not only among uprooted peasant steelworkers in the Monongahela Valley but also among thousands of now upwardly mobile garment workers who could never forget the precariousness of life in the shtetl. The change was visible culturally; with its quantitative emphasis on numbers of new recreational facilities, choral groups, and sports teams, the "Report of the GEB on Cultural Activities" for 1939 was practically a parody of the union's cultural agenda for 1919. It was caustically dismissed by the veteran activist Hyman Isovitz as a meaningless assortment of "athletics, signing societies, and dramatic groups."

Isovitz was an unreconstructed anarchist and may have been driven by temperament to go too far. If the Amalgamated and the CIO were busily forging people fit for bureaucratic routine, they worked with human materials shaped for other times and purposes. "It was desirable," Jacob Potofsky ruminated in 1938,

> . . . to have cold-blooded social workers and bankers and we have them to a limited degree. With all due regard to their contributions, unless they fundamentally have an emotional feeling about the work they are engaged in, it is questionable from the labor point of view as to what contribution they can make . . . to give tone to a labor bank or housing venture they must have fundamental emotional feelings.[60]

Sidney Hillman would harbor such "fundamental emotional feelings" until he died, but retaining his privileged position among the powerful depended on suppressing them. He knew Lee Pressman was right when the CIO counsel warned that the CIO was becoming dangerously dependent on the NLRB to solve problems once confronted head-on on the industrial battlefield. Hostile actions by the courts, state legislatures, reactionary congressmen, and even "an indifferent Federal administration" spread gloom everywhere. The difference between Hillman and the rest of the CIO general staff, however, was that while people like Murray felt free to complain, Hillman more and more identified personally and politically with that "indifferent Federal administration." Soon the sobriquet "labor statesman" would take on a darker shade of meaning, and a question would arise as to whether in fact Hillman represented the needs of labor within the councils of national power or, on the contrary, the viewpoint of a self-aggrandizing state within the councils of the labor movement.[61]

SIXTEEN

∾

Wars, Foreign and Domestic

Phil Murray darkly warned the CIO Executive Board in 1939 that "we are living in a wave and an age of reaction." By the middle of 1940 Lee Pressman matter-of-factly reported to the same board: "Within the past few weeks we have had to shift our emphasis from attempting to obtain new legislation to bending all our efforts to defend the legislative protection which we now enjoy."[1]

Above all it was the war in Europe that put a period to the era of New Deal reform. Every *démarche* in foreign policy drawing the country closer to the brink of belligerence left the administration noticeably more dependent on the "Tories of industry" and less willing to support the aspirations of a militant labor movement. Lewis resisted, finally broke with Roosevelt in spectacular fashion during the 1940 presidential campaign, and lived out the war in truculent, embattled exile. But for Hillman the war became the occasion of his greatest personal triumph. Convinced that there were no other options for labor outside the precincts of the Democratic Party, he trusted the fate of the CIO to Roosevelt even though, or perhaps because, both the CIO and the New Deal had lost their forward momentum. For his loyalty he was rewarded with a presidential invitation to employ his labor statesmanship at the highest levels of government on behalf of national defense. This capstone of Hillman's career soon threatened to become his greatest liability, however, a disabling weakness that eroded his moral authority and prestige among his comrades in the labor movement and in the end left him clinging to life, the victim of a massive coronary brought on by the unbearable stress of his position.

441

For twenty-two months Hillman wrestled with the problem of representing labor within an exfoliating bureaucracy increasingly populated by interests determined to shut labor out. Much was at stake: not only the equity with which the war was conducted, but also who was to direct and for what purposes the vast new resources it called into being once the war itself was over. The royal road to power grew treacherous indeed: Was it better to live inside or outside the "iron cage"? Could Hillman master his new power or would he be mastered by it? Had he been anointed or cursed?

Two presidential conventions, one in Chicago, one in Atlantic City, preoccupied Hillman as the new year began. He was already fully committed to Roosevelt's reelection, but the cold war between the President of the United States and the president of the CIO turned every act of loyalty toward one into an act of betrayal to the other.

Hillman pressed ahead in his quest for "labor unity," a cause whose immediate purpose (as was obvious to everyone) had much more to do with the calculations for reelecting the President than with the hoary tenets of working-class solidarity. But it was a cause that lacked a constituency, and it left Hillman nearly alone in a no man's land waving a white flag.[2]

The deeper problem was not that Lewis felt personally slighted by the President but that he nurtured an abiding distrust of the administration. At the 1939 CIO convention Lewis delivered a veiled warning:

> Let no public representative or citizen underestimate the tremendous power and influence now being exercised by labor in the political realm of the nation, and let no politician assume that he can ignore LNPL, nor ignore the mandates and ideals and objectives of organized labor without being held to strict accountability in the inevitable day when elections come again.

Hillman huddled with Roosevelt and in an effort to soothe Lewis's nerves arranged for the two presidents to meet, but to no avail. Lewis followed up with praise for Burton Wheeler, hoping to liven up prospects for the Senator's dark horse candidacy. Early in the new year, at the UMW convention, Lewis raised the temperature of debate when he criticized the President, the Democratic Party, and the whole idea of a third term, predicting "ignominious defeat."[3]

Hillman addressed the convention the next day to endorse the President and then pressured state CIO councils in New York, New Jersey, and California to join him in decrying Lewis's impetuous outburst. He pleaded that the future of the CIO depended on the fate of the administration. Still, Hillman had to remain conciliatory, passing off the differences between himself and Lewis as "natural" in a "democratic" movement like the CIO, while at the same time emphasizing that in his view the loss of "liberties" to European dictators now loomed as a greater danger than domestic concerns like unemployment. When Lewis once again hinted he might retire, Hillman flattered the vainglorious miner with a resolution insisting that he was indispensable and his resignation unacceptable. A few months later Hillman busied himself selling the President on the idea of a national conference on expanded production as the best way to deflect Lewis's heated criticisms of the regime's failure to solve the unemployment crisis.[4]

Lewis was hard to mollify and only grew angrier as the Democratic Party convention approached, brooding in public about a third party. Rumors surfaced about a nascent alliance among Lewis, the American Youth Congress, the National Negro Congress, the Townsend movement, and other elements of popular disaffection. Increasingly the war supplanted older issues as the focus of his fury. He accused the regime of using the war emergency to renege on its pledge to the labor movement and of pursuing an interventionist foreign policy despite its pronouncements to the contrary. Meanwhile, as Lewis did all he could to deflate the third-term balloon, Hillman used the ACW convention in May as a staging ground for its reinflation. There, Ickes, Wagner, Lehman, and La Guardia sang the praises of the New Deal and before a spontaneously enthusiastic assembly of delegates demanded a third term for the President.[5]

The Amalgamated convention, staged in Madison Square Garden, became a love feast for the President. Pandemonium followed the call for his reelection. Delegates were reverential: "God has blessed America with Franklin Delano Roosevelt," Ida Warhof exulted. For others the President was "that great leader of humanity" or, in language redolent with an older, apocalyptic imagery, "that great humanitarian Messiah." It was less a working convention than a celebration of America as an island of liberty, well-being, and tolerance surrounded by the seas of fascism.

If Lewis and his followers had abundant reasons to be suspicious of the President, it is important to remember that those who supported him—and of course on election day that turned out to be a whopping 79 percent of the CIO vote—were not merely engaged in an act of political pragmatism but were committing an act of political faith, ready to attribute the same world-historic significance to the contest of 1940 that they once reserved for the "final conflict" between Labor and Capital.

Leo Krzycki promised a "spiritual revival" borne by "missionaries inspired to bring the light where there is darkness" and to drive out the "forces of greed, forces of selfishness, forces of untruth." An ACW pamphlet re-called the class antimonies of a faded era as it excoriated "the idle swanks, the other people's money changers, the sweatshop de luxe, the breeders of class hatred and bigotry" who "want Willkie." J. B. S. Hard-man described the ACW as "a regiment of the army of humanity engaged in a great war . . . for the human race being a free race."

The cosmology of socialism, with all its earthbound allegory about purity and sin, sacrifice, and greed, about freedom and slavery, was thus transposed and refurbished, because, as an *Advance* editorial bluntly as-serted, the election of Wendell Willkie "is an invitation to Hitlerism to entrench its bases in this country." Nor was this the stagy grandiloquence and bombast of a fawning leadership seeking official favor. The New Deal worked a remarkable transformation in the mental climate of millions of immigrant workers, nowhere more wondrously than among the Amal-gamated's Jewish rank and file. Their letters eloquently attributed their sense of economic well-being and security—their diminished fear of debt, of sickness, of homelessness, of unemployment, of vigilante and corpo-rate terror—to FDR, who "saved us all," who presided over a "dream come true." However much the strength of Hillman's attachment to the Roosevelt regime may be measured in units of self-promotion and polit-ical expediency, it also registered those deep sympathies that bound legions of industrial workers to the egalitarianism of the New Deal and to the charisma of its leader.[6]

The Lewis and Hillman factions mobilized furiously, anticipating an explosion at the next CIO convention in the fall. Naturally, Hillman could count on the delegates from the ACW and the TWUA as well as from the URW, where his influence remained intact from the days of the Akron strike. Bruising battles had to be waged elsewhere, however, against Lewis loyalists and his allies from the CP. With the signing of the Nazi–Soviet pact, Hillman instantly became *persona non grata* in the eyes of American Communists, an "agent of Wall Street," as the party-controlled District 65 paper labeled him, "the real fifth column in labor's ranks . . . the employers' representative in the CIO." Lewis's vast orga-nizational resources and moral stature, together with the party's disci-plined presence in a number of strategic unions, put Hillman and the administration at a distinct disadvantage, but Hillman was as experi-enced as anybody in the art of bare-knuckle factional brawling.[7]

The allegiance of the UAW was coveted by both sides, and Hillman quickly concluded an alliance with Reuther's Unity Caucus. Both Hill-man and Lewis attended the UAW convention. There the Hillman–

Reuther bloc engineered not only an endorsement of Roosevelt, against the strenuous objections of Mortimer and Lewis, but a ban on officers who maintained membership in "illegal organizations," a rhetorical victory even if of no practical significance. The recent debacle in France allowed Hillman to indulge the solecisms of social patriotism: "No worker can be loyal to his union, if he is disloyal to our country. No one can say that he is for labor if he is not ready to defend democracy to the uttermost." Elsewhere, in New York for example, where the Hillman and CP armies were at equal strength, the fighting was bloody. Potofsky and Hardman prepared months in advance for the state CIO convention, all the while devising roadblocks to the CP's plan to convene a New York City industrial union council, which they could not control. At the Rochester convention of the state CIO, Mike Quill of the Transport Workers Union (TWU) did his best to sabotage a pro-Roosevelt resolution introduced by Hillman. But Louis Hollander, a veteran of the factional wars of the 1920s, rammed it through. Abe Chatman, chairman of the credentials committee and an ACW apparatchik hand-picked by Hillman to deal with the left in Rochester, called for the expulsion of the National Maritime Union; the Newspaper Guild; the United Office and Professional Workers; the State, County, and Municipal Workers; and the Furriers. Quill claimed a majority and insisted that his own lieutenant, Austin Hogan, be made Secretary-Treasurer. Hillman responded by threatening to walk out. Quill backed down. Herbert Lehman spoke and was cheered by the right. When the CP left rejoined with boos for Roosevelt and Hillman, the police were summoned. In New York City, where the CP was quite powerful, Hillman simply kept the ACW out of the city CIO council, which was run by Quill and Joseph Curran of the Maritime Union. Similarly, in Wisconsin anti-Lewis locals from the UAW, the UE, and of course the Amalgamated refused to affiliate with the state CIO, creating a crisis for the state leadership.[8]

In many other state and city CIO bodies, however, Lewis's strength made even these sorts of messy victories impossible. Nasty quarrels and wild charges and innuendos about financial malfeasance and other skullduggery filled the air at CIO executive meetings. Moreover, the mineworkers' leader made sure that the LNPL, which otherwise would assuredly have become a vehicle for the President's renomination and election, stayed away from the campaign.[9]

Instead, administration insiders plotted with Hillman directly. After a visit from Tom Corcoran, Ben Cohen, and Hillman to discuss Hillman's efforts to convince FDR to run again, Harold Ickes confided to his diary that "Hillman is one of the ablest and straightest leaders in the whole country." To Cohen he made clear his appreciation of Hillman's strategic value: "This able Jew, who was not even born in the United States, may be in a position to snatch the New Deal chestnuts from the fire."[10]

Roosevelt operatives mainly needed Hillman to steer developments within the CIO. Gardner Jackson, a Frankfurter intimate and LNPL executive, wrote to the President in November about the delicate balance of power. Jackson's daily talks with Phil Murray revealed the importance of a public endorsement by the administration if Murray was to consolidate his position as Lewis's successor, if and when Lewis made good on his periodic hints about resigning. Both the Lewis and the Hillman factions were prepared to support Murray, Jackson predicted, but Murray desperately needed some assurances about his freedom of action, and nothing could be more reassuring than a friendly word from the White House. Jackson claimed to be speaking for Perkins, Wallace, and Francis Biddle as well as himself. Down in the trenches, in Ohio and Oregon, for example, Hillman ordered his armies to battle on behalf of the President. Monroe Sweetland, Executive Secretary of Oregon's Commonwealth Political Federation, complained to Hillman about how difficult it was to marshal Roosevelt support in the teeth of the hostility generated by Lewis and the "old guard" Democrats who favored Vice President Garner. Nonetheless, in Oregon the woodworkers', textile, and longshore unions vanquished the Harry Bridges faction. The CP was much stronger in Washington, however, and in California. From New Jersey, Carl Holderman reported to Hillman that the left was isolated and that the Roosevelt campaign benefited from the combined efforts of the URW, the UAW, and the shipbuilding and textile unions.[11]

On balance there was no doubt that the Lewis forces were in the ascendancy as the election approached. Even though the President remained personally popular, worry about the drift of the administration's foreign policy and anger about its accelerating retreat from domestic reform percolated through the ranks of the CIO. Despite accumulating evidence to the contrary, Hillman declared that "not only has the New Deal held fast to the gains of the first six years but . . . we have continued to move forward." He was bluffing and grasping at straws.

And then, on the eve of the election, Lewis, shocking millions, endorsed Wendell Willkie on national radio. In a fit of megalomania he gambled his otherwise impregnable position as the CIO's Caesar on the willingness of the rank and file to follow him down this political dead end. This was Lewis at his most vindictive and vainglorious. Roosevelt, he said, sought war to save his presidency. His reelection therefore would constitute a "national evil of the first magnitude" and might result in "a dictatorship in the land." "Sustain me or repudiate me," Lewis cried to the legions of the CIO. It was a stunning and disastrous piece of melodrama.[12]

Hillman was practically exultant. "John L. Lewis is through—this is really the end for him," he boasted to Ickes over lunch. Although he found Roosevelt and Hopkins depressed and scared when he visited the White House the day after Lewis's announcement, Hillman himself was, on the contrary, supremely confident. He immediately unleashed his lieutenants in the ACW and the TWUA, who now freely lambasted Lewis as a "new pal of Weir and Tom Girdler." Louis Hollander prophesied that Lewis would "go down in history as the Benedict Arnold of the American labor movement." Nearly all CIO unions repudiated, privately or publicly, the Willkie endorsement. Murray and Tom Kennedy, Lewis minions for years, quickly reaffirmed their support of Roosevelt. Gardner Jackson, also for years faithful to Lewis, was mortified and resigned from the LNPL.[13]

Once the election was won, the administration embroiled itself more directly, if surreptitiously, in the factional maneuvering leading up to the CIO convention, seeking to undermine Lewis permanently and further to transform industrial unionism into a mechanism of party and government policy. Hillman was a willing co-conspirator for any number of reasons, not the least of which was his acute sense that Roosevelt's victory was a dangerously soft one. Meeting with his own GEB just after the election, he stressed the alarming strength of the conservative bipartisan coalition in Congress and frankly admitted that the election "was in no sense of the word a Democratic Party victory," as analyses of state returns revealed mass desertions by the middle class. Despite the November victory, one could count on "the possibility of continued resistance on the part of Willkie, the economic royalists, and great industrialists." Atlantic City would not only decide Lewis's fate once and for all but would offer a chance to align CIO and administration policy at a most precarious moment. With much at stake, and in an atmosphere supercharged with intrigue and psychological intimidation, administration insiders prepared for the convention.[14]

Gardner Jackson telegraphed Roosevelt from Detroit: "The pressures brought to bear upon boys who supported you . . . are outside any code I live by or have before experienced except in Sacco and Vanzetti case." Lewis, once his idol, was now off the reservation. Jackson was convinced that Murray was best positioned to take over and keep the organization intact: "Attempted designation of Sidney for that function would only create wider dissension," as after all, Jackson maintained, many of Lewis's criticisms were correct. Here Jackson touched on what was sure to be Hillman's greatest liability at the convention, namely, his official complicity in the administration's defense program, since his appointment in June to the National Defense Advisory Commission, which many in the CIO, including Jackson himself, perceived as a real threat to labor's legitimate rights and interests. "Any sluffing off of our social and labor standards in the name of defense necessarily spells the beginning of totalitarian hell for our children and ourselves." After conferring with Henry Wallace, Jackson addressed this delicate issue again. The two men agreed, Jackson reported, that the biggest problem facing the administration's friends in the CIO, people like Murray and R. J. Thomas, in answering the "derisive taunts of J. L. and his communist-inspired supporters, "was the growing evidence that the administration was unwilling to make defense contractors—major corporations like Ford and International Shoe—obey federal labor laws. That was all bound to explode in the administration's face in Atlantic City unless the President could "do something immediate about Sidney and his associates like Lube [Isidore Lubin] and the Defense Commission" to defuse Lewis's criticisms of the Ford and other defense contracts.[15]

Whatever his reservations, Jackson, like Hillman, saw no realistic alternative, certainly not the absurd one opened up by Lewis. And so, in collaboration with others close to the White House, he circulated a semiconfidential "Plan of Action" around which it was hoped the Hillman–Roosevelt circles would coalesce. The "Plan" called for a more or less blanket endorsement of the administration's domestic and foreign policy, a resolution condemning communism designed to break up the Lewis–CP alliance, a repudiation of Lewis's Willkie démarche, and a conciliatory stance regarding unity with the AFL. Some gestures were offered in Lewis's direction, including a hint that labor would maintain its independence within the Democratic Party and outside it if necessary. On the question of defense mobilization, the program piously proposed the simultaneous expansion of military and civilian production and, more pointedly, called for an agency to oversee economic planning, price controls, the defense of labor's rights, and the inclusion of labor representatives on bodies charged with industrial conversion. In the arena of foreign policy, where fears of war gave Lewis great leverage, Jackson's "Plan" called for an emphasis on global economic cooperation rather than military preparation but defended aid to Britain and domestic rearmament while warning that the United States must "refrain from actual participation in war, and insist that the armed forces of this country must not be sent abroad to take part in battles beyond the seas." All in all, the "Plan" constituted a concerted effort to capture the organization for the President.[16]

Ill will hung like a shroud over the convention proceedings. Hyman

Blumberg and Murray Weinstein of the Amalgamated refused to serve on committees stacked with Lewis loyalists. Charges and countercharges of financial peculations fouled the air. From their position as a besieged minority, the Hillman group counterattacked, censoring the *CIO News*, edited by the CP sympathizer Len De Caux, for the bias of its coverage and accusing it of deliberately evading the issue of labor unity. To aggravate the relations between Lewis and his erstwhile communist allies, the Hillman faction authored a resolution condemning communism, Nazism, and fascism and calling for the expulsion of their fellow travelers. The "right" demanded new constitutional limits on the power of the CIO president and, in an attempt to embarrass Lewis's people further, an unqualified endorsement of administration policy. Lewis parried with a general antiwar resolution and succeeded in getting Joseph Curran, the communist president of the National Maritime Union (NMU), elected to a CIO vice presidency.[17]

At the height of the black festivities Lewis delivered a speech that caustically invited the Amalgamated group to leave the CIO. He vented his contempt for the leadership of the AFL and by extension those who, like Potofsky, demanded renewed talks to explore once again the prospects for labor peace: "[T]here is a limit to which the membership of my organization should permit me to waste my time and their money." The emotional fever of the delegates rose perceptibly as Lewis next excoriated the needle trades leadership for its faint-heartedness and hypocrisy. Dubinsky "has crept back into the AFL . . . And Zaritsky . . . He said, 'Me too.' And now above all the clamor comes the piercing wail and the laments of the ACW. And they say, 'Peace it is wonderful.' And there is no peace." Venomously and with undertones of anti-Semitism, he challenged the ACW delegates: "Dubinsky took the easy way. Zaritsky took the easy way. If there is anybody else in the CIO who wants to take the easy way, let them go on." Lewis's supporters burst into riotous applause, paraded around the convention hall, and used the occasion to demand once again that Lewis, despite his Willkie speech pledge to resign, be drafted into the CIO presidency.

Whether or not Lewis intended to arouse anti-Semitic sentiments is perhaps unknowable. Frances Perkins noted that "Lewis was very anti-Semitic," that his fury over Hillman's intimacy with the President led him to think that Hillman was "determined to be the big Jew in the labor movement." He explained: "There has to be a Jew, you know, everywhere in their idea." But even if Lewis harbored no such beliefs and never intended to arouse such passions in the delegates, it was inevitable under the circumstances that the Amalgamated people would react not only in anger but with real fear. Hillman certainly considered the tone if not the literal content of Lewis's remarks to be anti-Semitic. Lewis enjoyed a well-deserved reputation as a factional alley fighter. In this instance, Hillman believed, he was trying to isolate the unions opposed to him by labeling them "Jewish"-controlled; but the tactic may have backfired, Hillman later observed, as after the speech members of the "gentile" unions, like steel, auto, and plate glass, expressed their distaste for Lewis's innuendos.[18]

Hillman had deliberately stayed away from the convention so as not to present himself as a target for Lewis's obloquy. But the anti-Semitic rumblings and the "draft Lewis" hysteria provoked by the CIO president's speech panicked the Amalgamated delegates. Newsreel cameras stationed in the hotel lobby waited to record the rumored walkout by the ACW. Potofsky called Hillman in Washington to describe the emergency and urge his immediate intervention. Overnight Hillman rushed to Atlantic City with his daughter Philoine, and early the next morning, before the proceedings began, he surprised the assembled delegates by taking a seat on the dais, obviously prepared to speak. Although unscheduled, there was no way to deny him the floor.

Speaking extemporaneously, Hillman delivered the most sagacious if not the most eloquent oration of his life. He began bravely by defending his own behavior in the Washington defense bureaucracy. He had just informed Eugene Grace of Bethlehem Steel that the company must adhere to the labor policy of the NDAC, and he expected to be delivering the same message to Henry Ford. Then he gently warned the delegates that their own behavior was being closely scrutinized not only by their fellow workers but by citizens everywhere. He hoped therefore that the convention would "not indulge in the kinds of things that you will regret in the days to come." Briefly, he alluded to the nasty rumor-mongering of the day before: "[T]here has never been a suggestion of our organization leaving the CIO . . . There has been some wishful thinking outside, and maybe even inside the CIO." Again he turned to the great fear, which, like some restive volcano, filled the air with noxious fumes: What was the fate of labor to be in a global war that seemed to draw irresistibly closer? Acknowledging that the NDAC was open to much legitimate criticism, he pleaded with the delegates to be patient. In greater detail he recounted his own performance in the areas of job training and reemployment, in winning large appropriations for the NYA, in the adoption of a nondiscriminatory hiring policy, and in making the first inroads into the problem of housing for defense workers. He pledged renewed efforts to enforce the FLSA, Walsh–Healy, and the NLRA. Shifting focus once more, in statesmanlike tones, he denied that the issue between Lewis and

himself was personal. They were strategic and arose out of their conflicting assessments of what was at stake internationally. In France, Belgium, and Norway labor suffered under the heels of tyranny, and he
somberly cautioned his audience that it would be foolhardy to think it
couldn't happen in America. He lashed out at the calumnies against the
Amalgamated, an union whose self-sacrificing loyalty to the CIO was
beyond question. The real disloyalists lurked elsewhere, among "elements who cannot participate in the democratic process" because of their
outside loyalties—"whether their orders come from Rome, Berlin, or
Moscow, it is the same thing." Hillman's instinct for the jugular was as
finely honed as Lewis's. He reminded everyone that the UMW boasted
an anticommunist clause in its own constitution. But quickly he diluted
the venom of his remarks, recalling what a "great privilege" his association with Lewis had been. The speech became elegiac. Hillman regretted the public airing of their differences, which could only do harm.
Lewis was a mighty speaker, and "when I am in disagreement with him
I am scared of his effectiveness." Finally, as if paying his last respects to
a departed hero, Hillman reached the climax of his speech and the whole
point of his feverish nighttime train ride to Atlantic City: "I regret that
John L. Lewis will not be the leader of this organization," as he is a man
of incomparable courage; but bowing to the inevitable, "it is my considered judgment when John L. Lewis steps down there must be a demand
for Phillip Murray." Chants of "We want Murray" swept through the hall
as SWOC, ACW, and UAW delegates demonstrated their enthusiasm.
Hillman was done.[19]

Murray's election was assured. Hillman had deflated the "draft Lewis"
balloon. But it is doubtful there was much air in it to begin with. In all
other respects Hillman and the administration could consider the convention at best an unsatisfying stalemate. Although delighted with
Lewis's official dethronement, administration insiders privately acknowledged that he continued to operate from a position of strength. Clearly
Murray, Lewis's longtime lieutenant, remained his psychological vassal;
indeed, he embarrassingly admitted as much in his acceptance speech,
where in an overwrought public soliloquy with his own tormented ego he
insisted that "I know I am a man," thereby convincing many listeners
that Murray, at least, harbored some doubts on that score. Moreover,
Lewis's position promised to grow stronger and Hillman's weaker unless
the government managed a more robust response to labor's festering
grievances. Above all, the penumbra of the war in Europe darkened
domestic politics. An administration scout informed Eleanor Roosevelt
and Lauchlin Currie that the CIO would continue to stand against all

signs of actual military involvement while adamantly insisting on its protections under the law and its right to participate fully in the mobilization bureaucracy.[20]

Hillman and his Washington friends had exaggerated their own strength or, rather, had underestimated their single most glaring weakness. Hillman was vulnerable, acutely so, because of his official association with the administration's foreign policy and, in particular, with its program of domestic mobilization. With good reason the CIO was intensely suspicious that labor would be excluded from policy-making positions, placing in jeopardy those rights and standards recently achieved. Apart from his charisma, this was an abiding source of Lewis's appeal, and he was shrewd enough to make use of it even while astonishing the world with his endorsement of the utilities lawyer from Illinois:

> In the last three years labor has been given no representation in the Cabinet nor in the Administration or policy-making agencies of the government. The current administration has not sought nor seriously entertained the advice or views of labor upon the question of national employment or lesser questions affecting the domestic economy . . . Labor today has no point of contact with the Democratic Administration in power.

On the face of it, these words were outrageously inaccurate and no doubt were meant to be insulting. They were, after all, delivered five months after Sidney Hillman had been appointed as one of the five members of the NDAC, arguably the highest national policy-making position ever occupied by any labor leader, with the possible exception of William Wilson, President Wilson's Secretary of Labor. As Labor Commissioner, Hillman was charged with assuring an adequate supply of manpower to meet defense production objectives and enjoyed the authority to monitor labor standards and labor relations. In theory, at least, it was a post of enormous responsibility and sensitivity. And yet, however purposely unbalanced, Lewis's words salted an open wound.[21]

Never, throughout Hillman's tenure in Washington, first on the NDAC, later in 1941 as Associate Director of the Office of Production Management, and finally in 1942 as head of the Labor Division of the War Production Board, did any of these agencies use their considerable power over industrial priorities and the issuing of lucrative government contracts to enforce social policy, especially labor policy. Thus, at the CIO convention Hillman was vulnerable to the charge that notorious violators of the labor laws, of which Ford and International Shoe were only the most recent and notorious examples, continued to be rewarded with handsome government contracts. Not only did the contracts make Hillman unpopular, they made him seem irresponsible as well. Gardner Jackson incredulously remarked to the President that Isador Lubin admitted he and Hillman "have scarcely seen any of the contracts before they were signed, that they didn't know anything of the Ford contract until after it was announced."[22]

It is the underlying irony of this phase of his career that Hillman's actual power to determine the contours of public policy declined in inverse proportion to his official position and prestige. Roosevelt had invited him to become part of a government of national unity, bipartisan in composition, in theory deaf to the pleadings of special interests. In reality, the agencies of economic mobilization were honeycombed by such interests, and as the defense crisis evolved the voices of the corporate old guard drowned out all other contending parties. The war turned out to be the gravedigger of domestic economic and social reform; indeed, it revivified efforts to undo the New Deal and the advances of organized labor. Even to the degree that he tried conscientiously to prevent that from happening, Hillman's task was ever more hopeless. He was caught between his commitment to Roosevelt and the "national interest" on the one side and his anxiety over the mounting attacks on labor and the "Keynesian" welfare state on the other. Criticized by the leadership of both the AFL and the CIO, undermined by fellow bureaucrats in the defense apparatus and the Department of Labor, sabotaged by Army and Navy directives running counter to ostensible government labor policy, targeted by businessmen out to garner unconscionable profits, besieged by strikes on the part of a resentful rank and file, and vilified by congressional reactionaries seeking to cripple labor legislatively, Hillman found himself increasingly isolated and politically paralyzed.

No one in the labor movement, not even John L. Lewis or William Green, was notified beforehand of Hillman's appointment to the NDAC in late May. Although neither said so publicly at the time, both objected. Lewis no longer trusted Hillman; Green never had. Lewis was incensed. The senior labor federation meanwhile let it be known that it considered Hillman unqualified for the post. In fact, when Green visited the White House to complain, he reminded the President of Hillman's suspect dealings with the Bolsheviks during the 1920s. According to Ickes, Roosevelt replied that had his health permitted he would have been in Russia too.

Opposition was not confined to the ranks of the professionally jealous. Secretary Perkins protested Hillman's appointment as labor's sole representative, questioning his qualifications as the president of a relatively small union in a light industry and arguing that it would anger the

AFL. She would spend many sleepless nights worrying about Hillman's overweening ambition, his maneuvering to become a kind of labor czar in the interests of which she believed him cynically prepared to mouth patriotic platitudes. On the other side of the aisle, Wall Street was not much happier; its pronouncements carried haughty implications that only captains of industry were competent to carry on the work of defense mobilization. Congressional revanchists were unsparingly malicious. Representative Eugene Cox of Georgia observed that Roosevelt had entrusted the training of the nation's workers to "Reds." He told the House that "the organization of the youth of the country under Sidney Hillman means Communism in the years to come. He is more dangerous than Earl Browder and a thousand times more dangerous than 10,000 Harry Bridges."[23]

Yet at first the landscape hardly seemed so bleak. Hillman felt supremely flattered by the appointment, although only his closest friends and relatives were allowed to know that. While critics carped in private or out loud, Elliot Janeway, for one, called the appointment a particularly shrewd instance of Roosevelt's celebrated talent for symbolic politics. The President risked nothing, Janeway said, by which he meant that more than anyone else Hillman seemed most disposed, by virtue of his past associations and ideological inclinations, to adopt a global definition of labor's interests, ready to conflate them with the more abstract purposes of the nation. Harold Ickes agreed and voiced an optimism about Hillman's appointment shared by the dwindling coterie of New Dealers. He found Hillman "quiet, serene, optimistic, and yet forceful. He has worked with Stettinius and Knudsen and he does not regard either of them as strongmen." Ickes recorded in his diary his hope and conviction that "Hillman will be willing to help us all that he can to hold back the economic royalists and he is confident that we will be able to hold all the labor gains that have been made during the last seven years."[24]

At first Hillman seemed to accomplish a good deal despite his rather uncongenial surroundings. The NDAC was composed principally of industrialists like Edward Stettinius of USS and William Knudsen of GM (who could afford to "live" on their dollar-a-year government salary, while Hillman had no choice but to depend on his $12,500 a year from the Amalgamated). They were aided and abetted by representatives of the Army and Navy (themselves with extensive connections to business, corporate law, and Wall Street investment bankers), who, while not necessarily hostile to labor, felt the wisest way to produce for the national defense was to provide business with as many incentives and with as few obstacles as possible. Among the Commission members, only Leon

Henderson was committed to both "Keynesian" economic policies and the New Deal's social welfare agenda.[25]

Labor laws protecting standards of hours, wages, and the right to organize, as well as union contracts with their plethora of work rules and other constraints on the uninhibited use of labor, were exactly the sorts of "obstacles" many on the NDAC were eager to live without. For many months government contracts had been issued with little if any attention paid to whether the corporate beneficiaries were in compliance with the nation's labor laws. Many, in fact, were not, as for example Ford and Bethlehem Steel. Hillman immediately turned his attention to the problem, arguing that the NDAC required an explicit labor policy of its own, one that would make clear that the government would not allow the foreign threat to democracy to be used as an excuse to defeat democracy at home.

It all seemed rather elementary and unobjectionable—in effect, it was asking the business community not to break the law. Yet it provoked an extended battle within the NDAC.

The political arithmetic of national defense had already registered a fundamental change. The war opened wide the portals of power to the whole phalanx of infrastructural and heavy industrial interests, along with their fiduciary associates, providing them the instruments with which to abort the gestation of "Keynesian" social democratic alternatives. Industrial mobilization was to be conducted as a joint enterprise between business and government, a government denuded of extraneous and disturbing social influences, mainly represented by a pliable military and with labor consigned to the margins of public policy debate.[26]

The strange struggle to persuade the government to enforce its own laws confirmed this shifting political ecology. Shortly after Hillman's appointment, Phil Murray wrote to complain about Bethlehem Steel, notorious for its profiteering and flagrant disdain for the labor law. The company was guilty of violating the Walsh–Healey Act requiring that it pay prevailing regional rates on government work; moreover, for some time it had conspicuously disregarded the NLRB's ruling that it disband its company union. Lewis importuned Hillman to declare open season on these corporate delinquents, but oddly Hillman refused to do so, even though at that very moment he was waging precisely the same fight inside the Commission.[27]

Day after day in Commission meetings he registered his complaints and criticisms: He wasn't being consulted on war plant construction and as a consequence was deluged with protests from the building trade unions; he was denied an opportunity to inspect the labor provisions of new contracts; the Army and Navy were simply not cooperative in enforcing national labor policy—putting to one side for a moment the vexed question of just what national labor policy was.

For the next twenty-two months this became Hillman's special dilemma: whether to risk an "embarrassing public break with his presidential benefactor, or instead to persist in the interminable skirmishes of bureaucratic guerrilla warfare. Hillman decided to persist, but wrestling the Commission into adopting a coherent labor policy proved exhausting and ultimately rather pointless.[28]

The military was represented by two Wall Street warriors, Assistant Secretary of War Robert Patterson and Secretary of the Navy Frank Knox. Both bristled at Hillman's suggestion that contracts ought to be distributed only to those who obeyed the law and in accordance with the shortages and surpluses of the labor market, public transportation, housing, raw materials, and so on. Such a policy threatened to disrupt relations with those favored large firms with which the military was accustomed to dealing. Industrialists on the Commission concurred. Knudsen's aide, John Biggers of Libby-Owens-Ford, and his counsel, Fred Eaton, a Wall Street lawyer with ties to Morgan and General Motors, along with another Wall Street lawyer, Blackwell Smith, organized the resistance. But initially, thanks to Roosevelt's support, to Lewis's ceaseless complaining, and to the increasingly likely prospect of major labor unrest, Hillman won. In September the NDAC announced a clear policy, first drafted by Hillman, Henderson, and Stettinius with the help of Lubin and Donald Nelson, essentially in line with Hillman's main objectives. Contracts were not to be awarded to companies currently in violation of labor laws; new plant sites were to be selected in part to reduce local and regional unemployment, and subcontracting was to be encouraged to create job opportunities and to utilize local labor pools. All reasonable efforts were to be made to keep the work week at forty hours, to pay time and half for overtime and Saturday, Sunday, and holiday work, and to provide adequate housing and health care for defense workers.[29]

Hillman was pleased. In a carefully rehearsed radio interview with Drew Pearson he boasted of his harmonious relations with the Commission's industrialists. He noted with pleasure that while labor legislation remained intact, the Labor Division had deftly headed off trouble in the copper, aircraft, and shipbuilding industries.[30]

As a practical matter, however, policy statements like these were quickly forgotten, unless those responsible for implementing their commands were prodded into remembering. The Quartermaster Corps, for example, again and again refused to abide by prevailing pay and overtime rules. It was not alone; other departments, like the Corps of Engineers and Ordnance did their best to vacillate, undermine, and evade. A Navy captain named Fisher flatly told Isidor Lubin in regard to substandard employment conditions in Jacksonville and Corpus Christi that the Navy would not use its negotiating leverage to win social improvements. NLRB findings of unfair labor practices were ignored until the combined pressures of Hillman on the inside and Lewis on the outside produced a ruling by Attorney General Robert Jackson that such findings were binding on government contractors. Again Hillman thought he had won. He announced to the press early in October that "Army and Navy contracts will no longer be given to companies violating federal labor laws." But the legal cabal from Wall Street—Eaton, Biggers, and Smith—were masters of bureaucratic obstruction and litigious delay. Hillman's statement was attacked by the businessmen on the Commission—Knudsen rallied a group of executives by telling them, "We don't want any part of that Russian system over here"—and by Representative Howard Smith at hearings where Navy Secretary Patterson trivialized the Commission's labor policy and asserted the freedom of the armed services to deal with whomever they pleased. The Attorney General quickly backed away from his own ruling. Finally, under intense pressure from the White House to bury the whole issue until after the election, Hillman beat a pathetic retreat, denying it was anybody's intention to withhold defense contracts from labor law violators. Knudsen immediately proceeded to negotiate a new contract with Ford despite a litany of NLRB complaints.[31]

As Hillman's pained pledge at the CIO convention revealed, little changed even after the election. The Army violated its own directives and awarded another contract to Ford, whose contempt for both organized labor and the NLRA were legendary. Gardner Jackson told Roosevelt, "the time has come for Sydney [sic] and him [meaning Lubin] to conduct an open campaign against sabotage in the Army and Navy on these problems." The President helped a bit with a memo to the Commission expressing his concern about the Ford and other contracts. Secretary of War Henry Stimson tried to work out a compromise, with Felix Frankfurter functioning as a private intermediary between Hillman and the brass hats. But with the elections over and Lewis on the warpath, the UMW president, together with the NMU, called on Hillman to resign his CIO vice presidency. In response Hillman toughened his stance against the latest $2 million award to Ford. He let the Commission know he was "disturbed by the lack of appreciation of this Commission for the seriousness of the labor problem." Finally, early in the new year, the War Department, conceding the issue, negotiated a $10 million contract with Chrysler rather than Ford, despite Ford's lower bid. In the future, Patterson announced, department contracts would contain a clause specifying compliance with the nation's labor laws.[32]

It was a gray and dolorous affair, this bureaucratic trench warfare, fought with rapier-like memos and lawyerly circumlocutions, where victory and defeat were measured in codicils and commas won and lost, dragging on irresolutely for months until petering out in uncertain stalemate. Certainly it augured poorly for Hillman's future. No matter how finely honed his bureaucratic dexterity, in the context of American politics the task of labor statesmanship was bound to be thankless. A labor movement nearing the apex of its industrial strength remained nonetheless politically frail and internally fractious. To be a "labor statesman" in those unpromising circumstances, without a source of reliable and independent political support, was proving far worse than being a minister without portfolio. It meant that Hillman served on the suffrance of other corporate, bureaucratic, and congressional elements who were determined to treat organized labor as a political pariah.

The war between Hillman and his host of enemies took place on many fronts. It raged most bitterly over the question of strikes, both those authorized by the trade union leadership and those that erupted more spontaneously, sometimes against the express wishes of the leadership.

That was not much of a problem through most of 1940, but it became more and more serious as growing labor shortages, together with inflation and war profiteering, raised the odds in favor of striking and multiplied the reasons for doing do. There was no more basic service Roosevelt expected of Hillman than to prevent or at least drastically reduce the actual interruption of production by strikes. Consequently, Hillman established an elaborate mediation machinery, judiciously staffed by representatives from both the CIO and the AFL, which did manage to forestall and settle many would-be strikes. It was in these instances that Hillman was able to practice successfully those arts of mediation and creative administration mastered over a lifetime. But once strikes were under way, his diplomatic magic seemed less potent.

Hillman was trapped in a maddening paradox. His power derived not from the tangible and intangible resources of a minatory movement but, on the contrary, rested ultimately on presidential confidence in his ability to police and pacify the restive. All through his years at the head of the Amalgamated and the CIO, Hillman's most notable victories were anchored in the irreducible realities of open social struggle. Now he had allowed himself to float free of those moorings, to depend for his survival on the thin atmosphere of official favor and bureaucratic intrigue. A deadly social logic unfolded. As workers displayed less and less willingness to engage in acts of grossly unequal sacrifice, Hillman became more and more strident and scolding, thereby cutting away at his diminishing credibility as a partisan of the disadvantaged and as a trustworthy architect of national concord.

As the war economy heated up, simmering discontent was visible everywhere. Worker morale deteriorated steadily in the face of overwork, speedups, and racial discrimination, while resentment accumulated over war profiteering and the gingerly way American business approached conversion to defense production so as not to endanger its civilian markets. At the same time tightening labor markets naturally acted to relax labor discipline and left prevailing incentive pay schemes suddenly less appealing. A crisis of authority and productivity loomed. An influx of younger, inexperienced workers aggravated the volatility of labor relations even in places as staid as the IAM local at Boeing, where older cadre lost control long enough for a strike to erupt in the fall of 1940.[33]

Even before the strike situation became truly critical, Hillman was racked with anxiety. Isador Lubin remembered about his boss: "Every time there was a threat of a strike or a strike took place, the heavens were going to fall." Hillman at first achieved some promising results in dampening incipient insurgencies. While Perkins jealously reproached him for "poaching," Hillman immediately established an informal, and subsequently a formalized, Labor Relations branch that managed to avert all but two of 241 potential defense strikes in 1940, some of them at vital installations. Every settlement was reportedly "a matter of jubilation to Sidney Hillman and his colleagues." Hillman was in his element, racing from hot spot to hot spot, exerting pressure backstage, exuding his own exotic charm, and parading the prestige of his office.[34]

Every sign of labor militance, however, struck the War Department as a form of intolerable insubordination. Mediation was hardly the favored military remedy. The War Department pressed for tougher measures, including at times direct military intervention, as for example at the Boeing facilities in Seattle, where the IAM locked horns with the UAW. Hoping to inveigle the brass hats in an unfamiliar world of talk and countertalk, Hillman invited a War Department representative to join the mediation process. That turned out to be a mistake, because it merely opened the door to more direct and unilateral action in a field for which the military had no talent. During a twelve-day UAW walkout at the Vultee Aircraft Corporation in November, the Army pushed unsuccessfully for compulsory arbitration and privately let it be known that "Hillman is a sissy on this one." The Attorney General declared the strike communist-inspired. Indeed, the "red" question increasingly served as a lightning rod attracting all the atmospherics associated with labor-baiting. Even in the fall of 1940, when there were scarcely enough strikes to fuel this hysteria, J. Edgar Hoover of the FBI was supplying Stettinius (who in turn conveyed them to Hillman) with reports on alleged CP responsibility for slowdowns at Bendix's aircraft division, at Consolidated Aircraft in San Diego, at Diesel Engineering in Detroit, and elsewhere. Increasingly, personnel at the Labor Relations branch expended their energies in subterranean bureaucratic civil wars, frantically trying to curb and derail the provocations of the War Department.[35]

Venomous internal rivalries, however, undercut these efforts at organizational hygiene. Adolph Germer wrote a warning to Hillman from the Pacific Northwest: "I need not tell you that the AFL bigwigs out here are particularly vicious. They are under the domination of the notorious Dave Beck, and I know I need not tell you that he will pull every string to submerge any and all CIO recognition." Meanwhile, Hillman was fending off accusations by Lewis that he had deliberately kept a UE representative off the Labor Relations committee. According to the UE's James Matles, Hillman told him the union was "tinged with red" and that it wasn't his, meaning Hillman's, fault that the UE "doesn't find it advisable to square ourselves politically."[36]

In those uncertain months of war scares and defense preparations, the tempo of labor unrest remained stately enough for Hillman to maneuver past the shoals of political and institutional rivalry. But everything changed in 1941, when there were more strikes than in any other year in American history except 1919 and 1937.[37]

Oddly enough, Hillman's predicament grew both better and worse in 1941. He was elevated to the highest government position he was ever to hold as Associate Director of the Office of Production Management (OPM), which replaced the NDAC in December 1940. He discovered, however, that his actual capacity to control labor unrest was substantially reduced. By the middle of the year, faced with strikes in shipyards, repair shops, aircraft plants, lumber yards, and elsewhere, Hillman was practically beside himself. He declared that "these strikes reflect adversely upon the integrity and patriotism of the American labor movement" and that he "unqualifiedly condemn and denounce the foregoing strikes."[38]

As was typical of Roosevelt's highly political approach to matters of administration, ultimate authority at the OPM was deliberately divided between Hillman and the director, William Knudsen. Hillman seemed to have the chief responsibility when it came to matters affecting labor, but Knudsen seemed to have the last word in running the agency. Although the two men got on remarkably well under the circumstances, Hillman was constantly treading an invisible line separating the outer limits of his own authority from the prerogatives of power that in effect emanated from Knudsen and finally from the President. Time and again he chose to defer to these higher authorities, a decision that diminished his stature in the eyes of both the labor movement and the intrigue-ridden hierarchy of the defense apparatus.

To be sure, Hillman and Knudsen did not represent the magnetic North and South of American politics, and over the next year they would work more in tandem than at odds. Still, Roosevelt had managed to freeze in institutional limbo a relationship of dual power destined to dissolve in the heat of class conflict. The great strikes of 1941 challenged the very presumption of a coherent national interest, calling into question Hillman's bureaucratic raison d'être as an engineer of social conciliation.[39]

A storm of strikes, cresting in June, swept across the country. Some were defensive attempts to ward off the stresses of accelerated output. Others expressed a new institutional boldness as trade unions launched organizing drives in once impregnable places like Ford. A sizable number were all but deliberately provoked by the obdurate resistance of managements still in thrall to fantasies of omnipotence. Homely workmen's hatreds were conflated with global confrontations. Thus the announcement scrawled across a blackboard in a conference room at the ALCOA plant in Cleveland:

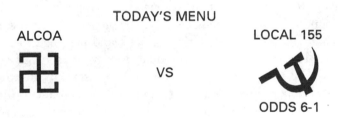

TODAY'S MENU

ALCOA   LOCAL 155

VS

ODDS 6-1

Strikes during the first half of 1941 affected the production of destroyers, cruisers, turbines for power plants, machine tools, gun mounts, tanks, ammunition, explosives, bombs, boats, boilers, machine guns, airplane engines, propellers, motors, and magnets—nearly all the paraphernalia of combat. The defense economy was a precisely reticulated, interconnected network, where severing even a minor link in the chain could have enormous repercussions. A strike of one thousand at Universal Cyclops stopped the delivery of a small amount of specialty steel, which in turn prevented the Stewart–Wagner Company from manufacturing one-third of the Army's total fuse program. A walkout by 2,800 at American Car and Foundry cut off the Army's whole supply of light tanks. A jurisdictional strike at Wright Airfield by 190 men interrupted the construction of the nerve center for testing items of strategic importance to the Air Corps, including a wind tunnel, an aircraft radio lab, and a dynamometer building.[40]

Dire predictions of national calamity and defeat filled the air, mostly disingenuous outpourings designed to poison the atmosphere against any continued role for organized labor in the higher councils of national defense. Representative Hatton Summers, chairman of the Judiciary Committee, was typical in the intemperate violence of his reaction, declaring that he "would not hesitate one split second to enact legislation to send [strikers] to the electric chair" if necessary. War Department personnel, spying an opportunity, huddled with congressional promoters of antistrike legislation. As emotions boiled over, twelve different labor-restraining bills competed for attention in the Congress. Most proposed statutory cooling-off periods of varying lengths; some would authorize the President to seize struck plants. The most comprehensive, the Smith bill, which was not enacted until 1943, outlawed strikes for the closed shop and deprived violators, who struck illegally or engaged in boycotts or jurisdictional strikes, of the protections afforded by the Wagner and Norris–La Guardia acts, protections they would also forfeit if a union officer held joint membership in the CP, the Bund, or the Young Communist League.[41]

Hillman, along with the CIO, lobbied tirelessly against all such legislative intervention. He pointed out to its myopic sponsors that such bills were more likely to encourage strikes by providing formal and highly visible channels for the registering of rank-and-file anger; at the very least, official coercion of this sort would destroy the spirit of voluntary cooperation he was working so assiduously to foster. In an appearance before the Truman Special Committee on Defense Production in April, Hillman was subjected to a round robin assault by Senators Carl Hatch, Owen Brewster, and Tom Connally, who indicted the OPM for its failure to do anything about the coal strike, about strikes in general, and especially about the nefarious doings of communists in defense plants. Privately, Hillman told the President that pending legislation would do nothing to address the really "troublesome situation of a wildcat, outlaw, or subversive in nature" and advised him that the President should not usurp injunctive powers and that compulsory cooling-off periods would have the effect of bringing on strikes earlier than they might otherwise occur. Meanwhile, Hillman prepared a fallback position. He had his chief aides draft milder legislation, calling for various forms of mediation and presidential intervention only in dire emergencies. He managed also at least to bury the egregious ideas cooked up in the War Department to amend the Sabotage Act of 1918 so as to make slowdowns a criminally subversive offense.[42]

As best he could, Hillman tried to keep his left flank covered as well by hurling rhetorical missiles at the fraying veil of national amity: "When large profits are reported in the press, labor justly feels it is entitled to some fair share of them. When labor is denied various rights guaranteed to it by law, labor cannot be expected to sit by without protest . . . no one can reasonably assume that these stoppages are entirely the fault of labor."[43]

But his enemies persisted, together blaming Hillman for underestimating and understating the crisis. All of these pressures prodded the President into creating the National Defense Mediation Board (NDMB), a tripartite agency of labor, management, and public representatives. Both the AFL and the CIO considered it a bad idea and a threat to the integrity of the collective bargaining process. It was also bound to drain away some of Hillman's own authority as the nation's supreme conciliator. Yet he loyally supported its creation and even compromised his own stature by getting involved in the Board's most hapless undertakings. During the "captive mine strike" of 1941, for example, he became so embroiled in the jurisdictional argument over what constituted a union shop, so sure he could search out some subtle, heretofore imperceptible third way to settle the strike, that he failed to see clearly how truly unassailable Lewis's position was.[44]

There were certainly those who appreciated Hillman's self-sacrificing fealty. Stimson confided to his diary, in words that also revealed his inbred condescension, that "Hillman is a pretty good little fellow and pretty fair and I think on the whole it is wise to give him a chance." When Hillman succeeded in getting Navy Secretary Knox to persuade Grace of Bethlehem Steel to bargain in good faith with the USW in return for a promise of union cooperation, Stimson expressed both his pleasure and the reigning conceit of a patrician elite: "Hillman is showing up very well in these matters. He is conservative and keeps his eye on the ball of the national interest." What Stimson perhaps sensed, and Hillman undoubtedly knew, was that unions like the USW were increasingly appreciative of the security of institutional routine as against the less predictable forms of rank-and-file activism. *In extremis*, Hillman's high regard for institutional stability could also be shared even by those managerial and military circles ordinarily insensitive to the exhausting stresses of war work.[45]

But such forbearance was rare and growing rarer as the strike wave surged. Knudsen became irritable: "I must admit the attitude of labor is at last getting my goat. I was one of those who felt after the first flurry labor would get down to business; but I believe now there is something more sinister than mere labor trouble behind some of these strikes." Like Stimson, Knudsen was prepared to scapegoat somebody if all else failed, especially when there were enough "goats" visible within the field of fire to lend this kind of avoidance reaction the odor of reality. And it was especially in those instances that Hillman's statesmanship became most problematical.

Assistant Secretary of War Patterson, for example, received alarmist communications about the crisis at Great Lakes Steel, where, his subordinate reported, the situation "can only be described as one of anarchy." Hillman and USW leaders looked on helplessly in the face of a seemingly endless series of wildcats. Patterson fired off a tart letter to Hillman lodging his agitated complaint. A similar strike at Mack Truck, the sole source of transmissions for medium-size tanks, provoked a peremptory demand from Patterson that Hillman settle the business immediately.[46]

Turmoil at the Allis-Chalmers plant in Milwaukee became a national scandal. UAW local 248 and the Allis-Chalmers president, Max Babb, were at loggerheads. Babb was driven to distraction by the presumptions of his workforce. Local 248 was not only run by a CP member, Harold Christoffel, its local president, but was aflame with the grievances and the wounded dignity of its skilled metalworkers, men with syndicalist inclinations and a great fear that the shift from specialized batch production to standardized mass production, in part occasioned by defense contracts, would undermine their status and security. In this instance, there was no question that Allis's output was vital. The company's $45 million in defense contracts included the manufacture of turbine generators and electrical equipment, which in turn governed work in thirty other plants. Indirectly it affected one-third of all government defense contracts, including Du Pont's munitions facilities, Bendix Aviation, and the production of twenty-five destroyers.

Hillman brought Babb and Christoffel to Washington, where he got them to agree, or so he thought, that from then on all members of the UAW would remain so for the lifetime of the contract—a desire that would later be called a "maintenance of membership" clause. But when he returned home, Babb declared he would have nothing to do with the "closed shop," while Christoffel intimated that was exactly what they had shaken hands on, all of which had nothing to do with what Hillman had proposed. And so the strike continued.[47]

It was a stunning repudiation from which Hillman fled in exhaustion to Florida. Caught between two obdurate opponents, he could find no way to finesse their differences. Taking advantage of his embarrassment,

Knudsen and Knox then ordered the strikers back to work and urged Roosevelt to seize the plant, without discussing it with Hillman or even notifying him in advance. That infuriated local 248, as well as Murray and R. J. Thomas, and provoked a three-day riot requiring the state militia to quell. Hillman was deluged with demands that he honor the maintenance of membership agreement from CIO unions in and outside of Wisconsin. Stimson gratuitously roiled the waters by telling the President that the "strike does not seem to be a legitimate controversy between labor and capital but a deliberate attempt by a communistic leader with a notorious record to foment disturbances." The President ultimately turned over the mess to the NDMB, which took seventy-six days to resolve it. The stain on Hillman's reputation as a facilitator of labor peace was permanent. [48]

A wildcat strike of UAW workers at the North American Aviation Company in Inglewood, California, in June proved even more damaging. The California aircraft industry, part of the massive reconfiguration of the national economy, with defense and defense-related production at its core, compacted together a set of bedeviling problems. The rush to turn out fighting planes upset the labor market, generating acute shortages, the pirating of skilled cadre by rival manufacturers, black market wages, and a chaotic shattering of customary job hierarchies. Young workers, often unfamiliar with cities, factories, and trade unions but made militant by the deranged circumstances of the job market, streamed into the centers of aircraft production and further unsettled a sensitive situation that the government was determined to stabilize.

The half-year preceding the explosion at Inglewood was filled with threats of strikes and actual "quickie" strikes up and down the West Coast at Vultee in Los Angeles, Ryan Aeronautical in San Diego, and elsewhere as old-timers and new recruits protested pay rates, exhausting overtime, and punishing shift schedules. Manufacturers squabbled among themselves, defeating Hillman's diligent efforts to get them to cooperate and standardize their labor policies. On top of that, the UAW local at North American was particularly unstable. During the faction fight with Homer Martin, the local sided with Martin. Later on the CIO just barely beat out the IAM in a representation election.

Wyndham Mortimer, a veteran of Flint and the CP, ran the UAW's organizing drive on the West Coast at a time when the party was least inclined to defer to the "national interest." Thus no one was genuinely surprised when an outlaw strike shut down North American Aviation. [49]

Hillman found himself in a no-win predicament. Constrained by his official responsibilities, he reluctantly sided with a decision by Roosevelt and Knudsen to send in troops to break the strike. For this he was roundly condemned by the CIO despite the fact that he had struggled for weeks to avoid precisely this military solution, and despite the fact that the strike itself was disavowed by the national leadership of the UAW and the CIO. Lewis used the occasion to convene a session of 250 CIO leaders in Washington to condemn Hillman and the President for their resort to force.[50]

An atmosphere of hysterical overreaction enveloped the strike. Everybody was irate about the CP and radicals generally. Hillman had become increasingly exercised since Allis-Chalmers. Knox sent him intelligence about an alleged NMU–CP undercover movement to foment a seaman's strike on all coasts, especially in New York, Baltimore, Boston, San Francisco, and New Orleans. Maxwell Brandwen documented the party's surreptitious attempts to undermine the umpire system at GM. Forrestal informed Knudsen about an alleged Socialist Workers' Party (SWP) plan to strike several sensitive Minneapolis manufacturers, including Honeywell, and Knudsen in turn asked Hillman to investigate. The investigation revealed, as in so many of these cases, the hollowness of the rumor. The air was thick with outlandish accusations. Hillman received wild communications pretending to uncover covert CP plans to take over key industries should the Congress pass antisubversive legislation. From the other shore, Gerald L. K. Smith circulated a petition at Ford's River Rouge plant stigmatizing Hillman as an ally of the CP and the Soviet Union and as a fast friend of Lenin, demanding the President fire him. For all these reasons, by the time Mortimer marshaled his troops Hillman had run out of patience. Not only did he accuse North American local 683 of doing "immediate and irreparable damage," but he used the occasion to curse others guilty of criminal disloyalty, including the International Woodworkers of America, whose leadership persisted in striking "unjustifiably" and issuing "violently false and inflammatory attacks upon the National Government."[51]

Right after the North American events, Hillman searched doggedly for ways to purge Communist Party members from defense industries. He recommended that Roosevelt create a board to investigate subversives. The President went so far as to have Attorney General Francis Biddle pursue the suggestion, but Biddle candidly observed that Hillman was indifferent as to the methods used and cared only about solving a problem "he considers pressing." Murray, however, preferred quieter internal purgations and the counterintelligence operations of the ACTU, which avoided provocative government intrusions into CIO affairs. His opposition to Hillman's suggestion left the plan stillborn.[52]

Once the decision was taken to send in the Army, unanimity evaporated within the ranks of the CIO. Murray joined Lewis in condemning the decision, along with Hillman's complicity. In a vitriolic exchange with Potofsky at a high-level CIO get-together in July, Lewis damned Hillman for his perfidy at North American: "Sidney Hillman stood at the elbow of the President of the U.S. when he signed the executive order that sent troops into the Inglewood plant." Meanwhile, R. J. Thomas felt compelled to resign from Hillman's OPM labor council, acidly characterizing it as no more than management front.[53]

There was a certain studied hypocrisy in all of this, as the Army's ostensible purpose in intervening was to uphold the authority of Richard Frankensteen and the CIO leadership. Nonetheless, the actual deployment of armed men traumatized the labor leadership and inflamed the aircraft workers. For weeks it was hard to restore order as Mortimer's martyrdom inflated the credibility of the CP. Welders went back to work reluctantly as they "were greatly incensed at the actions of the Army and also because of the throwing of tear gas." They might be working, Lubin was informed, but in their eyes the stature of the "Defense Administration" had dropped drastically while that of the CP was enhanced. Even "Dutch" Kindelberger, President of North American, while boasting, "Things are pretty damn quiet now," had to acknowledge that the welders remained obstreperous. Colonel Branshaw, who, together with Hillman's man on the scene, Eric A. Nichol, was charged with getting the plant back in operation, wired Patterson that "until we catch these radicals and absolutely stamp these insidious undermining elements preying on the minds of the men in these plants," turmoil would continue. Branshaw asked Hillman and Frankensteen to send a half-dozen loyal organizers, because at present "they don't dare to call a mass meeting because they are afraid they would be hooted off the stage . . . We are still sitting on a powder keg." Even after the left was beheaded and subdued, when the inflammatory radio broadcasts ceased and the CP groups were driven underground, Branshaw noted to Hillman the knotty problem of restoring social relations between radical and conservative workers. And this state of incipient rebellion persisted despite the fact that Hillman, together with the military brass and the NDMB, were more than ready to accept the basic wage improvements and job classifications demanded by the union and to impose them uniformly on the rest of the industry in order to eliminate one major cause of chronic labor upheaval.[54]

Cut adrift by his only natural fraternity, Hillman found refuge among bureaucratic mandarins and military functionaries who at bottom were hostile to his very presence. Stimson recorded the econonmium: "Sidney Hillman acted very well and was more vigorous almost than anyone else

against the strike and in favor of taking over the plant." Perkins over-
came her gnawing jealousy and congratulated Hillman for his courage.
The Army was irked that Hillman persuaded Roosevelt to assign a civilian labor adviser from Hillman's division to the commanding officer of
the plant, but the basic decision to use troops, after all, only legitimated
the service's eagerness to break strikes with bayonets.

In the end Hillman had no remedy for the general problem of the
"wildcat" strike. His preferred solution was to fashion a concert of interests, beginning with the CIO and the AFL, and then more broadly
between business and organized labor, which would provide the latter
with the sense of security it required to exercise discipline over its own
membership. Thus he became a chief architect of the labor–management
conference called by Roosevelt soon after Pearl Harbor.[55]

It was Pearl Harbor itself that instantly transformed Hillman's bureaucratic ruminations into reality. At the labor–management conference in January, the trade union leadership took the no-strike pledge
(the AFL with more gusto than the CIO). Not long afterward the newly
created National War Labor Board (NWLB) promulgated the "maintenance of membership" provision as official government policy. As the
rest of the nation went to war, the labor movement disarmed. Officially
sanctioned strikes were taboo. But the trench lines running across the
factory floor did not vanish so easily; indeed, as the war economy became
a businessmen's economy, rank-and-file disappointment and unauthorized strikes grew. By that time, however, Hillman was gone from government and no longer shouldered the official burden of pacification,
leaving behind a record blemished to be sure, but not without a string of
notable accomplishments in the art of social détente.[56]

Most artful of all, and linked to his other critical responsibilities for
ensuring a reliable, varied, and plentiful supply of labor, were the stabilization agreements Hillman masterminded in the strategically sensitive
construction and shipbuilding industries. Here his administrative inventiveness and his negotiating finesse paid off handsomely. These agreements were designed to equalize and standardize wages, hours, grievance
procedures, and other conditions of employment throughout the country. The point too was to stop the pirating of skilled workers and to quell
other forms of disruptive competition among the rival regional centers in
which these industries were located. While the whole issue of shortages
of labor and materials was perpetually enveloped in clouds of hysterical
exaggeration, the dimensions of the skilled shortfall in shipbuilding was
truly frightening. In the whole country, according to an NDAC survey,
there were only ten template makers, forty-six loftsmen, two hundred
three ship's electricians, thirty-five marine draftsmen, ninety-four marine

architects, one hundred fifty-six caulkers, and two hundred ninety-three shipfitters, totaling less than the number needed by the Boston Navy yard alone. "Pirating" or "scamping" in such circumstances was epidemic. Everything was made more complicated by the explosive demand for ships, defense cantonments, and housing; by the highly fragmented state of the construction industry; and by the presence of a quarrelsome group of suspicious, turf-conscious craft and industrial unions.[57]

Hillman turned first to shipbuilding and to his old comrade in social engineering, Morris Cooke. A commission established late in 1940, under Cooke's chairmanship, gathered together all the major and minor producers and the affected trade unions in each of four zones: the Atlantic, Pacific, Great Lakes, and Gulf Coast. Hillman and Cooke began on the West Coast, where they hammered out policies to standardize skilled rates and work rules governing overtime, shift premiums, and limits on production, as well as grievance and arbitration machinery and a pledge not to engage in strikes or lockouts. A series of secret meetings in San Francisco and the threat of an AFL-sanctioned strike finally produced a two-year agreement, which was then reproduced on the Great Lakes and the Atlantic Seaboard, and lastly on the Gulf Coast, where negotiations were stalled by racial tensions and squabbles between the AFL and the CIO. The shipbuilding stabilization agreements covered 400,000 workers and were enforced by a commission composed of representatives of the affected AFL and CIO unions and the principal shipyards as well as delegates from the Navy and the U.S. Maritime Commission. There were occasional breakdowns: A seven-week strike by the Machinists local in the San Francisco area, joined by a CIO shipyard local, ignited a momentary uproar, but Hillman, Green, and John Frey denounced it in concert (although conceding substantial wage hikes, which disrupted the market for machinists working in nonunion shipbuilding shops). Later a more serious strike erupted against Bethlehem in Oakland, but there the OPM decisively intervened, as did Frey, who led the nonstrikers back to work. Hillman thanked him. At the Federal Shipbuilding and Drydock Company in Kearney, New Jersey, a strike of 17,000 led the President, with Hillman's encouragement, to order the yard's seizure by the Navy and to impose a maintenance of membership rule, which the company vehemently opposed. On balance, however, the stabilization mechanisms worked well.[58]

Hillman next appointed Joseph Keenan of the AFL's IBEW to flesh out an analogous apparatus for the construction industry. Here, of course, the old-line craft unions were predominant, and Hillman acceded to their power, tacitly agreeing to freeze out Denny Lewis (John L.'s brother) and his United Construction Workers Organizing Committee.[59]

Stabilization agreements like these were ingenious adaptations to the shift in the balance of industrial power and were reminiscent of the more credible forms of plant representation and the system of shop committees fashionable during World War I. For months Hillman attempted to impose the same system in the aircraft industry, but it was too volatile. The workers were newer, the CIO more obstreperous and stronger, and the rate of expansion even more dizzying. Hillman got nowhere until the North American upheaval shocked the OPM into approving Hillman's scheme. The North American settlement then unsettled labor relations everywhere else in the industry. Rivalries among the UAW, the IAM, and an independent aircraft welders' group were rubbed raw. A gathering of all the major West Coast manufacturers fell apart in confusion. In the end, some companies assented, some did not; some unions agreed, but others wouldn't. Despite this failure, and notwithstanding occasional charges, some quite vehement, that Hillman showed favoritism in deciding which unions were to be granted *de facto* jurisdiction in these sectors, in the main the stabilization agreements worked well. Hillman was proud of them. They were, in effect, an application of the "new unionism" in conditions of martial law, mildly administered.[60]

The successes in shipbuilding and construction were promising, but they were, after all, only subsectors in an economy whose rate of expansion was accelerating from month to month, placing enormous strains on all those visible and yet to be tapped sources of labor. In some respects, the problem of labor supply lent itself to those techniques of social engineering for which Hillman was celebrated. That is, it was possible to view the issue as a problem in social statistics: How many workers would be required, in what occupational categories, of what levels of skill, where were they located, when were they needed, was there adequate transportation to get them to work sites and adequate housing to shelter them once they arrived? One could arrive at a rough approximation of the social demand and match it against available supply.

As Hillman did so, he immediately realized that despite the enormous reserves of unemployed workers still on the scene in 1940, the Depression had left behind the opposite social catastrophe as well. By making the nation's most technically skilled and versatile workers superfluous, it had severely undermined the nation's ability to staff those high-tech industries of the day upon which the war economy depended with adequate numbers and kinds of skilled workers, including tool designers and toolmakers, marine mechanics, and ship carpenters and electricians, to name but a few. The Depression not only rusted away industrial skills but drove many skilled cadre back to farms and other outposts of survival while demolishing hundreds of corporate training programs. It was estimated that of the 6 million workers in 1930, 12 percent were lost to the Depression.[61]

The deceptively simple answer was to train and replenish the deficit of skilled workers out of the pool of unemployed, a vast pool even in 1940, numbering at least 9 million. Working at an exhausting pace, Hillman, together with Lubin and Owen Young of GE, who had been asked by Roosevelt to help, designed a sprawling vocational education program, drawing on every government agency having anything to do with the supply or training or manpower, as well as public and private vocational schools, and, most important, on the "training-within-industry" (TWI) programs conducted by major corporations. Hillman appointed Channing R. Dooley of Socony Vacuum (who had created a highly regarded employee representation plan at Socony) and J. Walter Dietz of Western Electric to oversee a great expansion of TWI, a popular program that paid workers while they learned. By the end of 1941 Dooley and Dietz could report that TWI programs were in place at 1,800 contractors and subcontractors.

The experience of Lockheed in Burbank, California, exemplified the TWI mission. Its workforce increased from 12,000 to 51,000 in a single year. More than 20,000 enrolled in supplemental training in vocational schools, and all new workers were enrolled in the TWI program, including 2,300 supervisors; indeed, the company's whole complement of skilled toolmakers functioned as instructors and supervisors, as midwives really, of a newborn subspecies of industrial laborer, the "unit skill operator," trained to run a single machine.[62]

Suddenly the Civilian Conservation Corps (CCC) and the National Youth Administration (NYA) each received a new lease on life, their resources and responsibilities enlarged. The CC camps in particular were slated to turn out motor vehicle operators, auto mechanics and repairmen, radio operators, cooks and bakers, medical aides, and so on. Other agencies, including the Social Security Board and the Federal Security Administration, were enlisted as well. By the end of 1941 Hillman could report that 2.5 million were enrolled in all forms of training in 1,200 public vocational and trade schools, 155 colleges and universities, and 10,000 public school shops, and 835,000 were learning in TWI.[63]

To coordinate the activity of so many varied institutions, subject to so many diverse authorities, comprising widely differing constituencies, and to do so in a way that stood a reasonable chance of delivering on time the right mix of skills and occupations was no mean organizational feat. If it had been only that, a daunting piece of administrative architecture, it might have provided Hillman with an enduring sense of gratification, an exercise of "labor statesmanship" that bore fruit. But the fatal illusion of social engineering had always been that one might supravene political and social antagonisms through the magic of objective "social science." The "labor question," no longer a challenge to the moral economy of the social order, might become instead strictly a technical question of inventory control, an exercise in the management of a vast system of interchangeable parts.

But the question of labor supply, however rigorously it might be defined by the geometry of supply and demand, however free it might seem of the passions and interests that inflamed every other facet of labor relations, was at bottom a profoundly contentious business. Ultimately it became a feature of what was perhaps the most fundamental social question of the era: Who was to control and direct the vast expansion of productive facilities occurring under government auspices and at government expense?

If industry, for example, were to have a free hand in the training, recruiting, positioning, and transfer of skilled and semiskilled labor, it would threaten the elaborate set of procedures defining apprenticeship, the skill content of occupational categories, seniority, and a host of other work rules that unions had built up and had jealously guarded for many years. TWI, which enjoyed on the whole an excellent reputation, was nonetheless criticized for its lack of trade union participation, a complaint that echoed and reechoed throughout the maze of committees and agencies and boards and divisions that in one way or another jockeyed for influence over labor supply and priorities.[64]

Moreover, in circumstances of existing and imminent shortages there was great pressure to solve the problem of skilled labor, at least in part, by actually diluting the levels of technical competence customarily considered prerequisite for the performance of a great number of jobs. New machinery, especially a huge stock of special-purpose machine tools, was deployed to subdivide skilled tasks systematically into their semiskilled components. Factories were reorganized from top to bottom, generating unheard-of gains in productivity—a merchant vessel took thirty-five weeks to produce in 1937 but needed only fifty days in 1943. TWI, also committed to "skill dilution," charged its functionaries with developing elaborate job breakdown sheets with which to train new hires for simplified, single-operation tasks.[65]

The war emergency was an irresistible argument in favor of this deliberate degradation of skill, but the process also coincided with the desire of management to regain control over the shop floor. Naturally it bred resistance to even Hillman's most efficacious programs. In the long term, the labor movement worried about a postwar glutting of the market for skilled labor. More immediately, craft groups like the International Die-Sinkers Conference, and the metal trades in general, resisted the insidious dilution of skill introduced by speeded-up apprenticeship programs. The die-sinkers dealt from strength, for they were in short supply and vital for turning out dies, without which there would be acute shortages of aluminum and steel forgings. Hillman met repeatedly with the manufacturers and the die-sinkers, caught between the craft's determination to stop "dilution" and the military's even more insistent need for more die-sinkers.[66]

As the case of the die-sinkers illustrates, the war economy was an intricate piece of machinery that depended on the most exquisite synchronization of its components. Labor supply problems could never be taken up in splendid isolation but only in their messy interaction with shifting and often cross-cutting industrial and social priorities. With every passing month as the emergency grew, so did the strangulating sensation that there was less and less capacity to meet the combined manpower needs of the armed services and arms manufacturers without drastically cutting away sectors of civilian production once deemed essential. The specter of "rigorous controls" over the labor market, the freezing of wages, the immobilization of labor pools, and the explosive eradication of all barriers to race, age, and sex haunted the offices of the OPM, especially as the reserves of unemployed were at last absorbed by a parched labor market and the production targets of the "Victory Program" seemed increasingly utopian.[67]

So it was that the power to set industrial priorities carried enormous social consequences. A decision by the priorities branch of OPM could turn a thriving community into a ghost town, or do the exact opposite; it could throw thousands out of work, at least temporarily, or put thousands previously unemployed back to work and drive up local wages; it could determine the availability of consumer goods, disrupt families, devastate union locals, and force people to live in quonset huts on the sites of industrial "parks." Responsibility for maintaining and regulating the labor supply therefore ought to have carried with it some influence over such related matters as industrial priorities, contract placements, housing construction, the ordered phasing-out of consumer goods production, and a host of other vital questions. But this was the nub of the problem. Hillman's actual authority never measured up to his responsibilities. Until near the end of his government service, moreover, he was unwilling to make a bold effort to extend his influence.

For example, he did not forthrightly champion the "Murray Plan," which called for the creation of joint labor–management industrial councils with authority to make critical decisions regarding labor supply, priorities, defense housing, training, the deployment of plant and machinery, and related matters regarding the conversion to full-time war production. The "Murray Plan," along with analogous proposals by Walter Reuther for the auto industry in particular, represented the only serious attempt to institutionalize labor participation and some meaningful measure of control over the operation of the economy. Many of Hillman's business and brass-hat colleagues (Knudsen particularly) were adamantly opposed. All talk of government ownership or the sort of tripartite management suggested by Murray they dismissed as incompetent.

But not everybody reacted that way. In the summer of 1940 Hillman first saw Reuther's plan to use the idle capacity in the auto industry to manufacture tanks and bombers by pooling corporate equipment and manpower under the joint supervision of labor, management, and government. He seemed impressed and brought the plan to Knudsen, who claimed the auto industry was incapable of moving at the rate Reuther projected. Reuther returned with hard data demonstrating the plan's feasibility. Patterson actually liked its audacity, and it became an openly debated issue at the OPM early in the new year. Jerome Frank was "very impressed." John Carmody, Lauchlin Currie, Leon Henderson, Frankfurter, Harry Dexter White, and a whole regiment in the dwindling army of the New Deal defended it against Knudsen's ever more strenuous efforts to bury it. Hillman took up what was becoming his customary position somewhere in the pointless middle. He vacillated, first arguing in alliance with Frankfurter and against GM's Charles E. Wilson in favor of pooling productive resources, especially machine tools, circumventing corporate boundaries if necessary; but as resistance to his assault on the sanctity of property titles stiffened on the part of Wilson and Paul Hoffman of Studebaker, Hillman's conciliatory juices flowed liberally, and he allowed the question of labor participation to fade. Even while Hillman engaged in these evasions, however, he kept himself well apprised of the industry's scandalous, self-interested delays in converting to defense production. He knew the big firms were deliberately bottling up critical design, tooling, and plant resources. Hillman suggested deferring a decision while conducting a tour of the plants to see concretely what might be done. Action, if it could be called that, was most safely limited to fact-gathering and dissemination. Auto managements, however, had no doubts; they might "pool" ideas but not resources or prerogatives, as they despised the idea of relinquishing advantages to their competitors and their employees. Slowly the Reuther Plan receded from public view.[68]

A similar fate befell the even more ambitious "Murray Plan." According to its authors, each industrial council would be informed of the government's production requirements, would bear the responsibility of maintaining price levels, and would be endowed with full executive authority. In addition to democratizing the structure of industrial management, the "Murray Plan" would promote "industrial peace through the perfection and extension of sound collective bargaining relations." The CIO boldly projected these councils past the period of wartime emergency and into the postwar world as the principal instruments of democratic planning and stability.

But the "Murray Plan" remained stillborn, and only in part because of Hillman's foot-dragging. Neither Lewis nor the AFL worked up much enthusiasm for it either. As for Hillman, he was alternately defensive and hectoring. Responding to criticisms from SWOC cadre that industrial councils were the only way to guarantee labor's influence in the defense setup, Hillman reminded them, "Labor's plea in the defense program is being made from day to day," and he had the ear of the President. Moreover, he said, creating councils would diminish the government's authority and might induce labor and management to collude together to curtail production. At gatherings of union activists, Hillman's subordinates belittled the "Plan" and contrasted it unfavorably with the work of the Labor Division. Pearl Harbor momentarily revived interest in the "Plan," but when asked for his views by the President, Hillman again demurred, sensing yet another threat to his own bureaucratic well-being. "No one not wholly responsible to the government can be expected to have the necessary information and detachment. In short, 130,000,000 people cannot delegate to any combination of private interests final decisions in matters of basic policy."[69]

There was a certain irony in Hillman's backdoor bureaucratic maneuvering to blockade the "Murray Plan," since it was in many respects modeled after the form of "industrial democracy" upon which his own reputation and that of the "new unionism" rested. But now he saw it as a challenge to his own bureaucratic fiefdom. The "Murray Plan" would have established an officially sanctioned position within the economy for the organized labor movement and thereby reduced its need to rely on Hillman as the broker of its interests.

Hillman preferred to pursue labor participation and "industrial democracy" by other means, namely by defending and extending his own administrative reach. And for that purpose he sought allies not in the labor movement but in the bureaucratic labyrinths of Washington among groups of fellow New Dealers and sympathetic businessmen. He strove to get labor representatives from his own Labor Division placed on critical priorities committees, only to see them systematically ignored by the businessmen in charge.

Priorities decisions were inevitably unsettling, but by the middle of 1941 they were precipitating acute unhappiness among pockets of workers suddenly cut adrift when civilian production shut down and war orders went elsewhere. In the bureaucracy's argot this was called "priorities unemployment." Other workers, favored with new jobs, nonetheless found themselves homeless, without a rational way to get to work, bereft of the elementary amenities of urban living. All of these "labor problems" were organically tied to the production system. Curtailing civilian automobile output, for example, naturally left thousands jobless, a problem that in turn might be remedied through modified competitive or negotiated contracts; by awarding higher priority ratings to trucks and buses; by speeding up Army orders for vehicles of all sorts; or by joint labor–management collaboration to speed up the conversion process— that is, by methods that necessarily implicated the contracts, purchasing, and priorities subdivisions of the OPM.[70]

Yet remedies were never considered in concert with the rest of OPM's administrative machinery. In the social geography of the defense bureaucracy, labor was rarely allowed to wander freely beyond the perimeters of its own spare terrain. Industrial advisory committees, and Stettinius's Industrial Materials Division, were run by executives from major corporations and trade associations, who turned a blind eye to the social disruptions brought on by procurement decisions. They had little sympathy for workers who lost precious seniority privileges, who sought only the right to be reemployed, or who wanted the government to pay the costs of relocation. James Carey of the UE complained: "All the operating divisions, including priorities committees, are really dominated completely by representatives of management."[71]

Turning to Congress for help on the "priorities unemployment" problem was equally discouraging. Although he managed to get a bill introduced late in 1941 calling for supplementary unemployment benefits for those willing to train for defense jobs, the bill was defeated, and Hillman was accused of "trying to socialize the whole country."[72]

Hillman tried a series of poorly conceived bureaucratic end runs, which in the end only institutionalized his ambivalence. He created a "Labor Priorities Branch" within his division to police the problem and appointed his former LNPL deputy, Eli Oliver, to run it. Oliver immediately reported that contracts were routinely released without even the pretense of consulting the Labor Division. Always the "half-intellectual," Hillman created a Labor Supply branch, staffed by academic economists under J. Douglas Brown of Princeton and recruited from the Ivy League, the University of Wisconsin, and think tanks like Brookings and the National Resources Planning Board (NRPB). Brown applauded his boss's "half-intellectual" qualities, his "unique combination of a genuine intellectual, as introspective and idealistic philosopher, and a vigorous and shrewd negotiator." But the näive faith in social engineering characteristic of these economists drove to distraction the more hard-boiled trade unionists who manned Hillman's Labor Relations branch. Complaints were legion about imperious economists who never bothered to consult their brethren in the Labor Relations branch before approving hefty war orders.[73]

This constant skirmishing within his own bureaucratic army spoiled efforts to mount a united front against the military and industry, and was further aggravated by festering suspicions within the Labor Relations branch itself among rival representatives of the CIO and the AFL. In some instances AFL and CIO appointees refused to serve on the same committee.[74]

Meanwhile Knudsen made sure that Hillman's "labor advisory committees" (LAC) never enjoyed parity with the "industrial advisory committees" in influencing priority decisions. Indeed, most of these labor advisory committees were inert by 1942. That was also the fate of the labor–management shop committees Hillman initiated as a way of deflecting sentiment away from the "Murray Plan" and in the hope that they might intrude themselves into the arena of day-to-day production decisions. Hillman envisioned them as the nucleus of "the soundest basis for joint efforts by labor and industry to increase production." That they became, with a vengeance. While they did address problems of housing, health, and safety, mainly they were policemen of production, monitoring turnover, transfers, and absenteeism, watching out for carelessness, waste, and slippages in quality control. The committees were not so much ignored as they were converted into cheerleaders for intensified production, morale boosters, propagandists of patriotic sweating, bond salesmen, and blood collectors. Otherwise they were held in contempt by government and corporate functionaries alike. Once America became an active combatant, all social and political pretensions about their role were unceremoniously dropped. Donald Nelson, the head of the War Production Board, the successor to the OPM set up right after Pearl Harbor, told a meeting of CIO leaders that labor–management plant committees existed to increase production, period, and were not there "to put labor into management . . . nor help any union's organizing campaign, either. They're not grievance committees or pay scale committees or collective bargaining committees."[75]

If Hillman allowed the labor–management committees to devolve into engines of patriotic propaganda, then in part it was because he naturally assumed, as OPM Associate Director, a ceremonial function as galvanizer of the national will. He toured industrial centers, inspected defense plants, and extolled the virtues of social cooperation in nation-wide addresses, along with Roosevelt and with Churchill's Labour Minister, Ernest Bevin. He also organized war production conferences of professors, labor and management representatives, and civic leaders at leading universities and delivered uplifting remarks to occupied Europe and Britain via short-wave radio broadcasts. But, of course, he knew all too well the backstage rancor and discord that turned every day into a trial.[76]

Thus, in the teeth of the indifference of his fellow commissioners on the NDAC, Hillman doggedly raised and re-raised the housing crisis until he was placated with the chairmanship of a Commission subcommittee, only after fending off the efforts of Biggers to absorb the housing issue into Knudsen's bailiwick. The subcommittee struggled mightily against swarms of real estate speculators, construction profiteers, and rent gougers, pushing vigorously, but always within the limits and tempo of bureaucratic life, for a massive housing program as a vital element in the labor supply equation. But, of course, it was not to be.[77]

Since he was charged with marshaling all the nation's potential labor reserves, Hillman was also bedeviled by the race question. Here too his approach was to equivocate and placate. Complaints poured into the White House about rampant discrimination in defense work. As early as July 1940 Hillman appointed Robert Weaver as an administrative assistant to facilitate Negro training. The NDAC, and later the OPM, liberally dispensed an equal opportunity rhetoric, as did the CIO and the AFL. But within many AFL unions segregation and discrimination were untouchable custom. Even the TWI system was rife with racism. At Newport News Shipbuilding, for example, although 35 percent of the workforce was black, no blacks were trained as electricians or machinists. Hillman could hardly pretend ignorance. A report from a TWI field representative in Connecticut noted a reluctance to hire Italians "because of their emotional content," and observed that "Negroes are, of course, at the bottom of the list and receive last consideration."

Aubrey Williams, head of the NYA, told Eleanor Roosevelt that Hillman was doing nothing. She invited black leaders (Will Alexander, Walter White of the NAACP, and Robert Weaver) to a lunch with Hillman, Lubin, and Paul V. McNutt, where it was proposed that the President issue an executive order banning discrimination. But Hillman was reluctant, insisting that the problem would work itself out through private transactions among enlightened bureaucrats. He deliberately avoided any vigorous effort to enforce the government's nondiscriminatory policy in construction, fearing it would delay the building of cantonments. But the problem grew uglier, especially after Gerald Tuttle of the Vultee Corporation was quoted in *Fortune* as candidly acknowledging that "it is not the policy of this company to employ people not of the Caucasian race." Then the president and general manager of North American Aviation, J. H. Kindelberger, assured the *Kansas City Star* that its new plant in Fairfax, Kansas, would not employ Negroes. Hillman had to do something. He asked Robert Weaver to develop a program for integrating Negro workers and placed Will Alexander in charge of minority employment. Still, he tried his best to defuse the issue. On the same day he appointed Weaver and Alexander, he instructed all defense contractors that they were obliged to hire all *qualified* applicants.[78]

Even this rather timid letter might never have been sent without unremitting pressure from liberals, the press, and various black organizations. But Hillman was alone, abandoned by his corporate colleagues at OPM. Knudsen did not sign Hillman's letter to defense contractors, further antagonizing the black leadership. Knudsen did all he could to forestall more decisive steps, reassuring the President that "we will quietly get manufacturers to increase the number of Negroes on defense work. If we set a percentage it will immediately be open to dispute; quiet work with the contractors and the unions will bring a better result." The *Amsterdam News* made note of Hillman's occasional rhetorical boldness but expressed doubts as to whether any concrete action would follow. An NAACP "Negro Labor Committee" statement of early May 1941 slammed Knudsen for refusing to meet black spokesmen, while Hillman was judged well-intentioned but ineffectual.

Negro unemployment rose. Hillman's construction and shipbuilding stabilization agreements froze in place the all-white practices of the craft unions. Still, Hillman boasted to a conference of Negro leaders in Boston that integration was well under way, failing to note the minuscule numbers so far affected. A. Philip Randolph's threatened march on Washington drastically increased the political stakes. Hillman confessed to the OPM council in June that he could do nothing without the cooperation of industry and the armed services.[79]

Roosevelt then endorsed Hillman's earlier letter to defense contractors and ordered the OPM to take immediate steps. Soon thereafter the President issued Executive Order 8802 establishing the Fair Employment Practices Committee (FEPC) within Hillman's Labor Division. Even then the NAACP's *Crisis* argued that only intense pressure resulted in two rather than one Negro appointment to the FEPC "over the considerable opposition of Sidney Hillman of OPM." In fact, soon after its creation, Randolph and Walter White were pressing the FEPC chairman, Mark Ethridge, to dislodge the Commission from Hillman's division.[80]

In retrospect it is painfully obvious that the political economy of racism was not vulnerable to bureaucratic parry and riposte. At the time, however, the vast, nearly insatiable neediness of the war machine seemed actually to open up a route of attack down the broad avenue of the nation's dwindling labor supply. But if, in this area at least, the war seemed full of social promise, however illusory, in most other respects it seemed to be the gravedigger of whatever social democratic longings lingered on from the previous decade. Nowhere was this clearer than in the accelerated tendency toward industrial concentration.

Fostered by the government's prime contractors, aided and abetted by the customary procurement practices and political preferences of the armed services, corporate empire building not only obstructed Hillman's day-to-day responsibilities for ensuring an adequate and efficient labor force but loomed over the industrial landscape, threatening to recon- figure permanently the nation's postwar economic geography and social structure. It was a formidable dilemma, touching on the most sensitive issues of power and property, for which Hillman concocted a typically devious and oblique solution. He once again called in his old friend, Morris Cooke, to develop a program, quaintly dubbed "farming out," for decentralizing industry so as to lessen the disruptive impact of overly congested production, to weaken the power of industrial goliaths, and to prepare for a more socially and geographically balanced postwar econ- omy. The problem was a straightforward matter of wealth and politics, but the proposed solution would elide those realities through the more näive wisdom of a social engineering bureaucracy.[81]

By the middle of 1941 the concentration of defense contracts and "priorities unemployment" had joined forces, generating an embarrassing amount of idle capacity and idle men, littering the industrial hinterland with smaller companies, superannuating once-thriving industrial com- munities, and turning them into industrial "ghost towns." At meeting after meeting Hillman pursued his quixotic crusade: subcontracting and the dispersal of facilities, along with a program of priority unemployment insurance and wage standardization. He toured "ghost towns" like Pad- ucah, Kentucky; Cambridge, Ohio; and Harrisburg, West Virginia, as well as a series of blighted locales in Pennsylvania, in order to stir up sympathy for the "farming out" program. Meanwhile, Cooke was sup- posed to figure out a way of pooling the modest resources of these smaller towns and businesses so that they might be fit to handle government orders, which first of all had to be pried away from the grasping fingers of the *Fortune* 100, who often preferred patronizing their own subcontracting clients or dependents. Hillman's mandate to Cooke was both circumspect and precise. "Farming out" was meant to ensure the economic stability of the local community and its workforce. Moreover, it had to meet the high-precision requirements of airplane engine manufacturers or machine tool fabricators, a level of technical proficiency often beyond the technical and financial capabilities of many medium-size producers. An anglophile since the days of the Whitley Councils and the Labour Party's wartime manifesto, Hillman seized on the ingenious British approach of "bits and pieces," that is, the government would so simplify standards that parts of a larger, more technically complex job might be handled by ordinary foundries and machine shops.

Cooke was eager. He argued that "farming out," applied in concert with the Reuther and Murray plans, was a way to break the bottleneck in the machine tool industry. He launched a survey of unused facilities and labor resources in neglected regions and "ghost towns," which included detailed proposals for pooling tools, plants, and labor so as to qualify for defense contracts. He was fired by missionary zeal, claiming that "farming out" also "happens to be best adapted for safeguarding our after-the-war economy and social set up. There is considerable apprehension as to what our after-the-war world will be like if we cannot devise methods of keeping our smaller plants active." "Farming out" also promised to widen the constituency for reform by appealing to small businessmen shut out of the defense economy. Donald Nelson, head of the Supplies Priorities and Allocations Board (SPAB) and later of the War Production Board, was sympathetic to the longer-term structural purposes of the program. He did what he could to encourage a wider diffusion of contracts in labor surplus areas and among smaller manufacturers.[82]

The sympathies of Nelson and the self-interest of petty entrepreneurs notwithstanding, "farming out" was overrun by a contrary social logic and turned out to be another idea whose time never came. By the end of 1941 a Hillman aide reported that subcontracting and pooling programs were stagnating and in danger of takeover by "a class of racketeers." Above all, for the armed services and for Patterson especially, the question of industrial concentration was a nonissue. By the middle of 1941 six corporations held one-third of all private military contracts. By 1943 there would be 500,000 fewer businesses than in 1941.[83]

This was the birth of the "military–industrial complex," entailing a vast recycling of the country's industrial geography and industrial politics, which would underpin the Cold War economy for the next forty years. All those infrastructural and raw materials industries so recently savaged by the Depression flourished once again. Their economic renewal restored their political power, as representatives of the old "securities bloc," industrialists and financiers, together with their legal advisers, appeared everywhere throughout the upper echelons of the defense bureaucracy. Within the warrens of the NDAC and the OPM they assiduously lobbied to protect the industrial *status quo ante*, encouraged the further cartelization of the economy, and resisted pressure for regulatory controls. In the aluminum industry, for example, an adviser to FDR confessed that ALCOA set national priorities and functioned in effect as a surrogate government. For all its good intentions and engineering shrewdness, "farming out" hardly stood a chance.[84]

In those circumstances, the number of bureaucratic false starts, detours, and dead ends, like "farming out," grew embarrassingly large. The commingling of industrial, financial, and military elites, the linkages of interest and belief that gave them a unity of purpose, rapidly converted the defense mobilization apparatus into a branch of corporate America, curtailing the freedom of action of the New Deal's civil service bureaucracy. If Hillman had entered the government to win the allegiance of the labor movement to the higher purposes of the nation, CEOs and Wall Street lawyers took up their posts more often to win over the regime to the higher purposes of business. Inevitably then, Hillman found himself presiding over an administrative ghetto of ever diminishing significance.

He wasn't alone. The whole tribe of New Dealers felt themselves cut adrift. Leon Henderson and Donald Nelson were the most prominent figures willing on occasion to resist the corporate blitzkrieg. Both were old acquaintances of Hillman. A second tier of lawyers and economists, some in and some outside of Hillman's division, who looked to Henderson and Nelson for leadership, thought of themselves as the loyal "Keynesian" opposition. The group included Lauchlin Currie, Edward Prichard, Isidor Lubin, Robert Nathan, Joseph Rauh, Phil Graham, and Richard Gelber. Hillman's choice to run TWI, William Batt of SKF Industries (ball bearing manufacturers), was a patrician, a Union League Philadelphia Republican impressed, however, by the Swedish welfare state and therefore an enthusiast of the New Deal. Outside the defense bureaucracy itself were "all the usual suspects": Perkins, Wallace, Eziekel, Ickes, and, when he could afford to turn his attention to domestic affairs, Hopkins.[85]

Within the mobilization apparatus members of this loosely defined circle were at first known as the "all-outers" because of their insistence that business cut back its civilian production in favor of preparedness. Hillman, Henderson, and Nelson found themselves on the same side of the barricades on most matters of labor policy. In mid-1941 the "all-outers" won an apparent victory when Roosevelt created the SPAB. Hillman was a Board member, and Nelson was named Executive Director. The Board seemingly was empowered to fix priorities and allocate raw materials, fuel, power, and so on. But in fact the SPAB turned out to be another stillborn creature of bureaucratic stalemate, paralyzed by conflicting lines of authority. Nelson found himself in the anomalous position of being both Knudsen's superior and his employee, and ultimately subordinated to the OPM, where the "all-outers" were a besieged minority. The OPM was more a political arrangement designed to fend off contending social interests—labor, the military, private enterprise, and the "public"—than it was an administrative agency capable of really steering the economy.

Nelson confessed to a growing "sense of futility of everything we are doing. I could not throw off a feeling of impending calamity." To Ickes, Hillman seemed "laughably optimistic" that Roosevelt would make the drastic changes he desired. Gloomy New Dealers could no longer escape a sense of their own exclusion from the inner councils of power and policy. A presidential assistant informed Roosevelt that Henderson, who was threatening to resign, was "sulking in his tent," preferring to leave rather than face a showdown with the business faction he knew he would lose. The once-charmed circle of New Deal reform suffered from "hurt pride," aware that they were "no longer the king pins and they don't like it." The friction and *frisson* of defense mobilization politics were expressed in the raw by Knudsen's lawyer, Fred Eaton: "When the New Dealers were in power they didn't include us; now that we are in power we won't include them."[86]

Finally, Hillman attempted to break out of this bureaucratic *cul-de-sac*, but he did so within the ground rules of bureaucratic politics and too late for it to do any good. After Pearl Harbor the President established the War Production Board to replace the OPM, which immediately entailed a demotion from Hillman's position of "dual power" (more cynical observers might have said "dual impotence") with Knudsen to a post as head of the Labor Division of the new agency, reporting to Donald Nelson. Hillman saw what was in the offing and in feverish haste began working more intensely than even he was accustomed to. He gathered together the shrinking group of social democratic and "Keynesian" New Dealers still left in the administration to wage a kind of bureaucratic guerrilla war.

The creation of the WPB was a mortal wound. Hillman was humiliated, both personally and officially, by his demotion. The creation of the War Labor Board days later was an aftershock, further stripping him of influence and prestige. It would take more than a favorable word from on high to recover. Eli Oliver advised Hillman, even before the WPB defeat, to repair his frayed relations with Murray as part of a broader plan to restore the CIO's flagging clout within the defense apparatus. If Murray could squelch the pandemic of raiding and jurisdictional stoppages, without going so far as reunification with the AFL, then the "Murray Plan" might be "brought down out of the clouds" and set to work—perhaps not in name, but in specific industries—while the Congress remained flexible.[87]

But Frankfurter shrewdly observed, and told Roosevelt, how much wounded vanity and paranoid suspicion stood in the way of such a sensible compromise. He decried the bickering among Hillman, Murray, and Lewis, which had muddied the perspective of the movement and left it relying on the President to defend it instead of systematically organizing labor's own program on inflation, wages, and price policy, on the allocation of manpower, and so on. Murray, according to the Justice, suspected and was jealous of Hillman as FDR's "chosen" labor leader. Murray feared as well a break with Lewis, which would undoubtedly follow an unambiguous act of cooperation with the government. In Frankfurter's view, Murray turned to Hillman for help only when he feared Lewis more. He urged the President to call Hillman and Murray together and force them to cooperate.[88]

Marshaling the CIO's resources for an open confrontation with the military–industrial bloc was not, however, what Hillman had in mind. Mainly, he tried to mount an offensive within the civil service, hoping against hope to reverse the drift of events. In February 1942 he prepared a series of exhibits for the President, together with an outline for action, highlighting his predicament: "Up to three months ago, with very little difficulties, my responsibility for labor policy in the defense effort was not questioned. It was taken for granted that an appeal from me would go to you. Now, with the picture changed, Nelson has properly the full power and responsibility for production. It is necessary for labor to be in the same position."

While pleading his case before FDR, he tried as well to shore up his position in Congress, defending the WLB, arguing against additional labor legislation, and denouncing ill-founded proposals to scrap the forty-hour week by demonstrating that 75 percent of all defense workers labored at least forty-two hours, and in strategic sectors much more—fifty to seventy hours in machine tools, forty to seventy hours in aircraft. His testimony became less and less defensive. Early in April he tooted his own horn before the Senate Committee on Education and Labor. The Labor Division had supplied 172,000 new workers each week since Pearl Harbor, which was better than the Nazis were managing, he boasted to the Senators. Proudly, he recorded the truly remarkable accomplishments of the training program: Only 700 of 22,000 workers at the California Shipbuilding Company had any previous experience, and only 100 of the 6,500 employed by Consolidated Shipbuilding. Already, the Labor Division had trained 3.4 million outside of industry, not including those enrolled in TWI.[89]

At a WPB meeting in March, he presented a fourteen-point program to remedy the maldistribution of contracts and the interconnected labor surpluses and shortages that inevitably followed. Calamitous statistics were trotted out for their shock value: Between the end of 1940 and 1942, it was projected that the number of defense workers needed to rise by 15.8 million, and the number in the armed services by 3.4 million; more specifically, the aircraft industry would require seven times, shipbuilding six times, and ordnance thirty-five times more employees. As of March the demand for tool designers exceeded supply by 51 to 1; toolmakers by 25 to 1; marine machinists by 22 to 1; boring-mill operators by 12 to 1; ship carpenters by 7 to 1; ship electricians by 7 to 1; and turret lathe operators by 5 to 1. Yet there were still 5 million unemployed, and vast pools of labor remained untapped in the Appalachian highlands, in the Ozarks, in the Great Lakes "cut-over" region, and in parts of the old "cotton South." Given the enormous and competing demands for labor by the army, industry, government, and agriculture, Hillman pleaded, the Labor Division needed more than the power to coordinate: "Definite authority now needs to be granted by executive order and legislation may be required later." Nelson endorsed the recommendations and agreed to present them to the President. At the same time, Wallace suggested to Hillman that he issue a pamphlet to counteract the propaganda deluge about strikes and labor racketeering and the incessant calls to abolish the forty-hour week and overtime pay. Hillman enlisted Archibald MacLeish's help in turning out this piece of counterintelligence. Hillman told the President he and his aides had devised a better alternative to the current "Production Victory" campaign, which he dismissed as a "pure publicity stunt" run by high-powered press agents rather than through labor organizations, as it ought to be.[90]

All of this was but a prelude to the final confrontation. After weeks of intramural debate, Hillman and his allies drafted a comprehensive program and submitted it to Roosevelt. It called first of all for a kind of super manpower agency with vastly expanded authority to regulate the supply, allocation, and conditions of labor. But it did more than simply provide for Hillman's own bureaucratic aggrandizement. Indeed, it was Hillman's bid, at the midnight hour, to come forward as the champion of the New Deal, of the "Keynesian" fiscal revolution, and of social democratic reform. "The time is ripe for a national policy of economic stabilization," he informed the President, one designed to prevent inflation and strengthen the national will to victory through the social principle of equality of sacrifice. The memorandum outlined a series of specific measures: (1) a blanket order by the OPA freezing all prices and a general price ceiling that would include repeal of the agricultural exemption under the Price Control Act; (2) rationing to help enforce the price ceiling and prevent hoarding; (3) price subsidies for the poor to guarantee fair distribution of necessities; (4) a tax program based on the ability to pay and targeted at war profiteering by raising the excess profits rate to 100 percent over the 88.5 percent recommended by the Treasury, designating the difference as a fund for postwar reconstruction; (5) closing the gap between income and available civilian goods through voluntary siphoning off of the excess into "victory" bonds together with a compulsory savings plan, suggested by Keynes, to "sterilize" purchasing power during the emergency, which might then provide a "kitty" to cushion the anticipated postwar slump; (6) a "new wage policy" based on stabilization agreements in aircraft, ordnance, and machine tools, which would maintain the prevailing level of industrial wages except where they were lower than necessary, where there were insupportable inequities within an industry or region, or where an increase would help accelerate the output of vital supplies; and (7) a dispensary of union security devices to immunize the trade union bureaucracy as it went about enforcing an unpopular national wage stabilization policy.

Hillman concluded his "call to arms" optimistically. This program, he confidently assured the President, would end the chronic demand for punitive labor legislation, would "banish the spectre of inflation," and would release the energies of the people for "an all-out, unstinted production drive."[91]

It was, in its own way, a stunning document, full of promise and fight. But it was, after all, only a memo to the President, and the heroic possibilities of such an interoffice memorandum were, especially by that late date, extremely limited. The memo was sent on April 2, and Hillman awaited the President's pleasure. On April 18 Roosevelt created the War Manpower Commission but appointed as its director not America's first "labor statesman" but rather the ex-Governor of Indiana and head of the Federal Security Agency, Paul V. McNutt.

Rumors and omens of Hillman's demise had, for many months, added a ghoulish edge to the daily ritual of bureaucratic backbiting. By mid-1941, as the OPM revealed itself to be a creature of industrial–military strategy, there were whisperings among his own appointees in the Labor Division that Hillman ought to resign rather than continue on as a captive-cosmetic figurehead. Harold Ickes, Hillman's ally but a man given to quick and absolute judgments of character, had already decided by August 1941 that "Hillman is turning out to be a weak man in that combination. His activities should have been confined strictly to labor." Ickes's skepticism was shared by others. FDR was advised that many people were disappointed in Hillman's performance even while acknowledging he was engaged in an impossible mission. Most ominous were those signs that even his CIO comrades were not prepared to defend him—indeed, might even prefer to see him dethroned. Lewis's wounded vanity remained an open sore. He could scarcely contain his contempt for Hillman's Hamlet-like predicament. The irony was palpable. Lewis, a defender of capitalism and foe of the left for many years, was condemning Hillman for his slavishness to the *status quo*. Vainly, he tried to ram through a condemnation of Hillman and Roosevelt at the CIO convention. It fizzled after igniting some noisy fisticuffs outside the convention hall. But Lewis was more successful in fanning the flames of scandal, which further discredited Hillman's final months of statesmanship.[92]

In October 1941 Hillman was forced to appear before Senator Truman's Special Committee to Investigate the Defense Program to answer humiliating charges originating with John L. Lewis and his brother Denny. Hillman had conspired, so the Lewis brothers testified, together with officials of the AFL construction unions, to block the awarding of a government defense housing contract to a Wayne, Michigan, builder, the Currier Lumber Company, because that company had signed a closed-shop agreement with Denny Lewis's UCWOC and despite the fact that Currier was the low bidder on the project. Currier demanded Hillman's resignation. Denny Lewis denounced him before the CIO. Even Murray, although anxious to chill the dispute before it embarrassed everybody, wrote a private letter of protest to the President. Many in the CIO, while repelled by Denny Lewis's bombast and bullying, believed that Hillman had secured the construction stabilization agreement by privately promising to freeze out the UCWOC, and they resented that. This sort of "statesmanship" was criminal in the eyes of the rival labor federation. Hillman denied ever having promised the AFL a monopoly. He had advised John Carmody of the FSA to deny Currier the contract because, he claimed, the company was a notorious antilabor troublemaker suspected in the recent death of a Teamsters member during a bitterly contested struggle to organize the firm's truck drivers. Currier's management had signed on with Denny Lewis only to stymie the five-year-old organizing drive of the AFL. Lewis was engaged in a blatant act of raiding, Hillman maintained, and awarding the contract to Currier would only invite further strife. The CIO's convention passed a mild resolution criticizing the OPM for the Currier decision without naming Hillman.[93]

Hillman's testimony before the Truman committee was not by any means a disaster. He defended his rationale for the decision and rehearsed Currier's unsavory reputation. Of course, he also denied any conspiratorial collusion with the AFL. They had the members, and that was a simple fact of life. Low price was not the only criteria for awarding contracts. Speed, efficiency, the decentralization of production, and other social objectives were also important. He genuinely believed that the building stabilization agreement would come apart if the Currier award went through. In fact, he told Carmody, it threatened "to blow up our whole construction program."[94]

Hillman mounted a credible case, but his position was crumbling anyway. Most newspapers denounced him. Only Drew Pearson sprang to his defense in the *Times-Herald* and *The New Republic*. Lewis was quick to exploit his embarrassment among the auto workers of Detroit, who faced an acute housing shortage. The Truman committee issued a devastating vote of no confidence, recommending that the two-headed OPM be replaced with a new board run by a single chairman. Senator Brewster of Maine called Hillman an "appeaser." As for Truman, he remembered it this way in his memoirs:

> I had already determined that Hillman would have to go as Associate
> Director of OPM along with Knudsen. I had told the Senate in October . . .
> of an attempt by Hillman to have a construction contract withheld from the
> low-bidder because he feared that the award to that firm would be followed
> by labor troubles.

Truman's actual words were more biting: "I cannot condemn Mr. Hillman's position too strongly," he told the Senate. "First the U.S. does not fear trouble from any source; and if trouble is threatened, the U.S. is able to protect itself. If Mr. Hillman cannot, or will not, protect the interests of the U.S., I am in favor of replacing him with someone who can and will."[95]

After the Currier affair the odor of scandal never entirely disappeared; it was kept alive by Hillman's enemies on the right and left. Michigan's Representative Albert J. Engel, together with Fulton Lewis,

Jr., a conservative columnist and radio commentator, circulated a story early in 1942 that Hillman had abused his power and connived with Donald Nelson to divert government clothing contracts to firms that dealt with the ACW and at the expense of those firms under contract with the ILG. John L. Lewis claimed credit for this "exposure" as well, and at a WPB meeting he was called a liar to his face by Hillman's lawyer, Maxwell Brandwen, whereupon Lewis stormed out. Fulton Lewis called for Hillman's removal over the Mutual Radio Network, in part, or so Hillman's aides believed, to divert public attention away from sordid revelations about the avarice of vested industrial interests in suborning WPB officials into allowing continued civilian production. Donald Nelson responded to Representative Engel by denying any collusion while noting that most of the items on Engel's list were manufactured in non-ACW shops.[96]

But the damage was done. John L. Lewis and Fulton Lewis were driving nails into a coffin constructed at least in part by Hillman's ostensible allies in the labor movement. Friends were already urging him to resign. He stopped attending most WPB meetings. As it became clear that a new manpower agency, outside the precincts of the WPB, was in the offing, AFL and CIO leaders alike advised Roosevelt against choosing Hillman as its director. A committee comprising Sam Rosenman, Harold Smith, William Douglas, and Anna Rosenberg deliberated. Isador Lubin told Rosenman that the rumored appointment of Paul McNutt would amount to an indictment of Hillman, but Lubin then learned that Green and Murray had already told McNutt the job was his. R. J. Thomas later confessed: "We pulled the rug out from under Sidney when the WPB replaced the OPM because he wouldn't fight Bill Knudsen in the open. We knew he'd fight him in OPM meetings, but he wouldn't go to Congress and holler." FDR made it plain to Donald Nelson that Hillman's days were numbered. Discussing how to launch a new patriotic production drive, Roosevelt told Nelson to talk it over with Green and Murray, "alone at first and then have Sidney come over. They do not love him too much." When Rosenman and the rest of committee made their final recommendation to the President, they emphasized that "politically Sidney Hillman is impossible," a position argued most forcefully by Anna Rosenberg and Harold Smith.[97]

Hillman was simply no longer usable as a manager of industrial unrest, and with America's new status as a belligerent the committee members felt it would in any event be easier to impose administration policy and elicit real acts of sacrifice. By then Harold Ickes was convinced that Hillman's dumping was inevitable and echoed the view of R. J. Thomas:

Hillman was not a heavy-handed enough man to hold his own with the big
business pirates, first at OPM and then on the SPAB. His disposition and
character being what they were, he should not have accepted appointment
as co-director of OPM with Knudsen. . . . He could not stand against
Knudsen and so he cannot escape at least joint responsibility with Knudsen
for permitting the auto manufacturers to be using steel and plant capacity in
turning out a record number of autos. . . . When Hillman got into WPB
Nelson undertook to take what was left of him.

William O. Douglas, who worried about the reaction of labor to
Hillman's firing, pleaded with the President to send Hillman a soothing
telegram, which he did. It notified him of McNutt's appointment and
therefore of the Labor Division's loss of its training and labor supply
functions. Because of this general downgrading of the Division,"I feel
very strongly that you properly will not want that kind of work with the
WPB." But, the President tactfully insisted, he continued to cherish
Hillman's advice, so "I am therefore appointing you 'Special Assistant to
the President on Labor Matters.' " This honorary position, Roosevelt
flattered him, meant Hillman's "relationship to me in the Government
will be very similar to that of Harry Hopkins."[98]

But Hillman knew the analogy was empty. While Hopkins's importance as the President's emissary increased in direct proportion to his
distance from all positions of official responsibility, Hillman, on the
other hand, suspended in midair as the President's "Special Assistant,"
would be ignored by Washington and trade union bureaucrats alike. He
courteously declined the President's offer, suggesting that he could best
serve the country by resuming his position in the labor movement.[99]

It was an absolutely crushing blow. The President's telegram was sent
to Doctors' Hospital in Washington, where Hillman was being treated
for a massive coronary. The twenty-two months in office had been physically punishing to an already frail constitution. A year earlier serious
illness had nearly expedited a palace coup against Hillman at the birth of
the OPM. Several months later Hillman was examined for gout, and his
doctor contemplated an operation on his feet, opting instead for rigorous
physiotherapy and diathermy. He was hospitalized again around the time
of the WPB's creation. It all seemed trivial, however, compared to this
collapse of his heart, which very nearly killed him and left him ailing
through the following July.

Hillman was sick in spirit as well. Joseph Keenan, an AFL functionary and head of the Construction Stabilization Board, considered Hillman's firing "one of the most shabby treatments of an individual by the
White House I ever encountered. Afterwards I visited with Sidney one
evening . . . and he was dismayed." Edward Prichard thought "the whole

thing had just about broken Hillman," and he wondered if he could survive it. "At the least he will be in the hospital for some time." David Niles visited the hospital as well, where Bessie broke down in front of Niles, and Hillman confessed he had "no desire to go on." Niles discounted some of this as Hillman's known penchant for the melodramatic, but he reported to Grace Tully how hard it was for Hillman, who was "very much devoted to the Boss." Bessie reminded Niles of Hillman's earlier deep depression in Florida back in 1937 and of how the President's phone call lifted his spirits. She plaintively asked if he could do it again. Niles suggested to Tully that "in view of the splendid relationship that has existed between Hillman and the President," it might be politic to do so. FDR then wrote to Hillman wishing him a speedy recovery and extending an invitation to pay him a visit once he felt up to it. Days later Hillman replied, evidently delighted.[100]

Certainly Hillman's failure marked a milestone in the political history of the CIO, as after that the CIO no longer enjoyed any formal position of significance within the regime. After taking account of all of Hillman's liabilities and failings, so long as he remained on the job the labor movement as a whole, not just the CIO, retained a certain influence by virtue of the prestige attaching to Hillman's office. He was replaced by a series of faceless civil servants in the WPB's Labor Production Division, for all practical purposes voiceless and inert. McNutt's WMC was excluded from the labor relations arena and rendered powerless to enforce its will over those matters of labor supply which remained within its limited jurisdiction. As a conciliatory gesture, McNutt named Clinton Golden as vice chairman of the WMC and his special labor adviser and established a Management–Labor Policy Committee. No one paid any attention.[101]

Hillman's firing thus signaled a new equilibrium in the nation's political chemistry. His fate was to a considerable degree beyond his control, a predictable outcome of the genetic makeup of the defense bureaucracy. The Labor Division was never endowed with power enough to come forward as the central labor administration of the federal government. Lacking an arsenal of weapons with which to perform as labor's white knight, the Division was at best tepidly supported by the AFL and the CIO. Without more muscular backing from the labor movement, the Division was at a decided disadvantage in combating the potentates of the Army and heavy industry.[102]

Yet Hillman can hardly be held blameless. If he was a "half-intellectual," attracted by the world of ideas but never entirely confident within it, he also proved to be a "half-bureaucrat," an architect of the iron cage but never as adept as others in the arts and crafts of administrative routine and intrigue. Despite his formidable title of Associate Director, he never tried to assert his prerogatives and to force his way into matters of production. Even his friendliest associates agreed that he was "a somewhat erratic administrator." Frankfurter, who had promoted and patronized Hillman for twenty years, acknowledged to Roosevelt in the days before the firing that Hillman's leadership of the preceding two years lacked boldness, that the AFL's suspicions, the CIO's militance, and Lewis's drumbeat of denunciations together aggravated Hillman's "inferiority complexes," leaving him uncharacteristically timid and inept. This surprising timorousness also allowed internal squabbles to fester as the "Director" refused "to stake a clear stand when disputes arose." A retrospective assessment of Hillman's tenure acutely observed that it was not so much that Hillman couldn't adjust to bureaucratic protocol, but that he "never fitted into a bureaucratic organization which he could neither dominate nor direct."[103]

For a while, however, he certainly tried. An observer later remembered him as actually far less suspicious of corporate "dollar-a-year" men than, for example, Leon Henderson, and less doctrinaire on policy matters than the beleaguered circle of New Deal economists. Although Hillman and Knudsen argued frequently, they were in private "very friendly." Indeed, they trusted each other even while their respective staffs sedulously worked to subvert that trust. Utterly different in style, the two men shared important character traits despite their social distance. Both evinced a passionate patriotism peculiar to the foreign-born grateful for their remarkable social elevation. Both were men "of great natural intellect," largely self-educated, self-made, "and consequently self-reliant." Although Hillman's was a powerful personality that had grown accustomed to dispensing great authority, "he refused absolutely to fight Bill Knudsen in the press and in Congress."

At OPM meetings Stimson was genteel and polished, Knox boisterous and emotional, Knudsen taciturn and blunt, while Hillman "worked in the Talmudic tradition and loved to talk at length, going into all the subtleties and refinements of a position." Perkins, who warred constantly if quietly with Hillman over jurisdictional boundaries, staff, and funds, doubtlessly exaggerated his polemical preeminence when she remembered: "After a little while they all learned and Knudsen began to take almost everything that Hillman wanted. Hillman could always beat him out in an argument." The lessons of the Kovno seminary and the Marxist *kolkhoz* had endured. That was to be expected, not only because he was bred to debate, but because again and again he found himself swimming against the current.[104]

But under duress Hillman's greatest strengths could become disabling weaknesses. He had always been a tireless organizer with a compulsive need to be forever busy. He brought that restless energy to Washington and threw himself into dozens of demanding tasks all at once. A typical itinerary during a West Coast trip included meetings with Frey about simmering discontent among the metal workers; intelligence-gathering sessions with Germer about the CIO; numerous conferences with local OPM officials; interviews with job candidates; inspections of shipyards; meetings with contractors and bureaucrats about a variety of supply problems; a tour of Boeing with the company president and union officials; peacemaking among AFL and CIO warlords; more rounds of negotiations to stave off a welders' strike; a speech in San Francisco about subcontracting; a get-together with Governor Olson and San Francisco's Mayor Rossi to discuss the labor situation in California; another round of inspections of Henry Kaiser's magnesium plant; a tour of Lockheed in Burbank with its president; a strategy session with Thomas, Frankensteen, and Leonard to review the UAW's status in the aircraft industry; meetings with Bethlehem and Consolidated Steel magnates to figure out why their TWI programs were failing to supply enough adequately trained welders for the shipyards; more tours with aviation executives of plants in San Diego; an on-site assessment of Federal housing projects; and innumerable consultations with hordes of technical and industrial relations personnel—all in ten days.[105]

Hillman invited all this responsibility, relished it, in fact. He never spared himself and was on call at all times. More was driving him, however, than his normal quotient of surplus nervous energy. He desperately wanted to please, not be fawning, but by making himself seem agreeably indispensable to a world in which, despite everything, he would always feel himself the foreigner. He confided to a friend that the secret of his high posts was his willingness to undertake unpopular and unpleasant tasks. Hillman loved the whirl of Washington power politics, but it was after all a milieu of gentile gentry saturated in anti-Semitism. No matter how agnostic, even irreligious, he might appear, no matter how aloof he held himself from the worlds of Jewish labor and Zionism, Hillman remained tainted, and he knew it. As the psychological regimen needed to survive in this atmosphere of intrigue and covert operations grew ever more grueling, Hillman confessed, "I must work harder. If I fail it will be the failure of the Jew Hillman."[106]

Trying to be all things to all people, he overreached himself. He became an "over-organizer . . . a driver and severe on his staff." He developed the fanaticism of the political commissar. "He was afraid of incompetence and defeat." Egotism and hubris, a tendency to hold court that was hardly visible before, became obvious even to his most devoted colleagues. Frances Perkins was convinced that he wanted to be labor czar even if it meant circumventing the law. Yet at the same time he was so overcommitted, so absorbed in fending off intramural and outside assaults on his position, that he "neglected details while Knudsen reveled in them." Guilty of "administrative disorderliness," he didn't hesitate "to organize division after division which duplicated everything in the place," dispersing his strained resources until they were exhausted. [107]

By April 1942 Hillman himself was exhausted. There were major accomplishments to his credit: McNutt inherited a well-lubricated machine for the training of manpower; open hostilities between the warring labor federations had ceased, a truce that Hillman had helped negotiate; mechanisms for stabilizing wages and labor relations that Hillman conceived were in place and working. Yet he was dying physically and spiritually, a casualty of the war. On its altar he had offered up his political credibility, his moral puissance, and his organizational genius. There seemed to be nothing left.

SEVENTEEN

⚛︎

"Clear It with Sidney"

While still convalescing in Doctors' Hospital, Hillman received a disquieting report from Archibald MacLeish on the state of morale in the trenches of American industry. An "in-depth survey" revealed serious symptoms of malaise and disaffection. At most, 51 percent of war workers in Pittsburgh and only 37 percent in Detroit displayed high morale. Less than half of all defense workers exhibited "high morale." The rest expressed a sense of futility about the value of their individual efforts and, more alarming, a deep hopelessness about what awaited them in the postwar world, where many anticipated renewed depression, declining wages, and unemployment. They were overwhelmingly cynical about management and were prepared to armor themselves in a shell of self-interest. Even those with high morale harbored doubts and criticisms of profiteering managements who were reluctant to convert. As in world War I, when, many were convinced, owners used the emergency as an excuse to plunder, management could be expected to use this new national crisis to destroy the social achievements of the past decade. Those victimized by "conversion unemployment" were of course particularly suspicious. Summing up, MacLeish noted that it was not a "heartening picture." Unless the government took concrete steps—the $25,000 salary cap, for example, which carried at least symbolic weight with workers angry about corporate greed—and gave real assurances about economic security after the war, morale was bound to deteriorate further.

The survey was full of grim, visceral forebodings: "Everything is going to be worse after the war. There won't be any work, people will be crippled, and in hospitals, and on welfare. Factories will close up, there'll be nothing to produce. The next generation will have nothing but taxes and crippled men to support." Cynicism was in season: "We don't feel that the bosses are interested in us, so why should we kill ourselves?" is how one man explained the rationale for slowdowns at his plant. An interviewer in Pittsburgh discerned the fear beneath the self-interest: "Many of these workers have the indelible line of the depression years written on their faces. They remember only too well the hunger of that period. . . . Now that they are fully employed they feel they have to make the 'dough' while they can." Black workers' premonitions of the postwar world were even harsher: "I might be fighting for democracy all right," a Detroit aircraft worker said, "but it won't be democracy for the Negro. That's what makes me mad." Others worried that the speedup that war production legitimated would become the rule in peacetime. A UAW official put it this way: "They want to make the sacrifice themselves. They don't want someone else to force the sacrifice on them."[1]

This popular disaffection was politically debilitating, as it further undermined a regime that had already had its hands full fending off its gathering foes on the right. Once he had recovered from the physical and emotional trauma of his dismissal, Hillman dedicated all his dwindling energies to shoring up what remained of the New Deal Democratic Party. For that purpose he invented the country's first Political Action Committee. And for his troubles he became, for a moment, a figure of fear and loathing, the symbolic center of a presidential campaign remarkably sour and paranoid for a country still deep in the throes of war.

The groundswell of sullen suspicion uncovered by MacLeish did more than jeopardize the government's ambitious plans to outproduce the Axis. It threatened as well the delicate concord between the trade unions and the defense mobilization bureaucracies. The WLB and the NLRB sought to centralize and nationalize bureaucratic authority over rank-and-file activity, especially strike activity, and at the same time to ward off encroachments on managerial prerogatives. In return the government guaranteed the institutional security of the labor movement through the "maintenance of membership" principle, whereby all union members were required to retain union membership for the life of the contract. The arrangement essentially enlisted the trade union leadership as the gendarmes of collective bargaining, an unenviable position to hold, as accumulating resentments on the shop floor leached away the moral authority of labor officials.

In 1943 the number of man-hours lost to strikes tripled over 1942, as wildcat actions against the WLB's "wage freeze" and inflation defied the commands of government agencies and trade union leaders alike. Quit rates rose from 1 percent in 1939 to 2 percent in 1941 to 3 percent in 1942, then exploded, approaching 6 percent in 1943–44. In May 1943 Lubin warned Hopkins about looming trouble: "It seems as if we are riding a fundamental swell of industrial unrest." The President, Lubin advised, ought to get in touch with the labor leadership and threaten that unless order was restored congressional reactionaries would be impossible to stop. Late in 1943 Hillman informed the President that dissatisfaction with the "little steel" wage formula was "practically unanimous." And 1944 was worse. One-half of all auto workers struck, and what first emerged as a sporadic set of disconnected, local events began to take on the character of a mass movement. Inside the UAW the leadership had to fend off a popular demand to repudiate the no-strike pledge. Responding to the strike wave, the WLB threatened to withhold the privilege of "maintenance of membership" and to cancel draft deferments if union members didn't control themselves.[2]

Caught between the machinery of the state and its own constituency, the CIO leadership lobbied the WLB to ease up on its wage allowances, denounced the freeze order of the WMC channeling workers into key industries, and threatened to leave the War Labor Board if it didn't act. But everyone knew this to be an idle threat, as the CIO and the AFL, unlike Lewis, who had characteristically pursued his own course in the teeth of government intimidation, were dependent psychologically and politically on the government for the health and well-being of their own institutions.[3]

Moreover, the restiveness that implicitly challenged the social patriotism of the trade union and defense establishment was by no means universally egalitarian, democratic, or anticapitalist in motivation. Industrial discontent fed on racial anxieties about the hiring, promotion, and housing of black workers; on misogynistic concerns about the present and future position of women in the workforce and at home; on elitist and nativist presumptions about just who deserved the protections of seniority and the rewards of higher wages; on territorial jealousies among rival claimants to institutional turf; and on dozens of other petty grievances, phobias, and misunderstandings, which often had little or nothing to do with the social frustrations specifically brought on by war production.

The war inflicted wound after wound on the New Deal's body politic. Its vital signs declined along with Hillman's. The rhetoric of patriotic unity and collective responsibility wafted high over the heads of a fragmented electorate showing symptoms of pathological malfunction. Alarms even went off within the home guard, among garment workers noted for their idolatrous devotion to FDR.

As early as 1939 Carlo Tresca, the reigning patriarch of Italian anarchism in America, confided to Luigi Antonini of the ILG that he was worried about the extent of "fascist, anti-Semitic propaganda among the Italians" throughout the needle trades. Inside the ACW, August Bellanca instructed Joseph Salerno to mobilize the "activity" for decisive action against fascist fanatics circulating among the rank and file. Roosevelt's "stab in the back" condemnation of Mussolini's declaration of war against France excited nationalist passions. The Amalgamated's GEB had to proceed with extreme caution when sending speakers or organizers from the Sons of Italy to places like Binghamton, both because workers there were divided into fascist and antifascist camps and because the Sons were themselves split along the same lines. Bellanca, along with Joseph Catalonotti and others, played a conspicuous role in the Free Italy Labor Council, working to counteract fascist sympathizers. But locals and joint boards faced trying predicaments. For example, the GEB was asked to fund a large-scale antifascist radio campaign aimed at the whole Italian community, in which union locals were reluctant to participate themselves for fear of inciting political turmoil. During the New York City mayoral election of 1941, thousands of Italians deserted La Guardia for the Democratic candidate, William O'Dwyer, venting their anger over Roosevelt's foreign policy, with which the "Little Flower" was closely identified.[4]

Thus, even while the war became the occasion for ritualistic celebrations of the country's democratic cultural pluralism, it also reinvigorated more primordial attachments not always friendly to the purposes of the Roosevelt war regime. Elements of the Polish-language press purveyed a reactionary cliconationalism that expressed hostility not only to the government's Soviet ally abroad but to its attempts at New Deal revivalism at home. The press did not speak for all Poles, to be sure, but the ACW's Leo Krzycki worked intensely through the American Polish Labor Council to neutralize its influence. Krzycki had to overcome the dogged resistance of the Polish Catholic Church to bringing together all the Slavic churches in the American Slav Congress in support of the war aims of the government. The congress took on the even more intractable task of quelling ethnic frictions between Poles and Czechs, Czechs and Slovaks, and Serbs and Croats, who often refused to work alongside one another in defense plants. Of course, the symptoms of nationalist right-wing disaffection were plainly visible as well among German and Irish workers, who had never been overly friendly to the New Deal. The

Church's conservative influence was felt as well among East European Catholic workers in the UE and the USW, where ACTU cadre, priests and laity alike, concentrated their efforts.[5]

These unmistakable signs of political disarray had worried Hillman ever since the 1940 presidential election, when he impressed members of the GEB with the importance of widening the range of trade union political activity to counteract the loss of middle-class voters and the growth of the bipartisan conservative coalition in Congress. As the 1942 congressional elections approached, New Deal strategists gloomily surveyed a landscape full of enemies and fair-weather friends.[6]

Indeed, it was the 1942 campaign that brought Hillman back to life, but under unseemly circumstances. While he was undergoing a rigorous course of physiotherapies at Doctors' Hospital, Hillman was nursed by his friends back to psychic health. Still recuperating at his modest summer bungalow in Point Lookout on Long Beach, Long Island, Hillman, in his first interview after the heart attack, told the New York Times that business was to blame for shortfalls in defense output and for shortages of vital materials like aluminum, steel, magnesium, and synthetic rubber. Labor's self-sacrificing behavior, on the other hand, had been exemplary. Weak as he still was, Hillman itched to join the fray.[7]

In September Hillman got in touch with Marvin McIntyre. He was ready to come back to work and sought an appointment with the President. Ignored at first, he relived the suffering of the past spring. Suddenly he was recalled from exile, but with a distasteful assignment that taxed his conscience and probed the psychic economy of resentment and ambition with which he had lived since his recent humiliation. Administration strategists, sensing their weakness in the coming elections, wanted to reactivate the CIO politically and in particular to restore Hillman to favor. In an effort to mend fences with conservative and machine-dominated sections of his own party, Roosevelt asked Hillman to secure the backing of the American Labor Party (ALP) for the New York gubernatorial candidacy of John Bennett. Bennett, the state's Attorney General since 1930, was a stereotypical Tammany hack, a favorite of the American Legion, enthusiastically despised by liberal democrats in and outside of the ALP. It was James A. Farley and his minions who rammed Bennett through, edging out James Mead, Roosevelt's preferred choice. For Farley the stakes were high; in effect it was a contest to determine who would control the state's delegation to the Party's 1944 presidential nominating convention.[8]

Roosevelt's support for Bennett was transparently tepid. He acknowledged in a letter to Hillman that some people didn't believe his endorsement was wholehearted. Still, he expected Hillman to release the letter to the press as a pretext for announcing his own support for Bennett. Hillman hesitated, made clear his irritation, squirmed, and stalled for time, until finally, just days before the election, he made the President's letter public through the *New York Times*. The *Advance* followed with an editorial endorsing Bennett and urging the electorate to rely on the President's judgement.[9]

All in all it was a discreditable if passing interlude in Hillman's life. But it signalled just how desperate he and the administration had become. Currying favor with the right in any event turned out disastrously. In New York the split occasioned by the Bennett candidacy not only opened the door for Dewey but severely weakened the Democratic Party. More generally, the President and the Democratic Party, especially its New Deal wing, took a bad drubbing in the midterm elections. Even the venerable Progressive George Norris went down to defeat, losing both his rural base and German support, despite a substantial financial contribution from the ACW. Voter turnout was dismal; 28 million out of a potential 80 million, 22 million less than in 1940. Republicans gained forty-four seats in the House and nine in the Senate, and won the governorships of New York, Michigan, and California. Delighted with their own resuscitation, they egged on embattled Southern Democrats to leave the party.[10]

The 78th Congress demonstrated the cohesiveness of the Southern Democrat–conservative Republican opposition. Harry Byrd of Virginia led the campaign to liquidate the NYA, the CCC, the FSA, the WPA, and the NRPB. A Senate filibuster quashed an anti–poll tax bill passed by the House and clouded the air with fulminations against the FEPC. Failure to carry through the "second reconstruction" plotted in 1937–38 now haunted the calculations of panicked party strategists, who cringed and looked for ways to placate Southern racial and labor prejudices as well as the region's hereditary fear of federal intrusion. But the disaffection of Southern elites was deep. Most of all they resented the decline of Southern influence in Washington and were truly alarmed when the Supreme Court ruled against the white-only primary in the summer of 1943. They hated the pressure to open up party structures to Negro participation through the poll tax bill and the soldiers' vote bill, granting federal regulatory power over what was customarily a jealously guarded state prerogative to determine voter eligibility. Racial preoccupations spilled over into a generalized sensitivity to all statist initiatives, including the President's State of the Union talk about cradle-to-grave social security.[11]

Together with their Republican allies, "Dixiecrats" worried about the war-induced revitalization of the CIO, frightened by its integrationist principles and practices, convinced that it would scare away the new industry so avidly courted by the region's commercial boosters. The conservative bloc was strong enough to override a presidential veto and pass Senator Tom Connally's antistrike bill. The bill passed amid the national hysteria in response to John L. Lewis's defiance of the President in a series of quickie coal strikes. Connally's law prohibited strikes in plants seized by the government, allowed for the jailing of strikers, required thirty days' advance notice and an NLRB-supervised strike vote first, and banned political contributions by trade unions in federal elections. The Smith–Connally Act was accompanied by a rash of state legislation limiting the right to picket, to engage in jurisdictional strikes, and to contribute to local political campaigns. The congressional opposition also managed to restrict federal aid to education, to prohibit consumer subsidies by the Commodities Credit Corporation, and to kill the Kilgore–Murray bill for federal control over unemployment compensation, the proposals for a federal economic planning agency, and the symbolic call for a $25,000 salary cap.[12]

Even personal grudges were remembered and pursued. The presidential adviser James Rowe alerted Roosevelt that Millard Tydings, having discovered that the ACW supplied much of the money for Roosevelt's attempt to purge the Senator in the 1938 primaries, was plotting to indict Hillman, along with Drew Pearson, for violating the Hatch and Income Tax acts.[13]

This crystallizing congressional party of resentment and revanchism, prone to rants about the diabolical conspiracy of New York Jewish communists and labor radicals to run the government, was more than enough to rekindle the Great Fear of 1936 in the minds of Hillman and the CIO. Moreover, it was accompanied and probably encouraged by what seemed to be the irresistible infiltration by the corporate old guard into all the commanding positions of state power. The ascendancy of Bernard Baruch within the inner councils of the war economy was indicative. Baruch's advocacy of state-sponsored cartelization of the military-industrial economy was receiving a wider hearing, as a tidal wave of industrial and financial concentration rolled over whatever frail obstacles stood in its way.[14]

The rightward draft of the business community was apparent everywhere. During the early years of the war the WLB found a sympathetic constituency among Keynesian-minded businessmen: Eric Johnston, head of a smallish building materials firm and president of the U.S. Chamber of Commerce, Cy Ching of U.S. Rubber, Walter Teagle of Standard Oil, Henry Kaiser, William Batt, Robert Johnson, Marion

Folsom of Kodak, and Paul Hoffman of Studebaker. But by 1944 intransigents within the NAM and the USCC, revivified by the antilabor exertions of "New South" industrialists like Humble of Humble Oil in Texas and Midwestern diehards like the infamous Sewell Avery of Montgomery Ward, were mounting serious opposition to the labor–management entente of the New Deal. Keynesianism itself took on a protective coloration. While some, like Alvin Hansen, continued to advocate structural innovations in the system of production and distribution and were avidly supported by the CIO, an alternative "commercial Keynesianism" surfaced among liberal business circles organized into the Committee for Economic Development, which eschewed such drastic measures in favor of state-coordinated countercyclical fiscal and monetary manipulations on behalf of an otherwise unrestrained system of corporate-led growth.[15]

This tidal drift of the country away from the social democratic vistas of the mid-1930s was alarming in the extreme both to Hillman and, in its own way, to the administration. For Hillman there was never a question about how to respond. It was a matter of converting the enormous but latent political and electoral strength of the CIO into a mighty machine for the salvation of Roosevelt and what was left of the New Deal.

Was any other course conceivable? John L. Lewis marshaled his coal miners in resolute belligerence and with strike after strike during 1943 grandiloquently decried a regime so hypocritical as to shed blood abroad for democracy while turning a blind eye to rampant injustice at home. But Lewis, stranded in minatory isolation, champion of labor militance and trade union independence, hardly embodied a sane alternative for men who had come to prize their own probity and reasonableness. Lewis's heroism amounted to less than it seemed, as the nation's stockpile of coal was several multiples of what the war effort actually required. However, a comparable wave of strikes in the munitions, shipbuilding, or aircraft industries would have soon presented a dire emergency. There the no-strike pledge, which Lewis treated so cavalierly, constituted a blood oath. Ironically, Lewis escaped more serious censure, in part, precisely because the administration knew that a frontal assault on the UMW would necessarily elicit an angry if reluctant rejoinder from Hillman, Murray, and even William Green.[16]

Above all, Hillman remained appalled at the specter of reactive backlash from the right, both within and outside of the Democratic Party. He worried about rebellious sentiments to his left to be sure, mostly in the form of separatist exhortations emanating from Detroit, New York, and New Jersey to convene third parties or labor parties. He would go out of his way to stigmatize such breakaway stirrings, but largely as dangerous nuisances threatening the unity of his own political calculations and not because they stood any serious chance of success on their own terms. After all, the prospects for a labor party in 1944 were immeasurably less promising than they had been in 1936, while the Great Fear from the right grew more ominous. If the New Deal coalition was unraveling, he knew it was coming apart on the right, that its working-class and minority constituents on the left truly had nowhere else to turn.[17]

Summing up this complex political arithmetic, Hillman concocted the country's first "Political Action Committee" (PAC), designed to penetrate the policy-making upper echelons of the Democratic Party while preserving the CIO's freedom of political action. Months before its actual formation, Hillman and his colleagues laid the groundwork. Within weeks of the 1942 electoral debacle, the CIO raised the decibel level of its demands for equitable rationing and price controls and its declamations against pending antistrike legislation, the Smith–Connally bill particularly. At the same time labor leaders like Reuther, Murray, and Zaritsky joined with middle-class Progressives, including Reinhold Niebuhr and Paul Douglas, and prominent New Deal politicians, including Wagner and La Guardia, to broaden the united front against reaction, creating the Union for Democratic Action. Meanwhile the CIO "legislative committee" issued a general directive to all locals urging them to create their own legislative committees and to establish close working relations with local congressmen.[18]

Hillman devoted himself exclusively to the creation of a permanent political organization. He invoked the specter of a postwar economic trauma and told a Massachusetts CIO convention that political action had become imperative: "Workers can no longer work out even their most immediate day to day problems through negotiations with their employers. . . . Their wages, hours, and working conditions have become increasingly dependent upon policies adopted by Congress and the National Administration. . . . Labor must bring its full influence to bear in shaping these decisions." While he hoped to collaborate closely with FDR from the outset, the President kept his distance, waiting to see how robust an organization would result.[19]

In July 1943 Hillman gleefully reported to the President that the CIO had created a Political Action Committee to provide the organizational muscle for united political action by the labor movement on the President's behalf. The birthing happened at a CIO Executive Board meeting on July 7 and 8, where Hillman assumed the chairmanship of the new organization. Hillman described the CIO's political predicament as a "deplorable state of affairs and it will not be cured by simply finding fault with Congress." The labor federation was, he feared, infected with "defeatism." He warned against any attempt to revoke the no-strike pledge or similar exercises in frustrated acting-out. "The country will not stand for strikes during wartime. Make up your mind that is the situation." He was painfully frank and typically blunt: "We have lost a great deal since 1942, we have lost position in the Congress and in the country since 1940. . . . Of course we have twelve to fourteen million organized workers and there is a tremendous amount of power there. What it needs is organization." He was convinced that the time was ripe for another LNPL, "but don't come along with any hifalutin organizations that may work out 25 years from now or may not. The time is very short."

R. J. Thomas followed to report that the committee appointed by Murray to consider a "Labor League" had unanimously agreed that a third party would be unwise. The committee members may have harmonized on this point, but as a matter of fact it remained a sensitive issue at a time when the CIO felt besieged, suffering from an acute sense of its own political decline and inertia. George Baldanzi of the dyers' union, responding to the cautionary prescriptions of Hillman and Thomas, cautioned them in turn that the CIO rank and file would vehemently oppose any reaffirmation of the no-strike pledge that would allow Congress and the President "to ride over us rough-shod." Samuel Wolchok, the man Hillman had once deposed as head of the department store organizing drive, defended the notion of a third party, if only as a device for venting the anger of disillusioned defense workers who might otherwise resort to more drastic measures, Wolchok feared, even mass strikes. All in all, it was a remarkably acrimonious and troubled gathering for one ostensibly called to inaugurate a bold political adventure and to anoint Hillman as its overlord.[20]

In those early days Hillman expended considerable rhetoric on the third-party issue, making it unmistakably clear that the PAC would have nothing to do with dangerous diversions, that he personally had forever interred such visions as delusionary and utopian for midcentury America. He first stated his position at the July PAC executive meeting, where he asserted: "It is definitely not the policy of the CIO to organize a third party, but rather to abstain from and discourage any move in that direction," as it would "serve to divide labor and the progressive forces."

That was the most unequivocal repudiation of his own past. By 1944 the landscape of American politics had changed again in ways for which Sidney Hillman was partly responsible, and he no longer even flirted with the idea of independent politics: "We have no desire to organize another political party. As a matter of fact, we are opposed."[21]

Hillman did more than talk. He played a vital role in Minnesota, arranging the long-sought mating of the Farmer–Labor and Democratic parties. Roosevelt viewed the Farmer–Labor Party as crucial to his 1944 electoral strategy, and so was anxious to induce Elmer Benson to surrender the party's independence. Hillman told Sander Genis, an ACW apparatchik and president of the Minnesota CIO, to pull every lever at his disposal to effect the merger. Genis contrived to get his old foes from 1940 in the CP, who dominated the UE and other unions in the state, to cooperate. Hillman traveled to the state himself to warm up the atmosphere for fusion, and in 1944 the two parties made everyone happy by merging. Similarly, in New Jersey Hillman was asked by his old nemesis, Frank Hague, speaking through a Roosevelt intermediary, to quell the political revolt led by Carl Holderman and Irving Abrahamson. Hillman obliged. He monitored rebellious stirrings elsewhere as well, wanting reassurances, for example, from the principal leaders of the Michigan Commonwealth Federation that they wouldn't run rival candidates when the PAC endorsed a figure from one of the two major parties.[22]

Labor parties, farmer–labor parties, and antimonopoly parties seemed always to stand on the fringes of bourgeois politics, to speak a language of pariahdom, to indict American society and its political system for fundamental failings of social injustice, economic exploitation, and moral corruption. Programmatically, therefore, they invariably offered up proposals for dismantling the substructures of the marketplace: private property, wage labor, concentrated capital. The Labor Non-Partisan League, however, had established a new threshold of ambivalence. It still excoriated "manipulators of other people's money and the exploiters of other people's labor." It continued to herald the "battle of the masses against the classes, of the people against the economic royalists." But the LNPL was the creature of the second New Deal, and its remedies for the Depression echoed the state capitalist, regulatory, and redistributive agenda of the Keynesian elite. Politically, the League was androgynous, a labor party and yet not a labor party. The PAC embodied some of the same ambivalence but was already more unequivocally committed to carving out a permanent and prominent place for itself within the national councils of the Democratic Party. Its fealty to Roosevelt became ever more unconditional even as the President's regime coddled the "economic royalists" it had once lambasted.[23]

Above all else the immediate fact of the war and the elemental

impulse to conform lowered the sights of social reform. Then, too, the
Depression, the New Deal, and the war together accelerated the nationalization of culture, dissolving those multiple pockets of local resistance
rooted in town, city, and regional social economies, which had so often
given rise to third-party rebellions. Moreover, precisely because of the
New Deal's considerable victories, it was for the first time possible for
despised and dissenting populations to treat the state as an independent
actor capable of offering relief, of succoring the oppressed and punishing
their oppressors. And the CIO too could count up its victories and credit
many of them, especially the quantum leap in membership during the
war, to its special relationship with the New Deal's party and state.
Furthermore, the CIO officialdom was acutely aware that a third-party
rupture with the Roosevelt regime would be poorly appreciated by the
legions of the faithful among its own rank and file. Finally, it registered
in the thinking of Hillman and others that large-scale corporate capitalism had not only arrived but had arrived for good and all, extending its
networks of production and distribution everywhere, reducing to insignificance or wiping out entirely all those rural, small town, and urban
forms of petty capitalism that for generations had supplied much of the
social energy and repertoire of symbols for dozens of "producer," "labor,"
"farmer-labor," "populist," and "antimonopoly" insurgencies.

Hillman kept the new organization focused on the enormous tasks of
economic, social, and political reconstruction that would immediately
follow the war and were already the subject of intense debate. He had
learned a great deal from his World War I experience, including how
easy it was to emerge with an apparent victory only to see it all slip away
in a fit of domestic political reaction. The PAC was to prevent that from
happening again:

> Yes, we will win the war. But men and women, many of us who participated
> in the war a quarter century ago, left it to others to make the peace. . . .
> As a result of this war and the victory that will be achieved at the conclu-
> sion of it we must move forward to a broader program of social and eco-
> nomic security for the men and women of this nation.[24]

The PAC announced its "People's Program of 1944," an amalgam of
Keynesian fiscal policy and social welfare reform which in its essentials
was to remain the platform of organized labor for the next thirty years. Its
long-term plans called for full employment at fair wages, a national
planning board with power to plan compensatory public works spending,
a guaranteed annual wage, federal aid to education, construction of 1.5
million public housing units a year for ten years, the extension and

improvement of social security coverage including medical insurance, active antitrust enforcement and incentives for small business, and permanent status for the FEPC. To address the more immediate if temporary domestic problems bound to accompany the end of the war, it demanded various kinds of aid for returning veterans: educational and vocational training, free hospital and medical care, guaranteed reemployment at their old jobs, farm and home loans, and rigorous enforcement of price and rent controls. In foreign affairs, PAC advocated the adoption of the proposed new international monetary and trading system promulgated at Bretton Woods, liberal industrial credits for all nations, and a significant role for organized labor in all the international planning and administrative bodies of the peace.[25]

The promises and proposals of the People's Program were hardly a revelation. Vice President Henry Wallace's "Century of the Common Man" speech, delivered shortly after Hillman left the government in 1942, first articulated this vision of a "global New Deal": international full employment as the basis of domestic prosperity and internationally recognized standards of living; the destruction of multinational cartels; the breakup of formal and informal colonial empires; free trade and equal access to raw materials; and a global investment fund with which to sponsor infrastructural development, including transportation systems and TVA-style power, land reclamation, and development projects. At home, the goal of a full-employment postwar economy—Roosevelt and the CIO boldly projected 60 million jobs—achieved through a hazily defined mixed economy, had already emerged as the *sine qua non* of economic reconstruction. PAC's perspective on planning was likewise already on the table. In 1943 Murray refloated his industrial council plan to institutionalize the labor movement's participation in reconversion planning. Murray's councils would be authorized to allocate raw materials and workers and even to decide the disposition of government plants—in theory, at least, the most ambitious reformulation of postwar economic life. Hillman's thinking about postwar reconstruction was influenced by a 1942 Marriner Eccles speech in which the Federal Reserve chairman argued that if state planning worked well to maximize production for war, it could work as well in peacetime.[26]

The PAC was inspired by, and borrowed many of its concrete policy recommendations from, the report "Security, Work, and Relief Policies" issued by the National Resources Planning Board early in 1943. The Board's work reflected the thinking of Keynesian circles within and outside of the state bureaucracy. Sharing a common fear about a likely postwar depression, the report stressed the need for rigorous planning and countercyclical fiscal management; close cooperation between business and government to ensure full employment; massive programs of public housing, education, and health care; and infrastructural and urban development. Most important, it called for the protection of labor through an Economic Bill of Rights, including the right to work; equal opportunity; decent standards of nutrition, shelter, and clothing; and the right to security against the ravages of old age, sickness, unemployment, and disability.

The NRPB's vision of a managed cooperative commonwealth, prosperous and secure, struck a chord in the CIO from top to bottom. Addressing a gathering of CIO functionaries, Hillman reiterated this overriding preoccupation with security and the tendency to conflate it with liberation. The New Deal must be preserved, he implored, "to give dignity to men and women, to give them security—yes, freedom, political, social, but above all economic. And unless you can give to men and women economic security, all the rest is fraud."[27]

The Keynesian provenance of the "People's Program" was explicit. Prosperity and security rested on volume production at lower unit profits, buttressed by expanded and government-supported purchasing power, hence the PAC's call for a 20 percent increase in basic wage rates, a 65-cent minimum wage, more generous unemployment compensation, and special termination pay for war workers. Rigorous rent and price controls would prevent the liquidation of savings and purchasing power. The Keynesian perspective over the longer haul depended first of all on a guaranteed annual wage, and secondarily on a program of public works and aid to business.

Even the PAC's overture to the American farmer was an exercise in Keynesian stabilization, emphasizing the disruptive impact on national markets of low farm income. It called for continued price supports, federal aid in the search for new foreign markets, and the promulgation of a national dietary standard as the means for shoring up the demand for farm products and in turn for industrial commodities, as well as for arresting the flood of displaced agrarians onto the urban labor market. This was a long way from that heroic age when workers and farmers seemed to share an eschatology of toil, to constitute two virtuous armies of productive labor allied in a holy war against capitalist greed and parasitism.[28]

In the PAC's view, if the business of America was not purely and simply business, business could no longer be the perennial foil of labor's opprobrium. To be sure, the PAC assumed the proper antitrust position, but that was a bloodless gesture. Hillman and Cooke lamented the wartime moratorium on antitrust prosecutions and called upon the FTC to resume the offensive against "big monopolistic industrialists." But the

PAC staked its real chips at the other end of the commercial ledger, where it demanded tax favors for new businesses and smaller entrepreneurs and extensive government credits to finance reconversion, to subsidize foreign markets, and to facilitate industrial rehabilitation. The future seemed heavily freighted with stagnationist impulses. Clinton Golden forecast a risk-averse business community, one that feared a postwar glutting of the markets resulting from the enormous growth in plant capacity and efficiency and one therefore unlikely to seek out new industries, new technology, and new markets unless prodded, reassured, and assisted by the government.

Some in the CIO (although no one in the AFL) found this solicitude for business and these panegyrics to "free enterprise" hard to swallow. Baldanzi objected that it contradicted the "Murray Plan" emphasis on planning and state enterprise, complaining that it didn't "smell very good." But Hillman defended it as expedient language, acceptable to the current Congress. Murray went further and denied any inconsistency between "planned utilization of our natural resources and genuine free enterprise." In the end Hillman, Murray, and Hillman's counselor, John Abt, agreed to eliminate the offending phrase.

Baldanzi also wanted the PAC to oppose unequivocally the sale of government assets to "monopolistic groups." Again Hillman responded from the standpoint of political expedience, afraid about raising alarms in Congress. He reminded Baldanzi of the CIO's commitment to Senator James E. Murray's War Contracts Termination bill, but Baldanzi contemptuously dismissed all the talk about equality and unity between industry and labor as "a farce" and "fraud and deceitful talk." When it came to a decision, however, only N. A. Zonarich voted no on the reconversion plank.[29]

The "People's Program of 1944" was a grand synthesis, a vision of an integrated economic order that was, to be sure, functional and rational, but at the same time ethical and morally ambitious. This found expression not only in its asseverations about racial equality but also in its defense of women's right to work, its demands for equal pay for equal work and federally subsidized child care, its inspirational calls for cradle-to-grave social security, and its concern for domestic workers, unprotected farm workers, and the millions living without decent housing. When Hillman spoke to a Russian War Relief dinner at the end of 1942, it might have been 1922 as he summed up what the world was worrying about: "We are not fighting and dying in order to re-enact that modern imperialist scramble for power. . . . We fight for the Four Freedoms and all that they imply."[30]

The "People's Program of 1944" was the CIO's version of the Keynesian cooperative commonwealth. It received its finishing touches at a Conference on Full Employment convened at the beginning of 1944 in New York. The conference included Democratic politicians, businessmen, Keynesian economists, delegates from farm organizations, and social workers. "Full employment" may have been its raison d'être, but the conference did not mean to waste any time chewing over the "labor question." On the contrary, "full employment," Henry Wallace's 60 million jobs and a $170 billion national income, would render that refractory question of prewar politics moot, dissolving its deepest social enmities in a salubrious sea of mass prosperity.

Still, the conference was combative enough. "Big monopolistic industrialists" who resisted the state's guidance were accused of selfishly seeking after tax rebates and unconscionable profits while gloating over the demise of the emergency unemployment compensation bill and other efforts to relieve innocent victims of the war economy. Hillman described the niggardly national income figure of $100 billion predicted by the NAM and Alfred Sloan as betraying a callous indifference to those 10 to 15 million workers such a half-speed economy would leave unemployed. Reuther used the occasion to proselytize on behalf of his prefabricated housing reconversion plan for the aircraft industry, and Murray demanded that government-owned plants be used for the public's benefit and not be auctioned off on the cheap to private interests.[31]

It was a rousing sendoff. But the "People's Program of 1944" was not yet the program of the Democratic Party in 1944. Nor was it likely to become so then or in the future unless the PAC and its allies managed to foil the coalition of Dixiecrats, machine bosses, and conservative corporate lobbyists. In Hillman's view one way to accomplish that task was to outperform the urban machines at their own traditional specialty, the mobilizing of the electorate on election day. That would place Roosevelt and the leadership of the administration in the PAC's political debt.

For that purpose the PAC established an elaborate parallel machinery of its own, based on the CIO unions, city and state industrial union councils, and those independent and AFL unions willing to cooperate. Its work of voter education, registration, polling, primary electioneering, and canvassing before and on election day was meticulously organized and perhaps even more lavishly funded than the local precinct-based and patronage-fueled operation of the big city machines. Moreover, Hillman created in the summer of 1944 the National Citizens Political Action Committee, a middle-class analog of the PAC, to make highly visible the extensive nonlabor support for labor's political program. In a remarkably short time, PAC and NCPAC mastered the nuts-and-bolts work of local electioneering as well as the more theatrical techniques of mass politics.

Hillman sped around the country at a grueling pace, making innumerable speaking and radio appearances, holding preliminary conferences, and establishing PAC offices in nearly every major industrial center. Fourteen regional offices were created, and special divisions were established to concentrate on Negro, women's, and youth matters, as were research, radio, and speakers' bureaus. Verda Barnes, director of the women's section, mobilized people around "women's issues" like health care and jobs for women after the war and presented the case for having housework treated like any other form of productive labor. Henry Lee Moon, head of the Negro division, acknowledged the racist and reactionary circles within the Democratic Party but defended Roosevelt's record, the FEPC, and the CIO's unqualified opposition to the racially inspired Philadelphia transit strike of 1943, and made the point that Negroes had little other choice. Moon's division agitated successfully around issues of housing, education, equal pay for equal work, abolition of the poll tax, and antilynching legislation.[32]

While Democratic Party apparatchiks were vastly more experienced at corralling voters, the urban machines, appearances to the contrary notwithstanding, were often lethargic and confused. In many places the PAC rivaled them in money and most of all in energy. Most of the CIO felt estranged from the party machinery. Where an opportunity to cooperate arose, it fell to Hillman, who always cultivated the widest possible network of influence, to deal directly with people like Frank Hague. Returning from a nationwide intelligence-gathering mission, Hillman reported to the CIO Executive Board that he had found many places where machines were ready to listen to the PAC not only on matters of policy but even about what it considered most precious, the selection of candidates. He had met with top-level Democrats and had confirmed this openness. Where the party was riven by faction-fighting, the PAC was often viewed as a unifying force; at least it was welcomed that way by the New Deal wing. Hillman had long since been at home in the world of elite deal-making, so he closed his upbeat progress report with the assurance that if the PAC could win over key figures—"big people," he bluntly labeled them—the rest would be easy.[33]

Hillman missed no chance for broadening the PAC's connections. While there was never any serious possibility of engaging the AFL and the railroad brotherhoods in a nationwide united front, real collaborations were established with some Teamster locals, the Hotel and Restaurant Workers, the ILG, and many AFL unions on the West Coast. Trying to cast its net as far afield as possible, CIO and PAC staffers also met frequently with people from the Committee for Economic Development (CED), seeking out points of agreement on postwar employment and trade policy.[34]

Hillman repeatedly raised the specter of postwar inflation and recession, urging CIO cadre not to limit their program and propaganda appeals to the labor movement, but to reach out to small business, farmers, and professionals. Of course, the PAC paid close attention to the ethnic complexities of American politics, especially among its most immediate constituents. Leo Krzycki did yeoman work for the PAC among the Poles as chairman of the National Slav Congress. The congress worked diligently to counter Republican-inspired red scare propaganda in critical "Polish" cities like Buffalo, Cleveland, and Detroit.[35]

On his first trip after the July executive board announcement, Hillman was pleased to discover local units already active in Cleveland and Toledo. By the time of the CIO convention in November, the PAC was well launched, and the delegates enthusiastically contributed $750,000 and a staff of full-time organizers.[36]

Hillman paid painstaking attention to the mechanics of electioneering. He ordered union membership lists reclassified to reflect the ward or precinct affiliations of the membership so as to expedite voter registration drives. Voter registration was a top PAC priority, especially after the disheartening turnout of 1942, when only one-third of those eligible went to the polls. Hillman hammered away at the need to set up grassroots, precinct-level organizations, to create an "army of registered voters." He pressured particular unions like the steelworkers to assign paid fieldworkers in large numbers to get out the vote in key "steel states" like Pennsylvania, Ohio, and upstate New York. If the PAC was not quite a smoothly oiled electoral machine, it was hardly amateurish either. The committee compiled and disseminated the voting records of congressmen on thirteen key issues, including overrides of the President's veto, roll calls on the soldiers' vote bill, positions on appropriations for UNRRA, and so on. Moreover, the PAC's organized attention to a reconstituted and segmented electoral field with special tactical approaches to women, Negroes, and nationality groups was actually as sophisticated as anything yet devised by the Democratic Party. Where local Democratic Party machines were actively hostile, local PACs were instructed to operate through the campaign committees of individual candidates or, on occasion, to run their own candidates in the Democratic primaries.[37]

PAC propaganda was slickly packaged and even precocious in its mastery of the art of recombinant image manipulation. Its literature deliberately avoided the class antimonies of the League's 1936 inflammatory prose. Indeed, it was pacific, celebratory, and consensual. On the cover of its campaign staple, "This Is Your America," a bucolic farm tableau signaled the PAC's determination to slough off the overdeveloped muscular imagery of the embattled "Labor Militant" and to display itself rather in the ever resplendent colors of mythic Middle America. The pamphlet addressed itself to workers "earning your living honestly," to farmers, small businessmen, and housewives. America was a good place to live "for the Common people," beautiful, rich, industrious, and free so long as everyone's material welfare was provided for, their rights as citizens respected. The PAC wanted nothing more provocative than "a more perfect union in a land bursting with opportunity for all."[38]

As part of its focus on voter registration, the PAC took its educational work with great seriousness. Flyers, papers, and pamphlets circulated in workshops and neighborhoods covered a broad range of momentous issues: the United Nations; the economic bill of rights; guaranteed full employment at decent wages; aid to farmers; government regulation of industry; cradle-to-grave social security; the GI education bill; and civil rights and the FEPC. The PAC published an illustrated taxonomy of the whole defense mobilization apparatus to demonstrate its infestation by the overlords of America's corporate oligarchy. PAC campaigns zeroed in on four themes it felt would most alarm or anger parts of the population and thereby reverse the electoral slippage of 1942: the inequities of inflation and the WLB wage freeze, made all the more intolerable by corporate America's profit-taking; the threat to civil rights; the anticipated economic and social hardship and chaos of a business-dominated recovery; and the Great Fear of another Republican-bred Depression. Indeed, "Depression" was the Democrats' equivalent of the bloody shirt, and the PAC ceaselessly reminded people that the Republican Party, after Willkie's defeat by Dewey in the Wisconsin primary, was once again a captive of the Hoover claque, subject to a "narrow nationalism and the stubborn insistence on a return to the laissez-faire past."[39]

Once the PAC got off the ground, the President and administration insiders quickly shed their earlier aloofness. In the middle of a forty-state tour in October 1943, Hillman conferred with Vice President Wallace on the status of labor's political organization. Frank Walker, a machine boss, was apparently impressed enough to want "to play closely with Hillman." A month later Hillman met for forty minutes with the President. Immeasurably more confident than he had been a year earlier during the Bennett affair, Hillman candidly told Roosevelt that labor was losing confidence in the administration; with the exception of Wallace, it seemed far too tolerant of the growing "Tory" presence in Washington. FDR in turn gave Hillman the green light to work closely with Frank Walker in order to ensure a favorable delegation at the following year's nomination convention. As the presidential campaign approached, Hillman sought and received personal assurances from FDR that he intended to run for a fourth term.[40]

Presidential and PAC campaigning converged as the election drew near. Roosevelt took steps to revive the New Deal coalition through his platform's emphasis on the "Economic Bill of Rights." The President's speech in October in Chicago, prepared by Alvin Hansen and Marriner Eccles, called for a postwar full employment budget and for the replacement of a military-driven economy by planned civilian demand, buttressed by public as well as private investment, resource development, international economic cooperation, and universal social security. The speech could have been lifted intact from the "People's Program." In Congress, Senators Murray, Truman, and Harley M. Kilgore sponsored legislation to create a single agency to plan demobilization, which would include an employment advisory board of labor representatives empowered to consult on all major policies, including the canceling of government contracts and extended unemployment insurance for veterans and excessed defense workers. In the summer the administration renewed its efforts to abolish the poll tax, a PAC priority.[41]

The PAC enjoyed some remarkable early successes during the 1944 primaries. Three members of the House Un-American Activities Committee, which had worked overtime at castigating the PAC, failed to win renomination thanks largely to PAC electioneering: the committee's chairman and *bête noire* of all liberal and labor reformers, Martin Dies of Texas, was forced to withdraw from the Texas primary; Joseph Costello of California (whom the AFL had also worked to defeat), and Joseph Starnes of Alabama, who faced a pro-labor candidate, Albert Raines, were both defeated. In addition, Cotton "Ed" Smith of South Carolina, Rufus Holmes of Oregon, Bennett Champ Clark of Missouri, Hattie Connoway of Arkansas, John Newsome of Alabama, Richard Kleberg of Texas, and D. Worth Clark of Idaho all lost to PAC-endorsed candidates. At the same time, the PAC's friends in the South, like Lister Hill and Claude Pepper, won renomination. There were disappointments: Hamilton Fish in New York, E. E. Cox in Georgia, and Gerald Nye in North Dakota all survived PAC attacks. But in New York, Michigan, California, and Washington, the PAC displayed enough strength to cause Wendell Willkie and other liberal Republicans to make uncharacteristic remarks about labor's rights and about the legitimacy of its worries about security in the postwar world. Republican veterans even toyed with the idea of nominating the AFL's Bill Hutcheson for Vice President in order to dilute the labor vote.[42]

Once the primary season ended, the PAC was prohibited by the

Smith–Connally Act from funneling trade union money into federal elections. In part for that technical reason, but more importantly because Hillman and his administration confrères sought new ways to extend PAC's social reach, he created the National Citizens Political Action Committee in June. Ickes told Charles Merriam how much he liked the idea after he had discussed it with Hillman, who conceived of it "on the model of the Labor Party that has been functioning in New York." Ickes alerted Merriam to its strategic purpose: It "will be the Hillman organization that will have to take on the job that the Corcoran group did so well four years ago." In Ickes's view, the CIO had contributed more to the President's reelection in 1940 than the Democratic National Committee. "And so I can see great possibilities and a wide play for the organization that Hillman proposes."[43]

The NCPAC did indeed get "wide play," as it provided an entree for the CIO into diverse segments of the population not reachable directly through the trade union movement. Hillman made full use of the NCPAC cachet, often arranging to appear with one of its celebrities as he raced around the country on Roosevelt's behalf. He retained his odd appeal as a public speaker, uneloquent but forceful, his voice, blunt and heavily accented, commanded attention. In contrapuntal harmony with the patrician periods of Eleanor Roosevelt or the polished elocution of Bruce Bliven, Hillman's earthiness lent the campaign a Runyonesque aura. The NCPAC seemed to give weight and body to the social abstraction of a united front against reaction.

Whatever tangible returns could be plausibly attributed to the NCPAC—and that is much harder to determine than it is for the PAC, where one can at least measure and compare vote totals from working-class precincts and neighborhoods—rebounded to the credit of the PAC and the CIO. Less tangibly perhaps, but of even greater logistical import in the battle to control the Democratic Party, was the way the NCPAC institutionalized the CIO's relationship to prominent opinion-making, policy-shaping, and power-dispensing circles in Washington and New York. Hillman made clear from the outset that he conceived of the NCPAC not as a mass organization but as an influence network with lines running straight to the headquarters of allied organizations. If the NCPAC could in fact do what Ickes predicted and perform the role once played by Thomas Corcoran's group in 1940, then, together with the PAC's methodical street-level mobilization, the "People's Program of 1944" might become something more than a pious hope and programmatic wish list.

The NCPAC quickly became a high-visibility organization, attracting the literati and glitterati, businessmen and bankers, publicists and

professionals, intellectuals and veteran reformers committed to the precepts of the Keynesian cooperative commonwealth and the visionary
promise of the global New Deal. Hillman served as its chairman, al-
though he would have preferred the venerable George Norris. "Beanie"
Baldwin, a Frankfurter protégé and part of the New Deal circle in the
Agriculture Department, became Hillman's second in command. The
NCPAC board and membership comprised a veritable roll of honor:
Elmer Benson, ex-Governor of Minnesota; Gifford Pinchot; Freda Kirch-
way, publisher of The Nation; Morris Cooke; Mrs. Marshall Field; Mrs.
M. M. Warburg; Will Alexander, vice president of the Rosenwald Fund;
Louis J. Reynolds of Reynolds Metals; Mary McLeod Bethune; Reinhold
Niebuhr; Oscar Lange; Max Lerner; Orson Welles; Edward G. Robinson;
Ben Hecht; Arthur M. Schlesinger, Jr.; Lillian Smith; Paul Robeson;
Dorothy Parker; and other luminaries from the arts and sciences as well
as the worlds of entertainment and politics lent its membership a certain
glamour. Twenty-two of the NCPAC's 142 board members were Ne-
groes. George Weaver, representing the CIO's Committee to Abolish
Racial Division, worked to coordinate the campaign efforts of the
NAACP, A. Philip Randolph, and others. Southern racial and eco-
nomic liberals sent Clark Foreman, chairman of the Southern Conference for Human Welfare (SCHW), and its executive secretary, James
Dombrowski, to sit on the NCPAC board. A bevy of fraternal ethnic and
nationality organizations were represented as well, including the United
Committee of Slovak Americans, the Serbian Vidovodos Congress, the
Croatian Fraternal Union, and the American Slav Congress. James G.
Patton, President of the National Farmers Union, also served on the
board. There was even a place reserved for "Religious Associates," filled
by the Congregationalist pastor Dr. Dwight J. Bradley.[44]

The NCPAC brought together the well-positioned and the well-
intentioned and combined their special talents and connections with the
muscularity of the CIO. But doing good and doing well would not be
enough. However impressive the PAC's performance at the ballot box
was, the conservative wing of the party was not going to retire from the
field without a bloody fight. Moreover, the rise of the PAC and the
NCPAC aroused phobic sentiments which settled around the figure of
Sidney Hillman and threatened to engulf the PAC and along with it the
President and what remained of his New Deal Democratic Party. In a
word, the presidential election of 1944 brought the Cold War home years
before it erupted abroad. Its opening salvo made Sidney Hillman a household name in American politics and the object of national hysteria. It
was a battle that enmeshed Hillman in moments of Machiavellian in-

trigue. And finally it was a battle in which organized labor met the enemy and first discovered that "they is us."

Trouble erupted first during the primary season out of long-simmering animosities—not, however, on the right, but on the left. The very same Labor Party in New York that Ickes so admired and hoped the NCPAC might emulate nearly destroyed itself during a virulent faction fight, which allied Sidney Hillman and the Communist Party against the same socialist praetorian guard that had periodically sniped at Hillman since the founding days of the Amalgamated. Once again, but with far greater abandon than in the early 1920s, Hillman found himself stigmatized for daring to consort with the CP. By 1940 communism was no longer the preoccupation of cloistered leftists and labor radicals. Anticommunism was bidding fair to become the new civil religion of American politics, a black box of all the fears and resentments about what the New Deal had done and might still do to a mythologized American republic; an obsession that despite the putative object of its wrath, had precious little to do with the Soviet Union. The donnybrook that tore apart the ALP between 1942 and 1944 resembled the undercard of a championship prizefight, providing observers with a foretaste of the grander gore to come.

In the beginning Hillman had welcomed the SP "Old Guard" into the embryonic ALP, principally because of their ties to influential newspapers—the *Forward* particularly—and ties to mass institutions like the Workmen's Circle. He had acceded to their demand to exclude the CP as an organization, which of course did not prevent CP members from joining in large numbers as individuals. No one in the ALP, either among the leadership or among its constituencies, who were by 1940 either loyal New Dealers or captivated by the charisma and ghetto populism of Vito Marcantonio, any longer thought of the ALP as an embryonic labor party. While Alex Rose of the Hatters and Israel Amter of the CP did occasionally trade insults, peace prevailed, if uneasily. But in the umbrage expressed by Cahan and Dubinsky when Hillman briefly flirted with the party's senatorial nomination in 1938, in which he was supported by the CP, one could already scent the aroma of bad blood.

The Nazi–Soviet pact immediately broke the ice. The Social Democratic Federation threatened to walk out of the ALP, infuriated by CP fellow-traveler encroachments, even though they risked a rupture with their own trade union allies, who were, for the moment, less exercised by the issue. Hillman's relations with the CP became suddenly more frigid, not only in the ALP but everywhere he encountered them in the CIO. Still believing he could control the situation, Hillman set up rival ALP clubs in CP-dominated areas. He conferred with Rose and Dubinsky, and together they reorganized the party's state hierarchy to exclude the CP. ACW and ILG cadres beat the bushes in an effort to beef up anti-CP enrollments.[45]

The CP remained strong in the Manhattan branch of the ALP, while the right wing, led by the "Old Guard," controlled the Bronx and, more important, the party's state executive committee. By and large the immigrant working class of the garment center, whose socialism had become a propitiatory rite of ancestral reverence, supported the "right." Second-generation, college-educated new professionals and working-class cadre more recently mobilized by the CIO constituted much of the "left." Despite the scandal and ostracism that followed upon its foreign policy convolutions, the left held its own, so that by 1940 the ALP was gripped by an armed stalemate. An aide to La Guardia speculated that the ALP was doomed, the breach too wide to heal.

"The Progressive Committee to Rebuild the ALP," the left's moniker, attacked Hillman's position in the war administration. "Progressive Committee" propaganda called for the formation of a labor party and denounced the "Hillman–Dubinsky–Antonini" element for encouraging antilabor legislation. They hammered away at the conscription issue, indicting Hillman and the "right" for their complicity in creating "a huge industrial enterprise under a peonage system where the workers will wear uniforms." The "Progressive Committee" coordinated its attacks with Lewis's LNPL.

Meanwhile, the "right's" "Liberal-Labor Committee to Safeguard the ALP" baited left-associated luminaries like Lillian Hellman and Dashiell Hammett and accused the "Progressives" of consorting with Republicans to defeat pro-Roosevelt candidates in New York. The "right" remained unchallenged upstate and in control of the party's top posts. For the moment, Hillman found himself in alliance with his erstwhile comrades from the SP. In any event, so long as he was in Washington, he kept his distance from intramural party squabbles, assigning Jacob Potofsky and Hyman Blumberg to slug it out with the Communists.[46]

This peculiar stalemate lasted only until the German armed forces invaded the Soviet Union. Immediately the left sued for peace but was rebuffed by the right, so that the stalemate persisted through La Guardia's reelection in 1941. Working through Potofsky and Louis Hollander, Hillman reopened relations with the CP, a course tacitly accepted by Roosevelt (although not by the President's wife, who favored the right). The Bennett debacle, along with the universally disappointing outcome of the 1942 elections, then convinced Hillman of the need to rebuild the ALP as a means of strengthening the President's hand in New York.[47]

But the "Old Guard" had its own ideas about how to revive the liberal–labor coalition. Determined never again to work with the CP, they refloated the idea of a national labor party, both as a warning aimed at conservative Democrats and as a friendly gesture to similar dissident groups in Michigan, Ohio, New Jersey, and Pennsylvania. From Hillman's point of view and from that of the CP, which was just as single-mindedly dedicated to Roosevelt's reelection and the preservation of the wartime united front, this talk of a third party was treacherous.

Just at this moment, in the early spring of 1943, an incident that under different circumstances might have passed away without doing great damage instead rekindled ancient and more recent suspicions and lacerated raw personal relations between Hillman and the house of Jewish socialism. The Red Army arrested and then executed two Polish-Jewish socialists, Victor Alter and Henryk Ehrlich, members of the same Bund to which practically all Jewish socialists in America, including Hillman and Dubinsky, traced their own political ancestry. Dubinsky and others quickly organized a memorial protest in New York, attended by many prominent liberals and leftists as well as numerous ex-Bundists and their sympathizers from the city's garment centers. Of course, the CP did not attend. Neither did Sidney Hillman. His absence outraged even some of his own closest comrades, not to mention those socialist godfathers who for nearly thirty years had resented Hillman's independence, his aloofness from Jewish politics, and his overweening ambition.

Decades later partisans still recalled the event as a consummate moment of cowardice and sycophancy on Hillman's part. At the time, Joseph Schlossberg and Charles Ervin ignored Hillman's example and appeared at the memorial demonstration. J. B. S. Hardman, Hillman's longtime aide and one of the main organizers of the protest, resigned as editor of the *Advance* and irrevocably broke with Hillman. But for Hillman, and for that matter for Philip Murray, who was also conspicuously absent, memory, sentiment, and righteousness took a back seat to matters of state and political expediency. The Soviet Union, a vital ally, ought not to suffer contumely while its armies absorbed the main blows of the Wehrmacht. And the American CP was too potent a force, not only in the ALP but in the CIO, to alienate at a time when its cadre could be counted on to help rescue Roosevelt and the Democratic Party from the threat of domestic reaction. Hillman was more reconciled to working with the CP than was Murray, but both men recognized defeating the Nazis and restoring CIO influence as overriding objectives that they shared with the Communists.[48]

The Alter–Ehrlich affair raised tempers to the boiling point. A few months later in internal elections Brooklyn fell to the left. The right,

now in control of only the Bronx, accused Hillman of cynical maneuvering. With the PAC's formation, however, Hillman was more determined than ever to open up the ALP to CIO influence at the top,
believing at the same time that he was more than a match for whatever
machinations the CP might try. He publicly called for trade union control of the ALP and endorsed Mike Quill's City Council candidacy in the
Bronx.

Rose and Dubinsky, whose visceral hatred of the Communists now
bordered on the obsessive, were closed to all possibilities of compromise.
They preferred to work through the AFL unions they controlled (including not only the needle unions but the American Federation of Teachers
run by George Counts) rather than invite the participation of the politically trained CIO, even though on the face of it that seemed to
contradict the most elementary premise of the Labor Party. As the new
year began, Hillman met with Rose and CIO representatives to propose
a joint slate for ALP offices consisting of trade union delegates in proportion to their membership. When the state committee rejected the
compromise plan, the fight took on renewed ferocity. George Counts and
Alex Rose insisted on the withdrawal not only of CP leaders but of
"lesser known communists regardless of their union affiliations." Hillman, refusing to hand the right an absolute veto power over the *bona
fides* of CIO unions, asserted: "What has always been a false issue in this
primary campaign is the issue of Communism."[49]

Hillman felt he had little to lose, as the right would have to support
Roosevelt and the ALP stood to benefit if the CIO entered en masse with
all its money and human resources. Hyman Blumberg was assigned to
build a "Committee for a United Labor Party," with Harry Chapman of
the Railroad Clerks as chairman. In January 1944 Hillman proposed a
common slate of candidates for the party's state committee, to include
liberal spokesmen and a full complement of CIO representatives. When
the right rejected this, Hillman responded with a new proposal that the
most visible CP associated trade union leaders, Mike Quill and Joseph
Curran, be excluded, as individuals, from running for state party office.
The CP chairman, Earl Browder, had previously agreed to this proposition, communicating his assent through Hillman's legal counsel, John
Abt. Abt, bright, ingenious, and energetic, functioned as a kind of
shadlichen between Hillman and the CP on those delicate matters having
to do with the Communists' role in the PAC. The withdrawal of Quill
and Curran was still not enough, however, to appease the right. Party
primaries scheduled for the end of March became the focus of the final
conflict.[50]

Murray, Thomas, and Rieve all endorsed Hillman's position. At first FDR remained neutral. Sam Rosenman, whom the President had sent to investigate, told him things were primed to explode and cited the dangers of a CP coup. Late in January Roosevelt conducted a series of fruitless meetings with Hillman and Dubinsky. Adolph Berle touted Dubinsky and the right to the President and tried to mediate the dispute but failed. Eleanor Roosevelt clearly preferred the red-free right wing as well, believing that the left was too answerable to the Russians. Based on a recent CIO survey, Eleanor feared the impact of the "red" issue on working-class ethnics, Irish, Polish, and Italian voters especially. Dubinsky did his best to heighten these worries, telling Henry Wallace that "Hillman has control of the communists—he is hurting the Roosevelt effort in New York." But FDR deflected his importunings, assuring Dubinsky that "I have talked to Sidney Hillman about it and Hillman has agreed to eliminate all Communists from running for office."[51]

The PAC was too vital a part of the President's reelection calculations. He was content to see Hillman win on the one condition that no CP member would be allowed to occupy high ALP office. The President had become convinced that, among other things, Dubinsky was being unreasonable and had unduly personalized the issues at stake. As the primary neared, the House Un-American Activities Committee (HUAC) released a noxious report labeling the PAC a CP-dominated organization. Hillman immediately suspected, incorrectly, that Alex Rose was responsible for calling out the political police. Potofsky raged that Rose "would deal with the devil himself so long as that would keep him in office." He snidely characterized Rose's sole claim to leadership as "his capacity for red-baiting." It was a sign of how fevered and paranoid the atmosphere had become. The state executive committee leveled charges that a group of CIO leaders had met secretly with Earl Browder to plot the capture of the ALP. Mayor La Guardia made a last-minute plea for unity, but the right again refused to listen.[52]

Finally, on March 28 the left registered an overwhelming victory at the polls. The "Committee for a United Labor Party" swept all five boroughs and won sixty of sixty-two Assembly Districts in New York City, winning almost 60 percent of the vote in the right-wing stronghold of the Bronx. Three hundred twenty CIO people, including 120 from the ACW, were elected to party office. The left now occupied 570 out of the 750 seats on the state committee. The right even failed to keep the faithful in traditional ILG and millinery strongholds like the 16th Assembly District in Brooklyn and in parts of the Bronx. Hillman took over

as state chairman, Blumberg as secretary, and Harry Chapman as treasurer. As agreed, the CP was barred from top party positions. Gone now
was all talk of third-party diversions. The ALP positioned itself to
staunch the outflow of ethnic working-class voters.[53]

Immediately, the right departed to form what later became the Liberal Party, fracturing the ALP once and for all. J. B. S. Hardman, who
had been left seething ever since the Alter–Erlich affair, finally quit the
Amalgamated over Hillman's dealings with the CP. As far as Hardman
was concerned, circumstances, not Hillman, had changed: "In 1944 I
quit the Amalgamated because I couldn't stomach any more of Sidney
Hillman's gaming with the Communists. Sidney Hillman was no more a
Communist than the man in the moon, but the measure of Sidney
Hillman's approach to things was: 'Do you gain power? Does it bring
power? Or does it not bring power?'"

Others were even less charitable. In the months that followed, the
"Old Guard" joined with gusto the red-hunting mania that swept the
country. Dubinsky proclaimed publicly that "Mr. Hillman can act as a
front man for the Communists; I never did and never will." There were
some who lost a grip on themselves entirely and urged Dubinsky to go
public with some ill-conceived exposé of Hillman's and La Guardia's
connections to a garment center murder of 1931. Dean Alfange, the new
chairman of the right's Labor and Liberal Committee to Safeguard the
ALP, declared in a radio broadcast that "Mr. Hillman is so hopelessly, so
inextricably enmeshed with his Communist allies that he could not
withdraw even if he would." Two hundred prominent liberals, including
Max Ernst, Reinhold Niebuhr, and John Childe, the president of Columbia University, joined the chorus of condemnation. Mark Stern, the
ILG Educational Director, urged restraint, arguing with George Counts
that it was naïve to believe it possible to build a new party on the basis
of single-minded anticommunism, especially given the enormous prestige
of the Red Army and the diligent grassroots activity of the CIO state and
city councils, along with the CP "base-building" in local PTAs, nursery
schools, churches, Russian War Relief committees, and so on. The potential labor party voter was not apt to approve, Stern pointed out, when
Dean Alfange spent more time attacking the CP than Martin Dies. "A
party cannot grow on being anti-something else," he sagely advised. But
in the overheated aftermath of the primaries no one was listening.[54]

Louis Waldman, lawyer and perennial SP candidate for governor
during the 1920s and 1930s, wrote a piece for the *Saturday Evening Post*,
later republished in condensed form by the *Reader's Digest*, which described Hillman as a new kind of political boss intent on creating his own

machine. The PAC was erected on the model of all "Communist-sponsored 'United Front' organizations." The CP, Waldman shrieked, was the PAC's "godmother," and the PAC was the Communist vehicle for infiltrating national politics. Earl Browder, Waldman grimly prophesied, might soon "emerge as the dominant political figure in PAC."[55]

Eerily and perversely, Waldman's prophecy fulfilled itself, at least within the national psyche. A good deal of this rhetorical violence was probably calculated by those in the right wing like Ben Davidson and Dubinsky, who had always sought to use the primary wars to justify the formation of a new party. But in equal measure the heat radiated from primal anxieties that were by no means the exclusive preoccupation of sectarian leftists with hyperactive memories. The blood first spilled over the "red" question during the ALP primaries would spread and cover the presidential campaign that followed like a toxic red discharge.[56]

Within the PAC, anticommunism became a festering sore, never the wild contagion it became within the ALP, but one requiring Hillman's periodic attention and finesse to keep it from infecting the union politic. Catholic, often ACTU-led circles in the UAW allied with Walter Reuther resented Hillman's close working relationship with the CP and expressed Catholic working-class anxieties about the secularizing logic of the New Deal. Hillman recognized the delicacy of the issue, and so did the CP. Naturally, they held no formal meetings together and communicated by "signals" through intermediaries like Abt and Lee Pressman. At no time did the CP challenge Hillman's authority. But the party's energy, its bureaucratic strength within strategically vital unions like the UAW and the UE, and its influence among Negro and liberal reform organizations lent it an undeniable importance. Abe Raskin, an admirer of Hillman and no friend of the CP, acknowledged: "It is incontestable that much of the work of PAC was done by Communists and their supporters" and furthermore that they "exercised a significant if not a controlling voice in its policies."

Consequently, during the electoral campaign anticommunist groupings within the PAC tended to lapse into inactivity unless regularly prodded by Hillman and his lieutenants. In Connecticut, for example, factional wars within the UE nearly paralyzed all political activity in the state. Adolph Germer spent much of his time traveling around the country as a troubleshooter for Hillman, putting out factional brush fires, rousing the apathetic, and clearing the air of political suspicions, much if not all of which were inspired by the "red scare."[57]

Beyond the borders of the CIO, these same incendiary emotions began to rage out of control. What had first emerged as a vicious and

ancient quarrel within the chronically feuding family of Jewish socialism
soon became daily fare on the nation's menu of political fisticuffs. Even
while American and Soviet diplomats at Teheran and Yalta managed
temporarily to submerge the geopolitics and ideological histrionics of the
Cold War, a domestic "cold war," which, all appearances to the contrary
notwithstanding, was in its essential motivations and purposes different
from the one that would soon reconfigure world politics, exploded at
home. In the middle of the maelstrom, Sidney Hillman weathered the
country's first experience with anticommunism as an all-purpose, manipulated mass sentiment. Much of its animus was directed, ironically, at
those tendencies in American public life—centralized corporate and government bureaucracies, planning, social engineering, government
regulation—which had very little to do with Soviet communism and
everything to do with twentieth-century capitalism.

Not surprisingly, Martin Dies and his HUAC acted as the anticommunist "movement's" midwife. HUAC's "Investigation of Un-American
Propaganda Activity in the U.S.," released to coincide with the ALP
primary, concluded that "Sidney Hillman has entered into a coalition
with Communists for the purpose of building the CIO PAC. This is not
the first time in his career that Hillman has found himself in league with
the Communists, but it is by far the most sinister of all his Communist
coalitions." Much was made of Hillman's dealings with the Bolshevik
leadership in the early 1920s; the creation of the RAIC; the Amalgamated's $3,000 donation to the *Freiheit*; donations to the *Daily Worker*,
the *New Masses*, and other suspect publications; and Hillman's service as
a board member of the notorious Garland Fund. As parts of its "findings," the Committee reprinted a *New York Post* editorial warning of "a
conspiracy hatched by the Communists and Sidney Hillman to seize the
ALP." Hillman called Dies "a liar" and refused to participate in the
HUAC investigation.

Revenge came quickly when PAC electioneering compelled Dies to
withdraw from the Texas primary. But the depth of animosity stirred up
by the bilious congressman is indicated by the fact that William Green
actually called for Dies's election, hoping to strike a blow at the CIO and
the PAC. The AFL, Green explained to the President, sought nothing
more than "the return of our economy to the controls of free
enterprise."[58]

Moreover, the congressional "party of resentment" was fully prepared to continue its assault even in the absence of Martin Dies. Representative Smith of Virginia filled the air with thinly veiled
accusations about PAC violations of the Hatch and Smith–Connally
acts. Attorney General Francis Biddle sent FBI agents to investigate

PAC finances. Hillman gave the agents his full cooperation. In return, Biddle issued the PAC a clean bill of health. But Smith howled about a whitewash, which was enough to force the Justice Department to reopen the investigation, only to confirm its original findings. From the standpoint of the "party of resentment," that was, in a sense, the whole point—namely, that the executive branch was riddled from top to bottom with the agents of the "red" New Deal, that the whole federal bureaucracy was becoming an enemy enclave. So Smith pushed instead for special House and Senate investigations. Once again, the FBI was ordered to do some follow-up sleuthing, and once again Bureau agents reported nothing amiss.

Now it was Hillman's turn to counterattack. He testified convincingly before the Senate Committee on Privileges and Elections that the Smith–Connally Act did not apply to primary elections and that the PAC was an organization of political education, exempt from provisions of the Hatch and Smith–Connally acts. But still Dies would not relent, determined to expose the infestation of the administration by PAC operatives. A three-man subcommittee held hearings whose whole point seemed to be documenting the fact that Beanie Baldwin and the PAC's regional director in the South, George Mitchell, were former employees of the FSA. For the "party of resentment," however, the FSA was hardly an innocent item on a résumé. Instead, it bore the stigma of corruption and subversion. How fitting, after all, that those now in league with the CP should have once employed their nefarious talents on behalf of a leviathan of government, one that had engorged numerous New Deal bureaucratic offspring and intruded itself into the well-being and social security of the American people.[60]

Of course, for the Southern wing of the "party of resentment" Hillman's CIO-PAC was a fearsome hydra, threatening not only moral corruption and political subversion but the near-unspeakable prospect of racial mixing. Representative Rankin of Mississippi, during an attack on the FEPC, propounded the following damning equation:

It [the FEPC] is sponsored by the CIO PAC headed by Sidney Hillman, a Russian-born racketeer whom the anticommunist Americans [sic] of his own race literally despise and who is raising money by the shake-down method with which he is trying to control our elections. He wants to be the Hitler of America.

Rankin articulated an amalgam of popular sentiments that had been congealing for some time. Southern diehards like Rankin blamed a cabal of New York Jewish communists and labor organizers for the poll tax bill, the soldiers' vote bill, and every other real and imagined assault on their region's racial oligarchy. And it was true that the "People's Program" demanded the abolition of the poll tax; the Sidney Hillman again and again called for the mobilization of the Negro vote in the South as well as the North; that CIO organizers, emboldened by the war, once again dared to challenge the labor and racial arrangements of the South's political economy; and that PAC workers seemed to be everywhere registering voters, even going so far as to give people money to pay their poll tax.[61]

Southern hatred of the PAC, the CIO, and Sidney Hillman was not, however, a strictly provincial passion. It was expansive enough to anathematize the whole Keynesian cooperative commonwealth and to decry the "second" or "Economic" Bill of Rights with its demand for publicly supported housing, education, health, and employment. For that reason Southern revanchists were able to make common cause with like-minded opponents of the New Deal among Democrats and Republicans all across the country.

Circumstances surrounding the selection of FDR's running mate galvanized these hostile legions and turned the presidential campaign into a cathartic outpouring of rage directed against Sidney Hillman, who, for a moment, seemed to embody everything about the New Deal that offended the pieties and prejudices of Middle America: its gaudy cosmopolitanism, its "Jewishness," its flirtations with radicalism, its bureaucratic collectivism, its elevation of the new immigrant, its statism, its intellectual arrogance, and its racial egalitarianism.

Thomas E. Dewey and his party attempted to discredit their opponents by suggesting that the Democratic Party had become the political hostage of the CIO. The evidence amounted to a widely circulated rumor that President Roosevelt had given Sidney Hillman veto power over the choice of Roosevelt's vice presidential running mate. According to Arthur Krock, who first gave the rumor credence by publishing it in the *New York Times,* the President had instructed party leaders with regard to the vice presidential nomination to "Clear it with Sidney."[62]

From the moment the story appeared, "Clear it with Sidney" became the leitmotif of a political *opera bouffe* conducted by the Republican high command and designed to arouse every nativist, anti-Semitic, anticommunist, and antilabor instinct in the electorate. A story in the *Boston Herald,* appearing two weeks before Krock's "revelation," anticipated the coming hysteria. Under a headline borrowed from the title of the movie that made Richard Widmark famous—"America Should Deliver 'Kiss of Death' to Hillman"—the paper informed its readers:

Today's primaries mark the first time in the history of the Birthplace of Liberty that the victors, many of whose forebears fought for the freedom of these colonies . . . have been given their orders by a national dictator who came here from Russia 37 years ago.

The reporter, Bill Cunningham, went on to label Hillman a "communistic refugee." William Randolph Hearst ordered all his papers, including the *Herald*, to "play up Hillman and his PAC on every occasion. It is really a political bribery committee." Hearst sponsored a "Sidney Limerick Contest." A typical winning versifier sounded a favorite anticommunist theme:

> Clear it with Sidney, You Yanks
> Then offer Joe Stalin your thanks
> You'll bow to Sid's Rule
> No Matter How Cruel
> For that's a directive of Frank's

Hearst's *New York Journal-American* ran a contest in which readers were asked to compose the last line of a limerick. One wit came up with this:

> Clear everything with Sidney, the Czar;
> Yes, your job, your family, and your car
> When he rules the nation
> Frank'll take a vacation[63]

Hearst was by no means alone. The Scripps-Howard, McCormick-Patterson, and Gannett journalism complexes joined the assault on the PAC and Hillman personally. The *New York Mirror* decried the "Hillman-Browder Communist conspiracy to take over the U.S. through the machinery of the alleged Democratic Party." The *New York Daily News* warned that a "victory of the PAC would constitute the greatest single political triumph ever achieved by the Communists." The *Minneapolis Tribune*, citing diatribes by Dewey and Dubinsky, concluded that Hillman was "the biggest political boss in the U.S. and in the words of David Dubinsky is a 'front for the Communists.' " In *Newsweek*, Raymond Moley zeroed in on Hillman and Murray as representing a leftist faction in the labor movement bent on capturing the Democratic Party, a conspiracy first hatched in 1936, according to the onetime New Dealer. In *Commonweal*, John Cort boiled biography and history into a single digestible clump, arguing simply that Hillman's Russian and Jewish origins were enough in themselves to prove he was a red.[64]

Editorials and news stories often struck an anticommunist or nativist note—"Sidney Hillman, Russian-Born Immigrant"—or made anti-Semitic insinuations about the "Lithuanian pants presser" and his "early rabbinical training," or went straight for the jugular: "The people who support the New Deal ticket this November," the *Chicago Tribune* editorialized, "are supporting the Communists and building them up for the day when they plan to bring Red Terror sweeping down upon America. . . . A New Deal vote is an invitation to murder." Westbrook Pegler used his column to expose the CIO–CP alliance built upon "naturalized but unassimilated European parasites."[65]

Republicans pursued the "Clear it with Sidney" red herring with unalloyed enthusiasm. The chairman of the party's campaign committee suggested that "Hillman and Browder want to rule America and enslave the American people." Herbert Brownell painted a frightening prospect of Hillman's "stranglehold" on the White House. Clare Booth Luce told the *New York Times* that Hillman and the PAC were part of a CP plot and then, in a harlequinade of aristocratic posturing, declared: "If my head rolls in the basket at the election, surely it is a more American head than Mr. Hillman's." Luce's flair for the murderous metaphor was on display as well in the pages of the *New York Daily Mirror*, where she asked rhetorically: "What are the facts about PAC, this newly-laid egg out of the Hillman hen by the red roosters?" Republican billboards across the country asked: "It's Your Country—Why Let Sidney Hillman Run It?" The Republican vice presidential candidate, John Bricker, was uninhibited and splenetic: "The great Democratic Party has become the Hillman–Browder communistic party with Franklin Roosevelt as its front." On the campaign circuit, Governor Dewey was more circumspect but still insinuated that the Democratic Party had been captured by the Hillman–Browder cabal. When that seemed insufficient, anonymous scandal-mongers within the Dewey entourage revived fossilized rumors about Hillman's alleged connections to Louis "Lepke" Buchalder and his complicity in a contract murder.[66]

Apostates from the Republican Party received their own special form of calumny. In Baltimore the Republican Representative Ellison was lacerated for "stringing along with Sidney Hillman's sinister program to bankrupt the country and pave the way for Communism, and for voting with the radicals and left-wingers in Congress." Ellison's opponents made disingenuous appeals to working people to leave the CIO for the more American confines of the AFL: "I wonder," one of Ellison's inquisitors speculated, "how many people realize how sinister that man's program is?"

> Don't be fooled about Sidney Hillman. He knows as much about the finances of this country as any banker. . . . Sidney Hillman is at heart a Communist. He came to this country and was naturalized. He went back where he came from and returned a Communist and began injecting Communism into the labor unions of this country. . . . His idea—their idea—is to sink this country into debt so deep it will bankrupt it and then step in . . . and offer us a new form of government.[67]

The Republican Party and press could claim no exclusive franchise to "Clear it with Sidney" as a political incendiary. It was a rubric of enormous emotional attraction, a palimpsest whose outer layer of anticommunism covered over strata of the politically unconscious where a bestiary of greedy financiers, conniving Jews, hypereroticized Negroes, supercilious intellectuals, violently deranged radicals, and misspoken, unclean immigrants copulated with abandon and to the peril of civil and national order. For Southern Democrats, "Clear it with Sidney" further inflamed racial resentments about the arrogance and presumptuousness of upstart New York Jews. Representative Dies used the slogan as a pretext to resume hearings into alleged coercion of the CIO rank and file by Hillman and the PAC high command. Joseph Camp's Constitutional Educational League published a pamphlet—"Vote CIO and Get a Soviet America"—that worked over Hillman's Russian-Jewish heritage until it seemed genetically predetermined that he would end up a creature of the wily Earl Browder. Charlotte Carry, the PAC's New York regional director, was similarly tainted, because she had once been associated with Hull House. The pamphlet, with an introduction by Westbrook Pegler, showed Hillman on the cover holding a red banner that said "Vote CIO," while a photograph inside, captioned "coercive methods," displayed workers being beaten and bloodied by thugs while the text explained that Hillman "lays down the law." If the Hillman–Browder cabal triumphed, "all credit will be claimed . . . and will be due, mainly to Schmuel Gilman, alias Sidney Hillman . . . to Richard Frankensteen, nee Frankenstein," and to Browder, of course.[68]

The contagion even threatened to infect the PAC's inner councils. In August Ickes and Wallace agreed that Hillman was probably not the right man to head the PAC and apparently were encouraged in that view by Murray, who objected to the fact that "Hillman's accent, despite the fact he had come to this country as a very young boy, is so broken that it seems to me it is bound to make a bad impression." A bit farther from

home, Adolph Germer reported that John L. Lewis was "ranting
against Earl Browder, trying to tie him up with Roosevelt and Hillman." And within the Democratic Party, first-tier strategists, who better than anyone else knew how grossly exaggerated the "Clear it with
Sidney" story really was, nonetheless fumed over the notoriety it was
bringing to its victim. Party chairman Robert Hannegan maliciously
told a confidant how disturbed he was "about friend Hillman's many
statements. If only said Hillman could have one of his heart attacks
which he has had in the past at convenient periods, it would help."
Some way had to be found to keep Hillman quiet, especially because
Democratic Party intelligence had learned of a Republican scheme "to
lure Hillman into speaking on a nation-wide hookup to get his foreign-
Jewish accent on the air."[69]

All the lurid rhetoric actually served to conceal rather than expose
what was an important change in the chemistry of the Democratic Party.
While it was patently scurrilous for Hearst to claim a "Hillman–Browder
Communist conspiracy to take over the U.S. through the machinery of
the alleged Democratic Party," Dewey was much closer to the truth in
stating that "Mr. Truman was cleared with Sidney." But to the degree
that he was right, the Governor also managed to miss the point. If
Hillman played a significant part in the selection of Truman as
Roosevelt's running mate, it represented not the capturing of the Democratic Party by the CIO, as the Republicans warned, but the further
subordination of organized labor to the political and economic consensus
that would soon come to define postwar America.

To this day some mystery surrounds the claim that Roosevelt ordered
the party chairman, Hannegan, and his colleagues to "clear it with
Sidney." Rumors of the President's ill health made the vice presidential
selection a highly sensitive issue, however. And there is no question
that Hillman was consulted seriously and often, and that in his capacity
as PAC chairman he had a voice not so much in choosing Truman but
in aborting the candidacy of James F. Byrnes. Byrnes, the author of the
"little steel" formula, was roundly hated by the trade union officialdom.
Roosevelt treated the labor opposition to Byrnes with great seriousness.
Friends of Byrnes, like Elliot Janeway and Bernard Baruch, took a particularly narrow and even nasty view of the unfolding events. Janeway
believed that Hillman sought revenge, not only for the CIO but for the
personal scarring he received at the hands of Byrnes and his warlord allies
in 1942. And Baruch was furious that CIO-PAC managed to derail
Byrnes. But it was clear to such seasoned observers as Senator Alben
Barkley, who briefly harbored his own vice presidential aspirations, that
even if Roosevelt wanted him, the South Carolinian's restorationist

record, and not only on labor but on civil rights matters as well, would have fractured the party on the left. [70]

Byrnes himself lent credence to this version of the "Clear it with Sidney" legend. He claimed Hannegan approached him about accepting the second spot on the ticket. By July it was obvious to Byrnes that labor and black opposition to his candidacy was intense. At a Sunday dinner meeting in Chicago, just before the convention, Byrnes conferred with Hannegan, Ed Kelley of Chicago, and other machine leaders who still liked his chances. It was there, according to Byrnes, that Hannegan reminded Kelley, "Ed, there is one thing we forget. The President said, clear it with Sidney," and Kelley agreed that this was his understanding as well. Byrnes was convinced that his bid was stymied by Hillman (and by Ed Flynn, who predicted mass defections by Negro voters in New York if Byrnes appeared on the ballot). [71]

Byrnes was right. Officially the PAC and the CIO were committed to Henry Wallace right up until his defeat at the convention. There is no reason to doubt the sincerity of this pledge on the part of Murray and the rest of the CIO leadership as they saw in Wallace the last best hope to continue the New Deal after the war and Roosevelt's death, which many assumed would come before he had a chance to serve a full fourth term. What is not entirely clear but highly probable is that Hillman, unbeknownst to Murray, realizing the futility of the Wallace candidacy, given the strength of the opposition, had for months been quietly negotiating with top party leaders to collaborate in dropping the Vice President in favor of a mutually acceptable alternative. [72]

Whatever Hillman's ultimate role, Harry Truman owed his nomination first of all to the party's Southern Bourbons and urban bosses, and not to Sidney Hillman. By 1943 Southern Democrats were determined to block Wallace's renomination in order to arrest the forward momentum of the trade union and civil rights movements. Moreover, Southern business circles were in the vanguard of the resistance to the kinds of government regulations and controls with which Wallace was identified. Revolts by party regulars in Texas, South Carolina, and Mississippi focused on Wallace. Hillman calculated the high cost of unquestioning fealty to the New Deal's last visionary. On the one hand, the President gave Hillman the green light, late in 1943, to begin lining up the "right kind" of delegates for the Democratic Party convention. But Wallace already suspected Hillman's motives: "I am sure that Sidney was not being as friendly, frank, and open with me as he appeared to be on the surface," he noted in his diary. [73]

Gradually, Truman emerged out of the political background as the perfect compromise: a pro-Roosevelt voting record in the Senate; close ties to conservative politicians, businessmen, and machine bosses, yet tolerable to the labor movement; a border state politician, yet not known as a race-baiter. Harry Hopkins was convinced that Roosevelt had privately settled on Truman early in the process, that he considered Wallace too great a political liability, and that he might have preferred William O. Douglas but acceded to Hannegan's dedicated lobbying for Truman, impressed particularly by Truman's influence among his fellow Senators.[74]

In June, Ickes told Hillman that Wallace's renomination might cost FDR the election. Hillman was hardly surprised and asked for the Secretary's suggestions. Ickes recommended Douglas, but Hillman reacted negatively, arguing, in the argot of the political professional, that he'd never been tested and that he was afraid of "these young intellectuals." Ickes then mentioned Truman, but again Hillman balked. Although the Missouri Senator was friendly enough to labor, he too lacked seasoning, and his unsavory ties to the Prendergast machine in Kansas City did not sit well. Hillman offered up Hugo Black instead. In any event, it is apparent that long before the delegates convened in Chicago, powerful voices in the party were engineering a coalition of Dixie Democrats and city chieftains to dump Wallace in favor of Truman. Several weeks before the convention, Hillman informed Wallace that Ickes had phoned to say Wallace's chances were fading fast. Wallace plausibly concluded that it was Hillman who was softening under the pressure.[75]

As all the interested parties gathered in Chicago, the atmosphere of intrigue thickened. Hillman arrived early to set up the PAC's convention headquarters. After a strategy session within the CIO, Hillman dutifully informed the press that the PAC would fight to the end for Henry Wallace. Murray did all he could to bolster this impression and even managed to win over the Pennsylvania delegation. But even as they lobbied and cajoled, deals were being sealed elsewhere. At a White House conference a week earlier that included Roosevelt, Hannegan, Frank Walker, Kelley, Sam Rosenman, the oilman Edwin Pauley, and George Allen of the Democratic National Committee, a final decision was made to eliminate Byrnes and Barkley and to go with Truman. Hillman was not involved. And so it may be that the *New York Times* columnist Arthur Krock, who for years was on the friendliest terms with the Republican business community, deliberately concocted a loaded piece of government apocrypha. But there was enough truth in the story to make it credible. Once the shift to Truman was clearly under way, the party leadership bent its efforts to win the PAC's approval. Above all, that meant Hillman's approval.[76]

At a breakfast meeting with party strategists Hillman remained noncommittal. Soon, however, stories appeared in the national press hinting that Hillman sensed the inevitable. In private he began touting Truman in order to head off Byrnes. On July 16 Ickes phoned with the gloomy news that Wallace's candidacy was doomed and the PAC needed to move fast or else miss the boat. Hillman was alarmed. Anxiously, he met with the President. When A. F. Whitney of the Railway Trainmen visited, Hillman indicated that he was for Wallace first, but Truman second. When Whitney naïvely surmised that Truman was out of the race, Hillman replied: "Well he may get back into the race." Hillman seemed determined, at least to Whitney, "to have the CIO name the Vice President." By the time of Whitney's exchange with Hillman, the PAC chairman had already conferred with Truman over breakfast. In his memoirs, Truman recalled asking Hillman if he was supporting Byrnes— on the face of it a preposterous question which casts doubt on Truman's memory of the event. Nonetheless, according to Truman, Hillman said that besides Wallace the PAC could countenance either Douglas or the Missouri Senator. Whatever the precise nature of the exchange was, clearly Hillman was preparing to abandon a sinking ship.[77]

Certainly, Wallace believed this, as did Beanie Baldwin, along with several of Hillman's closest colleagues. Wallace sensed how serious his predicament was when Ickes and Rosenman approached him as emissaries from the President with the message that although the President liked him personally, he was more and more convinced Wallace could win neither in Chicago nor in November. Wallace remained sanguine, however, thanks to a recent Gallup poll and an equally optimistic one by Hillman's people. Two days later Roosevelt acknowledged he was having trouble with segments of the party nervous about Wallace's "communist sympathies." Hannegan was pumping hard for Truman, while Biddle, Ickes, Corcoran, and Rosenman were pushing Douglas. The President issued a letter to the convention chairman, Senator Samuel Jackson, saying he would personally vote for Wallace if he were a delegate. But the draft of the letter was an artful equivocation, cautioning the delegates to consider whether "the nominee meet such opposition in so-called doubtful states as to hurt the ticket," a phrase ultimately struck from the final draft but clearly indicating the President's state of mind. Again, FDR told Wallace that the party pros wanted Truman even though he hoped "it will be the same old team."[78]

The PAC embodied Wallace's last best hope. When he arrived in Chicago, he met with Hillman, Beanie Baldwin, and R. J. Thomas. Hillman denied that he had said anything on Truman's behalf, but according to Wallace, Murray confessed that Hillman nearly did exactly that at a press conference, only to be cut off at the last minute by Murray.

Then the President published a second, fatal letter to Hannegan indicating his approval of either Truman or Douglas.

Wallace felt betrayed. Adolph Germer privately denounced the "Five Horsemen"—Hannegan, Hague, Flynn, Farley, and Kelley—calling Truman's candidacy "a rebuke not only to organized labor, but also to the several million farmers who admire and love Henry Wallace." Now the fight moved to the convention floor, where, after Wallace seconded FDR's nomination, a traditional delegate's parade turned into a massive demonstration for the global New Deal and, implicitly, for Wallace. For a moment the legions mobilized, but so too did the Kelley machine, which thwarted the CIO's attempt to bring 1,500 demonstrators inside the convention hall. The last Wallace bubble burst.[79]

In the aftermath, Murray confirmed Wallace's suspicions about Hillman's rooting about for a second choice weeks before the convention opened. And Hillman did tell a confidant after the election that neither he nor the CIO had any intention of supporting Wallace to the end, that he had never entirely trusted him but used him as a figure around which to rally during the campaign, a catalyst to galvanize Progressive support for whoever the final CIO candidate turned out to be. None of this is entirely implausible, but it hardly constitutes the smoking gun of Hillman's perfidy, nor does it in any way suggest anything as momentous as the rumor published by Arthur Krock.[80]

Even if Hillman had been unwavering in his support of Wallace, it is unlikely that the outcome would have been any different. Neither he nor the movement he represented commanded the sort of positive and decisive influence "Clear it with Sidney" implied. That he may have instead played a double game suggests not only how anxious he had become to stay close to the centers of power, but how relatively docile the CIO had become, Republican hysterics notwithstanding.

The Progressive community was outraged. Freda Kirchway of *The Nation* grimly recorded the ascendancy of the old guard and the "sadly demoralized state" of the liberal element. Only the PAC, she concluded, fought hard and well for Wallace, and she predicted, rightly, that the intraparty war would continue. Indeed, considering the ferocity of the storm precipitated by Krock's story, Hillman and the PAC weathered it well.[81]

Hillman displayed his customary vigor and nervous energy, despite the underlying fragility of his health. He scored points by cooperating fully with the FBI's investigation, knowing the Bureau was unlikely anyway to run directly afoul of the administration. He used the occasion of his appearance before the Special Committee of the House to Investigate Campaign Expenditures to excoriate the panoply of well-financed right-wing organizations supporting Dewey. And he turned aside Dewey's attacks by reminding the Governor that he had on several occasions himself solicited the ALP for political and financial help when he ran for District Attorney in 1937 and again in his race for Governor in 1940 and 1942. "What is the difference between the ALP groups whose financial and political support you solicited in 1937 and those identical groups you now call communist in 1944?" It was an embarrassing question. He tried to disarm the "red" issue by noting that the PAC's program was entirely consistent with basic Catholic doctrine as enunciated in recent encyclicals. In a stunning address at a Roosevelt rally in Rochester, he continued the counterattack, denouncing Dewey as a creature of pure ambition, utterly lacking in principle, forever blowing with the prevailing political wind, a willing tool of Herbert Hoover and the Republican old guard, hypocritical and fickle in all his domestic and foreign policies.[82]

Hillman's Progressive friends sprang to his defense. The publicist Max Lerner pointed out on national radio that the campaign expenditures of the NAM alone were three times greater than the PAC's. News stories and editorials refuting the "Clear it with Sidney" canard appeared in the *St. Louis Post-Dispatch*, *The Nation*, *The New Republic*, and the *Philadelphia Record*. Even Hannegan went on the radio shortly before election day to denounce Dewey's Boston reference to "Clear it with Sidney" as "an unmitigated lie." PAC literature tried to undo the damage by emphasizing the rights and duties of citizenship and the contributions of immigrants to the American way of life, defending the inherent "Americanism" of interest group politics.[83]

Election day results seemed to present the most irrefutable answer to Hillman's enemies. *Newsweek* announced that "Sidney's PAC" had proved itself a real force, that Roosevelt would have lost otherwise, and that chief credit belonged to Hillman. *Newsweek* was not alone in crediting the PAC with the victory. The President, for one, effusively praised Hillman:

One thing I want to make perfectly clear to you Sidney is my appreciation. It was a great campaign and nobody knows better than I do how much you contributed to its success. I was glad to learn that the CIO in Chicago authorized the continuation of the PAC. . . . I send you no condolences for the licks you took in the campaign. You and I and Fala have seen what happened to the people who gave them.[84]

The CIO was naturally ecstatic. At an executive board meeting a week after the election, Hillman called it a "terrific mass movement right from below." He was particularly pleased with the extent of AFL rank-and-file support despite what he characterized as the pro-Dewey inclinations of the leadership. He singled out as noteworthy the big inroads into the Negro vote achieved in part through Hillman's April conference with Negro leaders in New York, the work of the Chicago Political Education Conference, PAC print and radio propaganda, and the PAC-backed candidacies of Adam Clayton Powell in New York and William Dawson in Chicago. Hillman claimed success as well in mobilizing women voters through Verda Barnes's Women's Division, which excited the imaginations of civic, religious, and PTA groups.

Hillman received a one-hour ovation as he itemized the PAC's victories over Dies and the AFL "reactionaries" and congratulated the assembled delegates for helping to inter the bankrupt political agnosticism of William Green. He couldn't help gloating a bit:

> Our opponents attempted to isolate us, to cut us off from the main body of the American people. No slander was too base, no appeal to prejudice too bigoted, no tactic too unprincipled for them to employ. . . . They failed because we did not pursue a narrow or selfish course. Our program was not a program for labor alone.

He went on to catalog the community groups, churches, PTAs, and civic, business, minority, and professional organizations that massed beneath the PAC's banner.[85]

Such euphoria was to be expected in the aftermath of so bitterly conducted a contest. Sometimes believing is seeing, but there were signs everywhere that the PAC's victory was less than met the eye and that Arthur Krock's now legendary rumor would continue to corrode the innards of the New Deal Democratic Party.

Even before election day, astute and sympathetic observers detected real weaknesses. I. F. Stone reported in *The Nation* that although the PAC was showing good registration results in key states like Illinois (Chicago), Michigan (Detroit), and Ohio (Cleveland), there were alarming soft spots among working-class women and Negro voters. Back in the spring Henry Wallace reported troubling news to Eleanor Roosevelt on the New York situation, where there were serious signs of Irish, Italian, Polish, and even Negro disaffection, a fall in the Democratic majority, and a failure by the PAC to register enough voters nationwide.

As a matter of fact, in seventeen of the twenty-eight states where the PAC was truly active in congressional campaigns, it turned out not to be a major factor, including in five Southern states. It did particularly well in the industrial states of New England, especially in Connecticut and Rhode Island, but not in Massachusetts, where the regular party machinery remained much more energetic. The PAC displayed strength on the West Coast, in the urban centers of Washington and California. In the industrial Midwest, however, the PAC's appeal turned out to be spottier than expected, although impressive. Roosevelt lost Ohio only because he did poorly outside the cities. Wisconsin went Republican, but Michigan went to the President. Despite Wallace's early pessimism, the PAC's performance in New York was excellent, but less so in Pennsylvania. The 79th Congress was by no means a PAC Congress. The PAC's financial contribution was modest by prevailing standards despite wild press exaggerations to the contrary. NCPAC and PAC together spent $1.5 million out of a $7.5 million total Democratic campaign war chest, as against the Republican Party's $13 million. In general the statistical results were mixed. Roosevelt lost his decisive margin of supremacy in the mid-Atlantic and East North Central regions and lost the West North Central states, and there were profoundly worrying signs of a Southern revolt brewing in Texas. But the PAC's strategic contribution to Roosevelt's victory in the urban North, Midwest, and West Coast was undeniable.[86]

And even if the PAC's actual organizational work showed signs of sloppiness and incompetence, the election gave rise to the myth of the PAC juggernaut. The myth itself, whatever its basis in reality, was a power in its own right.

The 1944 election was less a victory than a holding action staving off defeat, but at some cost to the coherence and self-confidence of the "Peoples Program of 1944." In Hillman's remarks to the CIO convention, he went out of his way to eschew not only all hints of a future labor party but also any loose talk about capturing the Democratic Party. The intimidating hysteria on the hustings had done its work. There was no strategic alternative or even any questioning of the PAC's permanent role as a power bloc within the party. James Carey bluntly warned that if the PAC was not to alienate farmers or other nonunion populations, it would have to remain scrupulously nonpartisan. Any open expression of political ambition or flaunting of power would reawaken the night terrors so skillfully exhumed by the Republican opposition.[87]

There were some who even dreamed of detoxifying the enemy by removing Hillman as the easy target of its rage. Murray approached Henry Wallace about chairing the NCPAC, assuring the Vice President that Hillman was in the post only temporarily. Wallace came away feeling that Murray had become deeply suspicious of Hillman. Eleanor Roosevelt, who planned to attend the CIO convention after the elec-

tion, broached the same subject with Wallace, asking if he would be
willing to head a broadened PAC, confessing that she considered Hillman ill suited.[88]

And then there were those who were troubled by the creeping timidity that seemed to be overcoming the CIO and its PAC. At a testimonial dinner for Wagner, Emil Rieve commented on the worrisome
state of the labor movement in domestic politics:

> Too many of these second and third-string assistant presidents, it seems to
> me, have too little faith in the democratic process and too great confidence
> in the everlasting rightness of property. Are the economic royalists again in
> the saddle? Have the money-changers returned to the temple—or were they
> never really turned out? . . . What are they trying to do to us, these latter
> day Bourbons to whom our home front has been entrusted? If this sort of
> thing continues we will have won the military war on a dozen foreign fronts
> and lost the social and economic war on the home front.[89]

The enduring significance of the Wallace imbroglio was thus the way
it helped forge a consensus among Northern and Southern conservative
Democrats more attracted to Henry Luce's vision of an "American Century" than to the prospect of a global New Deal evoked by Henry Wallace's "Century of the Common Man." Hillman would spend the final
two years of his life caught between those two centuries.

EIGHTEEN

~

"American Century" or
"Century of the Common Man"

Despite the noxious mudslinging and the unceremonious dumping of Henry Wallace, the election of 1944 was a tonic for all those who sought to renew the New Deal, to perpetuate the global antifascist alliance, and to inscribe the "People's Program" across a "Century of the Common Man."

Days after the election Philip Murray delivered a panegyric to Hillman: "And then there is the 'Old Beard' himself, sitting here at the table. . . . And I don't know of any individual in our movement that has suffered more real filthy, scandalous, lying personal abuse than Sidney Hillman has during the course of the campaign." It was a veritable "crucifixion," the devoutly Catholic CIO President declaimed, full of "vicious, anti-Semitic attacks." As for Hillman, he couldn't help but gloat. Likening the enthusiasm aroused by the PAC to the evangelism of the CIO's first days, Hillman wryly observed:

> Of course you know only a few fell on the side. Of course it is painful one of the small group is not here, but no one can blame the people here, or say that they did not try to save him against himself. Some of us did not come from high-up places, some of us came from lowly vocations in life, such, for example, as pantsmaker, but you know that is rather an essential part of a man's apparel—and Brother John has been caught now and then with that particular part of his apparel down.[1]

"PAC is Here to Stay," Hillman announced in the *New York Herald-Tribune's This Week* magazine section. Only apathy, born out of com-

539

placency, might allow "a pernicious minority" to usurp the PAC's triumph, but mass political education and the legislative struggle to implement the "People's Program of 1944" would prevent that from happening. Hillman's optimism, at least according to some "technical surveillance" conducted by the FBI at CIO headquarters, spanned the Atlantic. He was equally confident that social liberalism would dominate postwar Britain and that the U.S. labor movement would not be intimidated by irresponsible congressional threats to "work or fight." He boasted of the PAC's great inroads on the West Coast and even conferred with people from the Warner Brother's public relations department about how to glamorize the PAC's publicity.[2]

But in fact the election was a riptide running against the deeper currents of domestic and international politics. Elation soon gave way to a more sober assessment of the balance of power. Clearly, the struggle for control of the Democratic Party and the national government was far from over. At stake was the distribution of wealth and power not only in postwar America but in a good part of the rest of the world as well. An alarming consensus seemed to be emerging that entailed a decidedly more modest role for the government. It relied far more heavily on corporate-led economic growth to take care of the material needs of American workers and to sustain the dynamic of mass consumption upon which the whole economy rested. By presuming itself the universal solvent of all outstanding political and social antagonisms, this corporate-led growth strategy consigned the labor movement to a subordinate role in national politics, hoping to exclude it from serious participation in the institutions of state and industry.

Hillman struggled to preserve the imperiled entente among labor, business, and government at home and the antifascist Grand Alliance abroad. But the Truman administration fell hostage to alien interests. It became more and more difficult to maintain amiable relations between the Wallace and Truman wings of the Democratic Party. The prospects for sustaining an analogous accord internationally grew even dimmer. Yet Hillman remained bound and determined somehow to marry the "American Century" to the "Century of the Common Man." Shortly before he died, Sidney Hillman had one last chance to play the "labor statesman," this time on the stage of world politics.

During the war Hillman had established contact with the leadership of the trade union movements in the principal allied countries, including Britain and the Soviet Union, and with the underground remnants of the labor movement in both Axis and Axis-occupied nations, including France, Italy, and Germany. In the last instance particularly his purpose was not merely to extend fraternal assistance, but in so doing to determine the political complexion of the postwar European labor movement.

The ACW channeled funds to French trade unionists, Socialists and Catholics, so that they might maintain their independence from the Communist Party and Gaullist organizations. Hillman was confidentially apprised of two vital considerations: "the democratic elements abroad must be kept alive so that they will figure in post-war Europe, and the fact that the Communist underground is receiving support from Moscow while the democratic trade union elements abroad are receiving very little from its own counterparts." Paul Vignaux, a one-time professor and now an underground leader independent of De Gaulle and spokesman in the United States for both the Confédération Générale de Travail and Christian unions, thanked Hillman for his financial help and complained that the Gaullists had failed to provide the French labor resistance with adequate guarantees. Vignaux considered it impossible to ally with the military government in exile as the republican commitments of both the French Confederation of Labor and the Christian trade unions would not permit it. Hillman was aware that the "National Front," devoid of much programmatic coherence, was based purely on patriotic emotion, so it was critical for the country's democratic politicians and trade unionists to establish their own programmatic identity. The character of the French labor movement particularly would help determine the future political stability of Europe. That stability would be at risk if the CP's influence proved overbearing; yet it was just as important for the democratic labor movement to keep free of any association with "reactionary forces."

Hillman was kept informed as well of CGT and Christian trade union efforts to establish contact with the growing mass of deported workers, seeding occupied territories with cadres ready to collaborate with the advancing Allied armies. As the war progressed, Hillman grew more sanguine about the extraordinary alliance of the CGT with the Catholic labor movement and began funneling aid to both in proportions that reflected their relative strength: two-thirds to the CGT. The French Communist Party was happy to let Vignaux function as its go-between. Indeed, politically the French Communists remained studiously reticent, shying away from talk of the class struggle and opposing all concrete programmatic initiatives beyond the defeat of fascism.[3]

The struggle to maintain an independent French trade union movement "may actually come down to an actual fight for survival," Hillman predicted. He made sure the necessary aid was delivered through elaborately clandestine means, and not only to French trade unionists but to their counterparts in Poland, China, and Germany. Hillman carried on discussions with the Polish underground labor movement regarding its financial needs and about its strategic chances for sabotaging the German army. With respect to the remains of the German trade union movement, Reinhold Niebuhr acted as an intermediary, arranging for Hillman to meet with SPD exiles who wanted money to encourage what resistance they could inside Germany. In China, Hillman funneled all aid through the Chinese Association of Labor, as it seemed most representative of industrial China and was capable of operating behind Japanese lines. When the Allied offensive resumed in Italy in the late summer of 1943, Hillman broadcast appeals to the Italian workers through the facilities of the Office of War Information, calling on them to rise against the Nazi war machine.

These were delicate and dangerous operations. There was a physical risk of Nazi and Japanese retaliation. The CGT cautioned Hillman and Matthew Woll not to announce publicly their aid to the French trade unions, but to disguise it as aid to the resistance; otherwise Nazi reprisals against trade unionists were sure to follow. Even trickier, however, was nurturing a fragile independent labor movement, one both pro-Western and social democratic in orientation, without offending either Soviet-supported communist trade unions or far more conservative nationalist and religious movements. The material well-being and political power of organized labor as well as the general shape of industrial society after the war depended to a large extent on the way in which the European labor movement was reconstituted.[5]

It was an ecumenical undertaking. In the minds of people like Hillman and Wallace, the good health of the New Deal was bound up with the triumph of democracy abroad, while the victory of the global anti-fascist alliance would count for far less than it might unless the principles of New Deal reform and redistribution were exported throughout Western Europe and the "third world." In his "Century of the Common Man" speech, first delivered in May 1942, the Vice President limned the contours of a new world economy based on full employment, a universally recognized decent standard of living, the dismantling of international cartels, free trade, equal access to raw materials, and a global investment fund with which to foster the reindustrialization of Europe and the infrastructural development of the postcolonial world. In the months and years that followed this vision of a global New Deal, a kind of international Keynesian cooperative commonwealth, became more robust and more concretely defined the outlook of all those who, like Hillman, wished to resurrect the "labor question" from the ashes of the fascist conflagration. It warmly anticipated anticolonial revolution as part of the eschatology of antifascism. It proposed a vast reconstruction of the global hinterland through a network of TVAs and REAs and RFCs, through international trade commissions and international investment agencies, through regional and cross-national public works and development agencies, and of course through an international labor standards commission to protect the rights and guarantee the purchasing power of the world's working classes. "Ever normal" agricultural, as well as industrial "granaries," would underwrite global prosperity, while the liquidation of the great cartels and monopolies and the installation of universally recognized regulatory standards would pacify the perennially troubled relationship between capitalism and democracy.

A new transnational political economy demanded an apposite response to multinational industry from a multinational working class. In a word, the "Century of the Common Man" was to be a century of managed social revolution, a feat of global social engineering, and the apotheosis of universalist social science.[6]

Late in 1944, when the outcome of the war was no longer seriously in doubt and when questions about the political complexion of the postwar world therefore vied with military news for front-page attention, Hillman came forward as the chief architect of a new working-class international, helping to convene a world conference of trade union representatives in London. Murray too wanted the CIO fairly represented in the international councils of labor and had earlier approached President Roosevelt with the request that the CIO receive equal representation with the AFL in the International Labor Organization. FDR was willing enough, but when the AFL threatened to resign and disrupt, Murray withdrew his request.[7]

From the outset the CIO's ecumenical call to fashion a trade union movement analog to the Grand Alliance was viewed as a declaration of world war by the AFL. Just a few weeks before the end of the war in Europe, George Meany made the AFL's position on postwar cooperation with the Soviet Union crystal clear: It would amount to "grovelling in the dust of a false unity which would simply replace one form of totalitarianism with another." In turn, this view presented an excruciatingly delicate problem for the British Trade Union Congress (TUC), whose historically close ties to the AFL Sir Walter Citrine, the TUC head, was reluctant to forfeit. Speaking for the TUC, Citrine told Murray that the British were happy to host a conference and to discuss how to help the war effort and the problems likely to face labor after the war, but wanted assurances that the conference would be no more than "exploratory and consultative in character." The Americans were far readier to act, but Murray agreed to Citrine's most tentative formulation. The 1944 Trade Union Congress convention ordered that an invitation be extended to all bona fide labor organizations to attend a world conference the following year. The AFL and the UMW received formal invitations but, as expected, declined to attend.[8]

Delegates finally assembled in London in February. There were 204 of them representing 60 million workers from thirty-five countries. The AFL was the only significant labor body to boycott the proceedings deliberately, a position it was never to change. But Citrine, like Churchill preoccupied with minimizing Soviet and CP influence, did what he could to slow the new organization's momentum. And there were others who pursued the same objective.[9]

For the U.S. State Department too the London Conference was a cockpit of the Cold War. A secret informational circular to American diplomatic and consular personnel included a telegram from George F. Kennan assessing Soviet attitudes toward the international labor movement. The Soviets, according to Kennan, considered the new world federation important and therefore were sending a large delegation headed by their trade union commissar, Kuznetsov. They wanted European and American trade unions included in all planning for postwar reconstruction but considered the "Amsterdam International" hopelessly reactionary and sought its speedy demise. Like Murray, whom the Soviets cited on this point, they wanted a new organization established immediately, all the better to press claims for labor representation at the peace conferences to come. Kennan thought the Soviets were counting on the powerful position of the CPs in the various European labor movements and that the top levels of the Soviet leadership viewed the international labor movement as a key vehicle of Soviet foreign policy, a vehicle through which it would be easier to exert Soviet influence than through the CPs themselves. Kennan was worried about the willingness of Western trade union leaders to accord their Soviet counterparts legitimacy as democratic institutions. He was especially concerned that Moscow, "whether by design or coincidence," was able to cite official declarations of the CIO in defense of its own position. Although the British were far less malleable, Moscow could count as well on the dominating influence of the French CGT and the captive trade unions of Eastern Europe, and stood an excellent chance as well in Italy, Finland, Norway, and perhaps in Czechoslovakia, and certainly in Mexico, Cuba, and among other Latin American trade unionists. All in all, Kennan concluded, the Soviets could hope, with good reason, to dominate the new labor federation and to use it to intrude Soviet views into almost all deliberations about the makeup of the postwar world, including such vital matters as German reparations. Thanks to its immeasurable sacrifices of blood and sweat, the prestige of the international labor movement was at its apogee and could be expected to exert enormous pressure on foreign governments everywhere. Moscow meant in this way to pursue Russian objectives, which Kennan summarized as "implacable Soviet opposition to cartels, international business organizations, to the international connections of high finance."[10]

Observers kept the State Department advised of developments in London. An informant from the American Embassy noted that while Citrine pursued every conceivable way of thwarting communist influence, Hillman, who incidentally and typically missed the opening days of the conference suffering from a bad cold, characteristically tried to mediate between the TUC and the Soviet delegation. Thus, the British wanted to exclude any representatives from Finland, Rumania, Bulgaria, Italy, and the Soviet-dominated "Lublin" Polish government-in-exile. The CIO also opposed the "Lublin Poles" but was at best indifferent to those other suspect delegations. It especially wanted the Italians to participate and felt there were no good grounds for excluding delegates from the other three ex-enemy nations. Next the Soviets insisted that all issues be decided by votes reflecting the majority of the workers represented. Citrine naturally objected. Hillman saved the day with a compromise proposal requiring a two-thirds vote by national trade union centers. When Hillman opened a discussion about the nature of the new organization, he adopted the outlook of the Mexicans, French, and Russians that the IFTU (the AFL-controlled "Amsterdam International") ought to be ignored, which annoyed Citrine, who wanted instead to discuss transforming the discredited Amsterdam group into an all-embracing federation, and in so doing to postpone a decision to institutionalize the London conference. Hillman, Citrine, and Kuznetsov held protracted talks, during which Hillman made it clear that the CIO could not afford to join a federation dominated by the Russians, but that he was confident the Russians, for their own reasons of state, were unlikely to seek such control. He told Kuznetsov that if in fact the Russians were so foolish as to try, the CIO would walk out. Kuznetsov assured him of the Soviets' good faith, and on that basis Hillman told Citrine he wanted to move ahead. He knew that for the CIO the new organization was politically impossible without the TUC, but he also counted, rightly, on Moscow's sharing this view. Indeed, the Soviets displayed great forbearance, backing off on any issue that might incite the TUC actually to leave. In the event, Citrine remained, albeit with reservations, and counted on the rabbinical Hillman to find the formula to meet both British and Russian purposes.[11]

For a while at least, the tide was running against the machinations of those precocious Cold Warriors within and outside of the State Department. The London conference was an emotional gathering, including war veterans, underground resistance fighters, and even concentration camp survivors. Hillman described it as "a great instrumentality for good" and the hope of the future. Despite occasional differences, "the British are as anxious as the Russians and as we are to make sure there is a permanent organization quickly." Agreement on the political complexion of the post-war world seemed to be near. The conference enthusiastically endorsed a generous policy of social welfare reform, including social insurance, public employment, the forty-hour week, full employment, rigorous price con-trols, and global economic cooperation to expand international trade and development. The "Call to All Peoples," issued as the conference ad-journed, heralded demands for denazification and the unconditional right of the new World Federation of Trade Unions to participate in all postwar economic and political deliberations. [12]

Some of the same extraordinary social excitement of 1919 was in the air again, as if the "labor question," like some inexhaustible phoenix, had risen once more. The "future of the world depends upon what labor will do," Hillman declared, as it "is the only real big constructive power." Proudly he recorded some tentative success in getting the big powers to pay attention to the fledgling organization. "I want to say to you," he told the CIO Executive Board upon returning from London, "there is no greater power today in Europe; the only power there is the power of organized labor." The new WFTU, sketched out by the London confer-ees, could provide both the programmatic coherence and organizational resources with which to fill that power vacuum. [13]

Hillman hardly exaggerated. Certainly policy-makers in the State Department were acutely conscious of the worrisome drift of events that threatened to make the WFTU a force to be reckoned with. The Euro-pean labor movement had moved steadily to the left during the war. The resistance record of the European communist parties was superb. In coun-tries like France and Italy the postwar position of organized labor would inevitably be enhanced thanks to its central role in the resistance. Trade union officials in Britain and France would soon hold high government office. Union membership was growing rapidly not only in Britain and France but inevitably in Germany and Italy as well. It was a sign of the times that Leon Jouhaux of the French Socialist Party, who had been titular head of the CGT since 1910, now was compelled to share power with Benoit Frachan of the CP, who had served as the CGT's General Secretary. The Christian trade union movement had similarly grown in numbers and moral authority because of its refusal to collaborate with Vichy's efforts to fashion a government-directed corporatist labor move-ment. Throughout Europe sentiment for restricting the operations of free enterprise was widespread, while communist parties studiously avoided forcing the issue of socialization for fear of alienating the peasantry and the middle classes. In Italy particularly, State Department watchers were surprised at the speed with which the free labor movement was reconstituted, with the equal representation accorded to the socialists, communists, and Christian Democrats.[14]

All of this made for auspicious circumstances indeed for the birth of a movement as ambitious as the one envisioned in London. Still, Hillman was wary. Just back from London, he addressed a mass rally at Madison Square Garden (at which a Soviet emissary, Andrei Gromyko, spoke as well) to urge an international popular front against "American Century imperialists." Hillman warned: "Powerful and unscrupulous forces are at work" who "do not want international cooperation" but instead, even as the war continued, "are jockeying for positions from which to launch a new imperialist scramble for power . . . they seek domination of world markets and dream of an 'American Century,' " and spread "subtle anti-Soviet and anti-British poison," contriving to subvert the Dumbarton Oaks and Bretton Woods agreements. Delivering the same basic speech a few weeks later at Fanueil Hall in Boston, Hillman personalized with acid sarcasm his references to the "American Century": "Like Mr. Frederick Crawford and Congresswoman Luce, I was the guest of the American Army in Paris. Like them I was quartered at the Ritz Hotel. Like them, I saw the tea room at the Ritz at teatime. I noted the costly furs, inhaled the expensive perfume and heard the cultivated chit-chat of France's privileged few. But unlike them I was able to get something more than a Ritz-eye view of liberated Paris." He went on to recount tales of the extreme privation, brutality, and heroism that had been the daily fare of the French underground.[15]

After London the existence of the new organization was no longer in doubt, whatever the misgivings of the State Department, or however obdurate the opposition of the AFL. Seven months later, in September at the Palais de Chaillot in Paris, the WFTU held its founding convention. Gathered there were sixty-three organizations from fifty-six countries, voicing the concerns of 66 million workers. Hillman led the CIO delegation, helped draft the Federation's constitution, and was elected one of the six vice chairmen of its Executive Bureau. Despite Citrine's reservations, Louis Saillant, who had been Jouhaux's lieutenant but who had drawn much closer to the CP during his heroic years in the resistance, was named General Secretary, while Citrine himself assumed the chairmanship.[16]

Reporting for the Administrative Committee, Hillman presented the draft constitution and emphasized in particular the struggle to win representation for international labor in all the various commissions and agencies created by the United Nations in San Francisco and now charged with institutionalizing the peace. All WFTU affiliates were urged to bring pressure to bear on their respective governments. Angrily, Hillman protested the decision in San Francisco to deny a vote and advisory status to the WFTU in the UN's Social and Economic Council, which was viewed as the critical public instrument of international economic reconstruction.[17]

With militant resolve, the Paris conferees called for the eradication of the roots of fascism—the liquidation of the military and industrial basis of German and Japanese war potential, the speedy trial of all war criminals, the dissolution of all fascist organizations, and the prompt removal from power of all German and Japanese military functionaries— essentially seconding the agreements arrived at by the great powers at Yalta. But the WFTU went further, urging that German heavy industry, banking, and transport, as well as the land and property of the German trusts and cartels and the Junker aristocracy, be placed under UN control and that these resources be utilized to rehabilitate the rest of Europe. Naturally, the Federation expected the liquidation of the Nazi "Labor Front" but admonished the occupying authorities against converting German workers into slave laborers, which would undermine labor standards everywhere. The same core principles and policies were to be applied in Japan as well.[18]

Resolutions also called on the allies to break diplomatic relations with Francisco Franco's Spain and with Juan Peron's regime in Argentina, for an investigation of the repression of workers in Greece, and for an examination of the political and economic conditions in colonial and semicolonial countries. The UN was expected to uproot the vestiges of colonialism everywhere, and the conferees demanded the immediate right of self-determination for the peoples of Indonesia and Indochina.

The Federation promised to help the German and Japanese working classes to rebuild free, democratic labor movements and demanded appointment to all commissions charged with investigating economic and social reconstruction in the Axis countries. In particular they sought access to the Allied Control Commission in Germany and the Occupation authority in Japan. To ease the transition to peace elsewhere, the delegates called on all postwar governments to provide funds for returning servicemen, for trade schools, and for insurance against sickness and unemployment as well as money for housing. Governments were also importuned to exercise "control of the prices and distribution of the prime necessities of life, food, clothing." All WFTU affiliates were instructed to fight for the freedom to organize and engage in collective bargaining, to establish cooperatives and mutual aid associations, and for full freedom of speech, press, assembly, religion, and political association. All forms of racial, religious, and sexual discrimination were condemned. The Federation demanded equal pay for equal work, full freedom of opportunity, and equality of education and technical training.[19]

Paris presented a picture of "complete unity," and Hillman was exuberant. At General Eisenhower's invitation he then traveled to Germany to meet with U.S. representatives and spent a day meeting jointly and individually with people from the Social Democratic, Communist, and Christian Democratic labor movements. He left convinced that German labor "is the only group that holds out a promise of fighting for a dynamic democratic program." Upon returning to America, he urged President Truman to coordinate government and CIO activity designed to reorder thoroughly the former Axis states. When he finally came home to the CIO, Murray paid homage to his peripatetic statecraft, recounting for his trade union comrades all the obstacles successfully hurdled in "London, Paris, Washington, San Francisco and back again to London and Paris."[20]

Hillman's reputation by this time had achieved international stature. Interviewed in *La Tribune Economique,* he downplayed all rumors of discord within the WFTU, dismissed the strike wave then building in the United States as a temporary reaction to the disruptions of demobilization and reconversion, and struck a pose of oracular confidence in the prospects for social harmony. Mary Heaton Vorse, writing in the *Paris Post,* gave Hillman full credit for protecting the chrysalis of the WFTU from external and internal shocks, especially Citrine's tireless delaying tactics. A British version of *Life* magazine, the *Picture Post,* ran a photographic spread under the preposterous caption, "The Man Who May Be America's Next President." With far more reason, the magazine concluded that Hillman had earned the "undisputed right to be called America's first Labor Statesman."[21]

However, maintaining an uneasy peace inside the WFTU and pronouncing diplomatic axioms about the terms of social concord proved less taxing than establishing the tangible presence of the new organization in the tumultuous world of international politics. There the going was considerably rougher, as the acids of anticommunism ate away at the fabric of antifascism. Against the WFTU's wish to prolong the wartime concord stood a set of harsher global realities: nation-state rivalries, imperial ambitions, and two hostile economic systems. Hillman might try to bury doubts under soothing rhetoric—"in Russia it is their business to build the government they want"—but even within the CIO reservations fermented. Murray never attended WFTU meetings; Brophy feuded with Saillant; privately Emil Rieve and James Carey voiced their criticisms of Soviet society.[22]

The German question turned out to be particularly galling. It became a barometer of how quickly the Grand Alliance was dissolving in mutual mistrust and a case study of the way U.S. foreign and domestic policy emerged in tandem out of the same set of interests and fears. At one time New Dealers like Harry Hopkins, Robert Morgenthau, and Harold Ickes, together with members of the Labor Department, the OSS, and lower levels of the State Department, viewed the problem of postwar Germany in terms very similar to those adopted by the WFTU. They sought root-and-branch denazification of industry, decartelization, and even deindustrialization, and favored the rebuilding of a democratic labor movement. They looked forward to collaborating with the Soviet Union for those purposes. Others, in and outside of the State Department and the intelligence community, including especially George Kennan, John McCloy, and General Lucius Clay, contended that U.S. national security and self-interest required a reindustrialized German economy, reintegrated into a capitalist Western Europe. They were determined that secondary social concerns—labor relations, the inequities of industrial concentration, the political purification of educational and economic institutions—would not interfere with that higher purpose. Naturally, they viewed cooperation with the Soviet Union as unlikely at best and as a dangerous snare and delusion at worst.[23]

In the U.S. zone of occupation, the Economic Division, operating under the authority of McCloy and Clay, was staffed by investment bankers and corporate executives who bristled at all measures that might retard industrial output or upset property rights or the prevailing distribution of wealth. In three critical areas—denazification, decartelization, and the reconstitution of the German labor movement—conflict was therefore inevitable. Officially the Division was committed to fostering a unified, democratic trade unionism. But the Labor Relations Branch of the military government, staffed by AFL and CIO officials as well as by professionals from the NLRB, was internally divided over just what such principles might mean in practice. CIO people, usually in league with NLRB staffers, were encouraged by Hillman to rebuild the German movement "from the bottom up," a radical approach with recourse to rank-and-file plant committees as the basic unit of organization. AFL apparatchiks preferred a "top down" tactic that relied on regional organizing committees constituted by established trade union elites.

Partisans of the "bottom up" strategy saw it as the best way to circumvent old anticommunist trade union bureaucrats, whom they blamed for the debacle of Weimar. As a counterweight they wanted to empower works councils with substantive rights to participate in plant level decisions customarily the prerogative of management. Late in 1945 the AFL staffers sought out anticommunist sympathizers in the State Department who feared the potential influence of the German CP and other radicals. The AFL went out of its way to exaggerate the strength of the German Communists. Joseph Keenan of the IBEW, who had worked with Hillman at the Labor Relations Branch of the OPM, persuaded General Clay that the "bottom up" approach threatened German economic recovery. The military authorities then proceeded to eliminate most "bottom up" advocates. New rules institutionalized regional organizing committees, thereby restoring the zone's anticommunist old guard and defanging the infant works councils.

Still, a stalemate persisted. Labor cadres in the U.S. zone reaffirmed their commitments to various forms of public ownership and "co-determination" of industrial management. They were bolstered by the support of like-minded radicals in the other three zones of occupation, where the anticapitalist labor left was measurably stronger than it was in the U.S. zone. General Clay, however, violently opposed "co-determination" and anything that hinted at nationalization. Hillman and others argued with him that contrary to popular rumor the American zone was producing far more than it was being given credit for, implying that the spread of trade union organization, even a more radical variant, which was the case in the American zone, was in no way counterproductive. "Bottom up" advocates were, moreover, unintentionally abetted by the relative complacency of business and political elites, who at first considered the German labor movement moribund and therefore allowed the Labor Relations Branch wide authority and autonomy despite the fact that most of its strategic posts were held by CIO people. Within the Branch a bitter factional war ensued, focusing principally on the Branch's director, Mortimer Wolf, an NLRB functionary and CIO sympathizer.[24]

So long as the stalemate lasted, both sides actively practiced their preferred version of trade union architecture. The "bottom up" faction encouraged shop steward elections at the workplace, out of which works councils were created, which themselves were to constitute the nuclei of larger industrial unions. Conservative fears mounted as German workers began to display a disconcerting restiveness. Sentiment welled up from below for a unified movement for economic democracy, committed to breaking up the power of financial and industrial elites and to creating agencies of state economic planning that would legalize workers' rights to enterprise participation and co-determination. The AFL dug in its heels, determined to exclude the German Community Party (KPD) and other radicals from the trade union movement, lobbying in fact for an apolitical, strictly bread-and-butter variety of unionism to be run by the old German Socialist (SPD) leadership. Hillman was extremely critical of this Weimar-tainted old guard and believed they deserved to be retired. His opponents, including George Meany of the AFL as well as anticommunist activists from the Reuther faction of the UAW, began a red-baiting whispering campaign directed against Mortimer Wolf. Keenan, a devout Catholic, a friend of General Clay, and a labor adviser to the U.S. Military Government, led the renewed opposition, assisted by the labor priest, Father Joseph Walsh of Georgetown. He temporarily succeeded in ousting Wolf and in filling the top spots of the Branch with his own people. Keenan fed Clay's fears about the influence of CP members within the U.S. occupation agencies and stressed the larger danger of the CIO's overtly political and social unionism.[25]

But Hillman was a practiced and tireless faction fighter. He persuaded Colonel McSherry, head of the Manpower Division, that it was bad politics to restore the old German trade union officialdom. Quickly Wolf was back. The factional war continued past the time of Hillman's death. Ultimately the right triumphed; Clay intervened and ordered McSherry to end the shop steward experiment and to fire Wolf. In the end, all the red hysteria proved typically groundless anyway, as only a handful of KPD stewards were elected. Most were either nonpolitical, left-wing social democrats, or Christian Democrats. By the end of 1946 McSherry and Wolf were gone; so too was Hillman. The left was silenced.[26]

Just as the manichean politics of the Cold War increasingly fixed the future of the German trade unions, so too did it warp the course of denazification, of which reconstituting the labor movement was but one feature. Shortly after returning from Paris, Hillman, in his capacity as WFTU vice chairman, asked Truman to appoint a commission to do a full investigation of economic and social conditions in all the occupied zones, to report on the liquidation of fascism and the establishment of a democratic trade union movement. He also requested that this commission serve in an advisory capacity to the four-power Allied Control Commission. Truman seemed willing. But State Department reservations about the WFTU were already serious. Soon enough State would embark on a deliberate attempt to destabilize the WFTU by prompting the AFL to create a rival anticommunist International Confederation of Free Trade Unions. So Hillman's request fermented a while, subjected to a bureaucratic filibuster and to the second-guessing of foreign offices elsewhere. Hillman told Saillant he was dismayed about the delays. He had discussed arrangements with General Clay in Berlin as well as with Truman. Both had assured him of their support. Hillman suggested that the WFTU bypass the respective foreign ministers and ambassadors and appeal directly to the four generals on the Allied Control Commission.[27]

The tactic worked. The WFTU commission, whose members included Hillman, Citrine, Jouhaux, M. Tarasov of the Soviet Union, E. Kupers of the Netherlands, and Evzem Erban of Czechoslovakia, arrived in Berlin at the end of January 1946. The commission spent several days in Berlin and then four days in each of the occupation zones. The members met with General Sokolovsky, Marshal Zhukov's deputy; with Lucius Clay, who reported to General McNarney; and with their military equivalents in the French and British zones. They also interrogated and conferred with city and regional commandants, labor officers, and various representatives of the military government, as well as local German officials, burgermeisters, and provincial labor ministers. (They even detoured to view the war crimes tribunal and to visit Dachau.) Mainly, however, they met with trade unionists in works councils and on the factory floor. They did so in the absence of censorious military personnel. Throughout their three-week inspection tour they received the full cooperation of all the occupying authorities, but the report they issued could hardly have cheered those responsible for the reclamation of Germany.

In the area of denazification, the commissioners discovered that progress varied widely from zone to zone. In general, the results were far from satisfactory. They were deluged with information about Nazis' retention of important posts in public administration and industry. German trade union leaders were far from convinced that the military authorities were serious about expunging Nazi cadre. Industry was in the worst shape—not, the commissioners argued, because Nazis there possessed indispensable managerial or technical skills, as even the military acknowledged that that was not so. Often enough Nazi leaders were dismissed from one enterprise only to be reemployed elsewhere. Predictably, the WFTU emissaries reported that the trade union movement was the only reliable and determined anti-Nazi force in Germany, and for that reason ought to be granted "predominant" authority over denazification of industry. But lamentably, and despite the fact that trade unionists were apt to possess the most intimate knowledge of who the local Nazis and their supporters were, they were accorded only a minor role in the process. The commissioners concluded this portion of their report by identifying denazification as the number one priority: "Retention of any active Nazi, even at the level of foreman, is incompatible with the extirpation of Nazism and the building of a democratic Germany."

On a happier note, the commissioners observed that the pre-1933 political and religious divisions that plagued the trade union movement no longer existed. Communists, Christians, and Social Democrats seemed ready to pay common allegiance to a united movement. With equal optimism the investigators looked forward to the reconstitution of the movement along industrial rather than craft lines. They did acknowledge some serious differences about whether to organize an industrial union federation modeled after the CIO, or instead "One Big Union" with a centralized administration and treasury. The commissioners preferred the former and confidently predicted it would prevail. In any event, and more important, they proudly proclaimed all the trade unions to be democratically organized and thoroughly denazified. Admittedly, circumstances demanded a rigidly regulated economy during the occupation period so that it was unrealistic to expect complete freedom of action for the trade unions. Still, they could engage in collective bargaining over wages, within limits prescribed by the military authorities, and they could file grievances over a wide range of work-related and nonwork issues, including working conditions, housing, food distribution, and social insurance. The trade unions were also prepared to play a major role in the reeducation of German youth.

Following this upbeat account, the commission dropped the other shoe. The military authorities were failing to offer full cooperation in the growth of the trade union movement. There was little visible progress in forming zonewide industrial unions except in the Soviet zone. Too many removable obstacles—lack of transportation, inadequate physical facilities, and bureaucratic logjams in granting clearances to organize, to hold meetings, and to publish union newspapers—blocked the way everywhere else.

While the commissioners surveyed the severe privations suffered by the German population and reported acute shortages of housing and food, they found no mass malnutrition and in general concluded that the situation was no worse than in the rest of Europe. What finally did cause the WFTU investigators great alarm was an underlying worry about the incapacity of the German labor movement in the past to prevent the rise of Nazism. Whatever hopes they now harbored for the future of that movement were not enough to allay those fears. Thus they demanded that the occupying powers deprive the German economy of the means to make war, remove all productive capacity beyond what was necessary to maintain a European "average living standard," and destroy as well the economic basis of Junkerdom whose militarist traditions they believed had abetted Nazi aggression.[28]

Throughout the three-week inspection tour, Hillman proved himself a dogged interrogator, far more thorough and relentless than Citrine, for example, when it came to questioning military and German trade union officials on the extent of denazification. He voraciously gathered data from trade union delegations and members of the works councils on standards of living and material needs. Nor would he be put off by the obfuscations of military bureaucrats, as, for example, one Colonel Armitage of the British zone in Hamburg, who shamelessly declared denazification a success while German trade unionists supplied a damning abundance of evidence to the contrary—that is, once the Colonel left the room—and bitterly complained that they were systematically ignored on matters of denazification, especially at the level of enterprise management. Similarly, Hillman pursued British generals in the Ruhr on whether denazification was proceeding with appropriate vigor and with sufficient and adequately trained staff. He did the same in the Bavaria-Nuremberg area, run by the U.S. authorities, where denazification moved at a glacial pace, although more expeditiously in public administration than in industry. Yet even as upset as he was about the delays and evasions of the military, Hillman retained a lively sense of the politically feasible. Hence, when he arrived in Frankfurt, in the U.S. zone, he admonished the local labor radicals for their overzealousness in pushing the "One Big Union" scheme and in agitating for the nationalization of industry as the best route to denazification.[29]

Hillman returned more convinced than ever of how important it was for the WFTU to establish its official presence in the councils of the emergent new world order. But it was an uphill battle. The same circles that were deliberately dragging their feet on denazification, doing what they could to discourage the revival of rank-and-file unionism, and balking at the mention of postwar state planning and regulation were hardly ready to invite a newly organized international labor federation, radical at its circumference if not at its core, to deliberate with them about the structures of power and wealth in postwar Europe or about the process of decolonization in the Third World. What was even more provoking was that their view seemed to be infecting even those in powerful positions Hillman once considered friends.

After FDR's death, relations between the WFTU and Washington grew frostier. But the estrangement did not originate with Truman. Rather it was the offspring of the same passions that had fulminated through the presidential campaign of 1944. At first, early in 1945, when Roosevelt was still alive, there seemed to be some hope that the embryonic WFTU might maneuver its way within hailing distance of the institutional centers of international power. Alger Hiss, then function-

ing as a kind of temporary secretary general of the United Nations assembly planned for San Francisco, met with Hillman at the State
Department to discuss the question of a WFTU representative's attending in an advisory capacity. Hiss told Hillman and Saillant to send all
memos on that issue directly to him and he would see that they were
distributed to all the delegates. Soon afterward a letter sent to the new
Secretary of State, Edward Stettinius, and the four chairmen of the San
Francisco conference, and signed by Hillman, Citrine, Saillant, and
Tarasov, formalized the WFTU request. In effect Hiss and his aides were
offering to act as a conduit for WFTU propositions. Hillman was naturally encouraged but apparently even then was nagged by suspicions. [30]

Some months later he met Frances Perkins in Paris. He was there to
attend the WFTU's founding, and she for a meeting of the ILO. Perkins
was abashed by Hillman's extravagant praise for Kuznetsov. In fact, at a
Cabinet meeting the previous March she had told Roosevelt to "watch
out for Hillman," whose international plottings she considered unrealistic, even dangerous. Just before the London conference in February the
two met in New York, where Hillman "raved," according to Perkins,
about the prospects of securing for labor a position of control over all
major global issues. The WFTU, he was convinced, would penetrate and
dominate the UN, would end all future wars, and would plan the world
economy. His ravings went so far, Perkins reported, as to confide absolute trust in Kuznetsov and the Soviets. Perkins claimed that she had
warned Hillman that the whole scheme would be greeted with fear and
hostility in the United States, where class politics were now abhorred.
She advised him to look to the government, not the international working class, to solve these problems. But Hillman, so Perkins remembered,
was out of patience. When she pleaded with him that Roosevelt represented labor's best hope, he responded with a chilling anger: "Roosevelt!
I have no use for Roosevelt. . . . He has absolutely turned his back on
us. . . . But he does not care about the World Federation. I tried to sell
it to him. . . . He does not see that this is the life of labor. . . . I am
through with Roosevelt. . . . We have used him, but he is through. He
is finished. I wash my hands of him." Hillman finished with a denunciation of the President's wife.

Perkins, of course, had for years resented Hillman's elevation. It is
hard to know how far to credit her memory. On the day FDR died, a
reporter for the *New York World-Telegram* noted Hillman's evident grief.
Three days later, at the funeral, Hillman was apparently so overcome
that he tottered to a bench in Jackson Park, where he sat alone for hours
thinking, "I would never be able to get up and walk again." Perkins could
not know this and instead was revolted by what she perceived to be

Hillman's "self-importance," his obsession with power. She even contemplated going public with the news of Hillman's grandiosity and ingratitude, but feared the scandal it would undoubtedly ignite. A month later, at the President's funeral, she confessed that she felt like spitting at Hillman. By the time she ran into him in Paris, she could scarcely conceal her rancor toward the WFTU. Disgusted by Hillman's plaudits for the execrable Kuznetsov, she told him that even Ernest Bevin of the Labour Party considered the WFTU hopelessly "red." More significantly, she lobbied with Secretary of State Stettinius against granting the federation even consultative status, insisting over Stettinius's hesitations (he still worried about alienating the Russians), that the ILO was the politically preferable institution. She even managed to persuade Tom Connally to denounce the federation at the Foreign Ministers' meeting.[31]

If neither Roosevelt nor Perkins could be counted on to befriend the WFTU, it was because the revanchist currents unleashed by the "Clear it with Sidney" campaign coursed through the body politic with undiminished strength, November's victory notwithstanding. Representation for the WFTU was thus never in the cards for reasons that had as much to do with the Cold War at home as it did with the one unfolding more slowly abroad. Hillman was admitting as much in voicing his hurt disappointment with Roosevelt, even if his actual utterances may have been less venomous and cynical than Perkins recollected. On occasion, President Truman consulted Hillman on matters of foreign policy, in particular about the WFTU's demand that the Franco regime be treated as a diplomatic excommunicant. But the new President, along with the British, proved unbudgeable when it came to opening the door to WFTU representatives. In the end it was a case of the CIO's increasingly besieged position at home rendering it incapable of working its will abroad.[32]

Not long after Roosevelt's death, Charles Ervin delivered a candid assessment of the balance of power in America. He told Hillman that 1944 was not a Democratic Party victory and certainly not one for the New Deal, but rather a Roosevelt victory. Otherwise, Ervin argued, 1944 merely continued the decline of the Roosevelt majority. Now that FDR was dead, the going was bound to get rougher.[33]

Signs of decline and reaction proliferated. The Battle of the Bulge provided a strange kind of emotional lift for congressional conservatives. By renewing fears of protracted war, it stalled the momentum toward full-employment reconversion planning, breathed new life into the demand for national service legislation that would compel workers to "work or fight," and made Roosevelt once again chary of anything that might fray the bipartisan coalition in foreign affairs. The bill sponsored by

Senators Murray, Kilgore, and Truman, empowering a single state agency to plan demobilization, lost out to a tepid substitute offered by Hillman's old nemesis, Senator Walter George, that eliminated labor or other functional group representation and with that any serious capacity to plan the economy.

While the CIO hoped to take advantage of various statutory curiosities, it knew the George bill to be "a pale imitation" of its predecessor. As the war drew to an end, the apparatus that might have been used for postwar planning was rapidly dismantled. Julius Krug, head of the WPB, relaxed controls as fast as was feasible, enabling large corporations to resume their civilian businesses. Resistance by Maury Maverick and Chester Bowles at the OPA, who feared private accumulations of power and depredations upon the American consumer, as well as pleas by organized labor to maintain controls, were increasingly ignored. Meanwhile Southern and Republican red-baiting of Aubrey Williams killed his nomination to head the REA despite CIO efforts to save him.[34]

Hillman did all he could to marshal PAC and NCPAC resources on behalf of Keynesian and social democratic objectives. In the summer of 1945 the PAC led the fight against attempts to kill the FEPC and to eliminate price and rent controls prematurely. It also called for federal legislation to cushion the impact of unemployment during the reconversion period. PAC and CIO legislative energies were devoted to anti–poll tax bills and to a bill offered by Senator Murray to create a Missouri Valley Authority as a way of realizing the 60 million jobs promised by the "People's Program of 1944." Hillman called on state and regional PACs to pressure Senators waffling over the campaign to raise the hourly minimum wage to 65 cents. It was the bare minimum, he insisted, needed to sustain mass purchasing power and forestall a spiraling descent into depression.[35]

For Hillman, Murray, and the rest of the CIO-PAC leadership, political and industrial objectives were to be pursued in tandem. They accorded priority to the political arena, for they all sensed the massing hosts of industrial counterrevolution gathering for an assault on the recently won prerogatives of industrial unionism. If they were being fired upon from Washington as well, at least they could plausibly persuade themselves it was "friendly fire."

Hillman's memory was long enough to recognize the descending shades of a counterrevolutionary thermidor. The events of 1919, he prophesied, would seem "merely child's play to what will happen now," as the unstoppable forces of either inflation or deflation were in place. Ten million, perhaps even as many as 15 million, were likely to be thrown out of work. Aside from the profit motive, he suspected what was driving the business community "is their opposition to us . . . many of them believe that there is the opportunity to break down everything that has been done in the last decade and get a situation that will give them Fascist powers under some other name." Abroad, and just "a little below the surface. . . . Fascist elements have not taken their defeat as final." So too in America. There was no middle way: Barbarism beckoned unless the United States led the world in erecting a full-employment, high-wage, mass-consumption economy. Hillman also raised alarms about a vast propaganda machine of "vested interests," which made it imperative for the CIO to convince people that its program was not merely a "labor program" but a program of national salvation.[36]

While popular discontent simmered at the surface of public life, the CIO sought to avoid a head-on collision with business reactionaries and to deflect that social energy instead into more manageable political channels. Murray cautioned against strikes and reminded everyone that a national wage policy and the no-strike pledge were inseparable. Without the latter, Murray's tête-à-têtes with Truman and his advisers would produce nothing. The vital issues of the day were in any event intrinsically political. The CIO had to respond to the mass cancellation of contracts with demands for federally mandated lower prices and higher wages, a tax on corporate profits, community and industrial planning agencies, and public construction of housing and other facilities. It was time even to resurrect a more ambitious version of the wartime "Murray Plan." In a corporatist scenario for administering the postwar economy, the new "Murray Plan" extended its reach beyond the realm of production. Industrial councils would enjoy authority over all phases of business operations, including production and development; pricing; trade practices, the division of proceeds among rent, interest, wages, and profits; investment planning; mechanization, plant location; and more. In the end, however, the CIO leadership relied on Senator James Murray's Full Employment Act, an ambivalent piece of legislation even in its pristine, unamended version, which called for full employment while neither seriously intruding on the normal operations of a free enterprise economy nor threatening it with competing government facilities.[37]

Hillman too treated the link between the no-strike pledge and a national wage policy as inviolable. Workers were suffering, to be sure, but the war against Japan remained a first priority, and the pledge could not be revoked. "If we fail at this time our enemies will take advantage of us. It is the last mile of the race which will come into the public's mind." It would be wiser, then, to focus on the Murray–Patman Full Employment bill, which offered a real if sketchy reconversion plan. Above all, Hillman warned his comrades, they must not let themselves "be provoked into situations that might be disastrous to our organizations."

Hillman was sanguine but also coldly realistic. There was sufficient support out there to get minimum wage legislation through, but only by selling out agricultural workers to keep the South in line. For this reason the bill was deliberately split into industrial and agricultural sections. That might have constituted bad faith, but Hillman was prepared to defend it based on his tortuous experience in getting the original FLSA passed. "I have learned one thing, I think. When a liberal group says they will get all or nothing, they get nothing."[38]

Neither Hillman's confidence nor his political practicality, however, could disallow the fact that on the matter the CIO considered most critical—the formulation of a national wages policy—there was no progress at all. The CIO had a lot invested in the effort. The Keynesian economist Robert Nathan had been brought on board in the spring of 1946 to prepare a brief demonstrating that the high profits of American industry permitted higher wages without any coincident rise in prices. While still Deputy Director of the Office of War Mobilization and Reconversion, Nathan had estimated a 24 percent wage increase as vital for maintaining aggregate demand. It was this essential premise the CIO hoped to make the focus of a national debate and the axis around which the rest of its welfare and redistribution demands revolved. Hillman testified before a subcommittee of the Senate Committee on Education and Labor to defend the Keynesian wisdom of minimum wage legislation. Behind the scenes he reconnoitered the possibility of an alliance with Progressive businessmen like Henry Kaiser, Robert Johnson, Eric Johnstone, and similarly sympathetic steel, textile, and auto industrialists, together with friendly elements of the AFL, bishops from the Council of Catholic Bishops, and representatives from the liberal Protestant establishment.[39]

Discussions with Truman and his aides began in August. The President issued Executive Order 9599 ending the WLB's wartime wage policy and urged peaceful negotiations to formulate a new one. But then the government coasted, offering no concrete formulation. The situation worsened with Perkins's resignation from the Cabinet, the official termination of the WLB, and the retirement of William Davis from the Office of Economic Stabilization. Murray grimly reported no successful collective bargaining anywhere and echoed Hillman in decrying a "Fascist type of mind that is being definitely developed here in the U.S. among many large employers." Strike sentiment continued to mount, while industry, Murray observed, was stockpiling its wealth, preparing for war, using the carry back–carry forward provisions of the 1942 tax law to offset currently taxable war profits.[40]

The administration's vacillation on the question of a national wage policy was characteristic of a regime infiltrated by hostile interests and views. When Truman assumed office the CIO greeted him warmly and at least half sincerely, seeing in him a friend of such New Deal proposals as the FEPC, the Missouri Valley Authority, Bretton Woods, price controls, and so on. For longer than many others, Hillman tried hard to believe in this myth, or at least to keep his doubts to himself. After all, Truman as President was, in a sense, Hillman's creation, and he could not relish watching him mutate into a political Frankenstein monster. But privately his doubts were there from the beginning, and they grew as the new President surrounded himself with such arch-conservatives as Edwin Pauley and Louis Snyder. Pauley was a right-wing California Democrat whom Truman appointed Ambassador to the Allied Reparations Commission over Hillman's good friend and ally, Isador Lubin. Snyder, a Missouri banker and party sachem who hated economic controls and deficit financing, replaced Fred Vinson as head of the OWMR, where he immediately proceeded to dismantle the Office of Economic Stabilization. By the end of 1945 he had managed to drive from government such stalwart New Dealers as William Davis, Lubin, and Robert Nathan.[41]

Yet for a while there did seem some credible basis for Hillman's conviction that Truman was not entirely feckless. Briefly, for example, the President lent support to the liberal–labor campaign to make war plants available to new entrepreneurs and seemed open to other structural reforms during the reconversion period. He urged Congress to continue price controls, endorsed the Full Employment bill and the Murray–Wagner–Dingell act, and added his voice to those calling for a permanent FEPC. In an address to Congress in September 1945 Truman adopted as his own the Economic Bill of Rights, seemed to pledge the government's credit to shore up national production and consumption, and called for higher unemployment benefits and minimum wages, as well as public housing and other public works.[42]

Rapidly, however, the Truman administration became a study in equivocation. Not only did it defer a decision on wage-price policy, but the President did precious little to mobilize Congress behind the rest of the New Deal program. The South reacted badly to Truman's September address, treating it as a capitulation to PAC and "communist planning." It was a declaration of war. Southern Congressmen pilloried the notion of a national production budget, and Southern cotton and fruit producers went after the OPA with a vengeance. At least one-fifth of the antilabor bills were introduced by Southern Democrats, and they lent their enthusiastic support to South Dakota Representative Case's bill calling for a mandatory cooling-off period. Scarcely a month after Truman's rousing speech, defeat loomed for unemployment compensation; the full employment bill was suffering a thousand cuts; and the chorus in favor of antistrike coercion was growing shriller. By the end of the year, defeat seemed imminent on the FEPC and on housing and health legislation. Meanwhile, new tax laws accelerated refunds and credits to business, eliminated the excess profits tax, and lowered corporate rates.

Truman oscillated erratically, one moment paying obeisance to the elders of American business, and the next huddling with Hillman and delivering an energetic defense of collective bargaining and the need for a large supplement to the national wage level. All through the latter part of 1945 Hillman resisted an open break with the President, but as the CIO's legislative hopes withered and political options seemed increasingly bleak, irresistible pressures built up from below pressing for direct action in the industrial arena.[43]

As the war wound down, rank-and-file militants in the TWUA and the UAW forced through resolutions condemning the abuses of the WLB and demanding that the CIO withdraw from its deliberations. In March the textile workers went so far as to rescind their no-strike pledge. Alarmed, Murray tried to engineer a compromise and complained that these provocations would only help the enemy, including the AFL. Hillman added his own chastisement: "I am not willing to take the gamble" of revoking the pledge just to pressure the government. It was a "blind alley" that would feed charges that the CIO was obstructing military operations. "We have considerable power in this country," he boasted, "political power and sources of public opinion . . . but let us not permit ourselves the luxury of doing the thing that may lead to disaster." But once the war ended, it was impossible to argue that labor bore some special moral responsibility for maintaining national concord. Hillman's boast about the CIO's political muscle was abraded on a daily basis in the halls of Congress.[44]

CIO leaders and Truman administration executives feared an open confrontation with American industry. At first blush that might seem odd, as the CIO, along with the rest of the trade union movement, had grown substantially during the war and had consolidated its position in the core industries of the nation's economy. But socially it was a less formidable institution. Many veteran cadre from its formative years were lost to the war. Racial resentments corroded the ethos of solidarity. Newer recruits from the farms and small towns of Appalachia, the South, and the West, along with women and blacks, were for the most part trade union innocents and enlisted in the ranks more often as a condition of wartime employment than to manifest a state of mind. The deep incursions of the state into the collective bargaining process accelerated a bureaucratic transformation already visible by the late 1930s that dried up the springs of self-activity and daring mass mobilization, opening up instead the sluice gates of legal maneuvering by regiments of lawyers, economists, and industrial relations professionals. Ironically, the CIO, born in the streets of bloody rebellion, depended more than the AFL, and certainly more than the UMW, on the solicitous attention of the state. Neither Lewis nor the AFL could be persuaded to join the CIO's political campaign for a national wage policy, as both felt strong enough to face their foes directly in the marketplace without the aid and comfort of the administration. Lewis bellowed his opposition to "a corporate state and all its manifestations as expressed in the CIO resolution." Thus, without reliable allies from within the movement, the CIO leadership felt all the more in need of the government's friendship. For its part, the administration, already precariously balanced between its contending factions, feared nothing more than an open industrial war that might force it to choose sides.[45]

Despite rhetorical fireworks from Hillman and Murray about the fascist mentality of American business, the CIO executive, together with Truman, lived in the hope that managerial, trade union, and public bureaucratic elites might hammer out the terms of a détente before class relations broke down completely. In April 1945 the CIO, together with the AFL, signed a "Charter for Labor and Management," which the USCC endorsed as well, calling for full production and employment and high wages, to be achieved within the basic framework of free enterprise and without excessive government controls, and with full guarantees to management about its prerogatives in the workplace. In negotiating the "Charter," CIO leaders counted on the prescience and good will of industrialists like Henry Kaiser, Paul Hoffman, J. D. Zellerbach, E. J. Thomas of Goodyear, and Eric Johnston, president of the Chamber of Commerce, as well as those mainstream industrialists who were prepared to accept the basic existence of modern unions.

But of course they also had to contend with the hostility of the smaller, more provincial businessmen of the NAM, who refused to endorse the "Charter," insisting that it first outlaw strikes against WLB decisions and ban jurisdictional walkouts and strikes against technological displacement. In signing the "Charter" the CIO placed itself in the anomalous position of simultaneously endorsing the free enterprise system while trumpeting the "Murray Plan" and calls for government ownership and operation. The latter turned out to be sacrificial rhetoric offered up to propitiate the restive and to frighten hardened enemies; everything depended on working out some real concert of interests among labor, industry, and government. The "Charter" was an inauspicious attempt, but not the last one.[46]

The Republican Senate leader, Arthur Vandenberg of Michigan, a Taft conservative in the process of becoming a factotum of bipartisanship, publicly raised the idea of a national labor–management conference to be convened by the government where eighteen representatives from each side, together with the new Secretary of Labor, Lewis Schwellenbach, and Secretary of Commerce Henry Wallace, would work out the terms of postwar industrial peace. Truman and Hillman eagerly embraced the idea, and Hillman was involved from the start in its planning. Truman made a special request that Hillman represent the CIO, hoping his celebrated powers of conciliation would work their magic. The President pleaded for an extension of the no-strike pledge and for no large wage hikes until the conference had done its work. The conference was scheduled for November, and everyone knew time was running out.

All sides prepared warily. The Commerce Department's Business Advisory Council (BAC) reviewed a report on "National Collective Bargaining Policy" prepared by Industrial Relations Counsellors, Inc., which managed to endorse free collective bargaining but then to fill the air with second thoughts when it came to every practical exercise of that freedom. It complained about alleged NLRB bias against unaffiliated unions; objected to all clauses requiring union membership; defended employer rights to make known their own union preferences; excluded all management functions—plant organization, layout and equipment, materials and processes, control of plant property, the size of the workforce, scheduling and assignment of work, subcontracting, quality control, work rules, discipline, job classifications, merit raises, and promotions and demotions—from the sphere of "free" collective bargaining; condemned the idea of unions for foremen; sought to proscribe mass picketing, sympathy strikes, secondary boycotts, and jurisdictional strikes; recommended stringent penalties for wildcatters; proposed to disfranchise trade unions by barring political contributions even during the primary season; sought disempowering amendments to the NLRA and its decentralization; and embraced the idea of resubjecting the trade unions to the authority and injunctive powers of the antitrust laws. And these were, after all, the recommendations of a Rockefeller-funded group known for its "permissive" approach to the "labor question."

The CIO came armed as well with dossiers on all the major and minor actors from the NAM and the USCC, seeking to identify potential friends and enemies. Biographical sketches described the subjects' family background, education, marriage, public offices, business connections, political and religious affiliations, and fraternal ties, and then concluded with a report on their attitudes toward collective bargaining and trade unionism and their stance, if known, on vital pieces of labor, welfare, and racial legislation. The dossiers included character analyses and assessed skills and vulnerabilities as negotiators.

With guarded optimism Hillman joined the conference's "Collective Bargaining" committee. But with so much mutual suspicion fouling the air, the conference was doomed. Management spokesmen were willing to do little more than acknowledge their legal obligation to bargain. Otherwise, they emphasized their determination to preserve and recover lost prerogatives; to restrict collective bargaining to matters of wages, hours, and conditions; and to place explicit limits on trade union freedom of direct action. Despite Hillman's statesmanship and his plea that union security contained the key to economic stability, the "Collective Bargaining" committee could come to no common understanding about mechanisms to forestall strikes. Differences were if anything more unbridgeable when it came to defining mutual contractual responsibilities and legislative remedies for violations. In the end the committee issued two separate reports. Management representatives essentially adopted as their own the various strictures recommended by Industrial Relations Counsellors. Any lingering hope that a consensus on a national wage and price policy might emerge was quickly dispelled. Clearly industry preferred to fend for itself in the free market, sensing that the balance of political power was shifting enough in its favor so that it could safely settle its own most pressing problems outside the political arena. Industrialists were fortified in this stand by the war chests they had managed to accumulate thanks to the government's tax rebates.[47]

However, in the end it was labor, not management, that delivered the *coup de grâce* to the Labor–Management Conference of 1945. While the conferees were still going through the motions of deliberating, Walter Reuther announced that the UAW was walking out at GM. The greatest strike wave since 1919 was under way, confirming Sidney Hillman's premonition and forcing him to face the depressing possibility that whatever exactly had transpired in Chicago's Blackstone Hotel in July 1944, the outcome was turning out to be more bitter than he could ever have imagined.

The breadth and depth of working-class discontent were impressive. It encompassed not only industrial strikes but mass demonstrations for veterans and unemployment insurance. The strikes were hotly contested affairs—the one against GM lasted 113 days—and some were reminiscent of the industrial civil wars of the 1930s. There were even municipal general strikes. But there the resemblance to 1919 ends. At the end of World War I, when the "labor question" challenged the foundations of Western society and supplied politics with its moral passion and social *frisson,* industrial rebellion seemed to call into question the efficacy, justice, and viability of the capitalist order. The strike wave of 1946 never ventured that far, never, even implicitly, called into question the existing order of things. Still, this display of raw power, coming at a moment when war-ravaged Western Europe depended utterly on the prowess of the American economy, was an undeniably awe-inspiring sight.

In 1945 there were 4,750 stoppages; in 1946 there were 4,985, involving 4.6 million workers. Strikes in the oil and longshore industries actually preceded the conference, the President's pleas notwithstanding. When Reuther called out the UAW and issued his provocative demand for a 30 percent wage increase without any rise in car prices, strike fever quickly spread to the rest of heavy industry, including not only steel-workers but electrical, meatpacking, and railroad workers as well—and, of course, Lewis's miners. Industry used the opportunity to demand that the OPA relax its price ceilings. Otherwise, steel executives complained, how could they possibly be expected to afford Philip Murray's demand for a $2-a-day increase in rates?[48]

Whatever was left of the edifice of state economic controls was crumbling, and Truman began a slow panic. He called for legislation to extend the mandatory thirty-day cooling-off period of the Railway Labor Act to the rest of American industry. The days of "charters," concords, and conferences were over. The UAW defied Truman's call for a return to work, and Murray labeled the President a union-buster. Truman confessed to his Cabinet that he was hurt to hear himself vilified as a "thief." Then, characteristically, he backtracked, seeming to side with Reuther's demand that GM open its books to public inspection to see if indeed the company could afford to raise wages while holding the line on prices. GM responded by walking out of the fact-finding hearing. Walkouts of one sort or another became epidemic. Companies contemptuously ignored the findings of fact and recommendations of various official and impartial agencies. At first Truman did nothing; then he conspicuously ignored the recommendation of Chester Bowles to seize the steel plants and instead granted a $5-per-ton increase, mortally wounding what remained of the price control mechanism.

While Truman vacillated, Hillman refrained from open criticism. Even as his CIO brothers excoriated the President, Hillman kept silent, fearing above all an open break with the regime and with the Democratic

Party. He went so far as to wire praises for the President's efforts to settle the steel strike. Unlike Murray, he refused to blame Truman for the Case bill, for which Truman privately thanked him. The President and the PAC chairman faced an analogous predicament: somehow to suture together the rupturing tissues of the wartime social truce. In the end, however, it was a task beyond the powers of the most persistent and cool-headed statesmanship.[49]

Finally, when the railroad workers and soft coal miners struck in the spring, Truman grossly overreacted. He seized every opportunity to deliver antilabor diatribes in a plainly political surrender to the swelling chorus of congressional reaction. The PAC could no longer keep silent. Hillman held a press conference to defend the strikes as a last resort in the struggle to maintain purchasing power and ward off a new depression. Still, he tried to remain conciliatory and denied all radical intentions, thereby revealing the PAC's underlying defensiveness, its timorousness even while CIO armies warred on a half-dozen industrial fronts.

In an angry address to Congress, seething with a sense of personal betrayal and a thirst for revenge, the President threatened to draft the railroad strikers and called for drastic antistrike legislation. Liberals everywhere recoiled in disgust and with universal opprobrium for such arrogant Presidential disregard of elementary democratic rights. The CIO immediately reacted in kind, declaring Truman "the number one strike-breaker of the American bankers and Railroads" and pledging political retaliation. For the first time Hillman publicly condemned the President as "autocratic" and called for the defeat of Truman's legislative proposals.[50]

In the background some rumblings could be heard in and around PAC, from people like Reuther, A. Philip Randolph, John Green of the Shipbuilding Workers, and David Dubinsky about promises, plans, or threats to organize a third party. It remained background grumbling, quickly squelched by Hillman and Murray. But the question would not go away: Just what, politically speaking, was to be done?[51]

As a matter of fact, practically from the moment of Truman's vice presidential nomination the PAC had been stirred by indecisive debate about its political future. Within weeks of the November election Hillman and Ickes pondered putting together a conference to examine the PAC's options. Early in 1945 Hillman conferred with PAC cadre in California about the sorry state of the liberal wing of that state's Democratic Party. They assessed the relative strength of the pro-Wallace and anti-Wallace forces with an eye to the 1946 and 1948 elections, even though Hillman acknowledged that it would be premature actually to launch a movement for Wallace's nomination in 1948.

The fluidity of the national political scene left Hillman uncomfortably equivocating about what to do. While many within the liberal-labor coalition accepted Truman's nomination as a distasteful reality, their hearts remained with Wallace and his "Century of the Common Man" vision. The appearance of Wallace's book *Sixty Million Jobs* in the fall of 1945 acted as a clarion call to the armies of the Keynesian cooperative commonwealth and seemed to confirm Wallace as potential Presidential timber. But Hillman was reluctant to jettison his relations with Democratic Party headquarters. Shortly before Roosevelt's death, he told Ickes he remained unsold on Wallace's candidacy for 1948 and advised waiting until 1947 to decide. Wallace, he intimated, could not count on the support of the CIO next time; moreover, he personally preferred Hugo Black.[52]

Hillman relished his new stature as a Democratic Party influential, liked being consulted on a regular basis by Hannegan and local party potentates, and knew that should he openly declare himself a Wallace partisan he would instantly jeopardize his entree. But his caution was nurtured by more than self-regard.

The phobias aroused by "Clear it with Sidney" were hardly interred with Dewey's defeat. Beanie Baldwin reported to Hillman that their erstwhile friends in the Democratic Party were proving totally unreliable, were as susceptible to the anti-red contagion as anyone else, and in too many cases, Baldwin believed, remained unaware that the world had changed in fundamental ways during the last twenty years. Remarkably, a man who had successively served as Secretary of Agriculture, Vice President, and Secretary of Commerce was already widely regarded as a fringe politician who many intuited, years before it became reality, might break the mold of consensual two-party politics. As it had been for at least a decade, this was an eventuality Hillman abhorred. It was one especially to be avoided in the new postwar world of incipient cold war and domestic reaction, where the CIO and the PAC were forced, temporarily anyway, into a defensive posture. Even while rallying the troops after the election, and while defiantly declaring the PAC a permanent fixture in American politics, Hillman went out of his way to make clear that "PAC will have have nothing to do with the creation or fostering of a third party on the national scene."[53]

Hillman took steps to build up the PAC's defensive armor by inviting the embrace of more respectable circles of liberalism. He asked Eleanor Roosevelt to assume the leadership of the NCPAC. Hillman wanted the NCPAC to bear the main burden of building alliances to non–working-class populations. The PAC was too vulnerable to attack by Republicans and was often deserted by local Democrats, who more and more sought to evade the tough class issues that still simmered on the surface of domestic politics. Getting the late President's widow to assume NCPAC leadership would constitute a political and public relations triumph. Mrs. Roosevelt deliberated, told Hillman that although she wanted no pay she must have full power to appoint people she trusted, and stressed that if she accepted she intended to be an active not an honorary chair, something she suggested Hillman might not welcome. Ultimately she declined the invitation. She confessed to Hillman that she worried about alienating the Democratic Party, which of course was precisely the point for Hillman—how not to alienate the Democratic Party without at the same time surrendering the programmatic and political integrity of the labor movement.

Unspoken, but undoubtedly a factor in Mrs. Roosevelt's demurral, was the "red scare." When she referred to people she could trust and couldn't, she meant Communists, and certainly Hillman knew that. Yet in laboring to preserve and extend the wartime antifascist coalition, Hillman shied away from any wholesale purging of CP cadre. Nervous about undue party influence, he resisted a proposed merger between the NCPAC and the Independent Citizens Committee of the Arts, Sciences, and Professions. The ICCASP, an organization in which Harold Ickes served as executive chairman but where CP members exercised great operational authority, was tainted enough for Hillman to keep at a polite distance. Yet Hillman was otherwise cooperative, so the CIO, NCPAC, and ICCASP established a joint committee to coordinate liberal political strategy for the 1946 elections. The afterglow of the Allied victory was still warm enough, the penumbra of the Cold War still faint enough, so that as long as Hillman lived it remained credible for the CIO-PAC to insist that fascism constituted the great danger, that the foreign policy of the Soviet Union was principally directed at that common foe, that spheres of influence were acceptable if they served that grander purpose, and that after all was said and done fealty to the essentials of the New Deal should be the only litmus test of home front political alliances. Moreover, those within the antifascist united front who might have preferred to flog the red question a bit harder—liberal intellectuals and publicists in the Union for Democratic Action and others—were at the same time acutely aware that the CIO enjoyed enormous financial and organizational leverage, that without the CIO there was really no liberal-labor united front to speak of. Pressing the communism issue would obviously produce great stress within the CIO and thereby weaken the resistance to congressional and presidential reaction.[54]

Straddling the antipodes of domestic politics, as Hillman continued to attempt, proved ever more difficult. The evolution of the ALP in New York was a case in point. By 1945 the party acted as little more than a pressure group, vetting Democratic Party nominees and policies. With the endorsement of William O'Dwyer for mayor, the age-old feud with Tammany Hall seemed at an end. Both Hillman and the CP concurred on this course of action. The ALP presented a picture of perfect popular front harmony through 1945. But then CP strategy shifted. Communists gave voice to a more militant, anti-imperialist, and class struggle outlook, and rumblings about making over the ALP into a real third party were heard once again. Hillman and the CP locked horns as the CP's attitude toward Truman flared into open hostility, while Hillman did what he could to keep differences within the family. Hannegan pressured him to maintain the bloc with the Democrats and in return okayed the nomination of lesser ALP figures for minor state and municipal offices. In the months before his death Hillman and the CP were on a collision course over the question of a third party as Hillman pursued the role of party fixer.[55]

The political costs of preserving the popular front were becoming prohibitive. In Detroit, for example, Richard Frankensteen of the UAW appeared at first to be an unbeatable candidate for mayor. Yet he lost. His defeat registered the social conservatism fostered by the war, as Polish and Appalachian voters, disturbed by the shifting racial complexion of Detroit factories and neighborhoods, deserted Frankensteen in crippling numbers. The same anxieties were aroused, among those voters and among others from more middle-class precincts, by the NCPAC's association with the red-tainted ICCAPS. Race and red-baiting, which had mated so well during the presidential campaign, once again aborted an embryonic labor–Democratic Party alliance.[56]

In the face of these trying problems, Hillman redoubled the PAC's propaganda and organizing efforts. The "People's Program" for 1946 showed no signs of programmatic backsliding or of the disintegration of the antifascist alliance. Always alert to the latest innovations in mass politicking, Hillman announced a four-day school of "Political Action Techniques" in Washington, where such celebrated "teachers" as Ben Shahn and Pete Seeger were to instruct CIO and PAC cadre in everything from ghostwriting to the proper deployment of sound trucks. In the spring Hillman, Murray, and Ickes met to plot the 1946 campaign. Hillman "wants to go ahead and support candidates with programmatic principles wherever they can be found and supported with any chance of success," Ickes reported, and noted as well that Hillman and Murray pledged to raise a $150,000 war chest for the coming primary campaigns. Stories circulated that Hillman planned an amalgamation of PAC,

NCPAC, and ICCAPS, but Ickes, aware that such a fusion would only strain relations with the Administration further and limit his usefulness to the Keynesian left, vehemently denied those rumors and ruefully concluded to his diary that "Sidney Hillman certainly has the conservatives in a jittery state of mind."[57]

Then, as the strike wave crested and the PAC ran after every political opening within and on the circumference of the Democratic Party, the CIO turned its attention once again to the South, the most formidable obstacle barring its road to power. While in 1938 the CIO had joined with the Roosevelt administration in a combined industrial and political assault on the Southern oligarchy, in 1946 the Truman administration lacked the will. And so, on its own, the CIO launched "Operation Dixie," in the form of a campaign for industrial unionism, but with purposes no less political. David McDonald of the steelworkers put it well:

> The necessity of this campaign of course cannot be over-emphasized. We all know the political situation in the South, we know how deplorable it is, and we know how very fortunate we have been in being able to beat back those reactionary forces in Congress. We have been very fortunate in view of the make-up of that Congress, that we have not had some awfully bad legislation passed. As you know, the backbone of reaction is the South. We are firmly convinced that the only way to change that situation is by building unions.

"Operation Dixie," launched with much fanfare and high hopes, would nonetheless immediately find itself bedeviled by the same social frictions and ideological phantoms undermining CIO and PAC initiatives everywhere else. The AFL began its own organizing drive in the South, openly appealing to Southern conservatives and industrialists by red-baiting the CIO and by proudly pointing to its own pristine political agnosticism and strict business unionism. Once again Sidney Hillman functioned as a convenient emblem of evil, the Yankee, immigrant Jew, and red labor radical who would, if not checked, overturn the South's racial, social, and political order.[58]

In the South, in Detroit, in New York, and everywhere, communism, the doppelganger of American social nightmares, haunted Hillman's political calculations. In a telephone conversation with Wallace in the spring of 1946, Hillman referred cryptically and critically to Winston Churchill's "Iron Curtain" speech in Fulton, Missouri. It had caused great trouble abroad, Hillman observed, but even more vexing troubles at home. Wallace confessed that his friends were alarmed about his speaking before organizations suspected of CP affiliations. Hillman tried to assure him that those fears were grossly exaggerated and, speaking for himself, he refused to be intimidated and said that "it is silly for anyone to get involved in factionalism which divides the various progressives; that it does not become some people who have the responsibility of leadership to get involved in little things not of national significance." Wallace in turn thought now might be the time to plan for "a progressive American Democratic Party," but Hillman was unwilling to commit himself.[59]

As spring turned to summer, Hillman's indecision and ambivalence persisted and mirrored the disorientation of the whole "progressive" community. Truman had proved disingenuous and unreliable, and the search for his replacement was well under way. Yet a third party seemed unfeasible and unwise. Meanwhile, Hillman had privately concluded that Henry Wallace was unelectable. The CIO had flexed its industrial muscle with impressive results, but its political future was shrouded in uncertainty.[60]

For Sidney Hillman especially the strain of living with such daily ambivalence and precariousness must have been painful. Yet he seemed to rise to the occasion. After lunching with Hillman, Harold Ickes remarked that he had "become a man of affairs . . . fully able to stand on his own feet. He has keen judgment and initiative." Ickes praised Hillman's "character," speculated that added responsibility had lent him a new stature, and, to his surprise, found him looking quite healthy. But to intimates Hillman, who was always high-strung, tense, and driven, "seemed to be carrying a tremendous burden, frequently a trial even to those closely associated with him and those who loved him." Others, less enamored acquaintances, complained that Hillman had become a domineering personality who stripped his underlings of any independence of judgment and action. Always a forceful presence, it was as if he now hoped somehow to hold things together by the sheer exertion of his will.[61]

The war, with its aftermath, had exacted its toll. While superficially the occasion for his own personal triumph, it had become the medium of his professional and political disappointment. It had undermined, if only temporarily, his credibility and authority in the labor movement while leading to his rejection by a President he admired and defended. It had frustrated his best efforts to practice the arts of labor statesmanship whether among bureaucrats in government, in party caucuses, or at congresses of international labor. And it had destroyed his health.

The strain proved too great. Ickes was mistaken. Hillman was not healthy and in fact had never regained his strength since suffering the massive heart attack in 1942. Three less severe episodes followed. At 8:40 A.M. on July 10, while vacationing at his modest cottage in Point Lookout on Long Island, he was felled by a fourth coronary thrombosis. He died an hour and ten minutes later. He was fifty-nine years old.

News of his death interrupted regular radio broadcasts and commanded eight-column front-page banners in most metropolitan dailies. Rabbi Stephen Wise officiated at his funeral in Carnegie Hall, where his body lay in state as thousands came to pay final respects. Henry Wallace wrote to Bessie, "Your husband was one of the greatest labor statesmen of all time." The State Department commandeered a plane to fly Hillman's daughter Philoine and her husband from Czechoslovakia, where he was on Department assignment, back to New York for the funeral. President Truman issued a statement lamenting the nation's loss and praising Hillman as a "great humanitarian and an outstanding statesman in the field of labor–management relations." Progressives hailed him as "the most respected and feared labor leader in the country."

It was an impressive ending indeed. Even ten years earlier such a public tribute would have been unthinkable, not only for Hillman particularly, but for any American labor leader. It was easy enough to conclude, as one Progressive newspaper did, that the pomp accompanying his death "was not only an implicit tribute to his own achievements . . . but a significant index to labor's coming of age as a vital force in the community." But it was an ambiguous triumph at best, both for Hillman and for the labor movement with which he was identified.[62]

If there was a pathos to Hillman's life, it might be that as he drew ever closer to the center of power, he tended to forfeit his birthright, that obsidian sense of Yiddish irony vulcanized through centuries of shtetl privation and persecution. With it went the ability to tell the difference between the role of the courtier and that of the labor statesman. Not until Roosevelt died did Hillman acknowledge to himself, as one observer later wrote about the President, that "labor found him helpful when its political artillery was loaded and well-aimed, but merely friendly when it seemed outgunned in the battle for votes." Shrewd, self-possessed, and capable of coolly realistic calculations under trying circumstances, he was nonetheless prone to exaggerate the significance of his unique relationship with Roosevelt. And such delusions not only induced him to overvalue his entree to the White House, but conversely blinded him to whatever possibilities remained for enhancing the institutional independence of organized labor and thereby his real source of strength as a labor statesman.

In a sense no doubt different from the one Hillman intended, he had

become, after his ancestors, a rabbi, a secular rabbi of the labor movement, applying balm to its many wounds. But he was at the same time
the man in the "iron cage." For decades he had woven the skein of his
own bureaucratic confinement in party, state, and trade union. It was a
"velvet prison," mindful of its inmates' material well-being, respectful of
their democratic entitlements, and erected where once there had been
raw tyranny, numbing exhaustion, and endless degradation. The "new
unionism" and the New Deal, the CIO and the welfare state were, it
might be said, *mikvahs*. But for those who, like Hillman, at one time or
another had dreamed other dreams, enjoyment of them was also an act
of renunciation.

Once an ecstatic reverie, socialism, in all its various subspecies, had
become an advertisement for modernity, a promise to realize the pleni-
tude of the old order without imposing a new calculus of human desire.
The trajectory of Hillman's life—from Russian revolutionary to chairman
of the CIO-PAC—expresses as well a great sea change in American life,
which might be called the passing away of the "labor question." Sidney
Hillman came of age amid world war and global social revolution when
the very foundations of Western capitalism seemed on the brink of collapse, undermined by an insurgent proletariat. He died on the cusp of a
new world. The "labor question," which had spoiled the equanimity of
the American political and social order since at least the Civil War, had
at last found its answer in the insatiable cravings of mass culture and
consumption and in the phobic repressions of anticommunism.

At the last Amalgamated convention Hillman was to attend, in
May, A. H. Raskin and other journalists present, sensing his declining
strength, asked Hillman to make a statement, extemporaneously, about
his social philosophy and about what he foresaw for the labor movement.

> We want a better America, an America that will give its citizens, first of all,
> a higher and higher standard of living so that no child will cry for food in
> the midst of plenty. We want to have an America where the inventions of
> science will be at the disposal of every American family, not merely for the
> few who can afford them. An America that will have no sense of insecurity
> and which will make it possible for all groups, regardless of race, creed, or
> color, to live in friendship, to be real neighbors. An America that will carry
> its great mission of helping other countries to help themselves.[63]

Hillman died just before the Cold War and domestic anticommunism
became the overwhelming preoccupations of American life. He was still
young when he died, so it is especially hard to say that the timing of his
death was somehow fitting. And yet it was. The world had changed a

great deal between the time of his first challenge to the Czar in the invisible shtetl of Zagare and his emergence as a national and international leader of the modern labor movement. He had adapted his beliefs and behavior in innumerable ways in response to the social tectonics of the twentieth century. But through it all it was the "labor question" that animated his being. As his last words to his Amalgamated comrades suggest, he never surrendered his commitment to the idea that the labor movement uniquely embodied a vision, a generosity of spirit, and the political courage to rescue society from selfishness, exploitation, and organized violence. Not so very long after his death it would become harder and harder to imagine the labor movement aspiring to that same redemptive role in our national life.

Notes

Note: Papers of Sidney Hillman and the ACWA are now housed at the Labor–Management Documentation Center of the Martin P. Catherwood Library of the New York State School of Industrial and Labor Relations at Cornell University. However, I used the Papers while they were still at the Union's headquarters in New York City. They have since been reorganized by the archivists at Cornell so that the old file references are no longer usable. Thus, I shall refer simply to the H-ACWA Papers throughout these notes.

A work cited more than once in any chapter is identified with a full citation at its first mention in the chapter and by a short title in all references thereafter. When the short title falls more than ten note numbers past its previous appearance, the location of the full citation is added as follows: (note 3 above).

ONE: *Rabbi or Revolutionary*

1. Charles Madison, "Sidney Hillman: Labor Leader of the Amalgamated," *American Scholar*, Autumn 1979, p. 459.
2. S. L. Stark to Sidney Hillman, November 20, 1941, in Papers of Sidney Hillman and the Amalgamated Clothing Workers of America. Abraham S. Sachs, *Worlds That Passed* (New York, 1975; orig. pub. by Jewish Publication Society of America, Philadelphia, 1928), and *Encyclopedia Judaica*, 16 (Jerusalem, 1971): 915–16.
3. Salo W. Baron, *The Russian Jew Under Tsars and Soviets* (New York, 1964), p. 114, and Susan Anita Glenn, "The Working Life of Immigrants: Women in the American Garment Industry, 1880–1920," Ph.D. dissertation, University of California, Berkeley, 1983, p. 102.
4. Sachs, *Worlds That Passed*, pp. 82–83, and Simon Kuznets, "Immigration of Russian Jews to the U.S.: Background and Structure," *Perspectives in American History*, 9 (1975): 78. In 1898, 19 percent of all Jewish families received assistance on Passover.
5. Matthew Josephson, *Sidney Hillman: Statesman of American Labor* (New York, 1952), ch. 1, and Moses Rischin, "From Gompers to Hillman: Labor Goes Middle Class," *Labor History*, vol. 13, 1953.
6. Kuznets, "Immigration of Russian Jews," p. 77; Arcadius Kahan, *Essays in Jewish Social and Economic History*, ed. Roger Weiss (Chicago, 1986), pp. 3, 9, 15; and Baron, *The Russian Jew*, pp. 113–14.

7. Sachs, *Worlds That Passed*, p. 63. Max Weber has remarked that it was permissible for Jews to receive interest from foreigners and that "the traditionalist precepts of the Jewish economic ethics naturally applied in their full scope only to one's fellow religionists, not to outsiders, which was the case in every ancient ethical system." Max Weber, *General Economic History* (New Brunswick, N.J., 1982), p. 360. See also Robert J. Brym, *The Jewish Intelligentsia and Russian Marxism: A Sociological Study of Intellectual Radicalism and Ideological Divergence* (New York, 1978), p. 27, and Nora Levin, *While Messiah Tarried: Jewish Socialist Movements, 1871–1917* (New York, 1977), p. 225.

8. Lucy S. Dawidowicz, ed., *The Golden Tradition: Jewish Life and Thought in Eastern Europe* (Boston, 1967), pp. 179–85; author's interview with Philoine Fried, New York City, July 1978; *Encyclopedia Judaica*, 16: 915–16; and "Jacob Potofsky Notes on Hillman," H-ACWA Papers. Other notable Hillman relatives included a rear admiral, Ben Marcell, and the publisher David Alfred Smart, according to Ella Auerbach to Hillman, April 2, 1940, H-ACWA Papers.

9. Baba Meziah IX, 12, as cited in Mark Wischnitzer, *The History of Jewish Crafts and Guilds* (New York, 1965), pp. xvii–xix, 255–72. Baron, *The Russian Jew*, however, notes that *kahels* were officially abolished by the Czar in 1844.

10. Kuznets, "Immigration of Russian Jews," pp. 58–59; Glenn, "Working Life of Immigrants," pp. 28–31; and Sachs, *Worlds That Passed*, pp. 54–55.

11. Brym, *Jewish Intelligentsia*, p. 81; Dawidowicz, *Golden Tradition*, pp. 83–84, 86; and Arthur Liebman, *Jews and the Left* (New York, 1979), p. 8.

12. *Encyclopedia Judaica*, 16: 915–16.

13. *Encyclopedia Judaica*, 5: 1006; see also vols. 11, 13, 14.

14. *Ibid.*, vol. 11, and Dawidowicz, *Golden Tradition*, pp. 33, 85, 179–85.

15. Interview with Philoine Fried, July 1978; "Potofsky Notes on Hillman"; Glenn, "Working Life of Immigrants," pp. 13–15 (note 3 above); and Mari Jo Buhle, *Women and American Socialism, 1870–1920* (Urbana, Ill., 1981), pp. 1178–79.

16. Dawidowicz, *Golden Tradition*, pp. 179–85; Mark Zborowski and Elizabeth Herzog, *Life Is with People: The Culture of the Shtetl* (New York, 1952), pp. 96–97, 98, 230; and Sachs, *Worlds That Passed*, pp. 251–52.

17. Brym, *Jewish Intelligentsia*, pp. 55, 58; "Potofsky Notes on Hillman"; A. H. Raskin, "Sidney Hillman, 1887–1946," *American Jewish Yearbook*, 49 (1947–48): 1–14; "Potofsky Notes on Hillman"; and Rischin, "From Gompers to Hillman" (note 5 above).

18. Raskin, "Sidney Hillman"; Josephson, *Sidney Hillman*, ch. 1; interview with Philoine Fried, July 1978; and "Potofsky Notes on Hillman."

19. "Potofsky Notes on Hillman"; Josephson, *Sidney Hillman*, p. 31; Raskin, "Sidney Hillman"; and Madison, "Sidney Hillman: Labor Leader" (note 1 above).

20. Ezra Mendelsohn, *The Class Struggle in the Pale: The Formative Years of the Jewish Workers' Movement in Tsarist Russia* (New York, 1970), pp. ix, 41, 67.

21. Josephson, *Sidney Hillman*, ch. 1.

22. Liebman, *Jews and the Left*, p. 133 (note 11 above); and Gerald Sorin, *The Prophetic Minority: American Jewish Immigrant Radicals, 1880–1920* (Bloomington, Ind., 1985), p. 13.

23. "Potofsky Notes on Hillman"; Raskin, "Sidney Hillman"; Madison, "Sidney Hillman: Labor Leader"; and Josephson, *Sidney Hillman*, ch. 1.

24. Dawidowicz, *Golden Tradition*, pp. 179–85, and Sorin, *Prophetic Minority*, p. 26.

25. Liebman, *Jews and the Left*.

26. Henry Tobias, *The Jewish Bund in Russia: From Its Origins to 1905* (Stanford, Calif.,

1972); Kahan, *Essays in Jewish Economic History* (note 6 above), p. 9; Leonard Schapiro, "The Role of the Jews in the Russian Revolutionary Movement," *Slavonic and East European Review*, vol. 40, December 1961; Wischnitzer, *History of Jewish Crafts* (note 9 above); Mendelsohn, *Class Struggle in the Pale*, p. 88; Levin, *While Messiah Tarried* (note 7 above); David Lane, *The Roots of Russian Communism* (University Park, Pa., 1968), p. 167; and Sachs, *Worlds That Passed*, p. 82.

27. Liebman, *Jews and the Left.*
28. Schapiro, "The Role of the Jews"; and Tobias, *The Jewish Bund in Russia.*
29. Charles Woodhouse and Henry Tobias, "Primordial Ties and Political Process in Pre-Revolutionary Russia: The Case of the Jewish Bund," *Comparative Studies in Society and History*, vol. 8, 1965–66; Max Weber, *Economy and Society*, ed. Guenther Roth and Claus Wittich (Berkeley, Calif., 1978), 2: 1111, 1122, 1146–47, 1149, 1155–56; and Tobias, *Jewish Bund in Russia*, pp. 35–36, 69.
30. Josephson, *Sidney Hillman*, ch. 1.

TWO: *"Pauper Against Pauper"*

1. Author's interview with Philoine Fried, New York, July 1978, and Matthew Josephson, *Sidney Hillman: Statesman of American Labor* (New York, 1952), ch. 2.
2. "B. Bisno Notes," September 18, 1950, H-ACWA Papers.
3. "Jacob Potofsky Notes on Hillman," H-ACWA Papers.
4. *Ibid.*
5. Josephson, *Sidney Hillman*, ch. 2; A. H. Raskin, "Sidney Hillman, 1887–1946," *American Jewish Yearbook*, vol. 49, 1947–48; and "Labor Can Lead: The Story of Sidney Hillman," *The World Tomorrow*, November 1929.
6. Sidney Hillman to Charles Paiken, November 1908 and October 28, 1907, H-ACWA Papers.
7. "Potofsky Notes on Hillman."
8. *Ibid.*; "B. Bisno Notes," and Joseph Barondess, "From Sweatshop to Stability: Jewish Labor Between Two World Wars," *YIVO Annual of Jewish Social Science*, 16 (1976): 3.
9. Sidney Hillman, "Statement Before the U.S. Commission on Industrial Relations," Washington, D.C., 64th Cong., 1st Sess., Senate Document 415, vol. 1, pp. 566–71, April 1914, in H-ACWA Papers; Hillman to Jacob Potofsky, August 23, 1914, H-ACWA Papers; and Hillman note to himself, July 24, 1909, H-ACWA Papers.
10. Author's telephone interview with Elizabeth Eudey, May 31, 1985; "Potofsky Notes on Hillman"; Gerald Sorin, *The Prophetic Minority: American Jewish Immigrant Radicals, 1880–1920* (Bloomington, Ind., 1985), p. 57; interview with Philoine Fried, July, 1978; and Hillman, "Statement Before U.S. Commission."
11. Extract of Testimony of Joseph Schaffner, *Final Report of U.S. Commission on Industrial Relations*, vol. 1: 564–65, H-ACWA Papers; Hillman, "Statement Before U.S. Commission"; and N. Sue Weiler, "Walkout: The Chicago Men's Garment Workers' Strike, 1910–1911," *Chicago History*, vol. 8, Winter 1979–80.
12. Leon Stein, *Out of the Sweatshop: The Struggle for Industrial Democracy* (New York, 1977), citing Florence Kelley testimony before the U.S. Industrial Commission, May 3, 1899, p. 25, and Arthur Liebman, *Jews and the Left* (New York, 1979), pp. 171–72.
13. Jane Addams, *Twenty Years at Hull House* (New York, 1929).

14. Henry Tobias, *The Jewish Bund in Russia: From Its Origins to 1905* (Stanford, Calif., 1972), p. 101.

15. William Leiserson quoted in Benjamin Stolberg, *Tailor's Progress: The Story of a Famous Union and the Men Who Made It* (New York, 1944), p. 13, and Florence Kelley quoted in Dorothy Rose Blumberg, *Florence Kelley: The Making of a Social Pioneer* (New York, 1966), p. 128.

16. "Final Report and Testimony, Submitted to Congress by the Commission on Industrial Relations," Senate Document 415, 64th Cong., 1st Sess., 1916, 2: 2018 and 2: 1963–2050 *passim*.

17. Steven Fraser, "Combined and Uneven Development in the Men's Clothing Industry," *Business History Review*, Winter 1983, esp. p. 537.

18. "Report on the Conditions of Women and Child Wage-Earners in the U.S.," vol. II: "Men's Ready-Made Clothing," Senate Document 645, 61st Cong., 2d Sess., 1911, pp. 23–25, 415–16.

19. *Ibid.*, 2: 106–8, 132, 139, 229–30, 290–303; Susan Anita Glenn, "The Working Life of Immigrants: Women in the American Garment Industry, 1880–1920," Ph.D. dissertation, University of California, Berkeley, 1983, p. 46; and Edith Wyatt, "Garment Workers at Home," from Reel 12, "Handbook of the Chicago Industrial Exhibit," 1907, National Women's Trade Union League Papers, Margaret Drier Robbins Collection, Library of Congress.

20. "Final Report and Testimony," 2: 1991, 1995; Jesse Eliphalet Pope, *The Clothing Industry in New York* (St. Louis, 1905), esp. pp. 29–30; Wyatt, "Garment Workers"; *Women at Work: The Autobiography of Mary Anderson as told to Mary N. Winslow* (Minneapolis, 1951), p. 38; "Official Report of the Strike Committee," Women's Trade Union League (Chicago, 1911), p. 8, H-ACWA Papers; and "Extracts from Chicago Joint Board, ACWA, pp. 19, 21–28, 30–33, 38, H-ACWA Papers.

21. Glenn, "Working Life of Immigrants," pp. 39–40, and James R. Green, *The World of the Worker: Labor in 20th Century America* (New York, 1980), p. 22.

22. "Personal Testimony taken by a Court Reporter at the Breakfast Given by the WTUL," November 2, 1910, Emilio Grandinetti Papers, Box 1, Immigration History Research Center, University of Minnesota.

23. Hillman, "Statement Before U.S. Commission on Industrial Relations" (note 1 above).

24. Fraser, "Combined and Uneven Development," p. 538.

25. Jenna Weissman Joselit, *Our Gang: Jewish Crime and the New York Jewish Community, 1900–1940* (Bloomington, Ind., 1983), pp. 108–10.

26. James A. Schmiechen, *Sweated Industries and Sweated Labor: The London Clothing Trade, 1860–1914* (Urbana, Ill., 1984), p. 109.

THREE: *The Americanization of "Hilkie"*

1. The U.S. Commissioner of Labor reported in 1906 that no fewer than 500,000 men and women were out of work as a result of strikes and lockouts in the men's clothing industry between 1881 and 1905. Joan M. Jensen, "The Great Uprising in Rochester," in Joan M. Jensen and Sue Davidson, eds., *A Needle, a Bobbin, a Strike: Women Needleworkers in America* (Philadelphia, 1983), p. 86; Harry Best, "The Men's Garment Industry in New York and the Strike of 1913," University Settlement Studies, New York, 1914, H-ACWA Papers; and "Annual Report of the U.S. Commissioner of Labor on Strikes and Lockouts, 1906," Washington D.C., 1907.

2. "Jewish Workers' Victory—1890," *Die Arbeiter Zeitung,* May 1890, reprinted in *Jewish Life,* April 1953, Archives of the Jewish Bund, New York City.
3. Joseph Schlossberg, "The Rise of the Clothing Workers," ACWA Educational Pamphlet (New York, 1921), H-ACWA Papers, and Gerald Sorin, *The Prophetic Minority: American Jewish Immigrant Radicals, 1880–1920* (Bloomington, Ind., 1985), p. 90.
4. Abraham Shoul, "Unrest and Secession in the Men's Garment Trades in New York City," pp. 11–12, unpublished manuscript, June 1918, H-ACWA Papers.
5. Benjamin Stolberg, *Tailor's Progress: The Story of a Famous Union and the Men Who Made It* (New York, 1944), p. 36.
6. Sorin, *Prophetic Minority,* p. 77; Will Herberg, "The Jewish Labor Movement in the U.S.," *American Jewish Yearbook,* 1952, p. 5; Thomas Kessner, *The Golden Door: Italian and Jewish Immigrant Mobility in New York City, 1880–1915* (New York, 1977), pp. 56, 62, 73, 75, 76–77; Irving Howe, *World of Our Fathers: The Journey of the East European Jews to America and the Life They Found and Made* (New York, 1976), pp. 77–84; Melech Epstein, *Jewish Labor in the U.S.A.,* vol. 1: *1882–1914* (New York, 1950), pp. 224, 226, 236, 237; and Moses Rischin, *The Promised City: New York's Jews, 1870–1914* (New York, 1962), pp. 175–90.
7. "Some Truths Plainly Told," pamphlet, H-ACWA Papers; "Reports of the Committee on Manufactures on the Sweating System," 52d Cong., 2d Sess., January 20, 1893, pp. 223–24; and *The Garment Worker* (quarterly journal of the United Garment Workers), August 1901 and August 1903, H-ACWA Papers.
8. N. Sue Weiler, "Walkout: The Chicago Men's Garment Workers' Strike, 1910–11," *Chicago History,* vol. 8, Winter 1979–80, and Howard Barton Meyers, "The Policing of Labor Disputes in Chicago: A Case Study," Ph.D. dissertation, University of Chicago, 1929, pp. 655–57.
9. Sorin, *Prophetic Minority,* p. 82.
10. Samuel Liptzin, *Tales of a Tailor* (New York, 1965), p. 71; Mabel Hurd Willet, *Women in the Clothing Trade* (New York, 1902), p. 68; and Sorin, *Prophetic Minority,* p. 127.
11. Weiler, "Walkout"; Jacob Potofsky, "Reminiscences," *Advance,* July 22, 1927; and Sidney Hillman, "Statement Before the U.S. Commission on Industrial Relations," 64th Cong., 1st Sess., Senate Document 415, 1 (Washington D.C., April 1914): 566–71.
12. Author's interview with Beatrice Bornstein, June 7, 1979, and author's interview with Laurence Levin, June 8, 1979.
13. Hillman, "Statement Before U.S. Commission," pp. 566–71.
14. Extracts from *The Clothing Workers of Chicago, 1910–1922,* Chicago Joint Board, ACWA (Chicago, 1922), H-ACWA Papers.
15. "Official Report of the Strike Committee—Chicago Garment Workers Strike Oct. 29, 1910–Feb. 18, 1911," Women's Trade Union League of Chicago, p. 9, H-ACWA Papers.
16. "Some of the Results of the Hart, Schaffner & Marx Agreement," Reel 12, Margaret Drier Robbins Papers of Women's Trade Union League Collection, Library of Congress; Earl Dean Howard report to Joseph Schaffner, 1911, Box 17, Otto Beyer Papers, Library of Congress; and unpublished autobiography of Rebecca August, cited in Susan Anita Glenn, "The Working Life of Immigrants: Women in the American Garment Industry," Ph.D. dissertation, University of California, Berkeley, 1983, p. 309.

17. Weiler, "Walkout"; Anna Sondweiss, unpublished memoir, in possession of Steven Fraser; and extracts from *The Clothing Workers of Chicago.*

18. Howe, *World of Our Fathers* (note 6 above); Rischin, *Promised City* (note 6 above); Ezra Mendelsohn, *The Class Struggle in the Pale: The Formative Years of the Jewish Workers Movement in Tsarist Russia* (New York, 1970); Arthur Liebman, *Jews and the Left* (New York, 1979); Nora Levin, *While Messiah Tarried: Jewish Socialist Movements, 1871–1917* (New York, 1977); Henry Tobias, *The Jewish Bund in Russia: From Its Origins to 1905* (Stanford, Calif., 1972); and David Lane, *The Roots of Russian Communism* (University Park, Pa., 1968), are all useful in describing the work and political backgrounds of people like these early Amalgamated leaders.

19. "Speeches, Articles, and Reminiscences, ACW," Folder 17, Emilio Grandinetti Papers, Immigration History Research Center, University of Minnesota; "Biographical Data," Sam Levin, H-ACWA Papers; author's interview with Laurence Levin, June 8, 1979; "Biographical Data," Anzuino Marimpietri, H-ACWA Papers; "Biographical Data," Jack Kroll, H-ACWA Papers; author's interview with Delia Gottlieb, May 20, 1979; Jacob Potofsky Papers, then in possession of Gottlieb and subsequently donated to H-ACWA Papers; author's interview with Philoine Fried, January 25, 1979.

20. Rebecca Sive-Tomachevsky, "Identifying a Lost Leader," *Signs,* Summer 1978; Glenn, "Working Life of Immigrants," pp. 246–47; and Weiler, "Walkout."

21. Quoted in Moses Rischin, "From Gompers to Hillman: Labor Goes Middle Class," *Labor History,* vol. 13, 1953.

22. Mary Anderson, *Women at Work: The Autobiography of Mary Anderson as told to Mary N. Winslow* (Minneapolis, 1951), p. 38. This was a phenomenon repeated throughout much of American industry, even in railroading, otherwise noted for its invention of the modern bureaucratic business organization, according to Walter Licht, *Working for the Railroad: The Organization of Work in the 19th Century* (Princeton, N.J., 1983).

23. Extracts from *Clothing Workers of Chicago.*

24. Joseph Schaffner, "Testimony Before the U.S. Commission on Industrial Relations," extract in H-ACWA Papers.

25. Harry Hart, "Miscellaneous File," radio talk WCFL, June 12, 1937, Hart, Schaffner & Marx papers in possession of company; Weiler, "Walkout"; and Steven Fraser, "Dress Rehearsal for the New Deal," in Michael H. Frisch and Daniel J. Walkowitz, eds., *Working Class America: Essays on Labor, Community and American Society* (Urbana, Ill., 1983).

26. "Items in the *Chicago Daily Socialist,*" extracted in H-ACWA Papers.

27. *Ibid.*

28. Mary Field, "On Strike: A Collection of True Stories," *The American Magazine,* October 1911, in Reel 4, "Subject Files: Strikes Through World War I," WTUL Papers, Library of Congress.

29. *Chicago Daily Socialist,* December 16, 1910, and Weiler, "Walkout."

30. Field, "On Strike," and Jane Addams, *Twenty Years at Hull House* (New York, 1929), pp. 222–23.

31. Epstein, *Jewish Labor in the U.S.A.* (note 6 above), 1: 173.

32. George Creel, "A Way to Industrial Peace," *Century Magazine,* July 1915.

33. Earl Dean Howard, report to Joseph Schaffner, Otto Beyer Papers.

34. *Chicago Daily Socialist,* October 26, 1911.

35. Ellen Gates Starr to Jacob Abt, November 23, 1910, H-ACWA Papers. Starr's final

words were indeed prophetic: Abt's son, John, would go on to be a highly contro-
versial and radical legal adviser to Hillman in the late 1930s and the 1940s.

36. Weiler, "Walkout" (note 8 above).
37. Stolberg, *Tailor's Progress* (note 5 above), pp. 87–88.
38. Barry D. Karl, *Charles E. Merriam and the Study of Politics* (Chicago, 1974), esp. pp. 66 and 135.
39. Weiler, "Walkout."
40. Anderson, *Women at Work* (note 22 above), pp. 52–53, 54, and Allen F. Davis, *Spearheads of Reform: The Social Settlements and the Progressive Movement, 1890–1914* (New Brunswick, N.J., 1984), p. 108.
41. Eugene M. Tobin, *Organize or Perish: America's Independent Progressives, 1913–33* (Westport, Conn., 1986), pp. 17–18; "Official Report of the Strike Committee" (note 15 above); and Karl, *Charles E. Merriam.*
42. "Official Report of the Strike Committee," and Anderson, *Women at Work,* pp. 40–42.
43. "Official Report of the Strike Committee."
44. *Ibid.*; Margaret Drier Robbins, "Unidentified Fragment," from WTUL Strike Summary, Chicago 1909–1913, Reel 12, WTUL Papers; and Margaret Drier Robbins speech to WTUL Convention, June 12, 1911, in WTUL of Chicago Scrapbook, folder 1, September 8–15, 1911, The University Library, University of Illinois at Chicago.
45. Katherine Coman, Gertrude Barnum, and Ellen Gates Starr, "Participants in the Strike," pamphlet, Reel 4, December 14, 1910, WTUL Papers.
46. "Official Report of the Strike Committee."
47. Bruno Ramirez, *When Workers Fight: The Politics of Industrial Relations in the Progressive Era, 1898–1916* (Westport, Conn., 1928), pp. 4–5.
48. Coman, Barnum, and Starr, "Participants in the Strike."
49. Jane Addams to Mary Rozet Smith, November 22, 1910, "Letters Dec. 1–19, 1910," Jane Addams Memorial Collection, The University Library, University of Illinois at Chicago.
50. Addams, quoted in *Chicago Examiner,* October 31, 1910, extract in H-ACWA Papers, and "Jacob Potofsky statement," January 1963, H-ACWA Papers.
51. "A Call for Action," leaflet issued by the Committee of Italian Garment Workers, in possession of Beatrice Bornstein; Eugene Miller and Gionna Panofsky, "Radical Italian Unionism: Its Development and Decline in Chicago's Men's Garment Industry: 1910–30," conference paper, October 9–10, 1981, in author's possession; "Potofsky Notes on Hillman," H-ACWA Papers; and A. H. Raskin, "Sidney Hillman, 1887–1946," *The American Jewish Yearbook,* vol. 49, 1947–48.
52. "B. Bisno Notes," September 18, 1950, H-ACWA Papers, and Jacob Potofsky "Memoir," Oral History Collection of Columbia University (hereafter OHCCU), p. 48.
53. Joseph Schaffner to Potofsky, April 26, 1916, H-ACWA Papers, and "ACWA Convention Proceedings," May 1940, pp. 418–19, H-ACWA Papers. Ickes was of course gilding the lily for political purposes.
54. Agnes Nestor, *International Socialist Review,* January 11, 1911, and Anzuino Marimpietri, "From These Beginnings," 1944, H-ACWA Papers.
55. Anzuino Marimpietri, "Tailor Revisited," H-ACWA Papers, and Weiler, "Walkout" (note 8 above).
56. Marimpietri, "From These Beginnings," and Weiler, "Walkout."

57. Weiler, "Walkout."
58. Marimpietri, "Tailor Revisited," p. 31.
59. Chicago Joint Board of the ACWA, *The Clothing Workers of Chicago, 1910–1922* (Chicago, 1922); Steve Fraser, "Landslayt and Paesani," in Dirk Hoerder, ed., *Struggle a Hard Battle* (De Kalb, Ill., 1986); "Daily Trade Record," September 27, 1919, H-ACWA Papers; and Potofsky, "Memoir," OHCCU, p. 48.
60. John A. Dyche testimony before U.S. Commission on Industrial Relations, January 15, 1914, cited in Leon Stein, ed., *Out of the Sweatshop: The Struggle for Industrial Democracy* (New York, 1977); Glenn, "Working Life of Immigrants" (note 2 above), pp. 338–39; and Howard Report to Schaffner (note 33 above).
61. Potofsky "Memoir," OHCCU, p. 103; Sam Levin to Hillman, June 6, 1918, H-ACWA Papers; Hillman to Joseph Schlossberg, May 10, 1917, H-ACWA Papers; *Hart, Schaffner & Marx Labor Agreement, Cases Decided by the Board of Arbitration, Direct and Appealed, 1913–1925* (hereafter HSM Arbit.), Cases 5, 6, 8, and 13; *Board of Arbitration Men's Clothing Industry—Chicago Market, 1920–31* (hereafter Chic. Arbit.), Case 1.
62. Epstein, *Jewish Labor in the U.S.A.* (note 6 above), 1: 377; Folder 2, General Correspondence, 1911–32, Emilio Grandinetti Papers; Meyers, "Policing of Labor Disputes" (note 8 above), p. 696; "Summary Strike" culled from the *Chicago Daily Socialist*, H-ACWA Papers; "A Call for Action," leaflet in possession of Beatrice Bornstein; George Soule, *Sidney Hillman: Labor Statesman* (New York, 1939), pp. 29–40; Chicago Locals Minutes, 1911, H-ACWA Papers; *Chicago Tribune*, November 7, 1911; and Chicago Locals Minutes, 1912, H-ACWA Papers.
63. Paul Avrich, *The Russian Anarchists* (Princeton, N.J., 1967), pp. 18, 40, 42–49; Jenna Weissman Joselit, *Our Gang: Jewish Crime and the New York Jewish Community, 1900–1940* (Bloomington, Ind., 1983), p. 37; and author's interview with Leopold Gross, January 18, 1980. The sensationalist press in the late nineteenth century went so far as to define arson as "Jewish lightning," betraying a lurid anti-Semitism, but drawing as well on the impressive fact that 44 percent of all arson cases in the 1890s were tied to Jews. Of course, most of this was insurance fraud perpetrated especially by marginal property-owners.
64. Fraser, "Dress Rehearsal for the New Deal" (note 25 above).
65. Hillman, "Statement Before U.S. Commission" (note 11 above); Margaret Drier Robbins to Raymond Robbins, March 29, 1913, and March 9, 1912, and "Summary of Threatened 1913 Strike at HSM," "Correspondence Between MDR and RR, October 1911–March 1915," WTUL Papers; reprint of *Streater-Independent Times* article, "The Russian Jew," June 28, 1913, H-ACWA Papers and in Jacob Potofsky, ed., *John E. Williams, An Appreciation with Selections from His Writings* (published by ACWA, 1930); Matthew Josephson, *Sidney Hillman: Statesman of American Labor* (New York, 1952), p. 79.
66. Reprint of "The Russian Jew."
67. "Chicago Locals—Minutes, 1911," H-ACWA Papers; S. M. Franklin to Executive Board, National Women's Trade Union League, October 24, 1911, Reel 1, Container 1, WTUL Papers; and "Some of the Results of the HSM Agreement," WTUL Papers.
68. Howard Report to Schaffner (note 33 above) and Soule, *Sidney Hillman*, p. 31.
69. Margaret Drier Robbins to "Mieze," February 4, 1914, Reel 23, MDR Correspondence, WTUL Papers; "Some of the Results of the HSM Agreement," WTUL Papers; and Howard Report to Schaffner.

70. Joseph Schaffner, "Testimony Before U.S. Commission on Industrial Relations," extract in H-ACWA Papers, and "The Experience of Hart, Schaffner & Marx with Collective Bargaining," prepared by HSM for U.S. Industrial Relations Commission, April 1914, H-ACWA Papers.

71. Potofsky, *John E. Williams*, pp. 10, 20.

72. John E. Williams, "Testimony Before U.S. Industrial Relations Commission," 64th Cong., 1st Sess., 1: 697 ff.; Williams to Hillman, September 30, 1913, H-ACWA Papers; and *Streator-Independent Times*, September 28, 1913.

73. Potofsky "Memoir," OHCCU.

FOUR: *The Protocols of Power*

1. Baruch Charney Vladek, "Autobiography," Collection 37, Reel 20, pp. 3–4, Vladek Papers, Tamiment Library, and John Herling, "Baruch Charney Vladek," *American Jewish Yearbook, 1940* (Philadelphia), pp. 79–93.

2. Testimony of John A. Dyche before U. S. Industrial Relations Commission, January 15, 1914, quoted in Leon Stein, ed., *Out of the Sweatshop: The Struggle for Industrial Democracy* (New York, 1977), and Louis Levine, *The Women's Garment Workers* (New York, 1969), p. 272.

3. Melech Epstein, *Jewish Labor in the U.S.A.*, vol. 2: *1914–52* (New York, 1960), p. 23; "Jacob Potofsky Notes on Hillman," H-ACWA Papers; and Melech Epstein, *Profiles of Eleven* (Detroit, 1965), p. 275.

4. "Potofsky Notes on Hillman"; Epstein, *Profiles of Eleven*, p. 274; Hillman to Potofsky, February 7, 1914, H-ACWA Papers; Hillman to John E. Williams, January 28, 1914, H-ACWA Papers; Williams to Hillman, February 9, 1914, H-ACWA Papers; and "Industrial Peace with Honor and Democracy," *The Survey*, March 7, 1914.

5. Benjamin Stolberg, *Tailor's Progress: The Story of a Famous Union and the Men Who Made It* (New York, 1944), pp. 87–88; Allen F. Davis, *Spearheads of Reform: The Social Settlements and the Progressive Movement, 1880–1914* (New Brunswick, N.J., 1984), p. 108; Margaret Drier Robbins to "Mieze," February 14, 1914, Reel 23, MDR Correspondence, Women's Trade Union League Papers.

6. Hillman to Charles Paiken, June 29, 1914, H-ACWA Papers; Potofsky to Hillman, September 20, and Hillman to Potofsky, September 23, 1914, H-ACWA Papers.

7. Stolberg, *Tailor's Progress*, p. 88.

8. Stein, *Out of the Sweatshop*, quoting Brandeis's decision for the Board of Arbitration, January 21, 1915, and Milton Derber, *The American Idea of Industrial Democracy, 1865–1965* (Urbana, Ill., 1970), pp. 134–35.

9. *The Clothing Workers of Chicago, 1910–1922*, Chicago Joint Board of the ACWA, p. 76; "Report of the Proceedings of the Joint Conference Committee," November 17, 1910, Reel 4, "Subject Files—Strike through World War I," WTUL Papers; and Arthur Liebman, *Jews and the Left* (New York, 1979), p. 271.

10. *Documentary History of the Amalgamated Clothing Workers of America, 1914–16*, H-ACWA Papers; Epstein, *Jewish Labor in U.S.A.*, pp. 112–22; and Will Herberg, "The Jewish Labor Movement in the U.S.," *American Jewish Yearbook, 1952*, pp. 15–16.

11. Epstein, *Jewish Labor in U.S.A.*, 2: 414–17; "Minutes" of WTUL Executive Board, May 22, 1913, Reel 2, "Minutes and Reports, 1913–1924," WTUL Papers; and Abraham Shoul, "Unrest and Secession in the Men's Garment Trades in New York City," unpublished manuscript, June 1918, H-ACWA Papers, pp. 22–23.

12. Harry Best, "The Men's Garment Industry of New York and the Strike of 1913," University Settlement Society, 1914, and Arthur A. Goren, *New York Jews and the Quest for Community: The Kehillah Experiment, 1908–22* (New York, 1970), esp. pp. 199–200.

13. David Saposs interview with David Wolff, March 1, 1919, H-ACWA Papers; Nancy Schrom Dye, *As Equals and as Sisters: Feminism, the Labor Movement, and the Women's Trade Union League* (New York, 1980), pp. 116–17; Epstein, *Jewish Labor in U.S.A.*, 2: 418: Shoul, "Unrest and Secession," p. 23; and Goren, *New York Jews*, p. 206.

14. Shoul, "Unrest and Secession," pp. 26–27.

15. Irving Howe, *World of Our Fathers: The Journey of the East European Jews to America and the World They Found and Made* (New York, 1976), pp. 292–93, 294–95, 315; Arthur Gorenstein, "A Portrait of Ethnic Politics: The Socialists and the 1908 and 1910 Congressional Elections on the East Side," American Jewish Historical Society; and Epstein, *Jewish Labor in U.S.A.*, 2: 307–14.

16. Shoul, "Unrest and Secession," p. 28, and Joan M. Jensen, "The Great Uprising in Rochester," in Joan M. Jensen and Sue Davidson, eds., *A Needle, a Bobbin, a Strike: Women Needleworkers in America* (Philadelphia, 1983).

17. L. Rothbart to Jacob Potofsky, October 12, 1914, H-ACWA Papers, and David Saposs interviews with B. Schweitzer and Ephriam Kaufman, March 31, 1919, H-ACWA Papers. Some years later two Jewish organizers for the UGW in New York could barely conceal their contempt for their coreligionists. Benjamin Schweitzer, a German Jew, confessed that the recent immigrants were beyond him, although he was loath to attack them publicly. Kaufman, an American Jew of German Jewish parentage, said "the recent Jews are un-American and a detriment to this country. They should not be allowed to come here unless they change their attitude."

18. Shoul, "Unrest and Secession," p. 34.

19. *Ibid.*, pp. 34–37; author's interview with Beatrice Bornstein, June 7, 1979; telegrams, October 11, 1914, quoted in *Amalgamated Historical Anthology*, H-ACWA Papers; Shoul, p. 43; and J. B. S. Hardman "Memoir," OHCCU, p. 70.

20. Sam Liptzin, *Tales of a Tailor* (New York, 1965), pp. 141–42.

21. The *Forward* group had, in addition, opposed the election of Schlossberg to the post of general secretary. General Executive Board (hereafter GEB), "Minutes," 1922, H-ACWA Papers; Howe, *World of Our Fathers*, pp. 351–52; Epstein, *Jewish Labor in U.S.A.*, 2: 414–17; Herberg, "Jewish Labor Movement" (note 10 above); Hillman to Sam Levin, November 12, 1914, and to Frank Rosenblum, December 10, 1914, and June 9, 1915, H-ACWA Papers; Brais to Schlossberg, May 12, 1915, H-ACWA Papers; John E. Williams to Potofsky, November 12, 1914, H-ACWA Papers; and Epstein, 2: 48–49.

22. Clarence Darrow to Hillman, December 5, 1914, H-ACWA Papers, and Samuel Gompers to Benjamin Schlesinger, July 1, 1915, Box 4, Schlesinger Correspondence, International Ladies Garment Workers Union Papers.

23. Louis Feldman to GEB, September 29, 1915; Lazarus Marcovitz to Joseph Schlossberg, June 15, 1916; Rochester Joint Board to GEB, February 3, 1918; Schlossberg to "Officers," January 2, 1916; and Schlossberg to Potofsky, October 18, 1916, all H-ACWA Papers. *Documentary History of the ACWA, 1922–24*, H-ACWA Papers. Augusto Bellanca to Hillman, September 9, 1915; Rosenblum to Schlossberg, June 9, 1916; and Augusto Bellanca to Hillman, July 10, 1916, all H-ACWA Papers. Saposs interview with Wolff; Liptzin, *Tales of a Tailor*, pp. 167, 168–69; *Documen-*

tary History of the ACWA, 1916–18 (note 10 above); Abraham Shiplacoff to GEB, June 5, 1916, H-ACWA Papers; Hillman to Vladek, April 15, 1915, Baruch Charney Vladek Papers, Tamiment Library; and *Documentary History of the ACWA, 1918–20*, H-ACWA Papers.

24. Gerald Sorin, *The Prophetic Minority: American Jewish Immigrants and Radicals, 1880–1920* (Bloomington, Ind., 1985), pp. 93, 95. Hardman has been credited with discouraging whatever Zionist inclinations Hillman may have harbored. Gerd Korman, "Ethnic Democracy and Its Ambiguities: The Case of the Needle Trade Unions," N.Y. State School of Industrial and Labor Relations, Cornell, no. 569, reprint.

25. *Documentary History and Convention Proceedings of the ACWA, 1914–16*, H-ACWA Papers (hereafter *Doc. Hist.*), pp. 52–55.

26. *Ibid.*, pp. 67–68, 70, 72, 74–75. Schlossberg, who wrote the Preamble, lifted most of it directly from that of the SLP.

27. Shoul, "Unrest and Secession."

28. Organizing Leaflet, H-ACWA Papers, and "Anthology of Historical Documents," H-ACWA Papers.

29. Sam Gillis to Joseph Schlossberg, November 1, 1914, H-ACWA Papers.

30. Aldo Cursi to Hillman, May 5, 1915; Eisen to Hillman and Brais, May 19, April 14, and June 1, 1915; M. J. Elstein to Schlossberg, August 10, 1915; Louis Feldman letter, August 19, 1915; Sam Gillis to Hillman, June 5 and July 1, 1915; Lazarus Marcovitz to Schlossberg, March 7 and July 1, 1915; Marcovitz to GEB, June 15, 1916; George Suder to Hillman, December 12, 1914; and Potofsky to Hillman, January 29, 1915, all H-ACWA Papers.

31. Sam Levin to Hillman, July 7, 1916, and Potofsky to GEB, October 6, 1916, both H-ACWA Papers. Susan Anita Glenn, "The Working Life of Immigrants: Women in the American Garment Industry, 1880–1920," Ph.D. dissertation, University of California, Berkeley, 1983, p. 325, and Aldo Cursi to Brais, February 8, 1915, H-ACWA Papers.

32. Nina Asher, "Dorothy Jacobs Bellanca: Women Clothing Workers and Runaway Shops," in Jensen and Davidson, *A Needle, a Bobbin* (note 16 above), pp. 195–226, and Dorothy Bellanca to Hillman, March 20, 1915, H-ACWA Papers.

33. Bessie Hillman to S. Hillman, November 20, 1914, H-ACWA Papers; author's interview with Esther Peterson, February 5, 1985; GEB "Minutes," August 27–29, 1915, H-ACWA Papers. Ironically, Ellen Gates Starr wrote a letter of congratulations to Bessie on the occasion of her marriage to say how "wonderful to have all your interests in life absolutely unified; no prospect of being pulled two ways." Starr to B. Hillman, April 21, 1916, H-ACWA Papers.

34. Sorin, *Prophetic Minority*, p. 158.

35. Hillman to Schlossberg, February 17, 1915, and Leo Mannheimer to Hillman, November 24, 1914, both H-ACWA Papers, and Sorin, *Prophetic Minority*, p. 102.

36. Olive Sullivan to Margaret Drier Robbins, October 4 and November 3, 1915, Reel 23, "MDR Correspondence," WTUL Papers.

37. Howard Barton Meyers, "The Policing of Labor Disputes in Chicago: A Case Study," Ph.D. dissertation, University of Chicago, 1929, p. 772, 781, 785; Jacob Potofsky, ed., *John E. Williams: An Appreciation with Selections from His Writings* (published by ACWA, 1930), p. 58; and *Doc. Hist. 1914–16* (note 25 above).

38. "Chicago Strike—1915," H-ACWA Papers; "Why Not Arbitrate?" pamphlet published by Citizens Committee for Arbitration in the Clothing Industry, 1915,

H-ACWA Papers; and Hillman quoted in *Daily Trade Record*, September 27, 1915, H-ACWA Papers.

39. Harry Golden, *Carl Sandberg* (Cleveland, 1961), pp. 102–3; "Why Do the Clothing Manufacturers Refuse to Arbitrate?" October 31, 1915, Anthology of Historical Documents, H-ACWA Papers; *Chicago Daily News*, October 27, 1915; *Chicago Herald*, November 16, 1915; *Chicago Tribune*, November 29, 1915; *Chicago Daily News*, December 6, 1915; and Ellen Gates Starr, "Reflections on the Recent Chicago Strike of Clothing Workers," Ellen Gates Starr Papers, Folder 10, The University Library, University of Illinois at Chicago.

40. *Chicago Tribune*, November 1, 1915.

41. *Doc. Hist., 1914–16*, and Hillman to Schlossberg, November 6, 1916, H-ACWA Papers.

42. "Biographical Data," H-ACWA Papers; Barbara Wertheimer interview with Sara Barron, "The 20th Century Trade Union Woman: Vehicle for Social Change," Oral History Project, Program on Women and Work, Institute of Labor and Industrial Relations, University of Michigan, 1978, pp. 54–55; and *Doc. Hist. 1914–16*.

43. Sigmund Sonneborn, "Price Factors in Men's Ready to Wear Clothing," *American Academy of Political and Social Science Annals*, vol. 89, May 1920.

44. Frank Bellanca, "Scabs and Scab-Agencies: Proven Facts of the Scandalous Scabbism of the I. W. W.," ACWA pamphlet, H-ACWA Papers; *Baltimore Sun*, August 12, 1916; Dorothy Bellanca to Schlossberg, April 14, 1916, H-ACWA Papers; and "AFL Tries to Boycott and Crush ACWA," H-ACWA Papers.

45. "AFL Tries to Boycott," and F. Bellanca, "Scabs and Scab-Agencies."

46. Liptzin, *Tales of a Tailor* (note 20 above). That this was not only a matter of ethnic solidarity but also a function of the work culture of petty capitalism is demonstrated by the widespread presence of similar practices throughout much of American (and European) industry. Even machine shops and steel mills were honeycombed with such work groups, which in part viewed their joint interests to be in opposition to those of plant and corporate management. Craig Littler, *The Development of the Labour Process in Capitalist Societies: A Comparative Study of the Transformation of Work Organization in Britain, Japan, and the U.S.A.* (London, 1982).

47. Dorothy Bellanca to Schlossberg, December 27, 1916; *Doc. Hist. 1914–16*; and Dorothy Bellanca to Schlossberg, April 14, 1916, all H-ACWA Papers. Epstein, *Jewish Labor in the U.S.A.* (note 3 above), 2: 200, 213, 215, and Irving Howe interview with Isidore Wisotsky, p. 4, YIVO Archives.

48. National Industrial Conference Board, "Experience with Trade Union Agreements: Clothing Industries," *Research Report #38* (New York, June 1921); Association of Boys Clothing Manufacturers to Schlossberg, February 16 and January 21, 1916; "Minutes—Baltimore District Council #3, 1916"; Leon Mann to George Bell, February 25, 1919; Hillman to Louis Feldman, August 17, 1915; George Bell to Hillman, October 10, 1919; and "Minutes of Baltimore Jt. Bds. and Locals," June 26 and July 3, 1916, all H-ACWA Papers. Author's interview with Abe Chatman, August 23, 1978. "Statistics on Stoppages"; Frank Bellanca to GEB, January 6 and 18, 1915; Dorothy Bellanca to Hillman, March 18, 1918; Hillman to Schlossberg, February 19, 1915; and Schlossberg to Potofsky, June 19, 1915, all H-ACWA Papers.

49. "Biographical Data"; Rosara Lucy Passero, "Ethnicity in the Men's Ready-Made Clothing Industry, 1880–1950: The Italian Experience in Philadelphia," Ph.D. dissertation, University of Pennsylvania, 1978, pp. 160–64, 151–56, 305–6, 314, 319; Edwin Fenton, *Immigrants and Unions, a Case Study: Italians and American*

Labor, 1870–1920 (1957, reprint New York, 1975), pp. 463, 467–68; David Saposs interview with Frank Bellanca, March 29, 1919, Box 21, Saposs Papers, Wisconsin State Historical Society; Schlossberg to Nicholas Klein, March 8, 1916, H-ACWA Papers; Robert F. Foerster, *The Italian Emigration of Our Times* (1919, reprint New York, 1969), pp. 347–48, 327, 381; Thomas Kessner, *The Golden Door: Italian and Jewish Immigrant Mobility in New York City, 1880–1915* (New York, 1977), p. 56; Eugene Miller and Gianna Panofsky, "Radical Italian Unionism: Its Development in Chicago Men's Garment Industry, 1910–30," conference paper, 1981, in possession of Steve Fraser; Louis Feldman to Hillman, December 28, 1915, H-ACWA Papers; and J. M. Budish and George Soule, *The New Unionism in the Clothing Industry* (New York, 1920), p. 64.

50. Barbara Klacznska, "Why Women Work: A Comparison of Various Groups— Philadelphia, 1910–30," *Labor History*, Winter 1976; Sorin, *Prophetic Minority* (note 24 above), pp. 130, 136, 137; Dye, *As Equals, as Sisters* (note 13 above), p. 111; National Women's Trade Union League *Proceedings*, 2d Biennial Convention, 1909, p. 17, WTUL Papers; National WTUL *Proceedings of Interstate Conference*, 1908, p. 21, WTUL Papers; Fenton, *Immigrants and Unions*, pp. 467–68; and Foerster, *Italian Emigration*, p. 381.

51. George Enrico Pozzetta, "The Italians of New York City, 1890–1914," Ph.D. dissertation, University of North Carolina, 1971, pp. 4, 21, 22, 24, 27, 95–96, 107–8, 342, 344, 354–55; Fenton, *Immigrants and Unions*, pp. 16–25; Miller and Panofsky, "Radical Italian Unionism"; and Richard Gambino, *Blood of My Blood: The Dilemma of the Italian-Americans* (New York, 1974), p. 248.

52. Augusto Bellanca to Schlossberg, February 12, 1914, H-ACWA Papers.

53. Paul Arnone to Schlossberg, June 9, 1917; Louis Feldman to Schlossberg, September 29, 1915; Feldman to Hillman, December 28, 1915; Artoni to Schlossberg, 1918; Louis Feldman report from Rochester, June 30, 1918; Abraham Shiplacoff to Hillman, June 5, 1916; Valenti to Schlossberg, September 6, 1917; Aldo Cursi to Schlossberg, August 23, 1917; Eli Oliver to Frank Rosenblum, May 5, 1925; Emilio Grandinetti to Potofsky, September 20, 1916; J. A. Bekampis to Schlossberg, March 1, 1919; and GEB "Minutes," September 1928 and September 1929, all in H-ACWA Papers. Fenton, *Immigrants and Unions*, p. 471.

54. Glenn, "Working Life of Immigrants" (note 31 above), p. 329. Valenti to Schlossberg, September 6, 1917, Sam Gillis to Hillman, July 5, 1917; and Valenti to Schlossberg, December 28, 1917, all in H-ACWA Papers. GEB "Minutes," May 1924; Fenton, *Immigrants and Unions*, pp. 477–80, 526–27; Foerster, *Italian Emigration*; Anthony Capraro to Potofsky, June 16 and May 6, 1922, Box 3, Anthony Capraro Papers, Immigration History Research Center, University of Minnesota; "The Man Without a Friend," leaflet by ex-scab about ethnic ostracism, Grandinetti Papers; strike leaflet, Box 4, Capraro Papers; Fenton, *Immigrants and Unions*, pp. 509–10, 515–16, 520; Frank Rosenblum to Hillman, December 6, 1916, H-ACWA Papers; and Saposs interview with Wolff (note 13 above).

55. Pozzetta, "Italians of New York City," pp. 355, 357, 358; Fenton, *Immigrants and Unions*, pp. 477, 487, 495, 502, 515–16, 517–19, 520, 527, 529, 530, 548–55; *Doc. Hist. 1914–16*; Artoni to GEB, January 25, 1917, April 25, 1919, H-ACWA Papers; GEB "Minutes," June 1921, H-ACWA Papers; and Anthony Capraro to Potofsky, August 5 and June 16, 1922, Box 3, Capraro Papers. I want to thank Nunzio Pernicone for graciously agreeing to translate some of the correspondence from the Italian. Potofsky to Grandinetti, January 19, 1921, and Rosenblum to Grandinetti,

August 17, 1921, Folder 2, Grandinetti Papers; *Doc. Hist. 1918–20*; GEB "Minutes," February 15–16, 1928, H-ACWA Papers; John Horace Mariano, *The Italian Contribution to American Democracy* (New York, 1975, reprint of 1921 edition), pp. 130, 154–55; John P. Diggins, *Mussolini and Italian Fascism: The View from America* (Princeton, N.J., 1972), p. 87; Paul J. Campisi, "The Italian Family in the U.S.," *American Journal of Sociology*, vol. 53, May 1948; Nicholas John Russo, "Three Generations of Italians in New York City: Their Religious Acculturation," in Silvano M. Tomasi and Madeline H. Engel, eds., *The Italian Experience in the U.S.* (New York, 1970); Silvano Tomasi, *Piety and Power: The Role of Italian Parishes in the New York Metropolitan Area* (New York, 1975), pp. 8, 10, 34, 140.

56. Mark Zborowski and Elizabeth Herzog, *Life Is With People: The Culture of the Shtetl* (New York, 1952), p. 247; Howe, *World of Our Fathers* (note 15 above), pp. 225–40; Ezra Mendelsohn, "The Russian-Jewish Labor Movement," *YIVO Annual*, 14 (1969): 90; Liebman, *Jews and the Left* (note 9 above), pp. 163–65; Herberg, "Jewish Labor Movement" (note 10 above), p. 4; and Simon Kuznets, "Immigration of Russian Jews to the U.S.: Background and Structure," *Perspectives in American History*, 9 (1975): 117.

57. Glenn, "Working Life of Immigrants," pp. 244–46; Liptzin, *Tales of a Tailor* (note 20 above), p. 68; and Epstein, *Jewish Labor in the U.S.A.*, 1: 96–97, 237.

58. "Biographical Data," H-ACWA Papers; Augusto Bellanca to Hillman, March 16, 1917, H-ACWA Papers; David Saposs interview with Elias Rabkin, February 12, 1919, Box 21, Saposs Papers; and M. J. Elstein to Hillman and Schlossberg, August 10, 1915, H-ACWA Papers.

FIVE: *"The Messiah's Footsteps"*

1. David Montgomery, "New Tendencies in Union Struggles and Strategies in Europe and the U. S., 1916–22," in *Work, Community, and Power: The Experience of Labor in Europe and America, 1900–1925* (Philadelphia, 1983), and Stanley Shapiro, "Hand and Brain: The Farmer Labor Party of 1920," *Labor History*, vol. 26, Summer 1985.

2. Stanley Shapiro, "The Great War and Reform: Liberals and Labor, 1917–19," *Labor History*, vol. 12, (1971), no. 3.

3. Daniel Nelson, *Managers and Workers: Origins of the New Factory System in the United States, 1880–1920* (Madison, Wisc., 1975), pp. 156–61; Stuart D. Brandes, *American Welfare Capitalism, 1880–1940* (Chicago, 1970), p. 127; Bruno Ramirez, *When Workers Fight: The Politics of Industrial Relations in the Progressive Era, 1898–1916* (Westport, Conn., 1978), pp. 171–72, 208; Jacob Potofsky "Memoirs," OHCCU, p. 103; and *Doc. Hist. 1920–22*, H-ACWA Papers, appendixes.

4. *New York Call*, August 17, 1917; Dorothy Jacobs, "The Woman Problem," Official Souvenir, 3d Biennial Convention, 1918, H-ACWA Papers.

5. Gordon S. Watkins, "Labor Problems and Labor Administration in the U. S. During the World War," *Studies in the Social Sciences* (University of Illinois), vol. 8, September 1919.

6. Alexander M. Bing, *War-Time Strikes and Their Adjustment* (New York, 1921), p. 58, and *Doc. Hist. 1916–18*, H-ACWA Papers.

7. Henry Moscowitz to Newton Baker, July 25, 1917, H-ACWA Papers.

8. William W. Brenner, *Depression Winters: New York Social Workers and the New Deal* (Philadelphia, 1985), pp. 15–19.

9. Hillman to Walter Lippmann, August 5, 1917, and Hillman to John E. Williams, July 3 and 11, 1917, both H-ACWA Papers.

10. Hillman to Newton Baker, October 16, 1917, H-ACWA Papers.

11. Hillman to John E. Williams, July 3, 1917, and Earl Dean Howard to Hillman, July 6, 1917, H-ACWA Papers; and R. Jeffrey Lustig, *Corporate Liberalism: The Origins of Modern American Political Theory, 1890–1920* (Berkeley, Calif., 1982), pp. 139, 29, 39, 209, 259.

12. Christopher Tomlins, *The State and the Unions: Labor Relations, Law, and the Organized Labor Movement in America, 1880–1960* (New York, 1985), p. 189; Mary Anderson, *Woman at Work: The Autobiography of Mary Anderson as Told to Mary N. Winslow* (Minneapolis, 1951), pp. 105–6; Hillman to John E. Williams, July 11 and September 7, 1917, H-ACWA Papers; Watkins, "Labor Problems and Labor Administration"; Hillman to Baker, October 16, 1917; Florence Kelly to Walter Lippmann, June 26, 1917; Hillman to GEB, August 31, 1917; Hillman to Sam Levin, July 17, 1917; and Hillman to Lippmann, July 5, 1917; all in H-ACWA Papers.

13. Robert Asher, "Jewish Unions and the AFL Power Structure, 1903–1905," *American Jewish Historical Quarterly*, vol. 3, March 1976; Valerie Jean Conner, *The National War Labor Board: Stability, Social Justice and the Voluntary State in World War I* (Chapel Hill, N.C., 1983), pp. 96, 27–28; Michael E. Parrish, *Felix Frankfurter and His Times: The Reform Years* (New York, 1982), pp. 91, 84–85; and David M. Kennedy, *Over Here: The First World War and American Society* (New York, 1980), p. 267.

14. Bing, *War-Time Strikes*, pp. 58–60; R. S. True to Louis Kirstein, "Report on Labor Organization in N.Y. Shops," December 19, 1917, H-ACWA Papers; *Doc. His. 1916–18*; Potofsky to Frank Rosenblum, August 10, 1917; Potofsky to Ike Goldstein, August 10, 1917; Hillman to Baker, October 16, 1917; William Z. Ripley to Hillman, August 23, 1917; Hillman to Potofsky, September 15 and October 1, 1918; Hillman to Alex Cohen, November 20, 1917; Sam Levin to Hillman, August 6 and October 24, 1918; Richard A. Feiss, Office of Quartermaster General, to Hillman, March 1, 1918; Marie S. Orenstein to Hillman, October 4, 1918; Ripley to Theodore F. Bauling Clothing Co., October 9, 1918; Hillman to William Z. Ripley, July 11, 1917; Hillman to Florence Kelley, September 7, 1917; Hillman to Captain Walter E. Kreusi, August 14, 1917; Potofsky to Captain Brown, U.S. Navy Clothing Supply Depot, September 14, 1918; Memorandum on Negotiations, April 23, 1918; Joseph Schlossberg to N. I. Stone, May 7 and June 2 and 5, 1918; Hillman to Louis Hollander, July 9, 1918; Hillman to Ripley, September 26, 1918; Ripley to Louis Kirstein, July 2, 1918; and Ripley to Hillman, August 8, 1918, all in H-ACWA Papers; and *Doc. Hist. 1918–20*.

15. Ruth True to Felix Frankfurter, January 19, 1919, Preliminary Inventory of the War Labor Policies Board Records, Entry 2, Correspondence of the Chairman of the Executive Secretary, Box 27, "Needle Trades" Folder, Record Group 1, National Archives.

16. Sidney Hillman, "Statement before the Advisory Board on New York Strike," January 17, 1919, H-ACWA Papers; *Advance*, March 22, 1918; testimony by William Leiserson during injunction proceedings of Michaels-Stern Company vs. ACWA, July 1922, H-ACWA Papers; *Doc. Hist. 1916–18*; Hillman speech to Chicago Arbitration Board, December 13, 1919, H-ACWA Papers; Hillman letters to *New York Tribune*, December 15, and *New York Times*, December 24, 1917, H-ACWA

Papers; and Hillman and Schlossberg, "Statement on War Against German Autocracy," March 17, 1918; H-ACWA Papers.

17. Bing, *War-Time Strikes*, p. 61, and New York Advisory Board "Hearings," February 1919, pp. 89–90, 91, 118–19, H-ACWA Papers.

18. "Wartime Policies on Wages, Hours, and Other Labor Standards in the U.S., 1917–19," U.S. Department of Labor, Wage and Hour Division, May 1942, H-ACWA Papers; "N.Y. Advisory Board Proceedings," H-ACWA Papers; Gerald Nash, "FDR and the Origins of Early New Deal Labor Policy," *Labor History*, Winter 1960; James Augustine Walsh, "The Political Ideas of Felix Frankfurter, 1911–39," Ph.D. dissertation, American University, 1976, pp. 57, 69, 72–73; John S. Smith, "Organized Labor and Government in the Wilson Era, 1913–21: Some Conclusions," *Labor History*, Fall 1962; Potofsky "Memoir," OHCCU, p. 130; *Doc. Hist. 1918–20*; Felix Frankfurter and Samuel Rosensohn, "Survey of the New York Clothing Industry," May 1920, H-ACWA Papers; Abraham Shiplacoff, "Report on Inside and Outside Shops," n.d., H-ACWA Papers; M. Drubin, "Contract Shops" and "Plan for Establishing Inside Shops," November 19, 1919, H-ACWA Papers; Lazarus Marcovitz to Hillman and Schlossberg, August 14, 1915; David Wald to New York Joint Board, October 30, 1915, H-ACWA Papers; Francis Joseph Haas, "Shop Collective Bargaining: A Study of Wage Determination in the Men's Garment Industry," Ph.D. dissertation, Catholic University, 1922, p. 54; Hillman Statement Before N.Y. Advisory Board, January 17, 1919, H-ACWA Papers; Arthur Liebman, *Jews and the Left* (New York, 1979), p. 232; and Larry Gerber, "The Limits of Liberalism: A Study of the Careers and Ideological Development of Josephus Daniels, Henry Stimson, Bernard Baruch, Donald Richberg and Felix Frankfurter," Ph.D. dissertation, University of California, Berkeley, 1979, p. 232.

19. Smith, "Organized Labor and Government," and Watkins, "Labor Problems and Labor Administration."

20. Kennedy, *Over Here*, p. 268; Guy Alchon, "The Invisible Hand of Planning: Business, Social Science and the State in the American 1920s," Ph.D. dissertation, University of Iowa, 1982, p. 58; Robert D. Cuff, *The War Industries Board: Business–Government Relations During World War I* (Baltimore, 1973).

21. Stephen Skowronek, *Building a New American State: The Expansion of National Administrative Capacities, 1877–1920* (New York, 1982), pp. 123, 200, 210–11.

22. *Bulletin of the Taylor Society*, vol. 4, no. 6 (December 1919), and Felix Frankfurter, "Social Unrest," *Current Affairs*, vol. 10, no. 35 (January 5, 1920).

23. Frankfurter, "Social Unrest," and *Bulletin of the Taylor Society*, vol. 3, no. 6 (December 1917).

24. Shapiro, "Great War and Reform" (note 2 above), and Eugene M. Tobin, *Organize or Perish: America's Independent Progressives, 1913–33* (Westport, Conn., 1986), p. 98.

25. Shapiro, "Great War and Reform"; *Public*, May 4, 1918; *Bulletin of the Taylor Society*, vol. 4, no. 6 (December 1919); and Robert D. Cuff, "The Politics of Labor Administration During World War I," *Labor History*, Fall 1980.

26. Cuff, "Politics of Labor Administration."

27. Melvyn Dubofsky, "Abortive Reform: The Wilson Administration and Organized Labor, 1913–20," in James E. Cronin and Carmen Sirianni, eds., *Work, Community and Power: The Experience of Labor in Europe and America, 1900–1925* (Philadelphia, 1983), and Tobin, *Organize or Perish*, p. 56.

28. Tobin, *Organize or Perish*, pp. 57–58; Montgomery, "New Tendencies in Union

Struggles" (note 1 above); Conner, *National War Labor Board* (note 13 above), p. 109; and Ramirez, *When Workers Fight* (note 3 above), pp. 175–80.

29. Irwin Yellowitz, *Labor and the Progressive Movement in New York State, 1897–1916* (Ithaca, N.Y., 1965).

30. Tomlins, *State and the Unions* (note 12 above), p. 94.

31. "Works Councils in the U.S.," *National Industrial Conference Board Research Report*, no. 21, October 1919; Daniel Rodgers, *The Work Ethic in Industrial America, 1850–1920* (Chicago, 1978), pp. 58–59; David Eakins, "The Origins of Corporate-Liberal Policy Research, 1916–22," in Jerry Israel, ed., *Building the Organizational Society: Essays on Associational Activities in Modern America* (New York, 1972); and Henry Guzda, "Industrial Democracy: Made in the U.S.A.," *Monthly Labor Review*, May 1984.

32. "Works Councils in the U.S."; "Experience with Works Councils in the U.S.," *National Industrial Conference Board Research Report*, no. 50, May 1922; and Paul Douglas, "The Relationship of Shop Committees to Trade Unions," *Pacific Review*, n.d., copy in Box 186, Felix Frankfurter Papers, Library of Congress.

33. Sanford Jacoby, "Union–Management Cooperation in the U.S.: Lessons from the 1920s," *Industrial and Labor Relations Review*, vol. 37, October 1983; Norman J. Wood, "Industrial Relations Policies of American Management, 1900–1933," *Business History Review*, Winter 1960; and Henry Eilbirt, "The Development of Personnel Management in the U.S.," *Business History Review*, Autumn 1959.

34. Steven J. Scheinberg, "The Development of Corporate Labor Policy: 1900–1940," Ph.D. dissertation, University of Wisconsin, 1966, p. 139, and Jacoby, "Union–Management Cooperation."

35. Alchon, "Invisible Hand of Planning" (note 20 above), pp. 13–14, 63, 66, and Gerald D. Nash, "FDR and the Origins of Early New Deal Labor Policy."

36. J. Michael Eisner, *William Morris Leiserson: A Biography* (Madison, Wisc., 1967), pp. 7, 24, and *New York Times*, February 26, 1921.

37. Eisner, *William Morris Leiserson*, and William Leiserson, "Constitutional Government in American Industry," *American Economic Review*, vol. 12, supplement, 1922.

38. Tomlins, *State and the Unions*, pp. 79, 81.

39. Jacoby, "Union–Management Cooperation"; Samuel Haber, *Efficiency and Uplift: Scientific Management in the Progressive Era, 1890–1920* (Chicago, 1964), pp. 32–33, 122, 131, 149–50, 162; and Daniel Nelson, *Frederick W. Taylor and the Rise of Scientific Management* (Madison, Wisc., 1980), p. 111.

40. Grecco to Hillman, September 16, 1919, H-ACWA Papers, and Mary Barnett Gilson, *What Is Past Is Prologue: Reflections on My Industrial Experience* (New York, 1940), pp. 94, 116, 118.

41. Haber, *Efficiency and Uplift*, pp. 122, 133, and Jean Christie, "Morris Lewellyn Cooke: Progressive Engineer," Ph.D. dissertation, Columbia University, 1963.

42. Morris Cooke to Sidney Hillman, April 15, 1920, File 89, Box 9, Morris Cooke Papers, FDR Library, Hyde Park, N.Y.

43. Ripley to Hillman, September 4 and 20, and November 18, 1918; War Department to Hillman, n.d.; and Frank Rosenblum to Potofsky, September 3 and 27, 1920, all in H-ACWA Papers. "Report of General Conditions in Contracting Shops Manufacturing Clothing for the U.S. Government," October 7, 1918, Box A16, Louis Kirstein Papers, Baker Library, Harvard University, and William Z. Ripley, "Bones of Contention," *The Survey*, April 29, 1922.

44. Ripley, "Bones of Contention"; Leon Mann to George Bell, February 25, 1919,

H-ACWA Papers; and author's interviews with Nathan Katzman and Leopold Gross, January 18, 1980.

45. Transcript of Hillman speech to City Club of Chicago, February 1, 1919, H-ACWA Papers.

46. David W. Levy, *Herbert Croly of The New Republic: The Life and Thought of an American Progressive* (Princeton, N.J., 1986), pp. 168–69, and Robert Bruere to Hillman, October 8, 1920, H-ACWA Papers.

47. Chicago Joint Board ACWA, *Clothing Workers of Chicago*, pp. 191, 230–31; Paul Blanshard, "Industrial Government in Rochester," *Outlook*, February 23, 1921; *New Republic*, May 6, 1920, and February 1, 1919; and J. M. Budish and George Soule, *New Unionism in the Clothing Industry* (New York, 1920), pp. 290–302.

48. Carmen Sirianni, "Workers' Control in Europe in the Era of World War I: A Comparative Analysis of the European Experience," *Theory and Society*, vol. 9, 1980; Eilbirt, "Development of Personnel Management" (note 33 above); and Hugh G. J. Aitken, *Taylorism at Watertown Arsenal: Scientific Management in Action* (Cambridge, Mass., 1960), p. 34.

49. Nick Salvatore, *Eugene V. Debs: Citizen and Socialist* (Urbana, Ill., 1982), and John L. Thomas, *Alternative America: Henry George, Edward Bellamy, Henry Demarest Lloyd and the Adversary Tradition* (Cambridge, Mass., 1983).

50. Andrea Graziosi, "Common Laborers, Unskilled Workers, 1880–1915," *Labor History*, Fall 1981, and Ewa Morawska, *For Bread and Butter: Life-Worlds of East Central Europeans in Johnstown, Pennyslvania, 1890–1940* (New York, 1985).

51. *Advance*, February 8, 1918.

52. *Doc. Hist. 1916–18*.

53. Tobin, *Organize or Perish* (note 24 above), p. 76; *New York Times*, December 12, 1917; *New York Tribune*, December 15, 1917; Hillman and Schlossberg statement on war, March 17, 1918, H-ACWA Papers; and David Joseph Goldberg, "Immigrants, Intellectuals and Industrial Unions: The 1919 Textile Strikes and the Experience of the Amalgamated Textile Workers of America in Passaic and Paterson, New Jersey, and Lawrence, Massachusetts," Ph.D. dissertation, Columbia University, 1984, p. 389.

54. "Personal Documents," H-ACWA Papers.

55. *Doc. Hist. 1916–18*.

56. Haas, "Shop Collective Bargaining" (note 18 above), p. 47; Norma Fain Pratt, "Morris Hilquit: A Political Biography of an American Jewish Socialist," Ph.D. dissertation, UCLA, 1976, pp. 106–15; *Doc. Hist. 1916–18*; and "Union Handbills," Folder 8, Grandinetti Papers.

57. Potofsky to Hillman, September 22, 1917, H-ACWA Papers.

58. Irving Howe, *World of Our Fathers: The Journey of the East European Jews to America and the World They Found and Made* (New York, 1976), pp. 537–45; David Montgomery, "Class and Nationalism: Nationalism, American Patriotism, and Class Consciousness Among Immigrant Workers in the United States in the Epoch of World War I," in Dirk Hoerder, ed., *Struggle a Hard Battle: Essays on Working Class Immigrants* (De Kalb, Ill., 1986); and Hillman to Williams, January 2, 1918, H-ACWA Papers.

59. Marimpietri to Hillman, July 13, 1917, H-ACWA Papers, and Frank L. Grubbs, Jr., *The Struggle for Labor Loyalty: Gompers, the AFL and the Pacifists, 1917–20* (Durham, N.C., 1968), pp. 94–97, 116.

60. Sidney Hillman to Philoine Hillman, January 1918, H-ACWA Papers.

SIX: *Bolsheviks and Technocrats*

1. "The Amalgamated Calendar," May 1, 1918, to April 1, 1920, H-ACWA Papers; Alexander M. Bing, *War-Time Strikes and Their Adjustment* (New York, 1921), p. 61; ACWA *Conv. Proc., 1918,* H-ACWA Papers; Bessie Hillman to Sidney, 1919 telegram, H-ACWA Papers.
2. Brandeis quoted in Philippa Strum, *Louis D. Brandeis: Justice for the People* (Cambridge, Mass., 1984), p. 103; Wilson quoted in John Milton Cooper, *The Warrior and the Priest: Woodrow Wilson and Theodore Roosevelt* (Cambridge, Mass., 1983), p. 264; Haggai Hurvitz, "Ideology and Industrial Conflict: President Wilson's First Industrial Conference of October, 1919," *Labor History,* Fall 1977; Howe quoted in Stanley Shapiro, "The Great War and Reform: Liberals and Labor, 1917–19," *Labor History,* vol. 12, no. 3, 1971; Stanley Shapiro, "Hand and Brain: The Farmer–Labor Party of 1920," *Labor History,* Summer 1985; and *The New Republic,* June 29, 1918.
3. Agnes Nestor, *Women's Labor Leader* (Rockford, Ill., 1954), p. 225.
4. Carmen Sirianni, "Workers Control in Europe in the Era of World War: A Comparative Analysis of the European Experience," *Theory and Society,* vol. 9, 1980.
5. David M. Kennedy, *Over Here: The First World War and American Society* (New York, 1980), pp. 272, 256–58, and Shapiro, "Great War and Reform."
6. Shapiro, "Hand and Brain"; Eugene Tobin, *Organize or Perish: America's Independent Progressives, 1913–33* (Westport, Conn., 1986), p. 103; Nathan Fine, *Labor and Farmer Parties in the U.S.,* p. 397, cited in Richard Oestreicher, "Working Class Political Behavior and Theories of American Electoral Parties, 1870–1940," *Journal of American History,* 1986; Kenneth Campbell McKay, *The Progressive Movement of 1924* (New York, 1947), p. 58; and Henry David, "Labor and Political Action After World War I: 1919–24," *Labor and Nation,* February–March 1946.
7. *The New Republic,* February 16, 1918.
8. Strum, *Louis D. Brandeis,* p. 192, and Brandeis to Robert Bruere, February 25, 1922, "Brandeis, 1878–1923," Box 26, Felix Frankfurter Papers, Library of Congress.
9. Arthur Liebman, *Jews and the Left* (New York, 1979), p. 221; and Irving Howe, *World of Our Fathers: The Journey of East European Jews to America and the World They Found and Made* (New York, 1976), pp. 326–28.
10. "Amalgamated Calendar"; *Doc. Hist. 1918–20;* Francis Joseph Haas, "Shop Collective Bargaining: A Study of Wage Determination in the Men's Garment Industry," Ph.D. dissertation, Catholic University, 1922, p. 61; and Sumner Slichter, *Union Policies and Industrial Management* (New York, 1969, reprint of Brookings Institution edition, 1941), pp. 504–6.
11. ACWA *Conv. Proceedings 1920.*
12. *The World,* July 27, 1919, and *Conv. Proc. 1920.*
13. *Doc. Hist. 1918–20,* and Tobin, *Organize or Perish,* p. 124.
14. Steve Fraser, "The 'New Unionism' and the 'New Economic Policy,' " in James E. Cronin and Carmen Sirianni, eds., *Work, Community and Power: The Experience of Labor in Europe and America, 1900–25* (Philadelphia, 1983), and Strum, *Louis D. Brandeis,* pp. 181–92.
15. *Conv. Proc. 1920.*
16. *Ibid.,* and *Doc. Hist. 1918–20.*
17. David Saposs interview with Thomas F. McMahon, James Starr, and John Golden,

February 25, 1919, Box 21, Saposs Papers, Wisconsin State Historical Society, Madison.

18. "Lithuanian Mass Meeting," Lawrence, Mass., April 4, 1919, Box 9, Anthony Capraro Papers, Immigration History Research Center, University of Minnesota, and GEB "Minutes," April 1919, H-ACWA Papers.

19. "Interview with Antonette Bolis," Lawrence, Mass., April 4, 1919; "Interview with Mary Grinka," Lawrence, Mass., April 2, 1919; and "Interview with Annie Trina," Lawrence, Mass, n.d., all in Box 9, Capraro Papers.

20. David Joseph Goldberg, "Immigrants, Intellectuals and Industrial Unions: The 1919 Textile Strikes and the Experience of the Amalgamated Textile Workers of America in Passaic and Paterson, New Jersey, and Lawrence, Mass.," Ph.D. dissertation, Columbia University, 1984), p. 176.

21. "The Lithuanians in America," extract, Box 22, Saposs Papers, and Goldberg, "Immigrants, Intellectuals and Industrial Unions," p. 532.

22. David Saposs interview with Matthew Pluhan, April 3, 1919, Box 21, Saposs Papers; Arcadius Kahan, *Essays in Jewish Social and Economic History*, Roger Weiss, ed. (Chicago, 1986), pp. 106–7; and Goldberg, "Immigrants, Intellectuals and Industrial Unions," pp. 122–23.

23. GEB "Minutes," April 1919, H-ACWA Papers; J. M. Budish and George Soule, *The New Unionism in the Clothing Industry* (New York, 1920), pp. 259–66; and Goldberg, "Immigrants, Intellectuals and Industrial Unions," p. 425.

24. A. J. Muste to Anthony Capraro, January 17, 1920, "Lawrence 1919," Box 2, Capraro Papers.

25. A. J. Muste to GEB, May 26, 1920, H-ACWA Papers.

26. Goldberg, "Immigrants, Intellectuals and Industrial Unions," pp. 303–4; Muste to Capraro, January 15, 1920, and Capraro to Muste, March 1, 1920, both "Lawrence 1919" folder, Box 2, Capraro Papers; William Leiserson, *Adjusting Immigrant and Industry* (New York, 1924), p. 204; Edwin Fenton, *Immigrants and Unions, a Case Study: Italians and American Labor, 1870–1920* (New York, 1975), pp. 552, 556–57; David Saposs interview with David Wolfe, February 27, 1919, Box 21, Saposs Papers; Capraro to Augusto Bellanca, January 16, 1920, "Lawrence 1919" folder, Box 2, Capraro Papers, translated by Nunzio Pernicone.

27. David Saposs, "The Place of the Amalgamated Clothing Workers in the Labor Movement and the Achievements of the Organization," Box 21, Saposs Papers; *New Solidarity*, February 28, 1920; Nathan Kleinman, "Report to GEB," April 28, 1920, H-ACWA Papers; and Goldberg, "Immigrants, Intellectuals and Industrial Unions," pp. 359–70.

28. Muste to George Roewer, March 11, 1919, H-ACWA Papers; Capraro to A. Bellanca, March 28, 1919, and January 16, 1920, translated by Nunzio Pernicone, and Capraro to Schlossberg, 1919, Capraro Papers.

29. Goldberg, "Immigrants, Intellectuals and Industrial Unions," pp. 492, 477.

30. Shapiro, "The Great War and Reform" (note 2 above); Melvyn Dubofsky, "Abortive Reform: The Wilson Administration and Organized Labor, 1913–1920," in Cronin and Sirianni, *Work, Community, and Power* (note 14 above); Steven J. Scheinberg, "The Development of Corporate Labor Policy: 1900–1940," Ph.D. dissertation, University of Wisconsin, 1966, p. 136; Michael E. Parrish, *Felix Frankfurter and His Times: The Reform Years* (New York, 1982), p. 116; David Montgomery, "The New Unionism and the Transformation of Working Class Consciousness in America, 1909–22," in David Montgomery, ed., *Workers' Control in America*

(New York, 1979); Sanford Jacoby, *Employing Bureaucracy: Managers, Unions and the Transformation of Work in American Industry, 1900–45* (New York, 1985), p. 172; Irving Bernstein, *The Lean Years: A History of the American Worker, 1920–33* (Boston, 1972), ch. 2; and Daniel Horowitz, *The Morality of Spending: Attitudes Toward the Consumer Society in America, 1875–1940* (Baltimore, 1985), pp. 127–28.

31. Jacoby, *Employing Bureaucracy*, pp. 176–78, 192–93; Sanford Jacoby, "The Development of Internal Labor Markets in American Manufacturing Firms," in Paul Osterman, ed., *Employment Practices in Large Firms* (Cambridge, Mass., 1984); and Scheinberg, "Development of Corporate Labor Policy," p. 139.

32. Harry A. Corbin, *The Men's Clothing Industry: Colonial Through Modern Times* (New York, 1970), p. 135, and Dee Garrison, ed., *Rebel Pen: The Writings of M. H. Vorse* (New York, 1986), pp. 78–82. Mary Heaton Vorse became a great admirer of the ACWA and of Hillman's particularly, whom she celebrated as one of the "movers and shakers" of the postwar world for his persistent advocacy of industrial democracy. June Sachen, *Movers and Shakers: American Women Thinkers and Activity, 1900–1970* (New York, 1973). Vorse was one of those whom the ACWA helped to "disappear" by hiring her to organize the shirtworkers in obscure hamlets of Pennsylvania's anthracite coal country.

33. *Doc. Hist. 1918–20*, "Report to the Committee," June 25, 1919, H-ACWA Papers.

34. *Doc. Hist. 1918–20*, and "Leiserson Flays Accusers of Amalgamated," *Daily News Record*, January 15, 1920.

35. *Doc. Hist. 1920–22*; Frankfurter to Hillman, March 30, 1920, and Hillman to Frankfurter, March 29, 1920, Box 67, Frankfurter Papers; and H. N. Hirsch, *The Enigma of Felix Frankfurter* (New York, 1981), p. 71.

36. "Reminiscences of Leo Wolman," OHCCU, pp. 92–94, and Guy Alchon, "The Invisible Hand of Planning: Business, Social Science and the State in the American 1920s," Ph.D. dissertation, University of Iowa, 1982, pp. 113–14.

37. William E. Akin, *Technocracy and the American Dream: The Technocratic Movement, 1900–41* (Berkeley, Calif., 1977), pp. 31–32.

38. *Felix Frankfurter Reminiscences*, p. 204, extract in H-ACWA Papers, and "Reminiscences of Wolman," pp. 20–21.

39. Author's interview with Teccia Davidson Brill, April 29, 1986.

40. "Testimony of Eli Strousse and Max Holtz in Michaels–Stern Case," Research and Publicity Department, ACWA, Box 125, Frankfurter Papers; "Hearings on Clothing Industry" before Senate Committee on Education and Labor, June 9, 1921, H-ACWA Papers; *The New Republic*, May 19, 1920; *The Nation*, June 5, 1920; and *Daily News Record*, July 22, 1920.

41. Horowitz, *Morality of Spending* (note 30 above), pp. 109–10; Paul Nystrom, *Economics of Fashion* (New York, 1928), pp. 42–43, 430; *Doc. Hist. 1918–20*; and Corbin, *Men's Clothing Industry*, pp. 119, 123.

42. *Bulletin of the Taylor Society*, vol. 4, no. 6, December 1919; Liebman, *Jews and the Left* (note 9 above), p. 230; *Doc. Hist. 1920–22*; *Doc. Hist. 1922–24*; and George Bell, "Structure of Industry," 1919, H-ACWA Papers.

43. Meyer Jacobstein, "Talk to Foremen," February 25, 1919, H-ACWA Papers.

44. "Speech of Sidney Hillman," Boston, December 29, 1920, H-ACWA Papers; Corbin, *Men's Clothing Industry*, p. 128; and Richard Feiss to Frankfurter, November 27, 1918, War Labor Policy Board Records, Box 27, National War Labor Board, Record Group no. 1, National Archives.

45. GEB "Minutes," 1920, H-ACWA Papers; *Doc. Hist. 1920–22*; and Joseph Brandeis,

"From Sweatshop to Stability: Jewish Labor Between Two World Wars," *YIVO Annual of Jewish Social Science*, 16 (1976): 47–48.

46. GEB "Minutes," July 1920, H-ACWA Papers.

47. "Speech of Sidney Hillman," Boston, December 29, 1920, H-ACWA Papers.

48. *New York Evening Post*, December 9, 1920; *The New Republic*, January 12, 1921; "The Case of the Union as Stated by Observers," pamphlet, H-ACWA Papers; and Brandeis to Frankfurter, February 11, 1921, and Frankfurter to Brandeis, February 24, 1921, both Box 25, and Max Lowenthal to Frankfurter, n.d., Box 150, Frankfurter Papers.

49. "Summary of the New York City Lockout, December 8, 1920–May, 1921," H-ACWA Papers; "The Case of the Union as Stated by Observers," H-ACWA Papers; and Frankfurter to Brandeis, February 24, 1921.

50. Mary Heaton Vorse, "How Do They Do It?" *Advance*, April 1, 1921.

51. *New York Evening Post*, December 9, 1920, and "Hillman to Clothing Manufacturers Association," December 3, 1920, H-ACWA Papers.

52. Craig R. Littler, *The Development of the Labour Process in Capitalist Societies: A Comparative Study of the Transformation of Work Organization in Britain, Japan, and the U.S.A.* (London, 1982), and Sanford Jacoby, "Union–Management Cooperation in the U.S.: Lessons From the 1920's," *Industrial and Labor Relations Review*, vol. 37, October 1983.

53. Gerald Sorin, *The Prophetic Minority: American Jewish Immigrant Radicals, 1880–1920* (Bloomington, Ind., 1985), p. 93; Michael Buraway, "The Anthropology of Industrial Work," *Annual Review of Anthropology*, vol. 8, 1979; and Morris Cooke to Sidney Hillman, April 15, 1920, H-ACWA Papers.

54. Alchon, "Invisible Hand of Planning" (note 36 above), p. 58, and William Leiserson, "Industrial Stability," *American Academy of Political and Social Science Annals*, July 1920.

55. Morris Cooke, "Modern Manufacturing: A Partnership of Idealism and Common Sense," *American Academy of Political and Social Science Annals*, September 1919, and Leiserson, "Industrial Stability."

56. *New York Evening Post*, February 18, 1920, and William Hard, "Hillman and the Amalgamated," *The New Republic*, June 2, 1920.

57. Morris Cooke to Frankfurter, January 21, 1921, and Frankfurter to Cooke, January 25, 1921, Box 49, Frankfurter Papers; Akin, *Technocracy and the American Dream* (note 37 above), pp. 24, 31–32; and Brandeis to Robert Bruere, February 25, 1922, Box 26, Frankfurter Papers.

58. Commission on the Elimination of Waste in Industry of the Federated American Engineering Societies, *Waste in Industry* (New York, 1921), pp. 95–96, 98, 100, 101, 103, 108, 118, and Cook to Hillman, April 15, 1920, H-ACWA Papers.

59. Cooke to Hillman, June 18, and Cooke to H. K. Hathaway *et al.*, June 22, 1920, both H-ACWA Papers.

60. Max Friedman to Jacob H. Schiff, December 19, 1918, and Jacob Spitz to Potofsky, January 24, 1920, both H-ACWA Papers; Joseph Schlossberg, "Standards of Production," *Advance*, May 28, 1920; *Doc. Hist. 1916–18*; Will Herberg, "The Jewish Labor Movement in the U.S.," *American Jewish Yearbook 1952*; *Conv. Proc. 1920*; and Sam Liptzin, *Tales of a Tailor* (New York, 1965), pp. 256–57, 168–72.

61. *Advance*, May 28, 1920.

62. Interview with Sidney Hillman in *The World*, July 27, 1919.

63. *Advance*, May 28, 1920, and Judge Jacob M. Moses, "Labor Agreements with a

Powerful Union," *American Academy of Political and Social Science,* September 1919.

64. Francis Joseph Haas, "Shop Collective Bargaining: A Study of Wage Determination in the Men's Garment Industry," Ph.D. dissertation, Catholic University, 1922, p. 48; Meyer Jacobstein, "Can Industrial Democracy Be Efficient? The Rochester Plan," *Taylor Society Bulletin,* no. 2, 1919; and Paul Blanshard, "Industrial Government in Rochester," *Outlook,* February 23, 1922.

SEVEN: *A Strange Alliance*

1. Steven Fraser, "Dress Rehearsal for the New Deal," in Michael H. Frisch and Daniel J. Walkowitz, eds., *Working Class America: Essays on Labor, Community and American Society* (Urbana, Ill., 1983).

2. *Doc. Hist. 1920–22;* Melech Epstein, *Jewish Labor in the U.S.A.,* vol. 2: *1914–52* (New York, 1969), pp. 64–66, 89, 110–11; and J. B. S. Hardman "Memoir," OHCCU, pp. 54–56.

3. Fraser, "Dress Rehearsal."

4. *Doc. Hist. 1920–22;* GEB "Minutes," December 1921, H-ACWA Papers; J. B. Salutsky, "Constructive Radicalism in the Textile Industry," précis in "Needle Trades—1920s," Box 3, Daniel Bell Collection, Tamiment Library; GEB "Minutes," January 5, 1922, H-ACWA Papers; Will Herberg, "The Jewish Labor Movement in the U.S.," *American Jewish Yearbook 1952;* GEB "Minutes," May and July–August 1924, H-ACWA Papers; *Doc. Hist. 1922–24;* and GEB "Minutes," June 1921.

5. GEB "Minutes," August 1922, and Fraser, "Dress Rehearsal."

6. "An Appeal to the Lithuanian Amalgamated Tailors," H-ACWA Papers; K. Jurgelianis to Potofsky, January 20, 1919; and P. Grigaitis to ACWA, May 11, 1920, all in H-ACWA Papers.

7. Jurgelianis to Schlossberg, August 31, 1919; J. Buroydas to GEB, January 21, 1921; and DeLuca to Schlossberg, September 26, 1925, all in H-ACWA Papers. Charles Zimmerman file, November 13, 1964, Oral History Collection, Box 6, YIVO Archives, New York; GEB "Minutes," August 1922, June 1923, and July–August, 1924; Steve Fraser, "The 'New Unionism' and the 'New Economic Policy,'" in James E. Cronin and Carmen Sirianni, eds., *Work, Community and Power: The Experience of Labor in Europe and America, 1900–1925* (Philadelphia, 1983), p. 176; Irving Howe interview with Israel Breslow, Oral History Collection, YIVO Archives; *The Liberator,* July 1920 and June 1922; *Doc. Hist. 1920–22,* and *1922–24;* Salutsky, "Constructive Radicalism" précis; Daniel Bell interview with Earl Browder, June 22, 1955, "Goldsmith–Browder 1955 August file," Box 9, Bell Collection; "Notes on TUEL Minutes, 1923–27," March 7, 1924, June 10, 1925, and May 1, 1924, Box 3, Bell Collection; Charles Zaretz, *The Amalgamated Clothing Workers of America: A Study in Progressive Trade-Unionism* (New York, 1934), p. 258; and Melech Epstein, *Profiles of Eleven* (Detroit, 1965), p. 291.

8. *Doc. Hist. 1920–22,* and *Daily News Record,* November 18, 1921.

9. Fraser, "The 'New Unionism,'" pp. 178–79, 176.

10. Matthew Josephson, *Sidney Hillman: Statesman of American Labor* (New York, 1952), pp. 256, 258.

11. J. B. S. Hardman, "Oral History," p. 67, File 47A, Box 6, Hardman Papers, Tamiment Library.

12. D. M. Ladd to Herbert Hoover, June 22, 1946, File 61-9899; Victor J. Volgavec, "Bolsheviki Activities," December 15, 1922, File 61-9899, FBI files acquired under

FOIA; *New York Times*, April 13, 1922, and April 14, 1923; "American Fund for Public Service" extract from "Investigation of Un-American Propaganda Activities in the U.S.—Special Committee on Un-American Activities," House of Representatives, 78th Cong., 2d sess., Appendix Part IX, Communist Front Organizations first section, in "1921–27 Queries on Political Committee of TUEL," Box 8, Bell Collection.

13. Fraser, "The 'New Unionism,' " pp. 179, 180, 177–78, 182, 183, 187, 188.

14. Carmen Sirianni, "Workers' Control in Europe in the Era of World War I: A Comparative Analysis of the European Experience," *Theory and Society*, vol. 9, 1980.

15. Steven Fraser, "Dress Rehearsal" (note 1 above). To follow the intricate maneuverings of both the ACWA and CP leaderships over the La Follette campaign, the Daniel Bell and Charles Zimmerman collections are especially valuable, as are the papers of J. B. S. Hardman and the Anthony Capraro Papers.

16. R. Alan Lawson, *The Failure of Independent Liberalism, 1930–41* (New York, 1971), p. 40.

17. Kenneth Campbell Mackay, *The Progressive Movement of 1924* (New York, 1947).

18. Eugene Tobin, *Organize or Perish: America's Independent Progressives, 1913–33* (Westport, Conn., 1986), pp. 102, 109, and Mackay, *Progressive Movement*, p. 58.

19. Edward Filene to Newton Baker, January 30, 1923, "Liberal Groups—History," Edward A. Filene Papers, Credit Union National Association, Madison, Wisconsin. For the shopcraft unions particularly, it was specifically an act of retaliation against the Harding administration, which stood behind the Railway Labor Board's sanctioning of a wage cut and later its use of an antistrike injunction. Mackay, *Progressive Movement*.

20. Mackay, *Progressive Movement*, pp. 122–24, 153.

21. Tobin, *Organize or Perish*, pp. 135, 150; La Follette to La Guardia, November 24, 1922, Box 4153, La Guardia Papers, Municipal Archives, New York; Mackay, *Progressive Movement*, pp. 75–80, 122; Foster Rhea Dulles, "The La Follette Campaign of 1924," in Charles M. Rehmus, Doris B. McClaughlin, and Fredrick H. Nesbitt, eds., *Labor and American Politics* (Ann Arbor, Mich., 1978); and Fred E. Haynes, "The Significance of the Latest 3rd Party Movement," *Mississippi Valley Historical Review*, vol. 12, September 1925.

22. Mackay, *Progressive Movement*, p. 153; Dulles, "La Follette Campaign"; and Robert Zeiger, *John L. Lewis: Labor Leader* (Boston, 1988), pp. 199, 200.

23. Gwendolyn Mink, *Old Labor and New Immigrants in American Political Development: Union, Party and State* (Ithaca, N.Y., 1986), p. 241.

24. Mackay, *Progressive Movement*, p. 229; Henry David, "Labor and Political Action After World War I: 1919–1924," *Labor and Nation*, February–March 1946; and Norma Fain Pratt, *Morris Hilquit: A Political History of an American Jewish Socialist* (Westport, Conn., 1979), p. 193.

25. Tobin, *Organize or Perish*, pp. 124, 142; Mackay, *Progressive Movement*, p. 237; David, "Labor and Political Action"; Kenneth Waltzer, "The American Labor Party," Ph.D. dissertation, Harvard, 1977, p. 11; and American Labor Party papers, Tamiment Library.

26. "GEB Statement on the La Follette-Wheeler Campaign," appendix, *Doc. Hist. 1924–26*, and Pratt, *Morris Hilquit*, pp. 188–91.

27. Theodore Draper, *American Communism and Soviet Russia* (New York, 1960), pp. 36, 43–44; GEB "Minutes," July–August 1924, H-ACWA Papers; and Tobin, *Organize or Perish*, pp. 148, 149.

28. David, "Labor and Political Action"; *Conv. Proc. 1924*, p. 184; and Hillman speech at Cooper Union, September 16, 1924, H-ACWA Papers.

29. Donald A. Ritchie, *James M. Landis: Dean of the Regulators* (Cambridge, Mass., 1980), p. 21.

30. Thomas E. Vadney, *The Wayward Liberal: A Political Biography of Donald Richberg* (Lexington, Ky., 1970), pp. 73–74, 95–96; Larry Gerber, "The Limits of Liberalism: A Study of the Careers and Ideological Development of Josephus Daniels, Henry Stimson, Bernard Baruch, Donald Richberg, and Felix Frankfurter," Ph.D. dissertation, University of California, Berkeley, 1979, pp. 262, 270–71; and David M. Kennedy, *Over Here: The First World War and American Society* (New York, 1980), pp. 256–58.

31. Bruce Allen Murphy, *The Brandeis–Frankfurter Connection: The Secret Political Activities of Two Supreme Court Justices* (New York, 1982); H. N. Hirsch, *The Enigma of Felix Frankfurter* (New York, 1981), p. 77; and Gerber, "Limits of Liberalism," p. 335.

32. Murphy, *Brandeis–Frankfurter Connection*, pp. 91–92; Mackay, *Progressive Movement*, p. 229; and *Advance*, December 9, 1924.

33. Tobin, *Organize or Perish*, p. 158; Bert Cochran, *Labor and Communism: The Conflict That Shaped American Unions* (Princeton, N.J., 1979), p. 25; Gompers quoted in Irving Bernstein, *The Lean Years: The American Worker, 1920–33* (Boston, 1970), p. 97; and Mary Agnes Hamilton, "Sidney Hillman: The New Force in American Labour," *Contemporary Review*, February 1927.

EIGHT: *Socialism in One Union*

1. J. B. S. Hardman, *American Labor Dynamics in the Light of Post-War Developments* (New York, 1928), p. 10.

2. Irving Howe, *Dissent*, Winter 1956, p. 71.

3. Sam Liptzin, *Tales of a Tailor* (New York, 1965).

4. Author's interview with Sam Liptzin, February 2, 1980; "Report of Joseph Zack," Bell Collection; reports of "Trade Union Committee 1925–27," Box 3, Bell Collection; Irving Howe interview with Paul Novick, March 29, 1968, YIVO Archives; Howe interview with Charles Zimmerman, April 13, 1968, YIVO Archives; and "Report of the National Committee, Needle Trades Section of the TUEL," January 1925, Box 45, File 8, Charles Zimmerman Records, ILGWU.

5. Joseph Schlossberg to Elias Rabkin, October 27, 1916, H-ACWA Papers; interviews with Elias Rabkin, May 8 and December 20, 30, and 31, 1975, and January 1 and 4, March 6, 14, and 20, April 3 and 18, May 30, and June 6, 1976, conducted by his son; and author's interview with Rabkin's son, December 23, 1980.

6. Charles Elbert Zaretz, *The Amalgamated Clothing Workers of America: A Study in Progressive Trade Unionism* (New York, 1934), p. 258; *Doc. Hist. 1922–24* and *1924–26*; "Factionalism—1925" report, H-ACWA Papers; "Memo," 1926, unsigned, Box 6, J. B. S. Hardman Papers, Tamiment Library; "Amalgamated Diaries," 1927–28, H-ACWA Papers; "Amalgamated Clothing Workers of America," Box 5, Daniel Bell Collection; "Complaints and Investigations," H-ACWA Papers; Jacob Potofsky to Isovitz, January 6, 1915, H-ACWA Papers; Hillman speech to the New York Joint Board, 1924, "ACW Affairs," H-ACWA Papers; GEB "Minutes," February 9, 1925, H-ACWA Papers; "Report of the National Committee, Needle Trades Section, TUEL," Box 45, Zimmerman Records; Anthony Capraro reminis-

cence on Hillman, Box 5, and Capraro to Hillman, August 8, 1926, Box 5, Capraro Papers; J. B. S. Hardman, oral history, p. 74, Hardman Collection, Tamiment Library; GEB "Minutes," December 1926, May 3–5, 1927, January–February 1929, and August 1931, H-ACWA Papers; and Abraham Cahan to board of directors of *Forward,* December 23, 1926, Gus Tyler Papers, ILGWU.

7. "Local Histories," H-ACWA Papers; "Memo on Stoppages, 1925–26, Rochester," H-ACWA Papers; *Doc. Hist. 1924–26;* S. Kucharska to GEB, January 19, 1925, H-ACWA Papers; GEB "Minutes," October 13–15, 1927; *Doc. Hist. 1926–28;* and Steven Fraser, "Dress Rehearsal for the New Deal," in Michael H. Frisch and Daniel J. Walkowitz, eds., *Working Class America: Labor, Community and American Society,* (Urbana, Ill., 1983).

8. Fraser, "Dress Rehearsal"; Tesso Tomassini, "Tactics and Methods of the ACWA," Box 3, Capraro Papers; Capraro to Giovanitti, May 2, 1928, Box 1, Capraro Papers; unsigned letter to Gitlow, Krumbein, and William Weinstone, August 11, 1926, commenting on Capraro's plan to organize an Italian Trade Union Council of America, Box 1, Capraro Papers; correspondence between Capraro and Augusto Bellanca, April 14 and 11, and March 30, 1928, October 15, 1922, August 23 and September 2 and 10, 1923, and September 24, 1925, Box 6; correspondence with Frank Bellanca, August 22 and November 17, 1925, and January 17, 1924; Capraro to Hillman, August 8, 1926, Box 5; Peter Teem to Capraro, 1924, Box 2; Capraro to Teem, September 11, 1926, and Teem to Capraro, September 7, 1926, Box 2; Dorothy Bellanca to Capraro, June 14, 1928; A. Bellanca to Capraro, May 4, 1922, June 30, 1925, and November 2, 1923, Box 6—all in Capraro Papers. GEB "Minutes," February 1925, December 1925, and October 1927, H-ACWA Papers; "Report of Proceedings of the 4th Annual Conference, Needle Trades Section, TUEL-NYC, Jan. 1927," Box 45, Zimmerman Records; "Report of the Secretary on the Purposes of the Special Amalgamated Conference," January 3, 1927, Box 45, Zimmerman Records; Hillman to Sam Levin, June 4, 1925, H-ACWA Papers; A. Bellanca to Capraro, February 9, 1925; A. Bellanca to John Bongiovonni, June 1, 1925, H-ACWA Papers; GEB "Minutes," August 1926, H-ACWA Papers; William Z. Foster, "Report to Trade Union Committee of the Central Executive Committee," September 17, 1926, and January 14, 1927, Box 3, Bell Collection; "What Is and Why an Italian Labor Council of America," Box 1, Capraro Papers; and John W. Briggs, *An Italian Passage: Immigrants to Three American Cities, 1890–1930* (New Haven, 1978), pp. 75, 81–85, 90, 94, 106, 109.

9. Irving Howe, *World of Our Fathers: The Journey of the East European Jews to America and the World They Found and Made* (New York, 1976), pp. 355–56; *Conv. Proc. 1922,* p. 359; *Conv. Proc. 1924,* pp. 259–60; and *Advance,* July 15 and August 5, 1921. The ACW called work stoppages in New York, Chicago, Rochester, Cincinnati, and elsewhere on the day of their execution. *Doc. Hist. 1926–28.*

10. Peter Teem to Anthony Capraro, 1927, Box 2, Capraro Papers; "Minutes of the Trade Union Committee of the Central Executive Committee-TUEL," September 17, 1926, Box 3, Bell Collection; Licastro to Hillman, February 9, 1925, H-ACWA Papers; and GEB "Minutes," August 1926, H-ACWA Papers.

11. "Memo of the TUEL National Committee," August 27, 1924, Box 5, Bell Collection; "Amalgamated Clothing Workers of America" minutes of TUEL Central Executive Committee, 1925, Box 5, and "Minutes," September 13, 1926, Box 2, Bell Collection; "Minutes of Trade Union Committee of the Central Executive Committee-TUEL," September 17, 1926, Box 3, Bell Collection; H. D. Rosen-

bloom to Potofsky, March 9, 1925, H-ACWA Papers; "Statement by the New York Group," n.d., File 10, Box 40, Zimmerman Records; and Anthony Capraro to Central Executive Committee-TUEL, January 15, 1925, Box 4, Capraro Papers.

12. *Doc. Hist. 1926–28.*

13. Sanford Jacoby, *Employing Bureaucracy: Managers, Unions and the Transformation of Work in American Industry, 1900–45* (New York, 1985), p. 172, and Irving Bernstein, *The Lean Years: The American Worker, 1920–33* (Boston, 1970), pp. 97–103.

14. Selig Perlman, *A Theory of the Labor Movement* (Madison, Wisc., 1928); Jacoby, *Employing Bureaucracy*, p. 172; and Stanley Vittoz, "The American Industrial Economy and the Political Origins of Federal Labor Policy Between the World Wars," Ph.D. dissertation, York University, 1979, pp. 71–76.

15. Sanford Jacoby, "The Development of Internal Labor Markets in American Manufacturing Firms," in Paul Osterman, ed., *Employment Practices in Large Firms* (Cambridge, Mass., 1984), p. 44. Horsepower per worker rose 50 percent between 1919 and 1929 and the 63 percent increase in output per man-hour between 1920 and 1929 allowed for a 42 percent growth in industrial production without a rise in the number of factory workers and an actual 7 percent decline in man-hours worked. Vittoz, "American Industrial Economy," pp. 35–36, and Milton Derber, *The American Idea of Industrial Democracy, 1865–1965* (Urbana, Ill., 1970), p. 200.

16. Harry A. Corbin, *The Men's Clothing Industry: Colonial Through Modern Times* (New York, 1970), pp. 150–51; Steven Fraser, "Combined and Uneven Development in the Men's Clothing Industry," *Business History Review*, Winter 1983; Robert J. Meyers and Joseph W. Bloch, "Men's Clothing," in *How Collective Bargaining Works: A Factual Survey of Labor-Management Relations in Leading American Industries* (20th Century Fund, 1942); Paul Nystrom, *Economics of Fashion* (New York, 1928), p. 430; *Advance*, August 27, 1927; and Ludwig Stein to Hillman, May 18, 1922, H-ACWA Papers.

17. *Doc. Hist. 1924–26* and *1926–28*; "Membership—Industry Statistics," H-ACWA Papers; and Fraser, "Combined and Uneven Development."

18. Meyers and Bloch, "Men's Clothing," and *Doc. Hist. 1922–24.*

19. Arthur Liebman, *Jews and the Left* (New York, 1979), p. 240; Sumner Slichter, *Union Policies and Industrial Management* (New York, 1969; reprint of 1941 Brookings Institution Study), pp. 527–28; and "Membership—Geography," H-ACWA Papers.

20. Guy Alchon, "The Invisible Hand of Planning: Business, Social Science, and the State in the American 1920's," Ph.D. dissertation, University of Iowa, 1982, pp. 194–95, 199, 200; William J. Barber, *From New Era to New Deal: Herbert Hoover, the Economists, and American Economic Policy, 1921–33* (New York, 1985), p. 29; and Edward A. Filene, *The Way Out: A Forecast of Coming Changes in Business and Industry* (New York, 1924), pp. 145, 148, 141.

21. William Hard, "Hillman and the Amalgamated," *The New Republic*, June 2, 1920.

22. "Hillman Speech on International Tailoring Strike," August 19, 1925, H-ACWA Papers.

23. Sidney Hillman, "Labor Attitudes," draft of article later published in J. B. S. Hardman, *American Labor Dynamics* (New York, 1928), H-ACWA Papers; Sidney Hillman, "Labor in the United States," *St. Louis Post-Dispatch*, December 9, 1928; and Mary Agnes Hamilton, "Sidney Hillman: The New Force in American Labour," *Contemporary Review*, February 1927.

24. Phil Scranton, "Flexible Production and the Atlantic Corridor: Urban Manufactur-

ing, Prosperity and Decline, 1880–1950," manuscript draft, March 28, 1986, in possession of author.

25. *Ibid.*

26. Ripley, Marshall, and Rosensohn decision, Advisory Board of N.Y. Clothing Industry, March 4, 1919, H-ACWA Papers; Robert J. Meyers, "Occupational Readjustment of Displaced Skilled Workers," *Journal of Political Economy*, August 1929; and Earl Dean Howard to Hillman, January 8, 1925, and Hillman to Howard, February 2, 1925, H-ACWA Papers.

27. Thomas W. Holland, "The 'X' Plan in the Clothing Trade," *The New Republic*, August 27, 1929.

28. Slichter, *Union Policies and Industrial Management*, pp. 510, 512, 514, 518, 519, 522, 523; "Amalgamated Diaries," February 14, 1927, and August 18, 1929, H-ACWA Papers; and *Advance*, August 1927.

29. Robert Bruere, "Mr. Nash Does unto Others," *Survey Graphic*, January 1, 1926; Robert Littell, "Golden Rule Nash," *The New Republic*, March 10, 1926; *Daily News Record*, December 14, 1925; *Doc. Hist.* 1924–26 and 1926–28; Robert Bruere, "The Golden Rule Through Union Eyes," *Survey Graphic*, May 1, 1927; and Cincinnati Joint Board, "The Golden Rule as Applied in A. Nash Tailoring Co.," January 1922, H-ACWA Papers.

30. David Brody, "The Rise and Decline of Welfare Capitalism," pp. 54–57, in David Brody, *Workers in Industrial America: Essays on the 20th Century Struggle* (New York, 1980).

31. Morris Cooke to Hillman, December 29, 1919, Box 9, Cooke Papers; Cooke to Meyer Jacobstein, February 2, 1920, and September 27, 1921, Box 21, Cooke Papers, Library of Congress; and Hillman Speech at Conference of American Association for Labor Legislation, Hotel Astor, December 30, 1920, H-ACWA Papers.

32. Roy Lubove, *The Struggle for Social Security, 1900–35* (Cambridge, Mass., 1968), pp. 43–44, 158–59, and Leo Wolman, "The Future for Unemployment Insurance," *American Labor Legislation Review*, March 1923.

33. "The Reminiscences of Leo Wolman," p. 37, OHCCU; Bryce Stewart, "A Plan for Unemployment Insurance by Industry," *Bulletin of the Taylor Society*, vol. XII, August 1927; and Leo Wolman, *Locomotive Engineers Journal*, December 1923.

34. *The New Republic*, June 20, 1923. Although there was some sentiment for a flat rate, benefits were to be paid in proportion to wages received. *Doc. Hist.* 1924–26; Robert Bruere, "Cementing the Broken Year: Two Years of Unemployment Insurance in Chicago," *Survey Graphic*, April 1925; Leo Wolman to Bryce M. Stewart, April 10, 1926, and Wolman to Hillman, April 10, 1925, H-ACWA Papers.

35. Sidney Hillman, "Labor in the United States," *St. Louis Post-Dispatch*, December 9, 1928, and Jacoby, *Employing Bureaucracy* (note 13 above), p. 201.

36. "Cooperative League of America, 1923," H-ACWA Papers, and *New York Journal*, May 11, 1925.

37. *Doc. Hist.* 1926–28; Frederick Howe to Hillman, March 31, 1920, H-ACWA Papers; Jacob Potofsky interview with Roosevelt University, August 4, 1970, H-ACWA Papers; *New York World*, April 14 and May 19, 1923; *Current Opinion*, March 24, 1923; and GEB "Minutes," May 1920.

38. *Doc. Hist.* 1922–24, and Sidney Hillman, "The Labor Banking Movement in the U.S.," *Academy of Political Science*, 1925.

39. Hillman, "Labor Banking Movement."

40. Sidney Hillman, "Labor in the United States," *St. Louis Post-Dispatch*, December 9,

1928; "Memo to Henry Bruere," n.d., H-ACWA Papers; *New York Times*, September 16, 1927; *New York World*, December 15, 1927; and *Advance*, May 10, 1926. The "cooperative spirit" was not always in evidence. Abraham Kazan, a one-time ILG cloakmaker, took responsibility for organizing the ACW's new credit union and other cooperative ventures. He claimed Hillman was interested in the cooperative movement only insofar as it promoted his personal reputation for statesmanship, "but he did not think in terms of a cooperative and that membership would play the most important part." Kazan later refused to serve on the board of the Amalgamated Bank, quitting after three weeks because "it doesn't do anything for the average man." "Reminiscences of Abraham Kazan," OHCCU, pp. 77, 155.

41. Francis Joseph Haas, "Shop Collective Bargaining: A Study of Wage Determination in the Men's Garment Industry," Ph.D. dissertation, Catholic University, 1922, p. 48.

42. *Doc. Hist. 1922–24;* Jonathan D. Bloom, "Brookwood Labor College, 1921–33: Training Ground for Union Organizers," M.A. thesis, New York University, 1978, pp. 3, 7–8, 19; and David Saposs to William Leiserson, 1924, Box 36, William Leiserson Papers, Wisconsin State Historical Society.

43. Irving Howe, "The Significance of the Jewish Labor Movement," in *The Jewish Labor Movement in America* (Jewish Labor Committee, Workmen's Circle, 1957, copy in Archives of the Jewish Bund, New York).

44. *Doc. Hist. 1920–22; Conv. Proc. 1922,* pp. 259, 264; "A Brief Outline of Activities by the Education Department," H-ACWA Papers; author's interview with Beatrice Bornstein, June 7, 1979; and *Globe and Commercial Advertiser*, May 12, 1922.

45. William Leiserson to David Saposs, June 12, 1919, Box 21, Saposs Papers; "Digest of Statement of David J. Saposs of New York City—The Place of the Amalgamated Clothing Workers in the Labor Movement and the Achievements of the Organization," Box 21, Saposs Papers.

46. *Doc. Hist. 1920–22.*

47. James Harvey Robinson, *The New History* (Springfield, Mass., 1958), pp. 132–33, 139–43.

48. Jacques Donzelot, *The Policing of Families* (New York, 1979); Nina Asher, "Dorothy Jacobs Bellanca: Women Clothing Workers and Runaway Shops," in Joan M. Jensen and Sue Davidson, eds., *A Needle, a Bobbin, a Strike: Women Needleworkers in America* (Philadelphia, 1984); *Advance*, July 27 and September 28, 1917; Susan Anita Glenn, "The Working Life of Immigrants: Women in the American Garment Industry, 1880–1920," Ph.D. dissertation, University of California, Berkeley, 1983, pp. 345–46; R. Lomanassoff to Schlossberg, April 22, 1920, H-ACWA Papers; *Doc. Hist. 1926–28;* "Equal Rights in the Union," *The Survey*, February 15, 1927; and Mamie Santora to Dorothy Bellanca, September 2, 1924; Sarah Barinsky to Dorothy Bellanca, September 2, 1924; Mamie Santora to D. Bellanca, August 12, 1925; Santora to D. Bellanca, August 3, 1925; Bellanca to Santora, August 5, 1925; and D. Bellanca to Bessie Malac, September 2, 1925, all in H-ACWA Papers.

49. David Saposs interview with Sam Levin, December 26, 1919, Box 22, Saposs Papers.

50. J. M. Budish and George Soule, *The New Unionism in the Clothing Industry* (New York, 1920), pp. 219, 223, 227.

51. Daniel Bell, *The Cultural Contradictions of Capitalism* (New York, 1976), pp. xi–xii, 70, and Max Weber, *Economy and Society*, ed. Guenther Roth and Claus Wittich (Berkeley, Calif., 1978), 1: 515–16.

52. *True Story*, 1929, magazine cited in Glenn, "Working Life of Immigrants," pp. 4–5.
53. Daniel Horowitz, *The Morality of Spending: Attitudes Toward the Consumer Society in America, 1875–1940* (Baltimore, 1985), pp. 56, 122.
54. *Ibid.*, pp. 136, 137, and David Saposs, "The Place of the Amalgamated in the Labor Movement . . . ," Box 21, Saposs Papers.
55. Glenn, "Working Life of Immigrants," pp. 285, 286, 288, 289.
56. George Enrico Pozzetta, "The Italians of New York City, 1880–1914," Ph.D. dissertation, University of North Carolina, 1971, p. 242; Paul J. Campisi, "The Italian Family in the U.S.," *American Journal of Sociology*, vol. 53, May 1948; "Membership—Geographical," H-ACWA Papers; Silvano Tomasi, *Piety and Power: The Role of Italian Parishes in the New York Metropolitan Area* (New York, 1975), p. 140; Nicholas John Russo, "Three Generations of Italians in New York City: Their Religious Acculturation," in Silvano Tomasi and Madeline H. Engel, eds., *The Italian Experience in the U.S.* (New York, 1970).
57. *Doc. Hist. 1920–22.*
58. John Patrick Diggins, *Mussolini and Fascism: The View from America* (Princeton, N.J., 1972), pp. 95, 317–18; Steve Fraser, "Landslayt and Paesani: Ethnic Conflict and Cooperation in the Amalgamated Clothing Workers of America," in Dirk Hoerder, ed., *Struggle a Hard Battle: Essays on Working-Class Immigrants* (De Kalb, Ill., 1986).
59. David Saposs interview with Miss Friedman, May 7, 1930, Box 21, Saposs Papers.
60. Joseph Gollomb, "Sidney Hillman," *Atlantic Monthly*, July 1938, and Hillman, "Labor in the United States" (note 23 above).
61. Marshall quoted in Matthew Josephson, *Sidney Hillman: Statesman of American Labor* (New York, 1952), p. 318.
62. Author's interview with Virginia Hardman, June 11, 1985; A. H. Raskin, "Sidney Hillman, 1887–1946," *American Jewish Yearbook*, vol. 49, 1947–48; and author's interview with Teccia Davidson Brill, April 29, 1986.
63. Gollomb, "Sidney Hillman," and Hillman to Solomon Levitan, August 2, 1927, H-ACWA Papers.
64. Author's interview with A. H. Raskin, June 10, 1985; Hillman to Uncle Charles, February 15, 1924 and April 30, 1924, H-ACWA Papers; *New York Call*, December 24, 1922; Charles Ervin, "Personal Reminiscences," September 26, 1940, H-ACWA Papers; and author's interview with Teccia Davidson Brill, April 29, 1986.
65. Gollomb, "Sidney Hillman"; William Hard, "Hillman and the Amalgamated," *The New Republic*, June 2, 1920; and GEB "Minutes," November 10–13, 1924, H-ACWA Papers.
66. Author's interview with Brill; B. Bisno "Notes," September 18, 1950, H-ACWA Papers; and draft of "Labor's Attitudes," H-ACWA Papers, later published as Chapter 20 of J. B. S. Hardman, ed., *American Labor Dynamics* (New York, 1928).
67. Jacob Potofsky, "Personal Notes," September 13, 1934, H-ACWA Papers.
68. *Baltimore Evening Sun*, January 5, 1923, and *The Daily Worker*, January 22, 1924.
69. Author's interview with Brill; Mary Agnes Hamilton, "Sidney Hillman: The New Force in American Labour," *The Contemporary Review*, February 1927; and "Labor Can Lead: The Story of Sidney Hillman," *The World Tomorrow*, November 1929.
70. B. Bisno "Notes," H-ACWA Papers. Hillman refused, as a matter of socialist principle, to own the summer cottage in his own name, so it was recorded in Bessie's.
71. Hillman to Uncle Charles, May 31, 1922, Box 156, FF14 File, Hillman Papers, Martin P. Catherwood Library; Hillman to Uncle Charles, June 27, 1925, and

Hillman remittance of $500 to bank in Kaunas, February 9, 1929, H-ACWA Papers; Hillman to Armand Hammer, October 10, 1927, H-ACWA Papers; and J. H. Shaw to Hillman, March 5, 1921, and "Will" to Robert Szold, February 24, 1921, H-ACWA Papers.

72. Gollomb, "Sidney Hillman," and Max Weber, *Economy and Society*, ed. Guenther Roth and Claus Wittich, 2:1149.

73. "Labor Can Lead," and B. Bisno "Notes," September 18, 1950, H-ACWA Papers.

74. Hamilton, "Sidney Hillman."

75. *Chicago Daily News*, October 17, 1928.

NINE:"A Great Deal of Disaster"

1. *Doc. Hist. 1928–30.*

2. *Ibid.*; GEB "Minutes," September 20–22, 1928, September 1929, and February 15–16, 1928; La Follette quoted in *Congressional Record*, Senate, September 16, 1929, p. 3784; and Beulah Amidon, "Styles in Strikes," *Survey Graphic*, December 1929.

3. *Doc. Hist. 1928–30* and *1930–34*.

4. Hillman to William Leiserson, August 13, 1930, Box 1, William Leiserson Papers, Wisconsin State Historical Society, and GEB "Minutes," November 1930 and August 25–28, 1931. As late as 1939 average annual earnings in the industry were still 20 percent less than the level achieved in 1928. "Memo," Research Department, to Hillman, March 18, 1940, H-ACWA Papers; Matthew Josephson, *Sidney Hillman: Statesman of American Labor* (New York, 1952), ch. 15; Joseph Brandes, "From Sweatshop to Stability: Jewish Labor Between Two World Wars," *YIVO Annual of Jewish Social Science*, vol. 16, 1976; Hillman testimony before Senate Subcommittee of the Committee on Manufactures, 72d Congress, January 8, 1932, extract in H-ACWA Papers; "Reminiscences of Jacob Potofsky," pp. 208–11, OHCCU; *Daily News Record*, January 28, 1933.

5. Harry A. Corbin, *The Men's Clothing Industry: Colonial Through Modern Times* (New York, 1970), p. 166; "Hearings on Code of Fair Practices and Competition—Men's Ready to Wear Clothing Industry," April 26–27, 1933, Box 7112, National Recovery Administration Records, National Archives; Morris Gruenberg to Mark Cresap, May 8, 1935, H-ACWA Papers; H. K. Herwitz to Hillman, October 12, 1934, H-ACWA Papers; *Doc. Hist. 1930–34*; and GEB "Minutes," February 1–3, 1932.

6. Joel Seidman, *The Needle Trades* (New York, 1942), p. 187; *Doc. Hist. 1930–34*; "Report on Industrial Homework in Men's Clothing Industry," H-ACWA Papers; Robert P. Ingalls, *Herbert H. Lehman and New York State's Little New Deal* (New York, 1975), pp. 102–3; Kenneth Waltzer, "The American Labor Party," Ph.D. dissertation, Harvard University, 1977, p. 20; and "Child Labor," Box 129, Felix Frankfurter Papers, Library of Congress.

7. Hillman to Sylvan Kronheim, August 13, 1932, H-ACWA Papers; Hillman to Louis Kirstein, August 13 and December 19, 1932; Hillman to Lessing Rosenthal, December 19, 1932; and Hillman to General Wood, October 20, 1932, all in "Sidney Hillman" file, Case 4, Louis E. Kirstein Papers, Baker Library, Harvard University; *The New Republic*, August 13, 1932; and Corbin, *Men's Clothing Industry*, p. 167.

8. Hillman testimony before House Committee on Labor, April–May, 1933, on the 30-hour bill, Washington, D.C., extract in H-ACWA Papers; GEB "Minutes," February 1–3, 1932; Rosenthal to Levy, August 3, 1931, Hart, Schaffner & Marx material in Treasurer's Office; Rosenthal to Mark Cresap, December 5, 1932, HSM

material. These sources included the Commercial Factors Department, Macy's Department Stores, and various textile and railroad shipment statistics.

9. GEB "Minutes," February 1–3, 1932, and Mark Cresap to Rosenthal, November 28, 1932, HSM Material.

10. Corbin, *Men's Clothing Industry*, pp. 163, 164, and "ACWA Diaries," December 14, 1927, August 8, 1929, and January 30 and July 31, 1930, H-ACWA Papers.

11. Alan Block, *East Side, West Side: Organizing Crime in New York, 1930–50* (Cardiff, Wales, 1980), p. 163.

12. John Hutchinson, *The Imperfect Union: A History of Corruption in American Trade Unions* (New York, 1970), p. 70; Jenna Weissman Joselit, *Our Gang: Jewish Crime and the New York Jewish Community* (Bloomington, Ind., 1983), pp. 110, 148; and Sam Liptzin, *Tales of a Tailor* (New York, 1965), pp. 191–92, 268–69.

13. Albert Fried, *The Rise and Fall of the Jewish Gangster in America* (New York, 1980).

14. *Business Week*, August 31, 1957, and Joselit, *Our Gang*, pp. 168–69.

15. Liptzin, *Tales of a Tailor*, p. 68, and author's interview with Liptzin, February 2, 1980; GEB "Minutes," August 1922; Children Clothing Workers Joint Board "Hearings and Trial," September–October 1923, H-ACWA Papers; Joselit, *Our Gang*, p. 125; and GEB "Minutes," January 4, 5, 6, 1923, and September 20–22, 1928.

16. J. B. S. Hardman "Reminiscences," p. 74, OHCCU; Anthony Capraro critique of Josephson biography of Hillman, "Hillman" file, Box 5, Capraro Papers; Capraro to Hillman, August 8, 1926, "Hillman" file, Box 5, Capraro Papers; Amalgamated Pressers Club to American Civil Liberties Union and to Roger Baldwin, July 3, 1929, and to Grover Whalen, July 2, 1929, Box 40, Charles S. Zimmerman Records, ILGWU; TUEL Leaflets, Box 40, Zimmerman Records; Rose Wortis, "Needle Trade Struggle and Present Electoral Campaign," October 23, 1928, File 9, Box 45, Zimmerman Records; Hyman Isovitz to Hillman, 1930, H-ACWA Papers; "Report of the National Committee, Needle Trades Section, TUEL," October 1, 1924, File 7, Box 45, Zimmerman Records; and GEB "Minutes," May 8–10, 1930.

17. Leo Wolman "Reminiscences," pp. 133, 162, OHCCU; GEB "Minutes," July–August 1924 and January–February 1929; *Doc. Hist. 1930–34*; *Business Week*, August 31, 1957; Fried, *Rise and Fall of Jewish Gangster*, pp. 160–61; Block, *East Side, West Side*, p. 172; and Burton Turkus and Sid Feder, *Murder, Inc.: The Story of the Syndicate* (New York, 1951), pp. 338–43.

18. Joselit, *Our Gang*, citing *New York Times*, June 26, 27 and 29, 1931, and *Forward*, January 29, 1931, and *Doc. Hist. 1930–34*.

19. Block, *East Side, West Side*, pp. 164, 41–44.

20. *New York Times*, June 26, 1931; A. J. Muste to J. B. S. Hardman, December 17, 1931, Box 38, J. B. S. Hardman Papers, Tamiment Library; Hutchinson, *Imperfect Union*, p. 77; Fried, *Rise and Fall of Jewish Gangster*, p. 162; and GEB "Minutes," August 25–28, 1931. After his ouster, Beckerman went on to become general manager of the Fur Dressers' Factor Corp. and the Associated Employers of Fur Workers, Inc., where he brought in Lepke and Gurrah to enforce order among resistant manufacturers, dressers, dealers, and trade union officials. Block, *East Side, West Side*.

21. *Doc. Hist. 1930–34*, and author's interview with Maxwell Brandwen, March 9, 1979.

22. Joseph Spiotta to "Whom It May Concern," February 26, 1930, "Newark (local 24)" file, Box 1, Anthony Capraro Papers; "The Situation in Newark During the Administration of Harry Taylor," report by Louis Pennachia, 1930, "Newark (local 24) under Harry Taylor" file, Box 1, Capraro Papers; and Capraro critique of Josephson biography.

23. Joselit, *Our Gang*, pp. 124–25; Liptzin, *Tales of a Tailor*, pp. 182–83; and Block, *East Side, West Side*, p. 170.

24. Block, *East Side, West Side*, p. 172; Turkus and Feder, *Murder, Inc.*, pp. 335–43; Joselit, *Our Gang*, citing Thomas E. Dewey Collection, Box 2842, New York Municipal Archives; "Louis Buchalter: Notice of Criminal Record," March 27, 1940, Box 2500, William O'Dwyer Papers, New York Municipal Archives; A. J. Muste to J. B. S. Hardman, February 17, 1931, Box 38, Hardman Papers; and Fried, *Rise and Fall of Jewish Gangster*, pp. 164–65.

25. Statement of Harold E. Rosen in Reading, Pennsylvania, April 1941, to Kings County District Attorney, "Rosen Murder" file, Box 1, Kings County D.A. Files, New York Municipal Archives; "Investigations into the Death of Joseph Rosen," interrogation of Sylvia Rosen, October 16, 1936, Grand Jury Testimony, Box 1, D.A. Files, New York Municipal Archives; Joselit, *Our Gang*, pp. 127–28; *New York Post*, September 21, 1936; *New York Times*, September 14 and 15, 1938; William O'Dwyer "Reminiscences," 8: 236–39, OHCCU; Boxes 9243 and 9248, William O'Dwyer papers, New York Municipal Archives; and "Murder Inc.," Kings County D.A. Files, Box 1, New York Municipal Archives.

26. Fried, *Rise and Fall of Jewish Gangster*, pp. 225–26; *New York Daily Mirror*, December 5, 1941; and *New York World-Telegram*, December 17, 1943.

27. A. M. Whitehead to David Dubinsky, March 15, 1944, File 3b, David Dubinsky Collection, ILGWU, and Norman Thomas "Reminiscences," pp. 37–38, OHCCU.

28. Fried, *Rise and Fall of Jewish Gangster*, p. 159.

29. Richard Norton Smith, *Thomas E. Dewey and His Times* (New York, 1982), p. 163; "Lepke and the Death of Max Rubin—Esther Rosen's Statement," September 23, 1936, Kings County D.A. Files, Box 1, Murder, Inc., New York Municipal Archives; and statement taken by William McCarthy, assistant to Thomas Dewey, from Max Rubin, December 16, 1937, in which McCarthy promises immunity in return for help on the Rosen Case, same file.

30. "Memorandum re Samuel 'Sneaky' Levine," Murder Inc. file, Box 7, Kings County D.A. File; Executive Board Minutes, local 240, Box 7, New York Municipal Archives; "Memorandum" and "Atlas Cloth Sponging Company" files, Box 2842, Thomas E. Dewey, D.A. of Manhattan, Papers, New York Municipal Archives; and Fried, *Rise and Fall of Jewish Gangster*, pp. 225–26.

31. "Strikes and Stoppages, Men's Clothing Industry, 1931–35," H-ACWA Papers.

32. "ACWA Diaries," February 14, 1927, and January 30, 1930, and "Report to Honorable Howard W. Jackson on Working Conditions in the Garment Industry," submitted by Jacob H. Hollander, October 24, 1932, all H-ACWA Papers.

33. "Report of the Hearing by Dr. Jacob H. Hollander of Strikers from the Schoenman Shops in Connection with an Investigation of Conditions in the Clothing Industry," Baltimore, Maryland, October 13, 1932, H-ACWA Papers.

34. Hillman to Felix Frankfurter, January 16, 1933, Box 125, and Ben Cohen to Frankfurter, February 7, 1933, "Minimum Wage Law" file, Box 153, Frankfurter Papers, Library of Congress.

TEN: *In the Antechamber of Power*

1. Leo Wolman, "Economic and Social Planning in the Clothing Industry," report for the Bureau of Personnel Administration, January 7, 1932, H-ACWA Papers; Sidney Hillman, "Labor Leads Toward Planning," *Survey Graphic*, March 1932; and Sidney

Hillman, "The Shorter Working Day and a Minimum Wage," *Harvard Business Review,* July 1933.

2. Sidney Hillman, "Labor in the United States," December 9, 1928; Hillman, "Labor Leads Toward Planning"; Hillman, "Shorter Working Day"; and Hillman speech at dinner for Senator Robert Wagner at the New York Conference for Unemployment Legislation, April 8, 1931, H-ACWA Papers.

3. *Advance,* August 27, 1927; *Doc. Hist. 1930–34; New York Times,* October 17, 1926; *Daily News Record,* March 27, 1928; and Hillman, "Labor Leads Toward Planning."

4. Hillman, "Shorter Working Day"; Felix Frankfurter memo to Frances Perkins, Donald Richberg, and Robert Wagner, May 30, 1933, Box 159, Frankfurter Papers; Robert S. McElvaine, *The Great Depression: America, 1929–41* (New York, 1984), p. 92; Rexford G. Tugwell, *The Brains Trust* (New York, 1968), p. 20; and "Industrial Employment Code," tentative draft for discussion only, Box 283, William Jett Lauck Papers (#4742), Manuscript Division, Special Collections Department, University of Virginia Library.

5. McElvaine, *Great Depression,* pp. 37–38, and John Frey comments on "A Progress Report of the Commission on the Relationship of Consumption, Production and Distribution" to the American Engineering Council, February 5, 1932, Box 14, John Frey Papers, Library of Congress.

6. "Historical Anthology of Documents," H-ACWA Papers; William J. Barber, *From New Era to New Deal: Herbert Hoover, the Economists and American Economic Policy, 1921–33* (New York, 1985), p. 57; R. Alan Lawson, *The Failure of Independent Liberalism, 1930–41* (New York, 1971), p. 63; Kenneth S. Davis, *FDR: The New Deal Years, 1933–37* (New York, 1986), p. 119; and Hearings before the Senate Committee on Finance, 72d Cong., 2d Sess., 1933, extract in H-ACWA Papers.

7. Patrick D. Regan, "The Architects of American National Planning," Ph.D. dissertation, Ohio State University, 1982, esp. pp. 211–12, 215, 253; Edward Filene to Edgar Rich, February 10, 1928, "Unemployment" file, Edward A. Filene Papers, Credit Union National Association, Madison, Wisconsin; hearings on Senate Bill 6215 before Subcommittee of the Committee on Manufactures, U.S. Senate, 72d Cong., 1st Sess., p. 240, 1932; and Frey comments on "Progress Report."

8. Regan, "Architects of American Planning," p. 304; William W. Bremer, *Depression Winters: New York Social Workers and the New Deal* (Philadelphia, 1985), pp. 41–43, 53; Bonnie Fox Schwartz, *The Civil Works Administration, 1933–34: The Business of Emergency Employment in the New Deal* (Princeton, N.J., 1984), pp. 54–57; and Lucy Mason to Felix Frankfurter, December 7, 1932, Box 153, Frankfurter Papers.

9. Peter Friedlander, "Origins of the Welfare State," unpublished manuscript, contains critical ideas and information regarding the coalescing Keynesian milieu upon which much of the analysis of this chapter rests.

10. Philip H. Burch, *Elites in American History: The New Deal to the Carter Administration* (New York, 1980), pp. 18, 22–23, 27, 30, 31, 32, 33, 38; Michael Bernstein, "Long Term Economic Growth and the Problem of Recovery in American Manufacturing: A Study of the Great Depression in the United States, 1929–39," Ph.D. dissertation, Yale University, 1982; and Friedlander, "Origins of Welfare State."

11. Bremer, *Depression Winters,* p. 43; GEB "Minutes," September 20–22, 1928; Herbert Lehman "Reminiscences," pp. 488–89, 63–65, OHCCU; GEB "Minutes," September 1929; Hillman memo to Henry Bruere, n.d., H-ACWA Papers; and A. J. Muste to J. B. S. Hardman, December 17, 1931, "Conference for Progressive Labor Action," Box 38, J. B. S. Hardman Papers, Tamiment Library.

12. Lehman "Reminiscences," pp. 63–66, and Edward Filene Memo, January 17, 1929, Edward A. Filene Papers.

13. Lehman "Reminiscences"; George McJimsey, *Harry Hopkins: Ally of the Poor and Defender of Democracy* (Cambridge, Mass., 1987), p. 45; and Regan, "Architects of American Planning," p. 215.

14. Charles F. Roos, *NRA: Economic Planning* (New York, 1971), citing "Memorandum to a New Cabinet Member," December 1932, and memo to General Johnson, April 10, 1933, by Alexander Sachs; Frances Perkins "Reminiscences," p. 214, OHCCU.

15. Edwin T. Layton, *The Revolt of the Engineers: Social Responsibility and the American Engineering Profession* (Cleveland, 1971), pp. 156–57, 154; Jean Christie, "Morris Llewellyn Cooke: Progressive Engineer," Ph.D. dissertation, Columbia University, 1963; Harlow Person, "Scientific Management: An Analysis with Particular Emphasis on its Attitude Toward Human Relations in Industry," *Bulletin of the Taylor Society*, vol. 13, October 1928; and Morris Cooke to Robert Bruere, July 12, 1928, file 14, Box 2, and Cooke to Boyd Fisher, April 13, 1922, file 65, Box 8, Morris Cooke Papers, Library of Congress.

16. Friedlander, "Origins of Welfare State."

17. Morris Cooke, "Notes of Discussion at Conference Dinner of the Directors of the Taylor Society and Guests," April 28, 1927, file 8, Box 61, and "Some Observations on Workers Organizations," Presidential Address, 15th Annual Meeting of the Taylor Society, December 6, 1928, folder A, Box 62, Cooke Papers.

18. Christie, "Morris Llewellyn Cooke," pp. 124–25.

19. Friedlander, "Origins of Welfare State," and Philippa Strum, *Louis D. Brandeis: Justice for the People* (Cambridge, Mass., 1984), pp. 55, 58, 160–63, 166–67, 173–74, 178–82, 376, 383, 390–92.

20. Elliot A. Rosen, *Hoover, Roosevelt and the Brains Trust: From Depression to New Deal* (New York, 1977); Adolph A. Berle and Gardiner Means, *The Modern Corporation and Private Property* (New York, 1932); and Donald A. Ritchie, *James M. Landis: Dean of the Regulators* (Cambridge, Mass., 1980), pp. 21, 44, 54.

21. Ritchie, *James M. Landis*, p. 45; Jerome Frank to Tom Corcoran, September 26, 1933, Max Lowenthal to Corcoran, April 4, 1934, and July 12, 1935, and Lowenthal to "Tom" and "Ben" (Cohen), July 12, 1937, all in Box 204, Thomas Corcoran Papers, Library of Congress.

22. Frankfurter to Bruce Bliven, December 4, 1930, Frankfurter Papers.

23. Sidney Hillman statement at hearings of Senate Subcommittee on Manufactures, January 8, 1932, extract in H-ACWA Papers; Hillman to Morris Hilquit, December 31, 1931, and Paul Kellogg *et al.* to Hillman, January 31, 1931, both H-ACWA Papers; John Dewey telegram to Hillman, March 17, 1932, and Paul Kellogg to Hillman, December 1, 1932, both H-ACWA Papers; Irving Bernstein, *The Lean Years: A History of the American Worker, 1920–33* (Boston, 1972), p. 491; John Andrews to Hillman, September 19, 1930, H-ACWA Papers; Alfred B. Rollins, *Roosevelt and Howe* (New York, 1962), p. 300; Hillman testimony on Mastick–Steingut Unemployment Reserve Fund Bill, March 18, 1931, extract in H-ACWA Papers; Henry Bruere to Morris Cooke, May 9, 1930, Box 97, Cooke Papers; George Martin, *Madame Secretary: Frances Perkins* (Boston, 1976), pp. 215–16; Leo Wolman to William Leiserson, October 24, 1931, Box 1, William Leiserson Papers, Wisconsin State Historical Society, Madison; Matthew Josephson, *Sidney Hillman: Statesman of American Labor* (New York, 1952), ch. 15; Benjamin Cohen to Felix Frankfurter, February 7, 1933, and other letters, Container

11, "Minimum Wage Bills, 1923–33," Benjamin Cohen Papers, Library of Congress; and Sidney Hillman, "How to Meet the Problems Arising out of Unemployment," *Quarterly Bulletin of the New York State Conference on Social Work*, vol. 2, January 1931.

24. Josephson, *Sidney Hillman*, ch. 15; Hillman, "How to Meet Problems"; Hillman, "A Successful Experiment in Unemployment Insurance," American Academy of Political and Social Science, December 7, 1930, speech, H-ACWA Papers; J. Joseph Hutmacher, *Senator Robert F. Wagner and the Rise of Urban Liberalism* (New York, 1968), pp. 61–63, 67–69, 71–73; and Felix Frankfurter to Hillman, October 17, 1932, H-ACWA Papers.

25. Hillman testimony before Subcommittee of the Senate Committee on Manufactures, 72d Cong., 1st Sess., 1932, extract in H-ACWA Papers.

26. Jacob Potofsky, "Notes," H-ACWA Papers.

27. Bernstein, *Lean Years*; Milton Derber, "Growth and Expansion," in Milton Derber and Edwin Young, eds., *Labor and the New Deal* (Madison, 1957), p. 3; and J. B. S. Hardman, ed., *American Labor Dynamics* (New York, 1968), pp. 224–25.

28. Adolph Germer to James O'Neal, April 15, 1931, Adolph Germer Papers, Wisconsin State Historical Society, Madison.

29. Ruth L. Horowitz, *Political Ideologies of Organized Labor: The New Deal Era* (New Brunswick, N.J., 1978), pp. 83–87.

30. Author's interview with Teccia Davidson Brill, April 29, 1986.

31. *The Nation*, December 26, 1928; John Dewey *et al.* to Hillman, September 27, and Hillman to Dewey, September 30, 1932, H-ACWA Papers; "Minutes of Conference," League for Independent Political Action, September 2–3, 1933, "United Conference for Progressive Political Action, 1933" file, Box 38, J. B. S. Hardman Papers, Tamiment Library; Karel Denis Bicha, "Liberalism Frustrated: The League for Independent Political Action, 1928–33," *Mid-America*, vol. 48, no. 1, 1966; and Lawson, *Failure of Independent Liberalism* (note 6 above), p. 42.

32. Eugene Tobin, *Organize or Perish: America's Independent Progressives, 1913–33* (Westport, Conn., 1986), pp. 212–14.

33. Donald R. McCoy, *Angry Voices: Left of Center Politics in the New Deal Era* (New York, 1958), p. 30, and Hugh T. Lovin, "The Persistence of Third Party Dreams in the American Labor Movement, 1930–38," *Mid-America*, vol. 58, October 1976.

34. "Proceedings of a Conference of Progressives," March 11 and 12, 1931, Washington, D.C., H-ACWA Papers; Tobin, *Organize or Perish*, p. 214; and John Dewey to Senators Norris, La Follette, Cutting, Wheeler, and Costigan, April 8, 1931, Box 431A, Robert La Follette, Jr., Papers, Library of Congress.

35. Mark Leff, *The Limits of Symbolic Reform: The New Deal and Taxation, 1933–39* (New York, 1984), p. 109.

36. Patrick J. Maney, *"Young Bob" La Follette: A Biography of Robert M. La Follette, Jr., 1895–1953* (Columbia, Mo., 1978), pp. 85–87; "Proceedings of a Conference of Progressives"; *New York Times*, March 13, 1931; *Doc. Hist. 1930–34*; and Delbert D. Arnold, "The CIO's Role in American Politics, 1936–48," Ph.D. dissertation, University of Maryland, 1952, p. 8.

37. Robert La Follette to Leo Wolman, April 17, to Hillman, April 15, to Stuart Chase, April 15, and to George Soule, April 17, all 1931 and all in Box 431A, La Follette Papers, and "Proceedings of a Conference of Progressives."

38. Charles Ervin "Reminiscences," September 26, 1940, H-ACWA Papers; George Soule, *Sidney Hillman: Labor Statesman* (New York, 1939), pp. 158–62; Lewis Lan-

sky, "Isidor Lubin: The Ideas and Career of a New Deal Labor Economist," Ph.D. dissertation, Case Western Reserve, 1976, pp. 88–95; La Follette to Wolman, April 17, to Stuart Chase, April 15, to George Soule, April 17, and to Hillman, April 16, 1931; and Catherine Williams to La Follette, November 23, 1951, and La Follette to Williams, December 12, 1951, both H-ACWA Papers.

39. William H. Wilson, "How the Chamber of Commerce Viewed the NRA: A Re-Examination," *Mid-America*, April 1962, and Hillman testimony at hearings of Senate Subcommittee on Manufactures, 72d Cong., 1st Sess., October 22 through December 19, 1931, to establish a National Economic Council, extracts in H-ACWA Papers.

40. Wilson, "How Chamber of Commerce Viewed NRA"; Gerard Swope "Reminis-cences," pp. 20–22, OHCCU; J. George Frederick, ed. *The Swope Plan: Details, Criticisms, Analysis* (New York, 1931), pp. 21–25, 80–81; and Jacob Billikopf to Mrs. Gerard Swope, December 8, 1930, H-ACWA Papers.

41. Frederick, *The Swope Plan*, pp. 67–68, and Gabriel Kolko, *Main Currents in Modern American History* (New York, 1976), pp. 111–16, 119.

42. Barber, *From New Era to New Deal* (note 6 above), p. 123; Kolko, *Main Currents*, p. 119; Hillman transcript of radio talk, March 22, 1932, H-ACWA Papers; and Hillman testimony before Senate Subcommittee of Committee on Manufactures.

43. Louis Galambos, *Competition and Cooperation: The Emergence of a National Trade Association* (Baltimore, 1966), pp. 178–79, 190–95, 198; Robert F. Himmelberg, *The Origins of the NRA: Business, Government and the Trade Association Issue, 1921–22* (New York, 1976), pp. 63, 76, 83, 162; Hillman testimony at hearings on Federal Unemployment Relief, Senate Subcommittee of the Committee on Manufactures, 72d Cong., January 8, 1932, extract in H-ACWA Papers; Ellis Hawley, *The Great War and the Search for a Modern Order: A History of the American People and Their Institutions, 1917–33* (New York, 1979), pp. 95–96, 100–101, 103; and Adolph Berle, *Navigating the Rapids, 1918–1971*, ed. Beatrice Bishop Berle and Travis Beal Jacobs (New York, 1973), pp. 51–52.

44. Steve Fraser, "From the 'New Unionism' to the New Deal," *Labor History*, Summer 1984.

45. *Doc. Hist. 1930–34*; Josephson, *Sidney Hillman* (note 24 above), ch. 15; Jacob Potofsky "Reminiscences," pp. 208–11, 230–34, OHCCU; Hillman to Frances Per-kins, memo, December 21, 1932, Frances Perkins Special Manuscript Collection, Part I: Letters to Frances Perkins, OHCCU; Hillman to Felix Frankfurter, December 20, 1932, Box 125, Frankfurter Papers; Frankfurter to Hillman, January 5, 1933, H-ACWA Papers.

46. *Doc. Hist. 1930–34*; *Advance*, April 1, 1933; Frances Perkins "Reminiscences," vol. 4, pp. 302–21; GEB "Minutes," June 1933; Larry Gerber, "The Limits of Liberalism: A Study of the Careers and Ideological Development of Josephus Daniels, Henry Stimson, Bernard Baruch, Donald Richberg, and Felix Frankfurter," Ph.D. disser-tation, University of California, Berkeley, 1979, pp. 374–79; Himmelberg, *Origins of the NRA*, p. 192; Sidney Hillman, "A Proposal for Labor Boards as an essential in the Emergency," draft, March 31, 1933, H-ACWA Papers; Frankfurter to Perkins, April 15, 1933, H-ACWA Papers; and Frankfurter to FDR, April 14, 1933, cited in *Roosevelt and Frankfurter: Their Correspondence, 1928–45*, annotated by Max Freed-man (Boston, 1967).

47. Kenneth S. Davis, *FDR: The New Deal Years, 1933–37* (New York, 1986), p. 98; Raymond Moley, *The First New Deal* (New York, 1966), p. 287; Hillman, "Shorter

Working Day" (note 1 above); and Charles F. Roos, *NRA: Economic Planning,* citing Sachs, "Memorandum to General Johnson," April 27, 1933.

48. Lansky, "Isidor Lubin," pp. 156–57; Frances Perkins, *The Roosevelt I Knew* (New York, 1946), pp. 198–99; Jett Lauck memo, "Stabilization," to Philip Murray, John Lewis, Whitney, *et al.,* August 29, 1932, Box 283, William Jett Lauck Papers; Frances Perkins "Reminiscences," pp. 302–21, OHCCU; Freedman, *Roosevelt and Frankfurter,* p. 289; Arthur Meier Schlesinger, Jr., *The Coming of the New Deal* (Boston, 1957–60), pp. 96–98; Thomas E. Vadney, *The Wayward Liberal: A Political Biography of Donald Richberg* (Lexington, Ky., 1970), pp. 114–17; and Paul Mazur memo to FDR, May 19, 1932, cited in Rosen, *Hoover, Roosevelt, and the Brains Trust* (note 20 above). All this may exaggerate the degree of unanimity among those attracted by the broad contours of Keynesian and state capitalist remedies. Although the often publicized differences between "planners" and "antitrusters" has not only been inflated but more seriously missed the point, still real disputes over the extent and purposes of state intervention did exist and affected Hillman. Thus, Hillman's legal confidant, Max Lowenthal, was an original Brains Truster, but only briefly and only at Frankfurter's urging. Berle cultivated an abiding suspicion of the Harvard jurist as a free market fellow-traveler, whose argument for "a managed currency along the lines of Maynard Keynes" was a typically covert Frankfurter maneuver on behalf of archaic small business. Berle thus distrusted Lowenthal, speculating that his real motive was to foster inflation, "reflecting the views of the Amalgamated Clothing Workers or some similar group," or else he had been in touch with "some of the Jewish financiers, possibly Eugene Meyer of the Federal Reserve Board." Lowenthal, in Berle's eyes, was a "typical liberal on the make" with good intentions but no loyalty to anyone except to "Felix Frankfurter and the particular little group that revolves around him." Berle, *Navigating the Rapids,* pp. 51–53.

49. Jordan A. Schwartz, *The Speculator: Bernard M. Baruch in Washington, 1917–65* (Chapel Hill, N.C., 1981), pp. 241, 266, 288, 292–93; Albert U. Romasco, *The Politics of Recovery: Roosevelt's New Deal* (New York, 1983); Moley, *First New Deal,* p. 286; Himmelberg, *Origins of the NRA,* p. 112; and Lewis L. Lorwin, *Labor Relations Boards: The Regulation of Collective Bargaining Under the NIRA* (Washington, D.C., 1935), pp. 33–34.

50. Frankfurter to Perkins, Wagner, and Richberg, May 30, 1933, Box 159, Frankfurter Papers, and Jett Lauck, "Memo to Roosevelt," July 8, Box 283, and Lauck to Roosevelt, May 2, 1933, Box 285, Lauck Papers.

51. Sachs memorandum to New Cabinet Member, December 1932, and to General Johnson, April 10, 1933, cited in Roos, *NRA* (note 14 above).

52. Hillman, "Shorter Working Day."

ELEVEN: *"Washington Merry-Go-Round" or "National Runaround"*

1. *Fortune,* October 1933, and Donald Brand, *Corporatism and the Rule of Law: A Study of the National Recovery Administration* (Ithaca, N.Y., 1988).

2. Transcript of Sidney Hillman radio talk, "The Industrial Recovery Act and Labor's Change," WEVD, June 9, 1933, H-ACWA Papers; Solomon Barkin, "NRA Policies, Standards, and Code Provisions on Basic Weekly Hours of Work," Office of the National Recovery Administration, Division of Review, Box 7054, NRA Collection, National Archives; Raymond S. Rubinow, "Section 7a: Its History, Interpretation and Administration," Box 7055, NRA Collection; George Soule, *Sidney*

Hillman: *Labor Statesman* (New York, 1939), pp. 162–64; and GEB "Minutes," June 5, 1933. See also, for differences between Hillman and the AFL leadership over the power of labor in the recovery administration, "History of the Industrial Advisory Board," Record Group 9, Series 37, NRA Records, Miscellaneous Reports and Documents Section, Box 8336, NRA Collection.

3. Transcript of Hillman radio talk "Industrial Recovery Act"; GEB "Minutes," June 5, 1933; Jacob Potofsky, "Notes—Discussing the Wagner Bill," H-ACWA Papers.

4. "Bread and Roses: The Story of the Rise of the Shirtworkers, 1933–34," ACWA Pamphlet in collection of Delia Gottlieb, and Jacob Potofsky "Reminiscences," p. 216, OHCCU. Rieve was disgusted with the passivity of the AFL and approached Hillman with the idea of bringing the hosiery workers into the ACWA; Hillman was sympathetic to the proposal if a larger amalgamation of needle trade unions—an old dream that died hard—could be arranged. The hosiery workers of Philadelphia under Rieve were a particularly militant group within an otherwise feeble UTW. The Philadelphians had for some years engaged in independent politics along with other textile locals in the Northeast. Rieve worked closely with the ACW organizer Leo Krzycki, who was also a national officer of the SP and ran for local office on an independent–SP ticket. Rieve and Hillman attended the abortive Continental Congress together. GEB "Minutes," June 5, 1933; David Pivar, "The Hosiery Workers and the Philadelphia Third Party Impulse, 1929–35," *Labor History*, Winter 1964; and Hugh T. Lovin, "The Persistence of Third Party Dreams in the American Labor Movement, 1930–38," *Mid-America*, vol. 58, October 1976.

5. "Bread and Roses."

6. *Doc. Hist.* 1934–36; Jacquelyn Dowd Hall, Robert Korstad, and James LeLoudis, "Cotton Mill People: Work, Community and Protest in the Textile South, 1880–1940," *American Historical Review*, April 1986; James A. Gross, *The Making of the National Labor Relations Board: A Study in Economics, Politics and Law*, vol. 1: *1933–37*, (Albany, N.Y., 1974), p. 15; Sanford Jacoby, *Employing Bureaucracy: Managers, Unions and the Transformation of Work in American Industry, 1900–45*, (New York, 1985), ch. 9.

7. Leo Wolman "Reminiscences," p. 26; Isidor Lubin "Reminiscences," p. 76; and Frances Perkins "Reminiscences," pp. 327–28, all OHCCU.

8. *Doc. Hist.* 1930–34; William Green to National Labor Board, August 18, 1933, Labor Advisory Board Files, Box 8180, NRA Collection; and Hillman to Green, October 15, 1933, File 1A, Box 341, David Dubinsky Collection, ILGWU Archives.

9. Rubinow, "Section 7a"; Hillman address at proceedings of Cotton Textile Code hearing, June 28, 1933, extract in H-ACWA Papers; Louis Galambos, *Competition and Cooperation: The Emergence of a National Trade Association* (Baltimore, 1966); *New York Times*, June 29, 1933; and Barkin, "NRA Policies, Standards, and Code Provisions."

10. "Work Materials, NRA, Part C, Section 3," Office of the NRA, Division of Review, Box 7054, NRA Collection. The "Reemployment Agreement" was in part intended to offset the low precedent set by the textile code. It called for no less than $15 a week in cities of more than 500,000; no less than $14.50 in cities with populations between 250,000 and 500,000; no less than 40 cents an hour unless a code specifying less was adopted prior to July 15; and never less than 30 cents an hour. The goal of this "blanket code" was a thirty-five-hour week and a 40-cent minimum. Frances Perkins "Reminiscences," p. 214.

11. Wolman "Reminiscences," pp. 23, 172–73; Records of Labor Advisory Board meetings on August 8, 1933, sent to Leo Wolman by Leon Keyserling, Labor Advisory Board files, Box 8183, NRA Collection; Kim McQuaid, "The Frustration of Corporate Revival during the Early New Deal," *The Historian*, August 1979; "Minutes of the Joint Meeting of the Industrial Advisory Board and the Labor Advisory Board," August 3, 1933, Box 8415, Records Group 9, NRA Collection; and William Leiserson to Leo Wolman, September 8, 1933, Box 8182, NRA Collection.

12. Rubinow, "Section 7a"; National Labor Board stenographic report of hearing, St. Louis Clothing Strike, October 20, 1933, Box 7112, NRA Collection; and Frances M. Curlee to Robert Wagner, October 17, 1933, Box 8182, NRA Collection.

13. David O'Brien, "American Catholics and Organized Labor in the 1930's," *Catholic Historical Review*, October 1966, and Thomas E. Blantz, *A Priest in Public Service: Francis J. Haas and the New Deal* (Notre Dame, Ind., 1982), pp. 56, 61, 62, 73, 76.

14. Ordway Tead and Harry C. Metcalf, *Labor Relations Under the Recovery Act* (New York, 1933).

15. Irving Bernstein, *A Caring Society: The New Deal, the Worker, and the Great Depression* (Boston, 1985), pp. 93–106; and Felix Frankfurter to Donald Richberg, July 7, 1933, Box 159, Felix Frankfurter Papers.

16. Jacoby, *Employing Bureaucracy*, ch. 9.

17. Lubin "Reminiscences," pp. 20–21, and B. Bisno "Notes," September 18, 1950, H-ACWA Papers.

18. Gustav Peck memo, n.d., "Hartwell L. Brunson file," Box 8193, NRA Collection; Solomon Barkin to staff, April 30, 1934, "Brunson file"; Peck memo, July 14, 1934, "Brunson file"; "Petition and Brief of Labor Advisory Board for Reduction in Hours Without Decrease in Earnings on the 10/10 Principle," n.d., "Brunson file," Box 8193; and "Personal Files of Solomon Barkin," Box 8191, all in NRA Collection; and Leverett S. Lyon et al., *The NRA: An Analysis and Appraisal* (Washington, D.C., 1935), pp. 120–23.

19. "Meeting of Labor Advisory Board," August 31, 1933, and unpublished manuscript on the history of the LAB, ch. 6 and 10–12, both in National Recovery Administration, Labor Advisory Board, Reel 3083, Rose Schneiderman Papers, Tamiment Library.

20. John Frey to Labor Advisory Board, December 30, 1933, Reel 3083, Schneiderman Papers.

21. H. Weiss Report on Cotton Garment Code Compliance Machinery, September 15, 1934, Labor Advisory Board Files, Box 8182, NRA Collection; Jacob Potofsky to Burton Oppenheimer, September 26, 1934, H-ACWA Papers; H. Weiss to L. C. Marshall, August 27, 1934, H-ACWA Papers; and Gerald Markowitz and David Rosner, eds., *Slaves of the Depression: Workers' Letters About Life on the Job* (Ithaca, N.Y., 1987), pp. 172–73.

22. Potofsky to Oppenheimer, September 26, 1934, and Bessemer District Smelters' Council to Hugh Johnson, Robert Wagner, William Green, Hugo Black, George Huddleston, and George Googe, April 7, 1944, Box 423C, Robert La Follette, Jr., Papers, Library of Congress.

23. Lyon et al., *The NRA*, p. 443.

24. "History of the Industrial Advisory Board," volume 2, Box 8336, "Policies of the Industrial Advisory Board," Record Group 9, NRA Collection; Rubinow, "Section 7a" (note 2 above); "Labor's Role in the Administration of the Act," staff studies,

Division of Industrial Economics, Box 8126, NRA collection; Barkin, "NRA Policies, Standards, and Code Provisions" (note 2 above); William Lawson, "Policy on Wages Above the Minimum Under the NRA," Work Materials File, Box 7054, NRA Collection; and National Industrial Recovery Board "Minutes," March 25, 1935, Box 8448, NRA Collection.

25. Murray Edelman, "New Deal Sensitivity to Labor Interests," in Milton Derber and Edwin Young, eds., *Labor and the New Deal* (Madison, Wisc., 1957), and numerous letters to Hillman at the Labor Advisory Board, for example, from Thomas O'Brien of the Teamsters, Chauffeurs, Stablemen, and Helpers of America, December 7, 1934; from William Green, January 8, 1935; from L. W. Beman, October 15, 1934; from David Kurtz, December 8, 1934; from E. E. Little, April 6, 1935; from R. M. Neustadt, April 22, 1935; and from William Goldman, June 4, 1935, all in H-ACWA Papers.

26. Author's interview with Teccia Davidson Brill, April 29, 1986.

27. Hartwell L. Brunson File, Box 8193, NRA Collection; *Doc. Hist. 1930–34;* and "Men's Clothing Code Authority," H-ACWA Papers.

28. David Dubinsky to Hillman, March 25, 1935, H-ACWA Papers; Robert H. Connery, *The Administration of an NRA Code: A Case Study of the Men's Clothing Industry* (Chicago, 1938), pp. 11, 25; "Hearings on Code of Fair Practices and Competition: Men's Ready to Wear Clothing Industry," July 26–27, 1933, "Transcript of Hearings" File, Box 7112, NRA Collection; Barkin, "NRA Policies, Standards, and Code Provisions"; and "Miscellaneous Reports and Documents—NIRA/NIRB" file, Box 8448, NRA Collection.

29. Howard Meyers, "Labor's Experience Under Codes," H-ACWA Papers, and Bernstein, *Caring Society* (note 15 above), pp. 118–20.

30. "Hearing on Modification of the Code of Fair Competition in Men's Clothing," January 3, 1934, Box 7112, NRA Collection; Connery, *Administration of an NRA Code,* p. 54; "Homework and Other Problems" file, H-ACWA Papers; Morris Greenberg to Mark Cresap, May 8, 1935, H-ACWA Papers; and *The Nation,* August 15, 1934.

31. Lindsay Rodgers, memo of conversation with Mark Cresap, October 14, 1933, Hart, Schaffner & Marx papers, Treasurer's Office, and "Notes on meetings of Code Authority," November 8 and December 8, 1933, H-ACWA Papers.

32. M. D. C. Crawford to Hillman, May 9, 1935, and Crawford to R. Donald White, October 16, 1934, H-ACWA Papers. Hillman's criticism of the forty-hour provision was not only that it would hardly help reabsorb the unemployed but that in many of the codes that copied it the provision itself was mutilated by clauses permitting the averaging of hours over months or years; clauses that excluded large classes of workers; clauses with excessively generous tolerances for seasonal peaks; and so on.

33. James A. Hodges, *New Deal Labor Policy and the Southern Cotton Textile Industry, 1933–41* (Knoxville, 1986), p. 78, and "National Industrial Recovery Board Minutes and Agenda, September 1934–May 1935," October 1934, H-ACWA Papers.

34. Edelman, "New Deal Sensitivity to Labor Interests"; Hillman statement on President's executive order, August 22, 1934, H-ACWA Papers; Leon C. Marshall, notes of meeting, December 5, 1934, William W. Bardsley File, Series no. 7, Record Group 9, NRA Collection; and *Baltimore Sun,* January 23, 1935.

35. Hall *et al.,* "Cotton Mill People" (note 6 above); F. Ray Marshall, *Labor in the South* (Cambridge, Mass., 1967), pp. 167–68; *Doc. Hist. 1934–36;* Jacob Potofsky to Dorothy Bellanca, September 18, 1934, H-ACWA Papers; Frances Perkins "Reminiscences," 6: 1–20, OHCCU; and Rubinow, "Section 7a" (note 2 above).

36. Gross, *Making of the NLRB* (note 6 above), pp. 115–16. Hillman's confession came after Richberg emerged triumphant in a test of strength with the NLRB when he persuaded the President to side with the newspaper publishers against the Newspaper Guild.

37. Kim McQuaid, "Corporate Liberalism in the American Business Community, 1920–40," *Business History Review,* Autumn 1978; Robert M. Collins, "Positive Business Responses to the New Deal: The Roots of the Committee for Economic Development, 1933–42," *Business History Review,* Autumn 1978; and "Industrial Advisory Board Minutes of Dinner Meetings," October 12, 1934, IAB Minutes of Regular Meetings file, Box 8416, NRA collection.

38. R. M. Neustadt speech to Philadelphia Chamber of Commerce, March 11, 1935, and Paul H. Nystrom, "Dangerous Trends Under the NRA," March 12, 1935, both H-ACWA Papers; Brand, *Corporatism and the Rule of Law* (note 1 above); Ralph Flanders talk to Industrial Advisory Board, "An End to Unemployment," June 17, 1934, Box 231C, Robert M. La Follette, Jr., papers, Library of Congress; Ralph Flanders, "Social Effects of the Control of Hours and Wages," in "History of the Industrial Advisory Board," vol. 2, Box 8336, NRA Collection; "Report of Edward A. Filene's Cross-Country Study Tour, Jan.–Feb., 1934," Filene Papers; Joint meeting of the Business Advisory Council and Industrial Advisory Board, January 17, 1935, IAB Minutes File, Box 8416, NRA Collection; and Edward A. Filene, "Why We Must Have Codes," May 1935, Chamber of Commerce file, Filene Papers. Exemplary of the way the NRA disintegrated through the centrifugal forces of the market: In New England code authority chairmen lost confidence as shoe manufacturers violated wage codes because chain store distributors of cheap shoes reduced prices by buying from factories in Maine and New Hampshire that ignored the codes. Thus manufacturers in Lynn and Haverhill who once supported the codes couldn't afford to. Meanwhile, consumers gradually lost interest and paid no attention to NRA labels. All this unfolded amid growing pessimism about business generally, growing relief needs, stock market uncertainties, and a falling bond market. Memo to Edward Filene, September 5, 1934, Filene Papers.

39. Kenneth S. Davis, *FDR: The New Deal Years, 1933–37* (New York, 1986), pp. 314–16; Ronald A. Mulder, *The Insurgent Progressives in the U.S. Senate and the New Deal, 1933–39* (New York, 1979), pp. 78, 93–95; Records of the National Recovery Review Board ("Darrow Board"); and Sy Berman to Clarence Darrow, n.d., Box 1, NRA Collection.

40. *New York Times,* May 24, 1934.

41. Michael E. Parrish, *Felix Frankfurter and His Times: The Reform Years* (New York, 1982), pp. 220–21; Arthur M. Schlesinger, Jr., *The Politics of Upheaval* (Boston, 1960), p. 390; John Kennedy Ohl, *Hugh S. Johnson and the New Deal* (Dekalb, Ill., 1985), pp. 266–67, 280–81; Bernard Baruch to Marvin MacIntyre, June 18, 1934, NRA Folder, Box 158, President's Secretary File, FDR Papers; Donald Richberg to Marvin MacIntyre, August 16, 1934, Container 45, Donald Richberg Papers, Library of Congress.

42. Richberg to the President, September 14, 1934, Container 46, Richberg Papers; Richberg to MacIntyre, September 15, 1934, Container 46, Richberg Papers.

43. *New York Times,* September 28, 1934, and Hart, Schaffner & Marx "Scrapbook," Treasurer's Office, Company headquarters, Chicago. Hillman's vacated position on the LAB was assumed by Hyman Blumberg.

44. Robert Sobel, *The Age of Giant Corporations: A Microeconomic History of American Business* (Westport, Conn., 1972), pp. 107–8, and *New York Times*, September 28, 1934.
45. Hillman to Kirstein, September 29, 1934, File A12, Louis E. Kirstein Papers, Baker Library, Harvard University, and Drew Pearson and Robert S. Allen, "The Daily Washington Merry-Go-Round," December 12, 1934, H-ACWA Papers.
46. "NIRB Minutes and Agenda," October 5 and 19, 1934, H-ACWA Papers; "Minutes-NIRB," October 15, 19, and 23, 1934, Box 8448, NRA collection; Leon C. Marshall, "Office File of William W. Bardsley," Box 20, November 27, 1934, and early November, NRA Collection; and Barkin, "NRA Policies, Standards, and Code Provisions" (note 2 above).
47. *Buffalo Sun*, October 7, 1934; Hillman statement at hearings on Tobacco Code, October 8, 1934, H-ACWA Papers; "Statement of Board Members' Attitudes re Cigarette Code as Expressed at Meeting of Board," January 7, 1935, "Cigarette Code" folder, Records of the NIRB, Box 11, NRA Collection; Markowitz and Rosner, *Slaves of Depression* (note 21 above), p. 167.
48. "Memo," January 15, 1935, on cigarette code, Box 11, NRA Collection, and "NIRB Minutes," December 20, 1934, H-ACWA Papers.
49. Potofsky "Note," March 22, 1935, H-ACWA Papers.
50. Meyers, "Labor's Experience Under Codes"; *Doc. Hist. 1934–36*; "History of the Labor Advisory Board," unpublished manuscript in Schneiderman Papers; and "Labor Advisory Board recommendation to NIRB," Release no. 9287, December 17, 1934, LAB folder, "Official Policies and Suggestions by Labor Advisers," Box 8183, NRA Collection.
51. Donald Richberg to Marvin MacIntyre, March 19, 1935, Container 2, Richberg Papers; *The Nation*, April 13, 1935; and *New York World-Telegram*, April 4, 1935.
52. "Hearings on the National Recovery Administration" held before the Senate Committee on Finance, March 7–April 18, 1935, Volumes 10 and 11, pp. 756–73, 774–863, Washington D.C.
53. *New York Times*, May 22, 1935, and "Hearings on the National Recovery Administration."
54. Sidney Hillman, "The NRA, Labor, and Recovery," *Annals of the American Academy of Political and Social Science*, March 1934.
55. *Doc. Hist. 1930–34*; *Faribault Minneapolis News*, June 22, 1934; Hillman statement before the Pennsylvania State Federation of Labor, May 15, 1935, H-ACWA Papers; Hillman speech in New Haven, February 3, 1934, extract in H-ACWA Papers; Hillman testimony before the Senate Committee on Education and Labor, March–April 1934, extract in H-ACWA Papers.
56. Hillman speech in Faneuil Hall, May 27, 1935, extract in H-ACWA Papers; *Doc. Hist. 1934–36*; and "Address by Sidney Hillman," Madison Square Garden, May 23, 1935, H-ACWA Papers.
57. "President Hillman Speaks," address to local 4, March 29, 1935, appearing in *Advance*, April 1935.
58. Interview with Brill (note 26 above); Jacob Potofsky "Memoir," H-ACWA Papers; George McAneny to Hillman, April 24, 1934, H-ACWA Papers; and B. Bisno "Notes," May 1950, H-ACWA Papers.
59. Sidney Hillman, BBC radio address, "The Quest for Security," November 18, 1934, H-ACWA Papers, and Sidney Hillman, "Employer–Employee Relationships," draft of a speech to the Wisconsin Bar Association, December 7, 1934, H-ACWA Papers.

60. Adolph Berle, *Navigating the Rapids, 1918–1971*, ed. Beatrice Bishop Berle and Travis Beal Jacobs (New York, 1973), pp. 99–100.
61. Gross, *Making of the NLRB* (note 6 above), pp. 143–45.

TWELVE: *"We Are Going Ahead on Our Own"*

1. Sidney Hillman talk to the New York Joint Board, June 3, 1935, H-ACWA Papers.
2. "Bureau of Homework Inspection, Annual Report for 1936," Box 715, and Folder 58, Box 718, and Folder 26, Box 325, Robert F. Wagner Papers, Special Collections Division, Georgetown University Library.
3. Mark Cresap to Hillman, August 8, 1935; Hillman to Byres H. Gitchell, July 13, 1935; and Hillman to Percy Strauss, October 15, 1936, all in H-ACWA Papers. Louis Kirstein to National Retail Dry Goods Association, March 24, 1937, File A16, Case 7, and Kirstein to Fred Lazarus, January 13, 1937, both Louis Kirstein Papers, Baker Library, Harvard University; and *Doc. Hist. 1934–36*.
4. Delbert D. Arnold, "The CIO's Role in American Politics, 1936–48," Ph.D. dissertation, University of Maryland, 1952, p. 22; General File, Box 324, Folder 22, Robert F. Wagner Papers; *New York Times*, May 31 and October 21, 1935; "Resolution #204 on New NRA Legislation," introduced at the AFL 55th Biennial Convention, 1935, copy in H-ACWA Papers; and radio interview with Hillman at 1935 AFL convention in Atlantic City, extract in H-ACWA Papers.
5. *New York Times*, June 28, 1935; Mordecai Eziekel to Hillman and Hillman to Eziekel, both September 26, 1935, H-ACWA Papers; Arthur M. Schlesinger, Jr., *The Politics of Upheaval* (Boston, 1960), pp. 287–88; Eziekel to Hillman, October 22, and Hillman to Eziekel, October 31, 1935; and M. S. Rosenthal to Hillman, April 27, 1936.
6. The activities by the Filenes on behalf of the New Deal were numerous and varied and can be followed in detail by consulting the Edward A. Filene Papers at the Credit Union National Association in Madision, Wisconsin. Of particular interest are the files marked "Newton Baker," "Price Maintenance," "Massachusetts State Recovery Board," "Labor and Industry," "Recovery," "National Politics," "American Academy of Political and Social Science," "Report of E.A.F.'s Cross Country Study Tour," and "Chamber of Commerce." Lincoln Filene to Robert La Follette, Jr., December 16, 1935, Box 12C, Robert La Follette, Jr., Papers; *New York Times*, May 1, 1935; Albert U. Ramasco, *The Politics of Recovery: Roosevelt's New Deal* (New York, 1983), pp. 207–12; Adolph Berle, *Navigating the Rapids, 1918–1971*, ed. Beatrice Bishop Berle and Travis Beal Jacobs (New York, 1973), pp. 154–57; Robert M. Collins, "Positive Business Responses to the New Deal: The Roots of the Committee for Economic Development, 1933–42," *Business History Review*, Autumn 1978; "Will the Demands of Organized Labor Promote Recovery?"—a joint discussion by Sidney Hillman and James A. Emery, June 16, 1935, *America's Town Meeting of the Air*, NBC Radio, pamphlet of transcript in H-ACWA Papers; and "Is the American Worker's High Standard of Living a Myth?" CBS radio debate, April 16, 1935, extract in H-ACWA Papers.
7. Schlesinger, *Politics of Upheaval*, p. 419.
8. George Berry to Hillman, October 9, 1935, H-ACWA Papers; "Minutes of the Committee on National Industrial Policy," February 10–11, 1936; Seymour Dreschler, memo, April 28 and December 10–11, 1936; Berry to Hillman, December 8, 1935, and July 30, October 26, and November 6, 1936, all in H-ACWA Papers;

Washington Post, November 10, 1936; "Policy Statement," February 11, 1936, H-ACWA Papers; Dan Tracey to Hillman, February 14, 1936; W. L. Schurz to Hillman, February 14, 1936; and Raymond Reiss to Hillman, March 23, 1936, all in H-ACWA Papers. George Berry to Hillman, January 18, 1937, H-ACWA Papers.

9. *Doc. Hist. 1934–36*, and Cornelia Bryce Pinchot to Hillman, June 19, 1935.

10. Kristi Andersen, *The Creation of a Democratic Majority, 1928–36* (Chicago, 1979); Richard Keller, "Pennsylvania's 'Little New Deal,' " in John Braeman, Robert H. Bremner, and David Brody, eds., *The New Deal*, vol. 2: *State and Local Levels* (Columbus, Ohio, 1975); and Charles Garrett, *The LaGuardia Years: Machine and Reform Politics in New York City* (New Brunswick, N.J., 1961), p. 110.

11. Frances Perkins quoted in "He Fights for Labor," a Labor Non-Partisan League pamphlet, H-ACWA Papers.

12. Kenneth Casebeer, "Holder of the Pen: An Interview with Leon Keyserling on Drafting the Wagner Act," *University of Miami Law Review*, November 1987, Wagner quote on p. 294. Lubin, a Veblen student and a friend of Leo Wolman in the 1920s, was employed by La Follette's Education and Labor Committee in 1928 for its investigation of unemployment and was credited with its recommendations for countercyclical public works, a national unemployment service, and unemployment insurance. It was then that he became an adviser to Wagner. Later he became a friend of Hillman and a persistent critic of the NRA's labor codes. See Lewis Lansky, "Isidor Lubin: The Ideas and Career of a New Deal Labor Economist," Ph.D. dissertation, Case Western Reserve University, 1976, pp. 27–28, 73–74, 77–78, 80, 88–89; Christopher L. Tomlins, *The State and the Unions: Labor Relations, Law, and the Organized Labor Movement in America, 1880–1960* (New York, 1985), p. 119; Stanley H. Vittoz, "The American Industrial Economy and the Political Origins of Federal Labor Policy Between the World Wars," Ph.D. dissertation, York University, 1979, pp. 332–33; and Daniel Albert Sipe, "A Moment of State: The Enactment of the National Labor Relations Act, 1935," Ph.D. dissertation, University of Pennsylvania, 1981, pp. 160–61.

13. Newton Baker to Edward Filene, December 26, 1933; Filene to Baker, January 2, 1934; Baker to Evans Clark, April 26, 1935; and Filene to Baker, May 29, 1935, all Edward Filene Papers. Filene testimony before Committee on National Industrial Policy, December 9, 1935, H-ACWA Papers; Edward Filene, "What Price Prosperity?" address to annual convention of Wholesale Dry Goods Institute, January 16, 1936, H-ACWA Papers; and Folder 36, Box 717, Robert F. Wagner Papers. Cooke, who had been active in the public power movement since his days as Philadelphia's director of public works before the war, perceived both the REA and the Holding Company Act of 1935 as weapons against the great private utility interests often linked to financial circles run by Morgan; Kuhn, Loeb; Paine Webber, and others. He was joined in this view by Hillman's onetime legal adviser, Max Lowenthal, who worked as counsel to the Pecora Committee in its investigation of the stock exchange, and by Ben Cohen and Tom Corcoran, who helped fashion the act. The object was to break the stranglehold of the utility czars and their bankers by attacking monopoly rates, unsupported bond issues, absentee management, and the financial draining of operating companies. For Cooke, Carmody, and the Frankfurter lawyers, there was no better example of the deleterious effect of the securities bloc than its milking of public utilities. Breaking its grip would open up the infrastructural development of the country—that is, would promote broad economic development through the cheap diffusion of electric power and in particular would encourage the

mass market through the subsidized consumption of appliances, kitchens, bathrooms, and so on through the Federal Housing Agency and the Electric Home and Farm Authority. "Felix Frankfurter, 1932–33" file, Box 198, Thomas G. Corcoran Papers, Library of Congress; Philippa Strum, *Louis D. Brandeis: Justice for the People* (Cambridge, Mass., 1984), pp. 390–92; Jean Christie, "Morris Llewellyn Cooke: Progressive Engineer," Ph.D. dissertation, Columbia University, 1963, pp. 209–19; Donald A. Ritchie, *James M. Landis: Dean of the Regulators* (Cambridge, Mass., 1980), pp. 25, 44, 52–53, 54, 68; Bonnie Fox Schwartz, *The Civil Works Administration, 1933–34: The Business of Emergency Employment in the New Deal* (Princeton, N.J., 1984), pp. viii–ix, 54–57; "Brookwood Labor College" File, Box 6, J. B. S. Hardman Papers, Tamiment Library; and James A. Gross, *The Making of the NLRB: A Study in Economics, Politics and Law*, vol. 1: *1933–37* (Albany, N.Y., 1974), pp. 174–75, 177.

14. "Jett Lauck Memo to Mr. Lewis: Suggested Program for 1934–35," Box 40, and "National Policy Committee," Box 42, William Jett Lauck Papers, 4742, Manuscript Division, Special Collections Department, University of Virginia Library. Early in 1935 Lauck established a "National Policy Committee" to promote a program of government planning, industrial development, and political realignment. The Committee consisted of some familiar faces—Eziekel, Richard Feiss (Hillman's old friendly foe from Cleveland), Alexander Sachs, Ralph Flanders, and George Soule—as well as Alvin Hansen, Herbert Agar of the *Louisville Courier-Journal*, and various Taylorites and savings banks executives. Hillman participated in some of the Committee's deliberations. All agreed on the Keynesian fiscal principles but members were divided over the degree of necessary government intervention into pricing, product, and investment decisions. Correspondence between Morris Cooke and A. J. Muste and others in Folder 3, Box 25, and Clinton Golden to Cooke, December 9, 1929, and Golden to Hillman, April 24, 1920, Box 102, Morris Cooke Papers, FDR Library, Hyde Park, New York.

15. Irving Bernstein, *A Caring Society: The New Deal, the Worker, and the Great Depression* (Boston, 1985), pp. 102–3; Vittoz, "American Industrial Economy," pp. 351–70; and David Brody, "The Emergence of Mass Production Unionism," in David Brody, *Workers in Industrial America: Essays on the 20th Century Struggle* (New York, 1980).

16. L. A. Sherman to Hillman, April 25, 1935, H-ACWA Papers.

17. Frances Perkins "Reminiscences," pp. 432–37, OHCCU. For Perkins, Hillman and not Lewis was the real motive force responsible for the eventual split in the labor movement. Lewis functioned, in her eyes, as a kind of native American front man, so to speak. Her view betrays a certain rather widespread reading of Hillman's distinctively Semitic stealth and is woefully inadequate as an interpretation of Lewis's role, but it also contains an element of truth insofar as it was Hillman's connections and beliefs, going back over two decades, that most closely tied the CIO to the broader strategic purposes of the Keynesian elite.

18. Ruth McKenney, *Industrial Valley* (New York, 1937). Rose Pesotta, in *Bread Upon the Waters* (Ithaca, N.Y., 1987 reprint), recalls confronting the racist attitudes of transplanted Southern Appalachians, who hated Jews as much as blacks.

19. Brody, "Emergence of Mass Production Unionism," and John Frey to Hillman, July 5, and Hillman to Frey, July 1935, H-ACWA Papers.

20. Sidney Lens, *Left, Right, and Center: Conflicting Forces in American Labor* (Hinsdale, Ill., 1949), p. 316, and Hillman speech at AFL Convention, 1935, in "Anthology of Historical Documents—Part IV," H-ACWA Papers.

21. Tomlins, *State and the Unions*, p. 142; Melvyn Dubofsky and Warren Van Tine, *John L. Lewis: A Biography* (New York, 1977), p. 239; and Brody, "Emergence of Mass Industrial Unionism."

22. Morris Cooke and Philip Murray, *Organized Labor and Production: Next Steps in Industrial Democracy* (New York, 1940). David Gartman, *Auto Slavery: The Labor Process in the American Automobile Industry, 1897–1950* (New Brunswick, N.J., 1986), p. 173, notes that within the auto industry both craftsmen and laborers lost ground to the new class of semiskilled assemblers, machine tool and press operators, and "machine-minders."

23. Nelson Lichtenstein, *Labor's War at Home: The CIO in World War II* (New York, 1982); Ronald Schatz, *The Electrical Workers: A History of Labor at GE and West-inghouse, 1923–60* (Urbana, Ill., 1983), esp. p. 89; Peter Friedlander, *The Emergence of a UAW Local: A Study of Class and Culture* (Pittsburgh, 1975); Joshua B. Freeman, *In Transit: The Transport Workers Union in New York City, 1933–66* (New York, 1989); and Gartman, *Auto Slavery*, are all illuminating on this set of issues. See also Mel Piehl, *Breaking Bread: The Catholic Worker and the Origins of Catholic Radicalism in America* (Philadelphia, 1982), p. 61, and Ronald Edsforth, *Class Conflict and Cultural Consensus: The Making of a Mass Consumer Society in Flint, Michigan* (New Brunswick, N.J., 1987).

24. Robert A. Slayton, *Back of the Yards: The Making of a Local Democracy* (Chicago, 1986); Barbara Newell, *Chicago and the Labor Movement* (Urbana, Ill., 1961), pp. 115, 130, 150–51, 167–68, 180–81; and Edsforth, *Class Conflict*.

25. David Brody, "Labor and the Great Depression: Interpretive Prospects," *Labor History*, Spring 1972, and Josef J. Barton, *Peasants and Strangers: Italians, Rumanians and Slovaks in an American City, 1890–1950* (Cambridge, Mass., 1975). Most Italian and Slavic peasant immigrants hailed from areas of marginal small-scale, not latifundist, agriculture, where the sense of property rights remained strong. Ewa Morawska, *For Bread with Butter: Life-Worlds of East Central Europeans in Johnstown, Pennsylvania, 1890–1940* (New York, 1985).

26. Schatz, *Electrical Workers*, and Morawska, *For Bread with Butter*, p. 276. Skilled positions in the steel industry, including rollers, blacksmiths, and carpenters, were monopolized by Americans and West Europeans, whose racism helped block access to these jobs for East European immigrants and their offspring.

27. Silvano Tomasi, *Piety and Power: The Role of Italian Parishes in the New York Metropolitan Area, 1880–1930* (New York, 1975); Nicholas J. Russo, "Three Generations of Italians in New York City: Their Religious Acculturation," in Silvano M. Tomasi and Madeline H. Engel, eds., *The Italian Experience in the United States* (New York, 1970); Slayton, *Back of the Yards*, p. 62; quotation from Morawska, *For Bread with Butter*, p. 274; Lisbeth Cohen, "Learning to Live in the Welfare State," Ph.D dissertation, University of California, Berkeley, 1986; Humbert S. Nelli, *From Immigrants to Ethnics: The Italian-Americans* (New York, 1983); Barton, *Peasants and Strangers*; and Edsforth, *Class Conflict*.

28. Pressman cited in David Milton, *The Politics of U.S. Labor: From the Great Depression to the New Deal* (New York, 1982).

29. Irving Bernstein, *The Turbulent Years: A History of the American Worker, 1933–41* (Boston, 1971), p. 400; "CIO Minutes—1935–36," August 10, 1936, H-ACWA Papers; Hyman Schneid to Hillman, December 3, 1935, H-ACWA Papers; "Minutes" of CIO Meetings, December 9, 1935, April 14, August 2, and November 7–8, 1936, and March 9, 1937, kept by Katherine Pollock Ellickson, Ellickson Papers,

FDR Library, Hyde Park, N.Y.; letters between Hillman and Lewis in November and early December 1935 and Lewis to Hillman, December 21, 1935, H-ACWA Papers; and *New York Times,* August 7, 1936.

30. Adolph Germer "Diaries," December 1 and 4, 1935, Box 24, Adolph Germer Papers, Wisconsin State Historical Society, Madison; Hillman to Howard, February 7, 1936, cited in Walter Galenson, *The CIO Challenge to the AFL: A History of the American Labor Movement, 1935–41* (Cambridge, Mass., 1960), p. 9; CIO "Minutes," August 10, 1936, H-ACWA Papers; Ellickson "Minutes," November 7–8, 1936; and Edwin Young, "The Split in the Labor Movement," in Milton Derber and Edwin Young, eds., *Labor and the New Deal* (Madison, Wisc., 1957).

31. McKenney, *Industrial Valley* (note 18 above); John Brophy to Hillman, March 5, 1936, H-ACWA Papers; and Ellickson "Minutes," April 14, 1936.

32. Hillman is cited in Harvey A. Levenstein, *Communism, Anti-Communism and the CIO* (Westport, Conn., 1981), from Len De Caux, *Labor Radical: From the Wobblies to CIO—A Personal History* (Boston, 1970), p. 235.

33. Jacob Potofsky to Hillman, June 5, 1936; Hyman Schneid to Hillman, December 3, 1935; Clinton Golden to Joseph Schlossberg, August 17, 1936; Golden to Potofsky, September 25, 1936; and Potofsky "Notes," March 3, 1937, all in H-ACWA Papers.

34. George G. Kirstein, *Stores and Unions: A Study of the Growth of Unionism in Dry Goods and Department Stores* (New York, 1950); "Browder/Pressman Interview," Box 8, Daniel Bell Collection, Tamiment Library; and Louis Kirstein to Hillman, March 26, 1937, File A18, Louis Kirstein Papers, Baker Library, Harvard University. Soon after the creation of the DWSOC, however, Hillman became gravely ill, and the DWSOC withered away.

35. Sidney Lens, *The Crisis of American Labor,* (New York, 1959).

36. Julius Emspak "Reminiscences," pp. 138–40, OHCCU, and Ellinore Morehouse Herrick to Hillman, December 19, 1936, H-ACWA Papers.

37. R. J. Thomas "Reminiscences," p. 37, OHCCU; Homer Martin to Hillman, February 10, 1936, H-ACWA Papers; "Community Services" file, H-ACWA Papers; and Hillman to Germer, December 15, 1936, Box 3, Germer Papers.

38. Perkins "Reminiscences," pp. 148, 190–92, 197, 237–38, 241–44, and vol. 6, OHCCU; Perkins to FDR, February 5, 1937, "Labor Department," Box 77, President's Secretary's File, FDR Papers; and Lee Pressman "Reminiscences," pp. 90–92, OHCCU.

39. Frank Bowen to Robert Wagner and the NLRB, March 25, 1937, folder 53, Box 718, Wagner Papers, and "notes on telephone conversation" between Kirstein and Hillman, February 4, 1937, "Sidney Hillman (sweatshops)," A16 File, Kirstein Papers.

THIRTEEN: *"All Saw Ghosts"*

1. James A. Gross, *The Reshaping of the National Labor Relations Board: National Policy in Transition, 1937–47* (Albany, N.Y., 1981), pp. 11, 12, 13, 18–20, 177–79; James A. Gross, *The Making of the National Labor Relations Board: A Study in Economics, Politics and Law* (Albany, N.Y., 1974), pp. 200, 219–20; and "Memorandum on Conference with Secretary Perkins," October 11, 1937, "Secretary of Labor" file, Box 63, Father Francis Haas Papers, Catholic University.

2. Gross, *Reshaping of NLRB,* pp. 11, 18–20, and quoting John Frey, p. 247.

3. *Ibid.,* pp. 186–88. Justice Hughes, writing for the majority, credited the ACW as the

most important factor in bringing peace to the industry. Folder 53, Box 718, Robert F. Wagner Papers, Special Collections Division, Georgetown University Library.

4. Elinore Herrick to Hillman, December 19, and February 26, 1936, both in H-ACWA Papers. Clinton Golden was another case of the all-purpose cadre in transit. Field director of Brookwood Labor College and ACW organizer in Philadelphia in the 1920s, he went on to work for the Amalgamated in New England. Hillman recommended Golden to Gifford Pinchot during the mine strikes of 1933, and he became the Governor's labor adviser for the next eighteen months. In 1935 he was appointed regional director of the first NLRB in the Pittsburgh area. Hillman helped him get that job and, when the first NLRB died, another job with the new NLRB. Subsequently Golden moved to the SWOC, where he became a key organizer-strategist and a collaborator with Morris Cooke in introducing ACW-style industrial democracy and scientific management production reforms into the commercially hard-pressed specialty steel mills of the Midwest. The intimate collaboration between Board and CIO could easily turn into an insidious dependency, as Pressman himself eventually realized. By the middle of 1938 he was warning: "The number of cases filed with the Board has increased in recent months to the point where the wisdom of resorting to the Act is often questionable because of the length of time which is required for decisions. Unless excellent judgement is exercised in this connection, there is danger that organizing work may be seriously impeded by placing too much reliance upon the Board. All officers and organizers must understand that primary reliance must not be placed upon the Board for organizing work, and that the Board is to be used as an auxiliary weapon only." Clinton Golden to Potofsky, June 1, 1935; Jacob Billikopf to Potofsky, March 11, 1935; and Potofsky to Francis Biddle, March 12, 1935, all in H-ACWA Papers; *Saturday Evening Post*, February 19, 1944; Christopher L. Tomlins, *The State and the Unions: Labor Relations, Law, and the Organized Labor Movement in America, 1880–1960* (New York, 1985) p. 188.

5. Gross, *Making of NLRB*, pp. 115, 149–50, 155, 200, 218–20; Gross, *Reshaping*, pp. 18–20, 177–79; Gardner Jackson "Reminiscences," OHCCU, and author's interview with John Abt, July 10, 1979.

6. Patrick J. Maney, *"Young Bob" La Follette: A Biography of Robert M. La Follette, Jr., 1895–1953* (Columbia, Mo., 1978), pp. 172–73, 176, and Jerold S. Auerbach, *Labor and Liberty: The La Follette Committee and the New Deal* (Indianapolis, 1966).

7. R. Alan Lawson, *The Failure of Independent Liberalism, 1930–41* (New York, 1971), p. 72; Bruce Allen Murphy, *The Brandeis–Frankfurter Connection: The Secret Political Activities of Two Supreme Court Justices* (New York, 1982), pp. 154–56; and Frances Perkins, *The Roosevelt I Knew* (New York, 1946), p. 186.

8. Lawson, *Failure of Independent Liberalism*, p. 220, and Donald R. McCoy, *Angry Voices: Left-of-Center Politics in the New Deal Era* (New York, 1958), pp. 39–40, 43–44, 50–54, 56.

9. McCoy, *Angry Voices*, pp. 62, 66–67, 76–77, 80, 81, 83–84, 91, and Hugh T. Lovin, "The Fall of Farmer Labor Parties," *Pacific Northwest Quarterly*, January 1971.

10. Hugh T. Lovin, "The Persistence of Third Party Dreams in the American Labor Movement, 1930–38," *Mid-America*, vol. 58, October 1976; Joseph Schlossberg to Frank Rosenblum, August 26, 1936, and Schlossberg to Charles Weinstein, August 27, 1936, H-ACWA Papers; Delbert D. Arnold, "The CIO's Role in American Politics, 1936–48," Ph.D. dissertation, University of Maryland, 1952, pp. 23–24; and Bruce Bliven to Hillman, March 16, 1936, H-ACWA Papers.

11. Maney, *"Young Bob" La Follette*, p. 190.
12. Elliott Roosevelt, ed., *FDR: His Personal Letters*, (New York, 1970 reprint), 1:492, citing FDR to Edward House, February 16, 1935.
13. McCoy, *Angry Voices*, pp. 82, 108–11; and Thomas R. Amlie to Hillman, May 20, 1936, Alfred M. Bingham to Hillman, 1936, and Floyd Olson to Hillman, May 25, 1936, all in H-ACWA Papers.
14. Lovin, "Fall of Farmer Labor Parties."
15. John Earl Haynes, *Dubious Alliance: The Making of the Minnesota Democratic Farmer Labor Party* (Minneapolis, 1984), pp. 9, 15, 24; Lawson, *Failure of Independent Liberalism*, p. 220; Lovin, "Fall of Farmer Labor Parties," and "Persistence of Third Party Dreams."
16. Jacob Potofsky "Reminiscences," p. 277, OHCCU, and Matthew Josephson, *Sidney Hillman: Statesman of American Labor* (New York, 1952), p. 400.
17. Sidney Hillman speech at GEB Meeting, Atlantic City, April 19, 1936, H-ACWA Papers; Charles Ervin, "Notes," September 26, 1940, H-ACWA Papers; and *New York Times*, May 29, 1933.
18. Joseph Schlossberg, "Reviews and Perspectives," in *The Workers and Their World: Selected Essays by Joseph Schlossberg* (New York: American Labor Party, 1935).
19. *Doc. Hist. 1916–18*, and Gerd Korman, "Ethnic Democracy and Its Ambiguities: The Case of the Needle Trade Unions," *American Jewish History*, 75 (Ithaca, N.Y.: Industrial Labor Relations reprint, 1986): 422–23.
20. Schlossberg, "Reviews and Perspectives"; *Doc. Hist. 1934–36*; and Eric Davin and Staughton Lynd, "Picket Line and Ballot Box: Local Labor Parties in the 1930s," unpublished manuscript, 1979.
21. *ACWA Convention Proceedings 1936*, and Walter Galenson, *The CIO Challenge to the AFL: A History of the American Labor Movement, 1935–41* (Cambridge, Mass., 1960), p. 293.
22. People's Committee of the Farmer–Labor party to Schlossberg, July 3, 1936; New York Committee in Support of a Farmer–Labor Party and Trade Union Committee for a Labor Party, July 7, 1936; Illinois Labor Party Conference to Schlossberg, July 27, 1936; and Schlossberg to James O'Neal, August 19, 1936, all in H-ACWA Papers. Leo Krzycki to Hillman, May 22, 1936, H-ACWA Papers.
23. Hillman quoted in Galenson, *CIO Challenge*, p. 293.
24. Kenneth Waltzer, "The American Labor Party: Third Party Politics in New Deal–Cold War New York, 1936–54," Ph.D. dissertation, Harvard University, 1977, p. 72.
25. Melech Epstein, *Jewish Labor in the U.S.A.: vol. 2, 1914–52* (New York, 1969), p. 229; Herbert Lehman "Reminiscences," 8:15–16, and Special Project I, pp. 7–9, OHCCU; Frances Perkins "Reminiscences," 2:224–25, OHCCU; Box 70 of the Eleanor Roosevelt manuscript cited in Waltzer, "American Labor Party"; Warren Moscow, *Politics in the Empire State* (New York, 1948), pp. 104–5; James Farley "Reminiscences," p. 15, OHCCU; Ed Flynn "Reminiscences," pp. 20–21, OHCCU; and FDR to Colonel House, February 2, 1935, in E. Roosevelt, *FDR: His Personal Letters* (note 12 above). It should also be noted, however, that Berle, who functioned as a liaison between the Mayor and the new labor party, denied that La Guardia was actually involved at the outset. Kenneth Waltzer transcript of interview with Adolph Berle, November 12, 1968, in author's possession.
26. Waltzer, "American Labor Party," pp. 140–41; Louis Waldman to Hillman, August 19, 1936, H-ACWA Papers; Waltzer transcript of interview with Jacob Potofsky,

November 13, 1968, in author's possession; and "Material for Chapter 1—American Labor Party—of Memoir of Elinore M. Herrick," Folder 153, Box 10, Elinore M. Herrick Papers, Schlesinger Library, Radcliffe. Warren Madden of the NLRB gladly gave her leave from the Board to assume the post. Herrick to J. Warren Madden, July 30, 1936, Folder 49, Box 3, Herrick Papers; "Rough Draft of Memoir—Chapter 1," Folder 154, Box 10, Herrick Papers; and Herrick to Hillman, September 13, 1936, H-ACWA Papers.

27. "Labor's Non-Partisan League: Its Origins and Growth," pamphlet, p. 5, H-ACWA Papers, and Sidney Hillman, "Forward with American Labor," *Forward*, October 1936.

28. George Berry to Hillman and Dubinsky, September 12, 1936, H-ACWA Papers; Flynn "Reminiscences," pp. 20–21, and Farley "Reminiscences," p. 15; Dan Tobin memo to the President, February 18, 1936, President's Personal File (PPF) 3189, FDR Papers; and Lovin, "Persistence of Third Party Dreams" (note 10 above).

29. *New York Herald-Tribune*, August 14, 1936; Adolph Berle, *Navigating the Rapids, 1918–1971*, ed. Beatrice Bishop Berle and Travis Beal Jacobs (New York, 1973), pp. 115, 111; and Eleanor Roosevelt to FDR, July 16, 1936, cited in Waltzer, "American Labor Party," p. 73, f. 1.

30. Raymond Moley, *The First New Deal* (New York, 1966), p. 373; Charles J. Tull, *Father Coughlin and the New Deal* (Syracuse, N.Y., 1965), pp. 66–67, 91; and Alan Brinkley, *Voices of Protest: Huey Long, Father Coughlin, and the Great Depression* (New York, 1982).

31. Tull, *Father Coughlin*, pp. 151–52, and *New York Times*, October 9, 1936.

32. Ruth L. Horowitz, *Political Ideologies of Organized Labor: The New Deal Era* (New Brunswick, N.J., 1978), p. 211; Berry to Hillman, September 11, 1936, H-ACWA Papers; Berry to the President, June 22, 1936, PPF 3627; and Berry to Stephen Early, September 9, 1936, President's Official File (OFF) 2251, FDR Papers.

33. "Kn-La" file, Series 123A, Box 1, Labor's Non-Partisan League papers, Catholic University; Gardner Jackson "Reminiscences," OHCCU; Galenson, *CIO Challenge* (note 21 above), p. 294; and Arnold, "CIO's Role in American Politics" (note 10 above), p. 41.

34. "He Fights for Labor," LNPL Pamphlet, H-ACWA Papers; Arnold, "CIO's Role in American Politics," p. 34; McCoy, *Angry Voices* (note 8 above), p. 155; Sidney Lens, *Left, Right, and Center: Conflicting Forces in American Labor* (Hinsdale, Ill., 1949), pp. 316–17; and "Campaign Plan and Memorandum," August 11, 1936, H-ACWA Papers.

35. Mark Leff, *The Limits of Symbolic Reform: The New Deal and Taxation, 1933–39* (New York, 1984), pp. 160–64; *Economist* cited in Kenneth S. Davis, *FDR: The New Deal Years, 1933–37* (New York, 1986), p. 650; "Declaration of Principles" by Labor's Non-Partisan League of New York State, 1936, H-ACWA Papers; and Robert P. Ingalls, *Herbert H. Lehman and New York's Little New Deal* (New York, 1975), pp. 134–38.

36. Draft of Hillman speech and radio address on WEVD, September 30, 1936; ACWA telegram to FDR, May 29, 1936; Jouett Shouse to Hillman, May 26, 1936; and Hillman to Shouse, June 22, 1936, all in H-ACWA Papers. Hillman had the goods, because Charles Ervin had previously prepared for LNPL use sketches of the history, social composition, and activities of the Liberty League, the NAM, the USCC, and several right-wing sects, including the Sentinels, the Crusaders, the Southern Committee to Uphold the Constitution, the Farmers' Independent Council, and others.

37. William E. Leuchtenberg, *Franklin D. Roosevelt and the New Deal* (New York, 1963); Elinore Herrick to Charles Poletti, April 7, 1937, Folder 49, Box 3, Herrick Papers; Lehman "Reminiscences," p. 454; and *New York Sun*, April 4, 1936.

38. Directors of Council on Foreign Relations to Hillman, November 23, 1936; Raymond Buell to Hillman, April 1, 1937, all in H-ACWA Papers; Perkins "Reminiscences," 7:509–11.

39. Berry to FDR, November 11, 1936, PPF 3585, FDR Papers. Lee Pressman to Hillman, January 13, 1937; Pressman to SWOC, December 4, 1936; Frances Perkins to Hillman, October 28, 1936; Perkins to Hillman, November 27, 1936; and Merle D. Vincent to Hillman, November 16, 1936, all in H-ACWA Papers; *New York Times*, December 30, 1936.

40. Hillman to Philoine, October 18, November 9, and December 1936, all in H-ACWA Papers.

FOURTEEN: *Southern Exposure*

1. "Minutes" of CIO Meetings, March 9, 1937, kept by Katherine Pollock Ellickson, 1935–37, Ellickson Papers, FDR Library.

2. ACWA Press Release, February 14, 1937, H-ACWA Papers. By the fall of 1939 membership in the national trade union movement approached 7 million, an increase of nearly 4 million over 1935. Christopher L. Tomlins, *The State and the Unions: Labor Relations, Law, and the Organized Labor Movement in America, 1880–1960* (New York, 1985), p. 148.

3. *New York Times*, December 29, 1936, January 27, April 1, and May 22, 1937; and Jacob Potofsky "Notes—Wages and Hours," August 17, 1937, H-ACWA Papers.

4. Lee Pressman to Hillman, January 13, 1937; Berry to Hillman and John L. Lewis, March 15, 1937; and Berry to Hillman and David Dubinsky, September 12, 1936, all in H-ACWA Papers.

5. Max Lowenthal to Thomas Corcoran, April 4, 1934, July 12, 1935; Lowenthal to Ben Cohen and Tom Corcoran, July 12, 1937, Box 204, Thomas Corcoran Papers, Library of Congress, and Felix Frankfurter, 1932–33 file, Box 198, Corcoran Papers; David Stern to "Izzie," June 2, 1937, Box 212, Corcoran Papers; John Morton Blum, *From the Morgenthau Diaries: Years of Crisis, 1928–38* (Boston, 1965), 1: 321; Dean L. May, *From New Deal to New Economics: The Liberal Response to the Recession* (New York, 1981), pp. 83–84; and James A. Gross, *The Reshaping of the National Labor Relations Board: National Policy in Transition, 1937–47* (Albany, N.Y., 1981), pp. 18–20.

6. Jacob Potofsky, "Notes—Supreme Court," February 8, 1937, H-ACWA Papers; Charles Ervin, analysis of electoral results, November 8, 1936, H-ACWA Papers; and James A. Hodges, *New Deal Labor Policy and the Southern Cotton Textile Industry, 1933–41* (Knoxville, 1986), p. 143; Hillman second draft of speech on Supreme Court, March 5, 1937, H-ACWA Papers; Hillman to ACWA members, February 20, 1937; Berry to Hillman, March 25, 1937; "Packing the Court or Petting the Sweatshop," leaflet—all in H-ACWA Papers; "Supreme Court Calendar," Folder 14, Box 17, Adolph Germer Papers, Wisconsin State Historical Society, Madison, and Proceedings of Labor's Non-Partisan League Second Convention, March 8, 1937, Box 9, LNPL Papers, Wisconsin State Historical Society, Madison.

7. Delbert D. Arnold, "The CIO's Role in American Politics, 1936–48," Ph.D. dissertation, University of Maryland, 1952, p. 41; Hugh T. Lovin, "The Persistence of

Third Party Dreams in the American Labor Movement, 1930–38," *Mid-America*, vol. 58, October 1976; and LNPL *National Bulletin*, August 15, September 2, and October 1, 1937, H-ACWA Papers.

8. Kenneth Waltzer, "The American Labor Party: Third Party Politics in New Deal-Cold War New York, 1936–1954," Ph.D. dissertation, Harvard University, 1977, pp. 104, 117; Charles Garrett, *The LaGuardia Years: Machine and Reform Politics in New York City* (New Brunswick, N.J., 1961), pp. 265–66; Adolph Berle to Hillman, September 20, 1937, H-ACWA Papers; and Donald R. McCoy, *Angry Voices: Left-of-Center Politics in the New Deal Era* (New York, 1958), p. 160.

9. LNPL *National Bulletin*, September 2, 1937, H-ACWA Papers; and *New York Times*, September 15, 1937.

10. Mordecai Eziekel to Hillman, February 10, 1938, H-ACWA Papers; Eziekel to Jett Lauck, May 3, 1938, Box 35, William Jett Lauck Papers, University of Virginia; and Jean Christie, "Morris Llewelyn Cooke: Progressive Engineer," Ph.D. dissertation, Columbia University, 1963, pp. 213–19. Tom Corcoran thought the FLSA would shatter the monopoly on Southern Democratic politics held by older corporate interests—the railroads and public utilities especially.

11. Jacquelyn Dowd Hall, James Leloudis, Robert Korstad, Mary Murphy, LuAnn Jones, and Christopher B. Daly, *Like a Family: The Making of a Southern Cotton Mill World* (Chapel Hill, N.C., 1987), pp. 188–92; and Jacquelyn Dowd Hall, Robert Korstad, and James Leloudis, "Cotton Mill People: Work, Community, and Protest in the Textile South, 1880–1940," *American Historical Review*, April 1986.

12. Hodges, *New Deal Labor Policy*, p. 6, and Hall et al., *Like a Family*, pp. 296–300, 325–26, 354. Between August 1933 and August 1934, the Bruere Board received 3,920 complaints but authorized only ninety-six investigations and resolved only one wage and hour dispute in the workers' favor. It found no evidence of "stretchout" or of firings from union activity and ignored the National Labor Board's majority rule principle.

13. Francis Gorman to Len De Caux, October 25, 1937, H-ACWA Papers; UTW Executive Council "Minutes," September 13, 1935, June 18, March 13, and September 11, 1936, December 6 and October 10, 1935, and November 11, 1936, Box 674, Textile Workers Union of America Papers, Wisconsin State Historical Society, Madison; and UTW Executive Council "Minutes," January 29–30, 1937, and November 13, 1936, Box 647, TWUA Papers.

14. UTW Executive Council "Minutes," March 7, 1937, and Irving Bernstein, *The Turbulent Years: A History of the American Worker, 1933–41* (Boston, 1971), p. 617.

15. Hodges, *New Deal Labor Policy*, p. 148.

16. Hall et al., *Like a Family*.

17. Hodges, *New Deal Labor Policy*, pp. 12, 26, 29–30, 38–41.

18. Liston Pope, *Millhands and Preachers* (New Haven, 1942), and Philip J. Wood, *Southern Capitalism: The Political Economy of North Carolina, 1880–1980* (Durham, N.C., 1986), p. 122.

19. Wood, *Southern Capitalism*, pp. 67–71.

20. Hodges, *New Deal Labor Policy*, pp. 12, 16, 19. Nonetheless, outside participation was not unheard of. There was, for example, the case of the Cannon Mills, once a family company, the result of the consolidation of many mills into a modern, integrated facility employing 15,000, and listed on the NYSE. Berkshire Fine Spinning Associates, originally closely held, was merged in 1929 and subordinated to outside control. Similarly, surgical supply companies in the North—Johnson & Johnson and

Henry Kendall's firm—began buying up "captive mills" in the South and introduced an alien element into the Southern business culture, one decidedly more friendly to the New Deal. The postwar textile depression led many New England firms to rush south, fleeing the higher wage rates of the North (40 percent higher on average) and legislative regulation of hours. Between 1923 and 1935, 40 percent of New England factories closed and 100,000 workers lost their jobs, while the Piedmont's share of textile workers rose from 46 to 68 percent as the center of the industry migrated below the Mason–Dixon line. In other sectors of the industry, rayon particularly, foreign interests also established a presence: The Viscose Company was 95 percent owned by the British Courtaulds Ltd., and American Enka was Dutch. Here too, rents appeared in the fabric of regional antiunionism. Moreover, the very presence of synthetics represented a competitive threat to manufacturers of natural fibers; thus the silk trade shuddered when American Viscose started producing rayon in Virginia. "Textile Industries in the First Half of 1935—Part I: The Cotton Textile Industry," May 22, 1936, Box 215, Jett Lauck Papers; and "NRA Proceedings," Box 129, Dubinsky Collection, ILGWU Archives.

21. "Bulletin IV—The Textile Industry: Size and Organization," Textile Workers Organizing Committee, n.d., H-ACWA Papers.
22. "Report of the National Economic and Social Planning Association on the Textile Industry in the U.S.A.," May–June, 1937, Box 215, Lauck Papers; James C. Cobb, *The Selling of the South: The Southern Crusade for Industrial Development, 1936–1980* (Baton Rouge, 1982); "Bulletin IV—Textile Industry"; John Selby, "Industrial Growth and Worker Protest in a New South City: High Point, North Carolina, 1859–1959," Ph.D. dissertation, Duke University, 1984, p. 199; "Report" to Augusto Bellanca, February 5, 1938; Franz Daniel to ACWA Hq., November 5, 1936, H-ACWA Papers; and Solomon Barkin to Hillman, July 28, 1938, H-ACWA Papers.
23. Philip Scranton, "Flexibility, Routinization, and the Transformation of American Textile Manufacturing, 1880–1930," Business History seminar at Harvard Business School, Spring 1987; Barkin to Hillman, July 28, 1938; and Hall *et al.*, *Like a Family*, pp. 255–57.
24. Scranton, "Flexibility."
25. "Report of Meeting of the TWOC and the CIO," March 19, 1937, Series 4A, Box 1, TWUA Papers; Hodges, *New Deal Labor Policy*, pp. 150–51; UTW Executive Council "Minutes," June 18, 1936, Box 674, TWUA Papers; F. Ray Marshall, *Labor in the South* (Cambridge, Mass., 1967); "Summary of Information on the Progress of Unions Associated with the CIO," filed with Len DeCaux, October 7, 1937, Box 576, TWUA Papers; and "Memorandum on Conference of New England Representatives," March 17, 1937, Series 4A, Box 1, TWUA Papers.
26. Marshall, *Labor in the South*, pp. 169–70; Hodges, *New Deal Labor Policy*, pp. 151–52; "Applications to TWOC" in H-ACWA Papers; Jacob Potofsky to Clinton Golden, June 7, 1937, H-ACWA Papers; *Business Week*, August 20, 1937; Jett Lauck to Hillman, March 18, 1937, Box 36, Lauck Papers; and "Report of the National Economic and Social Planning Association," Box 215, Lauck Papers.
27. Carl E. L. Gill to McClurd, May 27, 1937, "Private—CIO Drive—Confidential," Box 31, Case Files, Record Group 9, NRA Collection, National Archives.
28. Martin Sosna, *In Search of the Silent South: Southern Liberals and the Race Issue* (New York, 1977), pp. 77, 90, 92; John A. Salmond, *Miss Lucy of the CIO: The Life and Times of Lucy Randolph Mason* (Athens, Ga., 1988); Lucy Randolph Mason to Po-

tofsky, November 30, 1937, H-ACWA Papers; and Hall *et al.*, *Like a Family*, p. 121.

29. Selby, "Industrial Growth and Worker Protest," pp. 224–25; Marshall, *Labor in the South*, pp. 170–71; Hodges, *New Deal Labor Policy*, p. 152; "Report of Meeting of TWOC and the CIO," March 19, 1937, Series 4A, Box 1, TWUA Papers; *Barron's*, September 20, 1937; *Business Week*, May 28, 1937; and Carl E. L. Gill to McClurd, March 14, 1937, "Private—CIO Drive—Confidential," Box 31, NRA Collection.

30. "Johnson & Johnson" file, Box 55, TWUA Papers; File 1A, NRA Proceedings, Box 129, David Dubinsky Collection; Frances Perkins, *The Roosevelt I Knew* (New York, 1946), p. 329; William Stix Wasserman to E. A. Filene, October 16, 1936, Filene Papers; *Fort Wayne Independent*, October 30, 1936; David Mendelsohn to Teccia Davidson, March 5, 1937; Mendelsohn to Hillman, March 17, 1937; and M. D. Crawford to Austin T. Levy and Robert West, March 17, 1937, H-ACWA Papers; Augusto Bellanca to Franz Daniel, February 15, 1937; Potofsky to Abe Chatman, June 18, 1937, H-ACWA Papers; Sol Stettin "Abstract of TWUA Oral History Project," TWUA Papers; and Jacob Billikopf to Hillman, June 24, 1938, H-ACWA Papers.

31. Stettin, "Abstract of Oral History Project," TWUA Papers.

32. Hodges, *New Deal Labor Policy*, p. 162; James A. Gross, *The Reshaping of the National Labor Relations Board: National Policy in Transition, 1933 47* (Albany, N.Y., 1981), pp. 14–16; David J. Saposs, Memorandum to Staff, "Current Anti-Labor Activities," Division of Economic Research, NLRB, March 1938, Robert F. Wagner Papers; TWOC "Newsletters," March 30, June 24, and July 2, 1937, H-ACWA Papers; and Marshall, *Labor in the South*, pp. 170–71.

33. Clinton Golden to Potofsky, March 25, 1937, H-ACWA Papers; *Textile Worker of New England* (published in Boston by the TWOC), October 1937, H-ACWA Papers; and Augusto Bellanca to Cornelia Pinchot, March 30, 1937, H-ACWA Papers.

34. Perkins, *Roosevelt I Knew*, pp. 248–53, and Container 11, "Minimum Wage Bills, 1923–33," Benjamin Cohen Papers, Library of Congress, contains extensive correspondence on this subject; see especially Cohen to Frankfurter, February 7, 1933.

35. Jonathan Grossman, "Fair Labor Standards Act of 1938: Maximum Struggle for a Minimum Wage," *Monthly Labor Review*, June 1978, quotes Hillman; Max Lowenthal to Tom Corcoran, July 12, 1935, and Lowenthal to "Tom and Ben," July 12, 1937, Box 204, Corcoran Papers.

36. Hillman to Robert Johnson, November 3, 1938; Johnson to Hillman, October 28 and November 4, 1938; Johnson to Hillman, July 6, 1938; George Berry to Hillman, September 25, 1936; and Johnson to Hillman, December 15, 1936, all in H-ACWA Papers. Johnson to FDR, January 23, 1938, Container 2, OFF 419, FDR Papers; David J. Mendelsohn to Hillman, March 17, 1937; and Johnson to Hillman, August 29, 1938, H-ACWA Papers.

37. Hillman to Merle Vincent, November 16, 1936; Vincent to Hillman, November 3 and December 28, 1936, and January 6, 1937, all in H-ACWA Papers; *New York Times*, December 29, 1936; and Vivian Hart, "The Fair Labor Standards Act of 1938: Statutory Reality and Minimum Wage Policy," paper delivered at the 1988 meetings of the Organization of American Historians.

38. *New York Times*, January 27, April 1, May 22, and June 15, 1937; Jacob Potofsky "Notes," March 25, 1937, H-ACWA Papers; and Hillman testimony before joint hearings of the Senate Committee on Education and Labor and the House Committee on Labor, 75th Cong., 1st. Sess., 1937, p. 943.

39. Franz Daniel to Augusto Bellanca, December 8, 1936, H-ACWA Papers. See Stokes articles in *New York World-Telegram*, December 30, 1936, and January 12 and 14, 1937; "Carpetbaggers of Industry," pamphlet in H-ACWA Papers; Hodges, *New Deal Labor Policy*, pp. 186–87; and Potofsky to Sam Levin, to Hyman Blumberg, to La Guardia, and to Jacob Asher, December 22, 1937, all H-ACWA Papers.

40. Gerald Markowitz and David Rosner, eds., *Slaves of the Depression: Workers' Letters about Life on the Job* (Ithaca, N.Y., 1987), pp. 76, 195, 77–79, 177–78.

41. Hodges, *New Deal Labor Policy*; Joseph Gollomb, "Sidney Hillman," *Atlantic Monthly*, July 1938; "TWOC Materials," H-ACWA Papers; Abe Chatman to Hillman, June 30, 1937; Blumberg, Salerno, and Mayo to Hillman, 1936; "Weekly Letters for Regional Directors," TWUA-TWOC file, Box A7-33, CIO Papers, Catholic University, esp. April 22, August 23, and September 11, 1937; and "Report of the TWOC and the CIO," March 19, 1937, Series 4A, Box 1, TWUA Papers.

42. Kerwin to McClurd, May 14, 1937, Box 127, NRA Collection; Carl Gill to McClurd, April 27, 1937, Box 31, NRA Collection; *The Textile Worker*, September 1937, H-ACWA Papers; and Franz Daniel to Potofsky, January 11, 1937, H-ACWA Papers.

43. Edward Levinson, *Labor on the March* (New York, 1938), pp. 240–41; and Tom E. Terrill and Jerrold Hirsch, eds., *Such as Us: Southern Voices of the Thirties* (Chapel Hill, N.C., 1978), pp. 167–68.

44. "Memorandum on Conference of New England Representatives," March 17, 1937, Series 4A, Box 1, TWUA Papers; Hodges, *New Deal Labor Policy*, pp. 162–63; and Selby, "Industrial Growth and Worker Protest" (note 22 above), pp. 219–20.

45. Hodges, *New Deal Labor Policy*, pp. 153–55, 159; Mason to Hillman, September 11, 1937, folder 2, Box 1, Lucy Randolph Mason Papers, Special Collections Department, Duke University Library; *Daily News Record*, October 9, 1937; Lucy Randolph Mason to Southern editors, July 10, 1940, Box 45, Jett Lauck Papers; *The Textile Bulletin*, cited in Hodges, *New Deal Labor Policy*, p. 158; *Bristol* (R.I.) *Herald Courier*, April 29, 1937; and Franz Daniel to Augusto Bellanca, October 23, 1937, H-ACWA Papers.

46. Charles Handy to A. Bellanca, October 6, 1937; Dorothy Bellanca to Hilda Cobb, March 22, 1937; Cobb to D. Bellanca, March 24, 1937; D. Bellanca to Zilla Hawes, January 13, 1937; Hawes to Potofsky, January 24, 1937; Nora Piore to D. Bellanca, October 29, 1937, all in H-ACWA Papers; Hodges, *New Deal Labor Policy*, quotes Barkin, pp. 178–79; Terrill and Hirsch, *Such as Us*, p. 189; and Hall *et al.*, *Like a Family*, (note 11 above), pp. 345–46.

47. Franz Daniel to A. Bellanca, November 21, 1937; and Dorothy Bellanca to Buck Borah, October 20, 1937, H-ACWA Papers; Robert P. Ingalls, *Herbert H. Lehman and New York's Little New Deal* (New York, 1975), pp. 117–18; James MacGregor Burns, *Congress on Trial: The Legislative Process and the Administrative State* (New York, 1949), p. 70; Congressman Martin Sweeney to the President, December 18, 1937, OFF 142, FDR Papers.

48. Burns, *Congress on Trial*, pp. 41, 72, 75; *New York Times*, August 21 and September 15, 1937; and "Bulletin" of Labor's Non-Partisan League, September 2, 1937, H-ACWA Papers.

49. Dean L. May, *From New Deal to New Economics* (New York, 1981), p. 4; Mark Leff, *The Limits of Symbolic Reform: The New Deal and Taxation, 1933–39* (New York, 1984), p. 209; and Donald T. Critchlow, "The Political Control of the Economy: Deficit Spending as a Political Belief," *Public Historian*, vol. 3, Spring 1981.

50. Hodges, *New Deal Labor Policy*, pp. 155, 170; and David Milton, *The Politics of U. S. Labor: From the Great Depression to the New Deal* (New York, 1982), p. 110.

51. Hodges, *New Deal Labor Policy*, pp. 170–71, 175; Solomon Barkin report to CIO Advisory Council, January 4, 1939, Box 576, TWUA Papers; "Report for the Conference of the Committee on the Experience During the Last Year," 1938, Series 4A, Box 1, TWUA Papers; Solomon Barkin report to Executive Committee, November 3, 1937, Box 567, TWUA Papers; "Daily Progress—Notes on Newspaper Clippings," 1938, Series 7A, Box 2, TWUA Papers; and Junius Scales and Richard Nickson, *Cause at Heart: A Former Communist Remembers* (Athens, Ga., 1987).

52. James T. Patterson, *Congressional Conservatism and the New Deal* (Lexington, Ky., 1967); Robert Johnson to Marvin MacIntyre, January 23, and to FDR, January 23, 1938, President's Official File 419, FDR Papers; and *New York Times*, December 31, 1937.

53. Nelson Lichtenstein, *Labor's War at Home: The CIO in World War II* (New York, 1982), pp. 17–21.

54. Adolph Berle, *Navigating the Rapids, 1918–71*, ed. Beatrice Bishop Berle and Travis Jacobs (New York, 1973), p. 139, and Hugh T. Lovin, "The Fall of Farmer Labor Parties," *Pacific Northwest Quarterly*, January 1971.

55. Gardner Jackson to Jett Lauck, August 12, 1937, and Gardner Jackson "Memorandum for Mr. Lewis on Public Relations Suggestions," "Gardner Jackson" file, Box 37, Lauck Papers.

56. Berle, *Navigating the Rapids*, pp. 154–57, 160.

57. James A. Gross, *The Making of the National Labor Relations Board: A Study in Economics, Politics, and Law, 1933–37* (Albany, N.Y., 1974), p. 247, citing Green's telegram to Madden, June 29, 1937, and p. 251.

58. Gross, *Reshaping of the NLRB*, p. 47; Paul Douglas and Joseph Hackman, "The Fair Labor Standards Act of 1938: The Background and Legislative History of the Act," *Political Science Quarterly*, vol. 53, 1938; Burns, *Congress on Trial*, p. 71; Hugh T. Lovin, "The Persistence of Third Party Dreams in the American Labor Movement, 1930–38," *Mid-America*, vol. 58, October 1976; Donald R. McCoy, *Angry Voices: Left-of-Center Politics in the New Deal Era* (New York, 1958); Sidney Lens, *Left, Right, and Center: Conflicting Forces in American Labor* (Hinsdale, Ill., 1949), quotes Wharton, p. 332; and *New York Times*, October 12, 1937.

59. Edwin Young, "The Split in the Labor Movement," in Milton Derber and Edwin Young, eds., *Labor and the New Deal* (Madison, Wisc., 1957); Dan Tobin to James Farley and Sam Rosenman, November 3, 1937, Box 1, OFF 407, FDR Papers; and Congressman Martin Sweeney to the President, December 18, 1937, OFF 2730, FDR Papers.

60. "Correspondence, 1935–37," Box 63, Secretary of Labor File, Father Francis Haas Papers, Catholic University, contains illuminating material on these formative peace negotiations.

61. *Daily News Record*, November 5, 1937; Charles Ervin, "Personal," September 26, 1940, H-ACWA Papers; "Personal" files and "Wife and Daughters" file, H-ACWA Papers.

FIFTEEN: *The Fall to Power*

1. Hillman to Philoine, n.d., Hillman to Bessie, n.d., and Dorothy Bellanca to Hillman, 1938, all in H-ACWA Papers; Joseph Schlossberg to all Joint Boards, January

31, 1938, H-ACWA Papers; Tom Corcoran to the President, January 27, 1938, "Tom Corcoran Folder," Box 141, President's Secretary's File, FDR Papers; and *New York Times*, March 30, 1938.

2. Joseph Gollomb, "Sidney Hillman," *Atlantic Monthly*, July 1938.

3. James T. Patterson, *Congressional Conservatism and the New Deal: The Growth of the Conservative Coalition in Congress, 1933–39* (Lexington, Ky., 1967), p. 211; and Mark Leff, *The Limits of Symbolic Reform: The New Deal and Taxation, 1933–39* (New York, 1984), pp. 213–14.

4. Robert Johnson to Tom Corcoran, October 22, 1937, "Robert W. Johnson" file, Box 202, Corcoran Papers, and Robert Johnson to Hillman, October 28, 1938, H-ACWA Papers.

5. David Stern to Marvin MacIntyre, October 18, 1935, H-ACWA Papers; and David Stern to the President, December 8, 1939, President's Personal File 2910, FDR Papers.

6. Robert M. Collins, "Positive Business Responses to the New Deal: The Roots of the Committee of Economic Development, 1933–42," *Business History Review*, Autumn 1978, and Kim McQuaid, "Henry S. Dennison and the 'Science' of Industrial Reform, 1900–1950," *American Journal of Economics and Sociology*, January 1977.

7. Mordecai Eziekel to Hillman, February 10, 1938, H-ACWA Papers; Theodore Rosenof, *Dogma, Depression and the New Deal: The Debate of Political Leaders over Economic Recovery* (New York, 1975), pp. 92–94; Eli Oliver to John Brophy, November 30, 1937, Labor's Non-partisan League Papers, Catholic University; and Patrick D. Regan, "The Architects of American National Planning," Ph.D. dissertation, Ohio State University, 1982.

8. Marriner Eccles to Tom Corcoran, March 12, 1940 "Stuart Chase file," Box 192, Corcoran Papers; CIO Committee on Housing Meeting, May 22, 1938, H-ACWA Papers; and Dean L. May, *From New Deal to New Economics: The Liberal Response to the Recession* (New York, 1981), pp. 142–45; Eccles's own empire in the Rocky Mountain West typified the sectoral interests likely to benefit: diversified investments and loans in real estate, furniture, lumber, metal castings and forgings, varied financial services and insurance, agriculture, and so on. See John Morton Blum, ed., *From the Morgenthau Diaries: Years of Crisis, 1928–38* (Boston, 1965), pp. 426–27.

9. Leff, *Limits of Symbolic Reform*.

10. "Wages and Hours—Congress" file, H-ACWA Papers; Folder 51, Box 3, Elinore Herrick Papers, Schlesinger Library, Radcliffe College; Paul Douglas and Joseph Hackman, "The Fair Labor Standards Act of 1938: The Background and Legislative History of the Act," *Political Science Quarterly*, vol. 53, 1938; and Eli Oliver to Hillman, June 12, 1938, H-ACWA Papers.

11. Jonathan Grossman, "The Fair Labor Standards Act of 1938: Maximum Struggle for a Minimum Wage," *Monthly Labor Review*, June 1978; "The Wages and Hours Law," Research Department memo, 1938, H-ACWA Papers; Ronnie Steinberg, *Wages and Hours: Labor Reform in the 20th Century* (New Brunswick, N.J., 1982), p. 159; Stanley Ruttenberg, "Report on Working Conditions," March 28, 1948, H-ACWA Papers; and Leaflet to BVD workers in Baltimore, H-ACWA Papers.

12. "Memo" to the President, unsigned, June 24, 1938, PPF 3585, FDR Papers; Tom Corcoran to Missy Le Hand, July 8, 1938, OFF 3295, FDR Papers; and Robert Johnson to Hillman, August 29 and July 6, M. D. C. Crawford to Hillman, June 29, Louis Stark to Hillman, July 7, Solomon Barkin to Hillman, July 22, Hillman to

John Andrews, August 5, and Donald Nelson to Hillman, September 30, 1938, all H-ACWA Papers.

13. Turner Catledge, "New Deal Councils Split over Choice of Foes for Purge," *New York Times*, June 29, 1938, and LNPL *National Bulletin*, n.d., H-ACWA Papers.

14. Jerold S. Auerback, *Labor and Liberty: The La Follette Committee and the New Deal* (Indianapolis, 1966), ch. 7; James A. Gross, *The Reshaping of the National Labor Relations Board: National Policy in Translation, 1937–47* (Albany, N.Y., 1981), p. 74; and Patterson, *Congressional Conservatism* (note 3 above).

15. Patrick J. Maney, *"Young Bob" La Follette: A Biography of Robert M. La Follette, Jr., 1895–1953* (Columbia, Mo., 1978), p. 208; Hugh T. Lovin, "The Fall of Farmer Labor Parties," *Pacific Northwest Quarterly*, January 1971; Donald R. McCoy, *Angry Voices: Left-of-Center Politics in the New Deal Era* (New York, 1958), pp. 172–76; Max Lowenthal to Tom Corcoran, October 27, 1938, Box 204, Corcoran Papers; Robert P. Ingalls, *Herbert H. Lehman and New York's Little New Deal* (New York, 1975), p. 231; and Delbert D. Arnold, "The CIO's Role in American Politics, 1936–48," Ph.D. dissertation, University of Maryland, 1952, p. 42.

16. Arnold, "CIO's Role," p. 47; Richard Keller, "Pennsylvania's Little New Deal," in John Braeman, Robert H. Bremner, and David Brody, eds., *The New Deal*, vol. 2: *State and Local Levels* (Columbus, Ohio, 1975); and Bernard F. Donahue, *Private Plans and Public Dangers: The Story of FDR's Third Nomination* (Notre Dame, Ind., 1965), pp. 96–97.

17. Gross, *Reshaping of the NLRB*, pp. 67–75; Memo to the President, June 3, 1938, President's Personal File 3585, FDR Papers; William Green speech, "How and Why We Want to Change the Wagner Act," March 18, 1939, Folder 68B, Box 719, Robert F. Wagner Papers, Georgetown University; "CIO-Executive Board Minutes," June 13, 1939; AFL-CIO Headquarters, Washington, D.C.; *New York Times*, July 27, 1939; and Hillman testimony, extract, from Hearings of the Senate Committee on Education and Labor, 1st Sess., July 26 and 31, 1939, on a bill to amend the NLRA, H-ACWA Papers.

18. File 1a, Box 339, David Dubinsky Collection, ILGWU Archives.

19. Nelson Lichtenstein, "Great Expectations: The Promise of Collective Bargaining and its Demise, 1935–65," paper delivered at the Woodrow Wilson Center, March 29, 1988, Washington, D.C.

20. Ronald Edsforth, *Class Conflict and Cultural Consensus: The Making of a Mass Consumer Society in Flint, Michigan* (New Brunswick, N.J., 1987); Irving Howe and B. J. Widick, *The UAW and Walter Reuther* (New York, 1949); Alan Brinkley, *Voices of Protest: Huey Long, Father Coughlin and the Great Depression* (New York, 1982), pp. 140, 200–202; David O'Brien, "American Catholics and Organized Labor in the 1930s," *Catholic Historical Review*, October 1966; Lichtenstein, "Great Expectations"; and transcript of Homer Martin radio broadcast, WJR Detroit and WGAR Cleveland, n.d., Box 20, Adolph Germer Papers, Wisconsin State Historical Society, Madison.

21. Lichtenstein, "Great Expectations."

22. Gabriel N. Alexander, "Impartial Umpireships: The General Motors–UAW Experience," in Jean McKelvey, ed., *Arbitration and Law: Proceedings of the 12th Annual Meeting, National Academy of Arbitrators* (BNA, Inc., 1959); *Detroit Free Press*, September 8, 1938; Wyndham Mortimer to Len De Caux, September 5, 1938, H-ACWA Papers; report of Hillman and Murray to the UAW membership, October 4, 1938, H-ACWA Papers; Mortimer to Hillman, November 30, memo by Philip

Murray, September 22, Harold Cristoffel to Hillman, December 10, James Murphy to Hillman, September 21, Maurice Sugar to Hillman, September 21, Frank Rosenblum to Hillman, September 23 and John Anderson to Hillman, September 28, all 1938 H-ACWA Papers. The Baltimore UAW was another center of Homer Martin strength and of persistent red-baiting, both by Martin loyalists and by the AFL's Baltimore Federation of Labor, even though the Amalgamated had been responsible for much of the CIO's progress in the city among steel and auto workers as well as taxi drivers and seamen. The local Amalgamated leadership, however, became increasingly timorous, fearing the reaction among Catholic workers whose parish priests, led by Archbishop Curley, attacked the CIO relentlessly. See Jo Anne Argesinger, *Toward a New Deal in Baltimore: People and Government in the Great Depression* (Chapel Hill, N.C., 1988), pp. 161–62, 172–73.

23. Adolph Germer to Phil Murray, December 13, 1938, box 24, Germer Papers; statement by Hillman and Murray on the factional situation, January 24, 1939, H-ACWA Papers; Hillman and Murray open letter to the CIO, January 25, 1939, H-ACWA Papers.

24. Hillman and Murray press release, September 24, 1939, supporting the new UAW international executive board, H-ACWA Papers; Harvey A. Levenstein, *Communism, Anti-Communism, and the CIO* (Westport, Conn., 1981), pp. 80–83; and R. J. Thomas "Reminiscences," 4: 24, 30–34, 5: 4, 9, 14, and 7: 9.

25. James A. Hodges, *New Deal Labor Policy and the Southern Cotton Textile Industry, 1933–41* (Knoxville, 1986), pp. 162–63, 170–71.

26. TWUA Executive Council Minutes, March 7, 1937, box 647, TWUA Papers, Wisconsin State Historical Society; Gary Gerstle, *Working-Class Americanism: The Politics of Labor in a Textile City, 1914–60* (New York, 1989); Mary Taccone to Solomon Barkin, June 28, 1938, H-ACWA Papers; Francis Gorman to John Brophy, February 9, 1938, Series A5, box 6, John Brophy Papers, Catholic University; Brophy to Emil Rieve, February 16, 1938, Series A5, box 6, Brophy Papers; Gorman to Hillman, May 16, 1938, box 67, TWUA Papers; and Providence and Wonnasquatucket Woolen and Worsted District Council to John Lewis, August 29, 1938, H-ACWA Papers.

27. Hodges, *New Deal Labor Policy*, pp. 176–77; "General Information" file, TWUA Papers; and Francis Gorman to All Unions of the UTWA, December 21, 1938, box 674, TWUA Papers.

28. Gardner Jackson to Hillman, January 27, 1939, H-ACWA Papers; TWOC Advisory Council Minutes, January 4–5 and April 20–21, 1939, and September 1939, Box 576, TWUA Papers; and TWUA Executive Board Minutes, June 8, 1939, Box 1, TWUA Papers.

29. Ewa Morawska, *For Bread with Butter: Life-Worlds of East Central Europeans in Johnstown, Pennsylvania, 1890–1940* (New York, 1985); John Bodnar, *Workers' World: Kinship, Community, and Protest in an Industrial Society, 1900–1940* (Baltimore, 1982); and Robert A. Slayton, *Back of the Yards: The Making of a Local Democracy* (Chicago, 1986), pp. 49, 50, 62, 76–79, 203–4.

30. Barbara Newell, *Chicago and the Labor Movement* (Urbana, Ill., 1961), pp. 115, 131, 142, 146, 167–68, 180–81.

31. Jacob Potofsky to Father Haas, July 8, 1937, and Haas to Monsignor Tourenhart, August 10, 1937, Box 63, Father Francis Haas Papers, Catholic University.

32. O'Brien, "American Catholics and Organized Labor" (note 20 above); Mel Piehl, *Breaking Bread: The Catholic Worker and the Origins of Catholic Radicalism in America*

(Philadelphia, 1982), p. 121; Herbert Lehman, "Reminiscences," pp. 477, 703, OHCCU; and Bruce Stave, "Pittsburgh and the New Deal," in Braeman, Brenner, and Brody, eds., *The New Deal*, vol. 2: *State and Local Levels*.

33. J. B. S. Hardman, ed., *The Amalgamated: Today and Tomorrow* (New York, 1939). Between 1936 and 1939, while ACW membership grew thanks to the union's aggressive inroads into new trades and industrial subsectors like pajamas, shirts, laundries, bathrobes, and buttons, there was a steady decline in all the major categories of workers organized by the union. Gladys Dickason to John L. Lewis, December 7, 1937; "CIO Survey," prepared by Dickason, February 2, 1940; and "Membership—Industry Comparison of 1936–38 and 1938–40," all in H-ACWA Papers; and Thomas Gobel, "Becoming American: Ethnic Workers in the Rise of the CIO," *Labor History*, vol. 29, Spring 1988.

34. David Brody, "Labor and the Great Depression: The Interpretative Prospects," *Labor History*, vol. 13, 1972.

35. David Gartman, *Auto Slavery: The Labor Process in the American Automobile Industry, 1897–1950* (New Brunswick, N.J., 1986); Tom Corcoran to Stephen Early, October 6, 1938, OFF 3295, FDR Papers; Lichtenstein, "Great Expectations" (note 19 above); and Howe and Widick, *UAW and Walter Reuther* (note 20 above).

36. Alexander, "Impartial Umpireships" (note 22 above).

37. Lichtenstein, "Great Expectations." The auto umpire was less broadly empowered than in the ACW system. He was a more passive functionary than his garment industry analog, who not only reacted to the grievances and demands of labor and management but creatively intervened with his own concrete proposals for rationalizing the work process and its supervision. In an industry as fractionalized as clothing, the impartial umpire was bound to come forward as its only coherent voice, but of course GM already assumed that position and would scarcely invite in a disinterested outsider to legislate its behavior. Thus labor relations in the auto industry remained noticeably more adversarial and less corporatist. Still, the jurisdiction of the auto umpire encompassed such matters as union discrimination, recognition, representation, grievance procedures, seniority, disciplinary layoffs and firings, hours, leaves of absence, unlawful strikes, and so on. Alexander, "Impartial Umpireships."

38. Robert E. Lane, *The Regulation of Businessmen: Social Conditions of Government Economic Control* (Hamden, Conn., 1966), p. 129; *New York Times*, July 27, 1939; Frances Perkins "Reminiscences," p. 173, OHCCU; Howell John Harris, "Getting Everybody Back on the Same Team: An Interpretation of the Industrial Relations Policies of American Business in the 1940s," Ph.D. dissertation, Oxford University, 1977, pp. 53–54; Carle Conway, address to the Annual Meeting of the Taylor Society, 1939; Clinton S. Golden and Harold J. Ruttenberg, *The Dynamics of Industrial Democracy* (New York, 1973 reprint); Henry P. Guzda, "Industrial Democracy: Made in the U.S.A.," *Monthly Labor Review*, May 1984; and Morris Cooke and Philip Murray, *Organized Labor and Production: Next Steps in Industrial Democracy* (New York, 1940). It would be easy to exaggerate how broadly and deeply this "new unionism" penetrated the collective unconscious of American management. An anomalous cowboy business culture persisted here long after it died away in Europe, and, as American business would later be chagrined to discover, even in places like Japan. Even major corporations like GE for years would never tire of trying to whittle away at the essentials of the new industrial unionism.

39. Frank Rising memo to Hillman, November 8, 1939, and Hillman speech to New England Council, November 24, 1939, H-ACWA Papers.

40. Sidney Hillman, "The Promise of American Labor," *The New Republic*, November 8, 1939.

41. Stephen Early memorandum for the President, October 8, 1938, PPF 2943, FDR Papers.

42. Tom Corcoran to the President, n.d., President's Secretary File, box 141, FDR Papers; Hillman to Philoine, November 1938 and December 1938, H-ACWA Papers; Francis Haas, "Memorandum on Conference with Secretary Perkins," January 11, 1938, "Secretary of Labor" folder, box 63, Haas papers; and Gross, *Reshaping of the NLRB* (note 14 above), citing AFL Executive Council Minutes, January 30–February 14, 1939, p. 127.

43. *New York Times*, February 23 and 26, 1939, and "Peace Proposals of the CIO—White House Conference," March 7, 1939, H-ACWA Papers.

44. CIO Executive Board "Minutes," June 13, 1939, Roll 1, AFL-CIO Headquarters, Washington, D.C.

45. Arnold, "CIO's Role in American Politics" (note 15 above), p. 50, and Drew Pearson and Robert S. Allen in Washington, D.C., *Times-Herald*, February 2, 1940.

46. John Brophy "Reminiscences," p. 832, OHCCU, and Len De Caux, *Labor Radical: From the Wobblies to CIO—A Personal History* (Boston, 1970).

47. Paul Douglas and Joseph Hackman, "Fair Labor Standards Act of 1938" (note 10 above); Ruth L. Horowitz, *Political Ideologies of Organized Labor: The New Era* (New Brunswick, N.J., 1978), pp. 196–98; Elizabeth Brandeis, "Organized Labor and Protective Labor Legislation," in Milton Derber and Edwin Young, eds., *Labor and the New Deal* (Madison, Wisc., 1957); *New York Times*, June 16, 1937; Hillman statement before the joint session of the House Committee on Labor and the Senate Committee on Education and Labor on the Black–Connery bill, June 15, 1937, H-ACWA Papers; Gardner Jackson "Reminiscences," pp. 745–48, OHCCU; and Robert Johnson to Tom Corcoran, June 25, 1937, "Robert Johnson" file, Box 202, Corcoran Papers.

48. Charles Ervin, "Personal Notes," September 26, 1940, H-ACWA Papers, and Melvyn Dubofsky and Warren Van Tine, *John L. Lewis: A Biography* (New York, 1977), p. 328. FDR to Hillman, November 15, 1937, PPF 3585; White House memos, July 2, 1938, and August 6, 1939, PPF 3585; and Tom Corcoran memo to the President, June 3, 1938, PPF 3585, all in FDR Papers. Gross, *Reshaping of the NLRB*, p. 226; "December 1938" file, H-ACWA Papers; Hardman, *Amalgamated: Today and Tomorrow* (note 33 above); and "National Youth Administration" file, H-ACWA Papers.

49. Lee Pressman "Reminiscences," p. 210, OHCCU.

50. Matthew Josephson, *Sidney Hillman: Statesman of American Labor* (New York, 1952), p. 400, and Dubofsky and Van Tine, *John L. Lewis*, pp. 319–23. Harvey Kitzman to Lewis, Hillman, and Murray, July 1, and John Abt to Hillman, May 2, both 1939, H-ACWA Papers.

51. Donahue, *Private Plans* (note 16 above); Richard Norman Chapman, "Contours of Public Policy, 1939–45," Ph.D. dissertation, Yale University, 1976; and Josephson, *Sidney Hillman*, p. 470.

52. Excerpts of letters by Teccia Davidson, September 1939, H-ACWA Papers, and George Soule, *Sidney Hillman: Labor Statesman* (New York, 1939).

53. *New York Times*, February 19, 1939; Virgil Jordan to Hillman, March 7, 1938; John A. Zeratsky to Hillman, April 4, 1938, H-ACWA Papers; and *Fortune*, October 1939.

54. Harold Ickes diary entry, September 23, 1939, pp. 3733–34, Harold Ickes Diaries, Library of Congress; *New York Times*, June 15, 1938; Jacob Potofsky to Gladys Dickason, September 16, 1938; and address of Sidney Hillman to New York Joint Board, April 24, 1939, H-ACWA Papers.
55. *New York World-Telegram*, January 11, 1938.
56. *New York Times*, July 2 and 5, 1938.
57. Walter Galenson, *The CIO Challenge to the AFL: A History of the American Labor Movement, 1935–41* (Cambridge, Mass., 1960), pp. 315–16; *New York Times*, June 29, 1938; Abraham Cahan, draft of article, probably for the *Forward*, June 28, 1938, file 37, Box 6, Papers of Mendel Osherowitch, YIVO Archives, New York; Melech Epstein, *Profiles of Eleven* (Detroit, 1965), p. 289; "Statement of New York Joint Board," June 29, 1938, Archives of the Jewish Labor Movement, Atran Center for Jewish Culture, New York; David Dubinsky and A. H. Raskin, *David Dubinsky: A Life with Labor* (New York, 1977), p. 270; and *Justice*, July 15, 1938.
58. Dubofsky and Van Tine, *John L. Lewis*, pp. 319–23, and *New York Times*, August 6 and November 13, 1939.
59. L. M. Rachofsky to Hillman, September 18, 1937, and August 20, 1940, and address of Sidney Hillman to New York Joint Board, April 24, 1939, H-ACWA Papers.
60. Gerald Sorin, *The Prophetic Minority: American Jewish Immigrant Radicals, 1880–1920* (Bloomington, Ind., 1985), p. 167, and Jacob Potofsky "Notes," H-ACWA Papers.
61. Christopher L. Tomlins, *The State and the Unions: Labor Relations, Law, and the Organized Labor Movement in America, 1880–1960* (New York, 1985), p. 188, and CIO Executive Board Minutes, June 13, 1939, AFL-CIO Headquarters.

SIXTEEN: *Wars, Foreign and Domestic*

1. CIO Executive Board "Minutes," June 3, 4, and 5, 1940, Reel 1, Book 1, AFL-CIO Headquarters, Washington, D.C.
2. James A. Gross, *The Reshaping of the National Labor Relations Board: National Policy in Transition, 1937–47* (Albany, N.Y., 1981), pp. 210–11, and Delbert D. Arnold, "The CIO's Role in American Politics, 1936–1948," Ph.D. dissertation, University of Maryland, 1952, pp. 50–52.
3. Lewis quoted in Walter Galenson, *The CIO Challenge to the AFL: A History of the American Labor Movement, 1935–41* (Boston, 1960), pp. 54–55; official memo, October 31, 1939, OFF 2546, Box 1, Franklin Delano Roosevelt Papers, Hyde Park, N.Y.; and Bernard F. Donahue, *Private Plans and Public Dangers: The Story of FDR's Third Nomination* (Notre Dame, Ind., 1965), pp. 117–18.
4. Donahue, *Private Plans*, p. 129; Bryant Putney, "Labor in Politics," *Editorial Research Reports*, vol. 1, 1940; *New York Times*, January 29, 1940; and CIO Executive Board "Minutes," October 8, 1939, Reel 1, AFL-CIO Headquarters.
5. Henry Wallace, "Diary," February 8, 1940, in "The Reminiscences of Henry Agard Wallace," OHCCU; Paul Appleby to Wallace, memo, September 19, 1940, in "Reminiscences of Wallace"; H. Ross, "John Lewis and the 1940 Election," *Labor History*, Spring 1976; and Donahue, *Private Plans*, pp. 158, 159.
6. *ACWA Conv. Proc. 1940*, pp. 457, 459–62, 464; Gallup poll cited by Irving Bernstein in "John L. Lewis and Voting Behavior of the CIO," *Public Opinion Quarterly*, vol. 5, June 1941; Committee on Political and Economic Information, ACWA, "They or We," 1940, H-ACWA Papers; ACWA N.Y. State Conference in Buffalo, September 14, 1940, pp. 51, 60–61, 63, H-ACWA Papers; "Proceed-

ings ACW Convention to Help Re-elect President Roosevelt," pp. 106, 108, 115, H-ACWA Papers; *Advance*, October 1, 1940; and rank-and-file letters of ACW General Office Department of Cultural Activity, "The People Speak: Letters from Clothing Workers in New York," 1940, H-ACWA Papers.

7. Lewis quoted in Aaron Levenstein, *Labor Today and Tomorrow* (New York, 1945), p. 166.

8. Harvey A. Levenstein, *Communism, Anti-Communism and the CIO* (Westport, Conn., 1981), pp. 89–90; Maurice Isserman, *Which Side Were You On? The American Communist Party During the Second World War* (Middletown, Conn., 1982), pp. 74–77; Hillman Speech at UAW Convention, July 31, 1940, H-ACWA Papers; Hardman to Potofsky, November 6, 1939, H-ACWA Papers; Lewis to Hillman, July 29, 1940, "David Dubinsky Correspondence," Box 340, File 1A, ILGWU Archives; author's interview with A. H. Raskin, June 10, 1985; *New York Times*, September 20 and 21, 1940; Bert Cochran, *Labor and Communism: The Conflict That Shaped American Unions* (Princeton, N.J., 1979), p. 149; and Henry Kitzman to Lewis, July 1, 1940, H-ACWA Papers.

9. CIO Executive Board "Minutes," 1938–1941, Roll 1, Book 1, AFL-CIO Headquarters, and Arnold, "CIO's Role," p. 57.

10. Harold Ickes, *The Harold Ickes Diaries*, May 4, 1940, Reel 4, p. 4361, and June 12, 1940, Reel 4, pp. 4489–90, Library of Congress.

11. Gardner Jackson to Franklin Delano Roosevelt, November 13, 1940, FDR Papers, and Monroe Sweetland to Hillman, April 8, 1940, and Carl Holderman to Hillman, October 11, 1940, both H-ACWA Papers.

12. Hillman speech to ACW, January 28, 1940, H-ACWA Papers, and Lewis quoted in Robert H. Zieger, *John L. Lewis* (Boston, 1988), p. 110.

13. Ickes, *Diaries*, November 9, 1940, Reel 4, p. 4962; Irving Bernstein, *The Turbulent Years: A History of the American Worker, 1933–41* (Boston, 1971), p. 720; Donahue, *Private Plans*, citing Josephson, p. 488; "We Disagree with John L. Lewis: Reaffirm Our Support of FDR," *Textile Labor*, special ed., 1940, H-ACWA Papers; *New York Times*, October 27, 1940; and Arnold, "CIO's Role" (note 2 above), p. 73.

14. *New York Times*, November 13, 1940; Hillman quoted in Jack Kroll, "Typescript of a Political Review," 1940, Jack Kroll Papers, Box 4, Library of Congress; and Hillman quoted in Ickes, *Diaries*, November 9, 1940, Reel 4, p. 4962.

15. Jackson to Roosevelt, November 8, 1940, FDR Papers.

16. Jackson to FDR, November 13, 1940, OFF 407, Box 2, and Gardner Jackson, "A Plan of Action," memo to FDR, November 15, 1940, both in FDR Papers, Hyde Park.

17. Isserman, *Which Side Were You On?*, pp. 78–79, and Arnold, "CIO's Role," p. 66.

18. Melvyn Dubofsky and Warren Van Tine, *John L. Lewis: A Biography*, (New York, 1977), p. 368. Dubofsky and Van Tine argue that ACW attacks on Lewis provoked the UMW President's "anti-Semitic" insinuations, but Lewis's feelings, however provoked, probably went deeper than that. Frances Perkins "Reminiscences," 8: 421–26, OHCCU, and Louis Breier to Leonard V. Finder, December 11, 1940, George Arents Research Library, Syracuse University.

19. Author's interviews with Lawrence Levin, June 8, 1979; with Beatrice Bornstein, June 7, 1979; and with Philoine Fried, January 25, 1979; and Hillman, "Address of Vice President Sidney Hillman" at 1940 CIO Convention, November 20, 1940, FDR Papers.

20. Lauchlin Currie to Eleanor Roosevelt, December 7, 1940, FDR Papers.
21. Arnold, "CIO's Role," p. 57, and Bruno Stein, "Labor's Role in Government Agencies During World War II," *Journal of Economic History*, 1957, p. 389.
22. Jackson to Roosevelt, November 13, 1940.
23. Arnold, "CIO's Role," p. 71; Irving Bernstein, *Turbulent Years*, pp. 718–19; and Ickes, *Diaries*, June 5, 1940, Reel 4, pp. 4452–54. To mollify the AFL, Roosevelt appointed Dan Tobin as his administrative assistant and made Dan Tracey of the IUE assistant secretary of Labor. Paul A. C. Koistinen, "The Hammer and the Sword: Labor, The Military, and Industrial Mobilization, 1920–1945," Ph.D. dissertation, University of California, Berkeley, 1964, p. 92; Perkins "Reminiscences," 7: 792, 801, and 8: 209–12; Frances Perkins, *The Roosevelt I Knew* (New York, 1946), pp. 355–56; James W. Fesler, "Labor Activity of the NDAC and OPM," p. 4, September 12, 1945, Policy Analyses and Records Branch, Office of the Executive Secretary—War Production Board; and Richard J. Purcell, *Labor Policies of the NDAC and OPM, May 1940 to April 1942*, Historical Reports on War Administration, WPB Special Study 23, October 31, 1946. *Business Week* joined Perkins in predicting a jurisdictional civil war between the AFL and the CIO. *Business Week*, June 18, 1940; *Washington Post*, July 7, 1940; Eugene E. Cox, "Extension of Remarks in the House of Representatives on Sidney Hillman," Appendix to *Congressional Record*, June 21, 1940, pp. 13400–13401, Washington, D.C.; and OFF 813–2, Boxes 6–7, FDR Papers.
24. Elliot Janeway, *The Struggle for Survival* (New Haven, 1951), p. 123, and Ickes, *Diaries*, June 15, 1940, Reel 4, pp. 4502–3.
25. Purcell, *Labor Policies*, p. 6.
26. Jordan Schwartz, *The Speculator: Bernard M. Baruch in Washington, 1917–65* (Chapel Hill, N.C., 1981), pp. 359–61; Koistinen, "Hammer and Sword," pp. 63–70; and Richard Norman Chapman, "Contours of Public Policy, 1939–45," Ph.D. dissertation, Yale University, 1976, pp. 151–54, 232. Chapman demonstrates that the Revenue Act of 1940, along with the shelving of the Attorney General's antitrust investigations and the assault on social services, signaled this change of direction.
27. Philip Murray to Hillman, August 14, 1940, H-ACWA Papers, and Leiserson to Hillman, August 13, 1940, William Leiserson Papers, Wisconsin State Historical Society, Madison.
28. "Minutes of NDAC," Box 88, September 11, 1940, Edward R. Stettinius Papers, 2723, Manuscripts Division, University of Virginia Library. Lewis supplied Hillman with a capsule documentary history of his attempts to get Roosevelt to take decisive action. Thus, as early as January 1939 he noted that Douglas Aircraft and Bethlehem, among other flagrant lawbreakers, were receiving large government orders. In March the CIO campaigned, along with Corcoran and Cohen, for the Barkley amendment to the military appropriation bill granting to military authorities the power to declare a contractor ineligible if found to be in violation of the NLRA. Rowe to Roosevelt, March 9, 1939, President's Secretary's File (PSF), Box 148, FDR Papers. Over the next year and a half, Roosevelt conveyed his general sympathies but claimed constitutional constraints on his power to issue an executive order to deal firmly with the violators. Hillman joined the correspondence in July 1940, arguing that he could not credibly ask the President to disregard the opinion of his legal advisers. Lewis to Hillman, July 15, 1940; Lewis to Roosevelt, January 18, 1939; Roosevelt to Lewis, January 30, 1939; Lewis to Roosevelt, February 21,

1939; Roosevelt to Lewis, March 20, 1939; Lewis to FDR, March 16, 1940; Hillman to Lewis, July 30, 1940; Lewis to Hillman, August 27, 1940; Hillman to Lewis, September 13, 1940; and Lewis to Hillman, July 3, 1940, all in H-ACWA Papers. Hillman to Lewis, OFF 2546, Box 2, and Arnold, "CIO's Role," p. 71.

29. John Biggers to Hillman, August 23, 1940, and Murray to Hillman, August 14, 1940, cited in Purcell, *Labor Policies*, pp. 34–41; communication from the President, "The General Principles Governing the Letting of Defense Contracts," September 13, 1940, filed with the House of Representatives 76th Cong., 3d Sess.; Stein, "Labor's Role," pp. 389–91; and "Minutes of the NDAC," Box 88, July 24, 1940, Stettinius Papers.

30. The interview was released and edited by Hillman's chief advisers, Lubin and Maxwell Brandwen, who struggled mightily to mute the clamorous plosives of Hillman's alien accent. "Every time we can avoid using a word that begins with a 'th' we ought to do so." Lubin to Brandwen, August 31, 1940, H-ACWA Papers.

31. Sidney P. Simpson to Potofsky, October 16, 1940; Amberg to Potofsky, March 3, 1941; Lubin to Hillman, July 18, 1940; Jackson to Hillman, October 2, 1940, Labor Policy Advisory Committee, all in H-ACWA Papers. *New York Times*, October 2, 1940; Koistinen, "Hammer and Sword," pp. 136–37; Purcell, *Labor Policies*, p. 47; Arnold, "CIO's Role," p. 73; and *Business Week*, December 21, 1940.

32. Jackson to Roosevelt, November 13, 1940, H-ACWA Papers; Purcell, *Labor Policies*, p. 51; Bruce Allen Murphy, *The Brandeis–Frankfurter Connection: The Secret Political Activities of Two Supreme Court Justices* (New York, 1982), pp. 231–32; Henry L. Stimson Papers, January 2 and 31 and February 1, 3, and 5, 1941, Yale University Library; *Washington Star*, December 13, 1940; *PM*, December 29, 1940, and January 31, 1941; "Minutes of NDAC," Box 88, December 6, 1940, Stettinius Papers; and Arnold, "CIO's Role," p. 75.

33. Howell John Harris, "Getting Everybody Back on the Same Team: An Interpretation of the Industrial Relations Policies of American Business in the 1940's," Ph.D. dissertation, Oxford University, 1977, ch. 3, and Sidney Simpson, memo to the Secretary of War, 1940, H-ACWA Papers.

34. Isador Lubin "Reminiscences," pp. 123–27, OHCCU; Koistinen, "Hammer and Sword," pp. 98–99; Purcell, *Labor Policies*, p. 168; and Joel Seidman, *American Labor from Defense to Reconversion* (Chicago, 1953), p. 43.

35. Koistinen, "Hammer and Sword," pp. 100, 120; Seidman, *American Labor*, p. 44; and J. Edgar Hoover to Stettinius and Hillman, memo, November 4, 1940, War Production Board Political Document File, 235.12–237.2, Box 1009, National Archives.

36. Adolf Germer to Hillman, July 10, 1940, Box 4, Adolph Germer Papers, Wisconsin State Historical Society, Madison, and James Matles to Lewis, July 22, 1940, "David Dubinsky Correspondence," Box 340, File 1A.

37. Richard Polenberg, *War and Society: The United States, 1941–45* (Philadelphia, 1972), p. 155.

38. Hillman Statement, June 6, 1941, Labor Policy Advisory Committee, H-ACWA Papers.

39. The executive order creating the OPM was dated January 7, 1941. Matthew Josephson, *Sidney Hillman: Statesman of American Labor* (New York, 1952), pp. 531–34. Actually, the original reorganization plan authored by Stimson, Patterson, Knox, and James A. Forrestal ignored labor completely, but objections by Frank-

furter and Murray led Stimson to propose a "collateral board" headed by Hillman. The final arrangements met with the approval of Stimson who was getting habituated to Hillman. "We have all tried Sidney Hillman out and felt pretty well satisfied with him." Henry L. Stimson Papers, December 17, 18, and 20, 1940, Yale University Library.

40. Koistinen, "Hammer and Sword," p. 104; diagram from Report on the Situation at the ALCOA Forging Plant in Cleveland, Ohio, October 17, 1941, Records of the WPB, National Archives; list of "Strikes in Defense Industries," May 26, 1941, figures from OPM, National Archives; and Edward McGrady to Roosevelt, March 8, 1941, H-ACWA Papers.

41. Koistinen, "Hammer and Sword," p. 106; Purcell, *Labor Policies*, p. 183; Seidman, *American Labor*, p. 28; and Murray to Congress, April 30, 1941, on Vinson Bill, H. R. 4139, Jett Lauck Papers, University of Virginia Library.

42. *New York Times*, February 21, 1941; Hillman testimony at the Hearings of the Special Committee investigation of the National Defense Program of the Senate, 77th Cong., 1st Sess., April 21, 1941, H-ACWA Papers; Hillman to Roosevelt, June 24, 1941, FDR Papers; Lubin to Brandwen, memo, November 18, 1941, H-ACWA Papers; Mary Norton to Roosevelt, November 14, 1941, OFF 407, Box 3; and *Congressional Digest*, April 1942.

43. Address to American Society of Newspaper Editors, April 19, 1941, H-ACWA Papers.

44. All through 1941 he defended the NDMB, despite the obvious contempt in which it was held by much of the labor movement. In part, he feared that more harmful antistrike legislation would result should the Board fail. As a result, Hillman was still halfheartedly defending the indefensible rulings of the NDMB even as its two labor members were resigning and the President was preparing to circumvent the Board's authority.

45. Koistinen, "Hammer and Sword," pp. 136–37, and Henry L. Stimson Papers, November 29 and October 2, 1940, and February 27, 1941. Thus the recalcitrance of management at a Bethlehem plant in Lackawanna, New York, led to a nasty and apparently unresolvable strike by the USW. Hillman and Knudsen brought company officials to Washington and ordered them to comply with the law. Bethlehem agreed to reinstate fired union organizers, to allow an NLRB election, and to bargain in good faith. *PM*, February 26 and March 14, 1941. In another case, Hillman managed to convince Forrestal, Knox, Myron Taylor, and William Davis, chairman of the NDMB, and through them the President, that government seizure of federal shipbuilding facilities, incorporating the rights of the USW, was essential if ships were going to get built. Federal Shipbuilding Strike, 1941, synopsis of conversations, August 17–23, 1941, H-ACWA Papers.

46. Donald M. Nelson to W. M. Jeffers, President of Pacific Railroad, Box 1024, "Labor Strikes 1939–41," War Production Board Papers; J. H. Ohley to Patterson, October 23, 1941, and Patterson to Hillman, August 14, 1941, both in Box 141, "Labor 1941," Robert Patterson Papers, Library of Congress.

47. Stephen Meyer, "The Uneasy Transition from Batch to Mass Production: Workers, Technology and Grievances at Allis-Chalmers in the 1930's," presented at AHA Convention, December 1988; Thomas E. Blantz, *A Priest in Public Service: Francis J. Haas and the New Deal* (Notre Dame, Ind., 1982), p. 195; Koistinen, "Hammer and Sword," p. 113; "Minutes of the Council of the OPM," March 17, 1941, Historical Reports on War Administration, WPB Document Publications no. 2,

Washington, D.C., 1946; H. W. Storey to Hillman and Knudsen, telegram, February 19, 1941, Box 242, "Labor Strikes and Disputes, 1939–41," WPB Records. Knudsen quickly undercut Hillman's position by wiring the company on February 19 that the agreement did not imply maintenance of membership and then told Hillman that he should convey the same message to the House Judiciary Committee. Knudsen to Hillman, February 20, 1940, WPB Records. Knudsen also told Governor Harold Stassen that under CIO pressure, Hillman had reversed his earlier position against the closed shop, indicating, inadvertently, that Knudsen too lived in ignorance of the distinction between a closed shop and a maintenance of membership arrangement. Knudsen to Stassen, March 21, 1941, WPB Records, National Archives. With some validity, then, company negotiators accused Hillman of equivocating. Storey to Knudsen, February 19, 1940, WPB Records.

48. Thomas E. Blantz, *Priest in Public Service,* p. 198; Knox to Babb, telegram, n.d., Box 1025, "Strikes Allis-Chalmers," WPB Records; Murray to Knudsen, March 27, 1941, WPB Records; Murray to Knudsen, telegram, March 1, 1941, H-ACWA Papers; and Stimson to FDR, April 15, 1941, Box 143, "Labor Folder 3," Patterson Papers. Hillman was kept apprised of that side of things by the FBI. A long memo from the Bureau examined the CP's influence throughout the Wisconsin CIO as well as local 248 and Cristoffel's CP and YPSL past. Memo from the FBI to Hillman, "Re: Strike at Allis-Chalmers Manufacturing Company Milwaukee, Wisconsin," March 10, 1941, Box 242, "Strikes, Allis Chalmers," WPB Records; Koistinen, "Hammer and Sword," p. 113; and Isserman, *Which Side Were You On?* (note 8 above), pp. 90–91.

49. Paul Shoup to Knudsen and Hillman, telegrams, January 1941, File 313.42, "Aircraft Labor Strikes," WPB Records and Cochran, *Labor and Communism* (note 8 above), pp. 176–81.

50. *New York Times,* July 7, 1941.

51. Knox to Hillman, confidential memo, April 14, 1941, Official File, 1940–42; Brandwen to Hillman, memo, February 20, 1941, Official File; Forrestal to Knudsen, March 29, 1941, Official File; Industrial Emergency Control Committee of North America memo to Hillman, April 1, 1941, Official File; Ed Levinson sends copy of petition by Smith to Hillman, February 26, 1941, Official File; and Hillman, Statement for Labor Policy Advisory Committee, June 6, 1941, LPAC File, all in H-ACWA Papers.

52. Biddle to Roosevelt, June 23, 1941, PSF Box 76, Justice Department File, and Biddle to Roosevelt, memo on "Subversive Employees," Justice Department File, both in FDR Papers; Levenstein, *Communism* (note 8 above), p. 169; and John Lord O'Brian to Hillman, July 10, 1941, Official File, H-ACWA Papers. Biddle floated a simpler scheme to establish an interdepartmental committee from Labor, Justice, War, and Navy; to pass on cases of Army and Navy intelligence and the FBI; and to seek cooperation from the CIO and the AFL for international sanctions against locals tainted with subversion. If that failed, employers would be asked to fire suspect workers. Hoover liked the idea, but its arbitrary and uncertain legal status invited labor movement opposition. Biddle to Roosevelt, June 23, 1941, Official File, H-ACWA Papers. Patterson, Knox, and John McCloy also used the strike to escalate their demands for tougher antisubversive measures, going so far as to suggest an outlaw "suicide squad" to operate free of legal constraints. The Attorney General warned the President that Naval Intelligence was tapping wires and listening in on the phone conversations of OPM officials. Roosevelt to Knox

and Patterson, June 4, 1941; Patterson and Knox to Roosevelt, May 29, 1941; and Jackson to Roosevelt, April 29, 1941, all in Box 141, Patterson Papers. Even after Pearl Harbor, Hillman pursued the issue. He told Francis Biddle it was improper for any labor organization to refuse to cooperate with the Justice Department in its ongoing efforts to prevent sabotage and promised he would speak to Phil Murray about the reported unwillingness of Harry Bridges and the California CIO to cooperate fully. Hillman to Biddle, January 9, 1942, Official File; Hoover to Knudsen, December 22, 1941, Official File; and Hillman to Murray, January 12, 1942, Official File, all in H-ACWA Papers.

53. Watson to Roosevelt, June 6, 1941, and Roosevelt to Murray, June 7, 1941, both in PSF Box 185, FDR Papers; *PM*, July 21, 1941; Koistinen, "Hammer and Sword," pp. 115–16; James Rowe, Jr., sent Hillman off-the-record interview with Lewis by the *Time* correspondent Eddie Lockett marked "confidential," August 5, 1941, Official File, H-ACWA Papers; and *New York Times*, July 8, 1941.

54. Cochran, *Labor and Communism*, pp. 176–81; John Packard to Lubin, June 11, 1941, Official File, H-ACWA Papers; Kindelberger to Merrill C. Meigs, June 10, 1941, "Transcript of Telephone Conversation," Box 313.42, "Aircraft Labor Strikes," WPB Records; Branshaw to Patterson in telephone conversation, June 20, 1941, Box 152, "North American Aviation Inc. Strike," Patterson Papers; Lieut. Col. Edward S. Greenbaum to Patterson, June 21, 1941, Box 152, Patterson Papers; Branshaw to Hillman in telephone conversation, June 18, 1941, and Branshaw Report, June 19, 1941, H-ACWA Papers; and Hillman to Roosevelt, Jackson, and Stimson, June 10, 1941, memo, Box 152, Patterson Papers.

55. Henry L. Stimson Papers, June 11–13, 1941, Yale University; Koistinen, "Hammer and Sword," p. 115; and Hillman to Roosevelt, November 24, and Lubin to Roosevelt, November 6, 1941, both in FDR Papers.

56. Koistinen, "Hammer and Sword," p. 153; "Government, Labor, Industry Conference, December 17–23, 1941," White House File of War Labor Conference, Frances Perkins Correspondence, Box 105, Record Group 174, Department of Labor, Office of the Secretary. Two days after Pearl Harbor a Hillman aide, Edward Prichard, Jr., prepared a memo on Hillman's behalf for the President, summarizing the pernicious and "vicious" provisions of the Smith Bill, proposing as an administration alternative that the NDMB be granted the power to stop strikes pending mediation, and authorizing the President to impose compulsory arbitration. "Analysis of Smith Bill" memo, February 24, 1941, Prichard File, WPB Records.

57. Purcell, *Labor Policies*, p. 215; Knox letter, October 31, 1940, and Acting Secretary of Navy to the Navy, July 1, 1940, both Box 1023, "Labor Pirating," WPB Records.

58. "Inception of Stabilization Idea," Shipbuilding Stabilization Agreements from Minutes of the NDAC, September 18, 1940, H-ACWA Papers. Here too, the shift from batch to mass production alarmed skilled metalworkers with syndicalist traditions and a jealous sense of their locals' autonomy. Richard Boyden, "Craft Consciousness and Labor Revolt: The Case of San Francisco Metal Workers, 1900–1941," paper presented at American Historical Association Meetings, 1988. Frey developed a new respect for Hillman as a result and appreciated that the CIO vice president scrupulously avoided awarding any advantage to CIO unions trying to organize the Bay Area yards. "An interview with John Frey," November 10, 1955, pp. 33–39, Daniel Bell Collection, Tamiment Library, New York University, and Purcell, *Labor Policies*, pp. 226–27.

59. Donald M. Nelson, *Arsenal of Democracy: The Story of American War Production*

(New York, 1946), p. 315; Purcell, *Labor Policies*, p. 237; and Galenson, *CIO Challenge* (note 3 above), p. 187.

60. Purcell , *Labor Policies*, p. 235. Douglas to Hillman, July 8, 1941; Cyril Chappellet to Hillman, August 7, 1941; and Hillman Statement of June 6, 1941, all in H-ACWA Papers. *Minutes of the Council of the OPM*, June 10 and 24 and July 8, 1941, Historical Reports of War Administration, WPB Documents Publications no. 2, Washington, D.C., 1946.

61. Purcell, *Labor Policies*, p. 94, and Leonard Adams, *Wartime Manpower Mobilization: A Study of the World War II Experience in the Buffalo-Niagara Area* (Ithaca, 1951), p. 25.

62. Polenberg, *War and Society* (note 37 above), p. 10. Even by the time of Pearl Harbor, 3 to 4 million remained unemployed and in need of training or retraining. Seidman, *American Labor* (note 34 above), p. 154; George G. Flynn, *The Mess in Washington: Manpower Mobilization in World War II*, (Westport, Conn., 1979), p. 7, and Owen Young to Hillman, July 10, 1940, H-ACWA Papers. Young to Roosevelt, May 27, 1940, and Roosevelt to Young, June 25, 1940, PPF Box 61, both in FDR Papers. John Collins to Hillman, October 9, 1935, H-ACWA Papers; Purcell, *Labor Policies*, pp. 115–17; and Sidney Hillman, "Problems of Labor Supply and Training: Labor Division War Production Board," March 3, 1942, H-ACWA Papers.

63. Hillman memo to NDAC staff, "Training Program for National Defense," July 26, 1940, Box 246, "Labor Training 1940–41," Records of the WPB. To overcome the ingrown hostility to the CCC on the part of anti–New Dealers, Hillman argued its value not only as an educator but as a socializer, and even militarizer, of young men. The whole organization was "similar and could be readily converted into a military organization," he told the NDAC in the July 26 memo. Enrollees were "toughened physically" and provided with the "elements of discipline in order to make possible group living in the barracks of the camps." A recruit not only learned the value of personal and public hygiene, but the right "social attitudes in order to get along with other enrollees with whom he is forced to live. He is taught how to take care of himself and how to give in when occasion demands," and, of course, the spiritual and material rewards of a "good day's work." See also NDAC Statement for the Press, June 24, 1940, H-ACWA Papers, Purcell, *Labor Policies*, p. 115.

64. "Summary of Meeting on the Effective Utilization of our Labor Supply," June 24, 1941, H-ACWA Papers.

65. Alan S. Milward, *War, Economy and Society: 1939–1945* (Berkeley, Calif., 1977), pp. 185–87; and Detailed Job Breakdown Sheet for TWI Program, n.d., H-ACWA Papers.

66. Stettinius to Young, July 26, 1940, Box 1036, "Training 1940–1941"; "Minutes of the OPM," December 2, 1941, Box 1111, "Aircraft Labor Strikes"; Letters, Box 1354, "Die-Casting and Molding Machines, Labor," all in Records of the WPB, Political Documents File. "OPM Digest Minutes," November 12, 1941, Box 26, Records of the WPB; and Hillman telegram to President Joseph T. Meiner, A. A. Handler, and Anson J. Sanford, December 12, 1941, Box 242, "Labor Strikes and Disputes, 1939–41," Records of the WPB.

67. Meeting no. 4 of the Supply Priorities and Allocations Board (SPAB), September 23, 1941, "Minutes of the meetings of SPAB," Record Group 179, Entry 6, National Archives, and A. F. Hinrichs to Stacey May, November 21, 1941, H-ACWA Papers.

68. I. F. Stone, "FDR Says Knudsen Board Is Studying Reuther Plan," *PM*, December 27, 1940; author's interview with Robert Nathan, November 9, 1984; Jerome Frank to Roosevelt, confidential memo, December 30, 1940, OFF 4234, FDR Papers; Subcommittee on General Problems in the Auto Industry, "Verbatim Transcript of the Joint Meeting Between Labor and Industry," January 6, 1942, H-ACWA Papers; J. Douglas Brown to Hillman, May 28, 1941, H-ACWA Papers; George R. Clark, "The Strange Story of the Reuther Plan," *Harper's Magazine*, May 1942; and Bruce Catton, *The War Lords of Washington*, (New York, 1948), p. 99.

69. Merton W. Ertell, "The CIO Industrial Council Plan: Its Background and Implications," Ph.D. dissertation, University of Chicago, 1955, p. 10; Philip Murray, "For Full Production," *The CIO and National Defense*, pamphlet (American Council on Public Affairs, Washington, D.C., 1940), H-ACWA Papers; OPM and Labor Department officials' meeting "On the Adjustment of Labor Disputes in Defense Industries," July 25, 1941, Perkins Correspondence File, Record Group 174, Papers of Assistant Secretary Daniel Tracey, Department of Labor, Box 380, Folder "Office of Production Management," National Archives; and Brooks to Oliver, November 22, 1941, Box 242.1, "Labor Strikes Mediation and Arbitration, 1940–42," Records of the WPB. Hillman felt pressure from constituent CIO unions. N. A. Zonarich, President of the International Union of Aluminum Workers of America, complained about labor's limited say over priorities. Zonarich to Hillman, July 2, 1941, H-ACWA Papers. CP member Reid Robinson of the Mine, Mill, and Smelter Workers Union conveyed the same message more harshly, accusing Hillman of cosmetically covering up industry's absolute supremacy. Robinson to Hillman, July 31, 1941, H-ACWA Papers. Hillman's replies for the President: Hillman to Rudolph Foster, August 20, and to Murray, February 10, March 5, and November 22, 1941, PPF Box 5640, "CIO File," FDR Papers, Hyde Park, N.Y., See also Catton, *War Lords*, p. 99; Hillman to Roosevelt, December 16, 1941, file 016.61, Records of the WPB; Koistinen, "Hammer and Sword" (note 23 above), p. 605; Purcell, *Labor Policies*, p. 152; Murray to Roosevelt, December 20, Roosevelt to Knudsen, December 26, and Roosevelt to Murray, December 28, all 1940, in file 631.0423, Records of the WPB; and Knudsen to Murray, January 8, 1941, file 240.1, Records of the WPB.

70. J. Douglas Brown to Hillman, August 4, 1941, H-ACWA Papers.

71. Koistinen, "Hammer and Sword," p. 599, and Edythe W. First, *Industry and Labor Advisory Committees in the NDAC and OPM, May 1940–January 1942*, Historical Report on War Administration, WPB Special Study no. 24, December 9, 1946, Records of the WPB.

72. Josephson, *Sidney Hillman* (note 39 above), pp. 556–57; Milward, *War, Economy and Society*, p. 51; and Seidman, *American Labor*, p. 154; Of course, the escalation of plant conversions following the Japanese attack generated a 100 percent rise in claims for unemployment benefits, finally inducing Roosevelt to ask Congress for emergency legislation to meet the crisis. John J. Corson to Hillman, January 21, 1942, H-ACWA Papers.

73. Biographical Data of the Personnel of the Priorities Branch, Labor Division, H-ACWA Papers; J. Douglas Brown, *The Industrial Relations Section of Princeton University in the World War II: A Personal Account*, published as Research Series 121 (Princeton, N.J., 1976), p. 43; and Oliver to Hillman, January 7, 1942, File 016.426, "Labor Priorities Branch, OPM Functions," Records of the WPB. The

Priorities Branch did produce meticulous analyses of the unemployment problem and detailed inventories of industrial skills, of regional wage levels, and of the local housing stock to establish objective criteria for certifying a community as threatened by priority unemployment. Once so certified, the Branch recommended remedial measures to the War and Navy departments, including company-by-company studies and reports on housing, transportation, the available pool of skills, and minority unemployment, as well as technical assessments of a company's capacity for defense work. Summary of contents of Political Document File Box 1023, File 241.71, "Labor, Unemployment, Certification," Records of the WPB.

74. Koistinen, "Hammer and Sword," p. 354, and Purcell, *Labor Policies*, p. 29.

75. Thanks to the aggressiveness of the rubber workers' LAC, however, an agreement was in place by late 1941 protecting the seniority rights of all those laid off to work in defense. The URW, fearing mass displacements due to priorities decisions, complained to Hillman that rubber workers were being ignored by government officials and management. Hillman then forced a meeting between the rubber LAC and OPM representatives to work out a fairer basis for allocating rubber, for protecting seniority rights, and for relocating displaced workers, as well as to prevent rubber companies from allocating work to lower-wage nonunion centers. Purcell, *Labor Policies*, pp. 22, 158–62; Brandwen revised draft of Hillman memo to Roosevelt, December 15, 1941, cited in Purcell, p. 29; Koistinen, "Hammer and Sword," p. 247; and Donald Nelson address at meeting of CIO representatives at the National Press Club, March 23, 1942, Washington, D.C., Box 644, File 245.13, Records of the WPB.

76. Purcell, *Labor Policies*, p. 81.

77. "Minutes of the NDAC," Box 88, July 10, 1940, Edward R. Stettinius Papers, University of Virginia Library; notes from "Defense Housing File," early August 1940, H-ACWA Papers; and Purcell, *Labor Policies*, pp. 11–12.

78. Louis Ruchames, *Race, Jobs, and Politics: The Story of the Fair Employment Practices Commission* (New York, 1953), pp. 11–13; R. J. Lever, "Report of trip to Connecticut, May 19–20, 1941", file 246.01 "Labor Supply and Training Program," Records of the WPB; John A. Salmond, *A Southern Rebel: The Life and Times of Aubrey Willis Williams, 1890–1965* (Chapel Hill, N.C., 1983), pp. 173–75; *Fortune*, March 23, 1941; and Hillman/OPM to "All Holders of Defense Contracts," April 11, 1941, Series A, Box 261, Folder FEPC Council 1941, NAACP Record Group II, NAACP Papers, Library of Congress.

79. Knudsen to Roosevelt, May 28, 1941, Box 1016, "Labor 1940–42," Records of the WPB; Statement of NAACP Negro Labor Committee, May 1941, partially printed in *New York Times*, Series A Box 265, folder "FEPC Mediation Board Appointments," NAACP Records Group II, NAACP Papers; Robert Weaver, *Negro Labor: A National Problem* (New York, 1946), p. 133; Ruchames, *Race, Jobs, and Politics*, pp. 18–20; and "Minutes of the Council of the OPM," June 10, 1941, Historical Reports on War Administration, WPB Document Publications no. 2.

80. Roosevelt to Knudsen and Hillman, June 12, 1941, memo in H-ACWA Papers; Purcell, *Labor Policies*, cites Executive Order 8802, June 25, 1941, p. 198; Polenberg, *War and Society* (note 37 above), pp. 103–4; Ruchames, *Race, Jobs, and Politics*, pp. 20–21; Roosevelt to Knudsen and Hillman, June 14, 1941, H-ACWA Papers; Herbert Garfinkel, *When Negroes March: The March a Week Movement in the Organizational Politics for FEPC* (New York, 1969), p. 74; and Walter White and A. Philip Randolph to Mark Ethridge, August 7, 1941, Series A, Box A261, folder

"FEPC General 1941," NAACP Records Group II, NAACP Papers. The FEPC was then allotted a pathetic budget and no enforcement powers, but its very existence, however perilous and impoverished, was enough to infuriate congressmen like Howard W. Smith of Virginia. See Robert A. Garson, *The Democratic Party and the Politics of Sectionalism, 1941–48* (Baton Rouge, 1974), pp. 16–17.

81. Jean Christie, "Morris Llewellyn Cooke: Progressive Engineer," Ph.D. dissertation, Columbia University, 1963, p. 275.

82. "Minutes of the Council of the OPM," May 6 and 13, 1941; First, *Industry and Labor* (note 71 above), pp. 173–74; Notes on October 1940 visits made by Hillman, Political Documents file 013.227, Box 15, "Labor Division, NDAC," Records of the WPB; Sidney Hillman, "The Problems and Organization of Farming Out," Farming Out Bulletin no. 4, NDAC/Labor Division, H-ACWA Papers; Cooke to Stettinius, November 14, 1940, Box 129, file 241.1, "Labor—Unemployment," Records of the WPB; I. F. Stone, "FDR Says Knudsen Board is Studying Reuther Plan," *PM*, December 27, 1940; Cooke to Hillman, July 15, 1941, H-ACWA Papers; and Nelson, *Arsenal of Democracy* (note 59 above), p. 126.

83. Prichard to Hillman, December 9, 1941, H-ACWA Papers, and Koistinen, "Hammer and Sword," p. 620. Over the course of the war two-thirds, or $117 billion, of the gross amount of defense contracts were let to one hundred companies; one-third of that total was absorbed by thirty-six giant corporations; two-thirds of all federal research contracts went to sixty-eight leading companies. The Defense Plant Corporation, operating under the auspices of the RFC, invested $7 billion of government money in aircraft, steel, oil pipelines, synthetic rubber, transportation, and chemicals, in the process eliminating the contractor's risk for the cost of these new facilities. Fully one-half of the DPC investment was for plant and equipment operated by the largest concerns: GM, Curtiss-Wright, Chrysler, Ford, Anaconda, ALCOA, USS. Most subcontracting, moreover, was handled directly by these corporations, while an even smaller number ran mammoth government-built plants for which service they received an option to purchase after the war. See Gerald T. White, *Billions for Defense* (Tuscaloosa, Ala., 1980), p. 48, and Koistinen, cited above, p. 664.

84. Koistinen, "Hammer and Sword," p. 680, and James Rowe to Roosevelt, May 22, 1941, FDR Papers.

85. Author's interview with Robert Nathan, November 9, 1984; *The New Republic*, May 11, 1942; and Catton, *War Lords* (note 68 above), p. 42.

86. Koistinen, "Hammer and Sword," p. 623; Presidential Executive Order creating the SPAB, August 28, 1941, H-ACWA Papers; Bernard L. Gladieux "Reminiscences," pp. 239–40, OHCCU; Schwartz, *The Speculator* (note 26 above), p. 370; William Leiserson, "Labor Relations and the War," speech delivered in New York, February 18, 1942, Box 540, file 240.1, Records of the WPB; Nelson, *Arsenal of Democracy*, p. 139; Ickes diary entry, May 10, 1941, Reel 4, p. 5500, Ickes Diaries; and James Rowe to Roosevelt, January 23, 1941, FDR Papers.

87. Purcell, *Labor Policies*, pp. 29–32, and Oliver to Hillman, December 9, 1941, H-ACWA Papers.

88. Max Freedman, annotator, *Roosevelt and Frankfurter: Their Correspondence, 1928–45* (Boston, 1967), pp. 52–54.

89. Sidney Hillman, "Problems of Labor Supply and Training," March 3, 1942; Hillman to Representative Ludlow, March 25, 1942; and Hillman testimony before

Senate Committee on Education and Labor, April 2, 1942, all in H-ACWA Papers.

90. "Minutes of the War Production Board," March 3, 1942, Historical Reports on War Administration, WPB Document Publication no. 4, National Archives; John J. Corson to Robert Nathan, February 26, 1942, file 241, box 241, Records of the WPB; Wallace to Hillman, March 25, 1942, file L10-791, Wallace Papers, Library of Congress; and Hillman to Roosevelt, February 18, 1942, H-ACWA Papers.

91. Hillman to Roosevelt, April 2, 1942, H-ACWA Papers. A month earlier Prichard had advised Hillman on the need to develop a national policy to solve the "little steel" wage dispute then preoccupying the WLB. Prichard warned about the need to guard against inflation and to promote an equitable sharing of national income, including a tax program to recover excess profits and unreasonably elevated personal income; a forced savings plan; and provisions for distribution on the basis of need, including the raising of substandard wages and stabilizing the levels of the more highly paid. By the end of 1941 inflation had made its spectral appearance; wholesale prices were up 26 percent from mid-1939, and retail prices more than 12 percent. See Prichard to Hillman, February 25, 1942, H-ACWA Papers, and Lester V. Chandler and Donald M. Wallace, *Economic Mobilization and Stabilization* (New York, n.d.), pp. 325–29.

92. Koistinen, "Hammer and Sword," pp. 610–11, and Ickes diary entry, August 2, 1941, Reel 4, p. 5817. The presidential aide in question, James Rowe, went on to recommend that David Niles, a veteran adviser, be asked to join Hillman's staff, despite Niles's view "that there is a blight on Jews to which his own friends in the Administration are contributing." See James Rowe to Roosevelt, May 22, 1941, PSF File, FDR Papers. In an off-the-record interview Lewis told the *Time* correspondent Eddie Lockett: "Even President Roosevelt said he was naming Hillman because he was halfway between John L. Lewis and Bill Green." Labor had no real voice in the government, Lewis insisted. He was convinced that Hillman was trying to drive a wedge between Murray and himself. During the remainder of the interview Lewis vented his rage about Hillman's role in the North American strike, his double dealings with the AFL building trades, and so on. See Rowe to Hillman, August 5, 1941, H-ACWA Papers, and Zieger, *John L. Lewis* (note 12 above), p. 130.

93. Brown, *Industrial Relations Section of Princeton* (note 73 above), pp. 41–42; Donald H. Riddle, *The Truman Committee* (New Brunswick, N.J., 1964), p. 59; Arnold, "CIO's Role in American Politics" (note 2 above), p. 87; Purcell, *Labor Policies*, p. 237; Hillman to Murray, December 11, 1941, H-ACWA Papers; *Detroit Times*, December 18, 1941; and R. C. Jacobson to Germer, October 30, 1941, Adolph Germer Papers, Wisconsin State Historical Society, Madison.

94. Sidney Hillman "Statement Before the Senate Committee Investigating National Defense," October 22, 1941, H-ACWA Papers; *New York Times*, October 9, 1941; and Hillman–Carmody telephone conversation, October 7, 1941, "Selected Notes of Policy File, 1941–46," H-ACWA Papers. Hillman blamed Carmody for making a precipitous decision in originally ruling in Currier's favor. He went so far as to intimate that there were people in Carmody's agency itching for this kind of incident. From the AFL's standpoint, one of the worrying side issues of the Currier dispute was that the company specialized in prefabricated techniques, which might jeopardize the jobs of skilled tradesmen.

95. Richard Rohman to Hillman, October 6, 1941, H-ACWA Papers; *New York Times*,

October 23, 1941; and Harry S. Truman, *Memoirs* vol. 1: *Year of Decisions* (New York, 1955), p. 180.

96. *New York Times*, March 3, 1942; John L. Lewis–Brandwen telephone conversation, March 11, 1942, transcript in H-ACWA Papers; notes on meeting of WPB Labor Division, March 13, 1942, H-ACWA Papers; notes on letters between Joint Board managers and manufacturers, 1940–42, H-ACWA Papers; Fulton Lewis radio broadcast on Mutual Radio Network, March 6, 1942, transcript in H-ACWA Papers; and Nelson to Representative Albert J. Engel, March 7, 1942, File 546.01–546.063, Box 1820, Records of the WPB.

97. Purcell, *Labor Policies*, p. 30; "G" to Roosevelt, March 18, 1942, PSF 152, FDR Papers; Koistinen, "Hammer and Sword," p. 610; Flynn, *Mess in Washington* (note 62 above), pp. 15–16; memo of conversation between Herbert Emmerich and Sydney Hyman, May 1949, H-ACWA Papers; Roosevelt to Nelson, February 26, 1942, PPF 5646, FDR Papers; *Business Week*, May 2, 1942; and *Washington Times-Herald*, April 17, 1942.

98. Arnold, "CIO's Role in American Politics," p. 88; Ickes diary entry, May 3, 1942, Reel 5, pp. 6593–94, Ickes Diaries; Gladieux "Reminiscences," p. 35, OHCCU; Flynn, *Mess in Washington*, pp. 15–16, citing Roosevelt to Hillman, April 18, 1942; Roosevelt to Hillman, April 18, 1942, H-ACWA Papers.

99. Hillman to Roosevelt, May 1, 1942, PPF, FDR Papers. Apparently some of Hillman's close friends actually expected him to accept the new position, but that was never a serious possibility. It was common if unspoken knowledge that the position carried no power or influence and was in fact but another if gentler means of purging the labor element from the war bureaucracy. See *Business Week*, May 2 and April 25, 1942.

100. Hillman's "health records and doctor's visits," January 27, 1941, April 1941, and May 1942, in H-ACWA Papers; Purcell, *Labor Policies*, p. 29; notes on Hillman's sickness, June and July 1942, "Personal File," H-ACWA Papers; William D. Hassett, *Off the Record with FDR* (New Brunswick, N.J., 1958), p. 38; Francis X. Gannon, *Joseph D. Keenan, Labor's Ambassador in War and Peace: A Portrait of a Man and His Times* (Lanham, Md., 1984), p. 43; Ickes diary entry, May 3, 1942, Reel 5, pp. 6593–94, Ickes Diaries; Niles to Tully, May 19, 1942, PPF 3585, FDR Papers; and Roosevelt to Hillman, May 23, 1942, and Hillman to Roosevelt, June 2, 1942, PPF 3585, FDR Papers.

101. Arnold, "CIO's Role in American Politics," p. 90; Koistinen, "Hammer and Sword," pp. 676–80; Polenberg, *War and Society* (note 37 above), pp. 20–21; and Flynn, *Mess in Washington*, pp. 110–12.

102. Robert Burr Smith, "Labor and Manpower Administration in War Production," report to Advisory Commission of National Defense, May 1, 1943, file 240.2, box 1134, Records of the WPB, and Koistinen, "Hammer and Sword," p. 354.

103. Koistinen, "Hammer and Sword," p. 611. Herbert Emmerich, secretary of the OPM, in fact criticized both his bosses, telling them that the agency couldn't function properly if they took up their time racing from one strike to another, trying to be "Taft and Walsh . . . when they should be Baruch." See Herbert Emmerich and Sydney Hyman conversation transcript, May 1949, H-ACWA Papers; Purcell, *Labor Policies*, p. 18; Freedman, *Roosevelt and Frankfurter* (note 88 above), pp. 52–54; Smith, "Labor and Manpower"; and James W. Fesler, "Labor Activity of the NDAC and OPM," preliminary report of the policy analysis and records branch, September 12, 1945, p. 4, Office of the Executive Secretary of the WPB.

104. Emmerich and Hyman conversation transcript, H-ACWA Papers; Gladieux,

"Reminiscences," pp. 99, 239, OHCCU; and Perkins "Reminiscences," pp. 875–78, OHCCU.

105. Itinerary and report on West Coast trip of Hillman, September–October 1941, H-ACWA Papers.

106. B. Bisno, "Notes on Sidney Hillman," September 18, 1950, H-ACWA Papers; author's interview with A. H. Raskin, June 10, 1985; author's interview with Teccia Davidson Brill, April 29, 1986; and Isidor Lubin "Reminiscences," OHCCU.

107. Emmerich and Hyman conversation transcript, H-ACWA Papers; author's interview with Esther Peterson, January 15, 1985; Perkins "Reminiscences," p. 814, OHCCU; and Perkins, *The Roosevelt I Knew* (note 23 above), pp. 357–58.

SEVENTEEN: *"Clear It with Sidney"*

1. Archibald MacLeish to Hillman, May 11, 1942; FBI "Survey of Intelligence Materials no. 22 on the Battle of Production," May 6, 1942, Office of Facts and Figures of the Bureau of Intelligence; and FBI "Report on Workers and the War, Division of Surveys Report no. 12," April 28, 1942, H-ACWA Papers.

2. Lester V. Chandler and Donald Wallace, eds., *Economic Mobilization and Stabilization* (New York, n.d.), pp. 152–53; *New York Times*, November 8, 1943; Maurice Isserman, *Which Side Were You On?: The American Communist Party During the Second World War* (Middletown, Conn., 1982), pp. 206–7; and Alan S. Milward, *War, Economy, and Society, 1939–45* (Berkeley, Calif., 1977), p. 242. The caucus insisted in addition that overtime and premium pay for weekend work be restored. Its impact was felt outside the union, as the Michigan CIO called for the creation of a labor party. Walter Reuther allied himself with the movement in 1943 as a stick with which to flay his opponents in the CP, but by 1944 the repercussions were worrisome enough to unite the leadership in the purging and disciplining of dissident rank-and-filers. See Irving Howe and B. J. Widick, *The UAW and Walter Reuther* (New York, 1949), and Joel Seidman, *American Labor from Defense to Reconversion* (Chicago, 1953), p. 139.

3. Seidman, *American Labor*, p. 160, and Bert Cochran, *Labor and Communism: The Conflict that Shaped American Unions* (Princeton, N.J., 1979), pp. 201–2.

4. Carlo Tresca to Luigi Antonini, August 24, 1939, file 1d, box 340, David Dubinsky Collection, ILGWU Archives; A. Bellanca to Joseph Salerno, October 18, 1940, and A. Bellanca to Julia Maretta, July 19, 1938, both in H-ACWA Papers; John P. Diggins, *Mussolini and Italian Fascism: The View from America* (Princeton, N.J., 1972), p. 407; A. Bellanca to the GEB, October 10, 1939, H-ACWA Papers; Ronald H. Bayor, *Neighbors in Conflict: The Irish, Germans, Jews, and Italians of New York City, 1929–41* (Baltimore, 1978), p. 143; Salvatore La Gumina, "Case Studies of Ethnicity and Italio-American Politicians," in Silvano M. Tomasi and Madeline H. Engel, eds., *The Italian Experience in the United States* (Center for Migration Studies, New York, 1970), p. 151; Kenneth Waltzer interview with Jacob Potofsky, November 13, 1968, transcript in possession of author; and Robert P. Ingalls, *Herbert H. Lehman and New York's Little New Deal* (New York, 1975), p. 142.

5. John Morton Blum, ed., *The Price of Vision: The Diary of Henry Wallace, 1942–46* (Boston, 1973), diary entry, February 22, 1944, p. 302; "Notes" on Leo Krzycki, H-ACWA Papers; and Len De Caux, *Labor Radical: From the Wobblies to CIO—A Personal History* (Boston, 1970), pp. 326–27.

6. "Political Review of 1940," typescript in box 4, Jack Kroll Papers, Library of Con-

gress, and Morris Cooke to Marvin MacIntyre, June 3, 1942, PPF 940, FDR Papers, Hyde Park, N.Y.

7. "Sidney Hillman Health, 1941–43" file, H-ACWA Papers; Cooke to Hillman, May 9, 1942, H-ACWA Papers; and *New York Times*, July 10, 1942.

8. MacIntyre to Roosevelt, memos, September 11 and 14 and October 3, 1942, PPF 8172, FDR Papers; MacIntyre to Roosevelt, September 19, 1942, President's Official File (OFF) 2546, FDR Papers; Richard Norton Smith, *Thomas E. Dewey and His Times* (New York, 1982), p. 346; Ickes to Harry Slattery, July 6, 1942, box 237, p. 67, Ickes Papers, Library of Congress; and Herbert Lehman "Reminiscences," pp. 710–15, OHCCU.

9. Roosevelt to Hillman, October 9, 1942, H-ACWA Papers; *New York Times*, October 29, 1942; Delbert D. Arnold, "The CIO's Role in American Politics, 1936–1948," Ph.D. dissertation, University of Maryland, 1952; A. Bellanca to La Guardia, October 22, 1942, box 2680, La Guardia Papers, Municipal Archives; and press release, October 29, 1942, H-ACWA Papers. Hillman phoned Pa Watson about the President's letter, which Flynn was urging him to release but which a discomfited Hillman wanted first to discuss with FDR. Transcript of Hillman call to Watson and memo to Miss Barnes, October 13, 1942, OFF 4910, FDR Papers; Smith, *Thomas E. Dewey*, p. 346; *Advance*, November 11, 1942.

10. Kenneth Waltzer interview with Potofsky, November 11, 1968; Hugh A. Bone, "Political Parties in New York City," *American Political Science Review*, vol. 40, April 1946; Richard Lowitt, *George W. Norris: The Triumph of a Progressive, 1933–1944* (Urbana, Ill., 1977), p. 425; Seidman, *American Labor*, p. 200; and Norman Chapman, "Contours of Public Policy, 1939–45," Ph.D. dissertation, Yale University, 1976, pp. 273–74.

11. Robert A. Garson, *The Democratic Party and the Politics of Sectionalism, 1941–48* (Baton Rouge, 1974), p. 22.

12. *Ibid.*, pp. 73–74; Richard Polenberg, *War and Society: The United States, 1941–45* (Philadelphia, 1972), p. 167; John Robert Moore, "The Conservative Coalition in the United States Senate, 1942–45," *Journal of Southern History*, vol. 33, August 1967; and M. H. Hinchey, "The Frustration of the New Deal Revival, 1944–46," Ph.D. dissertation, University of Missouri, 1965, pp. 42–43.

13. James Rowe to Roosevelt, July 19, 1942, President's Secretary File 148, FDR Papers.

14. Jordan A. Schwartz, *The Speculator: Bernard M. Baruch in Washington, 1917–65* (Chapel Hill, N.C., 1981), p. 52; Barton J. Bernstein, "The Debate on Industrial Reconversion: The Protection of Oligopoly and the Military Control of the Economy," *American Journal of Economics and Sociology*, vol. 26, April 1967; and idem, "The Removal of War Production Board Controls on Business, 1944–46," *Business History Review*, Summer 1965. According to a postwar summing-up by Maury Maverick's Smaller War Plants Corporation, by the war's end eight financial clusters dominated 29 percent of all nonfinancial and banking assets and a majority of the top 250 corporations. For example, the Morgan–First National City Bank of New York group allegedly controlled thirteen industrial corporations headed by USS and including most of the major primary materials producers in iron, coal, copper, and brass, as well as the key manufacturers of electrical and nonelectrical equipment, twelve utilities, eleven major railroads, and five financial institutions; the Mellon interests encompassed nine major industrial corporations, including such infrastructural suppliers as Jones & Laughlin and American Rolling Mills, one railroad, a utility, and two banks; and so on. The report cited Kuhn, Loeb railroad interests;

Rockefeller's oil and banking through Chase Manhattan; DuPont domination of three large industrials, including GM; a Chicago group of banks, meatpacking, and utility firms; a Boston banking, shoe machinery, and utilities behemoth; and a Cleveland-centered circle of banks and various steel companies, including Republic, Inland, Youngstown, and Wheeling. The precision of the report's groupings is open to question, but its underlying message is not. It found that the relative weight of big business, especially megalith-sized corporations, rose sharply during the war, while smaller businesses declined in importance. In 1938 smaller firms—those employing fewer than five hundred—accounted for 52 percent of total manufacturing employ- ment, but only 38 percent in 1944, with the steepest drops in the machinery and chemicals industries. The greatest concentration of assets occurred in iron and steel, nonferrous metals, ordnance, all kinds of machinery, transportation equipment, chemicals, oil, coal, and rubber. The report argued that the largest companies dominated not only particular manufacturing sectors "but the entire economy as a whole." Nor was this the working out of some inexorable law of progress. The systematic distribution of contracts to a small number of firms; favored access to raw materials, plants and parts; and generous amortization and carryback provisions under the tax code all were to blame. Research and development were conducted at government expense, and the eight largest corporations received two-thirds of that, while many companies walked away with patents developed under government aus- pices. The country's top hundred corporations monopolized two-thirds of the dollar volume of prime government contracts. The top ten corporations actually controlled 30 percent. Of the $26 billion of new plant and equipment built between 1939 and 1945, $20 billion was estimated as convertible to peacetime use, and the top 250 corporations potentially stood to control two-thirds of these assets, with even higher percentages in industries like iron and steel, shipping, aircraft, and fabri- cated metal products. See *Report of the Smaller War Plants Corporation* (Johnson Reprints, New York, 1972), pp. 18–42. The original report was prepared for a Special Commission to Study the Problems of American Small Business of the United States Senate, 79th Cong., 2d Sess., by John Blair, Harrison Haughton, and Matthew Rose on June 14, 1946. See also Paul A. C. Koistinen, "The Ham- mer and the Sword: Labor, the Military, and Industrial Mobilization, 1920–45," Ph.D. dissertation, University of California, Berkeley, 1964, pp. 721–22; Nelson Lichtenstein, *Labor's War at Home: The CIO in World War II* (New York, 1982), p. 91; and Donald M. Nelson, *Arsenal of Democracy: The Story of American War Production* (New York, 1946), pp. 391–400.

15. Howell John Harris, "Getting Everybody Back on the Same Team: An Interpreta- tion of the Industrial Relations Policies of American Business in the 1940s," Ph.D. dissertation, Oxford University, 1977, pp. 53–54, 64–66, 202, 207. The CED at its inception was a self-consciously elite organization. It deliberately excluded labor participation after preliminary discussions with Hillman and George Harrison. While it was prepared to accept the essentials of the New Deal's truncated welfare state and to deal with the responsible leadership of the AFL and the CIO, it rejected out of hand the stagnationist views of people like Hansen and Eziekel for fear they would invite an intolerable degree of state intervention. See Kim McQuaid, *Big Business and Presidential Power: From FDR to Reagan* (New York, 1982), pp. 109–10, and Robert Maurice Collins, "Business Responses to Keynesian Economics, 1929–64: An Analysis of the Process by Which the Modern Political Economy Was Defined," Ph.D. dissertation, Johns Hopkins University, 1975, pp. 220–30.

16. Robert H. Zieger, *John L. Lewis: Labor Leader* (Boston, 1988), pp. 136–37.
17. John A. Salmond, *Miss Lucy of the CIO: The Life and Times of Lucy Randolph Mason* (Athens, Ga., 1988), p. 107.
18. Richard Polenberg, *War and Society*, p. 204; Lowitt, *George W. Norris*, p. 445; and CIO Executive Board Minutes, February 5, 1943, Roll 2, AFL-CIO Headquarters, Washington, D.C.
19. Hillman remarks at CIO convention in Massachusetts, April 4, 1943, H-ACWA Papers; David Niles to General Watson, August 10, 1943, OFF 4910, FDR Papers; and Hillman to Wayne Coy, January 8, 1944, cited in Chapman, "Contours of Public Policy," p. 370.
20. The PAC executive included R. J. Thomas, Sherman Dalrymple of the rubber workers, Van Bittner from the USW, and Fitzgerald from the UE. The CIO endorsed the executive board action at its November convention. See James C. Foster, "1954: A CIO Victory?" in Charles Rehmus, Doris McLaughlin, and Frederick Nesbitt, eds., *Labor and American Politics* (Ann Arbor, Mich., 1978). There was some third-party sentiment inside the TWUA, articulated by Sol Stetin in New Jersey, but it was firmly opposed by Rieve at the 1943 convention, where Stetin lost badly. "Abstract of TWUA Oral History Project," Wisconsin State Historical Society, Madison, and CIO Executive Board Minutes, July 7–8, 1943, Roll 2, AFL-CIO Headquarters.
21. Joseph Gaer, *The First Round: The Story of the CIO-PAC* (New York, 1944), and "Sidney Hillman on Political Action: Excerpts from Speeches and Articles, 1924–1944," H-ACWA Papers. Murray, along with the PAC vice president Van Bittner, reinforced Hillman by announcing that "it is definitely not the policy of the CIO to organize a third party." See Garson, *Democratic Party and Politics of Sectionalism*, p. 58.
22. John Earl Haynes, *Dubious Alliance: The Making of the Minnesota Democratic Farmer Labor Party* (Minneapolis, 1984), p. 110; Memo summarizing Hague to Grace Tully, April 10, 1943, OFF 4910, FDR Papers; Hague to Tully memo, April 5, 1943, OFF 4910, FDR Papers; and August Scholle to Baldwin, March 21, 1944, FBI File 57–407, Section 7, acquired under the FOIA. Hillman was careful to cover his left flank as well. Thus, although he defended the no-strike pledge and the WLB when addressing a TWUA convention, he also demanded that the Board get back the power it recently lost to grant wage adjustments based on inequalities and inequities and criticized the manpower administration for failing to prevent hoarding, for the underutilization of women and Negro workers, for laxity in enforcement of seniority rules, and for its timorous attitude when it came to labor's rights. Hillman speech at TWUA convention, May 13, 1943, H-ACWA Papers.
23. New York State Labor Non-Partisan League "Declaration of Principles," July 16, 1936, H-ACWA Papers.
24. Hillman testimony before House Campaign Expenditure Committee, August 2, 1944, excerpt in H-ACWA Papers.
25. PAC Policy and Program 1944, "PAC 1943–44" file, H-ACWA Papers.
26. Alonzo L. Hamby, *Beyond the New Deal: Harry S. Truman and American Liberalism* (New York, 1973), pp. 26, 159; Merton W. Ertell, "The CIO Industrial Council Plan: Its Background and Implications," Ph.D. dissertation, University of Chicago, 1955, p. 6; Eziekel to Hillman, February 19, 1942, H-ACWA Papers; and Marriner S. Eccles, "Address Before the Annual Conference of Mayors," January 13, 1942, Washington, D.C., H-ACWA Papers.

27. "Security, Work, and Relief Policies," National Resources Planning Board, February 10, 1943, cited in Marion Clawson, *New Deal Planning: The National Resources Planning Board* (Baltimore, 1981), pp. 12–13, and Patrick D. Regan, "The Architects of American National Planning," Ph.D. dissertation, Ohio State University, 1982, pp. 345–46. The report's emphasis on state planning and cradle-to-grave social security enraged congressional conservatives. Under the leadership of Robert A. Taft, they attacked the report and killed the Board, mortally wounding at the same time the Wagner–Murray–Dingell bill for expanded social insurance. See Chapman, "Contours of Public Policy," p. 364, and Hillman testimony before the House Committee on Campaign Expenditures, August 2, 1944, excerpt in H-ACWA Papers.

28. "People's Plans for Reconversion," CIO-PAC pamphlet of the month no. 2, 1944, cited in Arnold, "CIO's Role in American Politics" (note 9 above), p. 104; Gaer, *First Round,* p. 204; *New York Times,* May 9, 1944; and "Proceedings of the Full Employment Conference," January 14–15, 1944, pp. 42–43, 87–89, cited in Arnold, "CIO's Role," p. 104, and in H-ACWA Papers. While the PAC condemned large-scale corporate farming, its own vision of a commercialized rural America replicated the approach of Morris Cooke and others at the REA and TVA. An agricultural RFC would extend rural electrification and government subsidized co-ops, soil conservation, irrigation, reforestation, and rural road-building projects to open up the hinterland to the delectations of mass merchandizing.

29. "Proceedings of the Full Employment Conference," January 14–15, 1944, pp. 24–25, 39, 87–90; "People's Plan for Reconversion," 1944 pamphlet; Arnold, "CIO's Role in American Politics," p. 114; Koistinen, "Hammer and Sword," p. 768; and CIO Executive Board Minutes, June 16–18, 1944, Roll 3, AFL-CIO Headquarters.

30. "Proceedings of the Full Employment Conference," pp. 133–34, 144, 156; "People's Plan for Reconversion" pamphlet; "The People's Program for 1944," p. 206, H-ACWA Papers; and Hillman speech at Russian War Relief dinner, December 22, 1942, H-ACWA Papers.

31. "Proceedings of the Full Employment Conference," pp. 16, 17, 12–13, 8, 6, 15, 38, 19–36; "Four Men Speak About Jobs for All," CIO-PAC publication no. 2, 1944, pp. 3, 16, 17, 34, H-ACWA Papers; and "People's Plan for Reconversion" pamphlet. Paul Hoffman's CED talked not of "full employment" but of "high levels" or "satisfactory levels." The National Planning Association pessimistically predicted that it would require a 40 percent increase in output over 1941 to soak up anticipated labor reserves after the war. See Aaron Levenstein, *Labor Today and Tomorrow* (New York, 1945), p. 205; Philip Murray, "Labor's Political Aims," CIO publication no. 102, cited in Arnold, "CIO's Role in American Politics," p. 19.

32. Gaer, *First Round,* p. 163.

33. Clark Clifford to Truman, 1947, cited in Bert Cochran, *Harry Truman and the Crisis Presidency* (New York, 1973), p. 13; and CIO Executive Board Minutes, October 28 and 29 and November 2 and 6, 1943, Roll 2, AFL-CIO Headquarters.

34. Cochran, *Harry Truman and Crisis Presidency,* p. 13; CIO Executive Board Minutes, October 28–29 and November 2 and 6, 1943, Roll 2; and *The New Republic,* October 9, 1944.

35. *Advance,* September 15 and October 1, 1943; *Detroit News,* September 15, 1943; *Minneapolis Tribune,* September 20, 1943; and GEB Report, 1940–44, May 1944, H-ACWA Papers.

36. Arnold, "CIO's Role in American Politics," p. 226. The ACW, USW, UE, UAW,

and CIO each chipped in $100,000; the shipyard workers donated $50,000, and $25,000 checks arrived from the textile, fur, and rubber workers. See Gaer, *First Round,* p. 177. The PAC raised $600,000 more during the 1944 primary season. Catherine Williams to Jerome Davis, May 7, 1962, H-ACWA Papers.

37. Polenberg, *War and Society* (note 18 above), p. 205; CIO Executive Board Minutes, January 27–28, 1944, AFL-CIO Headquarters; Robert Lamb to Murray, October 1944, "CIO-PAC 1944–45" file, Box 5, Philip Murray Papers, Catholic University; PAC Voting Records, FBI File 57-407, Section 15, acquired under the FOIA; F. P. Weber to Baldwin, February 10, 1944, FBI File 57-407, Section 17; and Fay Calkins, *The CIO and the Democratic Party* (Chicago, 1952), p. 115.

38. "This Is Your America," PAC pamphlet, July 1944, H-ACWA Papers, and Gaer, *First Round,* pp. 75–76.

39. "Big Business and Mobilization," PAC pamphlet, H-ACWA Papers; James C. Foster, *The Union Politic: The CIO Political Action Committee* (Columbus, Mo., 1975); and Hillman address as state chairman of the American Labor Party at state committee meeting, August 10, 1944, ALP press release, H-ACWA Papers.

40. Blum, *Price of Vision* (note 5 above), diary entries, October 21 and November 8, 1943, pp. 264–67, and February 16, 1944, p. 298; telephone conversation between Hillman and Niles, June 1944, OFF 4910, FDR Papers; and Hillman to Ickes, June 18, 1944, Ickes Diaries, pp. 9006–8, Library of Congress.

41. Hinchey, "Frustration of the New Deal Revival" (note 12 above), p. 13; Koistinen, "Hammer and Sword," pp. 761–62; and Garson, *Democratic Party and Politics of Sectionalism* (note 11 above), pp. 142–43.

42. Garson, *Democratic Party and Politics of Sectionalism,* pp. 73–77, 75–80; Gaer, *First Round,* p. 258; *New York Times,* June 16 and 22, 1944; and Arnold, "CIO's Role in American Politics" (note 9 above), p. 153.

43. In mid-June the CIO Executive Board discussed the need to shift campaign funds from union treasuries to individual contributions—strictly voluntary contributions that no one could show to be coerced. See CIO Executive Board Minutes, June 16–18, 1944, AFL-CIO Headquarters, and Ickes to Charles Merriam, July 3, 1944, Harold Ickes Papers, Library of Congress.

44. Arnold, "CIO's Role in American Politics," p. 234. Feeling his age, Norris declined the heavy responsibility and accepted the honorary chairmanship instead. Norris to Hillman, July 17 and August 1, 1944, H-ACWA Papers; *Washington Daily News,* June 19 and July 11, 1944; *Washington Post,* June 29, 1944; and *New York Times,* August 6, 1944. Norris took on the honorary post only after much prodding from Hillman. Gaer, *First Round,* pp. 217, 258; Cochran, *Harry Truman and Crisis Presidency,* p. 13; Garson, *Democratic Party and Politics of Sectionalism,* p. 66; and Report of the GEB, May 1944, H-ACWA Papers.

45. Kenneth Waltzer, "The American Labor Party: Third Party Politics in New Deal—Cold War New York, 1936–54," Ph.D. dissertation, Harvard University, 1977, pp. 91, f. 60, 223–25; Alex Rose to David Dubinsky and Hillman, June 19, 1940, File 2a, box 144, David Dubinsky Collection, ILGWU Archives; Paul Blanshard, Chairman of the Liberal and Labor Committee to Safeguard the ALP, leaflet, April 1940, file 2b, Box 144, Dubinsky Collection, ILGWU Archives; and *New York Times,* October 6, 1939.

46. Programmatically the two factions were indistinguishable in most respects. Everyone agreed on the Keynesian–social democratic agenda: planning for reconversion, rigorous enforcement of rent and price and rationing controls, the elimination of racial

and religious discrimination, the creation of a permanent FEPC, a menu of veteran assistance agencies, and vast public undertakings in the areas of low-cost housing and rural electrification. See "1944 State Program of the American Labor Party"; ALP flyers; and E. S. Epstein to La Guardia, December 21, 1939, all in H-ACWA Papers. See also press release of Progressive Committee to Rebuild ALP, April 18, 1941, Box 4, Labor's Non-Partisan League Papers, Catholic University; Progressive Committee to Rebuild the ALP mailing, August 7, and press releases, August 9 and 11, 1940, Box 4, LNPL Papers; "Notes" from 1941, LNPL General File, Box 4, LNPL Papers, Wisconsin State Historical Society; and Potofsky to Blumberg, June 10, 1941, H-ACWA Papers.

47. *New York Times*, August 6, 1942; Waltzer, "American Labor Party," p. 265; and *The New Republic*, August 21, 1944. For this reason, Hillman reaffiliated the ACW with the Greater New York State Industrial Council, controlled by the left.

48. Author's interview with Virginia Hardman, June 11, 1985; David Dubinsky and A. H. Raskin, *David Dubinsky: A Life with Labor* (New York, 1977), p. 273; and Maurice Isserman, *Which Side Were You On?: The American Communist Party During the Second World War* (Middletown, Conn., 1982), p. 160.

49. ACWA press releases, July 28 and October 23, 1943; Hillman to Rose, January 23, 1944; Counts and Rose to Hillman, January 25, 1944; and Hillman to Counts and Rose, February 9, 1944, all in H-ACWA Papers. Another largely bogus charge hurled back and forth by both factions was the issue of democratic control of the ALP. From first to last the party was run from the top down, and the only real question was who at the top was going to run it in the future. Kenneth Waltzer interview with Charles Zimmerman, August 7, 1969, transcript in possession of author, and Waltzer interview with Jacob Potofsky, November 13, 1968, transcript in possession of author.

50. Author's interview with A. H. Raskin, June 10, 1985; author's interview with Esther Peterson, February 1985; Melech Epstein, *Jewish Labor in the U.S.A.*, vol. 1: *1882–1914* (New York, 1950), pp. 236–37; and Waltzer,"American Labor Party," pp. 289–99.

51. Rosenman to Roosevelt, January 1, 1944, OFF 407, box 4, FDR Papers; White House memos, January 21 and February 1, 1944, OFF 4910, and Henry Wallace "Reminiscences," pp. 3255, 3110–11, OHCCU. For that matter, even leftists like the ALP's Eugene Connolly were voicing similar worries to Hillman about Democratic disarray and the prospect of defeat, even of Negro disaffection. By and large, the Irish rank and file of the TWU did not vote for the ALP ticket despite the popularity and notoriety of their picturesque leader, Mike Quill. Waltzer interview with Zimmerman, August 7, 1969, and Connolly to Hillman, March 24, 1944, H-ACWA Papers. Other presidential aides also prevailed upon Hillman to back down and sever his alliance with the left to avoid losing New York. *New York Times*, March 2, 1944.

52. White House memos, January 21 and February 1, 1944; General Watson telegram to Dubinsky, March 31, 1944; and David Niles to General Watson, March 21, 1944, all in OFF 4910, FDR Papers. Roosevelt to Hillman, February 7, 1944, PPF 8172, FDR Papers; Blum, *Price of Vision* (note 5 above), diary entry, March 3, 1944, p. 309; Potofsky speech at rally of Bronx County Committee for a United Labor Party, February 17, 1944, H-ACWA Papers; and Blumberg press release, 1944, H-ACWA Papers.

53. Jacob Potofsky "Notes," 1944, H-ACWA Papers, and Waltzer, "American Labor Party," p. 298.
54. J. B. S. Hardman "Reminiscences," p. 67, OHCCU. Statement by David Dubinsky, file 4a, Box 144; A. M. Whitehead to Dubinsky, March 31, 1944, file 3b, Box 143; Dean Alfange radio broadcast, March 27, 1944, file 4a, Box 144; and notes on election of March 28, 1944, file 4a, Box 144, all in David Dubinsky Collection, ILGWU Archives. Mark Starr to Ann Holmes, February 23, 1944, folder 8, Box B, and Starr to George Counts, March 30, 1944, folder 7, Box B, Mark Starr Papers, Tamiment Library, New York University. Nor were the victors much more judicious. The *United Labor News* ran a headline the following month—"Rose, Alfange Honor Fascist Agent, Use Hitler Propaganda Tricks"—about a dinner in honor of Genovese Pope that included a picture of Pope surrounded by fascist dignitaries saluting Mussolini. *United Labor News*, factional newspaper of Hillman and the PAC, 1944, file 4b, Box 144, Dubinsky Collection.
55. Louis Waldman, "Will the CIO Capture the Democratic Party?" condensed from August 26, 1944, *Saturday Evening Post* in the *Reader's Digest*, September 1944. Both Hillman and Dubinsky continued to plead their case before Eleanor Roosevelt for weeks after the primary. Hillman told the President's wife he sought only to strengthen her husband's hand by enlarging the trade union base of the party, that the charge of communism was a canard, evidently so once the right rejected the offer of the trade union leadership and the CP to eschew party office and La Guardia's last ditch unity plan. See Hillman to Eleanor Roosevelt, April 17, 1944, folder 2c, Box 376, Dubinsky Collection. Mrs. Roosevelt must have asked Dubinsky to respond, because a month later he wrote to vilify Hillman. He reminded the First Lady of the Hitler–Stalin pact, when Hillman shunned the CP, and then charged that Hillman deliberately allied himself with his onetime foe in 1943 purely to capture control of the ALP. The principal and principled issue, he insisted, was that the Communists "have no place or rights . . . since their political philosophy is diametrically opposed to ours." Spitefully, he predicted that although Hillman now "glories in his so-called victory," it was in truth a "phantom," as he had only "succeeded in pulling political chestnuts out of the fire for the Communists." Dubinsky concluded with an outburst of invective pillorying Hillman as "a major stockholder in the Communist Labor Party." See Dubinsky to Eleanor Roosevelt, May 23, 1944, file 2c, Box 376, Dubinsky Collection.
56. Waltzer interview with Zimmerman, August 7, 1969. PM speculated very early in 1944 that although the right would contest the primaries, its true purpose was to form a separate party. PM, January 13, 1944; Waltzer, "American Labor Party," p. 317; and House Committee on Un-American Activities, "Report on CIO-PAC," House report 13, pp. 78–79, March 29, 1944, 78th Cong., 2d Sess., Washington, D.C.
57. Bert Cochran, *Labor and Communism: The Conflict that Shaped American Unions* (Princeton, N.J., 1979), p. 257; A. H. Raskin, "Sidney Hillman, 1887–1946," *American Jewish Yearbook*, vol. 49, 1947–48; Thomas Burns to Joseph Salerno, April 27, 1944, file 57-407, Section 17, FBI Files, acquired under FOIA; and Germer to Allan S. Haywood, September 7 and 19, 1944, H-ACWA Papers.
58. HUAC "Report on CIO-PAC," p. 7; *New York Post*, January 14, 1944; Gaer, *First Round* (note 21 above), pp. 100–101; Harvey A. Levenstein, *Communism, Anti-Communism, and the CIO* (Westport, Conn., 1981), p. 191; and Green to Roosevelt, February 23, 1944, OFF 407, Box 4, FDR Papers.

59. *New York Times*, April 13 and June 10, 1944. Under special orders from FBI Director Hoover, the investigation was carried out at great speed. Assistant Attorney General Tom Clark wanted it conducted with the "utmost propriety" and with the "highest degree of discretion and tact." Hillman, Beanie Baldwin, and John Abt were interviewed at PAC headquarters, as were other national and local CIO leaders. FBI agents paid special attention to known and suspected Communists. Everybody testified to the purely educational and nonpartisan purposes of the PAC. The final report to Hoover concluded that the organization operated within the law, was mainly educational in nature, and had been entirely cooperative. Information supplied by Representative Dies was found to be of minimal use. See J. F. Buckley to D. M. Ladd, July 25, 1944, file 57-407, Section 8, FBI files; FBI report to Hoover, August 4, 1944, file 57-407, Section 13, FBI files; and D. M. Ladd to Hoover, August 19, 1944, file 57-407, Section 18, FBI files.

60. Gaer, *First Round*, pp. 233–34; "Report of the Committee on Presidential and Vice-Presidential and Senatorial Campaign Expenditures, 1944," June 13, 1944, pp. 142–43, 78th Cong., 2d Sess.; and HUAC investigation on Un-American Propaganda Activity in the United States, hearings, September 27–October 5, 1944, House Resolution 282, 78th Cong., 2d Sess.

61. Cochran, *Labor and Communism*, p. 94; *Congressional Record*, 78th Cong., 2d Sess., May 25, 1944, pp. 5054 *ff*; and Garson, *Democratic Party and Politics of Sectionalism* (note 11 above), pp. 108–16.

62. *New York Times*, July 25, 1944.

63. *Boston Herald*, July 11, 1944; H. O. Hunter to editors of all Hearst papers, September 12, 1944, H-ACWA Papers; Louis Overacker, "Labor Rides the Political Waves," *Current History*, December 1944; and Hearst contest, "Mail to Sidney Limerick Editor," *New York Journal-American*, n.d.

64. Arnold, "CIO's Role in American Politics," (note 9 above), p. 468; *New York Mirror*, September 29, 1944; *New York Daily News*, September 23, 1944; *Minneapolis Tribune*, November 2, 1944; *Newsweek*, September 25, 1944; and John Cort, "Hillman, OPA and PAC," *Commonweal*, October 20, 1944.

65. Polenberg, *War and Society* (note 18 above), p. 208; *Chicago Tribune*, August 6, 1944; Smith, *Thomas E. Dewey and His Times* (note 8 above), p. 410.

66. Smith, *Thomas E. Dewey and His Times*, p. 410; *New York Times*, October 1, 17, and 20, 1944; *New York Daily Mirror*, October 17, 1944; Polenberg, *War and Society*, p. 208; Republican Party speakers' manual, "What to Talk About," August, 1944, quoted in *The New Republic*, October 30, 1944; Isserman, *Which Side Were You On?* (note 48 above), p. 211.

67. *Baltimore Sun*, September 20, 1944.

68. Garson, *Democratic Party and Politics of Sectionalism*, p. 124; Arnold, "CIO's Role in American Politics," p. 171; and Joseph P. Camp and Westbrook Pegler, "Vote CIO and Get a Soviet America." The pamphlet went on to describe Hillman as "the suave and slippery front man. He is a diplomat of the smooth and sinister type . . . and he is dangerous. He gets around and has slept in both Moscow's Kremlin and the White House." Frank Gannett's Committee for Constitutional Government used similar Jew-baiting and red-baiting literature. See Arnold, "CIO's Role," p. 468.

69. Ickes meeting with Wallace, August 20, 1944, Reel 7, p. 9185, Ickes Diaries, Library of Congress; Adolph Germer to Herman Volk, September 13, 1944, H-ACWA Papers; and Niles to Tully, October 2, 1944, PPF 115, FDR Papers.

70. Robert J. Donovan, *Conflict and Crisis: The Presidency of Harry S. Truman, 1945–48*

(New York, 1977), p. xi, citing Oral History of James Rowe, transcript in Truman Library; Elliot Janeway, *The Struggle for Survival* (New Haven, 1951), pp. 348–49; Schwartz, *The Speculator*, p. 472; Alben W. Barkley, *That Reminds Me* (New York, 1954), pp. 190–91.

71. James F. Byrnes, *All in One Lifetime* (New York, 1958), pp. 227–28.

72. CIO-PAC Conference, June 16–17, 1944, resolution to endorse Wallace, cited in Arnold, "CIO's Role in American Politics," p. 149.

73. Donovan, *Conflict and Crisis*, p. xi; Garson, *Democratic Party and Politics of Sectionalism*, p. 37; Norman Markowitz, *The Rise and Fall of the People's Century: Henry A. Wallace and American Liberalism, 1941–48* (New York, 1973); Sidney Lens, *A Crisis of American Labor* (New York, 1959); and Henry Wallace diary entry, November 8, 1943, from Henry Wallace "Reminiscences," OHCCU.

74. Cochran, *Harry Truman and Crisis Presidency* (note 33 above), p. 13. Truman's was a slippery record on labor and social welfare: a supporter of Smith–Connally, but an advocate of relief; an opponent of the $25,000 salary cap, but a strong advocate of price controls. See Lens, *Crisis of American Labor*, and Robert F. Sherwood, *Roosevelt and Hopkins: An Intimate History* (New York, 1950), pp. 881–82. Early in 1944 a meeting in Hyde Park among Hannegan, Flynn, Kelly, and Dave Lawrence of Pennsylvania concluded that Wallace was a liability. Roosevelt remained noncommittal but was rumored to have told Ed Flynn that Truman was his choice. And indeed one less sinister version of the "Clear it with Sidney" story has it that Roosevelt intended to apprise Hillman of this decision in advance only so that he could do the necessary fence-mending with the CIO. See Warren Moscow "Reminiscences," pp. 8, 10, OHCCU.

75. Ickes diary entry, June 18, 1944, Reel 7, pp. 9006–8, Ickes Diaries, Library of Congress, and Wallace "Reminiscences," p. 3370, OHCCU.

76. *CIO News*, July 17 and 24, 1944; *New York Times*, July 18, 1944; Sam Rosenman, "What Makes a President?" *Ladies Home Journal*, May 1952; and Cochran, *Harry Truman and Crisis Presidency*, p. 15. Krock later denied he meant to imply that the convention decision was left in Hillman's hands. See *Editor and Publisher*, October 28, 1944, and *New York Times*, July 25, 1944.

77. *New York Times*, July 22, 1944, and *Newsweek*, July 19, 1944. Beforehand, he apparently told Ickes that he preferred Truman but was prepared to swing the PAC behind whoever the President wanted. Ickes quickly conveyed the news to Grace Tully so she could get the word to the President before Hillman arrived. See Ickes diary entry, July 16, 1944, Reel 17, p. 9088. Tom Corcoran credited Hillman's conversion to Truman to the efforts of Harry Hopkins, who in turn worked through David Niles, a trusted Hillman associate and presidential aide. See Ickes diary entry, July 30, 1944, Reel 17, pp. 9121–22; Byrnes, *All in One Lifetime*, pp. 227–28; and Harry S. Truman, *Memoirs*, vol. 1: *Years of Decision* (New York, 1955), p. 191. In another less credible version, Hillman is alleged to have said there was only one other person the CIO could support and that "I am looking at him now." Alfred Steinberg, *The Man from Missouri* (New York, 1962), p. 106, cited in Arthur F. McClure, *The Truman Administration and the Problems of Post-War Labor, 1945–48* (Rutherford, N.J., 1969), p. 41. It is unlikely that Hillman would have been so unequivocal in such an exploratory meeting and at a time when Douglas's name, appealing to many in the CIO, was still being talked about.

78. Blum, *Price of Vision* (note 5 above), Wallace diary entry, July 10, 1944, pp. 364,

367; and Roosevelt to Jackson, July 12 (draft) and July 14, 1944, PSF 143, FDR Papers.

79. Blum, *Price of Vision*, Wallace diary entry, July 19, 1944, pp. 367–71; and Germer to Murray, July 22, 1944, H-ACWA Papers.

80. Jacob Potofsky "Notes," H-ACWA Papers. Potofsky also remembered that Hillman was never overly impressed with Wallace and felt he was a strange and unpredictable man, but still the PAC's best option. See Jacob Potofsky "Reminiscences," p. 316, OHCCU. Baldwin was convinced that Hillman played a double game, one Murray never caught on to, in which publicly he remained a Wallace loyalist while privately dealing with the party's bosses. See Wallace "Reminiscences," pp. 3383–88, OHCCU. Years after the election, Baldwin caustically commented on the "amazing insight of city bosses" into Hillman's character, realizing they could get him to agree to a second-choice candidate while publicly never showing his hand, never forcing the issue among CIO delegates or pressuring the President to campaign for Wallace as he had promised. See "Report by C. B. Baldwin on Democratic National Convention of 1944," February 27, 1951, H-ACWA Papers. According to Wallace's diary, Murray told him that Hillman and the President together cooked up the Byrnes candidacy precisely in order to force Wallace to withdraw in exchange for Byrnes. Murray believed, so Wallace remembered, that if only he and Thomas had accompanied Hillman when he visited the President earlier in July, Wallace could have been saved. Bosses Hague and Kelly were not really opposed but merely carrying out the President's wishes. Rumors that the Catholic hierarchy was in the enemy camp were also unfounded, according to Murray, as Bishop Shiel of Chicago favored Wallace, and Frank Walker refused to participate in a Catholic anti-Wallace campaign. See Blum, *Price of Vision*, pp. 374–75. It is hard to know how much of this story to credit, but certainly given their mutual hostility and antithetical agendas, it is hard to conceive of a Hillman–Hannegan conspiracy of the sort described. Another story, by Oscar Chapman, Assistant Secretary of the Interior, blamed everything on Thomas Corcoran, who allegedly convinced Ickes that Wallace lacked support, mainly because Corcoran had it in for Wallace for refusing to appoint his legal cronies to the Agriculture Department. See Blum, p. 413.

81. Freda Kirchway, "The Battle of Chicago," *The Nation*, July 21, 1944.

82. Hillman statement before Special Committee of the House to Investigate Campaign Expenditures, August 28, 1944, transcript in H-ACWA Papers. In fact, although the whole New York trade union world was wary of Dewey from the outset of his career, Hillman did unreservedly endorse his place on the fusion ticket of 1937, and the ACW donated $5,000 to his campaign. In 1938 Dewey ran for Governor as the "New Deal Republican." See Smith, *Thomas E. Dewey and His Times* (note 8, above), p. 263; transcript of Hillman speech, September 9, 1944; press release, September 10, 1944; transcript of Hillman's Roosevelt rally address, October 26, 1944, Rochester; press release, October 27, 1944; and transcript of Hillman speech at UAW convention, September 14, 1944, Grand Rapids, all in H-ACWA Papers.

83. Radio address, "Town Meeting of the Air," September 21, 1944, cited in Arnold, "CIO's Role in American Politics" (note 9 above), pp. 171, 176–77; *New York Times*, August 11, 1944; Gaer, *First Round* (note 21, above), p. 170; William D. Hassett, *Off the Record with FDR* (New Brunswick, N.J., 1958), pp. 288–89; and Arnold, p. 231.

84. *Newsweek*, November 13, 1944, and Roosevelt to Hillman, November 25, 1944, OFF 4910, FDR Papers.

85. CIO Executive Board Minutes, November 16–17, 1944, roll 3; and Convention Proceedings of the CIO, November 1944, pp. 207 *ff*, H-ACWA Papers.
86. I. F. Stone, "The Eastern Seaboard," *The Nation*, October 14, 1944; Blum, *Price of Vision*, Wallace diary entry, April 5, 1944, p. 32; Foster, *Union Politic* (note 39 above); and Arnold, "CIO's Role in American Politics," p. 226.
87. Convention Proceedings of the CIO, November 1944, pp. 23–38, H-ACWA Papers.
88. Blum, *Price of Vision*, pp. 374–75, 390–91, and Wallace "Reminiscences," p. 3446, OHCCU. Wallace declined. He wasn't sure the plan would get Hillman's enthusiastic blessing and believed besides that liberalism needed to find its own voice within the Democratic Party and that if he left the PAC he'd be deserting his besieged friends.
89. Levenstein, *Labor Today and Tomorrow* (note 31 above), pp. 191–92.

EIGHTEEN: "American Century" or "Century of the Common Man"

1. CIO Executive Board Minutes, November 16, 17, 19, and 25, 1944, roll 3, AFL-CIO Headquarters, Washington, D.C.
2. *This Week*, January 14, 1945, and Special Agent R. B. Hood to J. Edgar Hoover, January 26, 1945, File 57-407, Section 19, FBI Files acquired under the FOIA.
3. Paul Vignaux to Hillman, December 28, 1942; Richard Rohman to Hillman, December 4 and January 29, 1942; Albert Guigi and George Buison to Hillman, April 22, 1943; Rohman to Hillman, May 11, 1943; Vignaux to Hillman, May 18, 1943; Hillman to Vignaux, June 25, 1943; and Rohman to Hillman, July 9, 1943, all in H-ACWA Papers.
4. Rohman to Hillman, December 4, 1942; Stephen P. H. Arsker to Hillman, March 27, 1943; Wladyslaw R. Malinowski to Hillman, September 16, 1943; Rohman to Hillman, April 26, 1943; Reinhold Niebuhr to Hillman, February 27, 1943; and Rohman to Hillman, June 14, 1943, all in H-ACWA Papers; Transcript of Hillman radio broadcast, 1943, through the Office of War Information, H-ACWA Papers.
5. Confédération Générale du Travail memo to Hillman and Matthew Woll, unsigned, 1943, H-ACWA Papers.
6. Alonzo L. Hamby, *Beyond the New Deal: Harry S. Truman and American Liberalism* (New York, 1973), pp. 23–26, and Norman Markowitz, *The Rise and Fall of the People's Century: Henry A. Wallace and American Liberalism, 1941–48* (New York, 1973), esp. p. 10.
7. CIO Executive Board Minutes, November 16, 17, 19, and 25, 1944, and March 10–12, 1945, AFL-CIO Headquarters.
8. George Meany to New York Central Trades and Labor Council, April 5, 1945, quoted in J. Goulden, *Meany* (New York, 1972), p. 125. As early as 1942 the AFL warned the TUC that if it openly negotiated with the CIO it would imperil relations with the AFL. Dennis MacShane, "International Labor and the Origins of the Cold War," unpublished ms. Thus Citrine, responding to an AFL threat to withdraw, resisted pressures to bring the CIO into the Anglo-Soviet-American Trade Union Committee. Murray and Hillman had earlier negotiated the creation of an American–Soviet trade union committee originally suggested by Soviet trade union leader, Kuznetsov. As for the Soviets, they did all they could to conciliate Citrine on this issue, hoping to prevent his bolting the committee and returning to the bureaucratic embrace of the old International Federation of Trade Unions. See CIO Executive Board Minutes, October 1–2, 1945, November 2, 1943, and January 27–28, 1944; Philip Murray to Walter Citrine, January 14, 1944, and Citrine to

Murray, November 2, 1943, roll 2, AFL-CIO Headquarters; and Peter Weiler, "Anglo-American Labor, the International Trade Union Movement, and the Cold War: The Break-up of the World Federation of Trade Unions," paper delivered at the 1982 meetings of the Organization of American Historians.

9. "Report of the CIO Delegates to the World Trade Union Conference," H-ACWA Papers; Murray to CIO Executive Board, March 10, 1945; CIO Executive Board Minutes, November 16, 17, 19, and 25, 1944; *New York Times*, November 14, 1944; and MacShane, "International Labor and Origins of Cold War."

10. "Information Circular Airgram to American Diplomatic and Consular Officers," February 16, 1945, from Grew, Department of State files, 800.5043/1-2645, National Archives.

11. American Embassy in London, Airgram, February 20, 1945, 277, State Department File 800.5043/2-2045, National Archives. Although the Soviets could legitimately lay claim to 40 percent of the WFTU membership, they allowed the British and Americans, with far fewer members, to control five seats, as opposed to the Soviets' three, on the new executive committee. Later they would endorse the British view that in the Western zones of occupation in Germany the labor movement should be reconstructed on the basis of autonomous industrial unions rather than as a centrally run federation of all workers, the model they otherwise implemented in their own zone. See MacShane, "International Labor and Origins of Cold War," pp. 173–75.

12. CIO Executive Board Minutes, March 10–12, 1945, Roll 3; "Report of the CIO Delegates to the World Trade Union Conference," n.d., H-ACWA Papers; "World Trade Union Conference Calls to All Peoples," n.d., H-ACWA Papers.

13. CIO Executive Board Minutes, March 10–12, 1945, Roll 3.

14. MacShane, "International Labor and Origins of Cold War," and "World Labor Developments," March 1946, Division of International Labor, Social, and Health Affairs, Department of State, copy of confidential report in H-ACWA Papers.

15. Draft of Hillman speech, Madison Square Garden, March 12, 1945, and draft of Hillman speech, Faneuil Hall, April 15, 1945, H-ACWA Papers.

16. CIO Executive Board Minutes, November 1–2, 1945, Roll 3; "Report of the CIO Delegation to the World Trade Union Conference," H-ACWA Papers; Hillman report to the CIO Executive Board, July 13–14, 1945, Roll 3. The others were Leon Jouhaux, Citrine, V. V. Kuznetsov, V. Lombardo Toledano from Latin America, Che Hsueh Fan of China, and A. Lindberg of Sweden. Hillman was himself worried about Saillant's elevation because of his friendliness toward the Soviets, and according to John Brophy he was even more disturbed about chronic Soviet versus anti-Soviet electoral battles over representation on various WFTU bodies, especially the Soviet attempt to disfranchise the Histadrut in favor a new Israeli labor organization. But in the end Brophy believed Hillman was too tolerant of Soviet machinations and left his post as assistant secretary convinced that Abt and Pressman exercised unhealthy influence over Hillman. Pressman, on the other hand, admired Hillman's ability to mediate between Citrine and Kuznetsov and noted that Hillman and Kuznetsov got along quite well. See CIO Executive Board Minutes, November 1–2, 1945, Roll 3; John Brophy "Reminiscences," pp. 964–67, 979–81, OHCCU; Lee Pressman "Reminiscences," p. 454, OHCCU; and MacShane, "International Labor and Origins of Cold War."

17. "Report of the Constitution Committee to the World Trade Union Conference"; "Draft of Constitution of the World Federation of Trade Unions"; and "The World Trade Union Conference Calls to All Peoples," all in H-ACWA Papers.

18. "World Trade Union Conference Declaration on the Trade Union Attitude to the Peace Settlement"; World Federation of Trade Unions: Resolutions of the Conference-Congress, September 25–October 8, 1945, H-ACWA Papers.
19. World Federation of Trade Unions: Resolutions of the Conference-Congress, and CIO Executive Board Minutes, November 1–2, 1945, Roll 3.
20. CIO Executive Board Minutes, November 1–2, 1945.
21. *La Tribune Economique*, 1945, copy in H-ACWA Papers; *Paris Post*, October 6, 1945; and "Sidney Hillman: World Trade Union Leader," *Picture Post*, February 17, 1945.
22. *Advance*, May 6, 1946, and MacShane, "International Labor and Origins of Cold War," pp. 169–70.
23. Weiler, "Anglo-American Labor" (note 8 above), and Carolyn Eisenberg, "Drawing the Line: The American Decision to Divide Germany, 1944–49," unpublished ms.
24. MacShane, "International Labor and Origins of Cold War," pp. 154–55, 295–96; summary of telephone conversation between Hillman and Henry Wallace, March 13, 1946, File Ia66-166, Henry Wallace Papers, Library of Congress.
25. Francis X. Gannon, *Joseph D. Keenan: Labor's Ambassador in War and Peace: A Portrait of a Man and His Times* (Lanham, Md., 1984), pp. 71–73, 77.
26. Eisenberg, "Drawing the Line." Wolf wrote the Army a scathing report accusing his opponents of trying to restore the discredited pre-1933 right-wing, anti-Soviet leadership.
27. Hillman to President Truman, November 8, and Hillman to "Comrade" Saillant, December 11, 1945, H-ACWA Papers. Hillman had already conveyed his puzzlement to Robert Murphy, U.S. Political Adviser for Germany, about the slowness with which the Allied Control Commission seemed to be acting. Robert Murphy to Hillman, November 27, 1945, H-ACWA Papers.
28. "Report of the Commission of the World Federation of Trade Unions to Investigate Conditions in Germany," H-ACWA Papers. Only 10 percent of German coal and steel capacity was beyond repair, and German factories were better stocked with vital materials than their British counterparts. See MacShane, "International Labor and Origins of Cold War," p. 289.
29. "Transcript and Notes on the German Commission Meetings," H-ACWA Papers.
30. Alger Hiss to Saillant, April 30, 1945, "WFTU Bulletin Clippings," FDR Papers; Hiss to Hillman, April 3, 1945; Hillman *et al.*, to Stettinius *et al.*, April 30, 1945; Hillman to Saillant, April 30, 1945; and Hiss to Saillant, April 30, 1945, all in H-ACWA Papers.
31. Frances Perkins "Reminiscences," pp. 747–57, 661–71, OHCCU; *New York World-Telegram*, April 13, 1945; and Matthew Josephson, *Sidney Hillman: Statesman of American Labor* (New York, 1952), p. 648, citing Maxwell Brandwen. The shock of the President's death was reinforced a few weeks later when news reached Hillman that his mother, his sister Sarah, and her whole family, as well as his sister Minna and her small son had been exterminated in Kovno by German executioners in October 1941. The belated report from his brother Mordecai left Hillman depressed and ill for days. See Josephson, pp. 649–50.
32. At a UN gathering in Lake Success, New York, early in 1946, the United States voted to deny the WFTU privileged access to the Economic and Social Council and to bar it from any role in formulating its agenda. Later both the WFTU and the AFL were granted a consultative affiliation despite stiff resistance by the Soviet delegation

to so favoring the AFL. *New York Times*, January 27, 1946; "Notes on UN Decision," February 13, 1946, cited in file 2b, box 173, David Dubinsky Collection, ILGWU Archives; Truman to Hillman, December 2, 1945, H-ACWA Papers; and "Report on UN Representatives," February 1946, "WFTU 1945–46" File, FDR Papers.

33. Charles Ervin, "What Really Happened in the National Campaign of 1944," June 1945, H-ACWA Papers.

34. M. H. Hinchey, "The Frustration of the New Deal Revival, 1944–46," Ph.D. dissertation, University of Missouri, 1965, pp. 13–43; Robert Lamb, "Reports on Legislation" as legislative representative of the United Steelworkers of America, January, February, March, and April 1945, H-ACWA Papers; Paul A. C. Koistinen, "The Hammer and the Sword: Labor, the Military, and Industrial Mobilization, 1920–1945," Ph.D. dissertation, University of California, Berkeley, 1964, pp. 761, 721–22; Richard Norman Chapman, "Contours of Public Policy, 1939–45," Ph.D. dissertation, Yale University, 1976, p. 389; CIO Executive Board Minutes, November 16, 17, 19, and 25, 1944, Roll 3, AFL-CIO Headquarters; and Barton Bernstein, "The Removal of War Production Board Controls on Business, 1944–46," *Business History Review*, Summer, 1965.

35. Robert Lamb, "Report on Legislation," February 1945, H-ACWA Papers; Hillman-PAC press release, August 14, 1945; and Hillman letter to local PACs, November 19, 1945, all in H-ACWA Papers. Hillman letter to local PACs, January 7, 1946, Jack Kroll Papers, Library of Congress.

36. *New York Times*, August 4, 1945, and CIO Executive Board Minutes, November 1–2, 1945, Roll 3.

37. CIO Executive Board Minutes, March 12 and July 13–14, 1945, Roll 3; Morton W. Ertell, "The CIO Industrial Council Plan: Its Background and Implications," Ph.D. dissertation, University of Chicago, 1955, pp, 8–10; and Aaron Levenstein, *Labor Today and Tomorrow* (New York, 1945), p. 207.

38. Hillman speech at meeting of CIO Executive Board, July 13–14, 1945, Roll 3. PAC's congressional marching orders ran as follows: revision of national wage policy to allow for generous adjustments to meet increased living costs; amendment of the FLSA to raise the minimum wage to 65 cents, and soon thereafter to 75 cents; supplementary unemployment benefits and extension of coverage to federal and maritime workers; permanent establishment of the FEPC backed by a healthy appropriation; passage of the full employment bill and the Murray–Wagner–Dingell social security bill; and quick approval of the UN Charter and Bretton Woods agreement.

39. Nelson Lichtenstein, *Labor's War at Home: The CIO in World War II* (New York, 1982), p. 219; author's interview with Robert Nathan, November 9, 1984; Hillman statement on amendment of the FLSA to Senate subcommittee of the Committee on Education and Labor, October 25, 1945, transcript in H-ACWA Papers; Gladys Dickason, Tilford Dudley, and Palmer Weber to Hillman, memo, August 1, 1945, H-ACWA Papers; and Henry Wallace "Reminiscences," diary entry, November 10, 1944, p. 3518, OCHHU.

40. CIO Executive Board Minutes, November 1–2, 1945, Roll 3.

41. Robert Lamb, "Report on Legislation," April 1945, H-ACWA Papers, and Joseph Davies diary, June 25, 1945, cited in Hamby, *Beyond the New Deal* (note 6 above), pp. 65, 57. Nathan went on to join the ADA's Committee for Economic Stability, which included a host of New Deal–Keynesian refugees: Lauchlin Currie, Galbraith,

Paul Porter, Leon Henderson, and Joseph Rauh. See Lichtenstein, *Labor's War at Home*, p. 192.

42. Hamby, *Beyond the New Deal*, p. 60; Robert J. Donovan, *Conflict and Crisis: The Presidency of Harry S. Truman 1945–1948* (New York, 1977), pp. 113–14; and Hinchey, "Frustrations of the New Deal," p. 112.

43. Arthur F. McClure, *The Truman Administration and Problems of Post-War Labor, 1945–48* (Rutherford, N.J., 1969), p. 83; Robert A. Garson, *The Democratic Party and the Politics of Sectionalism, 1941–48* (Baton Rouge, 1974), p. 158; Joel Seidman, *American Labor from Defense to Reconversion* (Chicago, 1953), pp. 255–56; Hinchey, "Frustrations of the New Deal," pp. 150, 192–93; Bert Cochran, *Harry Truman and the Crisis Presidency* (New York, 1973), p. 199; and Josephson, *Sidney Hillman* (note 31 above), p. 659.

44. Hillman speech to CIO Executive Board, March 12, 1945, CIO Executive Board Minutes, Roll 3.

45. Irving Richter, "The Decline of Organized Labor: A View from 1945," unpublished ms., 1984.

46. Howell John Harris, "Getting Everybody Back on the Same Team: An Interpretation of the Industrial Relations Policies of American Business in the 1940s," Ph.D. dissertation, Oxford University, 1977, p. 172; Levenstein, *Labor Today*, p. 236; and Koistinen, "Hammer and Sword," p. 755.

47. "Notes on Labor–Management Conference of 1945," H-ACWA Papers; Truman to Hillman, October 20, 1945, H-ACWA Papers; Donovan, *Conflict and Crisis*, p. 111; Hinchey, "Frustration of the New Deal," p. 177; "Report of the Committee on Labor Policy, October 1945," approved by the Business Advisory Council, October 26, 1945, General Records of the Department of Commerce, Record Group 40, Box 786, General Correspondence, Washington, D.C.; "Factual Information from 1944 Edition of Who's Who in Commerce and Industry and Private Reports About Delegates and Their Alternates from U. S. Chamber of Commerce and National Association of Manufacturers to National Labor Management Conference," Washington, D.C., November 5, 1945, H-ACWA Papers; Seidman, *American Labor*, pp. 224, 226; "Reports of the Collective Bargaining Committee, November 1945, at Labor Management Conference," November 20, 1945, H-ACWA Papers; Kim McQuaid, *Big Business and Presidential Power: From FDR to Reagan* (New York, 1982), p. 140; and Christopher L. Tomlins, *The State and the Unions: Labor Relations, Law, and the Organized Labor Movement in America, 1880–1960* (New York, 1985), p. 245.

48. James C. Foster, *The Union Politic: The CIO-PAC* (Columbia, Mo., 1975); Irving Howe and B. J. Widick, *The UAW and Walter Reuther* (New York, 1949); and Richter, "Decline of Organized Labor." The ACW contributed $100,000 to the GM strike fund. ACW press release, March 12, 1946, H-ACWA Papers.

49. John Morton Blum, ed., *The Price of Vision: Diary of Henry A. Wallace, 1942–46* (Boston, 1973), entry for December 13, 1945, p. 529, and Hillman's telegram to Truman, cited in Delbert D. Arnold, "The CIO's Role in American Politics, 1936–48," Ph.D. dissertation, University of Maryland, 1952. The telegram hailed Truman's "patient and constructive effort to effect a settlement of the pending steel controversy" in the face of steel company selfishness. Truman to Hillman, June 15, 1946, H-ACWA Papers.

50. *The New Republic*, April 29, 1946; John Cort, "Politics: AFL and CIO," *Commonweal*, May 10, 1946, and "Third Party," *Commonweal*, July 28, 1946; Hamby,

Beyond the New Deal, pp. 77–78; Hillman press release, May 29, 1946, H-ACWA Papers; Garson, *Democratic Party and Politics of Sectionalism,* p. 158; Donovan, *Conflict and Crisis,* p. 62; Hinchey, "Frustrations of the New Deal"; and Truman to Hillman, June 15, 1946, H-ACWA Papers.

51. Cort, "Politics," and "Third Party," and Garson, *Democratic Party and Politics of Sectionalism,* p. 158.

52. Hillman telephone call to Harold Ickes, December 2, 1944, p. 9374, Ickes Diaries, Library of Congress; J. R. Files to Hillman, January 22, 1945, file Ia 27-895, Henry Wallace Papers, Library of Congress; Hamby, *Beyond the New Deal;* and Henry Wallace conversations with Hillman, April 7, 1945, p. 9647, and July 14, 1945, p. 9884, Ickes Diaries.

53. In the midst of a congressional spasm of antilabor agitation, for example, Hillman huddled with Hannegan, who didn't want to see party relations with the PAC and NCPAC disintegrate on the eve of the 1946 elections. Hannegan assembled an informal brains trust comprising Henderson, Paul Porter, Robert Nathan, and Edward Prichard to advise the administration on reconversion policy. Hillman conferred with Hannegan on local matters as well. He conveyed his worries about the Democratic Party situation in New Jersey, and Hannegan offered to get him together with Frank Hague. Henry Wallace noted wryly to his diary: "Sidney certainly does get around." Similarly, it was rumored that Hillman had established excellent working relations with Boss Kelly of Brooklyn before that Party *capo* died. See Hamby, *Beyond the New Deal,* p. 81; Henry Wallace Diaries, March 15, p. 4646, and July 12, 1946, p. 4824, OHCCU; Beanie Baldwin to Hillman, August 31, 1945, H-ACWA Papers; and Sidney Hillman, "PAC Is Here to Stay," *New York Herald-Tribune,* January 14, 1945.

54. Arnold, "CIO's Role in American Politics," pp. 235–37. Ironically, Hillman's attempt at defensive camouflage for the NCPAC was first explored by Murray and directed against Hillman. A few days after the presidential election, Murray told Wallace he wanted him to replace Hillman as NCPAC chairman. Wallace conferred with Mrs. Roosevelt, who went so far as to suggest that Wallace ought to accept the leadership of a broadened PAC as she considered Hillman unsuited to the task. Wallace declined because, he touchingly confessed, he could not abandon his liberal friends in the Democratic Party. Eventually Hillman stepped down as NCPAC chairman in favor of the former Minnesota Governor, Elmer Benson. See Eleanor Roosevelt to Hillman, July 2 and 27, 1945, H-ACWA Papers; Blum, *Price of Vision,* Henry Wallace to Eleanor Roosevelt, November 10, 1944; Hamby, *Beyond the New Deal,* pp. 148, 154–55, 159; and Bert Cochran, *Labor and Communism: The Conflict that Shaped American Unions* (Princeton, N.J., 1979), p. 261. The merger did finally occur after Hillman's death at the end of 1946. The Progressive Citizens of America, which was the result, became the nucleus of the Wallace-for-President movement.

55. Kenneth Waltzer, "The American Labor Party: Third Party Politics in New Deal–Cold War New York, 1936–54," Ph.D. dissertation, Harvard University, 1977, p. 308; Hillman to Vito Marcantonio, November 12, 1945, Box 7, Vito Marcantonio Papers, New York Public Library; *New York Times,* February 14, 1946.

56. B. J. Widick, *Detroit: City of Race and Class Violence* (Chicago, 1972), ch. 8, and Foster, *Union Politic,* ch. 3.

57. "Political Action Committee Program of 1946," H-ACWA Papers; Hillman to CIO locals, June 1946, "CIO-PAC-D" file, Philip Murray Papers, Catholic Univer-

sity; and Harold Ickes diary entry, May 5, 1946, diary vol. 63.

58. Proceedings of the United Steelworkers of America Executive Board, April 1, 1946, p. 82, Pennsylvania State University Library, and Garson, *Democratic Party and Politics of Sectionalism*, pp. 187–88, 190–92.

59. Hillman telephone conversation with Henry Wallace, March 14, 1946, file Ia 66-168, Henry Wallace Papers.

60. *PM*, June 12, 1946.

61. Harold Ickes diary entries, April 26, 1946, diary vol. 63, pp. 4–5, and July 14, 1945, p. 9884; B. Bisno, "Notes," September 18, 1950, H-ACWA Papers; Henry Wallace diary entry, July 17, 1946, p. 4839, OHCCU; and Lee Pressman "Reminiscences," pp. 433–35, 397.

62. "Hillman biographical and personal file," H-ACWA Papers; Henry Wallace to Bessie Hillman, July 11, 1946, file Ia 41-556, Wallace Papers; author's interview with Esther Peterson, winter 1985; *Labor Unity*, March, 1987; and *PM*, July 11, 1946.

63. Author's interview with A. H. Raskin, June 10, 1985, and A. H. Raskin, "Sidney Hillman, 1887–1946," *American Jewish Yearbook*, vol. 49, 1947–48.

Index

671